The Botanical Garden I

Trees and Shrubs

The Botanical Garden I

Trees and Shrubs

The definitive reference with more than 2000 photographs

By

Roger Phillips
&
Martyn Rix

FIREFLY BOOKS

A FIREFLY BOOK

Published by Firefly Books Ltd., 2002

First Printing

National Library of Canada
Cataloguing in Publication Data

Phillips, Roger
    The botanical garden

Includes bibliographical references and index.
Contents: v.1. Trees and shrubs — v. 2. Perennials and
annuals.

ISBN 1-55297-591-6 (v. 1).—ISBN 1-55297-592-4 (v. 2)

1. Plants, Ornamental.   2. Gardening.   3. Plants,
Ornamental—Pictorial works.   I. Rix, Martyn   II. Title.

SB450.97.P48 2002   635.9   C2002-900216-8

Publisher Cataloging-in-Publication Data (U.S)

Phillips, Roger.
    The botanical garden volume I : trees and shrubs /
Roger Phillips ; and Martyn Rix. — 1st ed.
[492] p. : col. photos. ; cm.
Includes bibliographic references and index.
Summary: 510 genera of woody garden plants with full
details of how they are related, their origins and their uses.

ISBN: 1-55297-591-6

1. Woody plants.   2. Ornamental shrubs.
3. Ornamental trees.   I. Rix, Martyn.   II. Greenfield,
Pat.   III. Title.

635.976/ 097 21   CIP   SB435.5.P53 2002

Published in Canada in 2002 by
Firefly Books Ltd.
3680 Victoria Park Avenue
Willowdale, Ontario M2H 3K1

Published in the United States in 2002 by
Firefly Books (U.S.) Inc.
P.O. Box 1338, Ellicott Station
Buffalo, New York 14205

Color reproduction by Speedscan
Printed and bound in Great Britain by Bath Press

Acknowledgments

DESIGNER: Jill Bryan
ASSISTANT DESIGNERS: Gill Stokoe,
Debby Curry, and Gaia Chaillet Giusti
EDITOR: Candida Frith-Macdonald
PROOF READER: Jonathan Edwards
PRODUCTION: Chris Gibson and Lee Bekker

Most of the specimens came from the
following gardens, and we would like to
acknowledge the generous help we had from
them and their staff:

Marwood Hill Gardens, Dr Jimmy Smart and
Malcolm Pharoah; The Royal Horticultural
Society's Gardens at Rosemoor and Wisley,
Jim Gardiner, Jenny Holloway, John and
Sarah Chesters; Gorwell House, Dr John
Marston; Eccleston Square Garden, Kathryn
Maule; The Chelsea Physic Garden, Sue
Minter and Fiona Crumley; Bedgebury
Pinetum, Colin Morgan; The University
Botanic Garden, Cambridge; The Royal
Botanic Gardens Kew, Jessica Begon,
Rosmena Brown, and Helen Long in the
Gardens Development Unit.

We would also like to thank the following
individuals and gardens for their help,
encouragement, or for providing specimens
to photograph:

Harry and Yvonne Hay; Roger Clark at
Greenway Gardens; Guy and Emma Sissons
at The Plantsman Nursery; Nick and Karan
Junker at PMA Plant Specialities;
Rachel Martin at Trebah Gardens; Huw
Angus at Westonbirt Arboretum; Mary Anne
and Alastair Robb at Cothay Manor; John
d'Arcy at the Old Vicarage, Edington;
George Llewellyn; Carolyn Hardy; Alison
Rix; Nicky Foy; David McClintock;
Geoffrey Goatcher; and Dr James Compton.

Contents

Due to the number of plants covered, listings given here cannot be comprehensive but instead cover the major plants

Introduction

Our aim in this book is to provide new information and a new way of looking at plants and gardening from a more botanical viewpoint. The plant families are covered systematically, and the relationships between them are discussed; readers will be able to put the knowledge they have acquired piecemeal into a framework, and understand the botanical groups and the similarities and differences between them.

Genera and plant evolution

This book is based on the genus, genera in the plural, the Latin word for family, class, or race. Plants are classified in a hierarchy of many ranks, but the only three commonly used are family, genus, and species. To take an example, the black or water birch *Betula nigra* is a species in the genus *Betula* and the family *Betulaceae*. A genus is usually a very natural and familiar grouping, such as oak, beech, day-lily, or dahlia. Many genera are small and easily recognised by a combination of characteristics not found in another group of plants, for instance the green flowers, lobed leaves, and dry, winged seeds of *Liriodendron*, the tulip tree. Other genera are large, with tens or even hundreds of species, and can be further divided into subgenera; some botanists may consider these subgenera worthy of division into distinct genera, for example the division of *Cornus* into *Benthamidia*, *Chamaepericlymenum*, and *Swida*. Modern studies sometimes confirm these divisions, or sometimes show them to be artificial. The plant world can be imagined as a huge, chaotic, and multi-stemmed tree, branching repeatedly, with some branches dying, others thriving and waxing or waning in importance through the millenia. Some branches have survived almost unchanged for millions of years, others that were formerly very important have died out. A few have left just one or two remnants as isolated individuals on remote islands, in gorges, or in mountain forests; others have prospered and now exist as thousands of species.

The classical arrangement

Botanists are faced with the problem of showing in a list this complex result of millions of years of different lines of evolution. Linnaeus' system was based strictly on the sexual parts of the plant, the number of styles and stamens in each flower. This was convenient and worked quite well, but it was clearly artificial. Botanists soon began to work on more natural systems reflecting the evolutionary ancestry of plants, and ever since have continued the search for more natural groupings. The classical order of families was based on the premise that evolution of flowers was from the simple to the complex; thus magnolia and its relatives, with large, simple flowers, were considered especially primitive; daisies, on the other hand, with many flowers aggregated into a head that looks like a single flower, were considered advanced.

New developments

To classify modern plants accurately, we need to know their ancestry. Plant remains fossilize very poorly compared with bones or shells, but we can guess from fossils that trees in the coal-forming forests might have resembled giant clubmosses, horsetails, ferns, and conifers. Our knowledge of early flowering plants, probably appearing in the Jurassic, is even more scanty; it is likely many were aquatic herbs with no woody parts. Fortunately, we now have a new tool, DNA, to give clues to ancient relationships. DNA studies have confirmed the classical outline, but also show the true picture to be more complex. The relationships of several groups of plants that did not fit conveniently into any of the old schemes are now being clarified. Some of the major groupings and new evidence concerning their ordering are outlined on the following pages. Volume 1 follows broadly the order and relationships proposed by Kubitski and adapted by Mabberley in *The Plant Book* (1997); in Volume 2, I have been able to take into account more recently published DNA studies and have broadly followed the order proposed by Judd and co-workers in 1999. The monocotyledons are placed at the end in both volumes.

Ginkgo biloba

Tree ferns, ginkgo, and conifers

The ancient tropical swamp forests, which have ended up as coal today, were dominated by giant clubmosses, seed-ferns, and tree ferns, with primitive conifers. Few remnants of this flora have survived, probably because of the drastic changes in the world climate between the warm, wet Carboniferous and the dry Permian periods. Only some ancestors of *Osmunda* and relatives of the huge tropical fern *Marattia* survived from these warm forests; the modern ferns are a result of active evolution and divergence during the Triassic and Jurassic. Most of the tree ferns (see pp.16–17) are found in wet, cool tropical and subtropical forests, and the hardier ones come from the southern hemisphere. *Ginkgo biloba* (see p.18) is a remarkable survivor, the only one of its family. The leaves of this species and of many other, now extinct, *Ginkgo* species are found as far back as the Jurassic, and throughout the northern hemisphere in the early Tertiary. A second species, *G. adiantoides,* survived until the Miocene in North America, and into the Pliocene in Europe. *Ginkgo biloba* survived somewhere in China, where it was recognised as something special by early Chinese civilisation and widely planted in temple gardens. Other relicts such as the conifers *Metasequoia glyptostroboides* (see p.38) in China, and *Wollemia nobilis* in Australia also show how an ancient genus can survive in a small remote area. Conifers are today by far the most important group of ancient woody plants; they are thought to have originated as far back as the Devonian, but most of the present-day families can be traced back only as far as the Jurassic or Triassic.

Magnolia, bay, and Calycanthus

This group of families is interesting in having various combinations of primitive characteristics, that is, features that may have been present in the earliest flowering trees to grow on earth. Primitive wood anatomy, aromatic leaves, spirally arranged floral parts, and simple stamens with undifferentiated filaments are characteristics common in the group and thought to be primitive. In *Magnolia, Michelia,* and *Liriodendron* (the Magnoliaceae, see pp.56–59), the flowers are large and often showy, with numerous spirally arranged petals, stamens, and ovules. The related family Annonaceae (see p.65) is mainly tropical, and contains the custard apple, *Annona,* and the North American pawpaw, *Asimina triloba.* Winteraceae (see pp.60–61) which includes *Drimys,* is also primitive in many characteristics and probably belongs with the magnolia group. Also related to the Magnoliaceae are the small but interesting families Illiciaceae (see p.63) and Schisandraceae (see p.62); *Schisandra,* with its unusual red, fleshy fruits in hanging chains, and *Kadsura,* with similar fruits in a round head, are the only genera in the latter. The bay tree family, the Lauraceae (see pp.66–71), contains over 2500 species, mainly in the tropical forests. Most species have small flowers but sometimes large fruit, for example the avocado tree *Persea americana.* Others are aromatic, including the bay itself, *Laurus,* and *Cinnamomum,* the cinnamon. Related to Lauraceae is the Calycanthaceae (see pp.72–73), containing both the chocolate-brown flowered Carolina and California allspice, *Calycanthus,* and the lovely white-flowered *Sinocalycanthus,* recently discovered in China.

Sinocalycanthus chinensis

Witch hazel and Liquidambar

The witch hazel family, Hamamelidaceae (see pp.99–109), and the related Cercidiphyllaceae (see p.96) are superficially similar in many characteristics to the catkin-bearing plants such as hazels (Betulaceae, see below and p.119). *Hamamelis* itself has clusters of strongly scented flowers with ribbon-shaped petals; in *Corylopsis* the scented flowers are aggregated into hanging, catkin-like spikes; in *Sinowilsonia*, the flowers are even more catkin-like, scentless, unisexual and pollinated by wind. One of the outstanding features of most of the group is the fine red and golden colours produced by the leaves in autumn. Modern theories suggest that the similarities between the catkin-bearing plants and Hamamelidaceae are superficial, the result of evolution producing similar results from different ancestors, and that the Hamamelidaceae are related to the Saxifragaceae (see Volume 2).

Hamamelis × intermedia
'Hiltingbury'

Beech, oak, birch, and walnut

These catkin-bearing trees are dominant in temperate forests of both hemispheres. Most are wind-pollinated and have edible, nut-like seeds. The male flowers are massed together into catkins, primarily for wind-pollination, and the female flowers are usually reduced to scales with protruding stigmas to catch the pollen. Five well-known families make up most of the group. Fagaceae (see pp.110–118) includes the beech, oak, and sweet chesnut (*Fagus, Quercus,* and *Castanea*), and *Lithocarpus* and *Castanopsis*, in all of which the nuts are held in a cup or husk, which may be smooth or spiny. Dispersal depends on squirrels and mice hoarding the seeds, having found too many of them to eat at once.

The Betulaceae (see pp.119–123) have rather similar catkins, but often smaller seeds. There are two groups within the family; alders and birches (*Alnus* and *Betula*) have very small, often winged seeds, dispersed by wind or water, while hazel (*Corylus*), hornbeam (*Carpinus*), *Ostrya,* and *Ostryopsis* have larger seeds, often with wing-like bracteoles to help dispersal. The Juglandaceae (see pp.124–126), which include walnuts, hickories and pecans (*Juglans* and *Carya*), *Platycarya,* and *Pterocarya,* differ clearly in their pinnate leaves. Both large, heavy nuts and small, winged nuts are found in this family. Myricaceae (see p.127) and Casuarinaceae also have reduced flowers, and somewhat cone-like seed heads. Myricaceae, the bayberries or bog myrtles, produce aromatic wax. Casuarinas, the strangely named she-oaks, have jointed stems, reduced leaves, and nitrogen-fixing bacteria in the roots; originating in the Pacific area, they are now widely distributed in the tropics, particularly in sandy coastal areas, where some have become aggressive weeds. In spite of their reduced flowers and the presence of similar pollen in Tertiary deposits, DNA evidence indicates that these families are not primitive, as they were previously thought to be, but relatively advanced and most closely related to large-flowered plants such as melons and begonias (see Volume 2).

Alnus viridis

Mulberry, fig, and elm

The Ulmaceae (see pp.160–63) and Moraceae (see pp.164–67) are closely related. In the Ulmaceae, the elms, *Ulmus*, and the hackberries or nettletrees, *Celtis*, are close, the former with dry, winged fruit, the latter with small berries. The Moraceae contains mulberries and figs (*Morus* and *Ficus),* and the tropical *Artocarpus*, the breadfruit tree; all have milky sap and seeds embedded in sweet and juicy flesh. Modern studies link this group with the Rosaceae.

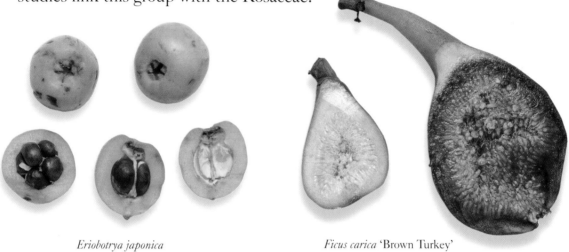

Eriobotrya japonica   *Ficus carica* 'Brown Turkey'

Rose, apple, and plum

The rose family, Rosaceae (see pp.228–71), contains most of the familiar temperate fruit trees, such as apples and plums (*Malus* and *Prunus*), and a range of edible fruit of differing structures, including strawberries and rasberries (see Volume 2). Apple-like fruits, so-called pomes, with soft seeds, are found in pears, quinces, and mountain ash (*Pyrus, Cydonia,* and *Sorbus*), while the stone fruits, such as plums, peaches, and cherries (all *Prunus*) have a single hard-shelled seed. Several hard seeds are found in hawthorn, *Crataegus*, eaten in both Mexico and Asia, where there are species with larger fruits than are usual in western Europe. Dry seeds of various types are found in *Exochorda* and *Spiraea* and in many familiar herbaceous plants such as meadowsweet, lady's mantle, and *Aruncus* (see Volume 2).

Dogwood, Nyssa, and Davidia

Recent accounts of the family Cornaceae (see pp.324–29) recognise two major branches; one contains *Cornus* and *Alangium,* the other *Nyssa* and *Davidia.* All are recognised by rather small flowers, sometimes advertised by conspicuous bracts. *Cornus* itself is interestingly diverse, and has been divided into several separate genera based on details of the flowers and fruit; it is common in both America and Eurasia. *Alangium* is a mainly tropical genus, widespread from Africa to Asia and Australia. *Nyssa* demonstrates the closeness of the floras of eastern North America and southeastern Asia; of its eight species, six are American, two are Asiatic. *Davidia* is an isolated genus of one species, and survives in the wild only as scattered trees in the mountains of western China. Studies of DNA suggest that *Hydrangea, Deutzia,* and *Philadelphus,* in the Hydrangeaceae (see pp.216–23), are related to Cornaceae rather than Saxifragaceae, with which they are usually linked.

Cornus alba

Maples and buckeyes

The family Aceraceae (see pp.354–59) contains just two genera. *Acer*, the maples and sycamore, is a genus of over a hundred mainly temperate trees and shrubs, renowned for their beautiful leaves, bark, and autumn colour. The flowers are small and either insect- or wind-pollinated, the leaves are opposite, usually lobed, and in one or two species deeply cut into separate segments. The fruits are characteristic pairs of seeds with a long wing on one side that acts as a propeller, slowing the fall of the seed and enabling it to be blown further by the wind. The second genus is *Dipteronia*, which contains a single species with pinnate leaves and a seed with a wing all the way round. The Aceraceae is sometimes included in the Sapindaceae (see pp.349–51), a family that includes a number of important trees and shrubs, such as are *Koelreuteria*, *Dodonea*, and the tropical fruits rambutan (*Nephelium*) and litchi. Also closely related, and sometimes included in this family, is Hippocastanaceae (see pp.352–53), containing *Aesculus,* the horse chestnut and buckeyes, with typical, big, brown, shiny seeds enclosed in an often spiky capsule.

Acer pentaphyllum

Viburnum and honeysuckle

The final group of advanced flowering plants often have heads of small flowers, clustered together and resembling a single flower; the daisy is the common and most extreme example of this, where the "petals" are part of the outer flowers, and the centre is made up of a mass of minute flowers. Many species of *Viburnum,* in the Adoxaceae (see pp.448–51), which belongs to this group, also show these larger outer flowers. Closely related to *Viburnum* is the honeysuckle (*Lonicera,* in the Caprifoliaceae, see pp.438–47), in which the flowers are in pairs, often crowded into whorls; the petals are joined and often form a long tube containing nectar for visiting bees, moths or birds. Recent research indicates that the ivies (*Hedera,* see Araliaceae, pp.380–81), with all the flowers in a rounded head, and the Umbelliferae, where the outer flowers in the flat head are often larger than the inner, and hollies (*Ilex,* see Aquifoliaceae, p.179), the relationships of which have in the past been uncertain, are all related to *Viburnum.*

Cordyline, palms and bamboos

The distinctness of the monocotyledons, which include grasses and bamboos (see pp.472–83), has been recognised for centuries. They cannot grow thick, woody trunks, so-called secondary thickening, so have produced few proper trees. Palms (see pp.464–65) are the main woody genera, and there are a few tree-like members of other families. In bamboos the grass-like stems become hard and tough, branching only where leaves are formed; all new shoots appear from the rootstock below ground. Palms build up a wide growing point before they begin much upward growth, so their trunks are parallel sided, continuing indefinitely upwards; only a few species branch. The most tree-like monocotyledons are the the dragon trees (*Dracaena*) and *Cordyline* from New Zealand, which make some secondary growth and build up thick trunks with many branches, reaching a great age.

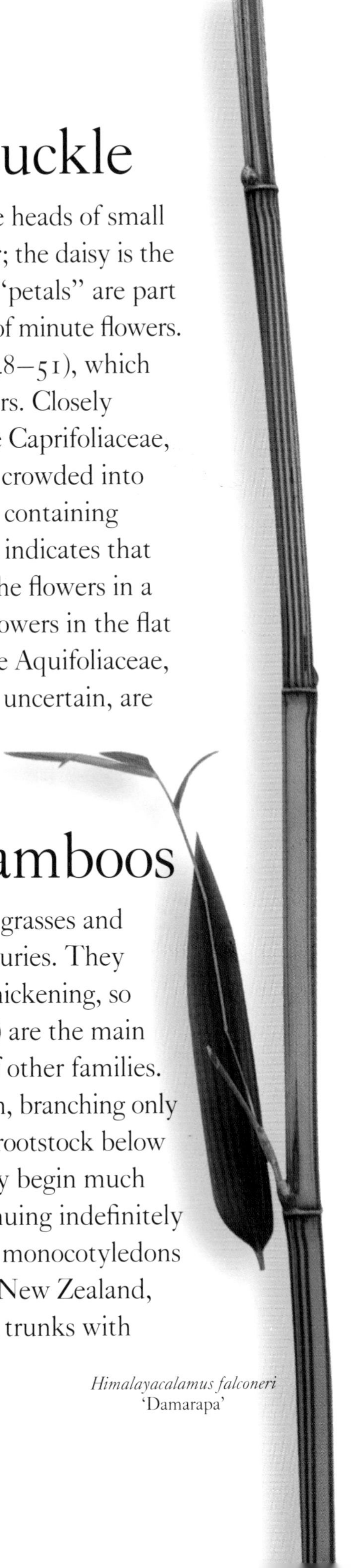

Himalayacalamus falconeri
'Damarapa'

Dicksonia antarctica
fertile pinnules, showing sori
3 × life size
October 25th

Dicksonia antarctica
⅓ life size
July 4th

Dicksonia

Dicksonia L'Herit. (1788) is a genus of around 25 species in the family Dicksoniaceae. The hardiest, *D. antarctica* Labill., is found on the Australian mainland and Tasmania, and is described here.

Description Tree ferns with trunks to 15m, unbranched, thick, and fibrous with masses of scales and roots. The leaves are evergreen, 2–4.5m long, 3- to 4-pinnate, with lobed segments. The sori, which contain the spores, are on the margins of the leaves and are protected by an indusium of 2 flaps.

Key Recognition Features Tree ferns with rather stout, hairy trunks, finally 50cm to 1m in diameter, the leaves spreading to 9m across.

Evolution and Relationships *Cyathea* J. Sm., another common tree-fern genus, generally has more slender, scaly trunks and wider fronds. *Cyathea dealbata* (Forst.) Schwarz, from New Zealand, is distinct in the white underside of the fronds.

Ecology and Geography *Dicksonia* species are found mainly in tropical, frost-free areas, growing in rainforest. *Dicksonia antarctica* is found in Queensland, New South Wales, Victoria, South Australia, and Tasmania, growing in gullies and cool, moist forests.

Comment Recent introductions to Europe from Tasmania have hopes of being hardier than the mainland forms, which are well established in Cornwall and the west of Ireland. The African *Cyathea dregei* Kunze, from grasslands in the high Drakensberg, should also be one of more frost-hardy tree ferns. Tree fern roots were widely imported in the past for use as a medium for growing orchids.

Dicksonia antarctica
young fronds
¹/₂ life size
May 1st

Dicksonia antarctica
¹/₃ life size
September 2nd

Ginkgo biloba leaves showing
autumn colour beginning
1/3 life size
October 9th

Ginkgo biloba
unripe fruit 2/3 life size
September 16th

Ginkgo biloba
male flowers and frosted
young leaves
2/3 life size, March 16th

Ginkgo

Ginkgo L. (1753) has one member, *G. biloba* L., the only surviving species in the family Ginkgoaceae. It was formerly found in many parts of the world, but survived only in China and there mainly as cultivated trees around temples.

Description The ginkgo can reach 45m in height, taking 100 years to reach 30m. The leaves are deciduous, fan-shaped, usually with one central cleft, deeper on leaves from elongating shoots. The male flowers are like short catkins; the female flowers are small, stalked, with 2–4 ovules. Male and female flowers are on separate trees, and pollination is by wind. The fruits are like large cherries, golden-yellow when ripe, with thin, sticky flesh that smells of sweet, rancid butter. The seed is a single large, pale brown nut.

Key Recognition Features The fan-shaped, 2-lobed leaves have simple dichotomous veins. Side shoots on the twigs are short, thick, and pointed.

Evolution and Relationships This is possibly the most ancient of all living trees, as leaves almost indentical to present day examples have been found in Jurassic deposits around 200 million years old; other species and at least 6 other genera have been identified from fossils in this period. *Ginkgo* shows many primitive features: the pollen produces motile sperms with spiral bands of flagella, which swim to the ovary, rather than a simple pollen tube as in other gymnosperms and flowering plants.

Ecology and Geography A tree of warm temperate forests, but tolerant of summer heat and winter cold. Possibly wild trees are reported in southeastern China in Zhejiang province (about 240 in Tian Mu Shan), but ancient trees are common around temples in many parts of China.

Comment Excellent as a garden specimen or as a street tree. Easily grown, hardy, disease- and pest-free, and very ornamental; the spring leaves are bright pale green, autumn colour is a lovely yellow. Male trees are preferred for street planting because of the unpleasant smell of the ripe fruits. The largest trees in Britain, now around 30m tall, were planted between 1760 and 1840. In China and Japan trees 1000 years old are still growing, and these ancient trees often show strange breast-like outgrowths from the trunk and lower branches. Ginkgo nuts are edible when roasted. Some compounds extracted from ginkgo are used in the treatment of Parkinson's disease, and extracts are said to hold back the effects of aging and be helpful against memory loss.

Araucaria

Araucaria Juss. (1789) is a genus of 19 species, the largest in the family Araucariaceae, found mainly in the southwest Pacific and in South America. *Araucaria araucana*, (Molina) K. Koch, the monkey puzzle or Chile pine, is the only species hardy in temperate climates.

Description Trees to around 30m after 100 years, with a girth of 3m. The leaves are evergreen, flat, stiff, scale-like, very sharp-pointed, spirally arranged around the shoot to give a diameter of around 8cm. The male cones droop in clusters at the ends of the upper shoots; the female cones are on the upper sides of shoots and take 3 years to ripen. Male and female cones are usually on separate trees; pollination is by wind. The mature cones are around 20cm long, and break up on the tree; the seeds are edible.

Key Recognition Features The thick, spiny shoots, short, rigid leaves, and rough, grey bark of the monkey puzzle are unmistakable. The branches are often clustered at the top of a tall, bare trunk.

Evolution and Relationships An ancient genus important in the Jurassic forests. The 2 other genera in the family are *Agathis* Salisb. with 20 species, including the New Zealand kauri pine, and the Australian genus *Wollemia* (W.G. Jones et al) discovered in 1994 in a hidden canyon in New South Wales, where only around 30 trees survive.

Ecology and Geography Forms pure stands in mountains; grows best in wet, windy climates. Monkey puzzle is native to Chile and western Argentina. 13 species are found only in New Caledonia.

Comment The monkey puzzle is common as an ornamental; it was popular in Victorian gardens, and is again in suburban gardens today. It is important for timber in Chile, and the seeds are edible. *Araucaria heterophylla* (Salisb.) Franco, Norfolk Island pine, has a very regular arrangement of horizontal branches; it is a common ornamental pot plant and often planted by the sea in mild areas. It has narrow, softer, incurved leaves. *Araucaria bidwillii* Hook. fil. from Queensland, Australia has softer leaves and huge cones with edible seeds. *Araucaria angustifolia* (Bertol.) Kuntze from southern Brazil and Argentina is the parana pine, a valuable timber tree, also with edible seeds.

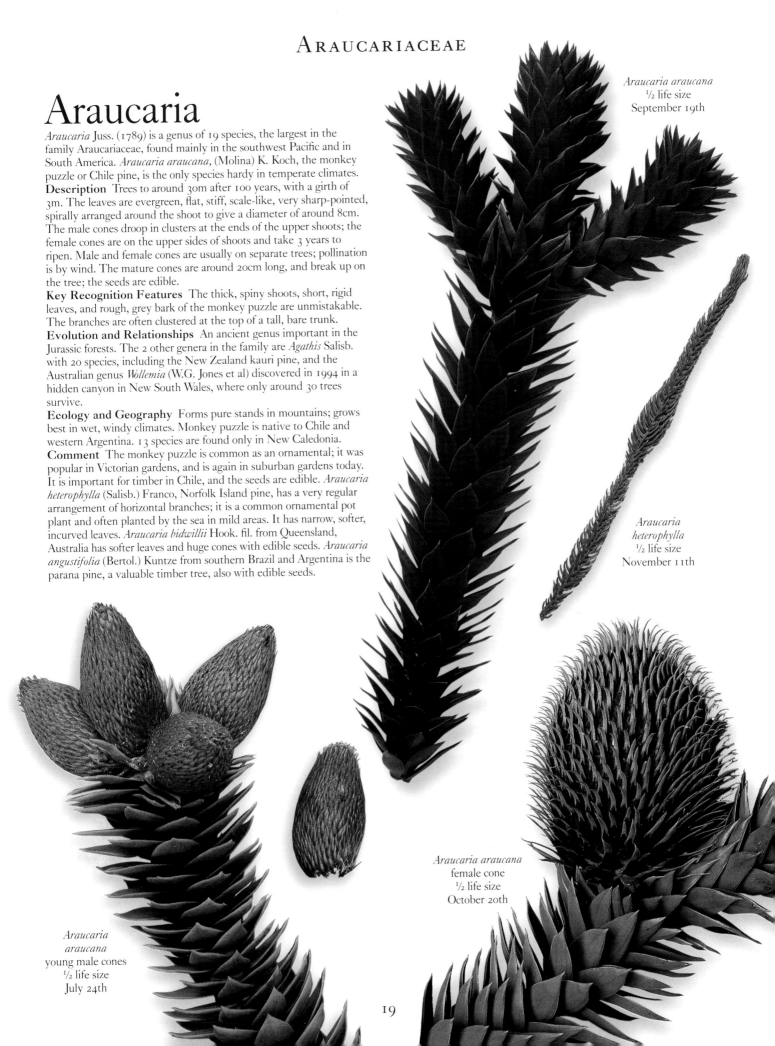

Araucaria araucana
½ life size
September 19th

Araucaria heterophylla
½ life size
November 11th

Araucaria araucana
female cone
½ life size
October 20th

Araucaria araucana
young male cones
½ life size
July 24th

Cephalotaxus

Cephalotaxus Sieb. & Zucc (1842) is the only genus of the family Cephalotaxaceae, with around 10 species in eastern Asia. *Cephalotaxus fortunei* Hooker is the one commonly cultivated.

Description Tree or large shrub to around 12m, evergreen. The leaves are narrow, flat, and leathery, with broad white or silvery bands beneath. Male flowers are formed in numerous small, short-stalked heads in the leaf axils, on separate trees from the female flowers, which are small, cone-like, and on stalks at the base of last year's shoots. Pollination is by wind. The fruits are 2—2.5cm long, the shape of small, green plums, ripening purplish-brown, usually with only 1 seed developing on each female cone.

Key Recognition Features Like very bold-leaved yews (*Taxus*, see p.52), but distinguished by the broad pale green or silvery bands on the undersides of the leaves, and the green fruit ripening pale brown. *Torreya* (see p.53) has similar but stiffer, spiny-pointed leaves.

Evolution and Relationships Close to the *Taxaceae*, and especially to *Torreya*, but differing in the fruit being in stalked, cone-like heads in leaf or shoot axils, not large fruits on the tips of shoots as in *Torreya*.

Ecology and Geography Understorey trees or shrubs in deciduous forests in northeastern India, China, Korea, and Japan to Malaysia; according to fossil evidence, previously more widely distributed.

Comment Long cultivated in Japan; *C. harringtonii* (Knight ex. Forbes) K. Koch is known only in cultivation: 'Fastigiata' is an ungainly, upright form, like a short Irish yew with robust shoots; var. *drupacea* makes an elegant shrub with a drooping form.

Cephalotaxus fortunei unripe fruits just over life size September 20th

Cephalotaxus harringtonii var. *drupacea* seed and ripe fruit 1 ½ × life size April 19th

Cephalotaxus harringtonii 'Fastigiata' ½ life size April 19th

Cephalotaxus harringtonii var. *drupacea* female flowers 1 ½ × life size April 19th

Cephalotaxus fortunei male flowers and needles 2 × life size, April 19th

Cephalotaxus harringtonii var. *drupacea* with male flowers ⅔ life size April 19th

Podocarpus

Podocarpus L'Herit. ex Pers. (1807) is a genus of around 110 species, by far the largest in the family Podocarpaceae.

Description Trees, to 30m or more in tropical species, or shrubs. The leaves are evergreen, usually flat, long, and often curved, with a strong midrib, but sometimes yew-like (*Taxus*, see p.52) and occasionally scale-like. The male flowers are like small catkins, the females minute. Males and females are usually on separate trees; pollination is by wind. The fruits are usually plum-like, green, ripening yellow, red, or blackish. Fruits of *P. macrophyllus* (Thunb.) Sweet and *P. totara* G. Benn. ex D. Don have red, fleshy stalks.

Key Recognition Features A diverse genus, but the large leaves, few seeds, and elongated catkins, are typical of most species.

Evolution and Relationships The scale-leaved species are often put into the genus *Dacrycarpus* (Endl.) Laubenf.

Ecology and Geography Generally found in moist forests. Important trees in the mountains of Africa, in South East Asia and Japan, southwards to New Zealand, and in South America to the West Indies, but absent from Europe and North America.

Comment Widely used for timber in tropical and subtropical areas. Some species are planted as ornamentals, notably *P. salignus* D. Don and the long-leaved *P. macrophyllus*, used for hedges in China and Japan, both of which grow well in the warmer parts of Europe and North America. *Podocarpus andinus* has twisted leaves and black fruits.

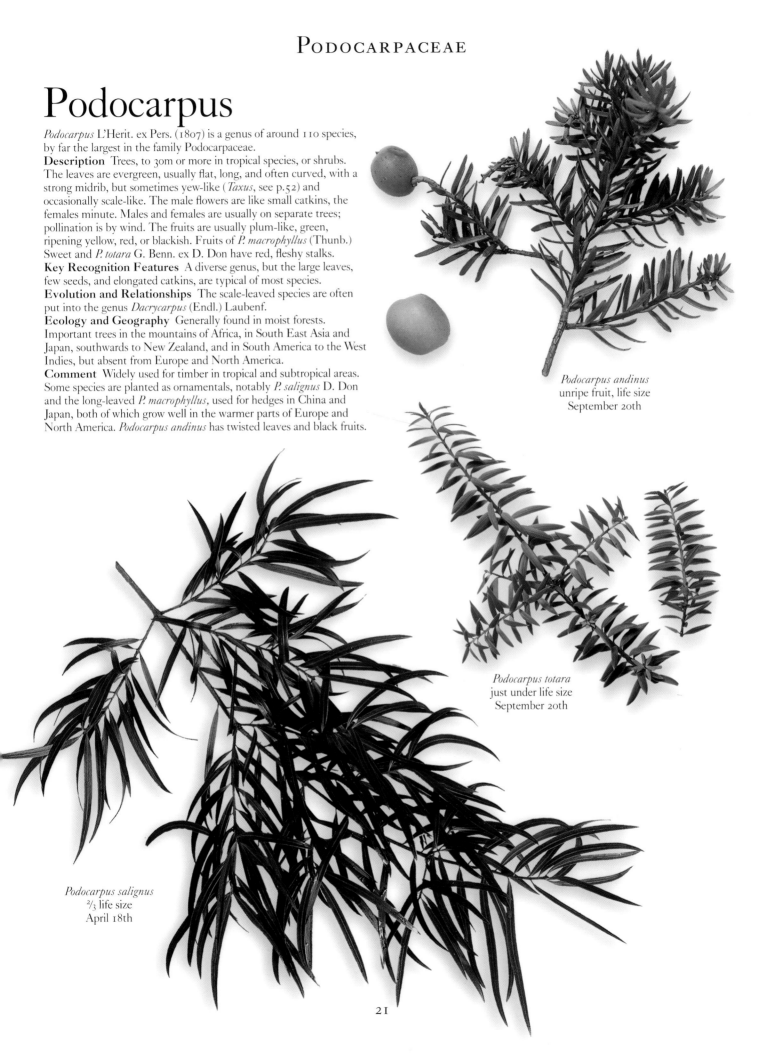

Podocarpus andinus
unripe fruit, life size
September 20th

Podocarpus totara
just under life size
September 20th

Podocarpus salignus
²/₃ life size
April 18th

Saxegothaea

Saxegothaea Lindley (1851) is a genus of only one species
S. conspicua Lindl., in the family Podocarpaceae, from southern
South America.

Description Trees to 30m in height in the wild, but only 20m in
cultivation, and often shrubby. The bark is dark brown, flaking to
leave reddish-brown patches, and the shoots are pendulous, with
whorls of 3–5 side shoots. The leaves are evergreen, curved, sharp-
pointed, with 2 white bands beneath. Male flowers are purplish-
brown, small, catkin-like, stalked, in pairs in the leaf bases. Pollination
is presumed to be by wind. The cones are at the ends of small shoots,
blue-grey, 5mm across, 10mm long, with spreading and downcurved
scales, fused into a fleshy mass enclosing a single nut-like seed.

Key Recognition Features Pendulous shoots with whorls of short
shoots on a tree with yew-like (*Taxus*, see p.52) leaves.

Evolution and Relationships The genus is close to *Podocarpus*,
(see p.21) especially to *P. andinus*, but has whorled shoots and stiff
leaves like *Araucaria* (see p.19).

Ecology and Geography *Saxegothaea* is found in moist rainforests
in Patagonia, in both southwestern Argentina and southern Chile.
It sometimes grows as an understorey in *Nothofagus dombeyi* (see
p.111) forest.

Comment This is very beautiful as a specimen tree, but grows well
only in cool, moist gardens. The name commemorates Prince Albert,
Duke of Saxe-Coburg-Gotha (1819–61), husband of Queen Victoria.

Saxegothaea conspicua
½ life size
April 19th

Saxegothaea conspicua
with immature male flowers
2 × life size, April 19th

Saxegothaea conspicua
female flowers, life size
September 20th

Dacrydium

Dacrydium Solander ex G. Forst. (1786) is a genus of around 21 species
in the family Podocarpaceae, from eastern Asia and Australasia.

Description Trees to 60m in height, evergreen, with slender,
cypress-like shoots, and male and female flowers on separate trees.
The leaves are small, scale-like, and overlapping on mature shoots,
which usually hang down; juvenile leaves are sparse and linear. The
flowers are small, the females on the tips of the shoots, the males, like
small catkins, in the axils of upper leaves. Pollination is by wind. The
fruits are egg-shaped, around 3mm long, surrounded by a usually
fleshy, cup-shaped aril, white in *D. bidwillii* Hook. fil. ex Kirk., red in
D. cupressinum Solander ex G. Forst.. In *D. franklinii* Hook. fil. the
cup is green and not fleshy. Flowers and fruit are rare.

Key Recognition Features The small, scale-like leaves on slender
shoots and the small fruit with cup-like aril are typical. *Dacrycarpus
dacrydioides* has similar scale-like leaves.

Evolution and Relationships *Dacrydium franklinii*, the Huon pine
from Tasmania, is sometimes separated in the genus *Lagarostrobus*
Quinn; *D. bidwillii* from New Zealand is sometimes listed as
Halocarpus bidwillii (Hook. fil. ex Kirk.) Quinn. *Microcachrys* Hook.
fil. ex Hook., a dwarf shrub from the mountains of Tasmania, has
similar scale-like leaves but tetragonal shoots and has seeds
surrounded by a large, scarlet aril to 8mm long.

Ecology and Geography *Dacrydium cupressinum* and *D. franklinii*
are forest trees, while *D. bidwillii* is an alpine shrub. The range extends
from the Malay peninsula to Borneo, Tasmania and New Zealand.

Comment *Dacrydium cupressinum*, the rimu or red pine, is an
important timber tree in the lowland forests of New Zealand, much
used for building, with beautiful reddish wood; *D. franklinii* and
D. bidwillii are sometimes planted as curiosities, especially in
southwestern England and Ireland.

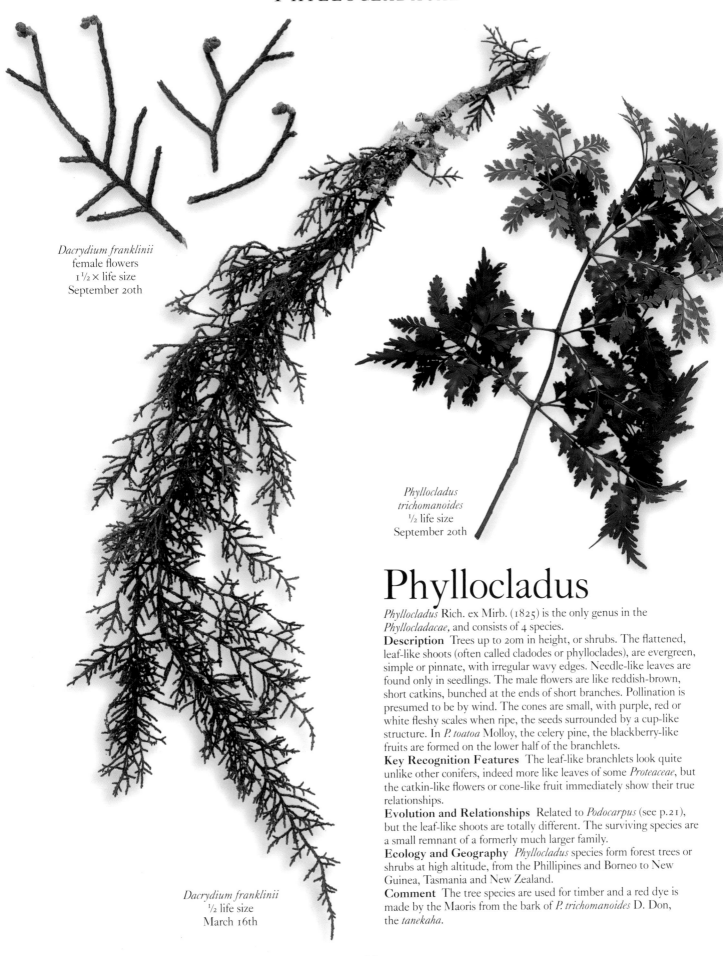

Dacrydium franklinii
female flowers
1 ¹/₂ × life size
September 20th

*Phyllocladus
trichomanoides*
¹/₂ life size
September 20th

Dacrydium franklinii
¹/₂ life size
March 16th

Phyllocladus

Phyllocladus Rich. ex Mirb. (1825) is the only genus in the *Phyllocladacae*, and consists of 4 species.

Description Trees up to 20m in height, or shrubs. The flattened, leaf-like shoots (often called cladodes or phylloclades), are evergreen, simple or pinnate, with irregular wavy edges. Needle-like leaves are found only in seedlings. The male flowers are like reddish-brown, short catkins, bunched at the ends of short branches. Pollination is presumed to be by wind. The cones are small, with purple, red or white fleshy scales when ripe, the seeds surrounded by a cup-like structure. In *P. toatoa* Molloy, the celery pine, the blackberry-like fruits are formed on the lower half of the branchlets.

Key Recognition Features The leaf-like branchlets look quite unlike other conifers, indeed more like leaves of some *Proteaceae*, but the catkin-like flowers or cone-like fruit immediately show their true relationships.

Evolution and Relationships Related to *Podocarpus* (see p.21), but the leaf-like shoots are totally different. The surviving species are a small remnant of a formerly much larger family.

Ecology and Geography *Phyllocladus* species form forest trees or shrubs at high altitude, from the Phillipines and Borneo to New Guinea, Tasmania and New Zealand.

Comment The tree species are used for timber and a red dye is made by the Maoris from the bark of *P. trichomanoides* D. Don, the *tanekaha*.

Sciadopitys

A genus of one species, *Sciadopitys verticillata* (Thunb.) Sieb. & Zucc., (1842), the Japanese umbrella pine, is the only member of the family Sciadopityaceae.

Description *Sciadopitys* grows to 28m in height, around 10m after 30 years, with shoots growing roughly 30cm per year in cultivation. Young trees are narrowly pyramidal, but old trees in the wild are wide and rounded. The bark is reddish-brown. Each leaf is in reality 2 leaves fused together; they are like flat, soft pine needles, 10—14cm long, 3—4mm wide, in whorls in the axils of small, scale-like leaves, which are also scattered along the shoots. The male flowers are rounded, in dense clusters on small shoots, the females fewer, also on short shoots, produced in spring. Pollination is by wind. The cones are rounded, with the edges of the scales curving down when ripe.

Key Recognition Features The separate whorls of soft, wide leaves are unmistakable.

Evolution and Relationships An isolated and ancient genus, traditionally included in the family Taxodiaceae, and now put into its own family, the Sciadopityaceae, with several unique features.

Ecology and Geography In moist forest in the mountains of Japan; found wild in only a few localities in Honshu, Kyushu, and Shikoku, but often cultivated. Much more widespread in the Mesozoic.

Comment A beautiful, distinctive tree, easily cultivated in a moist, cool position, but intolerant of drought and dry atmosphere and often short-lived in cultivation. A good specimen tree for an island in a lake.

Sciadopitys verticillata
male flowers (left) and young cone
½ life size, March 10th

Sciadopitys verticillata
½ life size
March 10th

Sciadopitys verticillata
seed and unripe cone (left)
and ripe cone (right)
life size, March 10th

24

Fitzroya

Fitzroya Hooker fil. ex Lindley (1851). A genus of only one species, *F. cupressoides* (Molina) I.M.Johnst., the Alerce, from Chile and Argentina, in the family Cupressaceae.

Description A tree to 50m in height in the wild, generally with weeping branches when young. The leaves are arranged in groups of 3, scale-like, keeled, usually spreading, 2.5–3mm long. Male flowers are small, 6–8mm long, cone-like, with numerous ovate, overlapping scales, solitary on the ends of short shoots. Pollination is presumed to be wind. The cones are rounded, 6–8mm across, with 2 or 3 whorls of 3 scales, each with a distinct hook, spreading when ripe, solitary on the ends of short shoots. Seeds 2–3mm across, each with 2 or 3 wings.

Key Recognition Features *Fitzroya* is easily recognised by the alternating whorls of 3 spreading, scale-like leaves.

Evolution and Relationships An ancient species, closest perhaps to *Pilgerodendron* Florin, which grows in the same area.

Ecology and Geography Found mainly on the coast of southern Chile, where it formed extensive ancient forests, often with *Saxegothaea* (see p.22), *Pilgerodendron*, *Drimys* (see p.60), and *Desfontainia* Ruiz & Pavon. It is also found in alpine valleys in Chile and Argentina along the Andes at up to 1500m, often with *Nothofagus dombeyi* (see p.111), *Austrocedrus* Florin & Boutelje, and *Saxegothaea* (see p.22). These areas all have very high rainfall and poor soils.

Comment The name commemorates Captain Robert Fitz-Roy of the *Beagle,* on which Charles Darwin sailed. Fine specimens of *Fitzroya* are still alive, though much reduced in number; one at least is estimated to be 3600 years old. New trees are being grown from seed in Chile to replenish the forests. The timber is exceptionally durable, and though living trees are protected, trees that have died are still used for timber.

Fitzroya cupressoides
¾ life size
September 20th

Fitzroya cupressoides
old cones
just over life size
September 20th

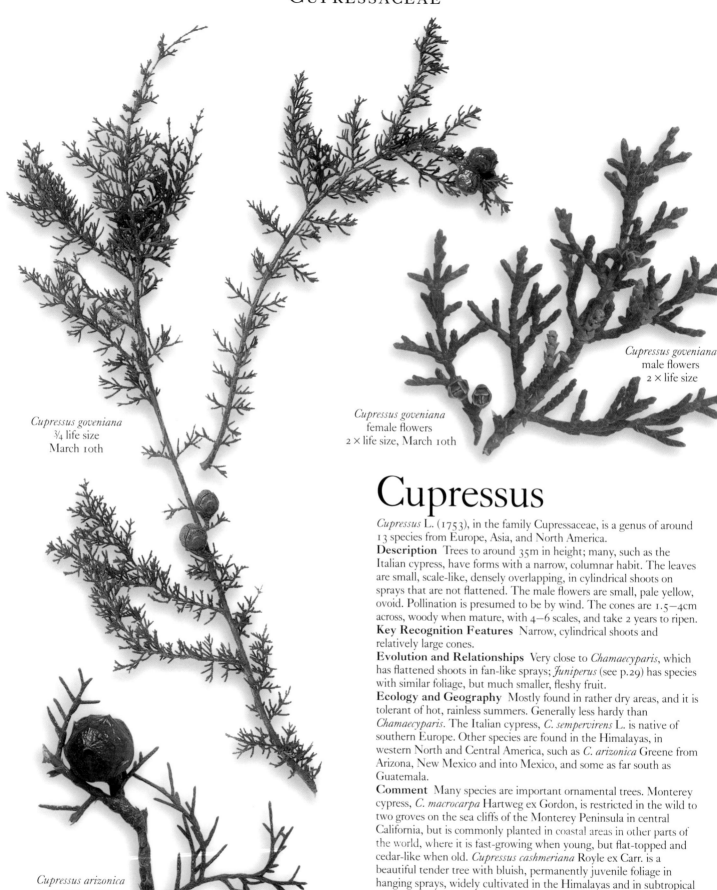

Cupressus goveniana
¾ life size
March 10th

Cupressus goveniana
female flowers
2 × life size, March 10th

Cupressus goveniana
male flowers
2 × life size

Cupressus arizonica
mature cone
just over life size
March 10th

Cupressus

Cupressus L. (1753), in the family Cupressaceae, is a genus of around 13 species from Europe, Asia, and North America.

Description Trees to around 35m in height; many, such as the Italian cypress, have forms with a narrow, columnar habit. The leaves are small, scale-like, densely overlapping, in cylindrical shoots on sprays that are not flattened. The male flowers are small, pale yellow, ovoid. Pollination is presumed to be by wind. The cones are 1.5–4cm across, woody when mature, with 4–6 scales, and take 2 years to ripen.

Key Recognition Features Narrow, cylindrical shoots and relatively large cones.

Evolution and Relationships Very close to *Chamaecyparis*, which has flattened shoots in fan-like sprays; *Juniperus* (see p.29) has species with similar foliage, but much smaller, fleshy fruit.

Ecology and Geography Mostly found in rather dry areas, and it is tolerant of hot, rainless summers. Generally less hardy than *Chamaecyparis*. The Italian cypress, *C. sempervirens* L. is native of southern Europe. Other species are found in the Himalayas, in western North and Central America, such as *C. arizonica* Greene from Arizona, New Mexico and into Mexico, and some as far south as Guatemala.

Comment Many species are important ornamental trees. Monterey cypress, *C. macrocarpa* Hartweg ex Gordon, is restricted in the wild to two groves on the sea cliffs of the Monterey Peninsula in central California, but is commonly planted in coastal areas in other parts of the world, where it is fast-growing when young, but flat-topped and cedar-like when old. *Cupressus cashmeriana* Royle ex Carr. is a beautiful tender tree with bluish, permanently juvenile foliage in hanging sprays, widely cultivated in the Himalayas and in subtropical gardens. In contrast, *C. dupreziana* A. Camus has survived in the now rainless mountains of the Tassili plateau in the Sahara by rooting deeply into groundwater under the dry wadis.

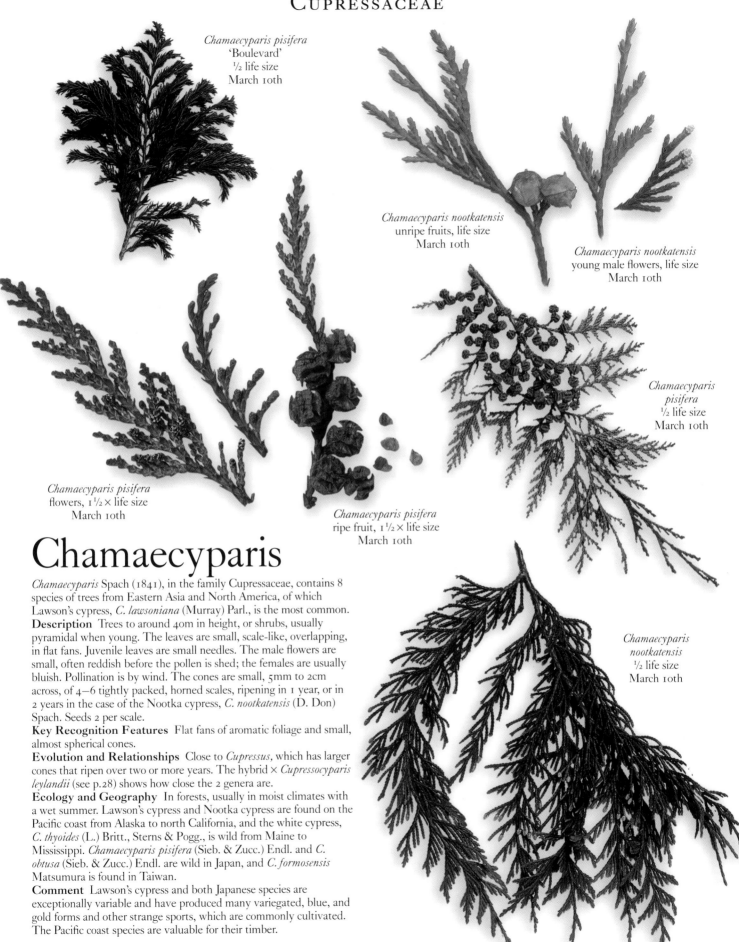

Chamaecyparis pisifera
'Boulevard'
½ life size
March 10th

Chamaecyparis nootkatensis
unripe fruits, life size
March 10th

Chamaecyparis nootkatensis
young male flowers, life size
March 10th

*Chamaecyparis
pisifera*
½ life size
March 10th

Chamaecyparis pisifera
flowers, 1½ × life size
March 10th

Chamaecyparis pisifera
ripe fruit, 1½ × life size
March 10th

*Chamaecyparis
nootkatensis*
½ life size
March 10th

Chamaecyparis

Chamaecyparis Spach (1841), in the family Cupressaceae, contains 8 species of trees from Eastern Asia and North America, of which Lawson's cypress, *C. lawsoniana* (Murray) Parl., is the most common.
Description Trees to around 40m in height, or shrubs, usually pyramidal when young. The leaves are small, scale-like, overlapping, in flat fans. Juvenile leaves are small needles. The male flowers are small, often reddish before the pollen is shed; the females are usually bluish. Pollination is by wind. The cones are small, 5mm to 2cm across, of 4–6 tightly packed, horned scales, ripening in 1 year, or in 2 years in the case of the Nootka cypress, *C. nootkatensis* (D. Don) Spach. Seeds 2 per scale.
Key Recognition Features Flat fans of aromatic foliage and small, almost spherical cones.
Evolution and Relationships Close to *Cupressus,* which has larger cones that ripen over two or more years. The hybrid × *Cupressocyparis leylandii* (see p.28) shows how close the 2 genera are.
Ecology and Geography In forests, usually in moist climates with a wet summer. Lawson's cypress and Nootka cypress are found on the Pacific coast from Alaska to north California, and the white cypress, *C. thyoides* (L.) Britt., Sterns & Pogg., is wild from Maine to Mississippi. *Chamaecyparis pisifera* (Sieb. & Zucc.) Endl. and *C. obtusa* (Sieb. & Zucc.) Endl. are wild in Japan, and *C. formosensis* Matsumura is found in Taiwan.
Comment Lawson's cypress and both Japanese species are exceptionally variable and have produced many variegated, blue, and gold forms and other strange sports, which are commonly cultivated. The Pacific coast species are valuable for their timber.

× *Cupressocyparis leylandii*
ripe fruits, 2 × life size
April 19th

× *Cupressocyparis leylandii*
female flowers
life size, April 19th

× *Cupressocyparis leylandii*
¹/₂ life size
April 19th

× Cupressocyparis

× *Cupressocyparis* Dallim. (1938) is the name given to hybrids between *Cupressus* (see p.26) and *Chamaecyparis* (see p.27), which first arose in cultivation in England in 1888. × *Cupressocyparis leylandii* (Dallim. & Jackson), Leyland cypress, is the most common of them.

Description Trees to around 30m in height, very fast growing, reaching 20m in 25 years, tall and narrow in shape, remaining green to the ground. The leaves are small, scale-like, and overlapping. The male flowers are small and yellow, usually found on × *Cupressocyparis leylandii* 'Leighton Green'. Pollination is by wind. The cones are spherical, 1–2cm across, dark brown, most common on 'Leighton Green', with around 8 scales. Seeds 5 per scale.

Key Recognition Features Very similar to *Chamaecyparis*, but more slender and less pyramidal with longer, narrower fans of less flattened foliage.

Evolution and Relationships Dallimore grew the original trees of × *Cupressocyparis leylandii* from cones of Nootka cypress, *Cupressus nootkatensis*, picked at Leighton Park near Welshpool, which then belonged to Mr Naylor. They were recognised as hybrids with Monterey cypress, *Cupressus macrocarpa*, only in 1925, 33 years after they had been planted at Haggerston Hall, the property of C. J. Leyland. 'Stapehill' has *Cupressus macrocarpa* as seed parent, and other hybrids have been formed using *Cupressus glabra* and *Cupressus lusitanica*.

Ecology and Geography Though both parents originate in western North America, they do not grow together in the wild.

Comment One of the fastest-growing of all conifers, easily grown from cuttings and commonly planted as a hedge or screen. Neighbours have fought over Leyland hedges which may be shelter for one, total shade for the other. Bossy politicians have even proposed that their planting be banned. Hedges can be kept in check by twice-yearly cutting of the new growth. The clone 'Castlewellan' is commonly planted and is golden in summer, brownish in winter.

Juniperus chinensis
female flower
life size
April 19th

Juniperus scopularia
'Blue Arrow'
just under
life size
April 1st

Juniperus virginiana
'Grey Owl'
¹/₂ life size, March 10th

Juniperus

Juniperus L. (1753), in the family Cupressaceae, contains around 60 species from the northern hemisphere southwards to tropical Africa.

Description Trees to around 30m in height, but usually less, and often prostrate shrubs. The leaves are either needle-like, whorled, and spreading, or scale-like, in 4 ranks, and appressed to the shoot as in a *Cupressus* (see p.26). The male flowers are small and cone-like, usually on separate trees from the females. Pollination is by wind. The cones are of 3–8 scales, which fuse and become fleshy when ripe. In most species they are purple or blackish, and less than 1cm across, but in some species are larger and reddish-brown when ripe. Unlike most conifer fruits, these are eaten by birds. Seeds 1–3 per scale.

Key Recognition Features The fleshy, berry-like cones and often also the whorled, needle-like leaves.

Evolution and Relationships In *Microbiota* the cones begin fleshy but break up at maturity. Foliage like both juvenile and adult *Cupressus* is found in the genus.

Ecology and Geography Habitats vary from cold, acid, subarctic mountains to hot, dry hills and warm, wet, mountain forests. Species are found wild from Siberia and Scotland to Mexico, at 5100m on Mount Everest, and in the mountains of tropical Africa.

Comment Many species are planted as ornamentals, particularly as dwarf or prostrate evergreens for ground cover. Fruits of *J. communis* L. are used to flavour venison and gin. In *J. drupacea* Labill., from Greece, Turkey, and Syria, the large, blackish fruit, to 2.5cm across, is edible. *Juniperus virginiana* L., the eastern red cedar, is commonly seen along hedgerows in the eastern United States; its scented wood is used for pencils and cedarwood chests.

Juniperus communis fruits, ¾ life size September 20th

Juniperus rigida male flowers life size April 19th

Juniperus chinensis 'Keetelerii' ½ life size March 10th

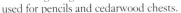

Juniperus chinensis 'Variegata' juvenile and adult foliage in white and green life size, March 10th

Microbiota

Microbiota Komarov (1923) is a genus of one species, *M. decussata* Kom., from Siberia, in the family *Cupressaceae*.

Description A shrub with prostrate branches to around 2m across, to 50cm in height. The leaves are arranged in opposite pairs, scale-like, incurved, around 3mm long, scented when crushed. The fans of foliage are held horizontally or curve downwards, and are often purplish in cold weather. The male flowers are small, ovoid, at the tips of the branchlets. Pollination is presumed to be by wind. The cones are berry-like when young, to 5mm long, 4mm across, with 4 fleshy scales that separate when ripe, and a single dark brown, shiny seed.

Key Recognition Features A spreading or prostrate, bright green, juniper-like shrub.

Evolution and Relationships Close to *Juniperus*, but distinct in its small cone which breaks up when ripe.

Ecology and Geography In exposed places on high mountains in southeastern Siberia.

Comment A recent introduction, now widely cultivated and popular for ground cover. It is very hardy and easily grown from cuttings.

Microbiota decussata with brown winter foliage, life size March 6th

Widddringtonia

Widddringtonia Endl. (1842) contains 4 species from southern Africa, in the family Cupressaceae.

Description Trees to around 30m in height, or shrubs. Upright, bushy, and pyramidal when young, but becoming flat-topped and cedar-like as old trees. The leaves are very small, alternate, scale-like, incurved, around 1.5mm long. The fans of foliage are dark green and rather lax. In the juvenile state the leaves are spirally arranged, needle-like, and spreading. The male flowers are small, 2—3mm long, at the tips of short, lateral branchlets. Pollination is presumed to be by wind. The cones are solitary or clustered, globular, woody when ripe, with 4 scales in 1 whorl and 5—10 winged seeds.

Key Recognition Features The loose fans of foliage and the 4 scales of the cone are characteristic.

Evolution and Relationships Close to *Callitris* from Australia and Tasmania, which has woody cones with 6 scales in 2 whorls.

Ecology and Geography Widddringtonias are found in mountain valleys. In montane forest in South Africa, *W. cedarbergensis* J. Marsh, the Clanwilliam cedar, grows in the Cedarberg, and *W. cupressoides* (L.) Endl. in the Drakensberg. In Malawi, on the high plateau of Mlanje Mountain, are the remnants of great forests of Mlanje cedar, *W. whytei* Rendle.

Comment The Mlanje cedars are exploited for their excellent timber: hard, scented, and exceptionally resistant to rot even in tropical conditions. Many of the largest trees in the wild are now dead or dying, and festooned with lichens, ferns, and *Streptocarpus* (see Volume 2), but plantations have been started in Malawi and Kenya.

Callitris

Callitris Vent. (1808) is a genus of 15 species from Australia and New Caledonia, usually called cypress pine, in the family Cupressaceae.

Description Trees to around 30m in height, or shrubs. Usually bushy and pyramidal when young, but becoming spreading as old trees. The leaves are very small, in whorls of 3, scale-like, incurved, around 1.5mm long. In the juvenile state the leaves are whorled, needle-like, and spreading, often bright green or glaucous. The male flowers are small, 2—3mm long, at the tips of the branchlets. Pollination is presumed to be by wind. The cones ripen in 1—2 years. They are solitary or tightly clustered, woody when ripe, 1.5—3cm across, usually globular with 6 scales (occasionally 4 or 8), often of 2 sides in whorls. The seeds are winged.

Key Recognition Features The 3-sided scale-leaves in a whorl and 6 scales of the cone are characteristic.

Evolution and Relationships Close to *Widddringtonia* in South Africa, but that has cones with 4 scales, and also to *Fitzroya* (see p.25) from South America, which has smaller cones with 6—9 scales in whorls of 3.

Ecology and Geography Most species are from dry, inland areas of Australia; *C. macleayana* (F. Muell.) F. Meull. is from the rainforest in New South Wales, and is probably the hardiest. Two species are also found in New Caledonia, a remarkable refuge of coniferous genera, and *C. rhomboidea* R. Br. ex Rich is widespread in eastern Australia.

Comment Many species are tolerant of drought, and are very useful garden trees and shrubs in Australia. The seeds keep their viability for several years under normal conditions. The timber of some species, notably *C. columellaris* F. Muell., is fragrant and resistant to termites.

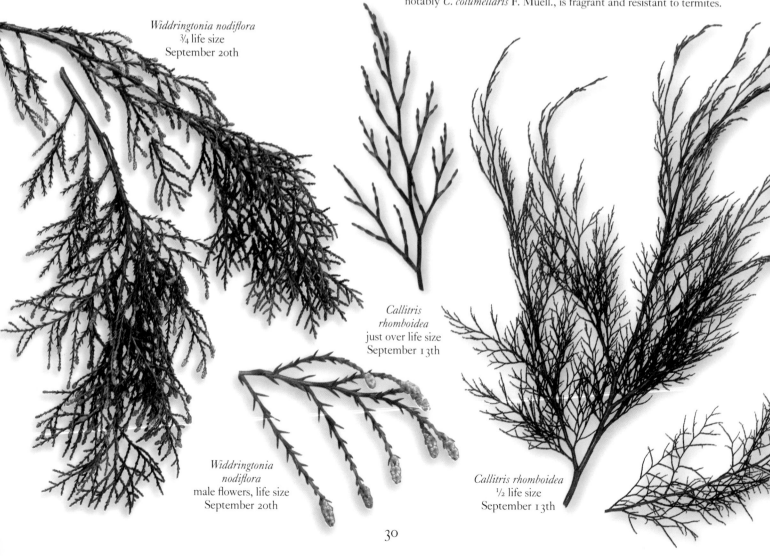

Widddringtonia nodiflora
¾ life size
September 20th

Callitris rhomboidea
just over life size
September 13th

Widddringtonia nodiflora
male flowers, life size
September 20th

Callitris rhomboidea
½ life size
September 13th

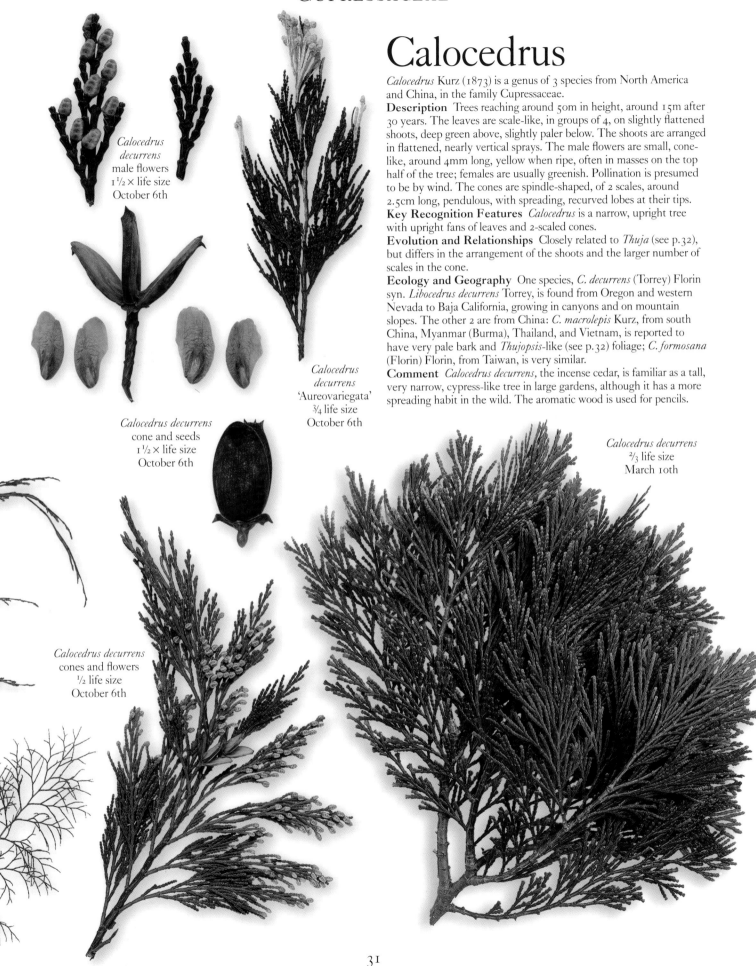

Calocedrus

Calocedrus Kurz (1873) is a genus of 3 species from North America and China, in the family Cupressaceae.

Description Trees reaching around 50m in height, around 15m after 30 years. The leaves are scale-like, in groups of 4, on slightly flattened shoots, deep green above, slightly paler below. The shoots are arranged in flattened, nearly vertical sprays. The male flowers are small, cone-like, around 4mm long, yellow when ripe, often in masses on the top half of the tree; females are usually greenish. Pollination is presumed to be by wind. The cones are spindle-shaped, of 2 scales, around 2.5cm long, pendulous, with spreading, recurved lobes at their tips.

Key Recognition Features *Calocedrus* is a narrow, upright tree with upright fans of leaves and 2-scaled cones.

Evolution and Relationships Closely related to *Thuja* (see p.32), but differs in the arrangement of the shoots and the larger number of scales in the cone.

Ecology and Geography One species, *C. decurrens* (Torrey) Florin syn. *Libocedrus decurrens* Torrey, is found from Oregon and western Nevada to Baja California, growing in canyons and on mountain slopes. The other 2 are from China: *C. macrolepis* Kurz, from south China, Myanmar (Burma), Thailand, and Vietnam, is reported to have very pale bark and *Thujopsis*-like (see p.32) foliage; *C. formosana* (Florin) Florin, from Taiwan, is very similar.

Comment *Calocedrus decurrens*, the incense cedar, is familiar as a tall, very narrow, cypress-like tree in large gardens, although it has a more spreading habit in the wild. The aromatic wood is used for pencils.

Calocedrus decurrens male flowers 1½ × life size October 6th

Calocedrus decurrens cone and seeds 1½ × life size October 6th

Calocedrus decurrens 'Aureovariegata' ¾ life size October 6th

Calocedrus decurrens cones and flowers ½ life size October 6th

Calocedrus decurrens ⅔ life size March 10th

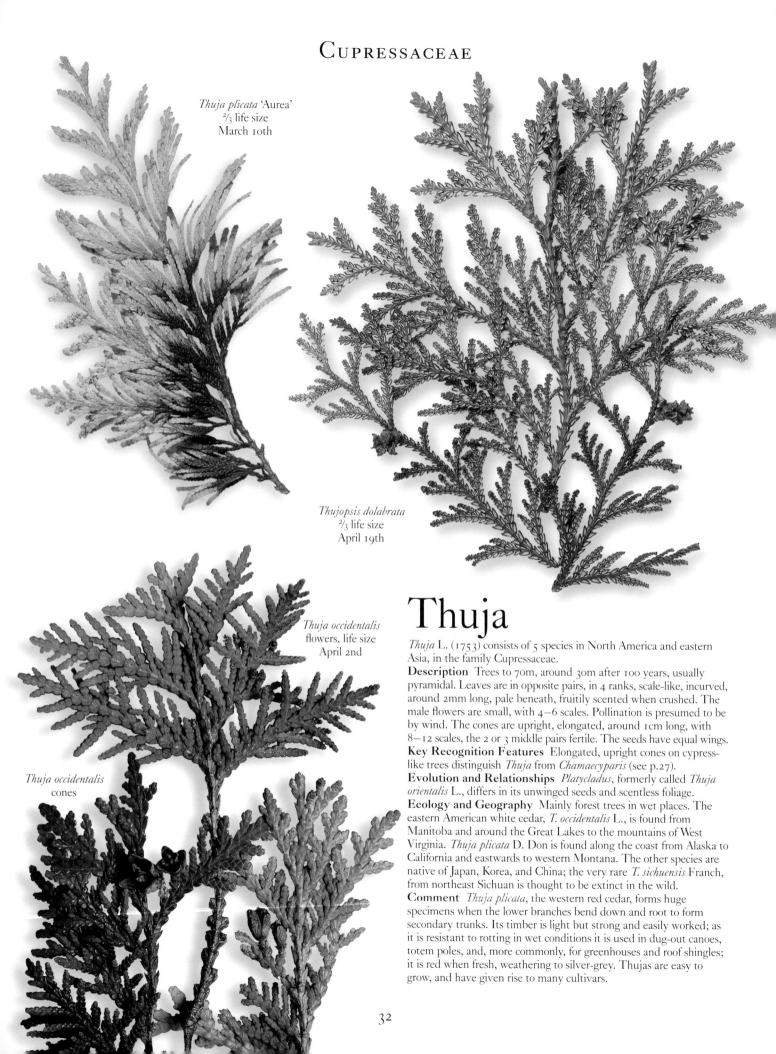

Thuja plicata 'Aurea'
²/₃ life size
March 10th

Thujopsis dolabrata
²/₃ life size
April 19th

Thuja occidentalis
flowers, life size
April 2nd

Thuja occidentalis
cones

Thuja

Thuja L. (1753) consists of 5 species in North America and eastern Asia, in the family Cupressaceae.

Description Trees to 70m, around 30m after 100 years, usually pyramidal. Leaves are in opposite pairs, in 4 ranks, scale-like, incurved, around 2mm long, pale beneath, fruitily scented when crushed. The male flowers are small, with 4–6 scales. Pollination is presumed to be by wind. The cones are upright, elongated, around 1cm long, with 8–12 scales, the 2 or 3 middle pairs fertile. The seeds have equal wings.

Key Recognition Features Elongated, upright cones on cypress-like trees distinguish *Thuja* from *Chamaecyparis* (see p.27).

Evolution and Relationships *Platycladus*, formerly called *Thuja orientalis* L., differs in its unwinged seeds and scentless foliage.

Ecology and Geography Mainly forest trees in wet places. The eastern American white cedar, *T. occidentalis* L., is found from Manitoba and around the Great Lakes to the mountains of West Virginia. *Thuja plicata* D. Don is found along the coast from Alaska to California and eastwards to western Montana. The other species are native of Japan, Korea, and China; the very rare *T. sichuensis* Franch, from northeast Sichuan is thought to be extinct in the wild.

Comment *Thuja plicata*, the western red cedar, forms huge specimens when the lower branches bend down and root to form secondary trunks. Its timber is light but strong and easily worked; as it is resistant to rotting in wet conditions it is used in dug-out canoes, totem poles, and, more commonly, for greenhouses and roof shingles; it is red when fresh, weathering to silver-grey. Thujas are easy to grow, and have given rise to many cultivars.

Thujopsis

Thujopsis Sieb. & Zucc. ex Endl. (1842), in the Cupressaceae, is a genus of only 1 species, *T. dolabrata* (L. fil.) Sieb. & Zucc.

Description The trees reach 40m in height in the wild, with horizontal branches arching downwards. In cultivation in Europe trees have reached around 15m after 50 years; young plants grow even more slowly and usually form many-stemmed shrubs. The leaves are scale-like, arranged in opposite pairs, in 4 ranks, the tips spreading or straight, the larger 4–6mm long, with distinct white patches beneath, on strongly flattened shoots. The male flowers are small, ovoid, blackish, on the tips of small side shoots; females are bluish-grey, in separate clusters on the same plant. Pollination is presumed to be by wind. The cones are 1–2cm long, bluish-green when fresh, ovoid, with 8–10 scales.

Key Recognition Features The very flat shoots with distinct white patches beneath on a spreading shrub, leafy to the ground.

Evolution and Relationships Close to *Thuja*, but differing in the much thicker, flatter shoots and larger scale-leaves.

Ecology and Geography In moist woods in the mountains in Japan, from southern Hokkaido to Kyushu. Those found from central Honshu to Hokkaido have smaller, denser foliage, and are called var. *hondai* Makino.

Comment An attractive ornamental, growing best in sheltered areas with high rainfall. A variety with a scattering of white shoots was often planted in old gardens. The timber is used for building and furniture-making in Japan.

Thujopsis dolabrata
underside of shoot
and old cone
just under life size
April 19th

Platycladus orientalis
old and young cones
just under life size
September 20th

Platycladus orientalis
²⁄₃ life size
September 20th

Platycladus

Platycladus Spach (1841) is a genus of only 1 species, *P. orientalis* (L.) Franco, still sometimes known as *Thuja orientalis* L. or *Biota orientalis* (L.) Endl., in the family Cupressaceae.

Description A tree to around 20m in height; around 10m, or often less, after 50 years. An upright bush when young, but more spreading as an old tree. The leaves are arranged in opposite pairs, in 4 ranks, scale-like, incurved, around 2mm long, scentless when crushed. The fans of foliage are held vertically, and are the same colour above and beneath. The male flowers are small, 2–3mm long, at the tips of the branchlets. Pollination is presumed to be by wind. The cones are blue-green when fresh, elongated, 2–2.5cm long, with 6–8 fleshy scales, each with a recurved horn. Seeds 5–7mm long, not winged.

Key Recognition Features The upright fans of foliage and the horned scales of the large cone are characteristic.

Evolution and Relationships Close to *Thuja*, in which it was formerly included, but distinct in cone and seed.

Ecology and Geography Long cultivated, and found apparently wild from central Asia to Japan, but probably native only in northeastern China, eastern Russia, and Korea.

Comment A sacred tree in China, commonly planted in cemeteries, including the imperial Ming tombs near Beijing, and in gardens. Long cultivated in Japan too. The slow-growing, upright young shrubs are frequently planted in Europe as ornamentals, and many dwarf and golden varieties are in cultivation.

Cryptomeria

Cryptomeria japonica (Thunb. ex L. fil) D. Don (1839), in the family Cupressaceae (formerly separated in Taxodiaceae), is the only species in the genus, sometimes called Japanese cedar, or *sugi* in Japanese.

Description Trees to around 65m; fast-growing, to around 20m in 50 years. Pyramidal when young, eventually a huge tree with buttressed roots and a rounded top and reddish-brown, stringy bark. The leaves are spirally arranged in 5 ranks, shining dark green, stiff, incurved or spreading at about 45 degrees to the shoot, with 4 bands of greyish stomata. The juvenile foliage of the cultivar 'Elegans' is soft, somewhat reflexed, and turns purple in winter. The male flowers are elongated, cone-like, to 1cm long, grouped near the tips of hanging twigs. Pollination is by wind. The cones are spherical, on short, scaly branches, 12mm to 2.5cm across, made up of around 20 spirally arranged scales, each with a single hook and 3–5 teeth, long and curved or short and straight, on the outside. Seeds 2–5 per scale, with 2 narrow, unequal wings.

Key Recognition Features An upright, loose-foliaged tree with spirally arranged leaves and almost leafy cones.

Evolution and Relationships Close to *Sequoiadendron* (see p.36), but that has smaller foliage and very different cones. *Taiwania* Hayata has similar but stiffer and bluer foliage, but elongated cones, closer to *Cunninghamia*.

Ecology and Geography Grows in moist forests in the mountains, perhaps native only in Japan, but widely cultivated in China since ancient times, and doubtfully native there; it is possibly wild in about 3 localities.

Comment The cultivar 'Elegans' is more common in cultivation than the proper tree, and forms large, floppy bushes with billowing masses of soft foliage, which go purple and brown in winter, appearing dead. The proper tree is widely grown for timber in Japan, with all the lower and middle branches removed to produce straight, knotless trunks. In the humid forests of Yakushima I have seen huge, ancient *sugi* with large trees of *Trochodendron* (see p.94) growing from and balancing their leaning trunks, while rhododendrons (see p.190), filmy ferns, and other epiphytes grow from their lower branches.

Cunninghamia

Cunninghamia R. Br. ex Rich. (1826) in the family Cupressaceae (formerly separated in Taxodiaceae), consists of 2 species from eastern Asia, with leaves like a soft, untidy monkey-puzzle (*Araucaria*, see p.19).

Description Trees to around 40m, fast-growing and straight in warm, wet climates, conical when young, with shredding, reddish-brown bark. The leaves are linear, flat, around 5cm long, tapering from the base to a point, with 2 pale bands beneath, in 2 uneven ranks. Short side branches are shed whole, giving the tree an untidy appearance. Male flowers are cylindrical, in tight bunches at the tips of branches. Pollination is by wind. The cones are rounded, to 4cm long; the numerous broad stiff scales have short, incurved, spiny tips.

Key Recognition Features The long, curved leaves on a rather dense tree, and the terminal rounded cones are characteristic. The branches of mature trees arch downwards.

Evolution and Relationships An ancient genus, known from Tertiary fossils in Europe.

Ecology and Geography *Cunninghamia lanceolata* (Lambert) Hook. is wild in forests in central and southeast mainland China, and commonly planted for forestry in other areas; *C. konishii* Hayata, with shorter leaves (2–4cm long), is found in Taiwan.

Comment Often seen in collections; though frost-tender when young, eventually makes a hardier tree. A fine specimen at Pencarrow, in Cornwall, was measured in 1980 and had reached 30m. 'Glauca' has bluish young leaves.

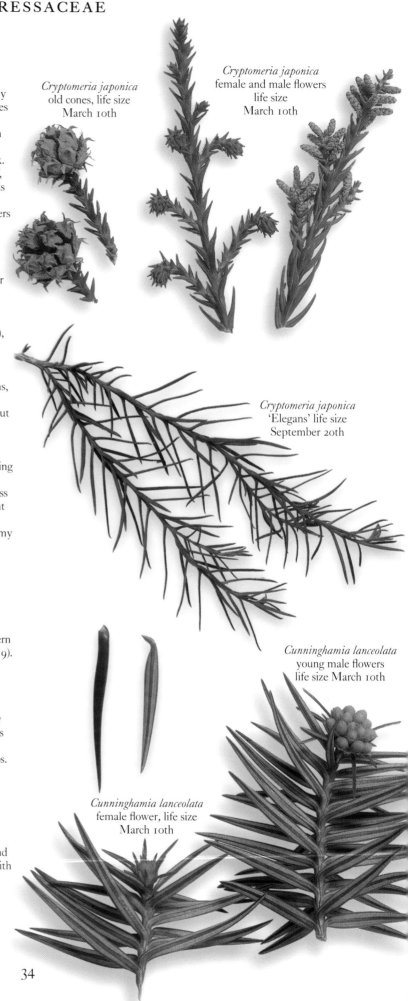

Cryptomeria japonica
old cones, life size
March 10th

Cryptomeria japonica
female and male flowers
life size
March 10th

Cryptomeria japonica
'Elegans' life size
September 20th

Cunninghamia lanceolata
young male flowers
life size March 10th

Cunninghamia lanceolata
female flower, life size
March 10th

Athrotaxis

Athrotaxis D. Don (1838), in the family Cupressaceae (though formerly separated in Taxodiaceae), contains 3 species from Tasmania, all called Tasmanian cedar.

Description Trees to around 40m in height, slow growing even when young, with shredding bark. The leaves range from scale-like and appressed to the cylindrical shoot in *A. cupressoides* D. Don to curved, needle-like, and somewhat spreading, 12mm long with white on the back in *A. selaginoides* D. Don. The male flowers are small, cone-like, and near the tips of the shoots. Pollination is presumed to be by wind. The cones are spherical, with 15–25 spine-tipped scales, 1–2.5cm across, open when mature. Seeds are oblong, 2-winged.

Key Recognition Features The spiky cones on foliage like that of *Cupressus* (see p.26) in *A. cupressoides*, *Sequioadendron* (see p.36) in *A. laxifolia* Hook., or *Cryptomeria* in *A. selaginoides*.

Evolution and Relationships The leaves resemble those of the 3 genera mentioned above, but the cones, which are quite like those of *Cryptomeria*, show the 3 species to be closer to one another.

Ecology and Geography The species range from the mountains for *A. cupressoides* to sea level for *A. selaginoides*, and are confined to Tasmania.

Comment These are rare plants in collections in Europe, where *A. laxifolia* grows better than the other two. *Athrotaxis selaginoides*, the King Billy pine, is exploited for timber in its native forests and is used for furniture and boats. Some specimens of *A. cupressoides* are reported to be over 1000 years old.

Athrotaxis laxifolia
old cone
$1\frac{1}{3}$ × life size

Cunninghamia lanceolata
cones, ½ life size
March 10th

Athrotaxis laxifolia
fruit, ⅓ life size
March 10th

Cunninghamia lanceolata
male flowers
½ life size
March 10th

Cunninghamia lanceolata
cone and seeds
life size, March 10th

Sequoiadendron

Sequoiadendron giganteum
male flowers
just under life size
March 10th

Sequoiadendron J. Buchholz (1939), in the family Cupressaceae (formerly separated in Taxodiaceae), has only 1 species, *S. giganteum* (Lindl.) J. Buchholz, called in America the giant sequoia, sierra redwood, or bigtree, and in England the Wellingtonia, a generic name coined by John Lindley in honour of the 1st Duke of Wellington.

Description Trees to around 90m, with huge trunks, the oldest speciemens over 1000 years old. In cultivation in Europe trees have reached 50m in around 110 years. The bark is reddish-brown, soft, and spongy. The leaves are narrow, 3–6mm long, incurved, and spirally arranged on the shoot. The male flowers are small, borne singly on the ends of short branchlets. Pollination is by wind. The cones are 5–8cm long, green, ripening to brown in the second year but persisting for up to 20 years, with numerous woody scales. Seeds have 2 unequal wings.

Key Recognition Features A very tall tree with a thick base and branchlets with incurved, narrow scale-like leaves.

Evolution and Relationships An isolated genus, close to *Sequoia*. but differing in its scale-like leaves and persistent cones, which stay green on the tree for several years; *Sequoiadendron* requires fire to regenerate from seed.

Ecology and Geography In coniferous forest on the western slopes of the Sierra Nevada in central California, at 900–2700m.

Comment The tallest specimens of *Sequoiadendron* have been cut down; one was recorded as 120m and 4000 years old, but the biggest alive now is "General Sherman", which is around 84m in height. The bark is about 60cm thick, which makes the trees invulnerable to fire. Trees are also exceptionally wind-resistant, but the tops are often killed by lightning, and sometimes the whole tree can explode after being hit.

*Sequoiadendron
giganteum*
1/3 life size
March 10th

Sequoiadendron giganteum
cones, life size
March 10th

Sequoia sempervirens
¹/₂ life size
March 10th

Sequoia sempervirens
a shred of bark
¹/₂ life size, March 10th

Sequoia sempervirens
young flowers and an
old cone
just under life size
March 10th

Sequoia

Sequoia Endl. (1847) in the family Cupressaceae (formerly separated in Taxodiaceae), is a genus of a single species, *S. sempervirens* (D. Don) Endl., the coast redwood from North America.

Description Trees to around 110m in height, and possibly 1000 years old, the tallest trees in the world, although some *Eucalyptus regnans* (see p.320) from Victoria have reached equal heights. In the extreme west of Europe trees have reached 40m in 100 years, and over 20m in 20 years. The bark is red, soft, and spongy. The leaves are evergreen, dark green above, pale beneath, in 2 rows on short shoots, 1–2.5cm long. The male flowers are small and terminal on short branchlets. Pollination is by wind. The cones are on the ends of short shoots, about 18mm long, with 15–20 spirally arranged scales, each with 5–7 ovules. Seeds have 2 wings.

Key Recognition Features The flat sprays of foliage and the very soft, spongy bark are typical.

Evolution and Relationships An ancient species, close to *Metasequoia* (see p.38) and *Sequoiadendron*. Unique among conifers in many characteristics: it is the only hexaploid, its mitochondrial DNA is paternally inherited, and the trees will resprout from cut stumps.

Ecology and Geography Found only on moist coastal hills in California, from Monterey northwards to Brookings in the extreme south of Oregon, usually below 300m. Its success here is thought to be due to the frequent sea fogs, which shroud the tree tops in thick mist, which condenses and effectively waters the trees.

Comment Almost as tall as *Sequoiadendron*, but more slender. Formerly much exploited for timber, but the largest trees are now preserved. The name commemorates Sequoyah, otherwise known as George Guess (c.1770–1843), the inventor and publisher of the Cherokee alphabet.

Metasequoia glyptostroboides
buds beneath the shoots
life size (trimmed)
September 10th

*Metasequoia
glyptostroboides*
old cones
1¼ × life size
December 15th

*Metasequoia
glyptostroboides*
½ life size
September 10th

*Metasequoia
glyptostroboides*
male buds
life size
December 15th

Metasequoia

Metasequoia Miki, in the family Cupressaceae (formerly separated in Taxodiaceae), was described from fossil material from Japan in 1941. Living specimens of its 1 remaining species, *M. glyptostroboides* Hu & Cheng, the dawn redwood, were discovered in China in 1945 and named in 1948.

Description Trees to around 45m, narrowly pyramidal when young, developing a wide, buttressed trunk in some climates. Fast growing when young, to 20m in 20 years. The leaves are flat and soft, opposite, on deciduous branchlets, which are formed in the axils of opposite buds. Each leaf is around 1.5cm long, green above and below. The male flowers are small, ovoid, around 3mm long, in pairs on drooping tassels, but not produced on young trees. Pollination is by wind. The cones are around 8mm long, with around 12 pairs of opposite scales, on the ends of short, leafy branches. Seeds 5mm, with 2 broad wings.

Key Recognition Features A *Taxodium*-like tree, recognised by the unique arrangement of the short shoots in the axils of opposite buds.

Evolution and Relationships Close to the evergreen redwood, *Sequoia sempervirens* (D. Don) Endl. (see p.37) in cone type. Other species of fossil *Metasequoia* have been found in deposits as early as the late Cretaceous, and from as far north as arctic Canada, so the living species is a true relict.

Ecology and Geography The dawn redwood grows in moist forests in ravines and by streams. It is known in the wild only in northwestern Hubei and northeastern Sichuan, but is now widely planted in China and in other temperate countries.

Comment An attractive and easily grown tree, which can be grown from both summer softwood and winter hardwood cuttings. The young leaves are susceptible to late frosts, but the trees soon recover. Autumn colour is a fine golden- or pinkish-brown. The Chinese name is *sui-sa*, meaning water spruce.

Taxodium distichum
½ life size
September 20th

Taxodium

Taxodium Rich. (1810), in the Cupressaceae (formerly separated in Taxodiaceae), is a genus of 1 species, *T. distichum* (L.) Rich., the bald or swamp cypress, from southeastern North America, Mexico, and Guatemala. The 3 varieties have been considered distinct species.

Description Trees to 50m, usually rather tall and narrow. Leaves are linear, around 1cm long, alternate, on deciduous branchlets, turning pinkish-brown, then reddish brown before falling. Male flowers are yellowish-green, elongated, in long tassels produced near the tops of the trees. Pollination is by wind. The cones are 1.5–4cm across, almost round, of few scales, each with 2 ovules. Seeds have unequal wings.

Key Recognition Features The soft, pale green leaves show this to be deciduous; the alternate leaves and buds in the axils of the branchlets distinguish it from the superficially similar *Metasequoia*.

Evolution and Relationships An ancient genus that has survived in the warmer parts of North America, but not in Asia.

Ecology and Geography In swamps, by rivers and lakes from Delaware southwards to Florida and Texas; var. *distichum* is the most common; var. *imbricatum* (Nutt.) Croom is found only from the coast of North Carolina to Florida; var. *mexicanum* (Carr.) Gord., syn. *T. mucronatum* Ten., extends from central Mexico to Guatemala and possibly southern Texas. *Taxodium ascendens* and *T. nutans* are synonyms of var. *imbricatum*.

Comment The roots often produce "knees", woody protuberances that stand up to 1m above soil level. These help them "breathe", and are especially common in wet areas; they are a feature of the Florida Everglades. Once established, this is a very hardy tree, both healthy and long-lived, surviving well in areas as different as southwest England and the Mediterranean. The famous tree in Santa Maria del Tule, near Oaxaca in Mexico, has the largest girth of any known tree, measured at 35.8m in 1982; the first mention of it was published in Seville in 1590, and even then it was said to have been much reduced in size by a lightning strike.

Taxodium distichum
cones
just under life size
September 20th

Taxodium distichum
just over life size
September 20th

Taxodium distichum
male flowers
life size
April 19th

Larix

Larix Mill. (1754), the larch, is a genus in the family Pinaceae, with 11 species found throughout the colder parts of the northern hemisphere.

Description Trees to 65m, pyramidal and fast-growing when young, regularly growing over 1m per year for 30 years. The leaves are 3–5cm long, deciduous, needle-like, bright green or greyish, with white bands beneath, in whorls on short shoots on the older branches and scattered on leading shoots. Autumn colour is a beautiful orange-yellow. The male flowers are small and often yellow, the females usually red; they are produced in early spring, before the leaves emerge on the long, hanging shoots. Pollination is by wind. The cones are generally small, with rounded scales, 3–4cm long, but to 8.5cm with exserted and reflexing pointed bracts in *L. griffithii* Hook. fil. Seeds have long wings.

Key Recognition Features The deciduous leaves in whorls and small cones are typical of larches. Bare twigs are pinkish, yellow-brown, or soft orange in winter.

Evolution and Relationships Similar in many characteristics to *Cedrus* (see p.43), but that is evergreen and has larger cones. *Pseudolarix* (see p.42) is closely allied, and is also deciduous, but has open, upright cones.

Ecology and Geography On mountain slopes and in northern bogs. The tamarack, *L. laricina* (Du Roi) K. Koch, is found all across North America from Newfoundland to Alaska. Other species are found in the Alps, in Siberia, and in the eastern Himalayas.

Comment Larch is valuable for timber, and commonly planted. Its wood is resistant to decay and especially valuable for building boats. It is also used for production of turpentine, and the bark is used in tanning. The hybrid between the European *L. decidua* Mill. and the Japanese *L. kaempferi* (Lamb.) Carr., now called *L. × marschlinsii* Coaz (formerly *L. × eurolepis* Henry) shows hybrid vigour and is often planted for quick shelter.

Larix × marshlinsii
male (left) and female flowers
life size
March 10th

Larix × marshlinsii
female flower and old cones
life size
March 10th

Larix gmelinii
¾ life size
March 10th

Pseudolarix amabilis
¾ life size
autumn colour, October 5th
(see p.42 for text and flowers)

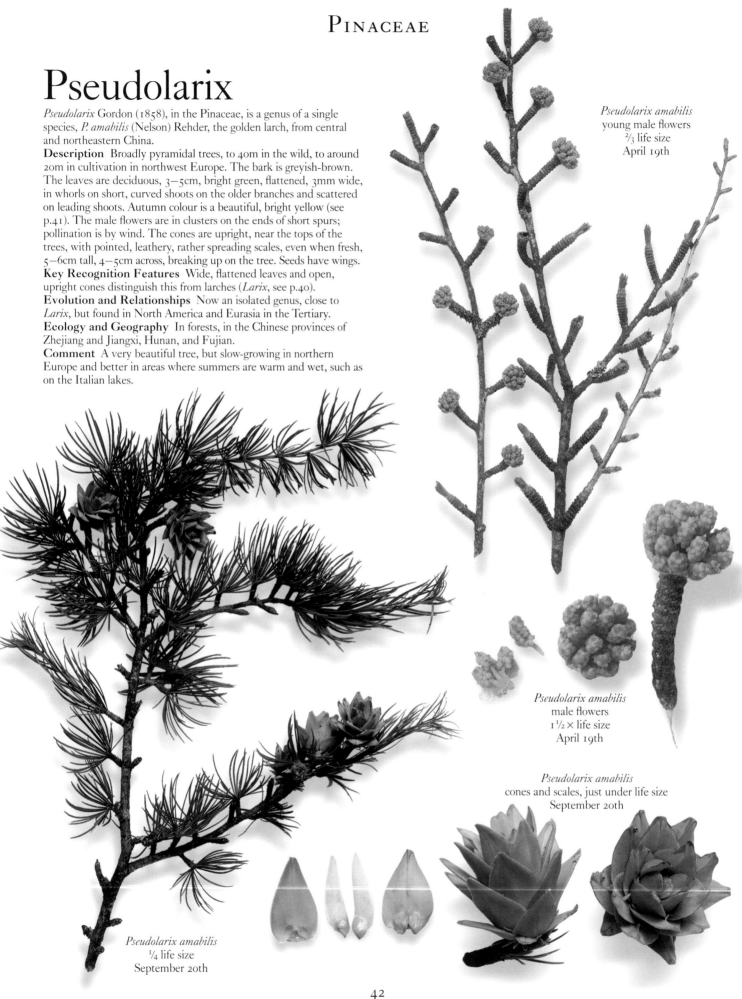

Pseudolarix

Pseudolarix Gordon (1858), in the Pinaceae, is a genus of a single species, *P. amabilis* (Nelson) Rehder, the golden larch, from central and northeastern China.

Description Broadly pyramidal trees, to 40m in the wild, to around 20m in cultivation in northwest Europe. The bark is greyish-brown. The leaves are deciduous, 3–5cm, bright green, flattened, 3mm wide, in whorls on short, curved shoots on the older branches and scattered on leading shoots. Autumn colour is a beautiful, bright yellow (see p.41). The male flowers are in clusters on the ends of short spurs; pollination is by wind. The cones are upright, near the tops of the trees, with pointed, leathery, rather spreading scales, even when fresh, 5–6cm tall, 4–5cm across, breaking up on the tree. Seeds have wings.

Key Recognition Features Wide, flattened leaves and open, upright cones distinguish this from larches (*Larix*, see p.40).

Evolution and Relationships Now an isolated genus, close to *Larix*, but found in North America and Eurasia in the Tertiary.

Ecology and Geography In forests, in the Chinese provinces of Zhejiang and Jiangxi, Hunan, and Fujian.

Comment A very beautiful tree, but slow-growing in northern Europe and better in areas where summers are warm and wet, such as on the Italian lakes.

Pseudolarix amabilis
young male flowers
²⁄₃ life size
April 19th

Pseudolarix amabilis
male flowers
1 ¹⁄₂ × life size
April 19th

Pseudolarix amabilis
cones and scales, just under life size
September 20th

Pseudolarix amabilis
¹⁄₄ life size
September 20th

Cedrus

Cedrus Trew (1755) in the family Pinaceae, the cedar, contains around
4 species or, according to some authorities, 1 species with 3 subspecies,
from around the Mediterranean and the western Himalayas.

Description Trees to 76m or more, usually pyramidal when young,
becoming typically flat-topped when old. Young trees of *C. deodara*
(Roxb.) D. Don grow around 1m per year in temperate climates, but
are faster in subtropical areas, where they are commonly planted. The
leaves are evergreen, needle-like, thin, in whorls 1–3.5cm long on
spur shoots. The male flowers are cone-like, upright on horizontal
branches, to 8.5cm long, opening in autumn. Pollination is by wind.
The cones are upright, rounded, to 12cm tall, of numerous thin,
rounded scales tightly pressed together, green, ripening to brown in
2–3 years and breaking up on the tree in summer. Seeds have wings.

Key Recognition Features The short, thin needles on short spurs
and large, rounded cones are typical.

Evolution and Relationships Close to *Pinus* (see pp.50–51), but
with thin-scaled cones.

Ecology and Geography Grows in mountain valleys and rocky
hillsides. *Cedrus atlantica* (Endl.) Carr., the Atlas cedar, is found in the
Atlas Mountains in Algeria and Morocco; *C. brevifolia* (Hook. fil.)
Henry is found in Cyprus; *C. deodara* (Roxb.) D. Don is found in the
Himalayas from eastern Afghanistan to Garwhal in northwestern
India. The cedar of Lebanon, *C. libani* A. Rich. is found from
southern Turkey at 1000–2000m, into northern Syria, as well as in
the famous forests in Lebanon, where some of the older specimens are
probably 2000 years old.

Comment Cedars of Lebanon are characteristic and beautiful trees
of old parks in Britain and Europe. The first specimens in England,
from seed brought from Aleppo by the Rev. Edward Pococke, were
planted at Childrey Rectory in Berkshire in 1646, but most large
specimens date from the 18th century. *Cedrus atlantica* 'Glauca', the
blue Atlas cedar, is a more recent introduction, planted since 1850 and
still very popular, reaching 20m in around 40 years. Cedar wood is a
rich reddish-brown, light, strongly scented, and resistant to rot.

Cedrus atlantica 'Glauca'
male flowers
1¾ × life size
September 20th

Cedrus atlantica 'Glauca'
female cone, ¾ life size
March 10th

Cedrus atlantica 'Glauca'
male flowers
½ life size
September 20th

Abies

Abies Mill. (1754), the fir, contains about 50 species from the northern hemisphere, in the family Pinaceae.

Description Trees to 80m, usually neat and narrowly pyramidal with stiff whorls of branches; many species are fast growing in good soils, reaching around 30m in 30 years. The leaves are evergreen, needle-like, usually spirally arranged but sometimes divided into 2 untidy ranks, with white lines of stomata beneath, mostly 2–5cm long. The foliage is often pleasantly aromatic. The male flowers are small, densely clustered on the shoots, and often red, blue, or purple; the females are generally green, sometimes purple. Pollination is by wind. The cones are upright, large, to 25cm high, usually high up, with rounded scales and often with exserted, pointed bracts, and breaking up on the tree. Seeds have wings.

Key Recognition Features The needles finally fall off leaving a smooth scar, rather than the peg-like scar left by the needles on *Picea* (see pp.48–49). The upright cones also contrast with the pendulous cones of *Picea*.

Evolution and Relationships A widespread genus, close to *Cedrus* (see p.43) in cone and *Picea* in leaf. Many species are reduced to small populations on isolated mountains in areas where the climate has become drier since the ice ages.

Ecology and Geography *Abies* usually grow on good soils in mountain forest, becoming stunted as they approach the top of the treeline. Several species are found in western North America and in China and Japan, fewer in Europe. Isolated species are *A. numidica* de Lannoy ex Carr., from Mount Babor in Algeria; *A. pinsapo* Boiss., from near Ronda in southern Spain; and perhaps the most rare, *A. nebrodensis* (Lojac.) Mattei from Sicily. *Abies bracteata* (D. Don) A. Poit., from the Santa Lucia mountains along the coast of southern California, has the longest leaves and distinctive long, exserted bracts with globules of resin.

Comment These are the finest trees of the Christmas-tree type, and regularly reach 30m in gardens. They are also often planted and harvested for timber. Many are very ornamental; *A. koreana* E.H. Wilson is an attractive dwarf, producing deep blue cones in profusion. *Abies concolor* (Gordon) Lindl. ex Hildebr. has distinctive, rather sparse foliage, with needles grey on both sides.

Abies cephalonica
male flowers
2/3 life size
April 19th

Abies pinsapo
1/2 life size
October 6th

Abies numidica
cone, 3/4 life size
September 20th

Abies delavayi var.
forrestii cone
1/2 life size
February 20th

PINACEAE

Abies koreana
young female cones
²⁄₃ life size, April 6th

Abies koreana
male flowers
²⁄₃ life size
April 6th

Abies koreana
male (left) and female
(right) flowers
1 ¹⁄₃ × life size
April 6th

Abies grandis
male flowers, ³⁄₄ life size
April 19th

Abies twig,
showing
smooth surface
after the
needles have
fallen
1 ¹⁄₃ × life size

45

Pseudotsuga menziesii
cone, just over life size
March 10th

Pseudotsuga menziesii
²/₃ life size
March 10th

Pseudotsuga japonica
male flowers
just under life size
April 19th

Pseudotsuga macrocarpa
female flowers
just under life size
April 19th

*Pseudotsuga
japonica*
½ life size
April 19th

Pseudotsuga

Pseudotsuga Carr. (1867), in the family Pinaceae, consists of 4 species in western North America and eastern Asia. *Pseudotsuga menziesii* (Mirbel) Franco is the Douglas fir.

Description Trees to 100m, untidily pyramidal or spreading; fast growing when young, reaching 30m in 50 years. The bark is usually corky, very rugged, and reddish-brown. The leaves are evergreen, soft, needle-like, 1.5–3cm long, and separating smoothly from the twig as in *Abies* (see p.44). The male flowers are small, conical, often reddish when young, and produced singly or in small groups along the twig; females are pinkish-green and borne in clusters. Pollination is by wind. The cones are 7.5–12.5cm long, pendulous, with rather few, rounded scales and narrow, 3-pronged, protruding bracts. Seeds have wings.

Key Recognition Features An irregular and untidy tree with *Abies*-like foliage, but slender buds and very different cones.

Evolution and Relationships Close to *Abies* and *Tsuga*.

Ecology and Geography Grows in mixed and coniferous forest from near sea level to 3000m in the Rockies. Of the 2 species in North America, *P. menziesii* is widespread from British Columbia to Mexico, with var. *menziesii* found along the Pacific coast, var. *glauca* (Mayr) Franco in the Rockies; *P. macrocarpa* (Vasey) Mayr is found only in southern California, and has large cones, sometimes to 20cm long. The other species are rarely seen; *P. japonica* (Shir.) Beiss. is found in southeastern Japan.

Comment The name Douglas fir commemorates David Douglas (1799–1834) who introduced the tree to gardens in Europe. In 1832 David Don named it *Pinus douglasii*, not knowing that Mirbel had already published the name *Abies menziesii* in 1825. Archibald Menzies (1754–1842), the surgeon and naturalist on Captain Vancouver's expedition, discovered the tree in 1793, but Douglas was the first to send back seed in quantity, in 1827. Douglas fir is a fine, tall timber tree, much planted both in North America and in Europe; one that measured 127m in height was felled in 1895 near Vancouver, but no equally tall ones are known today.

Tsuga

Tsuga (Endl.) Carr. (1855), the hemlock, consists of around 10 species in North America and eastern Asia, in the family Pinaceae.

Description Trees to 50m, pyramidal with arching tops when young, eventually wide spreading. Western hemlock, *T. heterophylla* (Raf.) Sarg. is particularly fast-growing when young, sometimes reaching 20m in 20 years. The leaves are evergreen, flat, and blunt, with white bands beneath, 1–3cm long, mostly in 2 irregular rows on the shoot. The male flowers are small, often reddish, on the ends of branchlets. Pollination is by wind. The cones are small, ovoid, with few, rounded scales, to 2.5cm, but to 7cm in *T. mertensiana* (Bongard) Carr. Seeds have 1 long wing.

Key Recognition Features The short, flat needles of different lengths and small cones immediately identify all but *T. mertensiana*. That is recognised by its forward-pointing, blue-grey leaves and hanging shoots.

Evolution and Relationships Closest to *Picea* (see p.48) in many features. *Tsuga mertensiana* in particular has chemical as well as morphological features intermediate to *Picea*, and may possibly have originated as a hybrid between the two genera. It has been put in the genus *Hesperopeuce* (Englm.) Lemmon. but is now generally retained in *Tsuga*.

Ecology and Geography Usually found in moist forests, often on rocky slopes. Four species are found in North America, of which *T. canadensis* (L.) Carr. is common in the northeast, and *T. mertensiana* is found mainly in the mountains from Alaska to northern California. The other species are scattered from the Himalayas to Japan, but there are none in Europe or western Asia.

Comment The name hemlock is derived from the smell of the leaves, held to be similar to that of the very poisonous umbellifer, *Conium maculatum* (see Volume 2). However, tsugas are not poisonous, and a tea can be made from the leaves of *T. canadensis*. *Tsuga heterophylla* is particularly shade tolerant, and can be planted as an understorey in deciduous woods; it is a valuable timber tree in Canada, and the bark is used for tanning.

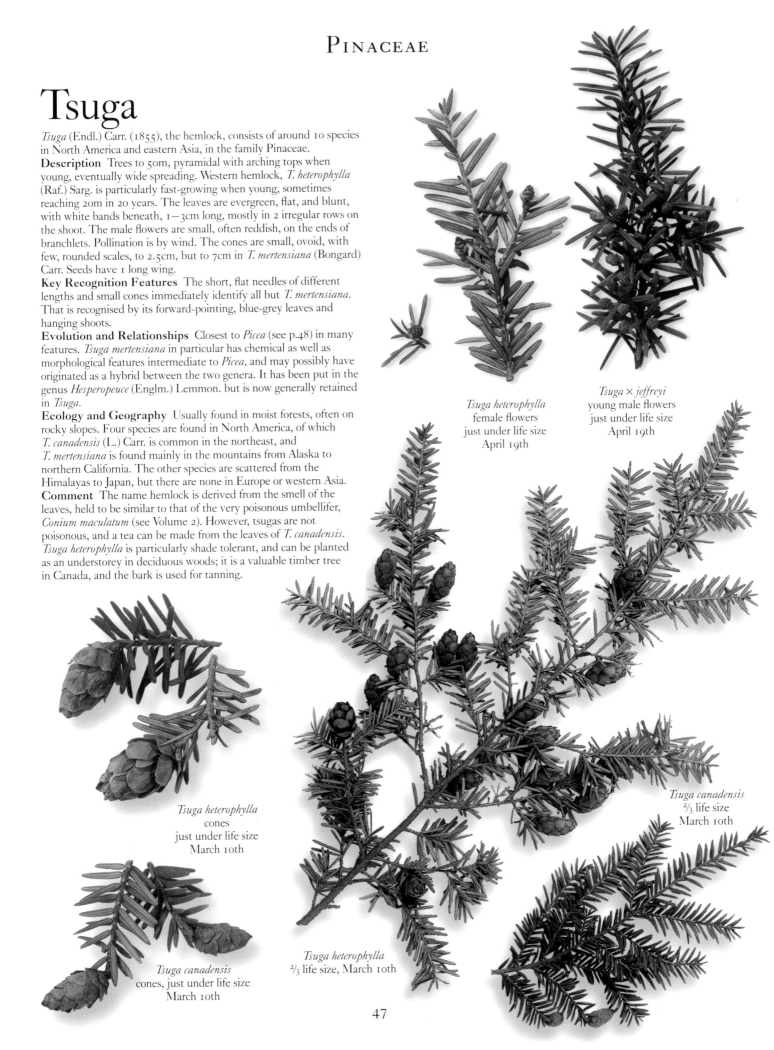

Tsuga heterophylla
female flowers
just under life size
April 19th

Tsuga × jeffreyi
young male flowers
just under life size
April 19th

Tsuga heterophylla
cones
just under life size
March 10th

Tsuga canadensis
²/₃ life size
March 10th

Tsuga canadensis
cones, just under life size
March 10th

Tsuga heterophylla
²/₃ life size, March 10th

Picea

Picea A. Dietr. (1824), the spruce, consists of about 35 species throughout the northern hemisphere, in the family Pinaceae.

Description Trees to 80m, usually narrowly pyramidal, and often with hanging branchlets. Fast growing, reaching 30m in 30 years. The leaves are evergreen, narrow, stiff, needle-like, spirally arranged, and mostly 1.5—3.5cm long. When they fall from the shoot they leave peg-like protuberances. Buds are 5—15mm long. The male flowers are elongated, at or near the ends of the branches, often red or purplish when young. The females are small cones. Pollination is by wind. The cones are pendulous, with numerous rounded or pointed, overlapping scales; they fall whole from the tree. They vary in length from around 15cm in the Norway spruce, *P. abies* (L.) Karst., to only around 3cm in the American red spruce, *P. rubens* Sarg. Seeds of all species have a single long wing.

Key Recognition Features The jingle "*Picea*, pegs, pendulous" is a reminder of the pegs left on the twig after the needles have fallen and the pendulous cones characteristic of the genus.

Evolution and Relationships *Tsuga* (see p.47) is close to *Picea* in having small, peg-like projections on the twig; *T. mertensiana* particularly so, with its narrow needles all round the shoot and relatively large cones. *Tsuga* differs, however, in having softer foliage and small buds, which are 1—3mm long.

Ecology and Geography *Picea* species are found mainly in montane forests near sea level in the far north. Eight species occur in North America, a few in Mexico and Europe, and several in China and the Himalayas.

Comment Most spruce are important as timber trees, and are commonly planted for quick-growing forestry for pulp and chipboard, as well as for Christmas trees. Some species are popular ornamentals, such as the blue spruce, *P. pungens* Englm., which originated in the southern Rockies from Wyoming to New Mexico, and *P. breweriana* S. Watson with its long, hanging side branches, which is found only in the Siskiyou Mountains on the border between California and Oregon.

Picea sitchensis
young female cones
life size
April 19th

Picea leaves and bare twig, showing pegs left after the leaves have fallen (*see Abies p.45*)

Picea orientalis
male flowers
just over life size
April 19th

Picea sitchensis
cone, 1⅓ × life size
November 15th

Picea likiangensis var.
montigena
leaves, April 19th

Picea likiangensis
var. *montigena*
flowers male (left) and
female (right)
just over life size
April 19th

Picea obvata
cones, life size
September 20th

Picea sitchensis
cones
¾ life size
September 20th

Picea polita
cone, life size
September 20th

Pinus

Pinus L. (1753), the pine, is the largest genus in the family Pinaceae, with around 100 species throughout the northern hemisphere.

Description Trees to 75m, broadly pyramidal when young, but mostly spreading when old; some species are only ever shrubs. *P. ponderosa* Dougl. ex Lawson can reach 72m, but at present the tallest specimens are of the sugar pine *P. lambertiana* Dougl., which is the tallest at 75m, with the longest cones to 50cm. The leaves are evergreen, needle-like, often stiff, 2–4cm long and solitary in *P. monophylla* Torr. & Frémont, but to 45cm long in *P. palustris* Mill.. Most species have leaves in bunches of 2, 3, or 5 on short shoots. The male flowers are in cone-like heads, usually clustered at the ends of the twigs, often reddish or purplish. Female flowers are small cones, usually red but occasionally green. Pollination is by wind. The cones are often very large, and are woody, of spirally arranged, narrow, overlapping scales, which often end in blunt teeth or claw-like hooks. Seeds sometimes with wings, sometimes nut-like and edible.

Key Recognition Features The long needles and woody cones make pines easy to distinguish from other conifers.

Evolution and Relationships A widespread and successful genus, closest to cedars, which however have shorter, thinner needles and thin-scaled cones that break up on the tree. Pines are generally divided into groups by the number of needles in the bunch, and by cone and seed type. The main groups are: 1. the white pines, which have 5 long, slender needles with 1 vascular bundle and soft, elongated cones, such as the North American *P. strobus* L. and the Himalayan *P. wallichiana* Jackson; 2. the Pinyon pines, such as *P. edulis* Engelm., which are usually shrubby and have 1–4 short needles and large, edible, nut-like seeds; 3. the rest of the genus have leaves in groups of 2 or 3, with 2 vascular bundles and ovoid cones, which are particularly large, hard, and viciously spiked in *P. coulteri* D. Don. Many of this group, such as *P. pinea* L., the Mediterranean umbrella pine, and *P. sabiniana* Dougl. ex D. Don, the digger pine from California, also have edible seeds.

Ecology and Geography Found in many habitats from moist mountain forests to coastal dunes, semi-deserts, and dry, rocky mountainsides. Pines range from Central America and the West Indies to Alaska, and in Asia from Siberia to Sumatra. They are particularly diverse in the southern United States and Mexico.

Comment *Pinus longaeva* D. K. Bailey, the intermountain bristlecone pine, is the longest-lived tree in the world; one in the White Mountains of Nevada is estimated to be 5000 years old, and by matching the rings with even older dead trees, a sequence going back over 8500 years has been established. Many species are used for turpentine, such as *P. pinaster* Ait. in Spain, and for medicines and flavourings, notably *P. halepensis*, used in retsina. Ponderosa pine, *P. ponderosa* Dougl. ex Lawson, is a very important timber tree in the western United States. Fire is important in the biology of some species: *P. palustris* has soft, short juvenile leaves and retains them until affected by fire, and the cones of *P. radiata* D. Don, Monterey pine, remain closed and keep the seeds viable for many years until they are released by the heat of a fire. The long, loose-leaved *P. patula* from Mexico and Nicaragua is widely planted in the tropics, particularly in southern Africa. The Scots pine, *P. sylvestris* L., is easily recognised by the foxy-red bark on its upper branches; it grows as far east as northeastern Turkey and eastern Siberia and is among the best for its durable timber.

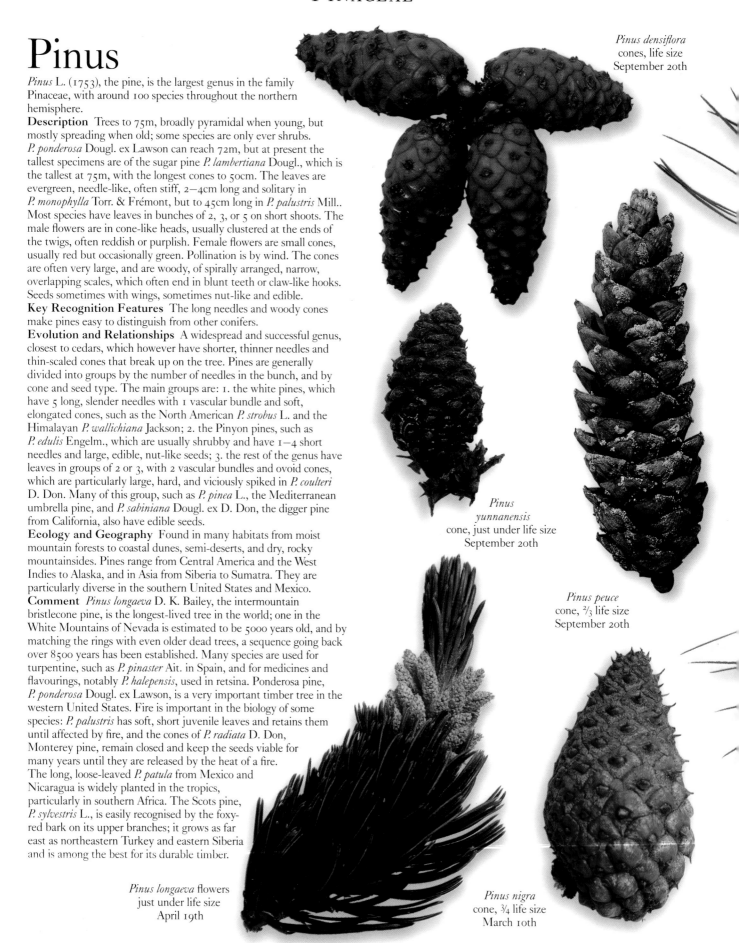

Pinus densiflora cones, life size September 20th

Pinus yunnanensis cone, just under life size September 20th

Pinus peuce cone, ⅔ life size September 20th

Pinus longaeva flowers just under life size April 19th

Pinus nigra cone, ¾ life size March 10th

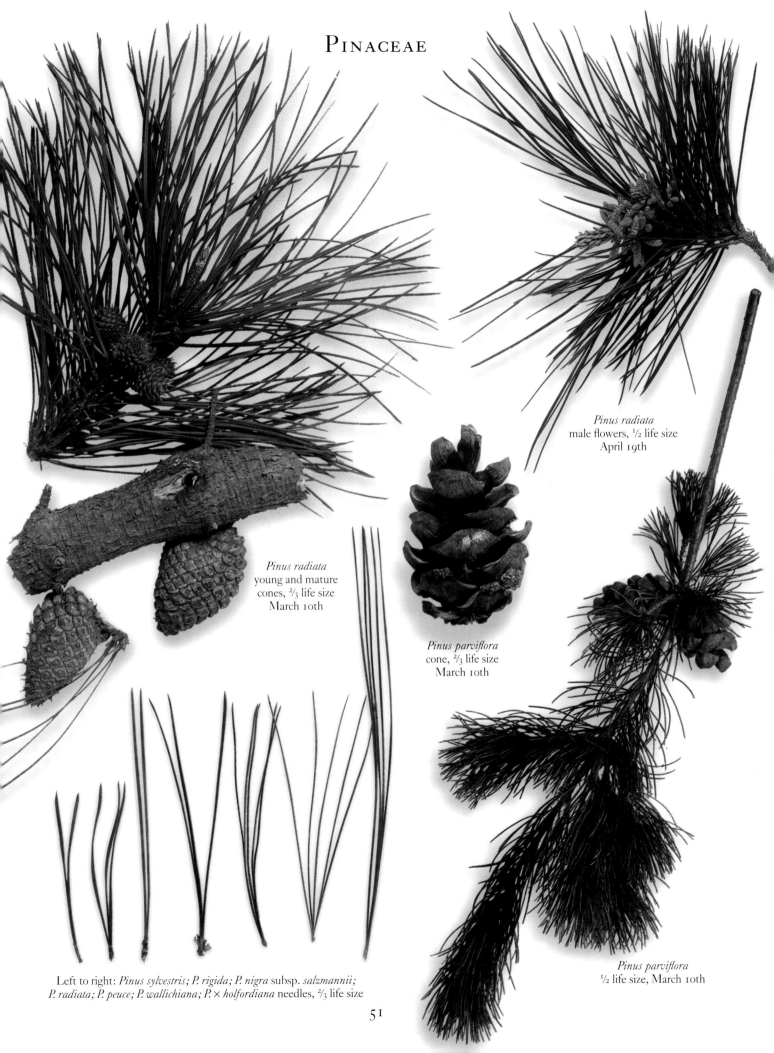

Pinus radiata
male flowers, ½ life size
April 19th

Pinus radiata
young and mature
cones, ⅔ life size
March 10th

Pinus parviflora
cone, ⅔ life size
March 10th

Pinus parviflora
½ life size, March 10th

Left to right: *Pinus sylvestris; P. rigida; P. nigra* subsp. *salzmannii;*
P. radiata; P. peuce; P. wallichiana; P. × *holfordiana* needles, ⅔ life size

Taxus

Taxus L. (1753) the yew, in the family Taxaceae, contains around 8 species in the northern hemisphere.

Description Trees to 26m, usually with wide-spreading branches. The leaves are evergreen, dark green above, paler beneath, flat, rather soft, and without a resin canal, 1–3mm wide, in 2 uneven rows on the sides of the twig. Yew leaves are particularly poisonous to horses and cattle, but regularly eaten by sheep and deer. The male flowers are small, around 4mm long, globular, and creamy yellow, opening in early spring. Females are small, green, near the tips of shoots, usually on separate trees. Pollination is by wind. The cones are single seeded, surrounded by a red, fleshy aril, which is sweet, sticky, and edible. The seeds are poisonous, 5–6mm long.

Key Recognition Features The flat, dark green, 2-ranked leaves are characteristic of most yews. *Torreya* differs in its much stiffer leaves. The red, fleshy fruit are found only in yews.

Evolution and Relationships The family Taxaceae contains 4 genera, one of which, *Austrotaxus* Compton, is confined to New Caledonia, a well-known repository for ancient conifers. *Pseudotaxus* W. C. Cheng, another relict, is found exclusively in southern China.

Ecology and Geography In forests and woods, sometimes as an understorey beneath deciduous trees, sometimes as pure stands. In North America *T. brevifolia* Nutt. is found on the west coast and *T. canadensis* Marshall in the northeast. A third, very rare species, *T. floridana* Nutt. ex Chapman is confined to the Apalachicola river in Florida. *Taxus globosa* Schlecht. is found in Mexico and Honduras. The European yew, *T. baccata* L. extends from western Ireland eastwards to Iran. The other species occur from the Himalayas to Japan and Sumatra, with one in Mexico.

Comment Ancient yews in Britain are nearly always found in old churchyards, and many are thought to pre-date the existing churches, and may even be Roman in origin, since they were used in Roman burial rites. The trunks of old yews are usually hollow, which makes them difficult to date accurately, but the famous tree at Fortingall in Perthshire is now thought to be 4000–5000 years old. The tree in Selborne churchyard in Hampshire was measured by Gilbert White (1720–93) in 1789 at 23ft (7m) in circumference. In 1987 it was 7.87m, before it was blown down in a gale in 1990. This increase of almost 90cm in 200 years suggests great age for the many ancient yew trees with girths of over 10m. Yew staves were used for English longbows, but most were imported from Spain, where yews grow faster and straighter; boxes of imported staves were found in the wreck of Henry VIII's flagship, the *Mary Rose*. Yew timber is now relatively rare, as it is not grown commercially, but has been used in table veneers and in small pieces in other furniture in England. Yew bark, especially from *T. brevifolia*, and the leaves *T. baccata* are sources of taxol, used with good effect to combat some cancers. Yews are often planted in gardens, especially for hedges and as specimens. Upright or Irish yews, both golden and green, are common; the original Irish yews were planted at Florence Court, County Fermanagh in 1778.

Taxus baccata
fruit of species and yellow-fruited form 'Lutea'
1 ¼ × life size, September 20th

Taxus baccata
male flowers
5 × life size

Taxus baccata
fruits, ½ life size
September 20th

Taxus baccata male flowers
1 ¼ × life size, February 20th

Torreya

Torreya Arn. (1838), in the family Taxaceae, contains around 6 species from North America, China, and Japan. Species are sometimes called California nutmeg or stinking cedar.

Description Trees to 35m, or shrubs. Young trees growing well can form a very wide-based pyramid. The leaves are evergreen, stiff, straight, with a central resin canal and 2 pale lines beneath, 1.5–8cm long, in rows on either side of the shoot. On good specimens the shoots can hang downwards. The male flowers are small, solitary, in the leaf axils; females are small and green. Pollination is by wind. The fruits are nut-like, usually single, green to purplish when fresh, with a leathery aril splitting to release the seed. Seeds are around 2.5–3.5cm long.

Key Recognition Features Stiff, yew-like leaves can belong to either *Torreya* or *Cephalotaxus* (see p.20), but in *Cephalotaxus* the leaves are curved and taper from near the base, while the leaves on *Torreya* are straight and parallel sided. Male flowers of *Cephalotaxus* are in tight bunches.

Evolution and Relationships An isolated genus, nearest to *Taxus*, but very different in fruit. Similarities to *Cephalotaxus* are superficial, as the male flowers, and females before they ripen, are very different.

Ecology and Geography In woods along streams and in canyons. *T. californica* Torr. is found in the coastal ranges and in the Sierra Nevada at up to 2000m. *T. taxifolia* Arnott is now very rare, found in Georgia and Florida, mainly along the Apalachicola river (as is *Taxus floridana*), and is endangered by a fungus disease. *T. nucifera* (L.) Siebold & Zucc. is common in the southern half of Japan, where it can form a large tree. *T. grandis* Fortune is found in eastern China, as is *T. jackii* Chun.

Comment The seeds of the Japanese *T. nucifera* are edible and used to produce cooking oil. It usually forms a tree, but there is a prostrate variety. *Torreya californica* is sometimes grown as an ornamental.

Torreya nucifera
fruit, just under life size
September 20th

Torreya californica
flowers, life size

Torreya californica
½ life size, April 19th

Ephedra equisetina
flower buds, life size
April 11th

Ephedra equisetina
just over life size
October 5th

Ephedra

Ephedra L. (1753), with around 60 species, is the only genus in the family Ephedraceae.

Description Wiry shrubs or climbers to 5m, but usually around 1m and spreading. The leaves are reduced to brown scales, which may form sheaths around the green, wiry stems. The male flowers are small, in dense spikes, with 2–8 strangely branching stamens. Pollination is by wind. The cones are solitary and yew-like (*Taxus*, see p.52) with yellow or red, fleshy inner bracts. Seeds are sometimes winged.

Key Recognition Features Wiry, horsetail-like shrubs with yellow, cone-like male flowers and yew-like fruit.

Evolution and Relationships Ephedraceae is a very isolated family, sometimes placed in the order Gnetales with two other single-genus families, the Welwitschiaceae, which includes the weird *Welwitschia* Hook. fil., found in the Namib desert, and the Gnetaceae, which contains *Gnetum* L., a genus of around 40 tropical climbers to trees with fleshy fruit.

Ecology and Geography In deserts and on dry hills. Twelve species are found in the drier parts of North America, with others in Mexico, South America, Europe, Asia and North Africa. One species *E. distachya* L. extends to northwestern France. *Ephedra fragilis* Desf. is a climber, native in the Mediterranean region.

Comment An uncommon plant in cultivation, usually grown as a curiosity. Many species contain ephedrine, long used as an antisyphilitic and antihistamine, and as a stimulant by athletes.

Ephedra equisetina
fruit, 2½ × life size
October 5th

54

Cycadaceae

Cycas

Cycas L. (1753), in the family Cycadaceae, sometimes called sago or false sago, is one of 11 families and 145 genera of cycads. *Cycas* itself consists of around 15 species, mainly from the tropics.

Description Stout, palm-like trees with trunks to 10m, knobbly, with scars left by the bases of old leaves. Leaves uncurling like fern fronds, evergreen, pinnate, with around 100 narrow segments, often very stiff and felted on the underside. The male flowers are usually solitary, large, to 80cm long, and cone-like, with tightly packed scales. The female flowers are short and frond-like, many in a whorl in the middle of the leaves, with ovules scattered along the margins. Pollination is by wind. Ripe female cones to 30cm long, with orange fruits on the margins. Seeds to 7cm long and nut-like.

Key Recognition Features Cycads are recognised by their palm-like habit, uncurling leaves, and the large, cone-like flowering stems and leafy female inflorescences.

Evolution and Relationships Cycads are very ancient group of plants, unique in many primitive features. In addition to the fern-like characteristics already mentioned, they have motile, flagellate sperm.

Ecology and Geography Found in tropical forests and on open grassland and rocks and cliffs in temperate areas. The range extends from East Africa to India, China, and Japan.

Comment Cycads are increasingly rare and threatened in the wild; although long-lived, they are slow-growing. Some *Cycas* species are eaten for the starchy pith in the stem, which is poisonous unless carefully prepared. The seeds are also edible. Many species, especially the dwarf *C. revoluta* Thunb. from Japan, are grown as ornamentals.

Cycas revoluta
¹/₂ life size
December 15th

Cycas revoluta
leaf base and leaflets
just over life size
December 15th

Magnolia

Magnolia L. (1753), the largest genus in the family Magnoliaceae, contains around 120 species, of which around 25 are hardy in cool temperate regions. Many species and hybrids are beautiful and popular garden trees and shrubs.

Description Trees to 30m in height, or shrubs, fast-growing in warm temperate climates. The leaves are deciduous or evergreen, alternate, usually ovate, not lobed, pinnately veined, and usually leaving a fine skeleton as they rot. Huge leaves to 60cm or more long are found in *M. macrophylla* Mich. in the southeastern United States. Winter buds are large, often with furry scales. The flowers are large, on the ends of the branches, often appearing in spring before the leaves, usually with 6–9 petals, but in some up to 33, in whorls of 3, white, pink, purple, or greenish, rarely yellow, usually scented. The stamens are numerous, spirally arranged, often with red filaments. Pollination is usually by beetles, which is common in primitive flowers, and also by honeybees, bumblebees, and flies. The fruits are often cone-like, with the seeds singly or in pairs, embedded in the receptacle. The seeds are suspended on thin threads, usually flattened, hard, and dark brown, with an orange or pink, fleshy aril.

Key Recognition Features Often huge flowers with whorls of smooth, fleshy petals, and numerous spirally arranged stamens and styles. Bark of the twigs usually aromatic, often lemon-scented.

Evolution and Relationships One of the most primitive genera of flowering plants; magnolia-like fossils from the mid-Cretaceous, called *Archaeanthus*, have been found in Dakota, Kansas. The simple stamens with pollen sacs on either side are a particularly primitive feature.

Ecology and Geography Magnolias are trees of moist forests. They are found in the northern hemisphere in eastern North America and Central America and in Asia ranging from the Himalayas to Japan and Sumatra.

Comment New yellow-flowered hybrids such as 'Elizabeth' are crosses between the green-flowered American *M. acuminata* L. and the white-flowered Chinese *M. denudata* Dersrouss. The timbers of some species are valued in Japan. The flowers of most species are edible, and the bark and flower buds of *M. officinalis* Rehd. & Wils. are used as a tonic in traditional Chinese medicine.

Magnolia wilsonii
life size
June 3rd

Magnolia × *loebneri* 'Merrill'
just under life size
March 12th

Magnolia × *loebneri* 'Leonard Messel'
showing spiral arrangement of
stamens and styles, just over life size
March 10th

MAGNOLIACEAE

Magnolia stellata
½ life size
March 10th

Magnolia 'Elizabeth'
½ life size
March 10th

Magnolia mollicomata
⅓ life size
March 12th

Magnolia wilsonii
fruiting heads,
ripe and (below)
unopened
½ life size
September 10th

Magnolia acuminata
½ life size
June 3rd

Seeds of *Magnolia wilsonii* cleaned
(left) and covered by aril (right)
2 × life size, September 10th

Michelia doltsopa
½ life size
March 9th

Michelia doltsopa
⅓ life size
March 9th

Michelia

Michelia L. (1753) contains around 45 species of mainly tropical trees in the Magnoliaceae. *Michelia figo* (Lour.) Spreng. is sometimes called banana shrub for the scent of its flowers.

Description Trees to 30m, or shrubs. The leaves are alternate, evergreen, simple, magnolia-like, shiny above, sometimes hairy beneath, to 18cm long in *M. doltsopa* Buch.-Ham. ex DC. The flowers are formed in the leaf axils, with 6–21 petals, in whorls of 3, white, yellow, orange, or purplish, heavily and sweetly scented. The stamens are numerous, with very short filaments; the stigmas are sessile on the carpels, with 2 or more ovules. Pollination is by insects. The fruits are either cone-like with separate carpels or sometimes fused into solid fruits. The seeds have a fleshy coat.

Key Recognition Features Similar to *Magnolia* (see pp.56–57), but with flowers in the leaf axils.

Evolution and Relationships Close to *Magnolia*, but more tropical. *Manglietia* Blume, of which only *M. insignis* (Wall.) Blume is hardy in temperate gardens, differs in having terminal flowers like a *Magnolia*, but separate carpels; its white, pink, or purplish flowers are scented.

Ecology and Geography In woods and scrub, from the Himalayan forests in Nepal and northern India to Ceylon, China, and Malaysia.

Comment *Michelia champaca* L. is used in India for its scented oil, called *champak* or *sabu*, and for its often orange flowers. *Michelia doltsopa* forms a large flowering tree in warm gardens; in England, it survives well only in the mildest gardens near the south coast. It has lovely scented wood. *Michelia compressa* (Maxim.) Sarg. makes a fine tree in southern Japan.

Liriodendron chinense
juvenile leaf
½ life size, June 23rd

Liriodendron

Liriodendron L. (1753), the tulip tree, contains 2 species in the family Magnoliaceae, 1 in North America, the other in China. Other names in North America are yellow poplar, poplar, and tulip poplar, which indicate the fast, straight growth made by the tree in the warm summer climate of the eastern seaboard.

Description Trees to 45m, fast-growing when young, growing 1m or more in a year, later slowing to around 1m in 3 years. The pith in the twigs is chambered. On old trees the base of the trunk is often swollen and gnarled. The leaves are alternate, deciduous, 4- to 6-lobed, the midrib ending at the base of the 2 central lobes, the blade to 30cm long, 40cm across, with pairs of rounded stipules. In *L. tulipifera* L., the American species, the lobes of the mature leaves are less deep than those found in the Chinese *L. chinense* (Hemsl.) Sarg., with leaves that have a distinctly pale underside. The flowers are large, upright, cup-shaped, yellowish-green, with an orange mark near the base, with usually 9 segments, the inner 6 petal-like, to 4cm long, the outer 3 green, sepal-like, smaller, and reflexed. The stamens are numerous (up to 50), whorled, 4–5cm long, with short filaments. The styles are simple, 60–100, on the ends of flattened ovaries. Pollination is by insects, probably usually by beetles. The fruits are dry samaras, spirally arranged, each with a single seed and a long wing.

Key Recognition Features The leaves of tulip tree, ending in a shallow or deep sinus, are unique. The persistent, dry-seeded, cone-like fruits and chambered pith identify the tree in winter.

Evolution and Relationships An isolated genus, closest to *Magnolia* (see pp.56–57) recognised by its leaves. Commonly found as far back as the Tertiary throughout the northern hemisphere; tulip-tree-like leaves have been found in the late-Cretaceous Dakota formation in central Kansas.

Ecology and Geography In moist woods, on low mountains and hills. The North American tulip tree is wild from Vermont and Ontario southwards to northern Florida and Louisiana. The Chinese species is reported from Shaanxi and Sichuan to Yunnan, Anhui, and Fujian, as well as in North Vietnam.

Comment Tulip trees are easy and fast growing, but do not usually begin to flower until 20 years after planting. The Chinese species is the most ornamental for its huge leaves and fast growth when young, but eventually it makes a smaller tree with smaller flowers. American Indians used the roots as a tonic and heart stimulant, and its timber was used by the early settlers for furniture.

Liriodendron tulipifera
mature fruiting heads
just over life size
September 5th

*Liriodendron
tulipifera*
seeds with wings
1⅓ × life size
October 12th

Liriodendron tulipifera
just under life size
June 3rd

Liriodendron tulipifera
½ life size, June 3rd

Drimys

Drimys J. R. & G. Forster (1789), in the family Winteraceae, contains around 30 species from South America and Australia to Malaysia and the Pacific islands.

Description Trees to 20m, or shrubs, often rather tall and narrow, fast-growing when young, later with pendulous branches. The bark and twigs are aromatic. The leaves are alternate, evergreen, simple, oblanceolate, usually dark green above and glaucous beneath. Flowers are rather small, on long, curved stalks, with numerous irregular, narrow petals and 2 or 3 sepals, and may be male, female, or bisexual. The stamens are short, about 20. Styles are absent; the stigmatic surface is along the inner edge of the carpels. Pollination is usually by flies. Fruits are usually 1–10 per flower, sometimes more, formed from the swollen carpels, often fleshy, and containing 1–10 seeds.

Key Recognition features The green, rather fleshy, aromatic twigs and narrow leaves are distinctive.

Evolution and Relationships The family Winteraceae is considered very primitive. This is shown in several traits: the wood lacks vessels, found in all other trees; the floral parts are all indefinite in number, and spirally arranged; and the stamens and carpels are of very simple construction. The leaves and leaf buds are also similar to *Magnolia* (see pp.56–57), and the twigs are aromatic, as they are in so many of these primitive genera.

Ecology and Geography Found in rainforests and mountain scrub: *D. winteri* J. R. & G. Forster in southern Chile and Argentina; *D. lanceolata* (Poir.) Baill. in New South Wales, Victoria, and Tasmania. Other species extend as far north as Mexico, and from Malaysia to Tahiti.

Comment *Drimys winteri*, Winter's bark, is named after Captain William Winter, who sailed around the world with Sir Francis Drake in 1578. He found the tree along the Straits of Magellan and used the aromatic bark as a flavouring and a treatment for scurvy. It makes an interesting tree in mild, humid gardens. The dwarfed and hardier var. *andina* Reiche flowers freely when young. The Australian *D. lanceolata* is a denser shrub with numerous black berries in autumn; its seeds have been used as a substitute for pepper.

Drimys winteri
bisexual flowers
½ life size, April 29th

Drimys lanceolata
bisexual flowers
life size, April 2nd

Drimys lanceolata
fruit, life size, October 6th

Drimys lanceolata
male flowers
2½ × life size, April 2nd

Drimys winteri
bisexual flowers
1⅓ × life size, April 29th

Pseudowintera colorata
flowers, 4 × life size
March 10th

Pseudowintera colorata
life size
March 10th

Pseudowintera colorata
bud, 4 × life size
March 10th

Pseudowintera colorata
life size, March 10th

Drimys lanceolata
just under life size
April 2nd

Pseudowintera

Pseudowintera Dandy (1933), in the Winteraceae, contains 3 species.
Description Trees to 8m, or shrubs. The leaves are evergreen,
leathery, simple, pungent to taste, brightly coloured in *P. colorata*.
The flowers are small and green, hidden among the leaves, opening
in early spring, aromatic. There are 5–6 simple petals, around 5mm
long. There are up to 15 stamens, in 3 series, shorter than the petals.
Styles are absent, with the stigmatic surface on the young carpels.
Pollination is presumed to be by insects. The fruits are black or red
berries, around 5mm across, with 2–6 black, angled seeds.
Key Recognition Features *Pseudowintera colorata* is easily
recognised by its brightly coloured leaves, reddish above and white
beneath in their first year.
Evolution and Relationships An isolated genus, close to *Drimys*.
Ecology and Geography Native to forests and scrub in New
Zealand, often common where large trees have been cut.
Comment *Pseudowintera colorata* is often cultivated for its
colourful leaves.

Schisandra

Schisandra Mich. (1803) contains 25 species in the Schisandraceae, with 1 in North America, the rest in eastern Asia.

Description Climbing shrubs to 20m or more, with twining stems. The leaves are deciduous or evergreen, simple, alternate, sometimes scented when crushed. The flowers are small, to 2cm across, and unisexual; the different sexes are usually on different plants, but sometimes on the same one. The petals are rounded, incurved, with 5–20 similar petals in 2 series, red or creamy-white. The stamens are numerous, 4–80, sometimes fused into a disc; the anthers have 4 cells. The styles are simple, 6–300 per flower, on an axis which elongates in fruit. Pollination is presumed to be by insects. The fruits are in hanging chains of juicy berries, red or sometimes black when ripe, with 1–3 kidney-shaped seeds.

Key Recognition Features The rounded petals in a cup-shaped flower are shared only by *Kadsura* (L.) Dunal, and that has a spherical cluster of berries.

Evolution and Relationships An isolated genus, close to *Kadsura* and, in spite of the very different fruit, to *Illicium*.

Ecology and Geography In scrub, often by streams. *Schisandra glabra* (Brickell) Rehd. is found in North America, scattered in the southeastern states. Most of the rest are found in China and Japan.

Comment Several species are cultivated for their long chains of bright red fruit. *Schisandra rubriflora* (Franch.) Rehd, & Wils., from the Himalayas and China, is the finest for its red flowers and fruit. It is best to plant both sexes to be sure of a good display of fruit. In China drugs from *Schisandra* are used to boost the immune system, treat hepatitis, and depress the central nervous system. Extracts have recently appeared in health drinks in the west.

Schisandra glaucescens
½ life size
May 19th

Schisandra rubriflora
female flower
½ life size
May 19th

Schisandra rubriflora
male flowers
½ life size, May 19th

Schisandra rubriflora
female flowers
just under life size
May 11th

Illicium

Illicium L. (1759), the star anise, is the only genus in the family Illiciaceae and contains 42 species in eastern Asia, southern North America, and Central America.

Description Trees to 18m, or shrubs. The leaves are evergreen, leathery, pointed, grouped towards the tips of the twigs. The flowers are short-stalked and usually slightly hidden among the leaves, white, yellow, red, or maroon, with numerous, usually narrow petals merging into sepals and bracts. The stamens are numerous. Styles are absent, the stigmas sessile on the tips of the carpels. Pollination is by various insects, including beetles. The fruits are star-like, composed of 8–15 segments, which may be fused or separate, each containing 1 often golden-brown seed. The seeds are sometimes ejected explosively.

Key Recognition Features The many-petalled flowers are rather similar to those of *Drimys* (see p.60), but the starry fruits are easy to recognise.

Evolution and Relationships An isolated family and genus, close to *Schisandra*, particularly in its wood anatomy. In pollen *Illicium* and *Schisandra* are close to *Drimys,* but DNA analysis suggests they are closer to Austrobaileyaceae C.T. White, a primitive family of a sole genus, *Austrobaileya*, containing 2 species from Queensland with large, green flowers, 5cm across, smelling of rotten fish. The range of the genus *Illicium* itself shows the connection between North America and eastern Asia.

Ecology and Geography In moist woods and along streams, often in rocky places. Two species, *I. floridanum* J. Ellis, and *I. parviflorum* Mich. ex Vent., are found in Georgia, Florida, Alabama, Louisiana, and northeast Mexico. Other species are found in China and Japan.

Comment *Illicium anisatum* L., syn. *I. religiosum* Sieb. & Zucc., is frequently planted near shrines in China and Japan; its oil is poisonous. *Illicium henryi* Diels is a decorative shrub from western China, with dark reddish flowers. Medicinally *I. verum* Hook. fil. is used to treat stomach pain, and the unripe fruit are a common flavouring in Chinese cookery and liqueurs.

Illicium anisatum
2½ life size
April 16th

Schisandra rubriflora
female flower, 1¾ × life size, May 11th

Illicium anisatum
½ life size
May 2nd

Atherosperma

Atherosperma Labill. (1806) is a genus of only 1 species, *A. moschatum* Labill., sometimes called southern sassafras or black sassafras. It is in the family Monimiaceae, but was formerly in the Atherospermataceae together with 4 other genera.

Description Trees to 25m, upright and fast-growing. Bark and leaves are aromatic. The leaves are opposite, evergreen, dull dark green above, glaucous beneath, with a few sharp teeth, 5–10cm long, and silky when young. The flowers are solitary in the leaf axils, pointing downwards, around 1cm across, white, with 8–10 petals, scented, appearing in autumn and winter. Female flowers are densely silky, with staminodes. There are 10–18 stamens, with long appendages on the filaments, fertile only in the male flowers. The styles are separate, each developing into a 1-seeded fruit. Pollination is presumed to be by insects.

Key Recognition Features The opposite leaves, glaucous beneath with few teeth, and the regular, opposite branches.

Evolution and Relationships Close to *Laurelia*.

Ecology and Geography Grows in moist, sheltered places in the forest from Queensland to New South Wales, Victoria, and Tasmania.

Comment A modest but attractive evergreen tree, often seen in collections on the Atlantic coast of Europe. In Tasmania the aromatic bark is used to make a tea. The wood is very springy, and has been used for clothspegs and toys. Most authorities give the flowers as up to 2.5cm across, but those I have seen are much smaller, around 1cm.

Atherosperma moschatum
male flowers and leaf underside
life size, February 14th

Atherosperma moschatum
female flower
1½ × life size
February 14th

Atherosperma moschatum
½ life size
February 14th

Laurelia

Laurelia Juss. (1809) is a genus of 2 species from New Zealand and South America, in the family Monimiaceae.

Description Trees to 35m, often with narrowly buttressed roots and hanging branches. The leaves are evergreen, rather pale, opposite, thick and leathery with coarse teeth, aromatic, to 8cm long. The flowers are small, around 5–10mm across, greenish or brownish, produced in clusters in the leaf axils, the males and females sometimes on separate trees, sometimes on the same tree. There are 5–12 stamens, with a cup-like gland at the base, opening by valves. The styles are numerous and plumose. Pollination is presumed to be by insects. The fruits are bottle-shaped, tapering to a narrow top, splitting to release the plumed seeds.

Key Recognition Features Opposite, thick, leathery leaves with coarse, blunt teeth.

Evolution and Relationships The family Monimiaceae is close to the Lauraceae (see pp.66–71), and encompasses a number of obscure genera, mostly from tropical South East Asia and the southern hemisphere.

Ecology and Geography One species, *L. novae-zelandiae* Cunn., the *pukatea*, is from New Zealand. The other, *L. sempervirens* (Ruiz & Pavon) Tul., which now includes *L. serrata* Bertero, comes from Chile and Argentina. They generally grow in wet, lowland forest.

Comment *Laurelia sempervirens* is sometimes grown as an ornamental in mild coastal gardens in western Europe, and is the source of Chilean or Peruvian nutmeg, a substitute for true nutmeg, *Myristica fragrans* Houtt., a native of the Moluccas.

Laurelia sempervirens
¹/₃ life size
September 13th

Asimina

Asimina Adans. (1763) contains 8 species in the family Annonaceae, found in North America, often called pawpaw. *Asimina triloba* (L.) Dunal, the dog-banana or Indian banana, is the most common.

Description Trees to 14m, or shrubs, usually wide spreading. The leaves are alternate, deciduous, obovate to oblanceolate, 6–30cm long. The flowers appear at the same times as the leaves; they are nodding, with 3 sepals, 3 or 4 maroon outer petals, and 3 or 4 curled inner petals, 3–4cm across, and foul smelling. The stamens are numerous, forming a ball. There are 3–7 styles, sessile or stalked. Pollination is by insects. The fruits are greenish or yellow, sweet and pulpy, elongated, 3–5 per flower, 5–15cm long, with a row of brown, bean-like seeds, each 1.5–2.5cm long.

Key Recognition Features Flowers with 2 distinct whorls of 3 petals and fleshy, bean-like fruits with several seeds.

Evolution and Relationships Related to the tropical custard apple, *Annona reticulata* L., and the sweetsop, *Annona squamosa* L., both of which have apple-like fruit with sweet pulp surrounding large, brown seeds. The true pawpaw or papaya is *Carica papaya* L., in the Caricaceae, an unrelated tropical family from South America.

Ecology and Geography Grows in woods and hedges. *Asimina triloba* is found from Ontario and New York to northern Florida and Texas. The other species are confined to Florida and Georgia.

Comment *Asimina triloba* is sometimes grown as a curiosity in Europe, where it was introduced by Peter Collinson in 1736. Many named varieties with improved fruit are available in America. *Asimina obovata* (Willd.) Nash from Florida has small leaves and large, lemon-scented flowers with outer petals 4–6cm long and red or pink inner petals. It flowers in early spring and makes a good ornamental in warm gardens.

Laurelia sempervirens
male flowers (above) and
female flowers (below)
2 × life size, April 11th

Laurelia sempervirens
²/₃ life size
April 11th

Asimina triloba
²/₃ life size
October 5th

Laurus

Laurus L. (1753), the bay or sweet bay, in the family Lauraceae, contains 2 species. One is native in the Mediterranean, the other in the Atlantic islands.

Description Trees to 15m, or shrubs, upright in habit when young, and resprouting quickly from ground level after fires or exceptional frost. The leaves are alternate, evergreen, leathery, aromatic, pinnately veined, 5–10cm long, oblong-lanceolate in *L. nobilis* L., broader, often almost round and hairy beneath in *L. azorica* (Seub.) Franco. The flowers are small, creamy-yellow, bisexual or unisexual, with 4 petals; buds formed in autumn, opening in spring. There are 12 stamens, opening by 2 flaps. Pollination is presumed to be by insects. The fruits are berry-like, 1–1.5cm long, and shining black.

Key Recognition Features The leathery, aromatic leaves are characteristic.

Evolution and Relationships The bay is the only genus of the family still to be found on mainland Europe; 3 other genera (including *Persea,* see p.68) have survived in the laurel forests of the Canary Islands, demonstrating how severely European flora was reduced by the ice ages. The family Lauraceae is mainly tropical and contains around 45 genera and over 2200 species.

Ecology and Geography The bay tree *L. nobilis* has long been cultivated, but is probably native only in the southern and eastern Mediterranean. It usually grows in scrub near the coast and in gorges, often by springs and streams. *L. azorica* is common in the laurel forests of Madeira, the Canaries, and the Azores.

Comment The bay tree was sacred to Apollo, and was called *daphne* in Greek. In myth, Daphne was changed into a bay tree by her father to escape the attentions of Apollo. Thereafter Apollo is portrayed crowned with bay, and bay leaves were used to crown the victors in the Pythian games held in his honour and also Roman emperors. Bay leaves are now commonly used in cooking; they keep their flavour well when dried. The oils are used in perfumery. A variety with small, narrow, very wavy leaves, *L. nobilis* f. *angustifolia*, is often cultivated.

Laurus nobilis
flowers, 1⅓ × life size
April 7th

Laurus nobilis
fruits, one with flesh removed
to show seed, 2 × life size
October 12th

Laurus nobilis
½ life size
April 7th

Umbellularia

Umbellularia (Nees) Nutt. (1842) is a genus of a single species, *U. californica* (Hook. & Arn.) Nutt. in the family Lauraceae, native of Oregon and California. It is variously called California bay, California laurel, California olive, myrtlewood, or pepperwood.

Description Trees to 45m, or shrubs. The leaves are evergreen, alternate, shiny, yellowish-green, narrowly oblong or narrowly elliptic, pinnately veined, to 10cm long, and aromatic but unpleasant. The flowers are bisexual, small, yellow, 5–10 in an umbel, with 6 petals, 12–16mm across. They open from autumn to spring. The stamens are short, usually 9, with 4 cells and 4 flaps. Pollination is presumed to be by insects. The fruits are berry-like, greenish to dark purple, 2cm across, with the swollen flower base forming a small cup.

Key Recognition Features The yellow-green, narrow leaves, like those of *Laurus*, on a large tree.

Evolution and Relationships In its cup-like, swollen flower base, 4-celled anthers, and pinnate veins, *Umbellularia* is close to *Litsea* (Lam.), which has around 400 species in tropical Asia, and 1 isolated along the southeastern coast of North America.

Ecology and Geography Found in canyons and valleys at up to 1500m, from southern Oregon to Baja California.

Comment The timber is used under the name pepperwood. It is said that to sniff the crushed leaves, or even to stand for long under the tree, can cause headaches.

Umbellularia californica
flowers, ⅔ life size
April 1st

Umbellularia californica
½ life size, October 5th

Umbellularia californica
fruit, life size
October 5th

Cinnamomum

Cinnamomum Schaeffer (1825), in the family Lauraceae, contains around 350 species, mainly in the tropics of South East Asia and the Americas. *Cinnamomum camphora* (L.) J. Presl, the camphor tree, is the only common temperate species and is described here.

Description Trees to 30m, wide-spreading with surface roots around the trunk, very well developed in old specimens. The leaves are evergreen, soft, alternate, oval, tapering to the base and into a long point, with 2–3 pairs of curved side veins, shining, aromatic, 7–10cm long, on a slender stalk. The flowers are small and green, in loose bunches on a long stalk, produced in the leaf axils in spring, with 6 segments, minutely hairy on the inside. The 9 stamens are in 3 whorls, with 4-celled anthers. The single style has a disc-like stigma. Pollination is presumed to be by insects. The fruits are round, black and fleshy, 7–10mm across, with a thick, green stalk formed by the swollen base of the flower, and a single seed.

Key Recognition Features The leaves with pairs of curved veins are typical of many genera in the Lauraceae. The soft young leaves with long points are characteristic of the camphor tree.

Evolution and Relationships A large genus, typical of the Lauraceae, which is a huge family in the tropics, with nearly 3000 species, and includes many important plants.

Ecology and Geography In woods and on rocks, especially near the sea, from Japan to China, Taiwan, and Malaysia.

Comment Commonly planted as a street tree in Los Angeles and the warm southeastern United States. It is very beautiful in spring when the new leaves are unfurling. The wood is used for boxes and distilled for aromatic oils used as a moth repellent and in aromatherapy, to rub on the chest and on bruises. *Cinnamomum verum* J. Presl from southwest India and Ceylon is the source of cinnamon bark, commonly used as a spice, and several other species are used as spice and incense.

Cinnamomum camphora
showing reddish young leaves
½ life size, May 5th

Persea americana
cultivated avocado fruit
½ life size

Persea ichangensis
½ life size, October 6th

Persea

Persea Mill. (1737) contains around 200 mainly tropical species of trees and shrubs in the family Lauraceae, including *P. americana* Mill., the avocado. Some species were formerly called *Machilus* Nees.

Description Trees to 20m, or shrubs. The leaves are evergreen, alternate, with many curved veins. The flowers are in loose, stalked bunches, small and green, bisexual or unisexual, with 6 segments. The stamens in the male flowers are 9, with 4-celled anthers. The styles are solitary, with a small, flattened stigma. Pollination is presumed to be by insects. The fruits are fleshy, to 25cm in large avocados, around 1cm in *P. thunbergii*. The seeds are solitary.

Key Recognition Features The fruit hang in long-stalked bunches on a tree with simple, evergreen leaves.

Evolution and Relationships Most species are in eastern Asia or the tropical Americas, but one is found in the laurel forests of the Canaries and the Azores, and probably occurred throughout Europe before the ice ages.

Ecology and Geography Found mainly in moist forests. The avocado is probably native of central America; it has been cultivated for around 10,000 years. The hardiest species are *P. ichangensis* (Rehder & Wilson) Kostermans from central China, and the closely related *P. thunbergii* (Sieb. & Zucc.) Kostermans from Japan, both formerly separated in the genus *Machilus*.

Comment Avocado pears are now cultivated widely in the tropics and subtropics. Other species are grown as curiosities. The wood of *P. nanmu* Oliver is used for coffins in China, that of *P. thunbergii* was used for solid cartwheels in Japan.

Neolitsea sericea
²/₃ life size
October 19th

Neolitsea sericea
flowers, 1 ¹/₂ × life size
October 19th

Neolitsea sericea
young leaves, ²/₃ life size
April 29th

Neolitsea

Neolitsea (Benth.) Merrill (1906), in the family Lauraceae, contains around 80 species from South East Asia. *Neolitsea sericea* (Blume) Koidz., with beautifully silky young leaves, is the only commonly grown temperate species and is described here.

Description Trees to 7m, or shrubs, upright and fast-growing when young. The leaves are evergreen, alternate, ovate-elliptic, 3-veined near the base, 5–7cm long, grouped near the tips of the branches, strikingly silky and pendulous when young. The flowers are small, greenish, with 4 petals, clustered at the apex of the shoots in umbels of 5–10, males and females on separate trees, opening in autumn. The stamens are conspicuous, usually 6, the inner 2 each with 2 glands at the base, with 4 pollen sacs. Pollination is by presumed to be by insects. The fruits are berry-like, yellow to red, around 12mm long, with the swollen base of the flower at the top of the stalk.

Key Recognition Features The 3-veined leaves and the silky young leaves.

Evolution and Relationships Two other mainly Asian genera, *Actinodaphne* Nees and *Litsea* Lam., are very similar, but have 9 stamens and 6 petals. *Neolitsea aciculata* (Blume) Koidz., also from Japan, has red flowers in spring and shining black fruit.

Ecology and Geography On hillsides and scrub, in deciduous or evergreen forests. *Neolitsea sericea* is found from Japan and Taiwan to Korea and China, *N. aciculata* is confined to Korea and Japan.

Comment An attractive evergreen, grown primarily for its young leaves. Both male and female plants are needed for berries to form.

Lindera

Lindera Thunb. (1783), in the family Lauraceae, contains around 100 species in North America and eastern Asia. *Parabenzion* Nakai is now included in *Lindera*.

Description Trees to 12m or shrubs, usually rather spreading. The leaves are usually deciduous, alternate, simple or 3-lobed at the apex, 3-veined or pinnate-veined, often aromatic. In the deciduous species autumn colour is often a lovely golden yellow. The flowers are small, yellowish, with 6 petals, males and females separate, in umbel-like, sometimes stalked clusters in the leaf axils at the tops of the twigs, in early spring. In the spicebush, *L. benzoin* (L.) Blume, the flowers are sweetly scented. There are usually 9 stamens, rarely 12, with 2-celled anthers with 2 flaps; female flowers have 9 sterile stamens. The styles have peltate stigmas. Pollination is presumed to be by insects. The fruits are fleshy or dry, green, black, or red, with 1 seed.

Key Recognition Features At flowering the young leaves point upwards, while the clusters of flowers hang beneath them at the tops of bare twigs. The leaves with 3 lobes towards the tip are distinctive, and only at all similar to *Sassafras*.

Evolution and Relationships A diverse genus, the species united by their umbels of flowers, the males with nine 2-celled anthers.

Ecology and Geography Found in woods and bogs, especially along streams. Two species are found in eastern North America, including the widespread and familiar spicebush, *L. benzoin,* and the rare *L. melissifolia* (Walt.) Blume, which is confined to the southeast. The other species are found in China and Japan.

Comment Several linderas, notably *L. obtusiloba* Blume, are attractive garden shrubs. Spicebush, *L. benzoin,* with small, yellow flowers in spring and red fruit combined with good autumn colour, is common in eastern North America from Ontario to Maine and southwards to northern Florida and Texas.

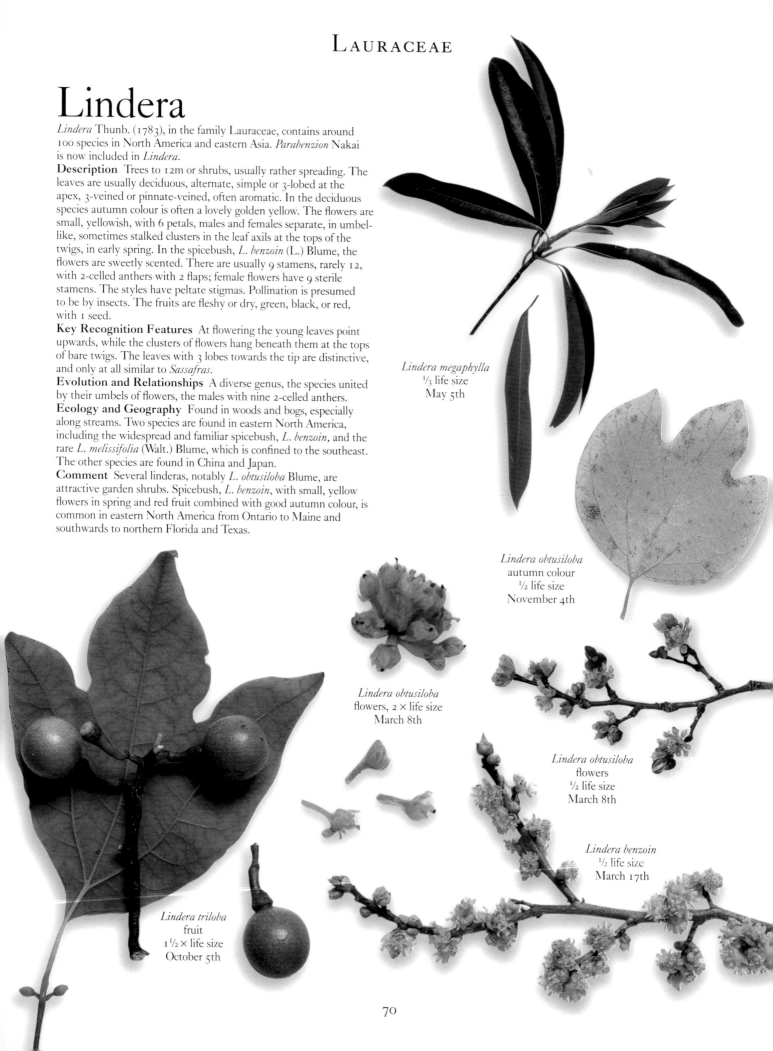

Lindera megaphylla
⅓ life size
May 5th

Lindera obtusiloba
autumn colour
½ life size
November 4th

Lindera obtusiloba
flowers, 2 × life size
March 8th

Lindera obtusiloba
flowers
½ life size
March 8th

Lindera benzoin
½ life size
March 17th

Lindera triloba
fruit
1½ × life size
October 5th

Sassafras

Sassafras J. Presl (1825), in the family Lauraceae, contains 2 or perhaps 3 species, 1 in North America and 1 or 2 in China.

Description Trees to 35m, or shrubs, with red-brown, aromatic bark and green twigs. When young the trees can grow very fast and upright. The leaves are alternate, deciduous, aromatic, ovate, and simple or 3-lobed towards the apex, pinnately veined, with the lowest pair of lobes much the strongest. They can reach about 20cm in length on strong shoots. Autumn colours are good orange and red. The flowers are small, in stalked bunches, appearing on the tips of the twigs before the leaves open, with 6 petals. Male and female flowers are on separate plants. There are 9 stamens in the male flowers, the inner 3 with 2 stalked glands at the base. The anthers are 4-celled, with 4 flaps. The styles are slender, with capitate stigmas. Female flowers have 6 flattened staminodes. Pollination is presumed to be by insects. The fruits are blue when ripe, in a shallow cup on a thickened, reddish stalk.

Key Recognition Features The green twigs and variably shaped, aromatic leaves are characteristic.

Evolution and Relationships The presence of pairs of closely related species in eastern North America and in western China is an indication that these areas shared the same woody flora before the ice ages and the opening of the Pacific.

Ecology and Geography In damp, rich woods, and in disturbed places, old fields, and hedgerows. *Sassafras albidum* (Nutt.) Nees is common from Ontario and Maine to northern Florida and Texas. *Sassafras tzumu* Hemsl. is found in western Hubei and Sichuan, and yet another species has been reported from China.

Comment The bark of sassafras roots was traditionally used to make tea. It was also one of the traditional constituents of root beer, but its use is now banned, as it has been linked to liver cancer. Oil of sassafras was used for killing lice.

Sassafras albidum
flowers, just over life size
April 11th

Lindera obtusiloba
½ life size
September 10th

Sassafras albidum
½ life size, July 28th

71

Calycanthus

Calycanthus L. (1753) is one of 4 genera in the Calycanthaceae. It has 2 species, both in North America.

Description Shrubs to 4m, rather upright and very leafy. The leaves are opposite, deciduous, aromatic, dark green, and rough to the touch on the upper surface, elliptic to ovate. The flowers are maroon or dark reddish-brown, strawberry- or pineapple-scented, to 7.5cm across, with numerous spirally arranged, rather narrow petals merging into sepals. There are 5–30 stamens, arranged in a spiral. The styles are long and slender, 5–35, each with 1 carpel, embedded on the inside of the young fruit. Pollination is by insects, attracted to the succulent, white substance on the tips of the inner petals, stamens, and staminodes. The fruits are dry and fibrous, flat-topped, with the 6mm-long seeds attached to the lower part of the wall.

Key Recognition Features The rough, opposite, aromatic leaves help identify the shrub without flowers. When in flower, the fruity scent and reddish-brown petals are typical.

Evolution and Relationships The spiral arrangement of the stamens and the undifferentiated floral segments are considered primitive characteristics. As well as *Sinocalycanthus* and *Chimonanthus*, the other genus in the family is the tropical *Idiospermum australiense* (Diels) S.T. Blake, the ribbonwood, from Queensland.

Ecology and Geography Found in woodlands and along streams and rivers. *Calycanthus floridus* L., the Carolina allspice, is from southeastern North America, flowering in late spring. *Calycanthus occidentalis* Hook. & Arn. is from California and Washington; its long-stalked flowers continue throughout the summer. *Calycanthus fertilis* Walt. is now considered to be merely a variety of *C. floridus*.

Comment *Calycanthus* contains the alkaloid calycanthine, which is very poisonous and similar to strychnine. It was used medicinally by American Indians.

Calycanthus floridus
flowers, ¾ life size
June 3rd

Sinocalycanthus

Sinocalycanthus Cheng & Chang (1964), in the family Calycanthaceae, contains 1 species, *S. chinensis* Cheng & Chang, from eastern China.

Description Shrubs to 5m. The leaves are deciduous, shining, elliptic to obovate, to 15cm long. The flowers are nodding, the outer 6 petals broad and white or sometimes pinkish, the inner, smaller petals yellow with maroon markings, arched over the stamens. There are 10–30 stamens, curled over the styles. Pollination is presumed to be by insects, possibly by beetles. The fruits are similar to those of *Calycanthus*.

Key Recognition Features The nodding white and yellow flowers are very distinctive.

Evolution and Relationships Close to *Calycanthus* and sometimes united with it.

Ecology and Geography In woods in eastern China.

Comment *Sinocalycanthus* was first described in 1957, and flowered for the first time in England in around 1994; it is slowly becoming more frequently planted in gardens.

Calycanthus floridus
seeds and capsules
just over life size
December 15th

Calycanthus floridus
⅓ life size
June 3rd

Sinocalycanthus chinensis
¾ life size, April 16th

Chimonanthus praecox
fruits, 1½ × life size
June 3rd

Chimonanthus praecox
leaves and unripe fruits
½ life size, June 3rd

Chimonanthus praecox
just over life size
January 28th

Chimonanthus

Chimonanthus Lindl. (1819), the wintersweet, contains perhaps 6 species from China in the family Calycanthaceae.

Description Shrubs to 6m, usually spreading. The leaves are opposite, deciduous or evergreen, slightly rough on the upper surface, but not aromatic. The flowers are very sweetly scented, to 3.5cm across, opening in winter and early spring before the leaves appear. They have irregular reddish, yellowish, or white petals, the inner, shorter ones sometimes marked with purple. The stamens are in 2 series; the outer 5–6 are fertile, the inner 5 are sterile. The styles are thin and separate. Pollination is by insects. The fruits are elongated, dry when ripe. The seeds are around 1cm long.

Key Recognition features The short, yellow flowers on bare twigs are characteristic in winter. In summer the rather thin, slightly rough, opposite leaves are easily recognised.

Evolution and Relationships Very different-looking in flower from *Calycanthus*, but with similar fruit, tapering to a long point.

Ecology and Geography On cliffs and on rocky hillsides. *Chimonanthus praecox* (L.) Link is common in western Hubei, in the Yichang gorges, and in northeastern Sichuan, where it is very variable in flower colour; Mikinori Ogisu reports seeing red-flowered forms there. *Chimonanthus nitens* Oliver and *C. yunnanensis* W. W. Sm. are nearly evergreen and have smaller flowers.

Comment Wintersweet is one of the loveliest shrubs for winter flowering. It needs warm summers to set buds and even at Kew Gardens in London is best grown against a wall. It has long been cultivated in both Japan and China.

Chimonanthus praecox
½ life size
January 28th

73

Akebia quinata
large female and small male
flowers, 1½ × life size
April 26th

Akebia quinata
¾ life size
April 26th

Akebia trifoliata
¾ life size
May 19th

Akebia

Akebia Decne. (1839), sometimes called chocolate vine, contains around 4 species in the family Lardizabalaceae. The name is derived from the Japanese *akebi*.

Description Woody climbers to 10m, with twining stems. The leaves are deciduous or evergreen, with 3–5 stalked leaflets. The flowers are vanilla-scented in some species, in spikes, the females at the base, long-stalked, the males towards the apex, smaller and short-stalked. Segments 3, chocolate-brown, rarely yellow. There are 6–8 stamens, and 5–10 ovaries. Pollination is presumed to be by insects. The fruits are 5–15cm long, sausage-shaped, 1–4 together, purple to brown when ripe, and splitting open to reveal white, edible but insipid pulp, in which are embedded the black or dark brown seeds.

Key Recognition Features The stalked leaves, deciduous in the commonly cultivated species, and the 3-petalled, chocolate-brown flowers are distinctive.

Evolution and Relationships Very different from the other members of the family in flower, but similar in fruit.

Ecology and Geography In rocky places and scrub, where it can scramble to the light, at up to 1500m, flowering in spring. All the species are from eastern Asia, and the most common, *A. quinata* (Houtt.) Decne. and *A. trifoliata* (Thunb.) Koidz. are found eastwards from Sichuan in China to Japan and Taiwan.

Comment The fruits of both the common species are eaten in China. They and their hybrid, *A. × pentaphylla* (Mak.) Mak., are grown as ornamentals for their unusual flowers. Fruit is rarely formed in England, but is common in North America, where summers are hotter and *A. quinata* has become naturalised from Connecticut to Georgia.

Stauntonia

Stauntonia DC (1818), in the family Lardizabalaceae, consists of around 24 species. Only *S. hexaphylla* (Thunb.) Decne. is commonly grown in gardens.

Description Woody climbers to 13m, with twining stems. The leaves are evergreen, with 3−7 ovate to elliptic leaflets, arranged palmately. The flowers are sweetly scented, purplish, males and females on separate plants, in bunches in the leaf axils. The female flowers have 3 ovaries, the males 6 stamens joined into a column; both have 6 fleshy segments, which in *S. hexaphylla* are narrow and curl backwards. Pollination is presumed to be by insects. The fruits are fleshy, edible, purplish, around 5cm long, with several seeds.

Key Recognition Features The leathery leaves, usually with 5−7 leaflets, and the pale purplish, scented flowers with narrow, pointed segments.

Evolution and Relationships Close to *Holboellia* (see pp.78−79), differing mainly in having stamens joined in a column.

Ecology and Geography Most species are found in eastern Asia; *S. hexaphylla* is native of Japan, Taiwan, and eastern China.

Comment Grown for its sweetly scented flowers in early spring. Female plants are sometimes reported to produce fruit in the absence of males.

Stauntonia hexaphylla
1/3 life size
October 5th

Sinofranchetia

Sinofranchetia (Diels) Henry (1907) is a genus of only 1 species, *S. chinensis* (Franch.) Hemsl., in the family Lardizabalaceae.

Description A woody climber to 15m, with vigorous, twining stems. The leaves are deciduous, with 3 leaflets, each 6−14cm long. The flowers are in drooping spikes, the males and females usually on separate plants. They are white with purple or brownish streaks, around 8mm across, with 6 segments and 6 nectaries, the males with 6 stamens, the females with 3 ovaries. Pollination is presumed to be by insects. The fruits are in chains to 20cm long, pale lavender-purple, with numerous flattened, dull blackish seeds. The pulp is edible, but watery and insipid.

Key Recognition Features The 3 ovate leaflets and the chains of pale bluish fruit.

Evolution and Relationships Of all the Asiatic genera, this shows the most similarities with the Chilean *Lardizabala biternata* (see p.76), which also has long spikes of flowers and 3-lobed leaves.

Ecology and Geography In woods and scrub at 1600−2800m in western and central China.

Comment This species is occasionally cultivated as a curiosity.

Sinofranchetia chinensis
unripe fruit
just under life size
September 20th

Sinofranchetia chinensis
1/3 life size
September 20th

Lardizabala

Lardizabala Ruiz & Pavon (1794) contains 1 or perhaps 2 species in the Lardizabalaceae; only *L. biternata* Ruiz & Pavon is cultivated.

Description Woody climbers to 10m, with twining stems. The leaves are evergreen, ternate or 2-ternate, with 3–9 leathery leaflets, dark green and shining above, 5–10cm long. The male flowers are in hanging racemes, the females solitary in the leaf axils, sometimes with the sexes on different plants. Male flowers have 6 fleshy segments that are green with purple edges, and 6 petaloid nectaries. Stamens 6, joined. Female flowers have 6 staminodes. Pollination is presumed to be by insects. The fruits are dark purple, sausage-shaped, to 7.5cm long, with many seeds.

Key Recognition Features The glossy, wavy-edged leaves with 3–9 leaflets.

Evolution and Relationships An isolated genus in a family that is found mainly in eastern Asia.

Ecology and Geography In rainforest in southern Chile, flowering in winter.

Comment A rare climber, sometimes grown as a curiosity.

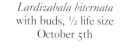

Lardizabala biternata
with buds, ½ life size
October 5th

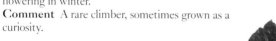

Lardizabala biternata
⅓ life size
April 11th

Decaisnea

Decaisnea Hook. fil. & Thoms. (1831) consists of 1 species, *D. insignis* (Griffith) Hook. fil. & Thomson, in the family Lardizabalaceae.

Description A shrub to 5m tall with few, rather thick, upright stems with very thick pith. The leaves are deciduous, 50–80cm long, pinnate, with 6–12 pairs of leaflets, 6–14cm long, glaucous beneath. The flowers are pendulous on long arching spikes, 2.5–3cm long, mostly male or female, but some bisexual, with 6 greenish, pointed segments, 6 stamens, and 3 ovaries, appearing in spring. Pollination is presumed to be by insects. The fruits are grey, greeny-blue, or golden-yellow, with small warts on the surface. They are up to 15cm long, solitary or in groups of 2 or 3, with a sweetish but insipid pulp, in which the black seeds are embedded.

Key Recognition Features The long, pinnate leaves, glaucous beneath, and the curious blue or yellow, bean-like fruit.

Evolution and Relationships *Decaisnea* is unusual for the Lardizabalaceae in being stiff and upright growing; all the other genera are climbers. The wood is very primitive in construction.

Ecology and Geography In damp woods and scrub at 600–2600m in China, from Sikkim to Yunnan, where the fruit is yellow, and in Sichuan, Shensi, and Hubei, where the fruit is blue. The blue-fruited form is still sometimes separated as *D. fargesii* Franch.

Comment The blue-fruited form is often grown as a curiosity; it fruits better in a position where the new shoots are not damaged by late frosts. E. H. Wilson records that on Mount Omei monkeys eat the fruit. In Sikkim the fruit were eaten by the Lepcha tribe.

Decaisnea insignis
flowers, ¼ life size
June 3rd

Decaisnea insignis
fruit and seeds
⅔ life size
September 8th

Decaisnea insignis
in fruit, ⅓ life size
September 8th

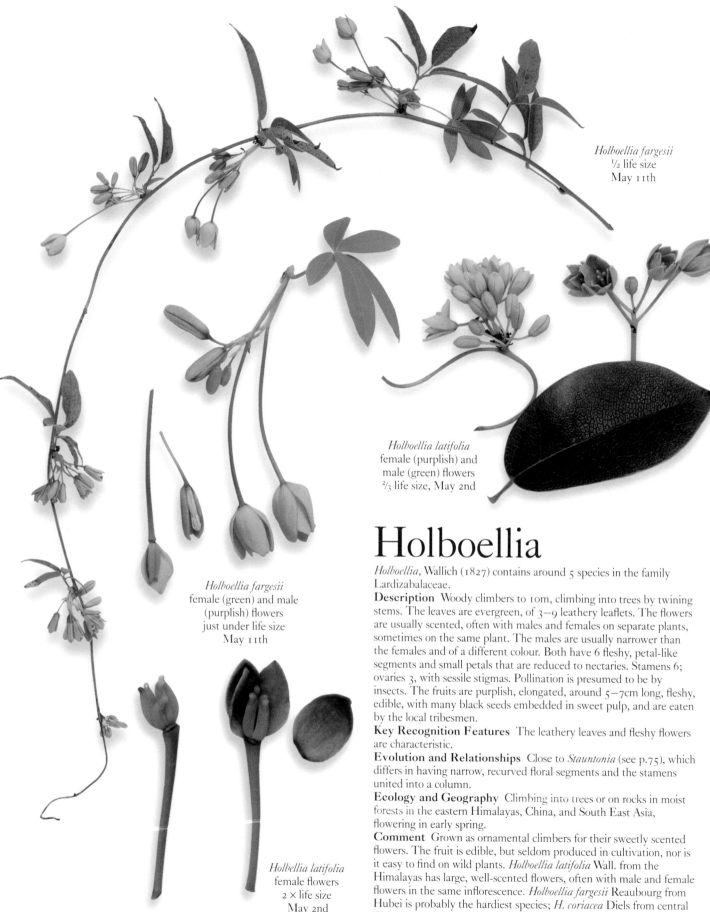

Holboellia fargesii
½ life size
May 11th

Holboellia latifolia
female (purplish) and
male (green) flowers
⅔ life size, May 2nd

Holboellia fargesii
female (green) and male
(purplish) flowers
just under life size
May 11th

Holbellia latifolia
female flowers
2 × life size
May 2nd

Holboellia

Holboellia, Wallich (1827) contains around 5 species in the family Lardizabalaceae.

Description Woody climbers to 10m, climbing into trees by twining stems. The leaves are evergreen, of 3–9 leathery leaflets. The flowers are usually scented, often with males and females on separate plants, sometimes on the same plant. The males are usually narrower than the females and of a different colour. Both have 6 fleshy, petal-like segments and small petals that are reduced to nectaries. Stamens 6; ovaries 3, with sessile stigmas. Pollination is presumed to be by insects. The fruits are purplish, elongated, around 5–7cm long, fleshy, edible, with many black seeds embedded in sweet pulp, and are eaten by the local tribesmen.

Key Recognition Features The leathery leaves and fleshy flowers are characteristic.

Evolution and Relationships Close to *Stauntonia* (see p.75), which differs in having narrow, recurved floral segments and the stamens united into a column.

Ecology and Geography Climbing into trees or on rocks in moist forests in the eastern Himalayas, China, and South East Asia, flowering in early spring.

Comment Grown as ornamental climbers for their sweetly scented flowers. The fruit is edible, but seldom produced in cultivation, nor is it easy to find on wild plants. *Holboellia latifolia* Wall. from the Himalayas has large, well-scented flowers, often with male and female flowers in the same inflorescence. *Holboellia fargesii* Reaubourg from Hubei is probably the hardiest species; *H. coriacea* Diels from central China always has 3 leaflets.

Holboellia coriacea
½ life size
April 29th

Holboellia coriacea
fruit, life size
September 16th

Holboellia coriacea
male flowers
just under life size
April 29th

Berberis calliantha
⅔ life size, April 29th

Berberis calliantha
flowers, 2 × life size
April 29th

Berberis darwinii
flowers, just under life size
April 25th

Berberis valdiviana
flowers, life size
April 25th

Berberis valdiviana
thorn, life size
April 25th

Berberis prattii var.
laxipendula
fruit, 1½ × life size
December 8th

Berberis

Berberis L. (1753) is a genus of around 400 species, by far the largest in the family Berberidaceae.

Description Shrubs to 5m, usually spiny, with yellow wood. The leaves are evergreen or deciduous, simple, often toothed, usually spiny, to 22cm long. On many stems the 3-pointed spines are modified leaves, and the normal leaves and flowers are formed on short shoots in their axils. The flowers are generally rounded, hanging, to 2.5cm across, produced singly or in umbels, simple clusters, or branching, grape-like bunches. The sepals and petals are usually yellowish or orange; the sepals usually in 2 whorls of 3, slightly spreading to reflexed, the petals also in 2 whorls of 3, forming a cup. Stamens 6, the anthers opening by valves. Ovary solitary, with a long to very short style, with 1–16 ovules. Pollination is by insects, usually bees. The stamens, which surround the ovary, are sensitive and spring inwards when touched. The fruits are berry-like, spherical to sausage-shaped; seeds are variable in number.

Key Recognition Features The yellow wood and the simple, spiny leaves or 3-pointed spines on the stems.

Evolution and Relationships The family Berberidaceae, in which woodiness is only poorly developed, is close to Ranunculaceae, which is an entirely herbaceous family with the exception of the subshrubby *Xanthorhiza*, (see p.85), which also has yellow wood, and the climbing *Clematis* (see pp.86–89). Within its family, *Berberis* is close to *Mahonia* (see p.82), with which it hybridises, but that has pinnate leaves. The new *Flora of North America* does not recognise *Mahonia* as a separate genus. There are several herbaceous members of the family, notably the evergreen, often bristly-leaved *Epimedium* (see Volume 2).

Ecology and Geography In many different habitats, from temperate rainforest to semi-desert, flowering mostly in spring. *Berberis* are found throughout the northern hemisphere and in South America, with concentrations of species in the Himalayan region and in southern Chile and Argentina.

Comment Many species are grown as ornamentals for their flowers and fruit, and are often planted in areas where vandalism is a threat to less tough and spiny plants. The fruits of most species are edible and can be made into jam. Many species of berberis are an alternative host to wheat rust, *Puccinia graminis* Pers., so their cultivation is banned in most of North America.

Berberis jamesiana
life size
October 5th

× Mahoberberis

× *Mahoberberis* Schneider (1906), in the family Berberidaceae, is a hybrid genus covering cultivated crosses between *Mahonia* and *Berberis* (see p.81).

Description Shrubs to 2m, the shoots not spiny. The leaves are evergreen, pinnate or entire, and toothed. The flowers are yellow, irregularly clustered. Fruits are not formed.

Key Recognition Features Entire and pinnate leaves carried on the same plant.

Evolution and Relationships These are garden hybrids. × *Mahoberberis neubertii* (Baumann) Schneider is between *Mahonia aquifolium* and *Berberis vulgaris*, and × *Mahoberberis aquisargentii* Krüssman is between *Mahonia aquifolium* and *Berberis sargentii*. A further hybrid, × *M. miethkeana* Melander & Eade, is between *Mahonia aquifolium* and another unknown evergreen *Berberis*.

Ecology and Geography The oldest of the hybrids, × *M. neubertii*, was raised in by M. Baumann at Botwiller in Alsace in 1854. × *Mahoberberis aquisargentii* was raised by H. Jensen in Sweden in 1943, and × *M. miethkeana* was found a Californian nursery at around the same time.

Comment These hybrids are sometimes grown as curiosities.

Mahonia

Mahonia Nutt. (1818) is a genus of around 100 species in the family Berberidaceae.

Description Shrubs to 5m, with yellow wood, the often thick stems not spiny. The leaves are alternate, evergreen, pinnate, with 3–41 leaflets, usually leathery and spiny. The flowers are somewhat rounded, often well scented, like lily-of-the-valley (*Convallaria*, see Volume 2), usually on long, upright or drooping spikes. The sepals and petals are usually yellowish or orange, rarely whitish or reddish-purple; the sepals in 2 whorls of 3, slightly spreading; the petals also in 2 whorls of 3, forming a cup. Stamens 6, the anthers opening by valves. Ovary solitary, with a short style and capitate stigma. The stamens surround the ovary and are sensitive, springing inwards when touched. Pollination is by insects, probably bees. The fruits are juicy, purplish-black, sometimes reddish, and rarely pale yellow or white, with few seeds. In one species, *M. fremontii* (Torr.) Fedde, the fruits are dry and inflated.

Key Recognition Features The stiff, pinnate leaves and spikes of flowers.

Evolution and Relationships Most of the Asiatic species are clearly distinct from *Berberis* (see p.81); some of the American species are distinct, while some lean towards *Berberis* in their stem structure, the arrangement of their flowers, and their susceptibility to rust. These usually have fewer leaflets as well.

Ecology and Geography Asian species are found from southern India and the Himalayas to China, Japan, and Sumatra; most of these species grow in or on the edges of forest, flowering in late autumn, winter, and spring. In North America and Mexico, the species are usually found in dry, open woods, chaparral, and semi-desert.

Comment Many species are planted as ornamentals: the Chinese species *M. japonica* (Thunb.) DC has been long grown for its excellent scent in winter. Cultivars of the hybrid *M.* × *media* C.D. Brickell are excellent large, winter-flowering shrubs. The fruit of most species are edible as jam. *Mahonia aquifolium* (Pursh) Nutt. is called Oregon grape, and is widely naturalised in Europe. The roots of many species were used medicinally by American Indians.

× *Mahoberberis
aquisargentii*
flowers, ½ life size
April 18th

× *Mahoberberis aquisargentii*
flowers, just over life size
April 18th

Mahonia japonica
fruit, ²/₃ life size
June 3rd

Mahonia japonica
¹/₂ life size
January 25th

Mahonia 'Moseri'
²/₃ life size
March 18th

Nandina

Nandina Thunb. (1781) consists of 1 species from eastern Asia, *N. domestica* Thunb., in the family Berberidaceae.

Description Shrubs to 3m, with upright, little-branched stems. The leaves are evergreen, much branched, with numerous leaflets, either in groups of 3 or pinnately arranged. The flowers are borne in pyramidal sprays, small, 6mm across, white, with numerous sepals and 6 petals. Anthers 6, opening by slits, with very short filaments. Ovary with 1 ovule, a short style, and minute stigma. Pollination is presumed to be by insects. The fruits are around 1cm across, red, or creamy yellow in var. *leucocarpa* Yanagawa, with 1 seed.

Key Recognition Features Upright stems and branching leaves.

Evolution and Relationships Not particularly close to other members of the family, and sometimes separated in the family Nandinaceae.

Ecology and Geography In woods and shady places. Native from central China to Japan, and long cultivated in both countries.

Comment *Nandina* is a useful evergreen for a shady corner, flowering and fruiting best in climates with warm, moist summers. In Japan it is often planted by the doors and under the eaves of houses to bring luck to the family, and was first recorded as a garden plant in the 13th century. By the late 19th century over 100 varieties were being grown in Japan, many variegated, some with thread-like, bamboo-like, or twisted leaves; it became associated with the tea ceremony and was also used in flower arrangements. In both China and Japan the berries have been used to treat asthma and whooping cough. It is sometimes called sacred bamboo.

Nandina domestica
fruits and seeds
3 × life size, December 15th

Nandina domestica
½ life size, December 15th

Nandina domestica
flower buds, ⅔ life size
December 15th

84

Menispermum

Menispermum L. (1753) consists of around 4 species of climbing shrubs in the family Menispermaceae. *Menispermum canadense* L., the Canada moonseed or yellow perilla, is the most common species.

Description Climbing shrubs to 6m, with twining stems. The leaves are variable in shape on the same plant, unlobed or with 3–7 lobes, usually wider than they are long. The flowers are small and white, in branched bunches, males and females on separate plants. There are 4–8 sepals in 2 rows, the petals 6–8, shorter than the sepals; the ovary has 2–4 styles. Pollination is presumed to be by insects. There are 12–24 stamens, with 4-celled anthers. The fruits are black, with unusual, spirally curved seeds.

Key Recognition Features Unusually shaped leaves and small fruits with spiral seeds.

Evolution and Relationships The Menispermaceae is a large, mainly tropical family, close to the Lardizabalaceae (see pp.74–79), but that family has mainly compound leaves and larger seeds with much endosperm. Other genera in eastern North America are *Cocculus* DC, the Carolina moonseed, and *Calyocarpum* Nutt., the cup-seed. *Sinomenium* Diels is a similar, hardy genus from China and Japan. All 3 are climbers with small, green flowers and red or black berries.

Ecology and Geography Growing in woods and along streams in eastern North America from Quebec and Manitoba to Georgia, and in eastern Asia.

Comment An unusual climber, sometimes grown for its attractive leaves. The roots have been used medicinally.

Menispermum canadense
⅓ life size
September 20th

Menispermum canadense
flowers, 2 × life size,
May 9th

Xanthorhiza simplicissima
flowers
2½ × life size
March 11th

Xanthorhiza simplicissima
flowers, ⅔ life size
March 11th

Xanthorhiza

Xanthorhiza Marsh. (1785), in the family Ranunculaceae, consists of 1 species from eastern North America, *X. simplicissima* Marsh., commonly called shrub yellow root.

Description A low shrub to 80cm, with yellow wood and suckering stems forming large patches. The leaves are mainly at the top of the stem, compound, pinnate or 2-pinnate, with toothed leaflets. The flowers are small, brownish-green, hanging in spike-like racemes, with 5 sepals, soon falling, and 5 petals, small and curved into nectaries. Stamens 5 or 10, ovaries 5–15, forming 1-seeded, light yellow pods. Pollination is presumed to be by insects.

Key Recognition Features Divided leaves on a short stem, yellow wood, and an acrid smell when crushed.

Evolution and Relationships Close in many ways to *Actaea* L., another Ranunculaceae with reduced flowers and compound leaves.

Ecology and Geography In woods from southern New York state to Kentucky and Florida.

Comment Sometimes grown for its attractive leaves, and in botanic gardens as one of the few shrubby members of the Ranunculaceae.

Xanthorhiza simplicissima
showing yellow bark
⅓ life size, October 12th

85

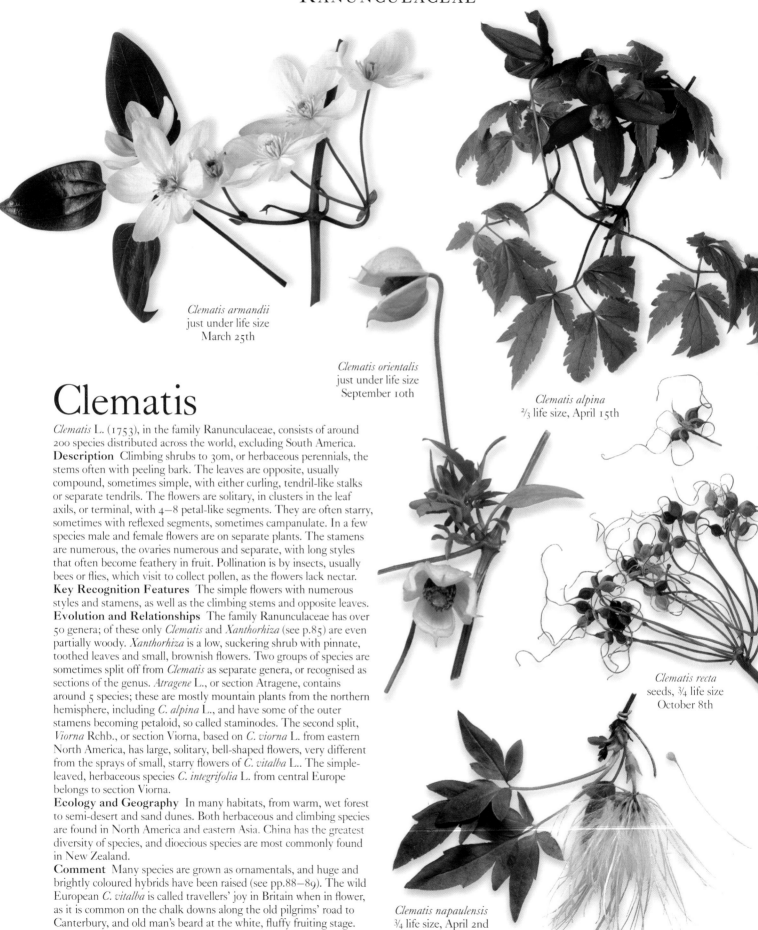

Clematis armandii
just under life size
March 25th

Clematis orientalis
just under life size
September 10th

Clematis alpina
²/₃ life size, April 15th

Clematis recta
seeds, ¾ life size
October 8th

Clematis napaulensis
¾ life size, April 2nd

Clematis

Clematis L. (1753), in the family Ranunculaceae, consists of around 200 species distributed across the world, excluding South America.

Description Climbing shrubs to 30m, or herbaceous perennials, the stems often with peeling bark. The leaves are opposite, usually compound, sometimes simple, with either curling, tendril-like stalks or separate tendrils. The flowers are solitary, in clusters in the leaf axils, or terminal, with 4–8 petal-like segments. They are often starry, sometimes with reflexed segments, sometimes campanulate. In a few species male and female flowers are on separate plants. The stamens are numerous, the ovaries numerous and separate, with long styles that often become feathery in fruit. Pollination is by insects, usually bees or flies, which visit to collect pollen, as the flowers lack nectar.

Key Recognition Features The simple flowers with numerous styles and stamens, as well as the climbing stems and opposite leaves.

Evolution and Relationships The family Ranunculaceae has over 50 genera; of these only *Clematis* and *Xanthorhiza* (see p.85) are even partially woody. *Xanthorhiza* is a low, suckering shrub with pinnate, toothed leaves and small, brownish flowers. Two groups of species are sometimes split off from *Clematis* as separate genera, or recognised as sections of the genus. *Atragene* L., or section Atragene, contains around 5 species; these are mostly mountain plants from the northern hemisphere, including *C. alpina* L., and have some of the outer stamens becoming petaloid, so called staminodes. The second split, *Viorna* Rchb., or section Viorna, based on *C. viorna* L. from eastern North America, has large, solitary, bell-shaped flowers, very different from the sprays of small, starry flowers of *C. vitalba* L.. The simple-leaved, herbaceous species *C. integrifolia* L. from central Europe belongs to section Viorna.

Ecology and Geography In many habitats, from warm, wet forest to semi-desert and sand dunes. Both herbaceous and climbing species are found in North America and eastern Asia. China has the greatest diversity of species, and dioecious species are most commonly found in New Zealand.

Comment Many species are grown as ornamentals, and huge and brightly coloured hybrids have been raised (see pp.88–89). The wild European *C. vitalba* is called travellers' joy in Britain when in flower, as it is common on the chalk downs along the old pilgrims' road to Canterbury, and old man's beard at the white, fluffy fruiting stage.

RANUNCULACEAE

Clematis hexapetala
⅔ life size
July 6th

Clematis urophylla
¾ life size
21st January

Clematis henryi
flowers, 1⅔ × life size
October 4th

Clematis henryi
½ life size, October 4th

RANUNCULACEAE

Clematis montana
½ life size
April 25th

Clematis 'Arabella'
½ life size
September 10th

Clematis
'Richard Pennell'
⅔ life size, July 3rd

Clematis 'Blue Belle'
just under life size
September 12th

Clematis 'Barbara Jackman'
⅔ life size, May 7th

Clematis 'Pearl d'Azure'
⅔ life size
July 14th

Clematis cultivars

Clematis hybrids are now among the most spectacular flowering woody climbers. Some rely on masses of small flowers for their effect, and the best of these are *C. montana* Buch.-Ham. ex DC and its forms, from China and the Himalayas, first introduced to Europe by Lady Amherst in 1831. The stems can reach 10m long, and the whole plant may be covered with pink or white flowers in late spring. The large-flowered hybrids are still associated with the name of Messrs Jackman of Woking, and the deep purple *C.* 'Jackmannii' is still one of the best hybrids. This first cross, between the European *C. viticella* L. and the Chinese *C. lanuginosa* Lindl., was made at their nursery in 1858, and they continued to produce new hybrids until the 20th century. Other large-flowered cultivars are hybrids of 2 other Chinese species long cultivated in China and Japan, *C. florida* Thunb. and *C. patens* Morr. & Decne. Modern hybrids are now found with flowers to 25cm across, in all shades from cream and white to pink, red, and purple.

Romneya

Romneya Harvey (1845), in the family Papaveraceae, consists of 2 very similar species from California.

Description Subshrubs to 2.5m, with hollow stems arising from far-creeping rhizomes. The leaves are divided, sometimes pinnate, sometimes deeply lobed, bluish-green, with a few bristly hairs. The flowers are on the ends of the stems and lateral branches. Sepals 3, green, falling separately, petals are 6, obovate, 4–10cm long. Stamens are numerous, the filaments yellow, purple at the base, and hinged below the anthers. The ovary is oblong to ovoid, with a short style and 7–12 stigmatic bands. Pollination is by insects, probably bees and beetles. The capsules are bristly, opening from the apex.

Key Recognition Features Large, white flowers and bluish-green, divided leaves. The sepals are beaked.

Evolution and Relationships *Argemone* L. (see Volume 2) has similar large, white flowers, but is always herbaceous and spiny.

Ecology and Geography In dry washes and canyons below 1200m in southern California and Baja California.

Comment A very attractive garden plant for a large, dry, sunny garden; the rhizomes can become invasive. In the name of the most familiar species, *R. coulteri*, W. H. Harvey (1811–66), author of *Flora Capensis* and Professor of Botany at Trinity College, Dublin, commemorated his friends Rev. T. Romney Robinson, an astronomer from Armagh, and Thomas Coulter, an Irish botanist who collected plants in Mexico and in California with David Douglas.

Dendromecon rigida
1½ × life size, June 24th

Dendromecon

Dendromecon Benth. (1835), in the family Papaveraceae, consists of 2 species from California.

Description Shrubs or small trees to 6m, with hollow, green twigs. The leaves are evergreen, leathery, lanceolate to elliptic or ovate, 2.5–10cm long. The flowers are yellow, poppy-like, on the ends of short branches. Sepals 2, falling as the flower opens; petals 4, 2–3cm long, obovate, with a satiny sheen. Stamens are numerous, the ovary superior, cylindrical, with a short style and 2 attached stigmas. Pollination is by insects. The fruits are curved capsules, 5–10cm long, with 2 valves. Seeds are small, brown or black.

Key Recognition Features The simple, greyish-green leaves and yellow, poppy-like flowers.

Evolution and Relationships Most of the family Papaveraceae are annuals or perennials, *Dendromecon* and *Romneya* being the only genera that are at all shrubby.

Ecology and Geography On dry slopes and washes, in scrub, especially after fires. *Dendromecon rigida* Benth. below 1800m in California and Baja California; *D. harfordii* Kellogg on Santa Catalina and the other Santa Barbara Islands.

Comment Attractive shrubs for dry gardens; in frosty areas *D. rigida* will survive better against a sunny wall.

Dendromecon rigida
½ life size, June 24th

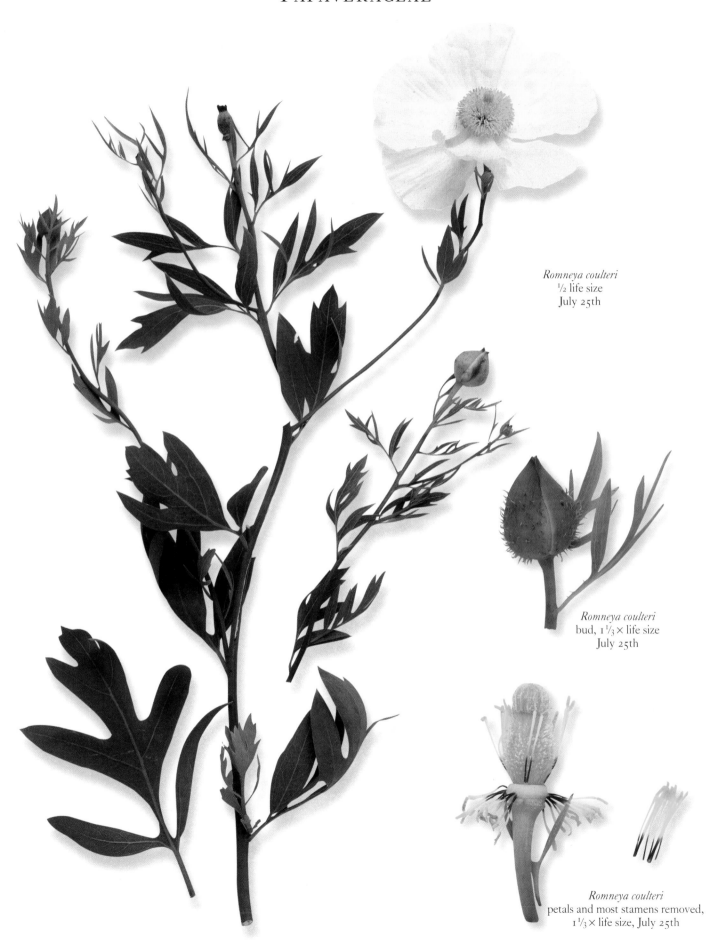

Romneya coulteri
½ life size
July 25th

Romneya coulteri
bud, 1⅓ × life size
July 25th

Romneya coulteri
petals and most stamens removed,
1⅓ × life size, July 25th

Atriplex

Atriplex L. (1753), in the family Chenopodiaceae, contains around 300 species, most of which are weedy annuals. A few shrubby species are cultivated for their silvery leaves.

Description Shrubs to 3m, with rather weak stems. The leaves are covered with silvery scales, undivided, and rather narrow in the shrubby species. The flowers are very small, green, and unisexual. Males have 5 segments and 5 stamens; females have 2 large bracteoles, usually no segments but sometimes 4–5, and 2 stigmas. Pollination is by wind. The fruits are dry, the bracteoles swelling and hardening around the seed.

Key Recognition Features Silvery, shiny stems and leaves and minute, green flowers with the bracteoles enlarging in fruit.

Evolution and Relationships The family Chenopodiaceae contains mostly annual or perennial herbs, including beet (*Beta* L.) and spinach (*Spinacia* L.), and a small tree, *Halostachys* C. A. Mey., from the saline steppes of central Asia. *Suaeda vera* J.F. Gmelin, often called *S. fruticosa*, is a small shrub with cylindrical, fleshy leaves, found in coastal southern England and around the Mediterranean.

Ecology and Geography In sandy, often saline ground in temperate and subtropical areas throughout the world, with many species in Australia.

Comment *Atriplex halimus* L., the tree purslane, is cultivated as an ornamental for its silvery leaves; it is especially good near the sea for its tolerance of salt. The orache, *A. hortensis* L., is an annual, often cooked like spinach, or grown for its red leaves. Other species are valuable as fodder in desert areas.

Ercilla volubilis
¼ life size, March 29th

Ercilla volubilis
⅔ life size, March 29th

Atriplex halimus
⅔ life size, October 5th

Atriplex halimus
¼ life size
October 5th

Ercilla

Ercilla A. Juss (1832), in the family Phytolaccaceae, consists of 1 species, *E. volubilis* A. Juss. from Peru and Chile.

Description Climbing shrubs to 6m, clinging by aerial roots with pad-like tips. The leaves are evergreen, fleshy, alternate, to around 5cm long. The flowers are small and pinkish, with 5 sepals, no petals, 4 long, white stamens, and a short style. Pollination is presumed to be by insects. The fruits are dark purple.

Key Recognition Features The fleshy, wavy-edged, toothed leaves on green stems.

Evolution and Relationships The family Phytolaccaceae contains 18 mainly subtropical genera. *Phytolacca americana* L., the pokeweed, is a large, leafy herbaceous perennial with spikes of small flowers followed by red-purple, juicy fruit. *Phytolacca dioica* (L.) Moq., the *ombu* or *bella sombra*, is an evergreen tree from the pampas of South America, sometimes planted in towns near the Mediterranean.

Ecology and Geography In rainforest in Chile, flowering in spring.

Comment An unusual climber, attractive when flowering well.

Plumbago

Plumbago L. (1753) is a genus of around 15 mainly subtropical species of annuals, perennials, and shrubs in the family Plumbaginaceae.

Description Shrubs to 3m, with green twigs scattered with scales of chalk. Leaves are alternate with rounded lobes (auricles) at the base, chalky beneath, generally oblanceolate. The flowers are usually in elongated heads at the ends of the branches, pale blue, purple, red, or white. The sepals are joined into a narrow tube with 5 ridges, scattered with long-stalked, sticky glands. Petals 5, joined into a long, narrow tube below, spreading above, with a strong midrib. Stamens 5, rarely 4, attached at the base of the tube. The style is solitary, with 5 spreading, papillose stigmas, the ovary superior. Pollination is by insects, visiting for the sticky nectar. Fruit is a 1-seeded capsule.

Key Recognition Features The long-stalked glands on the calyx, and the green twigs with alternate clusters of leaves.

Evolution and Relationships The relationships of the family Plumbaginaceae are uncertain. There are many similarities in flower structure with the Primulaceae, but also, especially in ovule type, with the Polygonaceae and with the Caryophyllaceae. The Plumbaginaceae are mainly herbaceous perennials (see Volume 2), which are successful cushion plants in harsh, often saline environments, for example sea thrift (*Armeria*), sea lavender (*Limonium*), and prickly thrift (*Acantholimon*), common on mountain steppes in southwest Asia. The genus *Ceratostigma* Bunge is often shrubby, like *Plumbago*, but differs in that its calyx lacks glands.

Ecology and Geography Usually in dry, rocky places, scattered in the tropics and subtropics, from South Africa and southern Europe to India, Australia, Mexico, and Peru.

Comment *Plumbago auriculata* Lam. is the common pale blue plumbago, planted everywhere in dry subtropical areas and in greenhouses. It will survive only a few degrees of frost. The name is derived from *plumbum*, lead, and is alluded to in the English name of leadwort; Pliny believed the plant to be an antidote to lead poisoning.

Fallopia

Fallopia Adans. (1763) in the family Polygonaceae, consists of around 9 species of annuals, shrubby climbers, and large herbaceous perennials. *Fallopia baldschuanica* (Regel) Holub, which is shown and described here, is the Russian vine, commonly grown to hide ugly fences and buildings.

Description Climbing shrubs to 5m or more, with twining stems that eventually become slightly woody. The leaves are deciduous, entire, usually heart-shaped. The flowers are small, pink or white, in narrow, branching spikes. There are 5 segments, the outer 3 larger, with keels or wings. Stamens 8, styles 3; flowers are often male or female in function, with either the stamens or the styles being sterile. Pollination is by perhaps by wind. The fruits are dry and nut-like, triangular in section, usually dark brown or black, and glossy.

Key Recognition Features The climbing stems, heart-shaped leaves, and triangular seeds.

Evolution and Relationships Polygonaceae is a mainly non-woody family that includes such familiar plants as docks (*Rumex*), buckwheat (*Fagopyrum*) and rhubarb (*Rheum*) (see Volume 2). Other slightly woody genera in the family include the climbing *Muehlenbeckia* Meissn. and the shrubby *Atraphaxis* L. from Europe and Central Asia.

Ecology and Geography *Fallopia* species are found in various habitats from Europe to Japan. *Fallopia baldschuanica* was first described from Baldschuan, in southern present-day Tajikistan, just north of the Afghan border. *Fallopia aubertii* (I. Henry) Holub. was described from Kanding in western Sichuan, 3000km to the east, but the 2 species differ in only very minor characteristics.

Comment *Fallopia* is often included in *Polygonum* L. or divided between other genera, but is at present recognised as a genus that includes both the mainly climbing species sometimes classed as *Bilderdykia* Dumort. and the giant, invasive herbaceous perennials previously classed as *Reynoutria* Houtt. which includes the potent pest Japanese knotweed, *Fallopia japonica* (Meissn.) Holub

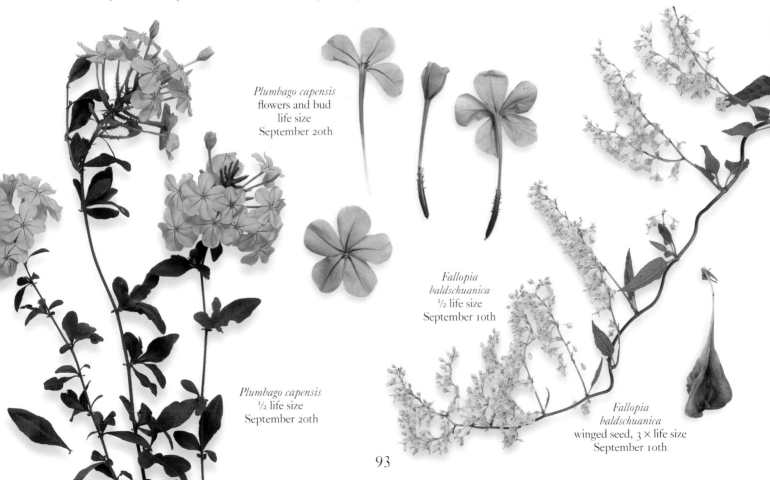

Plumbago capensis
flowers and bud
life size
September 20th

Plumbago capensis
½ life size
September 20th

Fallopia
baldschuanica
½ life size
September 10th

Fallopia
baldschuanica
winged seed, 3 × life size
September 10th

Trochodendron

Trochodendron Sieb. & Zucc. (1846) is the only genus in the family Trochodendraceae and consists of just 1 species, *T. aralioides* Sieb. & Zucc., from eastern Asia.

Description Trees to 25m or, as is usual in cultivation, dense shrubs, with green twigs ending in a large, pointed bud. The leaves are alternate, crowded at the ends of the shoots, evergreen, leathery, ovate to elliptic, 5–12cm long, stalked, with shallow, rounded teeth. The flowers are long-stalked, in elongated clusters at the tips of the shoots. Sepals and petals are absent; stamens 40–70, in 3 or 4 whorls around the ovary. The ovary is of 6–8 partly fused carpels, each with a single stigma. Pollination has not been recorded, but is probably by insects. The fruit is a capsule, made up of a ring of several-seeded, fused carpels with persistent stigmas.

Key Recognition Features The almost whorled, slender-stemmed evergreen leaves with a long curved point, and the heads of green flowers with numerous stamens.

Evolution and Relationships The family is very ancient and isolated; its nearest relatives are Tetracentraceae and, less closely, Cercidiphyllaceae (see p.96) and Eupteleaceae (see p.97), and it forms a link between Magnoliaceae (see pp.56–59) and Hamamelidaceae (see pp.100–109). Like some other primitive trees, including *Tetracentron*, the wood lacks vessels, but has tracheids. *Trochodendron*-like fossils are found in the late-Cretaceous.

Ecology and Geography In temperate rainforest, in Japan from northern Honshu southwards to the Ryu Kyu islands and Taiwan, in Korea, and on Quelpart Island. On Yakushima, where *Trochodendron* forms large trees, it grows epiphytically on the trunks of huge *Cryptomeria* trees (see p.34), rooted around 3m from the ground. The *Cryptomeria* leans one way, and the *Trochodendron* leans out in the opposite direction, balancing it.

Comment Birdlime was said to have been made from the bark in Japan. It is often grown as a curiosity in Europe, and makes a useful, hardy evergreen. The name *Trocho-* refers to the wheel-like arrangement of the radiating stamens.

Tetracentron

Tetracentron Oliver (1889), in the family Tetracentraceae, consists of 1 species, *T. sinense* Oliver, found from the eastern Himalayas to southwestern China.

Description Trees to 30m, with short, spur-like side-shoots as in *Ginkgo* (see p.18) and *Cercidiphyllum* (see p.96), and long, pointed buds. The leaves are deciduous, alternate, ovate, finely and sharply toothed, with 5–7 conspicuous, palmate veins; in Nepal and Bhutan the leaves have especially long, slender tips. The flowers are in catkin-like spikes of 10–15cm in length, 80–120 flowers per spike, in midsummer. The 4 sepals are small and green, the petals absent. Stamens 4; stigmas 4, attached at the base of the ovary. Pollination is perhaps by wind. The fruit is a 4-celled capsule; each cell has a spur-like appendage and up to 6 narrow seeds.

Key Recognition Features Strongly veined leaves and short, spur-like shoots.

Evolution and Relationships An ancient and isolated genus, sometimes put in Trochodendraceae. In appearance like a rather stouter *Cercidiphyllum* (see p.96), but differing clearly in its catkin-like flower spikes.

Ecology and Geography In forests, generally on damp slopes by streams, from Nepal, Bhutan, and Assam to southwestern China; recorded in Yunnan, Sichuan (on Mount Emei), Hubei, and Shaanxi.

Comment An elegant tree with upright and arching stems, colouring rich red in autumn, and also striking in midsummer with its yellowish-green catkins. The young leaves are often damaged by late frosts. The name *Tetracentron* refers to the floral parts in groups of 4.

Trochodendron aralioides
½ life size, May 2nd

Trochodendron aralioides
½ life size, May 2nd

Trochodendron aralioides
fruit, 3 × life size
November 4th

Trochodendron aralioides
in fruit, ⅔ life size
November 4th

Tetracentron sinense
⅓ life size
September 13th

Tetracentron sinense
fruit, 1½ × life size
September 13th

*Trochodendron
aralioides*
flowers, 2 × life size
June 12th

Trochodendron aralioides
½ life size, May 27th

95

Cercidiphyllum

Cercidiphyllum Sieb. & Zucc. (1846), with 2 very similar species, often called katsura or kadsura, is the only genus in the Cercidiphyllaceae.

Description Trees to 40m in height, fast-growing when young, around 4m after 5 years, 20m after 50 years. Very ancient trees are reported from China. The leaves are deciduous, opposite on long shoots, alternate on short shoots, almost round, smelling of burnt sugar, especially when frosted in spring or in autumn, when they are yellow to orange or red. The flowers are very small, produced before the leaves, with no petals but 4 scale-like bracts; the males have 15–20 pendulous, reddish stamens, the females 4–6 carpels, each with a long, crimson stigma. Pollination is by wind. The fruits are sausage-shaped, around 2cm long, in short-stalked clusters in the leaf axils. Seeds very small, flattened, winged.

Key Recognition Features The graceful, thin twigs and the rounded, opposite leaves are typical. The trees are often smelled before they are seen.

Evolution and Relationships An isolated family, usually linked with the Eupteleaceae and the Tetracentraceae (see p.94). Fossil remains from the late Cretaceous and from the early Tertiary at Joffre Bridge, near Red Deer, Alberta, link *Cercidiphyllum* to *Tetracentron* (see p.94) and show that the living Cercidiphyllaceae are but a small remnant of a formerly large and more diverse family.

Ecology and Geography In moist forests in the mountains, and deep soils in the lowlands. *Cercidiphyllum japonicum* (Sieb. & Zucc.) is found throughout Japan and in China, westwards to Sichuan and southeastern Gansu. The rarer species, *C. magnificum* (Nakai) Nakai is confined to Honshu, usually in the mountains. It has smooth bark and larger, more rounded leaves. In the past, *Cercidiphyllum* was also found in Europe and North America.

Comment *Cercidiphyllum japonicum* is a most attractive tree for a moist, sheltered position, where it is easy to grow, and often has lovely arching branches. The young leaves are easily damaged by late frosts. It is one of the earliest trees to change colour in the autumn. Selected garden cultivars have redder autumn tints, and 'Rotfuchs' is purple-leaved. In Japan the wood is used for furniture and indoor panelling, and the Ainu in northern Japan made dug-out canoes and mortars from it. The pendulous *Cercidiphyllum* is a variety of *C. magnificum*. The name refers to the leaf, which is like that of *Cercis*, the Judas tree.

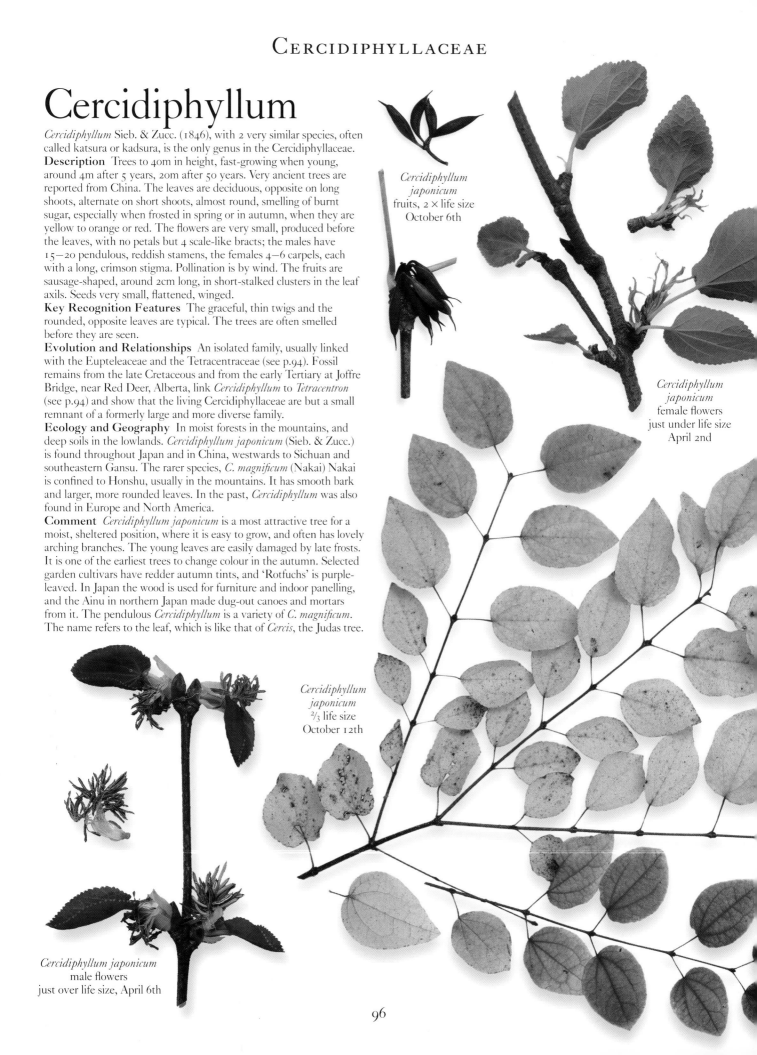

Cercidiphyllum japonicum
fruits, 2 × life size
October 6th

Cercidiphyllum japonicum
female flowers
just under life size
April 2nd

Cercidiphyllum japonicum
²⁄₃ life size
October 12th

Cercidiphyllum japonicum
male flowers
just over life size, April 6th

Euptelea

Euptelea Sieb. & Zucc. (1846), in the family Eupteleaceae, consists of 2 species in China and Japan.

Description Trees to 15m, or large shrubs, with slender twigs. The leaves are deciduous, alternate or in groups at the end of short shoots, irregularly toothed, with an abrupt, short point, reddish when young. The flowers are stalked, in small bunches in the leaf axils along the branches, the sepals and petals reduced to a minute cup. Stamens 8—18, the anthers hanging on slender filaments, developing before the styles, so the flowers pass through a male and then a female stage. Ovary is of 8—18 free, stalked carpels. Pollination is probably by wind as well as by insects. The fruits are slender-stalked, with narrow, papery wings, with 1—3 seeds, bright red and conspicuous along the branches when young.

Key Recognition Features Broad or rounded, toothed leaves with an abrupt, slender point.

Evolution and Relationships Close to *Cercidiphyllum* in floral structure.

Ecology and Geography In wet forests, with *E. pleiosperma* Hook. & Thoms. (syn. *E. franchettii*) from the eastern Himalayas to central China, *E. polyandra* Sieb. & Zucc. in Japan, from Honshu southwards.

Comment Attractive trees sometimes grown in collections; the leaves sometimes colouring red and yellow in autumn. The name is derived from *ptelea*, the Greek for elm.

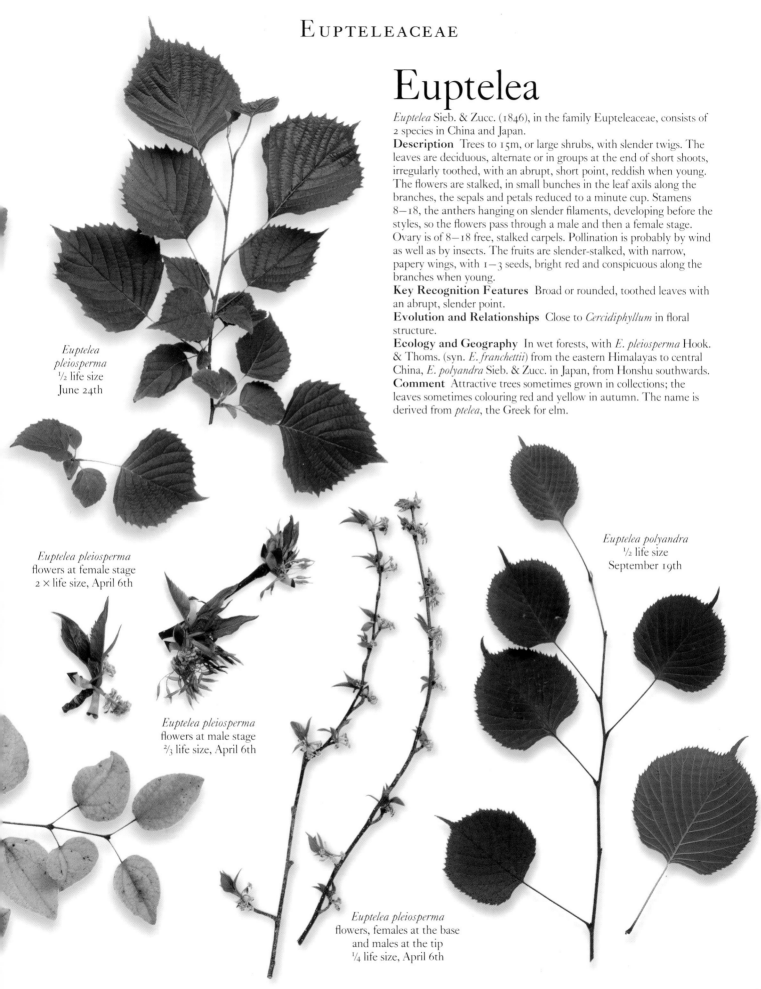

Euptelea pleiosperma
½ life size
June 24th

Euptelea pleiosperma
flowers at female stage
2 × life size, April 6th

Euptelea pleiosperma
flowers at male stage
⅔ life size, April 6th

Euptelea pleiosperma
flowers, females at the base
and males at the tip
¼ life size, April 6th

Euptelea polyandra
½ life size
September 19th

Platanus

Platanus L. (1753), in the family Platanaceae, consists of about 8 species from the northern hemisphere, commonly called the plane tree or, in America, the sycamore.

Description Trees to 50m or more, with silvery and often flaking bark. The leaves are deciduous, alternate, 3- to 7-lobed, to 30cm long, the swollen base of the leaf stem hiding the buds. The male and female flowers are in separate, spherical clusters, the males with 3 or 4 very small sepals, 3 or 4 minute petals, and 3 or 4 stamens; the females with 10–12 flowers in the cluster, each flower with 3 or 4 sepals, without petals, and with 5–9 styles, each with a long, red stigma. Pollination is by wind. The fruits hang in spheres, breaking into single achenes, each with a basal tuft of stiff hairs that aids dispersal by wind.

Key Recognition Features The maple-like leaves of most species, combined with alternate leaves, leafy stipules, and flaking bark.

Evolution and Relationships The family Platanaceae, of which this is the only genus, is close to the Hamamelidaceae.

Ecology and Geography In rocky valleys, often along streams or by lakes. Three species are found in North America, the most common of them, *P. occidentalis* L., from Ontario and Maine to central Mexico. *Platanus orientalis* L., the chenar tree, is native from eastern Europe to the Himalayas, and much planted both in Islamic gardens and in village squares, where it often reaches a huge girth.

Comment The London plane, *P. × hispanica* Mill., is often planted as a street tree. Its exact status is in some doubt, but it originated in Oxford Botanic Garden from seed sent from Montpellier in France. The timber, called lacewood, is used for veneers, cut radially to give a pale, silvery brown surface with regular darker rays. *Platanus* was also used medicinally by the American Indians. The name is derived from the Greek, *platanos*, mentioned by Aristotle and Plato, referring to its broad leaves.

Platanus × hispanica
½ life size, autumn colour
December 4th

Platanus × hispanica
with male and female
flowers and ripe fruits
½ life size, May 12th

Platanus × hispanica
female flowers
life size, May 12th

Platanus × hispanica
ripe fruit and seeds
1½ × life size, May 12th

98

Liquidambar

Liquidambar L. (1753), in the family Hamamelidaceae, contains around 5 species scattered across the northern hemisphere, called sweetgum in North America for their fragrant resin.

Description Trees to 41m, fast-growing, with stiff, spreading branches and often corky, winged twigs. The leaves are deciduous, alternate, maple-like (*Acer*, see p.354), 3- to 7-lobed, palmately veined, aromatic when crushed, to 20cm long. The flowers are unisexual, produced on the ends of the shoots, the males and females on the same tree. Sepals and petals are absent. The males are in upright, elongated clusters, 3–6cm long, with 4–8 stamens; females are in hanging, spherical heads, with 5–8 staminodes and a 2-locular ovary with 2 styles. Pollination is by wind. The fruits are spherical and spiny with hardened, curved styles. Seeds 8–10mm long, winged on 1 end.

Key Recognition Features The aromatic, maple-like leaves, which are alternate.

Evolution and Relationships The family Hamamelidaceae contains around 31 interesting and diverse genera, showing primitive chacteristics; many have scented resin. They are scattered in eastern North America, Central America, Asia, Africa, and Australia. All have persistent styles and hard-walled capsules opening to expose 1 or 2 bony seeds. *Liquidambar* itself is grouped with 2 other genera from South East Asia: *Altingia* Noronha., with narrowly lanceolate, evergreen leaves, and *Exbucklandia* R. W. Brown, with evergreen, heart-shaped leaves, both of which also have spherical fruiting heads and winged seeds. *Liquidambar* and *Altingia* are sometimes placed in a separate family, the Altingiaceae.

Ecology and Geography In woods and forest, often by streams and rivers, or in wet places. *Liquidambar styraciflua* L. is native from from New York to Texas in North America and through Mexico to Nicaragua. *Liquidambar formosana* Hance is found from Taiwan to Sichuan and Hubei, and southwards to Vietnam. *Liquidambar orientalis* Mill. is found in southwest Turkey and Rhodes, an unusual distribution for a relict tree; it or a very similar plant is known from fossil remains in Bulgaria, dating from the Pliocene.

Comment *Liquidambar styraciflua* is often planted as an ornamental, as its leaves colour well in autumn, being usually purplish, sometimes bright red. The gum and other parts of the tree were much used by American Indians for medicine, and the gum is now used especially for coughs and catarrh, as well as for chewing; the wood is used for furniture and panelling. The gum from *L. orientalis*, liquid storax, is used in friar's balsam and is the balm of Gilead of the biblical Psalms.

Liquidambar styraciflua
mature fruits
²⁄₃ life size
December 4th

Liquidambar styraciflua
autumn colour
¹⁄₃ life size
November 20th

Liquidambar
'Worplesdon'
¹⁄₃ life size
November 20th

Liquidambar styraciflua
flowers
just under life size
April 18th

Liquidambar orientalis
¹⁄₃ life size
November 20th

Parrotia persica
fruits, 1½ × life size
September 10th

Parrotia

Parrotia C.A. Mey. (1831), in the family Hamamelidaceae, contains
1 species, *P. persica* (DC) C.A. Mey, from northern Iran and
Azerbaijan, sometimes called Persian ironwood.

Description Trees to 12m, or spreading shrubs, with smooth,
flaking bark, and twigs with black, finely velvety buds. The leaves are
deciduous, alternate, oblong to ovate, with widely spaced veins,
asymmetrical at the base. The flowers are bisexual, without petals,
but with large bracts, appearing before the leaves. There are 5–7
stamens, red and conspicuous and 2 styles. Pollination is by wind.
The fruits are 2-celled, each cell containing 1 seed.

Key Recognition Features Asymmetrical leaves and smooth,
flaking bark.

Evolution and Relationships The small flowers without petals
and with red anthers are close to the evergreen *Distylium* (see p.108)
and *Sycopsis* (see p.109) from eastern Asia.

Ecology and Geography In forests, where it makes a large tree,
and forming mountain scrub at higher altitudes along the Caspian
coast in Iran and Azerbaijan.

Comment One of the best shrubs for autumn colour, the leaves
turning yellow, red, and purple; unlike many of the family, it is
tolerant of chalk and dry soils in full sun. Most of the clones in
cultivation form wide-spreading shrubs, but 'Vanessa' forms a
more-or-less upright tree.

Parrotia persica
showing flower buds and autumn
colour, just over life size
November 4th

Parrotiopsis

Parrotiopsis (Niedenzu) C. Schneid. (1904), in the Hamamelidaceae, contains 1 species, *P. jacquemontiana* (Dcne) Rehder.

Description Trees to 6m or shrubs, with greyish bark and twigs and finely velvety buds. The leaves are deciduous, alternate, often wider than long, finely toothed, with widely spaced veins, slightly rough beneath, with star-shaped hairs. The flowers are bisexual, in round clusters surrounded by 4–6 leafy, white bracts, appearing as the leaves unfurl. Petals are absent; stamens 15–24, conspicuous. The ovary has 2 cells and 2 styles. Pollination is perhaps by insects. The fruits are hard, crowded into heads, the capsules splitting into 4.

Key Recognition Features Thin, grey twigs and very broad, hazel-like (*Corylus*, see p.119) leaves.

Evolution and Relationships In vegetative characteristics close to *Parrotia*, but in flower closer to the American *Fothergilla* (see p.107).

Ecology and Geography In the undergrowth of coniferous forests and in deforested areas in the western Himalayas from Afghanistan to Kashmir and Himachal Pradesh.

Comment The specific name commemorates Victor Jacquemont (1801–32), who left France in 1828 to escape an unhappy love affair, and visited Simla, Tibet, and Kashmir collecting for the Jardin des Plantes. He died of cholera in Bombay, but not before he had collected many new species.

*Parrotiopsis
jacquemontiana*
unripe fruiting heads
1¾ × life size
November 24th

*Parrotiopsis
jacquemontiana*
ripe fruits, 1½ × life size
December 15th

*Parrotiopsis
jacquemontiana*
flowers and bracts
just over life size
April 20th

*Parrotiopsis
jacquemontiana*
⅔ life size
November 1st

Parrotia persica
flowers
just over life size
February 16th

Corylopsis sinensis
var. *calvescens*
f. *veitchiana*
flowers
¾ life size
March 12th

Corylopsis sinensis
flowers
1 ⅓ × life size
March 29th

Corylopsis sinensis
var. *willmottiae*
flowers, ¾ life size
March 12th

Corylopsis sinensis
seeds and capsules
1 ¼ × life size
September 24th

Corylopsis sinensis var.
calvescens f. *veitchiana*
½ life size
March 5th

Corylopsis

Corylopsis Sieb. & Zucc. (1835), in the family Hamamelidaceae, consists of 6 species from Bhutan to Japan.

Description Shrubs or small trees to 5m, with large, smooth buds. The leaves are deciduous, alternate, with palmate and pinnate veins that end in long-pointed teeth, smooth or with scattered hairs beneath. The flowers appear before the leaves and are scented, in spikes of up to 20, hanging from the leaf axils. There are 5 sepals, short, and 5 petals, conspicuous. Stamens 5, alternating with forked staminodes, sometimes longer than the petals, with yellow or reddish anthers. The ovary has 2 styles. Pollination is by insects. The fruits are hard, rounded capsules with a pair of curved, horn-like styles, splitting open to eject 2 hard, shining black seeds.

Key Recognition Features Thin leaves with strong ribs, smooth buds, and catkin-like flowering stems.

Evolution and Relationships The hanging flower spikes are similar to those of *Sinowilsonia*, but that has unisexual flowers with no petals and larger fruit. The individual flowers are closer to *Fortunearia* Rehd. & Wils..

Ecology and Geography On forest margins and in woods and scrub on steep hillsides from Bhutan, where *C. himalayensis* Griff. is found, to western China, where the very variable *C. sinensis* Hemsl. is widespread. Four species, including the commonly grown *C. spicata* Sieb. & Zucc. and *C. pauciflora* Sieb. & Zucc., are found in Japan.

Comment *Corylopsis* are quick-growing shrubs, very attractive in flower in spring, and graceful in leaf, with golden autumn colour. The early flowers, however, are easily damaged by spring frosts.

Corylopsis sinensis
autumn leaves
¾ life size
November 12th

Sinowilsonia

Sinowilsonia Hemsl. (1906), in the family Hamamelidaceae, contains 1 species, *S. henryi* Hemsl. from China.

Description Shrubs or small trees to 8m. The leaves are deciduous, alternate, with fine teeth, elliptic to ovate, to 15cm long. The flowers are in greenish catkins, with 5 sepals but without petals, the males hanging to 6cm, the females to 3cm, lengthening as the fruit ripens. Stamens 5; the ovary has 2 styles. Pollination is perhaps by wind. The fruit is an egg-shaped capsule with numerous black seeds.

Key Recognition Features The deciduous leaves and hanging, catkin-like flowers without petals.

Evolution and Relationships In flower and leaf, *Sinowilsonia* is remarkably like the catkin-bearing trees such as hazel (*Corylus*, see p.119). It is closely related to the Chinese *Fortunearia* Rehd. & Wils., which differs in having bisexual flowers with minute green petals and carried in erect spikes.

Ecology and Geography On the banks of mountain streams in northwestern Hubei in central China.

Comment The name commemorates 2 of the greatest plant collectors in China: Ernest Henry Wilson (1876–1930), who collected first for Veitch's nursery in 1899, and later for the Arnold Arboretum at Harvard University, Massachusetts, of which he was director from 1927 until his death, and Augustine Henry (1857–1930), who was a medical officer with the Imperial Chinese customs bureau, and later professor of forestry in Dublin.

Sinowilsonia henryi
female (small) and
male (large) catkins
just over life size, April 6th

Corylopsis sinensis
fruit and empty capsules
½ life size
September 24th

Sinowilsonia henryi
½ life size
October 10th

Disanthus cercidifolius
flowers
1 1/4 × life size
November 15th

Disanthus cercidifolius
autumn colour and flowers
2/3 life size
November 15th

Disanthus cercidifolius
2/3 life size
July 27th

Disanthus

Disanthus Maxim. (1866), in the family Hamamelidaceae, consists of 1 species, *D. cercidifolius* Maxim. from Japan and China.

Description Shrubs to 8m, with smooth twigs. The leaves are deciduous, alternate, smooth, and almost round, paler beneath, with palmate veins, turning purple, red, and orange in autumn. The flowers are back-to-back in pairs, like small, crimson starfish, faintly scented, produced in autumn as the leaves are falling. They are 1.5cm across, with 5 recurved, hairy sepals, 5 pointed, red petals, 5 very short stamens, and 2 short styles, Pollination is by insects. The fruits are 2-celled capsules with up to 6 black, shining seeds in each cell.

Key Recognition Features The smooth, round leaves, glaucous beneath, are only likely to be confused with *Cercis canadensis* L. (see p.273), and especially with the purple-leaved 'Forest Pansy', but those have pea-like flowers in spring.

Evolution and Relationships Very different in flower and leaf from all other genera in the family, and generally placed in its own subfamily, the Disanthoideae.

Ecology and Geography Native in moist woods in Japan, in central Honshu and Shikoku; possibly also in southeastern China.

Comment Planted for its wonderful early autumn colour.

Loropetalum

Loropetalum Rchb. (1818), in the family Hamamelidaceae, contains 1 or perhaps 2 species from the Himalayas to China and Japan.

Description Shrubs to 2m, wide-spreading with slender twigs. The leaves are evergreen, alternate, ovate to heart-shaped, 2–4cm long. The flowers are 6–8 in a cluster, produced in late winter or spring. There are 4 sepals, and 4 petals, linear, and white or deep pink. Stamens 4, very short, the anthers with 4 pollen sacs. Ovary with 2 styles. Pollination is by insects. The fruits are solitary, woody, splitting into 2 cells.

Key Recognition Features The small, evergreen leaves and narrow petals.

Evolution and Relationships Close to *Hamamelis* (see p.106) in the structure of the flowers.

Ecology and Geography On warm, sunny slopes and limestone cliffs, from Assam in India to southern China and northwards to Hubei, and in Japan, only on Honshu.

Comment An attractive small shrub for a warm climate such as the Mediterranean or California, or for a large pot under glass in cooler climates.

Loropetalum chinense
flowers, 2 × life size
April 20th

Loropetalum chinense
life size, October 25th

Hamamelis × *intermedia*
fruit and buds, 1½ × life size, October 1st

Hamamelis 'Arnold Promise'
autumn leaves
½ life size, October 20th

Hamamelis × *intermedia*
'Hiltingbury', flowers
life size, December 15th

Hamamelis

Hamamelis L. (1753), in the family Hamamelidaceae, contains 4 species and many garden hybrids, called witch hazels. All of them originate in China, Japan, or North America.

Description Shrubs or small trees to 11m, with grey bark and brown, velvety buds. The leaves are deciduous, alternate, and hazel-like (*Corylus*, see p.119), with parallel veins, asymmetric at the base, colouring well in autumn. The flowers are scented, in clusters on short shoots, usually on bare stems in late autumn, winter, or early spring. There are 4 sepals, the petals 4, linear, curled in bud and in frosty weather, pale yellow to orange and red. Nectar-bearing staminodes are 4; stamens 4, very short. The ovary is 2-celled, with 2 styles. Pollination is by insects. The fruits are velvety, hard, 4-lobed, splitting open to eject 2 hard, shining black seeds.

Key Recognition Features The hazel-like leaves (*Corylus*, see p.119) in summer with dull brown, velvety buds, and the yellow or red flowers with ribbon-like petals in winter.

Evolution and Relationships Similar to other members of the family in leaf and capsule, but very different in flower. *Hamamelis* shows the typical distribution of an ancient genus, with similar species in both eastern Asia and eastern North America. The diversity of flower types in the family and the scattered distribution of many of the genera suggest that this is an ancient family, probably ancestral to catkin-bearing genera such as *Corylus* on one side, but also close to the *Rosaceae* (see pp.228–271).

Ecology and Geography In woods, often by streams. In eastern North America *H. vernalis* Sarg. is confined to the Ozark plateau in Arkansas, Missouri, and Oklahoma, while the autumn-flowering *H. virginiana* L. is common from Quebec and Ontario to Florida and Texas. In Asia *H. japonica* Sieb. & Zucc. is found throughout Japan, *H. mollis* Oliver in China from eastern Sichuan to Hubei and Jiangxi.

Comment Witch hazels are among the best winter-flowering shrubs, either in light woodland or as specimens on a sheltered, partly shaded lawn. The bark and leaves of *H. virginiana* are the source of the distilled witch hazel of medicine, used to reduce the swelling of bruises and swollen veins.

Hamamelis
'Arnold Promise'
flowers, life size
March 25th

Hamamelis × *intermedia* 'Jelena'
autumn leaves, ⅓ life size
November 6th

Fothergilla

Fothergilla L. (1753), in the family Hamamelidaceae, consists of 2 species from eastern North America.

Description Shrubs to 6.5m, suckering from stolons, with star-shaped hairs on stems, buds, and leaves. The leaves are deciduous, alternate, shallowly toothed, with few, strong veins, often colouring well in autumn. The flowers are scented, in short, dense spikes, without petals. The sepals are reduced to a cup; the 12–32 stamens have long, stiff, white filaments and yellow anthers. The ovary has 2 long styles, which become curved and horn-like in fruit. Pollination is by insects. The fruits are in clusters, with 2 reddish-brown seeds per capsule.

Key Recognition Features Hairy, hazel-like leaves (*Corylus*, see p.119) and upright, white, brush-like flowers.

Evolution and Relationships The flowers are similar to those of *Parrotiopsis* (see p.101), but that has conspicuous bracts.

Ecology and Geography *Fothergilla gardenii* L. in swamps and sandy pine barrens on the coastal plains in Alabama, North and South Carolina, Georgia, and Florida; *F. major* Lodd. on riverbanks, rocky areas, and dry woods in the foothills and mountains of Alabama, North and South Carolina, Georgia, Tennessee, and 1 locality in Arkansas.

Comment Often grown as ornamentals for their flowers and autumn colour. Linnaeus named *F. gardenii* after John Fothergill (1712–80), a London doctor who had a private botanic garden near West Ham and a particular interest in American plants, and after Alexander Garden (1730–91), an Aberdonian who practised medicine in Charleston, South Carolina in 1752–83 and corresponded with Linnaeus.

Fothergilla gardenii
fruits, life size
September 16th

Fothergilla major
flowers, life size
April 2nd

Fothergilla major
autumn leaves, ¾ life size
November 16th

Fothergilla major
flowers, 1¼ × life size
April 18th

Distylium

Distylium Sieb. & Zucc. (1835), in the family Hamamelidaceae, contains 12 species of trees and shrubs from eastern Asia.

Description Trees to 25m, or shrubs, with star-shaped hairs on the twigs. The leaves are evergreen, alternate, elliptic to ovate. The flowers are unisexual, in short, upright spikes to 4cm long in the leaf axils, without petals. The males have 5 sepals and 5 stamens with large, red anthers; the females have 5 sepals, 5 staminodes, and 2 styles. Pollination is perhaps by wind. The fruits are woody, 2-pointed capsules.

Key Recognition Features The evergreen leaves and the short spikes of flowers in the leaf axils in early spring.

Evolution and Relationships Close to the other evergreen genus in the family, *Sycopsis*, which has stalkless flowerheads.

Ecology and Geography The common *D. racemosum* Sieb. & Zucc. is found in forests in Japan, Korea, and southern and central China. Other species are found southwards into Malaysia, and in Central America.

Comment Sometimes cultivated as an evergreen shrub in a shady position. The wood is used for furniture in Japan.

Distylium racemosum
flowers, life size
April 2nd

Distylium racemosum
fruits, life size
September 16th

Distylium racemosum
½ life size
April 2nd

Sycopsis

Sycopsis Oliver (1860), consists of 2 or 3 species of trees and shrubs from eastern Asia, in the family Hamamelidaceae.

Description Trees to 7m, or shrubs. The leaves are evergreen, alternate, elliptic to lanceolate, sometimes toothed, with short stalks. The flowers are male or bisexual, in stemless clusters in the leaf axils, without petals, but with softly hairy bracts. Males have minute sepals and 6—10 long stamens with large, orange-yellow or red anthers; in the bisexual flowers the stamens develop before the styles. Pollination is perhaps by wind. The fruits are woody, pubescent, 2-pointed capsules with 2 shining brown seeds.

Key Recognition Features The evergreen leaves and the stemless heads of flowers in the leaf axils in early spring.

Evolution and Relationships Close to *Parrotia* (see p.100) in flower, but to *Distylium* in general appearence.

Ecology and Geography *Sycopsis sinensis* Oliver is found in forests and along streams in eastern Sichuan and Hubei, central China.

Comment Sometimes cultivated as an evergreen shrub for a shady position.

× Sycoparrotia

× *Sycoparrotia semidecidua* Endress & Anliker (1968) is an interesting hybrid between *Parrotia persica* (see p.100) and *Sycopsis sinensis*. Its semi-evergreen habit is unusual, and it forms a large, strong-growing shrub, with *Parrotia*-like leaves and flowers. Some twigs often remain evergreen, while others lose their leaves. It is said to have been raised in Switzerland in around 1950, but was not named until 1968.

× *Sycoparrotia semidecidua*
flowers, 1½ × life size
February 12th

Sycopsis sinensis
flowers, life size
February 12th

× *Sycoparrotia
semidecidua*
⅔ life size
February 15th

Fagus

Fagus L. (1753), the beech tree, consists of 8–10 species from around the northern hemisphere, in the family Fagaceae.

Description Trees to 40m, with a smooth, grey trunk and twigs with long, pointed buds. The leaves are deciduous, alternate, with numerous parallel, straight side-veins, sometimes with short teeth, and usually with white, silky hairs. The flowers are unisexual, produced in the axils of the new leaves, the males and females on the same tree; the males are in oval, hanging clusters, with 4–7 joined sepals, no petals, and 6–16 long stamens. The female flowers are usually short-stalked, in pairs, with 3 slender styles. Pollination is by wind. The fruits consist of a softly spiny or scaly, 4-lobed husk, enclosing 2 or 3 shining brown, 3-cornered seeds, only 1 of which is fertile. The seedlings have characteristic fan-shaped cotyledons.

Key Recognition Features The long, pointed buds in winter, and the parallel-veined leaves in summer.

Evolution and Relationships The family Fagaceae, with 8 genera, is characterised by the cupule around the seed; an acorn cup in the oak (*Quercus*, see pp.112–15), a 4-lobed, woody husk in the beech, and a spiny husk, silky inside in the chestnut (*Castanea*, see p.118). The cupule has been shown to develop as an extension of the stalk below each flower. *Fagus* itself is close to the southern hemisphere *Nothofagus*, which generally has smaller leaves and seeds.

Ecology and Geography In forests in the mountains, where it often forms pure stands. One species, *F. grandiflora* Ehrh., is widespread in eastern North America, where it often occurs as an understorey shrub as well as a large tree. The common beech, *F. sylvatica* L., is found throughout Europe; subsp. *orientalis* (Lipsky) Greuter & Burdet, the oriental beech, is the largest tree, found in Greece, Turkey, and the Caucasus. The remaining species come from China and Japan, where *F. japonica* Maxim. has its fruits hanging on slender stalks to 4cm long.

Comment Beech is a valuable timber tree, traditionally used for chairs and other turned furniture, for which it was often planted on the chalk hills of southern England. Grey squirrels cause such damage to young trees that few are planted now. The seeds, commonly called beech nuts or mast, are edible and very tasty, though rather small. Beech makes a good hedge, responding well to frequent clipping and keeping its dead leaves in winter. Many varieties of *F. sylvatica* are cultivated as ornamentals, including various narrow-leaved cultivars, the copper beech with blackish-purple leaves, and fastigiate forms, including 'Dawyck'; the very fine weeping beech 'Pendula' can cover large areas by rooting at the tips of the branches to form a ring of secondary trunks.

Fagus sylvatica
fruits and seeds
²/₃ life size
September 15th

Fagus sylvatica
flowers
¹/₂ life size
May 10th

Fagus engleriana
autumn colour
¹/₂ life size
November 4th

Nothofagus

Nothofagus Blume (1850), in the Fagaceae, contains 35 species in the southern hemisphere, commonly called southern beech or *roblé*.

Description Trees to 35m, or shrubs, with short buds. The leaves are deciduous or evergreen, alternate, with up to 18 parallel, straight side-veins, and usually with irregular, shallow lobes and short teeth. The flowers are unisexual, produced in the axils of new and old leaves, the males and females on the same tree. Males are solitary or in groups of up to 3 or rarely 5, with sepals joined at the base, no petals, and 8–40 long stamens with yellow or red anthers. Females are usually short-stalked, usually in groups of 3, with 3 short styles. Pollination is by wind. The fruits consist of a small, softly spiny or scaly, 3- or 4-lobed husk, enclosing 2 or 3 brown, 3-cornered seeds, the middle seed flattened where 3 are present.

Key Recognition Features The usually small, parallel-veined, toothed leaves and small, beech-like fruit (*Fagus*).

Evolution and Relationships Close to *Fagus*, but much more diverse in flower structure, leaf, and habit.

Ecology and Geography In moist coastal to mountain forest, from New Guinea and New Caledonia to Australia and New Zealand, and in Argentina and Chile in South America.

Comment Many *Nothofagus* species are valuable timber trees in the southern hemisphere, and are frequently planted in the warmer, milder parts of western Europe and northwestern North America. They are generally fast-growing in cultivation, but liable to blow down in exceptional gales.

Nothofagus betuloides
male flowers
2 × life size
April 30th

Nothofagus betuloides
in flower, ½ life size
April 30th

Nothofagus antartica
female flowers and old
cupules, 2 × life size
April 30th

Nothofagus obliqua
open cupules and seeds
just over life size, September 16th

Quercus

Quercus L. (1753), the oak, contains around 500 species throughout the northern hemisphere, in the family Fagaceae.

Description Trees to 30m or more, or shrubs, with rounded buds. The leaves are deciduous or evergreen, alternate, lobed, holly-like (*Ilex*, see p.179), toothed, or with smooth edges. The flowers are unisexual, males and females on the same tree; the males on slender, hanging, usually interrupted catkins, with minute sepals, no petals, and usually 6 stamens surrounding a tuft of hairs. The female flowers are on short stalks, 1 per cupule, with 3 styles. Pollination is by wind. The fruits are solitary acorns, up to 6cm long in Q. lobata Née, set in a cup, which may be smooth, variously scaly, or with soft spines.

Key Recognition Features Acorns in a cup, combined with the male flowers on hanging spikes. In spite of the many exceptions, most species have recognisably oak-shaped leaves.

Evolution and Relationships Within the family Fagaceae, oaks are linked with the unusual and primitive genus *Trigonobalanus* Forman, which has 2 species in the mountains of northern Thailand to Borneo and the Celebes, and 1 in Colombia. They have primitive, scaly, lobed cups around nuts with 3 or more angles. Fossil Fagaceae are recognised as far back as the middle of the Cretaceous, and *Trigonobalanus* itself has been found in the Eocene in Europe. The genus *Quercus* is divided into subgenera or sections: in subgenus Cyclobalanopsis, sometimes recognised as a separate genus, which includes *Q. acuta* Thunb., the leaves are evergreen and not lobed, and the cup scales are in concentric rings; all are native of eastern Asia. In section Lobatae, the American red and black oaks, the leaves are varied in shape, but if lobed, the lobes end in long points. The acorn cups mostly have narrow, overlapping scales, and most have acorns that take 2 years to ripen. All are native from North America to Colombia, and include *Q. rubra* L., *Q. phellos* L., the willow oak, *Q. imbricaria* Mich., the shingle oak, and *Q. agrifolia* Née, the coast live oak. Section Protobalanus, the golden-cup oaks, contains 5 species found from Oregon through California to Arizona and Mexico; they have evergreen leaves and acorns maturing in 2 years, with the scales of the cup embedded in golden or glandular hairs. *Quercus chrysolepis* Liebm. is the most common of this group. Section Quercus, the white oaks, contains around 200 species throughout the northern hemisphere, the leaves mostly deciduous with rounded lobes, but sometimes evergreen and either holly-like or smooth-edged. The acorn scales are varied, but are not glandular. *Quercus dentata* from China and Japan, the rare chestnut-leaved *Q. pontica*, and the English species *Q. robur* L. and *Q. petraea* (Matt.) Liebl. belong to this group.

Two further sections are confined to Europe and Asia. In the Turkey oaks, section Cerris Loudon, the buds often have thread-like scales between them; leaf-shapes vary, and the acorns, which take 2 years to mature, usually have bristly cups. *Quercus suber* L., the cork oak, *Q. cerris* L., the Turkey oak, *Q. castaneifolia* C.A. Mey., and *Q. libani* Oliv. belong to this section. Section Ilex Loudon includes evergreen species in which the fruit matures in 1 year or 2, and the cup scales lie flat. *Quercus ilex* L., the holm oak, and *Q. coccifera* L. belong here.

Ecology and Geography In various habitats from Mediterranean semi-desert to subtropical rainforest, but mainly in deciduous or evergreen forest with summer rainfall. From Colombia in Central America to Canada, and in Asia as far south as Malaysia. Around 90 species are recognised in the United States and Canada, and even more in Mexico, but only 27 in Europe.

Comment Oaks have a large variety of uses. The timber, especially that of *Q. robur*, the English oak, is hard and strong, and is used for shipbuilding, rafters, wine barrels, and furniture; Irish bog oak, which has been pickled for thousands of years in acid peat, is used today for furniture and guitar fingerboards. *Quercus alba* L. and *Q. macrocarpa* Mich. previously provided similar timber in North America, but these species have now been replaced as commercial crops by the faster-growing red oaks, such as *Q. rubra*. Oak bark was much used in tanning, as were the huge cups of the Valonia oak, *Q. macrolepis* Kotschy. Bark from *Q. suber* L. is the source of cork; it is grown mainly in western Spain and Portugal, being peeled off the trunks and lower branches about every 8 years. Acorns were eaten in the past in times of famine, and as a substitute for coffee; some species are more edible than others but most are very bitter. Pigs were commonly put out to forage in the woods for them in autumn, a practice called *pannage*, which is still important in Corsica and parts of Spain. *Quercus coccifera*, the kermes oak, forms low, holly-like bushes in the Mediterranean *garrigue*. It produces a red gall, formed by the insect *Kermes vermilio*, the blood of which was the source of a vermilion dye used by the Spartans to dye their battledress scarlet so that blood stains would not show. A yellow dye was extracted from the American *Q. velutina* Lam., called quercitron bark. Galls from *Q. infectoria* Oliv. from Turkey were used to make ink. Many species of oak are cultivated as ornamentals, notably the American red oaks *Q. rubra* and *Q. coccinea* Münchh. for their fast growth, distinctive leaves and good autumn colour, the evergreen holm oak *Q. ilex* as a tough hedge or large tree, and *Q. macrolepis* for its particularly large, well-shaped leaves. There is a good variegated form of *Q. cerris* and several upright forms of *Q. robur*, as well as a purple-leaved form and the golden-leaved 'Concordia'.

The illustrations of Quercus *continue on pp.114–15.*

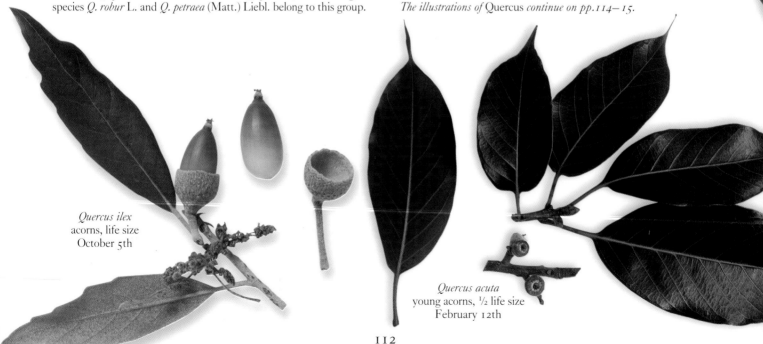

Quercus ilex
acorns, life size
October 5th

Quercus acuta
young acorns, ½ life size
February 12th

FAGACEAE

Quercus agrifolia
acorns
just under life size
December 5th

Quercus rubra
male flowers and female
flowers in the leaf axils
½ life size
May 11th

Quercus coccifera
¾ life size, November 12th

Quercus phellos
¾ life size
September 20th

Quercus phellos
autumn colour
¾ life size
September 20th

Quercus rubra
autumn leaves
¾ life size
October 12th

FAGACEAE

Quercus robur
male flowers
just over life size
April 28th

Quercus robur
acorns and cups
just under life size
October 14th

Quercus robur
female flowers
just over life size
April 28th

Quercus dentata
autumn leaves
½ life size
October 31st

Quercus castanifolia
acorns and leaves
¾ life size, September 20th

Quercus pontica
young male flowers
just under life size
May 11th

Quercus petraea
var. *pinnatifida*
½ life size
October 20th

Quercus petraea
¾ life size, September 15th

Quercus pontica
autumn leaves
½ life size
October 20th

Castanopsis

Castanopsis Spach (1842), in the family Fagaceae, contains around 100 species, mainly in subtropical eastern Asia.

Description Trees to 30m, or shrubs, with flattened buds. The leaves are evergreen, alternate, leathery, sometimes toothed, with unbranched, parallel side-veins. The flowers are in arching spikes, with females at the base, males covering the rest. Males have 5 or 6 distinct sepals and 10—12 stamens; females are 1—3 per cupule, each with 3 styles. Pollination is by wind and perhaps by insects. The fruits usually ripen in the second year and have a sometimes spiny, sometimes scaly husk, which splits unevenly when ripe.

Key Recognition Features The evergreen leaves and the chestnut-like fruit (*Castanea*, see p.118).

Evolution and Relationships Close to *Castanea*, but differing mainly in being evergreen, and in its nuts taking 2 years to ripen.

Ecology and Geography In woods and scrub from western China to Japan and southwards into Malaysia.

Comment From illustrations of the Japanese *C. cuspidata* (Thunb.) Schottky and from comments by E. H. Wilson on Chinese species, trees of *Castanopsis* are very striking when in full flower. They are however seldom cultivated in Britain, doing better in areas with warmer summers, such as Australia, New Zealand, and the southeastern United States. The seeds can be eaten like chestnuts.

Chrysolepis chrysophylla
¹/₃ life size
October 12th

Castanopsis cuspidata
¹/₂ life size, June 21st

Chrysolepis

Chrysolepis Hjelmquist (1948), in the family Fagaceae, consists of 2 species in western North America, often called western chinkapin.

Description Trees to 45m or shrubs. The leaves are evergreen, alternate, with parallel side-veins, usually golden beneath. The flowers are in spikes, with females at the base, males covering the rest, or sometimes all male. Male flowers have distinct sepals and 12 stamens; female flowers are 3 or more per cupule, each with 3 styles. Pollination is probably by insects. The fruits ripen in the second year after pollination; the cupule surrounding the nuts has 7 valves and is densely spiny, with branched spines; the nuts are light brown, edible, and sweet.

Key Recognition Features The evergreen leaves, golden beneath, and the spiny, chestnut-like fruit (*Castanea*, see p.118).

Evolution and Relationships Close to *Castanopsis*, with which it is sometimes united, but differing in the structure of the cupule.

Ecology and Geography In redwood forests, pine forests, and scrub from Washington and Oregon to California. The tall tree form of *C. chrysophylla* (Dougl. ex Hook.) Hjelmquist is found in coastal forest in the north. *Chrysolepis sempervirens* (Kellogg) Hjelmquist grows at up to 3300m in the Sierra Nevada.

Comment Sometimes cultivated as an evergreen shrub. The seeds can be eaten like chestnuts.

Lithocarpus

Lithocarpus Blume (1826), in the family Fagaceae, contains 1 species in North America and 100–200 species in eastern Asia.

Description Trees to 45m, or shrubs. The leaves are evergreen, alternate, leathery, not lobed but sometimes toothed, with parallel, unbranched side-veins. The flowers are unisexual or all male. The males are in narrow, upright spikes, with 12–18 or more stamens surrounding a sterile ovary; females are at the base of the spikes, 1 per cupule, with 3 styles. Pollination is by insects and perhaps also by wind. The fruits are acorn-like (*Quercus*, see pp.112–15) in a cup, or sometimes in a contorted cluster or dense head.

Key Recognition Features The upright, yellow male flower spikes and the crowded, acorn-like fruits.

Evolution and Relationships Although superficially similar to oak, especially in its acorn-like seeds, the flowers of *Lithocarpus* are closer to those of *Castanea* (see p.118). Around 100 species, including the Japanese *L. glaber* (Thunb.) Nakai and *L. edulis* (Makino) Nakai, are sometimes separated in the genus *Pasania* Oersted, but most authorities consider that *Pasania* differs so little from *Lithocarpus* that it is not worth separating.

Ecology and Geography In evergreen forest, usually subtropical or warm-temperate. *Lithocarpus densiflorus* (Hook. & Arn.) Rehder is found in California and Oregon, with var. *densiflorus* as a tree near the coast and var. *echinoides* (R. Br.) Abrams as a shrub in the northern Sierra foothills. The other species range from the eastern Himalayas to Japan and southwards to Java.

Comment A few of these fine evergreen trees are cultivated in specialist warm temperate gardens, but they are scarce because they do not often set viable seed in cultivation.

Chrysolepis chrysophylla
fruit, life size
October 12th

*Lithocarpus
variolosus*
²/₃ life size
May 18th

Lithocarpus pachyphyllus
¹/₂ life size, October 6th

Castanea

Castanea Mill. (1754), in the family Fagaceae, contains 8–10 species, including the European *C. sativa* Mill., the sweet or Spanish chestnut, and the American *C. pumila* Mill., the chinkapin.

Description Trees to 70m, or shrubs, often with deeply fissured, spiral bark. The leaves are deciduous, alternate, to 30cm long, with numerous parallel side-veins, which often end in a tooth. The flowers are scented, unisexual, and in long spikes produced after midsummer, females at the base of the spike, males covering the rest, or entirely male. The sepals are separate, petals absent, the stamens 12, surrounding a sterile ovary. Fertile female flowers 1–3 per cupule, with 6–9 carpels and styles. Pollination is by insects, especially bees; some wind pollination may also occur. The seeds are the edible sweet chestnuts; usually 3 in a spiny husk, usually with only 1 or 2 ripening.

Key Recognition Features The large leaves, 15–30cm long, with parallel veins, the spiny covering of the nuts, and the spiral, deeply fissured bark of old trees.

Evolution and Relationships The arrangement of male and female flowers on the same spike is considered more primitive than the unisexual spikes of oaks (*Quercus*, see pp.112–15) and beeches (*Fagus*, see p.110). The closest genus to *Castanea* is the evergreen *Chrysolepis* (see p.116) from western North America.

Ecology and Geography In forests and mountain valleys. The American *C. dentata* (Marshall) Borkh. was formerly common throughout the eastern states; the 2 chinkapins are more local. The European *C. sativa* is probably native only south of the Alps, but is widely planted northwards to Scotland and Ireland. Other species are found in Japan and China, where *C. henryi* Rehd. & Wils. is reported to reach 70m.

Comment The sweet chestnut is thought to have been introduced into northern Europe by the Romans, who used the nuts to make flour; today they are often candied as *marrons glacées* or roasted. The timber is very durable, easy to split, and widely used for fencing, laths, and in the past for hop poles, for which there are still large plantations on poor, sandy soils in Kent and Sussex. The American chestnut was formerly a dominant forest tree, but in the 1930s was infected by the Asian blight, *Cryphonectria parasitica*, which has destroyed practically all the large specimens.

Castanea sativa
½ life size
June 22nd

Castanea sativa 'Heterophylla'
immature fruit, ⅔ life size
September 16th

Castanea sativa
nuts, just over life size
November 24th

Corylus maxima
½ life size
September 15th

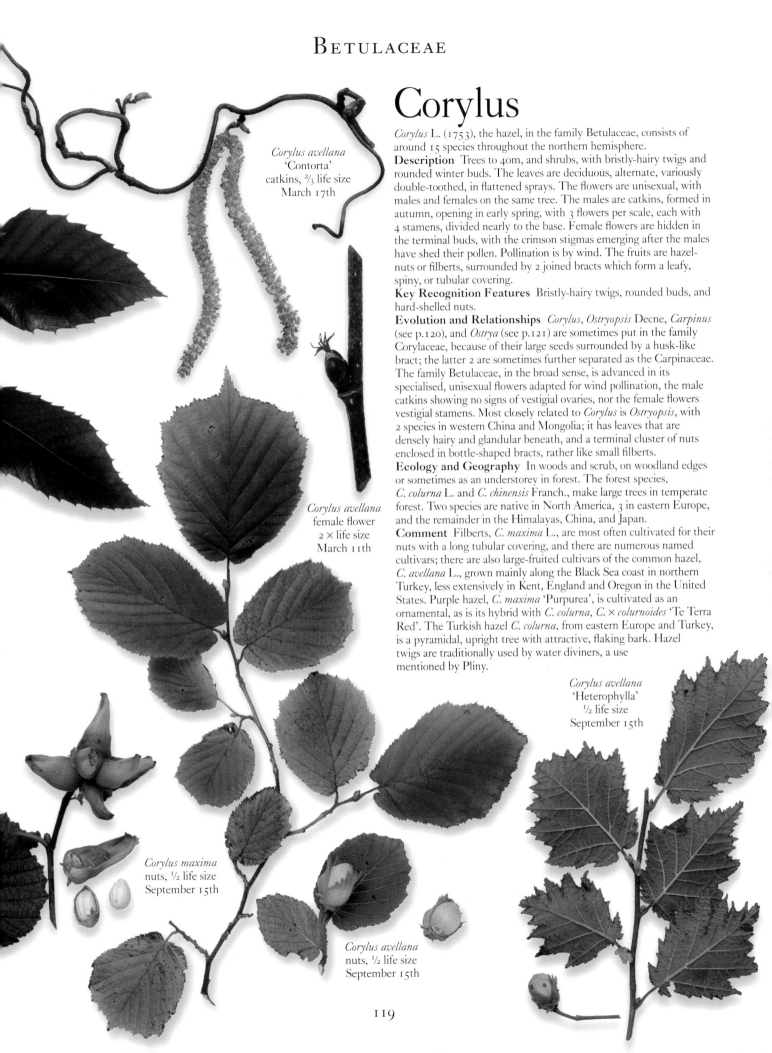

Corylus avellana
'Contorta'
catkins, ⅔ life size
March 17th

Corylus avellana
female flower
2 × life size
March 11th

Corylus

Corylus L. (1753), the hazel, in the family Betulaceae, consists of around 15 species throughout the northern hemisphere.

Description Trees to 40m, and shrubs, with bristly-hairy twigs and rounded winter buds. The leaves are deciduous, alternate, variously double-toothed, in flattened sprays. The flowers are unisexual, with males and females on the same tree. The males are catkins, formed in autumn, opening in early spring, with 3 flowers per scale, each with 4 stamens, divided nearly to the base. Female flowers are hidden in the terminal buds, with the crimson stigmas emerging after the males have shed their pollen. Pollination is by wind. The fruits are hazel-nuts or filberts, surrounded by 2 joined bracts which form a leafy, spiny, or tubular covering.

Key Recognition Features Bristly-hairy twigs, rounded buds, and hard-shelled nuts.

Evolution and Relationships *Corylus*, *Ostryopsis* Decne, *Carpinus* (see p.120), and *Ostrya* (see p.121) are sometimes put in the family Corylaceae, because of their large seeds surrounded by a husk-like bract; the latter 2 are sometimes further separated as the Carpinaceae. The family Betulaceae, in the broad sense, is advanced in its specialised, unisexual flowers adapted for wind pollination, the male catkins showing no signs of vestigial ovaries, nor the female flowers vestigial stamens. Most closely related to *Corylus* is *Ostryopsis*, with 2 species in western China and Mongolia; it has leaves that are densely hairy and glandular beneath, and a terminal cluster of nuts enclosed in bottle-shaped bracts, rather like small filberts.

Ecology and Geography In woods and scrub, on woodland edges or sometimes as an understorey in forest. The forest species, *C. colurna* L. and *C. chinensis* Franch., make large trees in temperate forest. Two species are native in North America, 3 in eastern Europe, and the remainder in the Himalayas, China, and Japan.

Comment Filberts, *C. maxima* L., are most often cultivated for their nuts with a long tubular covering, and there are numerous named cultivars; there are also large-fruited cultivars of the common hazel, *C. avellana* L., grown mainly along the Black Sea coast in northern Turkey, less extensively in Kent, England and Oregon in the United States. Purple hazel, *C. maxima* 'Purpurea', is cultivated as an ornamental, as is its hybrid with *C. colurna*, *C. × colurnoides* 'Te Terra Red'. The Turkish hazel *C. colurna*, from eastern Europe and Turkey, is a pyramidal, upright tree with attractive, flaking bark. Hazel twigs are traditionally used by water diviners, a use mentioned by Pliny.

Corylus avellana
'Heterophylla'
½ life size
September 15th

Corylus maxima
nuts, ½ life size
September 15th

Corylus avellana
nuts, ½ life size
September 15th

Carpinus orientalis
with fruits, ⅓ life size
July 1st

Carpinus japonica
⅓ life size, July 1st

Carpinus japonica
fruits, just under life size
July 1st

Carpinus orientalis
bracts and nuts
just under life size, July 1st

Carpinus turczaninowii
⅓ life size
July 1st

Carpinus fangiana
⅓ life size
July 1st

Carpinus betulus
male and female flowers
life size, April 2nd

Carpinus

Carpinus L. (1753), the hornbeam, consists of 26 species throughout the northern hemisphere, in the family Betulaceae.

Description Trees to around 30m with a spreading habit, or large shrubs, with bluntly pointed winter buds. The leaves are deciduous, alternate, with parallel veins, and generally with sharp teeth. The flowers are unisexual, with males and females on the same tree. The males are catkins, enclosed in the buds through the winter, opening in late spring, with 3 flowers per scale, each with 3 stamens, divided into 2, hairy at the apex. Females are 2 per bract. Pollination is by wind. The fruits are in hanging spikes, with leafy bracts partly enclosing a small, hard nut. The bracts aid dispersal of the seeds by wind.

Key Recognition Features The leaves resemble those of the beech (*Fagus*, see p.110), but are generally thinner, duller, and more toothed. The leafy and pendulous fruiting heads are also typical. The bark is generally smooth and greyish.

Evolution and Relationships *Carpinus* is closest to *Ostrya* and has the fruiting scale partially surrounding the fruit. These genera have larger seeds than the birches (*Betula*, see p.123) and alders (*Alnus*, see p.122), but smaller than the hazels (*Corylus*, see p.119), and are sometimes separated into the Carpinaceae.

Ecology and Geography In woods: 1 species with 2 subspecies in eastern North America; 1 species in Mexico and Central America; 2 species in Europe; the rest from the Himalayas to Japan.

Comment The wood of the common hornbeam, *C. betulus* L., is exceptionally hard and was used for tools, cog-wheels, and butcher's blocks, and in pianos. It is most common in southeastern England and western France, where it forms woods on sandy soils and is often used to form clipped hedges. Some other species are grown as ornamentals. *Carpinus turczaninowii* Hance, from northeastern China, Korea, and Japan, has small leaves up to 5.5cm long, while *C. fangiana* Hu has leaves to 27cm and fruiting catkins to 45cm long.

Ostrya

Ostrya Scop. (1760), the hop hornbeam, contains 5 species in the northern hemisphere, in the family Betulaceae.

Description Trees to 18m, or shrubs, with the bark breaking into strips and scales. The leaves are deciduous, alternate, with parallel side-veins and fine teeth, similar to those of *Carpinus*. The flowers are unisexual, with males and females on the same tree. Males are catkins, formed in autumn, remaining exposed through the winter to open in late spring, with 3 flowers per scale, each with 3 stamens, divided into 2, hairy at the apex. Females are 2 per bract. Pollination is by wind. The fruits are in hanging, hop-like clusters (*Humulus,* see Volume 2), with flattened, bladder-like bracts enclosing a small, hard nut.

Key Recognition Features The *Carpinus*-like leaves and the hop-like fruit clusters.

Evolution and Relationships Close to *Carpinus*, differing mainly in the exposed winter catkins and the bladder-like scale around the nut. These scales aid dispersal of the seeds by wind.

Ecology and Geography In dry woods and rocky places, with 1 species in southern Europe, 1 in eastern China and Japan, and 3 or 4 species in North America, Mexico, and Central America.

Comment *Ostrya virginiana* (Mill.) K. Koch is the ironwood, common from Canada to Florida, used for sleigh runners, wheel rims, mallet heads, and tool handles. *Ostrya carpinifolia* Scop. is an attractive small tree in the foothills of the Alps and mountains around the Mediterranean, the leaves particularly bright green in spring.

Ostrya virginiana
⅓ life size, July 1st

Ostrya virginiana
female flowers
and old catkins
⅓ life size
May 2nd

Carpinus caroliniana
catkins, ⅔ life size
April 6th

Ostrya virginiana
bracts, nuts, and
whole fruit
1⅓ × life size
July 1st

Alnus

Alnus Mill. (1754), the alder, consists of around 25 species around the northern hemisphere and southwards to Argentina, in the Betulaceae.
Description Trees to 30m, and shrubs, with often dark brown twigs and bark; winter buds usually with short stalks. The leaves are deciduous, alternate, often rounded to obovate, and usually toothed. The flowers are unisexual, with males and females on the same tree. The males are catkins, formed in autumn, and remaining exposed through the winter, opening in early spring or, in a few species, in autumn; there are 3 flowers per scale, each with 4 stamens, often reddish anthers, and undivided filaments. Female flowers are usually 2 per bract. Pollination is by wind. The fruits are in cone-like heads, with woody, scale-like bracts and small, narrowly winged seeds, dispersed by wind and water.
Key Recognition Features The often rounded leaves, the exposed winter catkins, and the cone-like fruits.
Evolution and Relationships Wind specialisation is taken a stage further in alders than in the larger-fruited genera of the family, putting them closest to *Betula*. *Alnus* is a diverse genus, some species, such as the Japanese *A. firma* Sieb. & Zucc., having hornbeam-like leaves (*Carpinus*, see p.120). Two groups flower in autumn: the subtropical subgenus Cremastogyne, and subgenus Clethropsis, which include the common Himalayan species *A. nepalensis* D. Don and the rare North American relict species *A. maritima* (Marsh.) Muhlenb. ex Nutt.
Ecology and Geography Usually near water, on river banks, in wet woods, and on lake shores. Eight species are found in North America, 5 in Europe, and 10 in Japan. One species, *A. acuminata* Kunth, is found through the Andes into South America.
Comment Alders are successful in open, bare areas such as were left after the retreating glaciers, on gravel banks in rivers, or on any bare soil close to water. All species can fix atmospheric nitrogen through actinomycete-filled cells in their roots, which may appear red and swollen, and these also help them to colonise wet, infertile ground. Alder wood was used in the past for piles, as it is resistant to rotting underwater, and is found both in old Amsterdam and in the Rialto in Venice. The wood was also used for violins and for carving. *Alnus cordata* Desf., the Italian alder, is fast-growing and much planted for shelter belts, especially since it keeps its leaves into early winter.

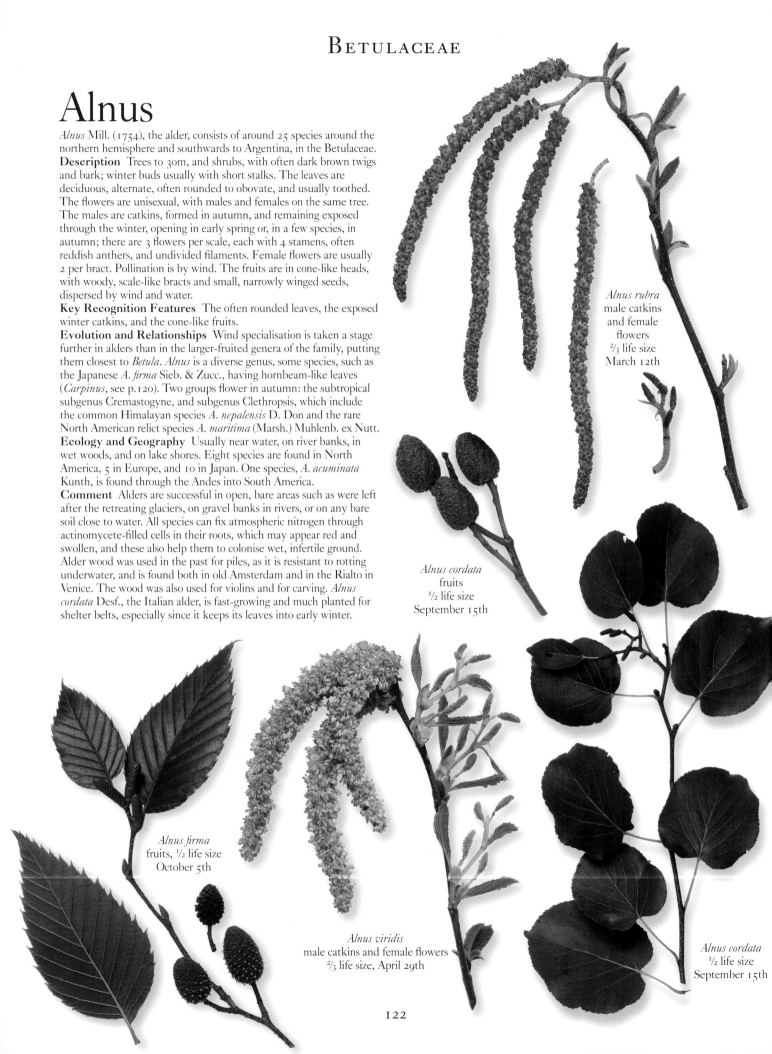

Alnus rubra
male catkins
and female
flowers
²/₃ life size
March 12th

Alnus cordata
fruits
¹/₂ life size
September 15th

Alnus firma
fruits, ¹/₂ life size
October 5th

Alnus viridis
male catkins and female flowers
²/₃ life size, April 29th

Alnus cordata
¹/₂ life size
September 15th

Betula uber with fruits
life size, September 16th

Betula

Betula L. (1753), the birch, in the family Betulaceae, contains around 30–35 species found throughout the northern hemisphere.

Description Trees to 30m, or shrubs, with white, pink, or reddish, often peeling bark. The leaves are deciduous, alternate, with parallel side-veins, usually toothed. The flowers are unisexual, with males and females on the same tree. The males are catkins, formed in autumn and remaining exposed through the winter to open in early spring; there are 3 per scale, each with 2 or 3 stamens, the anthers and filaments divided nearly to the base. Females are usually 3 per bract. Pollination is by wind. The fruits are in upright or pendulous, catkin-like heads, with trident- or fleur-de-lys-shaped, scale-like bracts and small, usually winged seeds, breaking up on the tree, dispersed by wind.

Key Recognition Features The peeling bark and the female catkins, which break up on the tree.

Evolution and Relationships Birches are close to *Alnus*, but less diverse, though also well adapted to wind pollination and dispersal. Birch-like fossils are known as far back as the upper Cretaceous, and fossil species from the Eocene are close to *B. lenta* L. and *B. utilis* D. Don. The more primitive species are thought to be those with numerous side-veins in the leaf and erect catkins, such as *B. lenta*, and especially the large-leaved *B. insignis* Franch. from southwestern China. The most derived are the dwarf, shrubby species from high latitudes, such as the arctic *B. nana* L. Hybridisation between species is common in the wild where 2 species grow close together, and birches have evolved partly by hybridising. The species often produce diploid pollen and egg cells, instead of the haploid cells usual in species, so resulting in fertile tetraploid seedlings that can form new species. All alders, in contrast, have retained the same chromosome number; the base number for both genera is 2n=28.

Ecology and Geography Most birches are colonists of dry, open habitats, dying of old age as oaks (*Quercus*, see pp.112–15) and other larger trees become established, though a few, such as *B. alleghaniensis* Britt. are common as large specimens in mature woodland. Pure birch woodlands are a common feature of cold-temperate areas, most conspicuously covering much of Siberia, and of high mountains in warmer parts. Of the 30–35 species recognised, 18 are found in North America, about 10 in China, and the remainder in Europe and Japan.

Comment Birches are commonly cultivated as fast-growing, graceful trees with ornamental bark. The wood of *B. pendula* Roth. is light and an excellent insulator, so is used for the inside of saunas in Finland. The wood of *B. alleghaniensis* is used for furniture, panelling, and plywood in north America. Birch sap, collected in spring when it pours from the tree, can be used to make beer. Various species have been used medicinally, and *B. lenta* was used as a source of oil of wintergreen, or methyl salicylate; American Indians used it to treat many ailments. Betulinic acid from the bark is reported to trigger cell death in melanomas in culture. The bark of *B. papyrifera* Marsh. is waterproof and was used for birch-bark canoes by American Indians, as well as for roofing in some parts of the world. Several species were used as paper, including *B. utilis*, which has been found in the form of 1800-year-old Buddhist manuscripts in Afghanistan. *Betula uber* (Ashe) Fernald is almost extinct in the wild, and is sometimes listed as *B. lenta* subsp. *uber*.

fruiting scales and seeds
Betula ermannii (top),
Betula cordifolia (centre),
Betula pumila (bottom)
2 × life size
September 16th

Betula uber
autumn leaves, life size
September 16th

Betula pumila
male catkins and
female flowers
just over life size
April 29th

Betula pubescens
fruits, ¾ life size
September 16th

Juglans

Juglans L. (1753), the walnut, in the family Juglandaceae, consists of around 21 species throughout the Americas and in Eurasia.

Description Trees to 50m, or shrubs, with glandular twigs with chambered pith; buds with scales. The leaves are deciduous, alternate, pinnate, with or without a single terminal leaflet. The flowers are unisexual, with males and females on the same tree. The males are in catkins, formed on 2-year-old twigs, opening with the leaves in late spring, sometimes with 4 sepals, and with 7–50 stamens, anthers usually pubescent. Females are in clusters on the ends of the current year's twigs, bottle-shaped, with 2 styles. Pollination is by wind. The nuts are enclosed in thick husks, with 2 often wrinkled shells.

Key Recognition Features The chambered pith in the branchlets, which can be seen if a young twig is cut lengthwise.

Evolution and Relationships Fossils probably ancestral to the Juglandaceae are found in the Eocene in North America, and pollen has been found in the upper Cretaceous in Sweden. The relationships of the family Juglandaceae are uncertain, but it is considered close to the oaks (*Quercus*, see pp.112–15) and other catkin-bearing trees. The current view regards the husk to be part of the calyx, and the nut analogous to the nut of a hazel (*Corylus*, see p.119). *Juglans* itself is closest to *Carya*, which differs in having solid pith in its twigs.

Ecology and Geography In woods and on dry, rocky slopes in the mountains, as well as along streams. Six species are found in North America, including *J. nigra* L., the American black walnut, and *J. cinerea* L., the butternut or white walnut; others are native through Mexico to the Andes in northern Argentina. One species, the common walnut *J. regia* L., is widely cultivated in Europe; it is probably native in Romania and the Balkans and eastwards to Central Asia.

Comment Walnuts are commonly planted for their nuts and their timber. Even in England, *J. nigra* can be fast-growing, reaching 15m in 30 years, but in areas with warm, wet summers it would grow faster; in the cooler parts of Britain, *J. regia* grows much better. The most sought-after timber with the best figuring is taken from the very base of the trunk below ground level and from burrs, from both *J. nigra* and *J. regia*. It was used for fine English furniture from the late 16th century until the large-scale importation of mahogany, which is resistant to woodworm, from the Caribbean in the 1730s. Walnut is still the preferred wood for gunstocks, and *J. nigra* is now being used for guitar fingerboards instead of mahogany. Many named varieties of walnut have been selected for their nuts, and these are propagated by grafting. Edible oil is extracted from the nuts; this industry is based in France. The name *Juglans* is said to come from *jovis glans*, the nut of Jupiter, and walnut or welshnut from the old English for foreign nut, *walh-hnutu*.

Juglans regia, with female flowers
½ life size, May 20th

Juglans regia
male catkin
1⅔ × life size
May 20th

Juglans nigra fruit
½ life size
September 16th

Juglans regia
female flower
1⅔ × life size, May 20th

Carya

Carya Nutt. (1818), the hickory, consists of 18 species, mainly in eastern North America, in the family Juglandaceae.

Description Trees to 52m, the twigs with solid pith, the bark often peeling away in large plates and strips. The leaves are deciduous, alternate, pinnate, with 3–17 leaflets, colouring a beautiful gold in autumn. The flowers are unisexual, with males and females on the same tree. The males are in catkins, on 1- or 2-year-old twigs, in groups of 3, opening with the leaves in late spring, sometimes with 4 sepals, and with 3–10 stamens. Females are in short spikes, on the ends of the current year's twigs, bottle-shaped, with 2 styles. Pollination is by wind. The nuts are enclosed in husks that split when ripe, with 2 shells, often wrinkled but usually smoother than *Juglans*.

Key Recognition Features The twigs with solid pith, the catkins in groups of 3, and the leaves with the terminal leaflet the largest.

Evolution and Relationships Close to *Juglans*, but more diverse, particularly in North America. Fossil remains are known from the northwestern United States, Europe, and western Siberia, and also from China and Japan, but only 1 species, *C. cathayensis* Sarg., is now found in South East Asia.

Ecology and Geography In woods, mainly in plains by rivers, but also in hills, with 4 species common in eastern North American woods, the rest mainly in the southern states, with some extending to Mexico.

Comment The pecan, *C. illinoinensis* (Wang.) K. Koch, is grown for in North America for its nuts. Varieties with thin shells have been selected, as most other species have very thick-shelled nuts, although *C. ovata* (Miller) K. Koch also has thin shells and edible nuts. *Carya cordiformis* (Wang.) K. Koch is called the bitternut. Hickory wood is very good for axe and mattock handles and hurley and lacrosse sticks, being very strong and shock-resistant.

Carya laciniosa
autumn leaf
½ life size
October 16th

Carya ovata
female flowers
¾ life size
June 15th

Carya ovata
male catkins
¾ life size, June 15th

Carya cordiformis
nut with husk splitting into 4 and clean nuts
⅔ life size
November 1st

Juglans regia, fruit with husk partly removed and with green husk
¾ life size, September 20th

Carya ovata
⅓ life size, June 15th

Pterocarya rhoifolia
young fruits
$1\frac{1}{3}$ × life size, July 1st

Pterocarya rhoifolia
$\frac{1}{3}$ life size, July 1st

Pterocarya

Pterocarya Kunth. (1824), the wing-nut, contains around 6 species from the Caucasus to Japan, in the family Juglandaceae.

Description Trees to 40m, often with suckers, and very fast-growing; most species without bud scales, so that the winter twigs end in small, brown, folded leaves. Twigs with chambered pith. The leaves are deciduous, alternate, pinnate, to 60cm long, with 7–21 leaflets, which increase in size towards the leaf apex. The flowers are unisexual, with males and females on the same tree. The males are in catkins, in groups of 3, opening with the leaves in late spring; each flower has 1–4 small sepals and 6–18 stamens. Female flowers are on long, loose spikes, each with a 2-lobed, fluffy, pinkish style. Pollination is by wind. The small nuts are enclosed in winged husks, in spikes to 50cm long.

Key Recognition Features The large, pinnate leaves and hanging spikes of winged nuts. In winter the small, brown, velvety leaves instead of bud scales and the chambered pith are easy to see.

Evolution and Relationships *Pterocarya* forms a group with *Platycarya* Sieb. & Zucc., *Engelhardtia* Leschen. ex Blume, and some other tropical genera, distinct from *Juglans* (see p.124) and *Carya* (see p.125). *Platycarya strobilacea* Sieb. & Zucc. from Japan has 4–12 erect male catkins surrounding an erect female inflorescence, which becomes cone-like with very small, winged nutlets. *Engelhardtia spicata* Leschen. ex Blume, from the Himalayas, has leaves without a terminal leaflet and long, hanging spikes of nutlets with 3-lobed wings.

Ecology and Geography In wet places in flood plains and by rivers. Several species are found in China, 1 in Japan, and 1 in the Caspian forest, in the southern Caucasus, and along the Black Sea.

Comment Several species are grown as ornamentals in large gardens, soon making huge trees. *Pterocarya rhoifolia* Sieb. & Zucc. from Japan has fruiting spikes to 30cm long and reaches 30m in height. *Pterocarya fraxinifolia* (Lam.) Spach, the Caucasian wing-nut, is even bigger, and a prolific producer of suckers. *Pterocarya* × *rehderiana* Schneid. (*P. stenoptera* × *P. fraxinifolia*) has hybrid vigour, and can grow 30m in about 40 years, in good years growing around 2m.

Pterocarya fraxinifolia
1 female and 2 male
catkins, $\frac{3}{4}$ life size
May 10th

Pterocarya fraxinifolia
sections through
male catkin
$1\frac{3}{4}$ × life size
May 10th

Myrica

Myrica L. (1753), the bog myrtle or wax myrtle, consists of around 50 species, found mainly in the Americas and South East Asia, in the family Myricaceae. *Comptonia* L'Hérit., sometimes included in *Myrica*, has 1 species in northeastern North America.

Description Trees to 25m, or shrubs, with aromatic twigs and leaves. The leaves are deciduous or evergreen, alternate, usually lanceolate, often toothed but not lobed. The flowers are small, in rounded clusters, produced before or with the leaves, usually unisexual, with the males and females on separate plants, but sometimes bisexual; the plants often change sex from year to year. Male flowers have 3–12 stamens partly enclosed by a bract, female flowers have an ovary surrounded by 2–6 small bracts, and a short style. Pollination is by wind. The fruits are often fleshy and covered with wax, but sometimes dry and spongy.

Key Recognition Features The scented leaves and the fruit clusters on the branches below the leaves.

Evolution and Relationships The family is small and isolated, generally considered close to Juglandaceae. *Comptonia peregrina* (L.) Coult., the sweet fern, is closely related, but has pinnate leaves, long male catkins, and linear bracteoles surrounding the fruit. Confined to northeastern North America, it is the only survivor of around 12 species of *Comptonia* identified in the Eocene in Europe as well as in North America. It is named after the Rev. Henry Compton (1632–1713), Bishop of London, who had a famous garden at Fulham Palace.

Ecology and Geography Usually in bogs and wet places, but also a forest tree. The genus has an unusual distribution: 7 species are found in North America, 1 of which, *M. gale* L. the bog myrtle, reaches western Europe and eastwards to St Petersburg, but not Greenland. One tree species is found in the Azores, Canaries, and Madeira, a relict of the Tertiary forest flora. Seven species are found in South Africa, but none in Australia or New Zealand, and the genus is also absent from the Mediterranean area, southwestern and Central Asia, and most of Siberia. It appears again in the Himalayas, and from China to New Guinea, with 1 species in New Caledonia. In northern Japan and eastern Siberia, *M. gale* is again the dominant species, but another tree species, *M. rubra* Sieb. & Zucc., is found from central Japan to China.

Comment *Myrica californica* Cham. is found along the coast from British Colombia southwards to Santa Barbara, *M. cerifera* L. is confined to the southeastern states, but extends southwards to Central America, and *M. pensylvanica* Mirbel is found in the northeast; their round fruits are covered with whitish wax, once used for candles.

Myrica californica
male and female flowers
just over life size, May 5th

Comptonia peregrina
male catkins
just over life size
May 14th
(see *Myrica* for text)

Myrica cerifera
young male flowers
2/3 life size, May 5th

Myrica californica
with catkins, 2/3 life size
May 5th

Eucommia

Eucommia Oliver (1890), in the family Eucommiaceae, consists of 1 species, *E. ulmoides* Oliver, from China.

Description Trees to 20m, or more, usually rather spreading, with rough, dark brown bark. The leaves are deciduous, alternate, ovate or oval, with a slender point. The flowers are unisexual, with both sexes on the same tree, opening in early spring before the leaves. The males consist only of 5–12 brown stamens, the anthers with long slits and a prolonged connective; the females are solitary in the axils of bracts, flattened, with a short style and 2 unequal stigmas. Pollination is by wind. The fruits are flat, winged, 1-seeded, rather like those of an elm (*Ulmus,* see p.160), notched at the apex, around 3.5cm long.

Key Recognition Feature The strange property of the leaves to hang together by almost invisible rubbery threads from the veins when pulled carefully apart.

Evolution and Relationships An isolated family and order, nearest perhaps to Ulmaceae (see pp.106–109), or Urticaceae (see Volume 2).

Ecology and Geography *Eucommia* is apparently unknown in the wild. In China it is grown near temples and houses, mainly in western Hubei and Sichuan.

Comment The bark, called *du zhong,* meaning silk thread, has been used for at least 2000 years for its medicinal properties, as a tonic and diuretic, against liver disease and arthritis, and as an aphrodisiac. The rubbery threads from extinct *Eucommia* have been found in German *braunkohle* deposits dating from the Tertiary.

Simmondsia

Simmondsia Nuttall (1844), in the family Buxaceae, or sometimes separated in its own family, the Simmondsiaceae, consists of 1 species, *S. chinensis* (Link) C.K. Schneid., from southwestern North America.

Description Shrub to 2m, spreading. The leaves are opposite, leathery, and dull green. The flowers are small, greenish, unisexual, in the leaf axils. There are 5 sepals, around 5mm long in the clustered male flowers, 1.5cm long in the solitary female flowers, which have 3 styles. There are 10–12 stamens. Pollination is perhaps by wind. The fruits are acorn-like, 3-sided, with 1 seed.

Key Recognition Features The dull, leathery, opposite leaves, 3–3.5cm long, without teeth.

Evolution and Relationships An isolated genus; there are a few stranded in southern California, such as *Carpenteria* (see p.220) and *Lyonothamnus* Gray in the Rosaceae.

Ecology and Geography In semi-desert, creosote-bush scrub, and chaparral in southern California and into Baja California.

Comment *Simmondsia chinensis* is grown for its valuable oil, called jojoba oil, a substitute for sperm whale oil that is used in cosmetics. It is also planted as a drought-tolerant, dwarf, evergreen shrub. The genus is named after T.W. Simmonds (d.1804), an English naturalist who went with Lord Seaforth on his 1800–1806 trip to the West Indies. Nuttall named the plant *S. californica,* but Link had already named it *Buxus chinensis,* presumably believing that it came from China.

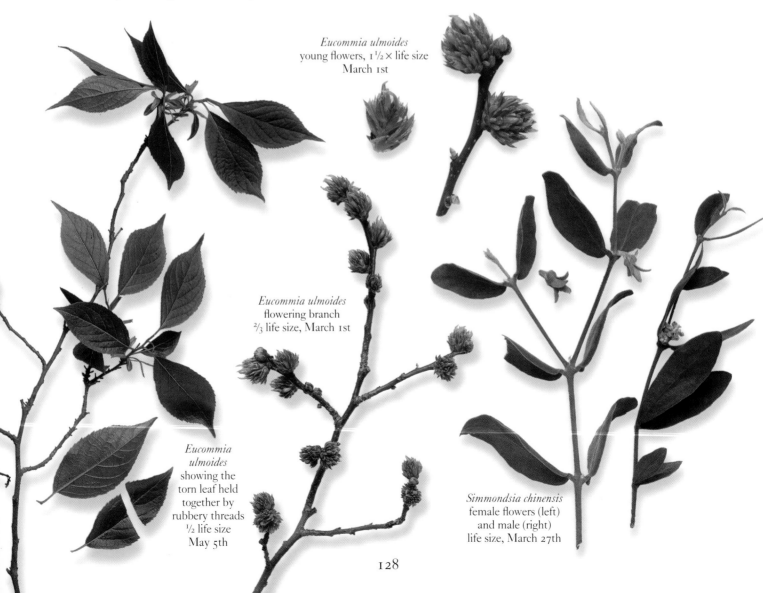

Eucommia ulmoides
young flowers, 1½ × life size
March 1st

Eucommia ulmoides
flowering branch
⅔ life size, March 1st

Eucommia ulmoides
showing the torn leaf held together by rubbery threads
½ life size
May 5th

Simmondsia chinensis
female flowers (left)
and male (right)
life size, March 27th

Buxus sempervirens
'Elegantissima'
life size, May 2nd

Buxus balearica
flowers, just under life size
April 1st

Buxus balearica
½ life size, April 20th

Buxus microphylla
young fruit
life size, August 1st

Buxus

Buxus L., (1753), the boxwood, consists of around 50 species in the Buxaceae, including the common English box, *B. sempervirens* L.

Description Trees to 8m, or shrubs. The leaves are evergreen, alternate, usually rounded, not toothed. The flowers are small, in rounded clusters in the leaf axils, unisexual, the males and females on the same plant and forming a compact inflorescence. The male flowers have 4 sepals and 4 stamens, and surround the female flowers, which have 3 fused ovaries surmounted by three 2-lobed styles. Pollination is presumed to be by wind. The fruits are hard, explosive capsules which eject the shining black seeds.

Key Recognition Features The rounded, opposite leaves with indistinct, parallel side-veins, on ridged, green twigs.

Evolution and Relationships There are several different opinions of the relationships of the family Buxaceae. Some consider it close to the spurges (Euphorbiaceae, see p.169), because of its flower structure and 3-carpelled fruit. In seed characteristics especially, it is close to Hamamelidaceae (see pp.100–109). In stamens and wood anatomy it is close to *Pittosporum* (see p.214). Other genera in the Buxaceae are *Sarcococca* (see p.130), *Pachysandra* (see Volume 2), and *Styloceras* Kunth ex A. Juss. from the northern Andes.

Ecology and Geography Generally grows in well-drained soils and as an understorey shrub in dry woods, in Europe and Asia along the Himalayas to Japan, in Central America, where there are 34 species in Cuba, and in Africa southwards to Natal, but not in the Cape.

Comment Boxwood is the heaviest of European timbers, heavier than water. Because of its very fine grain, it was used for woodblocks for engraving, as well as in marquetry and inlays. It was also used for croquet balls, flutes, and combs. Box is commonly planted for garden hedges; some cultivars, used to edge beds, are especially slow-growing and sprout well after clipping.

Sarcococca

Sarcococca Lindl. (1826), in the family Buxaceae, consists of around 11 species in eastern Asia, with scented flowers in winter.

Description Subshrubs to 1m, suckering to form large patches. The leaves are evergreen, mostly alternate, usually narrowly lanceolate and pointed, not toothed. The flowers are small, whitish, wonderfully scented, in loose clusters in the leaf axils, unisexual, the males and females on the same plant, sometimes in clusters of one sex, sometimes mixed, with the females below the males. The male flowers have 4 sepals and 4 stamens, the female flowers have 4–6 sepals and 2 or 3 styles. Pollination is presumed to be by insects. The fruits are fleshy and red, purple, or black, with 1–3 seeds.

Key Recognition Features Pointed leaves on a short, suckering subshrub; on warm winter days you generally smell the flowers before you see the plant.

Evolution and Relationships In its scented flowers and often fleshy fruit, *Sarcococca* is closer to *Pachysandra* (see Volume 2), which contains some shrubby species in China, than to *Buxus* (see p.129).

Ecology and Geography Found in forests and woods in the Himalayas from Afghanistan to central China.

Comment *Sarcococca confusa* Sealy is known only in cultivation, and is probably of hybrid origin. *Sarcococca hookeriana* Baill. is one of the best scented plants, and is excellent if brought indoors in winter, or planted close to a door.

Sarcococca confusa
male flowers (above), female flowers
(below), 1¾ × life size, January 20th

Sarcococca confusa
berries, 1⅔ × life size
December 4th

Sarcococca confusa
¾ life size
January 20th

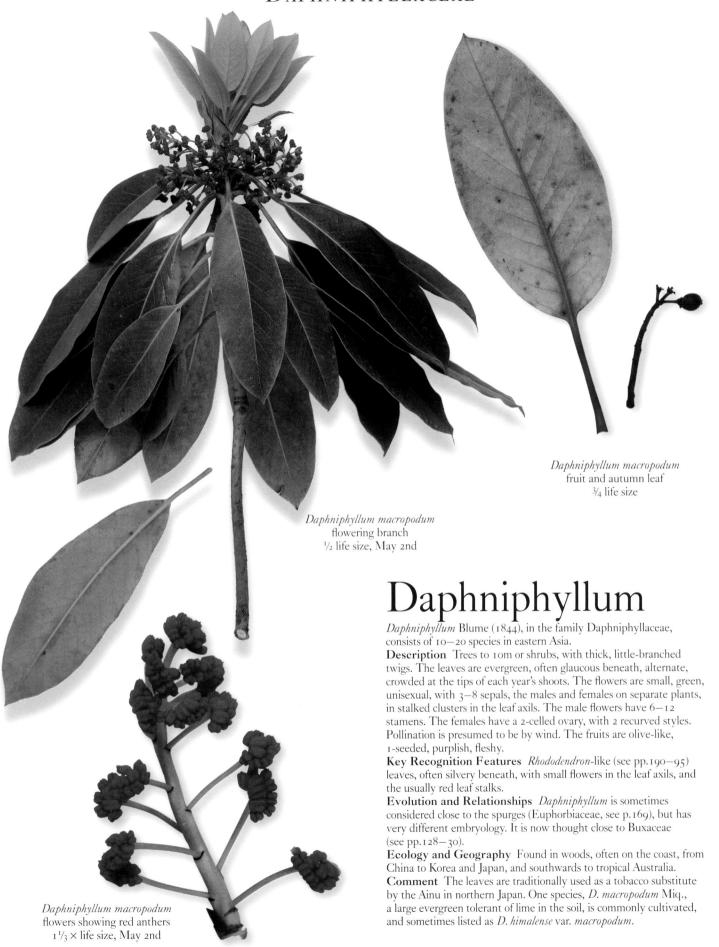

Daphniphyllum macropodum
fruit and autumn leaf
¾ life size

Daphniphyllum macropodum
flowering branch
½ life size, May 2nd

Daphniphyllum

Daphniphyllum Blume (1844), in the family Daphniphyllaceae, consists of 10–20 species in eastern Asia.

Description Trees to 10m or shrubs, with thick, little-branched twigs. The leaves are evergreen, often glaucous beneath, alternate, crowded at the tips of each year's shoots. The flowers are small, green, unisexual, with 3–8 sepals, the males and females on separate plants, in stalked clusters in the leaf axils. The male flowers have 6–12 stamens. The females have a 2-celled ovary, with 2 recurved styles. Pollination is presumed to be by wind. The fruits are olive-like, 1-seeded, purplish, fleshy.

Key Recognition Features *Rhododendron*-like (see pp.190–95) leaves, often silvery beneath, with small flowers in the leaf axils, and the usually red leaf stalks.

Evolution and Relationships *Daphniphyllum* is sometimes considered close to the spurges (Euphorbiaceae, see p.169), but has very different embryology. It is now thought close to Buxaceae (see pp.128–30).

Ecology and Geography Found in woods, often on the coast, from China to Korea and Japan, and southwards to tropical Australia.

Comment The leaves are traditionally used as a tobacco substitute by the Ainu in northern Japan. One species, *D. macropodum* Miq., a large evergreen tolerant of lime in the soil, is commonly cultivated, and sometimes listed as *D. himalense* var. *macropodum*.

Daphniphyllum macropodum
flowers showing red anthers
1⅓ × life size, May 2nd

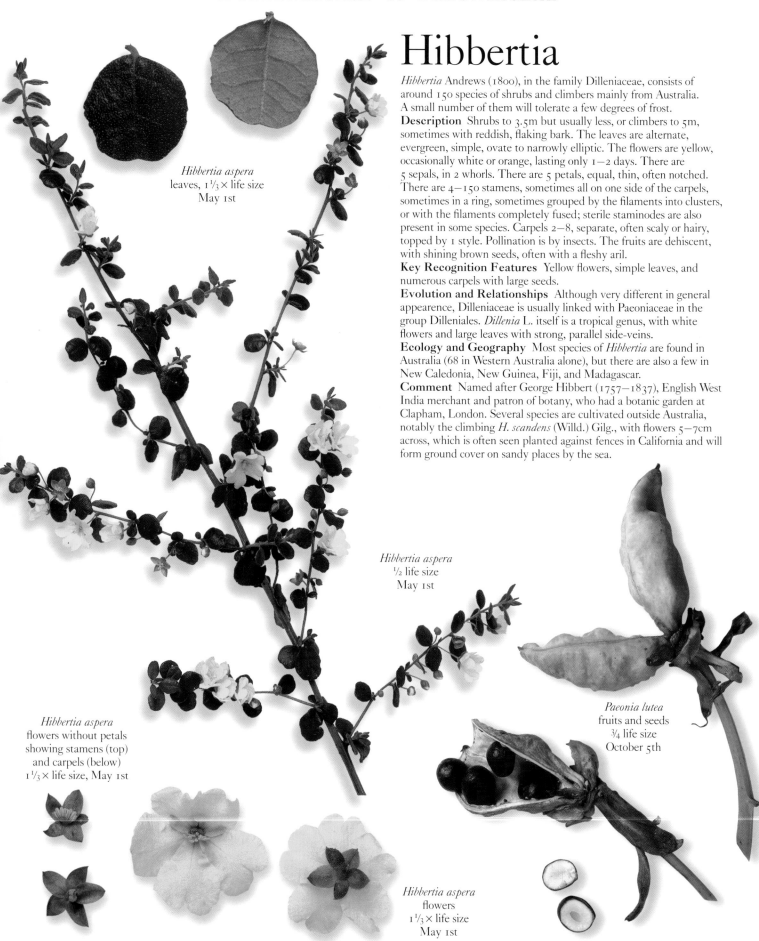

Hibbertia aspera
leaves, 1 1/3 × life size
May 1st

Hibbertia

Hibbertia Andrews (1800), in the family Dilleniaceae, consists of around 150 species of shrubs and climbers mainly from Australia. A small number of them will tolerate a few degrees of frost.

Description Shrubs to 3.5m but usually less, or climbers to 5m, sometimes with reddish, flaking bark. The leaves are alternate, evergreen, simple, ovate to narrowly elliptic. The flowers are yellow, occasionally white or orange, lasting only 1–2 days. There are 5 sepals, in 2 whorls. There are 5 petals, equal, thin, often notched. There are 4–150 stamens, sometimes all on one side of the carpels, sometimes in a ring, sometimes grouped by the filaments into clusters, or with the filaments completely fused; sterile staminodes are also present in some species. Carpels 2–8, separate, often scaly or hairy, topped by 1 style. Pollination is by insects. The fruits are dehiscent, with shining brown seeds, often with a fleshy aril.

Key Recognition Features Yellow flowers, simple leaves, and numerous carpels with large seeds.

Evolution and Relationships Although very different in general appearence, Dilleniaceae is usually linked with Paeoniaceae in the group Dilleniales. *Dillenia* L. itself is a tropical genus, with white flowers and large leaves with strong, parallel side-veins.

Ecology and Geography Most species of *Hibbertia* are found in Australia (68 in Western Australia alone), but there are also a few in New Caledonia, New Guinea, Fiji, and Madagascar.

Comment Named after George Hibbert (1757–1837), English West India merchant and patron of botany, who had a botanic garden at Clapham, London. Several species are cultivated outside Australia, notably the climbing *H. scandens* (Willd.) Gilg., with flowers 5–7cm across, which is often seen planted against fences in California and will form ground cover on sandy places by the sea.

Hibbertia aspera
1/2 life size
May 1st

Paeonia lutea
fruits and seeds
3/4 life size
October 5th

Hibbertia aspera
flowers without petals
showing stamens (top)
and carpels (below)
1 1/3 × life size, May 1st

Hibbertia aspera
flowers
1 1/3 × life size
May 1st

Paeonia

Paeonia L. (1753), the only genus in the family Paeoniaceae, consists of around 30 species, a few shrubs but mostly herbaceous perennials (see Volume 2), in Europe, Asia, and North Africa, with 2 species found in California.

Description Shrubs to 2.5m, with thick, soft twigs. The leaves are alternate, usually at the tops of the shoots, with 3 major divisions, and further subdivided into usually lanceolate lobes. The flowers are large, short-lived, with 1—12 leafy bracts, 5 unequal sepals, and 5—9 petals. There are 6 stamens, the numerous anthers, opening by longitudinal slits. There are 1—8 carpels, separate, often hairy, topped by a broad, short style. Pollination is by insects, often pollen-eating beetles. The fruits are dehiscent, with numerous purplish-black seeds with a fleshy aril, and also usually red infertile seeds.

Key Recognition Features Divided leaves and large flowers, to 30cm across in *P. suffruticosa* Haw.

Evolution and Relationships Formerly thought close to or even included in the Ranunculaceae (see pp.86—89), because of its numerous stamens and follicle-like capsules, but now recognised as being close to Dilleniaceae, in that its petals are derived from sepals rather than from stamens, in its persistent sepals, and in its aril-bearing seed.

Ecology and Geography In rocky places on cliffs and in scrub, the herbaceous species sometimes in open steppe. The shrubby species are found in western and central China and the eastern Himalayas, with *P. lutea* Franch. in southeastern Tibet. Herbaceous species are found mostly around the Mediterranean and in the foothills of the Caucasus.

Comment The cultivars of *P. suffruticosa*, the *moutan*, or *hua wang*, king of flowers, are one of the classic ornamental genera of China. Cultivation in China began in Chekiang the early 4th century, and by the early T'ang period in around 700AD. hundreds of varieties were grown. By the 11th and 12th centuries the centre of cultivation was in Sichuan, and there yellow-flowered varieties appeared. At present the centre of *moutan* culture is the city of Heze, where there is an annual festival in May. The cultivars of *P. suffruticosa* grow well in Europe and North America in areas with cold winters and warm summers. The taller but smaller-flowered *P. lutea* and *P. delavayi* Franch. are more easily grown in humid areas but are less spectacular in flower.

Paeonia suffruticosa
cross-section of flower
showing red styles and
stamens, 1 ½ × life size
May 1st

Paeonia lutea
¼ life size, April 21st

Paeonia suffruticosa
Japanese cultivar
¼ life size, May 1st

Azara serrata
flowers
1 ¼ × life size, April 29th

Azara integrifolia
just under life size
March 17th

Azara serrata
½ life size
April 29th

Azara

Azara Ruiz & Pavon (1799), in the family Flacourtiaceae, consists of around 10 species in South America.

Description Shrubs to 8m, with slender twigs. The leaves are evergreen, alternate, often toothed, in unequal pairs on the shoot, the larger to 7cm long. The flowers are small, yellow, scented, in stalked clusters in the leaf axils in early spring or summer. There are 4 or 5 sepals, somewhat downy; petals absent. Stamens up to 50, the outer sometimes sterile. The anthers open by slits. Narrow nectaries are sometimes present among the stamens. Style simple, sometimes 3-lobed, on an ovary with 1 locule and 3 rows of seeds on the wall, so-called parietal placentation. Pollination is probably by insects. The fruits are fleshy, greyish or orange berries, with a persistent style and up to 25 seeds, ripening in mid- to late summer.

Key Recognition Features The 2 sizes of shiny, green leaves, and the fluffy, yellow flowers made up of conspicuous stamens.

Evolution and Relationships Despite their differing appearance, the Flacourtiaceae is close to Dilleniaceae (see p.132) and Violaceae (see p.140); this is noticeable especially in the arrangement of fruits and seeds. Some authorities also link it to the Tiliaceae (see pp.150–51).

Ecology and Geography Found on the margins of rainforest and on damp, rocky slopes in Chile, southern Argentina, and Uruguay.

Comment Attractive shrubs for sunny, sheltered places in mild gardens. They should not be allowed to dry out in summer.

Azara integrifolia
fruit, life size
October 5th

Azara microphylla
'Variegata'
2/3 life size, March 17th

Azara uruguayensis
showing distinctly
different leaf shapes
1/3 life size, September 13th

Berberidopsis

Berberidopsis Hook. fil. (1862), in the family Flacourtiaceae, consists of 2 species. *Berberidopsis corallina* Hook. fil. from South America is described here; the other species, *B. beckleri* (Muell.) Veldcamp, from eastern Australia, is not widely cultivated.

Description A climbing shrub with twining stems to 6m. The leaves are evergreen, alternate, finely toothed, short-stalked, truncate at the base. The flowers are in terminal sprays and solitary in the axils of the upper leaves, red, fleshy, around 12mm across, hanging on slender, red stalks in late summer. Sepals and petals are both 9–15, the outer 3 small, the rest larger, incurved. Stamens 7–10, with very short filaments. Carpels 3, fused; the style thick, 3-lobed at the apex. Pollination is probably by hummingbirds, possibly also by insects. The fruit is a berry with many seeds, but seldom seen.

Key Recognition Features The alternate, rather holly-like leaves (*Ilex*, see p.179), with soft teeth, and the red, fleshy flowers, which look almost like berries.

Evolution and Relationships It is hard to imagine the steps by which *Azara* and *Berberidopsis* evolved to look so different, indeed Berberidopsis is isolated within the Flacourtiaceae, a particularly diverse family.

Ecology and Geography In evergreen rainforest, in Valdivia, Chile, behind the port of Coronel, from where it was introduced to England in 1862 by Richard Pearce collecting for Messrs Veitch.

Comment *Berberidopsis corallina* is frequently cultivated, but very rare or possibly extinct in the wild. It needs shelter and moist soil, with careful protection from drying winds in summer. The Australian species was formerly called *Streptothamnus beckleri* F. Muell.

Berberidopsis corallina
1/2 life size
December 10th

Idesia

Idesia Maxim. (1866), in the family Flacourtiaceae, consists of 1 species, *I. polycarpa* Maxim. from eastern Asia.

Description Tree to 20m, with spreading branches. The leaves are deciduous, the blade heart-shaped, 10–20cm long, whitish and papillose beneath; the stalks long, with conspicuous nectaries. The flowers are in much-branched sprays and unisexual or bisexual. Bisexual flowers have 5 yellowish, downy sepals, no petals, numerous stamens with downy filaments, and 3–5 styles on a 1-celled ovary with usually 5 fused carpels. Male flowers have a vestigial ovary and females have short staminodes and a normal ovary. Pollination is perhaps by insects or perhaps by wind. The fruits are conspicuous, red or black berries with numerous seeds.

Key Recognition Features The long-stalked, large, heart-shaped leaves with 2 nectaries, and the branching sprays of flowers and fruit.

Evolution and Relationships Both *Carrieria* Franch. and *Poliothyrsis* have rather similar leaves and flowers with numerous stamens, but both have capsules.

Ecology and Geography Found in woods and scrub, often by streams, from western Sichuan in China eastwards to Taiwan, on Quelpart Island, and in Japan.

Comment An attractive, quite fast-growing tree, hardy as far north as New York and southern England. Though usually reported to be dioecious, our specimen has both bisexual and male flowers. The downy leaved var. *vestita* Diels is likely to be hardier than the type. The name commemorates E.Y. Ides (fl. 1720), a Dutch traveller in China.

Idesia polycarpa
twig and flower spray
¼ life size, July 1st

Poliothyrsis sinensis
dehisced capsules
2 × life size, May 5th

Idesia poliocarpa
flowers, 1¼ × life size
July 1st

Poliothyrsis sinensis
young fruit
2 × life size, October 6th

Poliothyrsis sinensis
¾ life size
October 6th

Poliothyrsis

Poliothyrsis Oliver (1889), in the family Flacourtiaceae, consists of 1 species, *P. sinensis* Oliver from China.

Description Tree to 15m, or shrub, with grey bark and spreading branches. The leaves are deciduous, the blade heart-shaped, 8–15cm long, hairy but not papillose beneath, the stalks without nectaries. The flowers are scented, whitish, in much-branched sprays, unisexual, with males and females in the same inflorescence, produced in late summer and early autumn. Male flowers have 5 yellowish, downy sepals, no petals, and numerous stamens of different lengths; female flowers have very short staminodes and three 2-lobed, spathulate styles reflexed along the 1-celled ovary. Pollination is presumed to be by insects. The fruits are downy, spindle-shaped capsules, to 2.5cm long, opening by 3 or 4 teeth and containing numerous winged seeds.

Key Recognition Features The heart-shaped leaves, hairy beneath, smaller and thinner than those of *Idesia*, and the 2-lobed, spathulate styles.

Evolution and Relationships Close to *Idesia*; also close to *Carrieria* Franch., but that has a large, woody capsule with usually winged seeds.

Ecology and Geography In woods and scrub in China from western Sichuan eastwards to western Hubei, and further south.

Comment An easily grown tree, flowering when quite young.

Populus

Populus L. (1753), the poplar or aspen, in the family Salicaceae, contains 35–40 species around the northern hemisphere.

Description Trees to 50m and shrubs, fast-growing, often sprouting from the roots, with pointed buds with several scales. The leaves are deciduous, usually triangular or heart-shaped, rarely willow-like, often white beneath, with long stalks. The flowers are in hanging catkins, unisexual, with the males and females on different trees, usually opening in spring. Male flowers have a thin, toothed or fringed scale, and usually numerous stamens with red anthers. Female flowers are in a small cup, with a 1-celled ovary with 2–4 stigmas. Pollination is by wind. The fruits are small, flask-shaped capsules, splitting into 2 or 3 segments, with small seeds attached around the lower part; each seed is surrounded by long, cottony hairs to aid dispersal by wind.

Key Recognition Features The usually triangular leaves on often flattened stalks; in early spring the woolly catkins are conspicuous, as are the seeding catkins which give the trees their American name of cottonwood.

Evolution and Relationships The differences between poplars and willows (*Salix* see pp.138–39) are mainly connected with the change from insect to wind pollination; the intermediate genera are discussed under *Salix*.

Ecology and Geography In wet places, usually by streams or where ground water is near the surface, but not in waterlogged soil. The seeds need to fall on wet, open soil to germinate, and retain their viability for only 2 or 3 days. Poplars are found around the northern hemisphere, with the greatest number of species in China; 1 species, *P. ilicifolia* (Engl.) Rouleau, reaches as far south as Tsavo in Kenya.

Comment Many species are planted as fast-growing ornamentals; the males have attractive spring catkins. *Populus balsamifera* L. and its hybrids have sticky, scented buds, which perfume the air on wet days in spring. The commonly planted *P.* × *candicans* 'Aurora' has heavy white blotching on the leaves. Timber from poplars is light and often straight, and is slow to catch fire. It is used for plywood and matches. Several hybrids are grown for biomass, with stooled plants growing over 2m a year even in England; fast-growing trees can grow 20m in 12 years. The fastigiate variety of *P. nigra* L., 'Afghanica', has white bark and is used for roofing poles of flat-roofed houses across Asia; 'Italica' is the Lombardy poplar, which is said to have appeared in the Po valley around 1700. The name *Populus* is supposed to have come from the Latin for people, because it was commonly planted in village squares. However, the tree *populus* properly has a long *o* and, being a tree, is feminine, while *populus*, the people, has a short *o* and is masculine.

Populus lasiocarpa leaf with cottony filaments containing seeds ⅓ life size July 27th

Populus × *canadensis* male catkins ¾ life size March 10th

Populus × *canadensis* ½ life size, March 10th

Salix

Salix L. (1753), the willow, in the family Salicaceae, contains at least 300 species, mainly in the northern hemisphere.

Description Trees to 30m, or shrubs; in the arctic *S. herbacea* L. less than 1cm above ground. The leaves are alternate or, rarely, opposite, deciduous, usually lanceolate to ovate, undivided, to 20cm long in the Chinese *S. magnifica* Hemsl.. The flowers are in upright, catkin-like heads, unisexual, with males and females on different trees, usually opening in spring. The male flowers have a thin, often silky scale, 1 or more nectary scales, and usually 2 but up to 12 stamens, sometimes with fused filaments. Female flowers have a silky scale, nectar-secreting glands, and a 1-celled ovary with 2–4 stigmas. Pollination is by insects, particularly bees and moths, only rarely by wind. The fruits are small, flask-shaped capsules, splitting into 2, with small seeds attached around the lower part; each seed is surrounded by silky hairs to aid dispersal by wind.

Key Recognition Features The alternate leaves and 1-scaled winter buds. The upright male or female catkins are easy to recognise when the plants are in flower.

Evolution and Relationships The family Salicaceae is superficially similar to the catkin-bearing trees such as hazel (*Corylus*, see p.119), but is now considered an isolated family, closer to the Flacourtiaceae (see pp.134–36) in the order Violales, with which it shares some rust fungi. Of the 2 main genera, *Salix* are insect-pollinated while *Populus* (see p.137) are wind-pollinated. Two rarer and very closely related genera are found in Japan: *Toisusu* Kimura, syn. *Salix urbaniana* Seemen, has pendulous, willow-like catkins and is insect-pollinated; *Chosenia* Nakai, syn. *Salix arbutifolia* Pallas, is a large tree also found in Korea and eastern Siberia and has willow-like leaves but reddish, hanging male catkins, and is wind-pollinated. Hybrids between these 2 genera are found where they grow together.

Ecology and Geography Usually found in wet places by streams or rivers, as the seeds are very short-lived and shed in summer. Found throughout the temperate parts of the northern hemisphere; rare in South America and Africa, and absent as a native genus from Australia and New Zealand.

Comment Many species are grown for ornament, especially those with furry catkins on bare twigs in the spring, known as pussy willow, or palm, as they are often open on Palm Sunday. The weeping willows, *S. × sepulcralis* Simonkai, *S. pendulina* Wend., and the Chinese *S. babylonica* L., are planted for their gracefully hanging branches. Some species are grown for timber, notably *S. alba* L. subsp. *caerulea* (Smith) Smith, used for cricket bats. Many species, especially the osier, *S. viminalis* L., are planted for basket-making. Other fast-growing species and hybrids are now planted for biomass. Sallows, *S. capraea* L. and *S. cinerea* L., are used as a source of charcoal, both for drawing and for making gunpowder. Aspirin, acetylsalicylic acid, was originally extracted from willow bark, where it is in the form of salicine, an alkaloid similar to quinine. In the past the leaves were sometimes used as tea, and the bark dried for winter and mixed with oatmeal in times of famine.

Salix bockii
flowering in autumn
life size
October 8th

Salix gracilistyla
'Melanostachys'
male catkins
life size, April 1st

Salix atrocinerea
female catkin
1¼ × life size, March 29th

Salix hookeriana
male catkin
1¼ × life size
March 29th

SALICACEAE

Salix hookeriana, male flowers
2 × life size, March 29th

Salix exigua
just over life size
June 10th

Salix atrocinerea female flowers
2 × life size, March 29th

Salix hookeriana
male catkins
½ life size, March 29th

Salix moupinensis
female, young leaves
⅔ life size, April 18th

Salix alba subsp. *vitellina*
'Britzensis'
1¼ × life size, April 29th

Salix atrocinerea
female catkins
½ life size, March 29th

Melicytus alpinus
berries 2 × life size
October 5th

Melicytus dentatus
flowers, 1¾ × life size
May 1st

Melicytus ramiflorus
just under life size
April 11th

Melicytus alpinus
just under life size
October 5th

Melicytus

Melicytus Forster & Forster (1776), in the family Violaceae, consists of perhaps 10 species. Until recently, many were put in a separate genus *Hymenanthera* R. Br.

Description Trees to 10m, or shrubs, often with stiff, much-branched twigs. The leaves are evergreen, alternate, smooth-edged or toothed. The flowers are very small, 3–6mm across, unisexual, with males and females on different plants, starry or bell-shaped. Sepals are 5, fused at the base, petals 5, small, sometimes recurved, greenish, whitish, or pale yellow. Male flowers have 5 stamens, the filaments sometimes fused into a tube; female flowers have a 1-celled ovary of 3 fused carpels, the style with 2, 3, or up to 6 branches. Pollination is presumed to be by insects. The fruits are dark blue, purplish, or whitish berries, sometimes bluish on one side, white on the other.

Key Recognition Features Masses of often short-stalked purple or white berries on a very stiff shrub or small tree. *Coprosma* Forster & Forster has several superficially similar species, but opposite leaves.

Evolution and Relationships The family Violaceae contains the genus *Viola* (violets and pansies, see Volume 2), as well as several tropical and southern hemisphere shrubs and trees. Their affinities are thought to be with the Resedaceae (see Volume 2) and the Flacourtiaceae (see pp.134–36).

Ecology and Geography In rocky and stony places in mountains or on coasts, or in evergreen forests. From Fiji and the Solomon Islands to eastern Australia (*M. dentatus* (R. Br.) Garnock-Jones), with most species in New Zealand, where 10 have been described.

Comment A few species of *Melicytus* are grown for their ornamental berries. *Melicytus crassifolius* (Hook. fil.) Garnock-Jones is a coastal dwarf cushion shrub with white berries. *Melicytus angustifolius* (DC) Garnock-Jones is a taller shrub, to 1.75m, often with leafless stems and masses of blue-and-white berries.

Stachyurus

Stachyurus Sieb. & Zucc. (1835), in the family Stachyuraceae, consists of 5 or 6 species from the Himalayas to Japan.

Description Shrubs or small trees to 5m, with rather stiff twigs. The leaves are alternate, deciduous or partially evergreen, linear-lanceolate to ovate, long-pointed. The flowers are formed on stiff, downward-pointing spikes in autumn, and open in spring before the new leaves expand. Sepals 4, unequal; petals 4, yellow to cream or pinkish. Stamens 8, in 2 whorls; anthers arrow-shaped. Ovary 4-celled, of 4 fused carpels, the partitions not reaching the apex of the ovary, with numerous ovules on the wall, so-called parietal placentation. Styles undivided. Pollination is presumed to be by insects. The fruits are 4-celled berries, with a persistent style and numerous small seeds.

Key Recognition Features The stiff, downward-pointing spikes of usually yellow, bell-shaped flowers with 4 petals. The superficially similar *Corylopsis* (see p.102) has soft, hanging spikes.

Evolution and Relationships An isolated family of doubtful affinity, sometimes considered close to the Flacourtiaceae (see pp.134–36), sometimes to the Theaceae (see pp.172–77).

Ecology and Geography In scrub and on cliffs at up to 3000m, from central Nepal through southwestern China eastwards to Hubei and in Taiwan and Japan.

Comment Attractive shrubs, commonly grown for their early spring flowers. 'Magpie' is a good variegated clone of *S. chinensis* Franch., which is generally stronger-growing than the Japanese *S. praecox* Sieb. & Zucc. Some forms of *S. himalaicus* Hook. fil. & Thoms. have elegant, narrow, almost evergreen leaves.

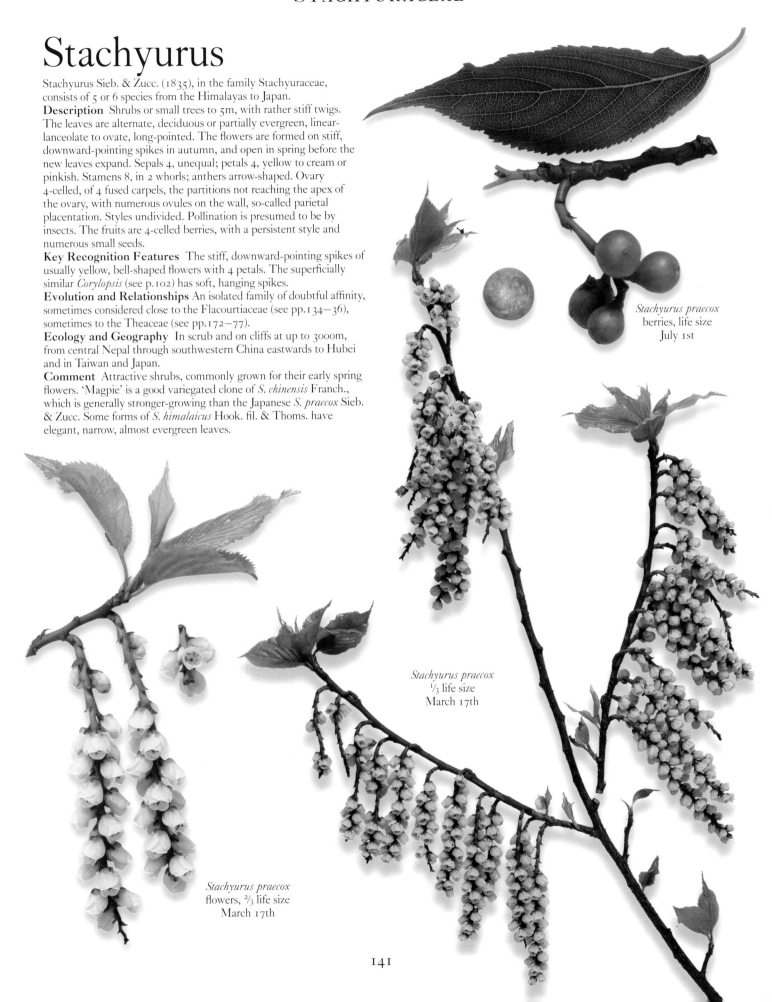

Stachyurus praecox
berries, life size
July 1st

Stachyurus praecox
⅓ life size
March 17th

Stachyurus praecox
flowers, ⅔ life size
March 17th

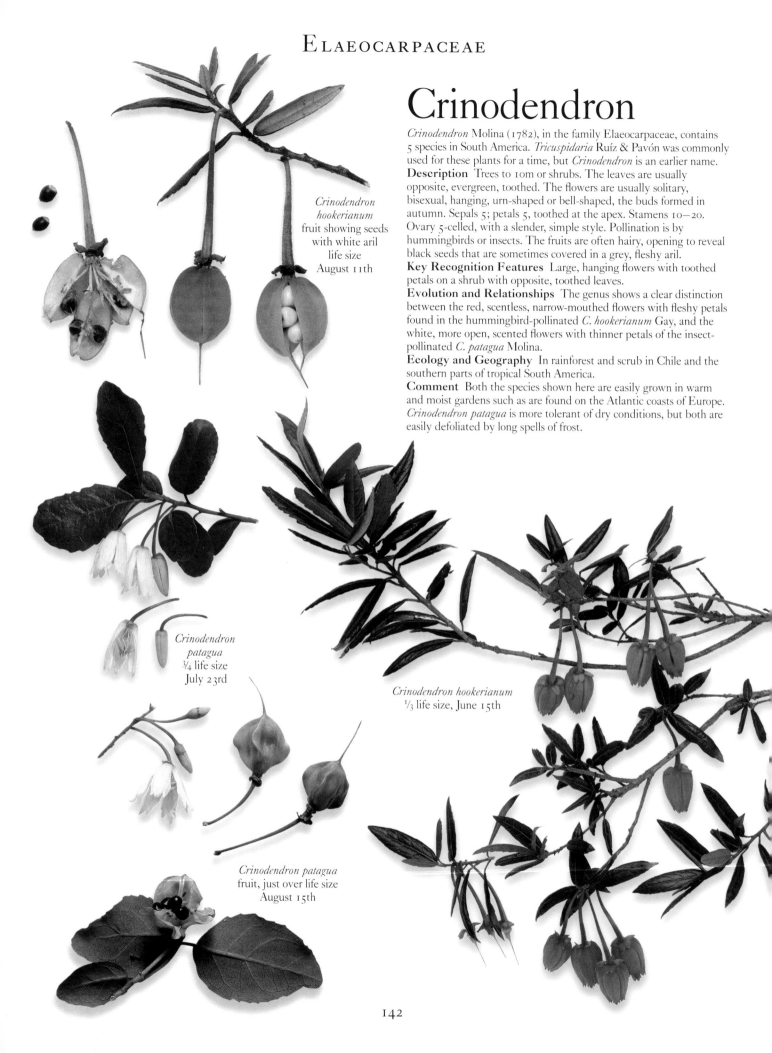

Crinodendron

Crinodendron Molina (1782), in the family Elaeocarpaceae, contains 5 species in South America. *Tricuspidaria* Ruíz & Pavón was commonly used for these plants for a time, but *Crinodendron* is an earlier name.

Description Trees to 10m or shrubs. The leaves are usually opposite, evergreen, toothed. The flowers are usually solitary, bisexual, hanging, urn-shaped or bell-shaped, the buds formed in autumn. Sepals 5; petals 5, toothed at the apex. Stamens 10–20. Ovary 5-celled, with a slender, simple style. Pollination is by hummingbirds or insects. The fruits are often hairy, opening to reveal black seeds that are sometimes covered in a grey, fleshy aril.

Key Recognition Features Large, hanging flowers with toothed petals on a shrub with opposite, toothed leaves.

Evolution and Relationships The genus shows a clear distinction between the red, scentless, narrow-mouthed flowers with fleshy petals found in the hummingbird-pollinated *C. hookerianum* Gay, and the white, more open, scented flowers with thinner petals of the insect-pollinated *C. patagua* Molina.

Ecology and Geography In rainforest and scrub in Chile and the southern parts of tropical South America.

Comment Both the species shown here are easily grown in warm and moist gardens such as are found on the Atlantic coasts of Europe. *Crinodendron patagua* is more tolerant of dry conditions, but both are easily defoliated by long spells of frost.

Crinodendron hookerianum
fruit showing seeds
with white aril
life size
August 11th

Crinodendron patagua
¾ life size
July 23rd

Crinodendron hookerianum
⅓ life size, June 15th

Crinodendron patagua
fruit, just over life size
August 15th

Aristotelia

Aristotelia L'Hérit. (1784), in the family Elaeocarpaceae, contains 5 species from the southern hemisphere.

Description Trees to 10m, or shrubs. The leaves are usually opposite, evergreen or deciduous, simple or pinnate, often toothed. The flowers are small, unisexual, with males and females sometimes on separate plants, in sprays or sometimes solitary in the leaf axils, often bell-shaped. Sepals 4 or 5, not joined; petals 4 or 5, generally toothed, fringed, or lobed, and green, white, pink, or reddish. Stamens 4 to many, the anthers opening by apical slits. The ovary is 2- to 4-celled, with 2 ovules per cell. Styles often curved backwards. Pollination is presumed to be by insects. The fruits are red berries, usually ripening black, with the seeds often angled.

Key Recognition Features The divided, notched, or toothed petals of the rather small flowers, usually produced in branching sprays.

Evolution and Relationships The family Elaeocarpaceae is said to be related to Tiliaceae (see pp.150–51), and to Rhizophoraceae Pers., the mangrove family. *Elaeocarpus* L. itself is a mainly tropical genus, with 5-lobed petals and fruits with 1 hard stone. *Vallea stipularis* Ruíz & Pavón is a similar attractive but tender shrub from the Andes with crimson flowers around 2.5cm across.

Ecology and Geography In scrub, often appearing in quantity where forest has been felled, in Chile and Argentina, and in Australia, Tasmania, and New Zealand.

Comment Wine is said to have been made from *maqui*, the fruit of *A. chilensis* (Molina) Stuntz in Chile, and also from *A. serrata* (Forst.) W. Oliver, the wineberry, in New Zealand. *Aristotelia fruticosa* Hook. fil. is a stiff, twiggy shrub like *Melicytus* (see p.140), but with opposite branches.

Aristotelia chilensis
1½ × life size
May 11th

Crinodendron hookerianum
flower parts, just under
life size, June 15th

Aristotelia chilensis
½ life size, May 11th

Passiflora

Passiflora L. (1753), in the family Passifloraceae, contains around 350 species of climbers, mostly in the tropics.

Description Climbing shrubs to 20m, often woody below. The leaves are alternate, evergreen or deciduous, usually lobed, with curling tendrils in their axils; the leaf stalks, bracts, or undersides of the leaves often have conspicuous nectariferous glands. The flowers are solitary in the leaf axils or in a hanging inflorescence, of distinct and complex form. Bracts 3; sepals 5, sometimes 4, often fused at the base; petals 5, sometimes 4 or absent; the corona consists of several rows of filaments, often with bands of colour. Stamens 5, sometimes 4, the anthers opening downwards, on a stalk above the corona. The ovary is above the stamens, with 3 styles and knob-like stigmas. Carpels usually 3, fused into a single cell. Pollination is by insects, perhaps butterflies, and by birds. The fruits are leathery and full of seeds surrounded by often delicious flesh.

Key Recognition Features The corona of filaments and the stamens and styles on a stalk above the rest of the flower, a so-called androgynophore, is distinctive. Without flowers, the lobed leaves with glands on the leaf-stalks are typical of most species.

Evolution and Relationships There are 16 other small genera in the Passifloraceae, some of which are shrubs, not climbers, and lack tendrils. These show similarities with Flacourtiaceae (see pp.134–36); there are also affinities with Cucurbitaceae Juss., the cucumber family, in leaf shape, tendrils, and fruit. One isolated climber, *Tetrapathaea tetrandra* (Sol.) Cheesm, with simple leaves and small, green, unisexual flowers, is found in New Zealand. The genus *Passiflora* itself is often divided into 22 subgenera: the hardy *P. caerulea* L. and the edible *P. edulis* Sims both come from subgenus Passiflora. The most distinct subgenus is Tacsonia, in which the hanging flowers have a long tube, pink or red sepals and petals, and merely a trace of a corona; in subgenus Distephana the flowers are upright and bright red. Both of these are probably adaptations to pollination by hummingbirds.

Ecology and Geography In forests and rocky places, often climbing over large trees. The range extends from the southern United States to subtropical South America, throughout tropical Africa, and from southern India through Indonesia to northern Australia.

Comment Most species are cultivated for their unusual flowers. John Vanderplank, who has collected passionflowers for many years, recorded in *Passion Flowers* (1991) the excitement felt by 17th-century monks when these strange flowers were first discovered in Mexico. In 1610 Jacomo Bosio was working on a treatise on the cross of Calvary when an Augustinian friar, Emmanuel de Villegas, arrived in Rome from Mexico and showed him drawings of a wonderful flower, "stupendously marvellous". Bosio was unsure whether or not to include these drawings in his book to the glory of Christ, fearing that they were greatly exaggerated, but further reports by Mexican Jesuits passing through Rome convinced him that the flower was indeed as it was shown. In Christian iconography, the 3 bracts at the base of the flower represent the Trinity; the 5 sepals and 5 similar petals represent 10 apostles, Peter and Judas being absent; the corona of narrow blue and white threads represents the crown of thorns, by tradition 72 in number; the 5 stamens represent the wounds; and the 3 styles represent the nails. Most species have edible fruit, and a few are grown for their pulp, notably *P. edulis* and the larger and more tropical *P. quadrangularis* L.. The banana-like fruit of *P. mollissima* (HBK) Bailey, is also produced commercially. Other species are also grown in butterfly houses, being the food plants of heliconid butterflies.

Passiflora caerulea
²⁄₃ life size
September 13th

Passiflora caerulea
fruit, 1¼ × life size
September 13th

Passifloraceae

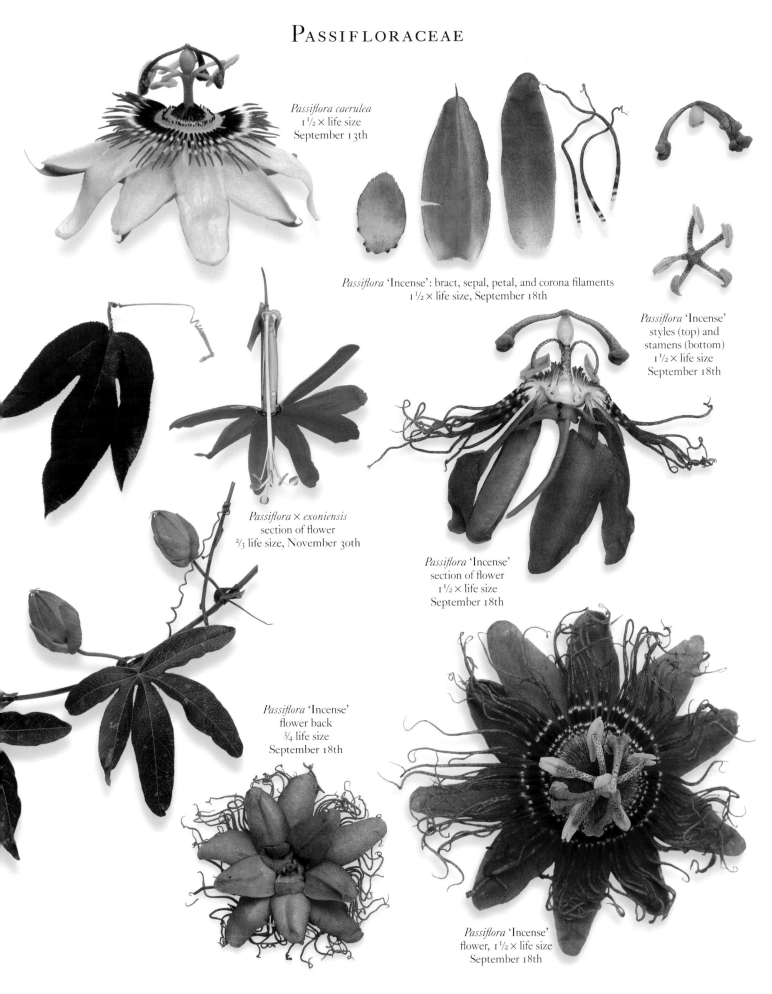

Passiflora caerulea
1½ × life size
September 13th

Passiflora 'Incense': bract, sepal, petal, and corona filaments
1½ × life size, September 18th

Passiflora 'Incense'
styles (top) and
stamens (bottom)
1½ × life size
September 18th

Passiflora × *exoniensis*
section of flower
⅔ life size, November 30th

Passiflora 'Incense'
section of flower
1½ × life size
September 18th

Passiflora 'Incense'
flower back
¾ life size
September 18th

Passiflora 'Incense'
flower, 1½ × life size
September 18th

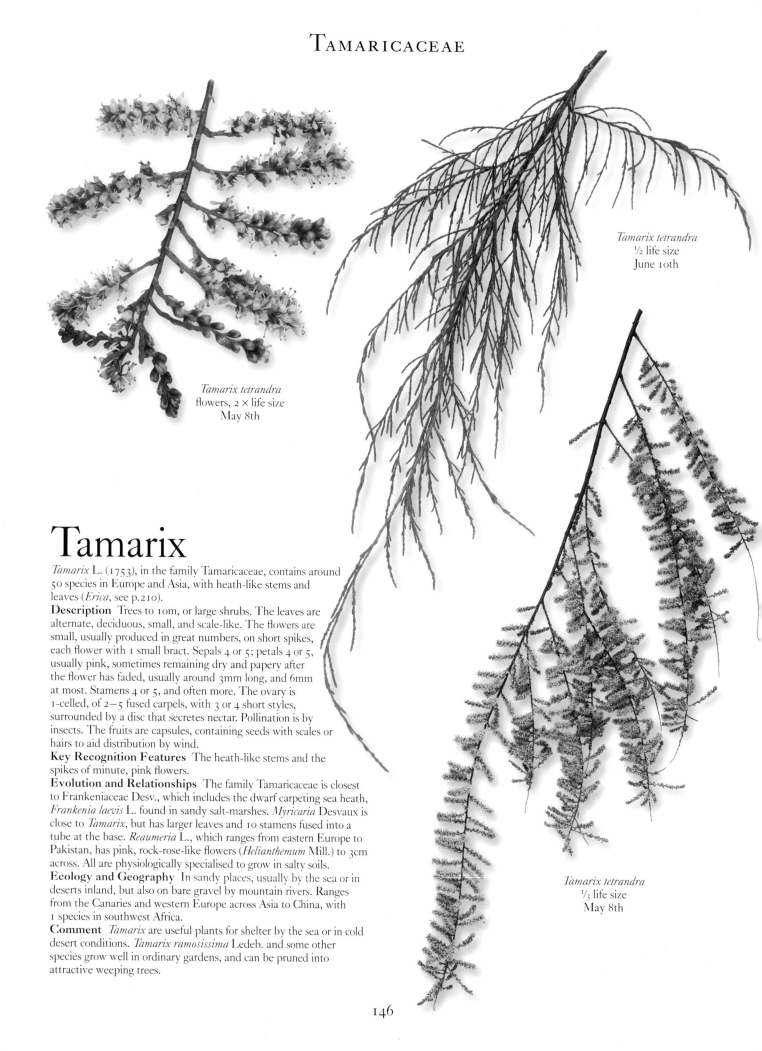

Tamarix tetrandra
½ life size
June 10th

Tamarix tetrandra
flowers, 2 × life size
May 8th

Tamarix

Tamarix L. (1753), in the family Tamaricaceae, contains around 50 species in Europe and Asia, with heath-like stems and leaves (*Erica*, see p.210).

Description Trees to 10m, or large shrubs. The leaves are alternate, deciduous, small, and scale-like. The flowers are small, usually produced in great numbers, on short spikes, each flower with 1 small bract. Sepals 4 or 5; petals 4 or 5, usually pink, sometimes remaining dry and papery after the flower has faded, usually around 3mm long, and 6mm at most. Stamens 4 or 5, and often more. The ovary is 1-celled, of 2–5 fused carpels, with 3 or 4 short styles, surrounded by a disc that secretes nectar. Pollination is by insects. The fruits are capsules, containing seeds with scales or hairs to aid distribution by wind.

Key Recognition Features The heath-like stems and the spikes of minute, pink flowers.

Evolution and Relationships The family Tamaricaceae is closest to Frankeniaceae Desv., which includes the dwarf carpeting sea heath, *Frankenia laevis* L. found in sandy salt-marshes. *Myricaria* Desvaux is close to *Tamarix*, but has larger leaves and 10 stamens fused into a tube at the base. *Reaumeria* L., which ranges from eastern Europe to Pakistan, has pink, rock-rose-like flowers (*Helianthemum* Mill.) to 3cm across. All are physiologically specialised to grow in salty soils.

Ecology and Geography In sandy places, usually by the sea or in deserts inland, but also on bare gravel by mountain rivers. Ranges from the Canaries and western Europe across Asia to China, with 1 species in southwest Africa.

Comment *Tamarix* are useful plants for shelter by the sea or in cold desert conditions. *Tamarix ramosissima* Ledeb. and some other species grow well in ordinary gardens, and can be pruned into attractive weeping trees.

Tamarix tetrandra
⅓ life size
May 8th

Halimium

Halimium (Dunal) Spach (1836), in the family Cistaceae, contains 9 species from around the Mediterranean.

Description Shrubs to 1.5m. The leaves are opposite and evergreen. The flowers are usually in sprays, opening mostly in early summer. Sepals 3 or 5, the outer 2 much smaller than the inner; petals 5, yellow or white, sometimes with a purple blotch. Stamens numerous. Style short or absent, with a capitate stigma. Pollination is by insects. The fruit is a 3-celled capsule with numerous seeds.

Key Recognition Features Similar to the more common *Cistus* (see p.148) but usually with yellow flowers; the white-flowered *H. umbellatum* (L.) Spach can be recognised by its numerous small flowers, around 1.8cm long, and its 3-celled capsules.

Evolution and Relationships The family Cistaceae has 7 genera, mainly around the Mediterranean, with 2 genera, *Hudsonia* L. and *Lechea* L., in North America. It is probably related to the Malvaceae (see pp.154–59), and possibly also to *Bixa orellana* L. from tropical Central America and *Cochlospermum* Kunth, both in the family Bixaceae Kunth.

Ecology and Geography In rocky and heathery areas, open pine forests, and sandy places on the coast, mainly in the western Mediterranean, Spain, Portugal, and Morocco.

Comment Some species are cultivated for their bright yellow flowers; they are somewhat less hardy than many *Cistus*.

Halimium lasianthum
flowers, 1 ¼ × life size
July 6th

Halimium
seed capsule
2 × life size
September 21st

Halimium lasianthum
½ life size, July 6th

Cistus

Cistus L. (1753), in the family Cistaceae, contains 16 species from around the Mediterranean.

Description Shrubs to 4m, the stems often sticky with aromatic resin. The leaves are opposite, evergreen, often hairy, linear to ovate. The flowers are usually on a branched inflorescence, but open singly in the morning, falling by early afternoon. Sepals 3 or 5, the outer 2 smaller than the inner; petals 5, pinkish-purple to white, sometimes with a purple blotch at the base. Stamens numerous. Style short, with a capitate stigma, elongating towards midday. Pollination is by insects, usually bees. The fruit is a capsule with 5, sometimes up to 10, cells containing numerous seeds.

Key Recognition Features The flowers have crinkled petals, which fall by early afternoon. The opposite leaves mostly have short, smaller-leaved shoots in their axils.

Evolution and Relationships *Cistus* contains the largest shrubs in the Cistaceae, and is very close to *Halimium* (see p.147). The largest genus in the family is *Helianthemum* Mill., the rock rose, with 120 species, but all are dwarf subshrubs. *Tuberaria* (Dunal) Spach is entirely herbaceous, containing both perennial and annual species.

Ecology and Geography In rocky areas; it is one of the main constituents of the *garrigue,* dwarf scrub of the dry hills. Most species are found in the western Mediterranean, Spain, Portugal, and Morocco, but a few extend eastwards to central Turkey. *Cistus* are not long-lived. They do not regenerate from the rootstock after fires, as do many Mediterranean shrubs: their leaves contain an actively flammable resin, and they rely on producing masses of seeds that germinate immediately after competition from larger shrubs has been burned away.

Comment Many species are cultivated for their long succession of flowers, and for the scent of their leaves, which is reminiscent of hot, dry hills. Hybrids are common in cultivation and, being largely sterile, they have a longer flowering season than many of the species. *Cistus ladanifer* L. and *Cistus creticus* L. are sources of the resin ladanum, used in scent.

× Halimiocistus

× *Halimiocistus* Janchen is the name given to hybrids between *Halimium* (see p.147) and *Cistus*, several of which are cultivated. × *H. wintonensis* O. & E.F. Warb. is a hybrid between *C. salviifolius* L. and probably *Halimium lasianthum* (Lam.) Spach, with mainly white flowers; 'Merrist Wood Cream' is a cultivar of this that bears creamy yellow flowers with red spots. Other crosses have white flowers, sometimes with a yellow base.

Cistus albidus
capsules and seeds
1 ¾ × life size
September 15th

Cistus × purpureus
½ life size
June 12th

Cistus ladanifer
var. *sulcatus*
½ life size
June 12th

× *Halimiocistus wintonensis*
'Merrist Wood Cream'
¾ life size, June 23rd

Cistus × cyprius
'Tania Compton'
½ life size
June 12th

Cistus albidus
½ life size
June 12th

Cistus populifolius
½ life size, June 12th

Cistaceae

Cistus × pulverulentus
½ life size
June 12th

Cistus ladanifer
½ life size
June 12th

Cistus ladanifer
var. sulcatus
½ life size, June 12th

Cistus albidus
½ life size
June 12th

Cistus salviifolius
⅔ life size
June 20th

Cistus × purpureus
½ life size
June 12th

Tilia × euchlora
¹/₂ life size
fruits and autumn leaves
October 17th

Tilia

Tilia L. (1753), the lime tree or basswood, contains 20–25 species from the northern hemisphere, in the family Tiliaceae.

Description Trees to 37m, with fibrous bark. The leaves are alternate, deciduous, asymmetric at the base, toothed but seldom lobed. Flowers are usually in umbel-like clusters, partially attached to a thin, narrow bract. Sepals 5, with nectaries covered by hair; petals 5, pale greenish-white to bright yellow; 5 petal-like staminodes are also present in some species, and these have more cup-shaped flowers than the rest. Stamens many, grouped into 5 bundles. Ovary 5-celled, each cell with 2 ovules. Style slender, with a 5-lobed stigma. Pollination is by insects. The fruit is solid, not splitting, staying attached to the wing-like bract, with 1–3 seeds.

Key Recognition Features The asymmetric leaves and the umbel-like cluster of flowers attached to the bract. In winter the stringy bark of the twigs and the round, shiny, reddish buds are characteristic.

Evolution and Relationships The genus is homogeneous and distinct, even from other members of the family.

Ecology and Geography In woods and on rocky hillsides. Limes are typical inhabitants of temperate, northern hemisphere deciduous woodlands, found in eastern North America, southwards to Mexico, throughout Europe to the Caucasus, and again in China and Japan. In England *T. cordata* Mill., the small-leaved lime or pry, is characteristic of ancient woodlands in England, and thrived when the climate was warmer than it is now.

Comment The dried flowers are often used for making a delicate herbal tea. The flowers of some species and cultivars, notably *Tilia* 'Petiolaris', the weeping silver lime, contain an abundance of the sugar mannose, which makes them intoxicating to bees, especially bumblebees. The wood is white and smooth-grained and was much used for fine carving in the 17th and 18th centuries, especially by such craftsmen as Grinling Gibbons. Bass or bast, used for matting and rope, was made from the fibrous bark of several species.

Tilia mongolica
²/₃ life size
June 24th

Tilia 'Petiolaris'
fruits, 1¼ × life size
September 16th

Tilia 'Petiolaris'
flowers, ³/₄ life size
August 4th

Sparrmannia

Sparrmannia L. fil. (1781), in the family Tiliaceae, contains 7 species from Africa and Madagascar. *Sparrmannia africana* L. fil., is the *Zimmerlinden*, a commonly grown house plant that will survive outside in mild areas.

Description Trees to 7m, or shrubs, with fibrous bark. The leaves are alternate, evergreen, toothed or 3- to 7-lobed, with stellate and simple hairs. The flowers are usually in umbel-like clusters, opposite the leaves. Sepals 4, white, petals 4, white. Stamens numerous, some or many of the outer ones sterile, but with bearded filaments. Style slender, with a 4- or 5-lobed stigma. Pollination is by insects. The fruit is a bristly, 4- or 5-celled capsule.

Key Recognition Features The large, softly hairy leaves and the numerous stamens, many of which are sterile.

Evolution and Relationships The family Tiliaceae is related to the Malvaceae (see pp.154−59). *Entelea arborescens* Brown, the New Zealand *whau*, is a single species very close to *Sparrmannia*; its leaves are similar, but it has smaller flowers without sterile stamens and very bristly fruit. The genus *Grewia* L., with 150 species mainly in Africa, South East Asia, and Australia, is deciduous with all the stamens fertile and a fleshy, few-stoned fruit.

Ecology and Geography In rocky valleys on the margins of forests in much of Africa, as far south as the Cape.

Comment The genus is named after Dr Anders Sparrmann (1748−1820), a Swede who accompanied Captain Cook on his second voyage. The floral biology of *S. africana* is unusual: in nature the flower, facing downwards with reflexed petals, catches rain in a cup formed by the petals, and lets it overflow drop by drop, keeping the stamens dry until they are disturbed by a pollinating insect, at which point they move outwards, dusting the insect with pollen.

*Sparrmannia
africana*
flowers
¾ life size
January 6th

*Sparrmannia
africana*
⅓ life size
January 6th

Tilia henryana
⅓ life size
September 10th

Tilia mexicana
⅔ life size
July 6th

Tilia oliveri
⅔ life size
July 6th

*Tilia
kiusiana*
⅔ life size
July 6th

Fremontodendron

Fremontodendron Coville (1893), in the Sterculiaceae, consists of 3 species in western North America.

Description Trees to 10m, with dark bark. The leaves are evergreen, alternate, sometimes 3- to 7-lobed, dark green above, white or pinkish and velvety-hairy beneath. The flowers are bisexual, solitary, covered with star-shaped hairs outside. Sepals 5, fused at the base, yellow to orange, with a nectary pit at the base; petals absent. Stamens 5, filaments fused for about half their length around the base of the style, with convoluted anthers. Ovary of 5 fused cells, style slender. Pollination is by insects. The fruit is a hairy capsule with 5 rows of ovules, surrounded by the papery remains of the sepals. Seeds are hairy or shining black.

Key Recognition Features The dark green, softly leathery leaves with pinkish scurf beneath, and the large, rich yellow flowers.

Evolution and Relationships *Fremontodendron* is one of those small and isolated genera found only in southern California. Others are *Carpenteria* (see p.220) and *Romneya* (see p.90).

Ecology and Geography On dry hillsides and in chaparral and open oak woods, at up to 1800m, in California from Shasta County southwards to Baja California.

Comment The species and several cultivars, such as 'California Glory', are grown for ornament. The bristly hairs on the fruits are particularly irritating. If given too moist or rich a soil the plants grow very fast but are short-lived. The genus is named after Col. John Charles Frémont, (1813–90), an early explorer of western North America.

Fremontodendron californicum
²/₃ life size
May 15th

Fremontodendron californicum
open capsule with dry, persistent sepals
2¹/₄ × life size, November 22nd

Fremontodendron californicum
1¹/₂ × life size, May 15th

Reevesia

Reevesia Lindl. (1827), in the family Sterculiaceae, contains 3 or 4 species from the Himalayas to Taiwan.

Description Trees to 10m, and shrubs. The leaves are alternate, evergreen, simple. The flowers are in flat-topped, many-flowered clusters and white or pink. Sepals 3–6, unequal; petals 5. The stamens and ovary are on a long tube, the stamens composed of 5 groups of 3 sessile anthers, alternating with 5 staminodes. Carpels 5, fused. Pollination is by insects. The fruit is a woody capsule with winged seeds.

Key Recognition Features The flattish clusters of flowers with the long, style-like staminal column, white in *R. thyrsoidea* Lindl., pink in *R. pubescens* Mast.

Evolution and Relationships The small flowers and long staminal column are specialised characteristics in the family.

Ecology and Geography Grows in rocky valleys and on wooded hills from Nepal through southern China to Taiwan. The trees are remarkable as they often seem to occur as isolated individuals.

Comment Rare and attractive ornamental trees. The genus is named after John Reeves (1774–1856), inspector of tea for the East India Company, who lived in Canton and Macao from 1812; he sent plants and a large collection of drawings of Chinese plants to the Royal Horticultural Society in London.

Reevesia thyrsoidea
½ life size, May 17th

Reevesia thyrsoidea
showing stamens and ovary on
the end of a long tube
life size, May 17th

Hoheria lyallii
⅓ life size, June 3rd

Hoheria lyalii
seed heads and unwinged segments
1½ × life size, September 8th

Hoheria

Hoheria Cunn. (1839), in the family Malvaceae, contains 5 species in New Zealand.

Description Trees to 10m or more, and shrubs, with fibrous bark. The leaves are alternate, evergreen or deciduous, triangular to ovate, toothed; the juvenile leaves are smaller and especially deeply lobed. The flowers are produced in clusters and singly in the upper leaf axils. Sepals 5, fused at the base into a calyx; petals 5, thin, white, rounded or notched at apex. Stamens numerous, fused into a column at the base, the filaments grouped above into 5 bundles, with small anthers. Carpels 5–15, each with 1 ovule, surrounding a central axis; styles with 5–15 branches. Pollination is by insects. The seed heads split into dry, often winged, 1-seeded segments.

Key Recognition Features The genus *Hoheria* is recognised by its numerous white flowers among the leaves, produced in mid- to late summer. *Plagianthus* Forster & Forster, with 2 species in New Zealand, is similar but has smaller, greenish flowers, each with 1 carpel.

Evolution and Relationships The Malvaceae has much in common with the Tiliaceae (see pp.150–51), but is a mainly herbaceous family, containing familiar plants such as okra (*Abelmoschus* Medik.) and mallow (*Malva*, see Volume 2). Most species have sepal-like bracts, called an epicalyx, just beneath the sepals. These are absent in *Hoheria*, suggesting that it is a primitive genus in the family.

Ecology and Geography Found on the edges of forest and in open areas by streams throughout New Zealand.

Comment Most species and some hybrids, such as 'Glory of Amlwch', are cultivated in gardens in areas with mild winters. In colder areas the shrubs need protection from freezing wind.

MALVACEAE

Hoheria sexstylosa
¾ life size, August 4th

Hoheria lyallii
life size, June 3rd

Hoheria sexstylosa
seed heads and
winged segments
2 × life size
October 25th

Hibiscus syriacus 'Hamabo'
1/3 life size, September 25th

Hibiscus syriacus
capsules and seeds
1 1/2 × life size, November 24th

Hibiscus syriacus
'Jeanne d'Arc'
1/3 life size, September 25th

Hibiscus syriacus
1/3 life size
September 25th

Hibiscus

Hibiscus L. (1753), in the family Malvaceae, contains about 300 species, mainly in subtropical areas.

Description Trees to 25m, shrubs, or herbs, the branches with stipules. The leaves are alternate, evergreen or deciduous, usually roughly triangular and toothed, sometimes 3- to 7-lobed. The flowers are large, colourful, usually solitary in the axils of the upper leaves. The bracts are often sepal-like. Sepals 5, fused at the base; petals 5, equal, attached to the stamen tube. Stamens numerous, with the filaments fused into a tube that is often long and slender, particularly so in *H. schizopetalus* (Mast.) Hook., and the anthers with short, free filaments near the stigmas. Carpels 5, the long style inside the stamen tube, with 5 stigmas. Pollination is by insects or birds. The fruits are 5-celled capsules with numerous seeds.

Key Recognition Features The long stamen tube is easily recognised; in *Hibiscus* this is combined with a 5-celled capsule and 5 simple styles.

Evolution and Relationships *Hibiscus* is the largest and showiest genus in the family; it is most closely related to *Gossypium* L., the cotton plant. The species with very long stamen tubes are probably pollinated by birds or large butterflies.

Ecology and Geography Some are found in scrub, on rocks, and in open woods, often near the sea; others, such as the American *H. moscheutos* L., in marshes. The range extends throughout the tropics and into temperate zones. Some species are annual weeds.

Comment Many species are grown as ornamentals. *Hibiscus rosa-sinensis* L. is the common tropical hibiscus which beauties put behind their ears in the South Seas; the original species has red flowers but it is now grown in yellow, orange, and almost blue. *Hibiscus syriacus* L. is the hardiest species, with generally reddish-purple, pink, blue, or white flowers; in spite of its name it probably originated in China. Several species, notably *H. cannabinus* L., have fibres in the stems which are used for matting and rope. The red, fleshy calyx of roselle, *H. sabdariffa* L., is edible, and its taste has been likened to sorrel; when dried, it is used as a herbal tea.

Hibiscus syriacus
1 1/4 × life size, September 25th

Lavatera

Lavatera L. (1753), in the family Malvaceae, contains 25 species across the northern hemisphere.

Description Shrubs to 4m, perennials, biennials, or annuals. The leaves are alternate, evergreen, lobed, often greyish and velvety-hairy. The flowers are usually solitary or few in the axils of the upper leaves. Bracts 3, sepal-like, fused at the base. Sepals 5, petals 5, equal. Stamens numerous, the filaments fused into a short tube. Carpels many, with long, slender styles and thread-like stigmas. Pollination is by insects or birds. The fruits are in a whorl and 1-seeded.

Key Recognition Features The 3 bracts, generally called epicalyx segments, fused at the base, and the whorl of numerous seeds. The flowers are generally pink.

Evolution and Relationships Close to the mallow (*Malva*, see Volume 2), but generally larger plants. *Malva* has the epicalyx segments separate at the base. The presence of a whorl of 1-seeded fruits is considered an advanced characteristic compared with other genera, such as *Malope* L., in which the fruits themselves are whorled.

Ecology and Geography On rocky coasts, cliffs, and dry meadows; 1 species, *L. assurgentiflora* Kell. on the Santa Barbara Islands, may be hummingbird pollinated, and the red-flowered *L. phoenicea* Vent. from the Canaries may have attracted bird pollinators in the past. Other species are found across Europe and around the Mediterranean, eastwards to Kashmir, and perhaps 1 species in Australia.

Comment The large, thick-stemmed *L. arborea* L., the tree mallow, is a biennial shrub of seaside cliffs and dunes in western Europe. *Lavatera olbia* L. 'Rosea' is commonly cultivated, forming a large shrub in one season. *Lavatera thuringiaca* L. is a woody-based perennial. Other probable hybrids between the two species are commonly cultivated. *Lavatera* commemorates Johan Heinrich Lavater (1611–91) a physician from Zurich.

Lavatera thuringiaca
fruit, 1¾ × life size
November 29th

Lavatera thuringiaca
seeds, 1¾ × life size
November 29th

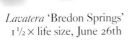

Lavatera 'Bredon Springs'
1½ × life size, June 26th

Lavatera 'Bredon Springs'
½ life size, June 26th

Abutilon

Abutilon Mill. (1768), in the family Malvaceae, contains 100 species distributed throughout the tropics and into temperate South America.

Description Shrubs to 10m, with fibrous bark. The leaves are alternate, evergreen, more or less triangular, often lobed. The flowers have no bracts, and are produced singly or in small clusters. Sepals 5, often coloured, almost forming a tube; petals 5, equal, often forming a hanging bell. Stamens numerous, the filaments fused into a short tube. Carpels many, with long, slender styles. Pollination is by insects or birds. The fruits have a whorl of 2- to 9-seeded capsules.

Key Recognition Features The hanging, bell-shaped flowers are typical of many species; flat, bluish or white flowers are typical of the temperate South American species, such as *A. vitifolium* Presl..

Evolution and Relationships *Abutilon* is closely related to *Sphaeralcea* A. St-Hil. and *Sida* L., in which the fruit is also a ring of capsules. The flat-flowered species are sometimes separated in the genus *Corynabutilon* (Schumann) Kearney.

Ecology and Geography In forests and rocky places. Most species are found in South America, from southern Chile northwards; a few in California and tropical Asia, and around 30 in Australia.

Comment Many species are grown as ornamentals, especially in frost-free climates. Those with hanging flowers are good for attracting hummingbirds, especially *A. megapotamicum* (Spreng.) A. St.-Hil. & Naudin, with its red calyx and yellow petals. The spotted leaves of *A. megapotamicum* 'Variegatum' are caused by a virus that commonly infects other species.

Abutilon 'Louis Marignac'
⅔ life size, September 29th

Abutilon 'Canary Bird'
⅔ life size
September 29th

Abutilon 'Nabob'
⅔ life size, September 29th

Abutilon × *milleri*
⅔ life size, June 22nd

Abutilon vitifolium
⅔ life size
May 11th

Malvaceae

Abutilon megapotamicum 'Variegatum'
½ life size, October 17th

Abutilon megapotamicum
½ life size, October 17th

Abutilon vitifolium
capsules and seeds
1 ½ × life size
September 16th

Abutilon 'Canary Bird'
capsule, 1 ½ × life size
November 24th

Abutilon × suntense
'Ralph Gould'
½ life size, May 18th

Ulmus thomasii
1¼ × life size
June 24th

Ulmus procera
flowers, life size
February 20th

Ulmus procera
young fruits, 1¼ × life size
April 25th

Ulmus

Ulmus L. (1753), the elm, contains around 30 species from around the northern hemisphere, in the family Ulmaceae.

Description Trees to 35m, or rarely shrubs, often suckering and regenerating from the roots. The leaves are alternate, usually deciduous, toothed, with pinnate veins, asymmetric at the base, and sometimes rough on the surface. The flowers are small, in short-stemmed bunches borne on bare twigs before the leaves, usually in spring. Sepals 5–9, fused at the base; petals absent. Stamens 3–9, the anthers usually red before they open. Carpel 1, with a deeply 2-lobed style. Pollination is by wind. The fruits are 1-seeded samaras surrounded by thin wings.

Key Recognition Features The rough, toothed leaves with pinnate veins, and in spring the small flowers along the branches, followed by the green, winged fruits.

Evolution and Relationships Ulmaceae contains 18 genera, some tropical. It is usually grouped with the Urticales, which includes the Urticaceae (see p.168), Cannabaceae (see Volume 2), and Moraceae (see pp.164–67); there are also similarities with the Eucommiaceae (see p.128). Two subfamilies are recognised; Ulmoideae (*Ulmus, Zelkova, Hemiptelea* see p.162, *Planera* Gmel.) with dry fruits, and 2n=28; Celtidoidae (*Aphananthe* see p.162, *Celtis* see p.163, *Trema* Lour.) with fleshy fruits and 2n=20, 30, and 40.

Ecology and Geography In woods and in hedgerows, nowadays often shrubby as large trees have been killed by disease in many areas. Six species are native in North America; the rest mainly in China. The wych elm, *U. glabra* Huds., is less susceptible to disease, and common in northern areas. *Ulmus americana* L. has also survived in many areas.

Comment Virgil described how grape vines were trained on elms, and this practice could until recently be seen in the countryside near Naples. The timber was used for piles and for wooden water pipes and drain pipes, because it is resistant to rot in wet conditions. Elms are common in hedgerows throughout southern England, and in parts of North America, being fast growing and often planted for shade, shelter, fodder, and firewood. Until the 1960s they were fine trees, a conspicuous feature of the landscape in lowland areas, but from 1965 onwards a virulent strain of Dutch elm disease, *Ceratocystus ulmi*, appeared and was spread quickly by elm bark beetles, *Scolytus* spp., and now hardly a single large tree remains. Dead trees often resprout and reach around 6m before succumbing to disease again. Many North American species are also affected by the disease, which reached America around 1930. This is not the first time that disease has decimated European elms; elm pollen is common in late post-glacial peats in southern England, but around 4000BC, about the time of the coming of Neolithic agriculture, about half the trees suddenly died. Other less devastating epidemics killed large numbers of European elms around 1500, in 1820–60, and in 1918–30.

Ulmus procera
flowers, 3½ × life size
February 20th

Ulmus procera
½ life size
April 25th

Zelkova

Zelkova Spach (1841), in the family Ulmaceae, contains 4 species from Europe and Asia.

Description Trees to 40m, or shrubs, with smooth and sometimes flaky bark. The leaves are alternate, deciduous, rough, often with coarse, blunt teeth, with pinnate veins, nearly symmetric at the base. The flowers are small, unisexual, appearing as the leaves unfurl. The males are in bunches at the base of the twigs, the females single in the leaf axils towards the tips. Sepals 4 or 5; petals absent. Stamens 4 or 5. Carpel 1, with a deeply 2-lobed style. Pollination is by wind. The fruits are 1-seeded, green, stalkless, and slightly fleshy.

Key Recognition Features The rough, coarsely toothed leaves, with pinnate veins, and the smooth bark, flaking in small pieces. *Zelkova serrata* Mak. and *Z. carpinifolia* (Pall.) K. Koch tend to have many tall, upright branches from a short, thick trunk.

Evolution and Relationships *Zelkova* is close to *Ulmus* in most characteristics, but the 1-seeded, fleshy fruit links it with *Celtis* (see p.163).

Ecology and Geography In woods and on rocky hillsides, with *Z. abelicea* (Lam.) Boiss., syn. *Z. cretica* Spach, in Crete; *Z. carpinifolia* in northern Turkey and the Caucasus; *Z. sinica* Schneid. in China, and *Z. serrata* in Japan.

Comment All the species are planted as ornamentals. *Zelkova serrata* is susceptible to Dutch elm disease (see *Ulmus*), but the others are resistant. *Zelkova carpinifolia* is especially striking in its upright main branches, and *Z. abelicea* is a particularly elegant small tree.

Zelkova schneideriana
with fruits, ¾ life size,
September 16th

Zelkova abelicea
with fruit, ¾ life size
September 16th

Zelkova abelicea
flowering branch
⅔ life size, May 11th

Zelkova sinica
flowers, 2 × life size
May 11th

Hemiptelea

Hemiptelea Planch. (1872) in the family Ulmaceae, contains 1 species, *H. davidii* (Hance) Planch. from northern China, Korea, and eastern Siberia.

Description Tree to 3m, or shrub, densely branched, with spiny branchlets. The leaves are alternate, deciduous, toothed, 2–5cm long, with pinnate veins, symmetrical at the base. The flowers are small, unisexual, in the leaf axils, in spring. Sepals 5–9, fused at the base; petals absent. The males have 4–5 stamens, the females 1 carpel, with a deeply 2-lobed style. Pollination is by wind. The fruits are 1-seeded samaras with the wing only half surrounding the nut.

Key Recognition Features The small leaves, resembling *Zelkova* (see p.161), and half-winged samaras.

Evolution and Relationships Close to *Ulmus* (see p.160) except for the fruit.

Ecology and Geography On dry hillsides, especially on the *loess* in northeastern China, from Zhejiang northwards to Korea, near Seoul and near Mukden.

Comment In northern China this is planted as a dense, thorny hedge. The specific name commemorates Père Armand David (1826–1900), French naturalist and missionary in China. Most of his plant discoveries, and the giant panda, were from Moupine, now Baoxing, in Sichuan.

Aphananthe

Aphananthe Planch. (1873), in the family Ulmaceae, contains around 6 species.

Description Trees to 30m, fast-growing. The leaves are alternate, deciduous, very rough, parallel-veined, oblique at the base. Flowers are small, unisexual, appearing as the leaves unfurl, the males in many-flowered bunches at the base of the twigs, the females singly in the leaf axils towards the tips. Sepals 4 or 5; petals absent. Stamens 4 or 5. Carpel 1, with a deeply 2-lobed style. Pollination is by wind. The fruits are 1-seeded, black, juicy, often hairy, with persistent styles, on stalks 7–8mm long.

Key Recognition Features The very rough, toothed leaves, with straight, pinnate veins ending in the teeth.

Evolution and Relationships The genus is very close to *Celtis*, differing mainly in the leaves.

Ecology and Geography In rocky places and by roadsides in the lowlands; 1 species in Mexico; 3 in Madagascar; *A. aspera* (Thunb.) Planch., the sandpaper tree, is found in Korea, Japan, and China, with a closely related species ranging through tropical South East Asia to northern Australia.

Comment *Aphananthe aspera* is sometimes planted as a fast-growing timber tree.

Hemiptelea davidii
$1\frac{1}{4}$ × life size, May 5th

Hemiptelea davidii
flowering branch
$\frac{1}{3}$ life size, May 5th

Aphananthe aspera
$\frac{2}{3}$ life size
October 12th

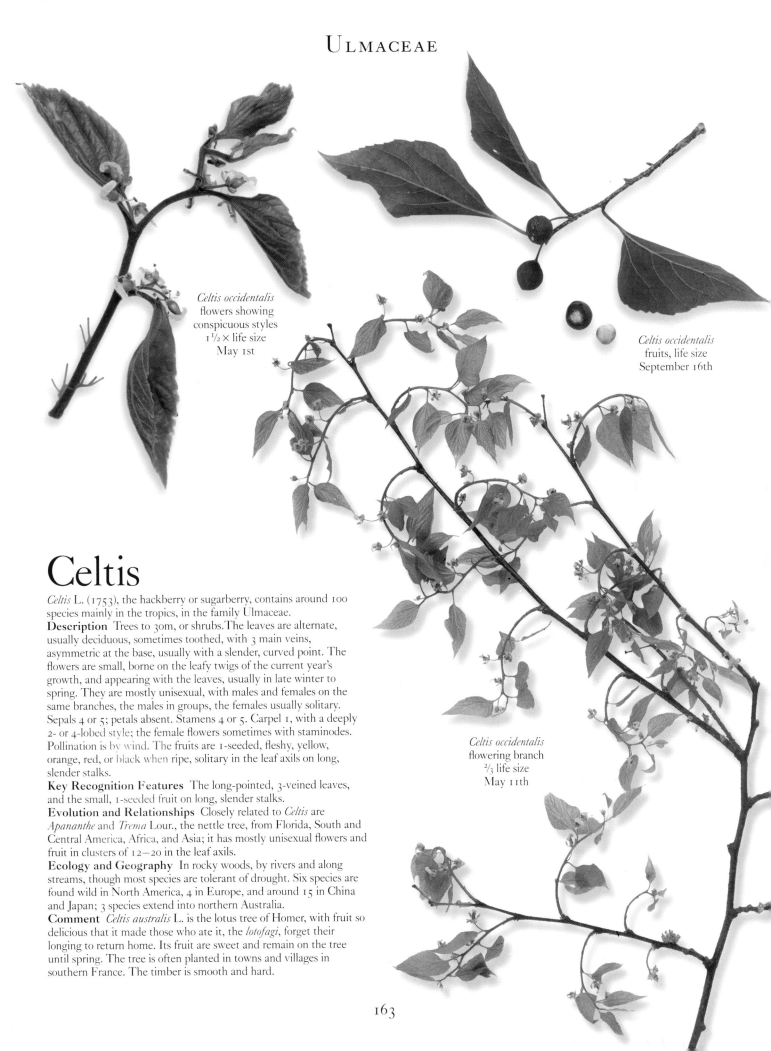

Celtis occidentalis
flowers showing
conspicuous styles
1 ½ × life size
May 1st

Celtis occidentalis
fruits, life size
September 16th

Celtis occidentalis
flowering branch
⅔ life size
May 11th

Celtis

Celtis L. (1753), the hackberry or sugarberry, contains around 100 species mainly in the tropics, in the family Ulmaceae.

Description Trees to 30m, or shrubs. The leaves are alternate, usually deciduous, sometimes toothed, with 3 main veins, asymmetric at the base, usually with a slender, curved point. The flowers are small, borne on the leafy twigs of the current year's growth, and appearing with the leaves, usually in late winter to spring. They are mostly unisexual, with males and females on the same branches, the males in groups, the females usually solitary. Sepals 4 or 5; petals absent. Stamens 4 or 5. Carpel 1, with a deeply 2- or 4-lobed style; the female flowers sometimes with staminodes. Pollination is by wind. The fruits are 1-seeded, fleshy, yellow, orange, red, or black when ripe, solitary in the leaf axils on long, slender stalks.

Key Recognition Features The long-pointed, 3-veined leaves, and the small, 1-seeded fruit on long, slender stalks.

Evolution and Relationships Closely related to *Celtis* are *Apananthe* and *Trema* Lour., the nettle tree, from Florida, South and Central America, Africa, and Asia; it has mostly unisexual flowers and fruit in clusters of 12–20 in the leaf axils.

Ecology and Geography In rocky woods, by rivers and along streams, though most species are tolerant of drought. Six species are found wild in North America, 4 in Europe, and around 15 in China and Japan; 3 species extend into northern Australia.

Comment *Celtis australis* L. is the lotus tree of Homer, with fruit so delicious that it made those who ate it, the *lotofagi*, forget their longing to return home. Its fruit are sweet and remain on the tree until spring. The tree is often planted in towns and villages in southern France. The timber is smooth and hard.

Morus alba
fruit, life size
September 16th

Morus alba
'Venosa', life size
September 16th

Morus nigra
fruit, 1½ × life size
September 18th

Morus nigra
male (left) and female (right) flowers
just over life size, June 3rd

Morus nigra
flowering branch
½ life size, May 21st

Morus

Morus L. (1753), the mulberry tree, contains around 12 species in tropical Africa and temperate Asia, in the family Moraceae.

Description Trees to 20m, or large shrubs, the young shoots with milky sap. The leaves are alternate, deciduous, toothed or variously lobed, sometimes slightly rough. The flowers may be bisexual or unisexual, on the same or different plants, small and green, the males grouped into catkin-like heads. Sepals 4, rarely 5; petals absent. Stamens 4, carpels 2, style with 2 branches. Pollination is by wind. Later the sepals of the female flowers become juicy and sweet, coalescing to form an elongated fruit; each flower contains 1 seed.

Key Recognition Features The rough, alternate leaves with irregular lobes, especially on juvenile branches, and the juicy, edible white, red, or black fruit are typical.

Evolution and Relationships The family Moraceae is close to Urticaceae (the nettle family, see p.168), but are mainly tropical trees with fleshy fruit, and include *Artocarpus* Forster & Forster, the breadfruit, in which the female inflorescence becomes like a giant mulberry. *Ficus* is the largest genus in the family. *Fatoua villosa* (Thunb.) Nakai, the mulberry weed or crabweed, is an annual from Asia now established as a weed in the southeastern United States. Its fruits are not fleshy, and the seeds are ejected explosively.

Ecology and Geography On rocky slopes, by streams, and in forests. Two species are native in North America, including the forest tree *M. rubra* L. The commonly cultivated *M. alba* L. and *M. nigra* L. are from China.

Comment *Morus alba* is often grown for silk worms, the trees being pollarded to produce ample leafy shoots. *Morus nigra* is most commonly grown in Europe for its fruit; it is an ancient cultivated tree, possibly derived from *M. alba*; the trees eventually become spectacularly gnarled and twisted.

Ficus

Ficus L. (1753), the fig tree, in the family Moraceae contains 750 species, mainly large trees in the tropics.

Description Trees to 30m, shrubs, or climbers, with milky sap. The leaves are usually alternate, usually evergreen, rarely deciduous, sometimes lobed. The flowers are very small and carried on the inside of the wall of the inflorescence, usually with males and females together, sometimes with the males and females on different trees. Sepals 2–6, petals absent. Stamens 2, carpel 1, with an unbranched style. Pollination is by small wasps which enter the flowering figs through the hole in the apex. The ripe figs consist of hundreds of 1-seeded female flowers embedded in the juicy wall of the inflorescence.

Key Recognition Features The fruits, all of which look like typical figs, are easy to see. The common fig, *F. carica* L., also has deeply lobed, rough leaves; in wild figs these may be lobed right to the central vein.

Evolution and Relationships The genus is very distinct from others in the family.

Ecology and Geography The wild type of the edible fig is found in rock crevices in gorges, often near springs. Other species are found throughout the tropics, often starting life as epiphytes on other trees before sending down roots to the ground and smothering their host tree, therefore called strangler figs.

Comment *Ficus carica* has been cultivated for 6000 years in Egypt, having probably originated in northern Iraq or Turkey; even today most dried figs are produced in Turkey, including ancient Caria, and exported from Izmir (formerly Smyrna). Many of the tropical species are grown as house plants, as they survive in low light conditions, not dissimilar from the floor of a tropical forest. *Ficus elastica* Roxb. ex Hornemann is the India rubber plant, which quickly makes a large tree in the tropics. *Ficus religiosa* L., the sacred fig, *peepul*, or bo tree, has characteristic leaves with long, slender drip tips; it also has a particularly complex interaction between fruit and pollinators. *Ficus benghalensis* L., the banyan, can cover areas up to 1.6 hectares with stilt-like roots that become secondary trunks. *Ficus pumila* L. is a small-leaved, ivy-like climber when young, becoming shrubby when mature, with larger leaves and large blue figs. It is nearly hardy, and a form with variegated leaves is grown as a house plant and often seen on walls in California or the Mediterranean.

Ficus carica
'Brown Turkey'
young fruit
life size
October 3rd

Ficus carica
'Brown Turkey'
ripe fruit, life size
October 3rd

Ficus carica
½ life size
late fruit and autumn leaf
September 29th

Ficus carica
'Brown Turkey'
⅓ life size, October 3rd

Broussonetia

Broussonetia L' Herit. ex Vent. (1799), in the family Moraceae, contains 8 species.

Description Trees to 16m, or shrubs, sometimes climbing, the twigs with milky sap. The leaves are alternate, usually deciduous, often lobed. The flowers are unisexual, with males and females on different plants. The male flowers are in pendulous, catkin-like spikes, with 4 sepals, fused at the base, no petals, and 4 stamens. Female flowers are in round heads, with 4 sepals, fused at the base to form a tube, 1 carpel, and a long, undivided style. Pollination is by wind. The fruits are round, red, with each seed surrounded by a fleshy covering extending from the enlarged sepal-tube.

Key Recognition Features The rough leaves, hairier and more delicate than those of a mulberry (*Morus*, see p.164), and the round, hairy female flowers, which become red fruit.

Evolution and Relationships *Broussonetia* and the related genera *Maclura* and *Cudrania* Tréc. are close to *Morus*, differing mainly in details of flower and fruit.

Ecology and Geography In rough, bushy places, by roads and in woods. One species in Madagascar, the rest in China and eastern Asia, with 3 found wild in Japan, including *B. papyrifera* (L.) Vent., the paper-mulberry tree, which is naturalised in North America.

Comment *Broussonetia papyrifera* and *B. kazinoki* Sieb. are cultivated for making tough paper in China and Japan. The genus name comemorates Pierre Marie Auguste Broussonet (1761—1807) a biologist from Montpellier, France.

Broussonetia papyrifera
branch with young fruit
2/3 life size, June 22nd

Broussonetia papyrifera
young catkins
3/4 life size, April 11th

Maclura

Maclura Nutt. (1818) contains only 1 species, *M. pomifera* (Raf.) C.K. Schneid., the osage orange, from North America, in the family Moraceae.

Description Tree to 20m, the twigs with spines in the leaf axils and milky sap. The leaves are alternate, deciduous, rounded at the base, slender-pointed, hairy, not toothed or lobed. The flowers are unisexual, with males and females on different plants. The male flowers are in catkin-like spikes, with 4 sepals, no petals, and 4 stamens. Female flowers are in round heads, with 4 sepals, the 2 inner narrower than the 2 outer, 1 carpel, and a long, undivided style. Pollination is by wind. The fruits are large, round, green, to 12cm across, with each seed surrounded by fleshy sepals.

Key Recognition Features The large, green fruits remain on the tree after the leaves have fallen, and then lie on the ground. They exude milky juice when cut open.

Evolution and Relationships *Cudrania* Tréc., from China and Japan southwards to Australia, is closely related to *Maclura* and sometimes united with it; it has similar but smaller fruits, which ripen orange. × *Macludrania*, the hybrid between *Maclura* and *Cudrania*, was raised in France; it has large, orange fruits.

Ecology and Geography In scrub and along hedges and roads; native of southwestern Arkansas, southeastern Oklahoma, and Texas, and naturalised elsewhere northwards to New York state.

Comment The genus is named after William Maclure (1763–1840) an American geologist. The wood was used for bows and war clubs, and the trees were planted as hedges in the midwest.

Maclura pomifera
ripe fruit, ½ life size
October 5th

Maclura pomifera
⅓ life size, June 21st

Maclura pomifera
female flowers
¾ life size, June 21st

Boehmeria spicata
female flowers
just under life size
October 5th

Boehmeria spicata
²/₃ life size
October 5th

Boehmeria

Boehmeria Jacq. (1760), in the family Urticaceae, contains 80 species, mainly in the tropics.

Description Trees or shrubs to 3m in the temperate species, and often perennials. The leaves are usually opposite, evergreen or deciduous, toothed, and sometimes lobed. The flowers are unisexual, small and whitish-green, in spike-like or pyramidal sprays, with males and females usually on the same plant. The males have 4 sepals, no petals, 4 stamens, and a rounded, sterile ovary. The females have 4 sepals and 1 carpel with a long style. Pollination is by wind. The fruits are single, dry seeds 1–2.5mm long.

Key Recognition Features The finely toothed leaves, which are usually opposite, and very small, whitish flowers.

Evolution and Relationships The nettle family Urticacaeae is close to the *Moraceae* (see pp.164–67), but many species are herbaceous, with stinging hairs. The flowers are always small and insignificant, and most species have small, dry seeds. *Debregeasia* Gaudich. is an exception; most species have the sepals becoming juicy as the seed ripens, and *D. edulis* (Sieb. & Zucc.) Wedd. from China and Japan, has masses of edible, orange fruit along the branches.

Ecology and Geography Open places in the mountains and hills, swamps, ditches, and woods, in the Americas from Argentina northwards to Labrador and Maine, and in the old world tropics northwards to Japan and China.

Comment *Boehmeria spicata* (Thunb.) Thunb. is a common subshrub in China and Japan. *Boehmeria nivea* (L.) Gaudich., the *ramie* or China grass, is sometimes cultivated for its very long, strong fibres. In China, fine cloth was made from it, which was then embroidered with silk; it was grown in North America and is now naturalised near the coast.

Euphorbia

Euphorbia L. (1753), in the family Euphorbiaceae, contains around 2000 species found throughout the world. Most are succulents, many are herbaceous, and a few are woody shrubs; of these a few, such as *E. mellifera* Aiton (described here), are temperate ornamentals.

Description Small tree or shrub to 15m, the twigs and leaves with milky juice. The leaves are alternate, evergreen, with a strong midrib, not toothed. The flowers are unisexual, both on the same plant, in flat-topped or rounded sprays at the tops of the shoots, often surrounded by petal-like bracts. Male flowers are very reduced, of 1 stamen and anther. Female flowers have a 3-locular ovary, 3 styles, and sometimes 3 flat glands, which may be round or horn-like, black, red, or yellow. Pollination is by insects, attracted by the sometimes conspicuous and glistening drops of nectar. The fruits are 3-lobed capsules with 3 seeds, sometimes splitting explosively to eject the seeds, which often have an oily appendage to attract ants.

Key Recognition Features The milky juice and the unusual flower structure are distinctive.

Evolution and Relationships The family Euphorbiaceae contains over 8000 species, many of which are important tropical trees, such as *Hevea brasiliensis* (A. Juss.), the source of much rubber. The most closely related family is *Buxaceae* (see pp.129–30), and it is possibly also close to *Tiliaceae* (see pp.150–51), *Daphniphyllaceae* (see p.131), and *Flacourtiaceae* (see pp.134–36). *Euphorbia* has the most specialised flowers in the family.

Ecology and Geography In many habitats throughout the world; *E. mellifera* is found in laurel forest in the Canary Islands and Madeira, a relic of forests that were widespread in Europe in the Tertiary. Other tree species in Africa are cactus-like succulents.

Comment Many herbaceous species are cultivated in frosty areas. *Euphorbia pulcherrima* Willd. ex Klotsch, a native of Mexico, is grown all over the tropics and is the common house plant called Poinsettia, sold in winter; the red bracts and flowers develop best with nights more than 14 hours long.

Euphorbia mellifera
flowers, 2 × life size
April 9th

Euphorbia mellifera
½ life size, April 9th

Daphne × napolitana
(above), *Daphne pontica*
(below), 1 ½ × life size
April 10th

Daphne bholua var.
glacialis 'Gurkha'
1 ½ × life size
February 20th

Daphne pontica
½ life size
April 10th

Daphne

Daphne L. (1753), in the family Thymelaeaceae, contains around 50 species in Europe and Asia.

Description Shrubs to 2m, with tough, fibrous bark. The leaves are usually alternate, evergreen or deciduous, usually narrow, and neither toothed nor lobed, with a strong midrib, usually grouped towards the ends of the twigs, with an acrid smell and taste. The flowers are generally sweetly scented, tubular at the base, with 4 coloured sepals and no petals. Stamens 8, attached to the inside of the tube in 2 whorls, the anthers on short filaments; carpel 1, style short, with a globular stigma. Pollination is by insects: bees and small moths in the species with green, concealed flowers; butterflies and moths in the species with showy, exposed heads of flowers. The fruits are juicy, usually ripening red, with 1 seed.

Key Recognition Features The small, 4-lobed, tubular, scented flowers and simple, untoothed leaves.

Evolution and Relationships The family Thymelaeaceae is mainly tropical; it is considered close to Euphorbiaceae (see p.169) and the Flacourtiaceae (see pp.134–36), with *Daphne* the largest temperate genus. *Elaeagnus* L. is superficially very similar in flower, with a 4-lobed, tubular calyx, but that has 4 stamens.

Ecology and Geography On rocks and screes, in woods, often on limestone. Seventeen species are found in Europe, and the genus extends through the mountains of Asia to China, and to Japan, where 4 species are native. One species is found in Kamtchatka, but none reached America. *Dirca* L., the leatherwood, is the only member of the family found in North America.

Comment Many species are grown for their scented flowers in winter or early spring. Paper is made from the bark fibres of some species in the Himalayas, notably *D. papyracea* Wall. ex Steud. and *D. bholua* Buch.-Ham., which is also one of the best ornamentals. *Daphne genkwa* Sieb. & Zucc., from northern China, unusual in its opposite leaves and almost blue flowers, is used in Chinese medicine to induce abortion.

Daphne bholua 'Alba'
life size, February 20th

Edgeworthia

Edgeworthia Meissner (1841), in the family Thymelaeaceae, contains 3 species in eastern Asia.

Description Shrubs to 2m, usually with many stems from near the ground. The leaves are alternate, evergreen or deciduous, 8–15cm long, lanceolate. The flowers are in nodding, spherical heads at the tips of the branches, sweetly scented, tubular at the base. Sepals 4, yellow, orange, or red; petals absent. Stamens 8, attached to the inside of the tube, the anthers on short filaments; carpel 1, style slender, with a long, papillose stigma. Pollination is by insects. The fruits are dry, surrounded by the base of the sepal tube.

Key Recognition Features The nodding, spherical heads of yellow or orange flowers, very silky outside.

Evolution and Relationships Other related genera are *Wikstroemia* Endl. with around 20 species in China and Japan, which has scales on the disk at the base of the flower and sometimes 5 sepals, and *Stellera* L., which is *Daphne*-like but has a stout rootstock and herbaceous stems.

Ecology and Geography In scrub and open forests, by streams, the deciduous *E. chrysantha* Lindl. in central and eastern China, and the evergreen *E. gardneri* (Wall.) Meissn. in the eastern Himalayas and western China.

Comment *Edgeworthia chrysantha* is cultivated in Japan, where it is called *mitsumata* and used for making a fine, strong, silky paper, and *E. gardneri* is used for paper in the Himalayas. An even finer, silkier Japanese paper is made from *Wikstroemia canescens* Meissn, called *gampi*. *Edgeworthia* is named after Michael Packenham Edgeworth F.L.S. (1812–81), an Irish botanist in the Bengal Civil Service.

Daphne mezereum
in fruit, life size
June 21st

Edgeworthia chrysantha
leaves, 1/2 life size
May 24th

Daphne mezereum
berries, 2 1/2 × life size
June 21st

Edgeworthia chrysantha
(top) and *E. chrysantha*
'Rubra' (bottom)
life size, February 20th

Camellia

Camellia L. (1753), in the family Theaceae, contains around 200 species, including the familiar Japanese cultivated camellias.

Description Trees to 15m, or shrubs, sometimes with smooth, reddish bark. The leaves are alternate, evergreen, leathery, toothed but not lobed. The flowers are usually without stalks, either solitary or a few together in the leaf axils. The bracts and sepals fall away as the flower opens. Petals generally 5 and joined at the base in wild plants, but often numerous and more or less separate in garden forms. Stamens numerous, the outer filaments fused at the base and sometimes joined to the petals; anthers versatile. Carpels 3, fused, each with 4–6 ovules. Style 1 or with 3 or 4 branches, slender. Pollination is by insects and perhaps also by birds, which often peck off part of the flower without damaging the style. The fruits have thick, leathery walls, and split into 3, with usually only 1 or 2 large seeds ripening in each fruit.

Key Recognition Features The leathery leaves and the flowers with several bracts and sepals, followed by large seeds.

Evolution and Relationships The family Theaceae is close to Aquifoliaceae (hollies, see p.179) and Styracaceae (see pp.180–85), and also to Dilleniaceae (see p.132) and several other tropical families.

Ecology and Geography In woods by streams and on rocky hillsides from the eastern Himalayas to Japan and Malaysia.

Comment Camellias have been cultivated in China and Japan for over 1000 years, first for the oil from their seeds, later for tea and for ornament. The tea plant, *C. sinensis* (L.) Kuntze, has small, white flowers and is usually grown in hedge-like rows, the tips of the shoots being carefully pinched off as they grow. Tea was first brought to Europe, specifically Holland, in 1610 and first auctioned in London in 1657. Today there are over 2000 named ornamental cultivars of camellia, mostly of *C. japonica*, raised mainly in the United States, China, Japan, England, and Australia. The seeds of several species, but particularly of *C. japonica*, L., *C. oleifera* Abel, and *C. sasanqua* Thunb. are processed for their oil, which is used as hair oil, for cooking, and as an ingredient in soap.

The illustrations of Camellia *continue on p.174.*

Camellia japonica
life size, March 20th

Camellia saluenensis
¹/₂ life size, March 7th

Camellia × *williamsii*
'E.G. Waterhouse'
¹/₂ life size, March 25th

THEACEAE

Camellia japonica
'Doctor Burnside'
⅓ life size, March 18th

Camellia japonica
'Rubescens Major'
⅓ life size, March 18th

Camellia japonica
'Hanafûki', ⅓ life size,
March 18th

Camellia japonica 'Furô-an'
⅓ life size, March 18th

Camellia japonica
'Lavinia Maggi'
⅓ life size, March 18th

Camellia japonica 'Arajishi'
⅓ life size, March 18th

Camellia 'Jury's Yellow'
½ life size, March 25th

Camellia japonica 'Jupiter'
⅓ life size, March 18th

Camellia japonica
fruit and seeds
life size, September 3rd

Camellia japonica 'Alba Simplex'
⅓ life size, March 18th

Camellia reticulata
½ life size, March 1st

Camellia salicifolia
¾ life size, March 1st

Camellia sasanqua
'Rainbow'
⅔ life size
November 12th

Camellia sasanqua
'Hugh Evans'
⅔ life size
November 1st

Camellia 'Francie L'
⅔ life size, March 20th

Cleyera

Cleyera Thunb. (1783), in the family Theaceae, contains 17 species, mainly in Central America. One species, *C. japonica* Thunb., is sometimes cultivated and is described below.

Description Trees to 12m, or shrubs. The leaves are alternate, evergreen, *Camellia*-like (see pp.172–74); in 'Fortunei' or 'Tricolor' variegated with yellow, reddish when young. The flowers are small, whitish, pink, or pale yellow, on slender stalks, singly or in pairs in the leaf axils, in midsummer. Bracteoles 2, spaced on the flower stalks, soon falling; sepals 5; petals 5, with the stamens attached at the base. Anthers bearded, attached at the base. Carpels 2 or 3, fused, style with 2 or 3 stigmas. Pollination is by insects. The fruits are red, ripening to black berries with stalks around 1cm long and many seeds.

Key Recognition Features The *Camellia*-like leaves, with small flowers in summer, followed by berries.

Evolution and Relationships *Cleyera* is close to *Camellia*, but has a berry-like fruit. It is also close to *Eurya*, but that has male and female flowers on different plants.

Ecology and Geography In rocky woods or by streams, *C. japonica* in Nepal, China, and Japan, the other species in Mexico, Central America, and the West Indies.

Comment *Cleyera japonica* is sometimes found under the name *C. fortunei* Hook. fil. or *C. ochnacea* DC, and sometimes under the genus *Eurya*; it is the sacred tree of Shintoism. The variegated form 'Fortunei' is most commonly cultivated.

Eurya

Eurya Thunb. (1783), in the family Theaceae, contains around 70 species, mainly in tropical eastern Asia.

Description Trees to 10m or more, or shrubs. The leaves are alternate, evergreen, leathery, sometimes rounded at the apex. The flowers are unisexual, the males and females on different plants, short-stalked, in groups in the leaf axils, around 5mm long. Bracteoles 2, minute, persisting. Sepals 5; petals 5, fused in the lower third to form a small, cup-shaped flower. Stamens 5–25, the anthers without hairs, attached at the base. Carpels 2–5 and fused, styles 2 or 3. Pollination is by insects. The fruits are many-seeded, blackish berries.

Key Recognition Features The masses of very small, bell-shaped, unisexual flowers along the twigs are characteristic.

Evolution and Relationships *Ternstroemia* L. fil. is rather similar, but has leaves grouped at the ends of the branches and flowers on curved stalks 1–2cm long and thickened at the apex, followed by red fruits.

Ecology and Geography In rocky woods in eastern Asia, from Sri Lanka eastwards. The hardiest species are found in China and Japan.

Comment A rather insignificant evergreen, sometimes grown as a curiosity.

Cleyera fortunei
²/₃ life size
December 8th

Eurya japonica
flowers, life size
May 17th

Eurya japonica
¹/₂ life size
May 17th

Stewartia pseudocamellia
just under life size
June 3rd

Stewartia pseudocamellia
fruit, ¹/₂ life size
September 16th

Stewartia malacodendron
²/₃ life size, June 23rd

Stewartia

Stewartia L. (1753), in the family Theaceae, contains around 8 species in eastern Asia and North America.

Description Trees to 20m, or shrubs, often with grey bark peeling to leave reddish patches. The leaves are alternate, deciduous, very slightly toothed, narrowly ovate. The flowers are white, usually solitary in the leaf axils. Sepals 5, fused at the base, persisting in fruit, with 2 small bracts beneath them. Petals 5, sometimes up to 8, fused at the base, usually rounded. Stamens numerous, the filaments joined at the base and attached to the petals, anthers attached by the middle. Carpels 5, rarely 4 or 6, fused. Styles 5, rarely 4 or 6, sometimes joined. Pollination is by insects. The fruits are pointed capsules with 2–4 seeds per cell. Seeds are rather flat, sometimes narrowly winged.

Key Recognition Features The deciduous leaves and white, *Camellia*-like (see pp.172–74) flowers, often combined with smooth or flaky bark, are distinctive.

Evolution and Relationships There are several closely related and rare genera, all with similar white flowers, and differing mainly in their capsules: *Hartia* Dunn, now sometimes united with *Stewartia*, is evergreen and has buds without scales, enclosed by winged stalks; *H. pteripetiolata* Dunn, from southwestern China, is sometimes cultivated. *Franklinia* Marshall, from Georgia, is now extinct in the wild but frequent in gardens in the eastern United States northwards to New York; it is a small, deciduous tree with a round, woody capsule that opens at both the base and apex. *Schima* Blume contains 1 very variable species, *S. wallichii* (DC) Korthals; it bears its flowers among a group of evergreen leaves at the ends of the branches and has a rounded capsule splitting into 5. *Gordonia* Ellis, from both South East Asia and southeastern North America, has around 70 species of evergreen trees and shrubs, including *G. lasianthus* L., the loblolly bay; the flowers are usually at the tips of the branches, the capsules slightly elongated.

Ecology and Geography In woods: 2 species are found in North America, *S. malacodendron* L. at low levels and *S. ovata* (Cav.) Weatherby in the mountains, and the remaining species are found in China, Korea, and Japan.

Comment Most species are cultivated for their attractive flowers in summer. *Stewartia malacodendron* and *S. ovata* f. *grandiflora* (Bean) Kobuski are particularly beautiful, having purple filaments that contrast with the white petals.

Stewartia pseudocamellia
²/₃ life size, June 3rd

Diospyros

Diospyros L. (1753), the persimmon, contains around 475 species, mostly in the tropics, in the family Ebenaceae. Only the temperate species are described here.

Description Trees to 25m, or large shrubs, with dark brown or blackish bark. The leaves are alternate, evergreen or deciduous, ovate undivided, without teeth. The flowers are small, white, yellowish, or reddish-brown, with very short stalks, hanging below the twigs, mostly unisexual. Sepals 4, enlarging as the fruit matures; petals 4, spreading or recurved, joined at the base. Stamens 6–20. Carpels 8, fused, each with 1 or 2 ovules. Pollination is by insects. The fruits are juicy and sweet, often flattened at the base, and bright orange or blackish when ripe. They are often produced in the absence of the male trees, and are then seedless.

Key Recognition Features The smooth leaves on slightly zigzag twigs, the small, hanging flowers, and the round, orange fruit with conspicuous sepals are characteristic.

Evolution and Relationships The family Ebenaceae and the Ebenales are of uncertain affinity, but are often considered close to the Theaceae (see pp.172–77) and the Styracaceae (see pp.180–85).

Ecology and Geography In fields and woods and on rocky hills by streams, *D. virginiana* L. in southeastern North America northwards to Connecticut, *D. lotus* L. and *D. kaki* L. fil. in Asia.

Comment *Diospyros kaki*, the Chinese persimmon or kaki, is widely cultivated for its fruit, sometimes called Sharon fruit. It hangs on the trees after the leaves have fallen and is best eaten after it has been frosted. The fruit of *D. lotus* is the date plum, very sweet when eaten dried. The tropical *D. ebenum* Koenig from India and Sri Lanka provides the hard, black wood, ebony, and other species from Asia provide zebra-wood or marblewood, used in marquetry.

Diospyros lotus
flowers, 1¾ × life size
June 22nd

Diospyros virginiana
fruit, ¾ life size
October 5th

Diospyros glaucifolia
flower parts
1¾ × life size
August 4th

Diospyros lotus
⅓ life size
June 22nd

Ilex

Ilex L. (1753), holly, contains around 400 species throughout the world, in the family Aquifoliaceae.

Description Trees to 25m, or shrubs, usually with smooth bark. The leaves are usually alternate, evergreen, less often deciduous, undivided but sometimes deeply spiny, stiff and leathery. The flowers are small and white, yellowish, green, purplish, or reddish, in clusters in the leaf axils, unisexual, the males and females usually on separate trees. Sepals 4–8, joined at the base; petals 3–8, joined at the base. Stamens 4–8, attached to the base of the petals. Carpels 2–9, fused, with 1 or 2 ovules each. Pollination is by insects. The fruits are fleshy berries, red or black when ripe, with 2–10, sometimes more, hard-coated seeds.

Key Recognition Features The small flowers and, in typical species, the leathery, shiny leaves.

Evolution and Relationships There is very little agreement on the position of this family. Many authorities put it close to Celastraceae (see p.334) and to Aceraceae (see p.354), in the order Sapindales, not in the Theales, as here.

Ecology and Geography In usually moist woods, and in swamps. Around 15 species are found wild in North America, about 20 in Japan, only 2 in Australia. Around 50 species and very many cultivars are cultivated in temperate gardens.

Comment Common or English holly, *I. aquifolium* L., has produced many garden varieties with striking leaves, while the deciduous North American *I. verticillata* L. is showy when the bare twigs are laden with shining red berries; its leaves can be made into tea. Cultivars of these with yellow fruits or bisexual flowers are also grown. *I. paraguayensis* A. St.-Hil. provides *maté*, a popular South American tea. Holly timber is white and hard, and was used for veneers.

Ilex aquifolium
female flowers (above)
and male flowers (below)
2 × life size
May 6th

Ilex 'Sparkleberry'
berries and seeds
1¾ × life size
October 5th

Ilex aquifolium
berries and seeds
life size
October 14th

Ilex
'Golden King'
½ life size
November 19th

Ilex verticillata 'Quitsei'
with bisexual flowers
¾ life size, June 23rd

Ilex aquifolium
½ life size, October 14th

Styrax obassia
½ life size
August 4th

Styrax japonicus
⅔ life size, June 3rd

Styrax

Styrax L. (1753), in the family Styracaceae, contains around 120 species, found throughout the world. Only 10 temperate species are commonly cultivated.

Description Trees to 16m, or shrubs, often with scented resin in the bark. The leaves are alternate, deciduous or, in some tropical species, evergreen, undivided, but sometimes lobed or toothed. The flowers are white or pale pink, often in clusters or hanging in elongated bunches. Sepals 2–5, fused at the base and often bell- or cup-shaped; petals 5–10, joined at the base, all equal. Stamens 10–16, alternating with the petals. Ovary superior. Carpels 3–5 and fused, style 3- to 5-lobed. Pollination is by insects. The fruits are dry or fleshy, with 1 or 2 large, oily seeds.

Key Recognition Features The flowers with 5–10 pointed, white petals, a cluster of stamens, and a long, slender style.

Evolution and Relationships The family Styracaceae contains 12 genera, mainly in subtropical Asia and tropical South America. It is considered close to Ebenaceae (see p.178) and the tropical family Sapotaceae, to which belongs *Palaquium gutta* (Hook.) Baillon, the source of gutta-percha.

Ecology and Geography In woods and on rocky slopes. One species, *S. officinalis* L., is found wild around the Mediterranean and in California (var. *californica* (Torr.) Rehd.); other species are found mainly in eastern Asia and Japan, and from southern North America southwards into South America.

Comment Most species, and especially *S. japonicus* Sieb. & Zucc., are attractive trees and shrubs for well-drained soils. *Styrax officinalis* is the source of gum storax, used medicinally and in incense, and the tropical *S. benzoin* Dryander from Sumatra produces benzoin, used in friar's balsam.

STYRACACEAE

Styrax japonicus
fruits and seed
¾ life size
September 16th

Styrax japonicus 'Otome'
just under life size
June 15th

Styrax hemsleyanus
fruits and seed
¾ life size
September 16th

Styrax hemsleyanus
¾ life size, June 3rd

Styrax japonicus 'Otome'
½ life size, June 15th

Sinojackia rehderiana
fruits, 2 × life size
August 4th

Sinojackia rehderiana
flowers, just under life size
May 18th

Sinojackia rehderiana
⅔ life size, May 11th

Sinojackia

Sinojackia Hu (1928), in the family Styracaceae, contains 3 species, all found in China.

Description Trees to 6m, or shrubs, the twigs with stellate hairs when young. The leaves are alternate, deciduous, toothed, long-pointed. The flowers are small, white, on short, leafy shoots. Sepals 5–7, joined at the base; petals 5–7, usually narrow, joined at the base. Stamens 10–14. Ovary inferior. Carpels 3 or 4, fused, the style longer than the stamens, persisting on the fruit. Pollination is by insects. The fruits are woody, usually with 1 seed.

Key Recognition Features The numerous stamens, extra petals, and inferior ovary distinguish this from *Styrax* (see pp.180–81).

Evolution and Relationships *Sinojackia* is intermediate between *Styrax* and *Pterostyrax*.

Ecology and Geography In rocky woods in the mountains in eastern China, and westwards to Sichuan.

Comment *Sinojackia rehderiana* Hu is sometimes grown in collections for its numerous flowers in early summer.

Pterostyrax hispida
fruits
1¼ × life size
September 16th

Pterostyrax hispida
⅔ life size, June 15th

Pterostyrax

Pterostyrax Sieb. & Zucc. (1835), in the family Styracaceae, contains 3 or 4 species in eastern Asia.

Description Trees to 15m, or shrubs, the twigs with stellate hairs when young. The leaves are alternate, deciduous, thin in texture, with bristly teeth. Flowers are small and white, in bunches, hanging on one side of the branches. Sepals 4 or 5, forming a cup; petals 5, barely joined at the base. Stamens 10, sometimes joined at the base. Ovary inferior. Carpels 3–5, fused, the style longer than the stamens, thickening and persisting on the fruit. Pollination is probably by insects. The fruits are dry and ribbed or winged, with 1 or 2 seeds.

Key Recognition Features The hanging bunches of small flowers, all pointing downwards, along one side of the branches.

Evolution and Relationships Close to *Halesia* (see p.184); differs in its 5 petals. *Alniphyllum* Matsum. in China has similar but upward-pointing flowers with the stamens joined for more than half their length.

Ecology and Geography In rocky woods in the mountains, *P. corymbosa* Sieb. & Zucc. and *P. hispida* Sieb. & Zucc. in Japan and China, *P. psilophylla* Diels ex Perk. in western China.

Comment Attractive shrubs and small trees bearing scented flowers in midsummer.

Pterostyrax hispida
flowers, 1⅓ × life size
June 15th

Halesia monticola
flowers, just over life size, April 18th

Halesia monticola
fruit, ⅔ life size
December 8th

Halesia carolina
fruit, life size
September 16th

Halesia

Halesia L. (1759), in the family Styracaceae, the snowdrop tree or silverbell, contains 5 species.

Description Trees to 28m, or shrubs. The leaves are alternate, deciduous, shallowly toothed. The flowers are white and hang down along the branches. Sepals form a cup with 4 faint ribs; petals 4, joined at the base. Stamens 8—16, with hairy filaments. Ovary inferior. Carpels 2—4, fused, the style long and slender, persisting on the fruit. Pollination is by insects. The fruits are dry, with 2 or 4 longitudinal wings and a hard stone with 1—3 seeds.

Key Recognition Features The hanging, 4-petalled flowers and the winged fruits.

Evolution and Relationships The genus is closest to *Rehderodendron* which differs in its 5- to 10-ribbed fruits and 5 petals.

Ecology and Geography In woods and on rocky hills and plains. Four species are found in eastern North America, from West Virginia and North Carolina southwards, and 1 species is reported from eastern China.

Comment The genus *Halesia* is named after the Rev. Stephen Hales, F.R.S. (1677—1761) an early physiologist, author of *Vegetable Staticks* (1727), and inventor of a bellows to pump air down to the lower decks of ships. The American species are hardy and attractive small garden trees.

Halesia monticola
⅔ life size, April 18th

Rehderodendron

Rehderodendron Hu (1932), in the family Styracaceae, contains 9 or 10 species in southern China and South East Asia.

Description Trees to 9m, or shrubs. The leaves are alternate, deciduous, with fine teeth. The flowers are white, on leafless, branched stems at the base of the new shoots, lemon-scented. Sepals very small, reduced to 5 small lobes; petals 5, joined at the base. Stamens 10, the filaments joined at the base. Ovary mostly inferior. Carpels 3 or 4, fused, with the style longer than the stamens. Pollination is by insects. The fruits are woody capsules, with 5–10 ribs and 1–3 long, narrow seeds.

Key Recognition Features The large, woody fruits are characteristic.

Evolution and Relationships The genus is an isolated one, possibly closest to *Halesia*.

Ecology and Geography In rocky woods in southwestern China from Sichuan southwards to northern Vietnam and Thailand.

Comment *Rehderodendron macrocarpum* Hu, the most commonly grown species, is an attractive tree, flowering when still young, the young leaves, shoots, and autumn colour often reddish. The name commemorates Alfred Rehder, (1863–1949), born in Sachsen, Germany, but for many years curator of the Arnold Arboretum at Harvard University in Massachusetts; a specialist on woody plants, he named many of E.H. Wilson's Chinese collections (see p.103).

Rehderodendron macrocarpum
fruiting branch, ½ life size
September 10th

Rehderodendron macrocarpum
flowers, 1¼ × life size
May 1st

Rehderodendron macrocarpum
½ life size, May 1st

Rehderodendron macrocarpum
cross-section of fruit
2 × life size, September 10th

Hypericum

Hypericum L. (1753), St John's wort, contains around 400 species of trees, shrubs, and herbaceous plants, in the family Guttiferae, sometimes called Clusiaceae.

Description Trees to 12m, or shrubs. The leaves are opposite, evergreen or deciduous, rounded, with a prominent midrib, often dotted with glands. The flowers are usually yellow, cup-shaped, with 4 or 5 sepals, often glandular, usually persisting on the fruit, and 4 or 5 asymmetric petals. Stamens numerous, usually in 4 or 5 equal bundles opposite the petals. Ovary superior. Carpels 3–5, fused, styles 2–5. Pollination is by insects. The fruits are dry capsules or sometimes fleshy berries, with numerous small seeds.

Key Recognition Features The yellow flowers with numerous slender stamens fused into bunches are typical.

Evolution and Relationships The family is mainly tropical and includes *Garcinia* L., containing the mangosteen, *G. mangostana* L., with edible fruit, and *G. xanthochymus* Hook. fil. ex T. Anderson, which produces gamboge yellow dye. The Guttiferae are related to Theaceae (see pp.172–77) and perhaps Myrtaceae (see pp.313–21). *Hypericum* is the only genus in the family common outside the tropics.

Ecology and Geography In many habitats, but the woody species are usually found in open woods and on mountainsides. Shrubby and tree species are common on high mountains in the tropics, and the large-flowered shrubby species are most numerous in western China.

Comment Many species and cultivars are cultivated for their showy flowers in summer and autumn. One of the most common is 'Hidcote', a complex hybrid named after the garden in Gloucestershire where it originated. Some species are used to treat depression in herbal and homeopathic medicine. The black berries of the shrubby European *H. androsaemum* L., called tutsan (from *toute saine*), were used as a diuretic and its leaves were applied to wounds.

Hypericum androsaemum
¾ life size, June 15th

Hypericum androsaemum
fruits and seeds
life size
September 29th

Hypericum bellum
young fruit, ⅔ life size
September 2nd

Hypericum bellum
⅔ life size, September 2nd

Hypericum bellum
seed capsules
$1\frac{1}{3}\times$ life size
November 25th

Hypericum 'Rowallane'
$\frac{2}{3}$ life size, June 23rd

Hypericum 'Rowallane'
just over life size, June 23rd

Actinidia pilosula
⅔ life size, May 16th

Actinidia deliciosa
hermaphrodite form
½ life size, June 3rd

Actinidia kolomikta
½ life size
May 11th

Actinidia deliciosa
fruit, ¾ life size
September 16th

Actinidia

Actinidia L. (1753), in the family Actinidiaceae, contains 40 species.

Description Woody climbers to 20m or more, with twining stems. The leaves are alternate, deciduous, sometimes bristly-hairy, sometimes marked with patches of silver or pink. The flowers are unisexual, produced in the leaf axils, solitary or clustered, the males and females usually on separate plants, and often well scented. Sepals 5, petals 5 and white, reddish, or yellowish. Stamens numerous. Ovary superior, with 3–30 fused carpels and numerous styles. Pollination is by insects. The fruits are fleshy, juicy berries with numerous small, black seeds.

Key Recognition Features Climbers with white male or female flowers with numerous styles and stamens, and large, juicy, greenish berries with numerous small seeds.

Evolution and Relationships In many systems of classification, Actinidiaceae is associated with Eucryphiaceae. In the system followed here, Eucryphiaceae is put close to the Rosaceae, and Actinidiaceae is considered close to Ericaceae (see pp.190–210), but the seeds suggest affinities also with Theaceae (see pp.172–77). *Clematoclethra* is a related genus with 1 species, *C. scandens* (Franch.) Maxim. in China; it has flowers with 10 stamens, 1 style, and 5 fused carpels in the ovary.

Ecology and Geography In woods and scrub, climbing into large trees, in China and Japan southwards to Indonesia.

Comment The species with variegated leaves are attractive ornamentals, and there have been reports that male plants develop better-coloured leaves. *Actinidia deliciosa* (Chev.) Liang & Ferguson is the current name for the edible kiwi fruit or Chinese gooseberry, formerly but erroneously called *A. chinensis* Planch. Other species, such as *A. arguta* (Sieb. & Zucc.) Miq., have smaller edible fruit.

Clethra

Clethra L. (1753), in the family Clethraceae, contains around 64 species, mainly in America and eastern Asia.

Description Trees to 11m, or shrubs. The leaves are alternate, evergreen or deciduous, with a strong midrib and stellate hairs. The flowers are usually in spikes, white or pinkish, often scented. Sepals 5 or 6, overlapping, joined at the base, persisting on the fruit; petals 5, joined at the base. Stamens 10–12, sometimes joined at the base to the petals, the anthers often blackish, opening by pores. Ovary inferior, of 3 fused carpels; ovules many, placentation axile; style slender, 3-fid at the apex. Pollination is by insects. The fruits are dry capsules, opening to release the very small, usually winged seeds.

Key Recognition Features The roughly hairy leaves and long spikes of white, bell-shaped flowers, with 10–12 often long stamens.

Evolution and Relationships Clethraceae is close to the Ericaceae (see pp.190–210), and sometimes included in the Cyrillaceae, in the order Ericales; both have rounded capsules with numerous small seeds. *Cyrilla* L., the leatherwood, consists of 1 species, *C. racemiflora* L., found in swamps in North and Central America.

Ecology and Geography In woods and on rocky hillsides; also in swamps, especially *C. alnifolia* L., the sweet-pepper bush. Several species are found in China, including *C. barbinervis* Sieb. & Zucc. and *C. delavayi* Franch., others in North America and southwards to the tropical Americas. One species, *C. arborea* Ait., is found in Madeira and the Azores; it is an interesting relic of the Tertiary forests, and very close to the Sumatran species *C. pulcherrima* Ridley.

Comment Attractive ornamental shrubs flowering in late summer.

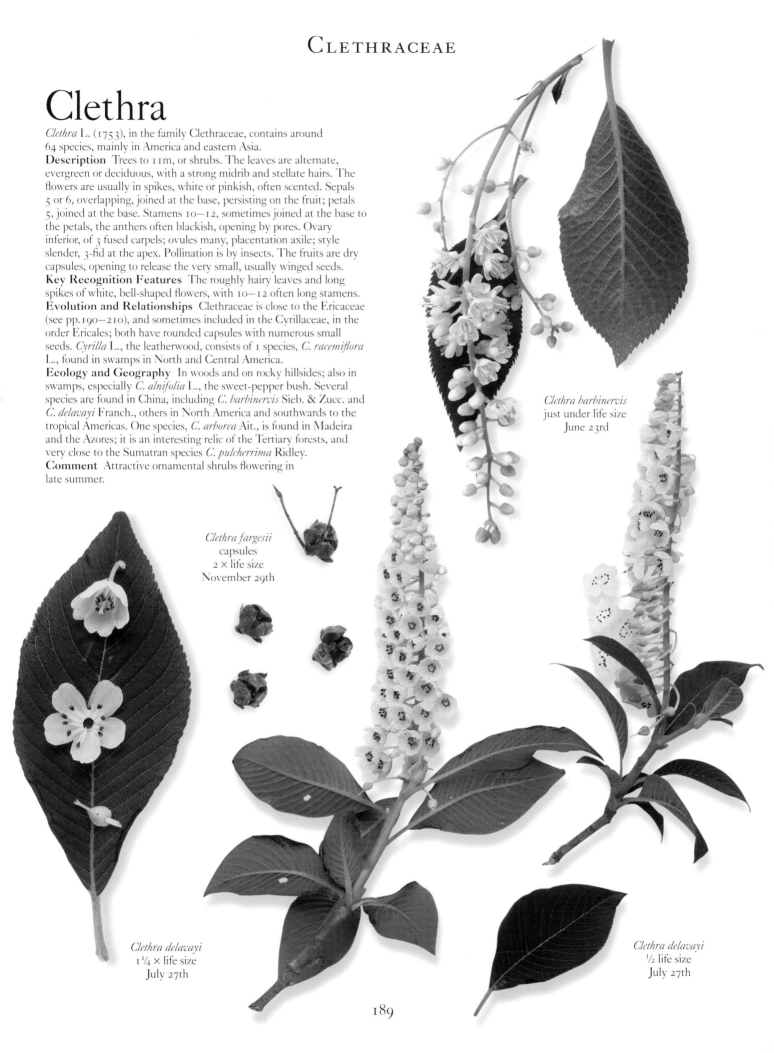

Clethra barbinervis
just under life size
June 23rd

Clethra fargesii
capsules
2 × life size
November 29th

Clethra delavayi
1¼ × life size
July 27th

Clethra delavayi
½ life size
July 27th

Rhododendron

Rhododendron L. (1753), the azalea or rhododendron, in the family Ericaceae, contains around 800 species, mostly in the northern hemisphere.

Description Trees up to 50m (*R. arboreum* Smith) to creeping shrubs. The leaves are alternate, usually grouped towards the ends of the shoots, evergreen or deciduous, undivided, often with scales or many-celled hairs beneath. The flowers are generally in groups called trusses, at the ends of the branches, surrounded in bud by numerous scales. Sepals 5, often joined and cup-shaped at the base, forming a calyx; petals usually 5, sometimes up to 10, equal, joined at the base and often tubular, forming a corolla. Stamens usually 10, but may be up to 27, the anthers opening by pores, the pollen sticking together in thread-like masses. Ovary superior. Carpels 5, fused, with numerous ovules; style usually long and curved, with a sticky stigma at the tip. Pollination is by insects, or by birds in some Chinese and Himalayan species, such as *R. spinuliferum* Franch. The fruits are dry capsules that split to release the small, often winged, wind-dispersed seeds.

Key Recognition Features The large flowers with a tubular or trumpet-shaped corolla and long, slender stamens with anthers opening by pores, producing sticky threads of pollen.

Evolution and Relationships *Rhododendron* is easily the largest genus in the family and is split into 4 large and 4 small subgenera, described opposite. The leaves show remarkable diversity and are very important in the classification and identification of the species. *Azalea* L. and *Ledum* L. are now included in Rhododendron: they were described by Linnaeus in 1753 from European species, and discoveries in the Himalayas together with later research have shown that the distinctions he used do not work for the genus as a whole. For *Azalea*, these distinctions included being often deciduous, with fragrant, rather flat, deeply lobed flowers with typically 5 stamens.

Ecology and Geography Usually on humus-rich, acidic soils, on hillsides and rocks, and in swamps, as well as epiphytic on trees; sometimes on limestone in areas of heavy rainfall, such as *R. decorum* Franch. in China or *R. luteum* (L.) Sweet in the Caucasus. Around 20 species are found in North America as far south as Florida, around 12 species in Europe and western Asia, and the rest in eastern Asia, especially in the Himalayas on the borders of India, Myanmar (Burma), and China, where the genus is most diverse. Another centre of diversity is New Guinea, where the so-called Vireyas grow both in the forests and on mountain heathland, with 2 species just extending as far south as Australia.

Comment This is perhaps the largest temperate woody genus that is valuable for cultivation in climates with wet summers. Hybrids are easily formed between species in the same subgenus, and this has led to thousands of cultivars suitable for gardens, and many commonly called azaleas for winter flowering indoors. In Britain, "azalea" is used for deciduous plants with hairy leaves and scented flowers in orange, yellow, pink, or white, while in North America, Japan, and Australia, it covers evergreens with seldom hairy leaves and unscented flowers in purple, red, pink, or white. Few species have economic uses, being mostly poisonous to animals, producing intoxicating honey, and seldom growing large enough to be useful for timber.

The Subgenera of Rhododendron The genus *Rhododendron* has been divided by botanists into 8 subgenera, listed opposite; the first 2 contain the rhododendrons and those previously classified as *Ledum*; the next 2 contain the majority of the plants commonly called azaleas; the remaining 4 small subgenera contain 34 obscure and little-cultivated species from the Pacific region. Hybrids within a subgenus are often very easy to produce, hybrids between subgenera very difficult. The species and hybrids illustrated here are named beneath their respective subgenera.

Rhododendron venator
½ life size, April 21st

Rhododendron aberconwayi
'His Lordship'
½ life size
April 21st

Rhododendron orbiculare, ½ life size

Rhododendron williamsianum
½ life size
April 21st

ERICACEAE

Rhododendron griffithianum
½ life size, April 21st

Rhododendron auriculatum
½ life size
August 4th

Rhododendron rex
subsp. *fictolacteum*
½ life size
April 21st

Rhododendron pseudochrysanthum
½ life size
April 2nd

Subgenus Hymenanthes Includes most of the large, evergreen, non-scaly rhododendrons, which often have dense, hairy indumentum on the undersides of very large leaves. *R. aberconwayi* Cowan 'His Lordship', *R. auriculatum* Hemsl., *R. bureavii* Franch., *R. falconeri* Hook. fil., *R. griffithianum* Wight, *R. lacteum* Franch., *R. orbiculare* Decne., *R. pseudochrysanthum* Hayata, *R. rex* subsp. *fictolacteum* (Balf. fil.) D.F. Chamb., *R. makinoi* Tagg, *R. venator* Tagg, *R. wasonii* Hemsl. & E.H. Wilson, *R. williamsianum* Rehd. & E.H. Wilson, *R. yakushimanum* Nakai, see pp.190-91 and p.193 for leaves.
Subgenus Rhododendron Includes most of the scaly-leaved, evergreen rhododendrons and many epiphytic types, those previously classified as Ledum, and the subtropical Vireyas from Malesia and New Guinea. *R. augustinii* Hemsl., *R. christianae* Sleumer, *R. cinnabarinum* Hook fil. subsp. *cinnabarinum*, *R.* 'Fragrantissimum', *R. lutescens* Franch., *R. neoglandulosum* Harmaja, *R. spinuliferum* Franch., *R. yunnanese* Franch., see p.192 and some leaves on p.193.
Subgenus Pentanthera Includes the deciduous azaleas. *R.* 'Corneille', *R.* 'George Reynolds', *R. luteum* Sweet, *R.* Mollis azalea, *R. viscosum* (L.) Torr., see p.194.
Subgenus Tsutsusi Includes the evergreen azaleas. *R.* 'Ambrosia', *R.* 'Amoenum', *R.* 'Hinomayo', *R.* 'Kure-no-yuki', *R.* 'Pippa', *R.* 'Amoenum Splendens', *R.* 'Vuyk's Scarlet', see p.195.
Subgenus Azaleastrum Includes around 30 species in South East Asia, including *R. hongkongense* Hutch.
Subgenus Candidastrum One species, *R. albiflorum* Hook., in northwestern North America.
Subgenus Mumeazalea One species, *R. semibarbatum* Maxim., in southern Japan.
Subgenus Therorhodion Two species in northeastern Asia and Alaska, including *R. camschaticum* Pall.
The illustrations of Rhododendron *continue on pp.192–95.*

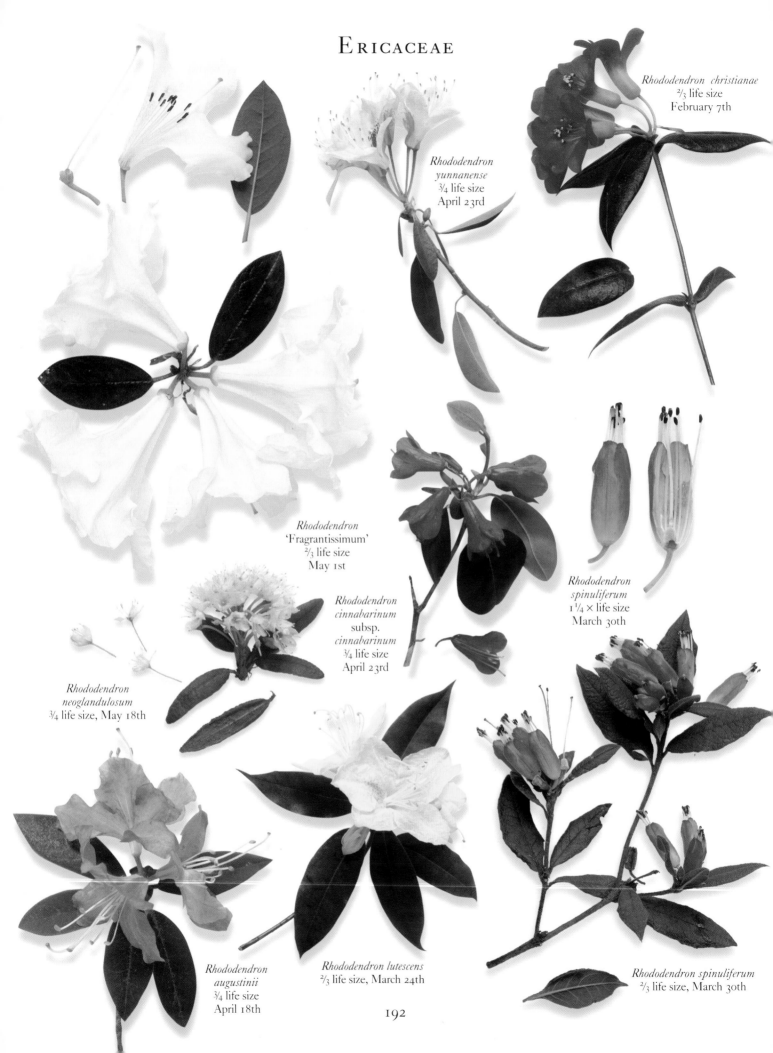

ERICACEAE

Rhododendron christianae
²/₃ life size
February 7th

Rhododendron yunnanense
¾ life size
April 23rd

Rhododendron 'Fragrantissimum'
²/₃ life size
May 1st

Rhododendron cinnabarinum subsp. *cinnabarinum*
¾ life size
April 23rd

Rhododendron spinuliferum
1 ¼ × life size
March 30th

Rhododendron neoglandulosum
¾ life size, May 18th

Rhododendron augustinii
¾ life size
April 18th

Rhododendron lutescens
²/₃ life size, March 24th

Rhododendron spinuliferum
²/₃ life size, March 30th

ERICACEAE

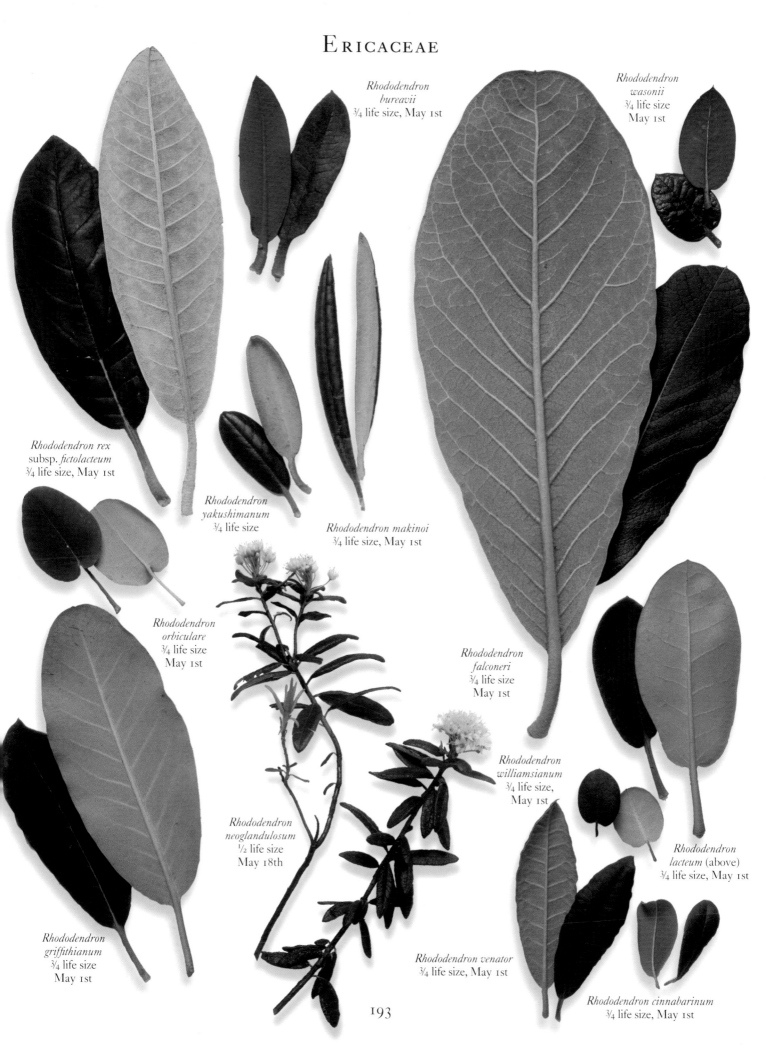

Rhododendron bureavii
¾ life size, May 1st

Rhododendron wasonii
¾ life size
May 1st

Rhododendron rex
subsp. *fictolacteum*
¾ life size, May 1st

Rhododendron yakushimanum
¾ life size

Rhododendron makinoi
¾ life size, May 1st

Rhododendron orbiculare
¾ life size
May 1st

Rhododendron falconeri
¾ life size
May 1st

Rhododendron neoglandulosum
½ life size
May 18th

Rhododendron williamsianum
¾ life size,
May 1st

Rhododendron lacteum (above)
¾ life size, May 1st

Rhododendron griffithianum
¾ life size
May 1st

Rhododendron venator
¾ life size, May 1st

Rhododendron cinnabarinum
¾ life size, May 1st

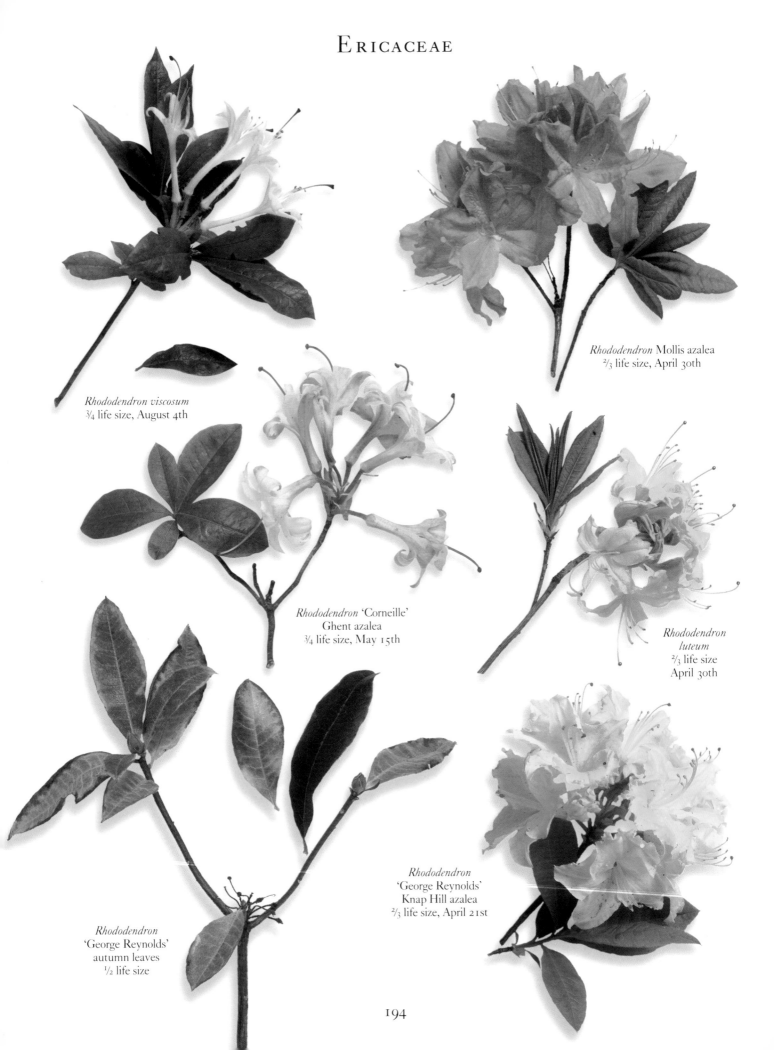

Rhododendron Mollis azalea
⅔ life size, April 30th

Rhododendron viscosum
¾ life size, August 4th

Rhododendron 'Corneille'
Ghent azalea
¾ life size, May 15th

Rhododendron
luteum
⅔ life size
April 30th

Rhododendron
'George Reynolds'
Knap Hill azalea
⅔ life size, April 21st

Rhododendron
'George Reynolds'
autumn leaves
½ life size

ERICACEAE

Rhododendron
'Amoenum Splendens'
²/₃ life size, May 18th

Rhododendron evergreen azalea
²/₃ life size, May 18th

Rhododendron
'Kure-no-yuki'
²/₃ life size, May 18th

Rhododendron
'Amoenum'
²/₃ life size, May 18th

Rhododendron
'Pippa'
²/₃ life size, May 18th

Rhododendron
'Hinomayo'
²/₃ life size
May 18th

Rhododendron
'Vuyk's Scarlet'
²/₃ life size, May 15th

Rhododendron
'Ambrosia'
²/₃ life size, May 18th

Epigaea

Epigaea L. (1753), in the family Ericaceae, contains 3 species.
Description Creeping shrubs to 10cm tall. The leaves are alternate, evergreen, flat, with stiff hairs. The flowers are pinkish, in bunches of 1–5 at the tips of the shoots. Sepals 5, not joined at the base, petals 5, equal, joined at the base, forming a flattish or tubular corolla. Stamens 10, the anthers opening by slits, the pollen in sticky threads. Ovary superior. Carpels 5, fused, with numerous ovules; style long and curved. Pollination is by insects. The fruits are greenish, globose, with the seeds embedded in a fleshy placenta.
Key Recognition Features The flat, ovate leaves with stiff, brownish hairs on a creeping plant.
Evolution and Relationships *Epigaea* is close to *Rhododendron* (see pp.190–95), differing in the absence of bud scales. *Phyllodoce* Salisb. and *Daboecia* D. Don are also grouped with *Rhododendron*, in spite of their heather-like appearance, (*Erica*, see p.210). So are the small genera *Tripetaleia* Sieb. & Zucc. from Japan and *Elliottia* Muhl. from North America (which now includes *Cladothamnus* Bong.), which both have unusual flowers with 3 or 4 reflexed petals.
Ecology and Geography In rocky woods. The 3 species are interestingly scattered across the northern hemisphere, with *E. repens* L. found in eastern North America, *E. asiatica* Maxim. in Japan, and *E. gaultherioides* (Boiss. & Bal.) Takht. in northeastern Turkey and Georgia, formerly in the separate genus *Orphanidesia* Boiss. & Bal..
Comment These attractive and interesting shrubs are difficult to grow successfully.

Kalmia

Kalmia L. (1753), in the family Ericaceae, contains 7 species from North America.
Description Trees to 12m, or shrubs. The leaves are usually alternate, sometimes opposite or in groups of 3, evergreen, narrowly ovate. The flowers are usually in umbels or short bunches, pink to red, purplish, or white. Sepals 5, petals 5, equal, joined nearly to the top, forming a saucer-shaped corolla. Stamens 10, the anthers pressed into pouches in the petals, opening by pores, the pollen sometimes sticky. Ovary superior. Carpels 5, fused, with numerous ovules; style long and curved. Pollination is by insects, usually bumblebees, which are heavy enough to spring the stamens and be dusted with pollen. The fruits are dry, rounded capsules with numerous seeds.
Key Recognition Features The pinkish flowers with anthers pressed into pouches in the petals.
Evolution and Relationships *Kalmiopsis* Rehd., with 1 species in Oregon, is closely related but does not have the anthers in pouches on the petals.
Ecology and Geography *Kalmia latifolia* L. prefers dry, rocky woods, where it can form an understorey beneath deciduous trees; the other species are mostly found in bogs and pine barrens. All are found today in North America, from Newfoundland and Hudson Bay to Alaska and southwards to Florida and Cuba; fossil *Kalmia* is reported from the lower Miocene in Germany.
Comment *Kalmia latifolia*, the mountain laurel or calico bush, is one of the most attractive of flowering shrubs, the flowers looking as if they are made of icing. Many new hybrids with larger and brighter red flowers with interesting markings have been raised in the United States. The wood is hard and smooth, sometimes used for turning. The genus was named by Linnaeus after his pupil Peter Kalm (1715–79), who spent 3 years from 1748 travelling in America. As well as collecting plants for Linnaeus, he wrote an interesting journal on the early settlers.

Epigaea repens
¾ life size, March 8th

Epigaea repens
life size
March 8th

Epigaea repens
flowers
1½ × life size, March 8th

Epigaea repens
fruiting calyx
1½ × life size
March 8th

Ericaceae

Kalmia latifolia
fruits, 1¼ × life size
December 12th

Kalmia latifolia
⅔ life size, June 3rd

Kalmia latifolia
1¼ × life size
June 3rd

Kalmia latifolia
'Nipmuck'
1¼ × life size
June 3rd

Kalmia latifolia
'Nipmuck'
⅔ life size, June 3rd

Menziesia

Menziesia J.E. Smith (1791), in the family Ericaceae, contains 8 species from eastern Asia and North America.

Description Shrubs to 2m. The leaves are alternate, deciduous, often grouped at the ends of the branches. The flowers are bell-shaped, sometimes narrowed at the mouth, in umbel-like bunches, usually pinkish. Sepals 4, joined at the base; petals 4 or 5, equal, joined to form a corolla. Stamens 5–10, the anthers opening by apical slits. Ovary superior. Carpels 4, fused, with numerous ovules. Pollination is by insects, probably bees. The fruits are leathery capsules, without a persistent style and with numerous narrow, elongated seeds.

Key Recognition Features The bell-shaped flowers with bristly stalks on a small shrub, the parts mostly in groups of 4.

Evolution and Relationships The genus *Menziesia* is close to *Rhododendron* (see pp.190–95), especially in the way the capsules split along the ribs.

Ecology and Geography In rocky mountain woods, with 1 species in eastern North America, 2 in the northwest, and 4 in Japan.

Comment Very attractive small shrubs. The genus is named after Archibald Menzies (1754–1842) from Aberfeldy, Perthshire, who visited the Pacific coast of the Americas as surgeon and naturalist under Captain Vancouver in 1791–95.

*Enkianthus
perulatus*
1¼ × life size
April 2nd

Menziesia ferruginea
with old capsules and flowers
½ life size, May 18th

Menziesia ciliicalyx
flowers, ¾ life size
May 12th

Menziesia ciliicalyx
var. *purpurea*
¾ life size
June 1st

*Enkianthus
campanulatus*
life size, June 1st

Enkianthus chinensis
¾ life size, June 1st

Enkianthus

Enkianthus Lour. (1790), in the family Ericaceae, contains around 13 species in eastern Asia.

Description Trees to 6m, or shrubs. The leaves are alternate, deciduous, generally clustered at the ends of the branches, often colouring brilliant red in autumn. The flowers are small, hanging in bunches, bell-shaped or urn-shaped, often brownish-green or reddish. Sepals 5, joined at the base; petals 5, equal, joined to form a sometimes narrow-mouthed corolla. Stamens 10, the anthers opening by pores; pollen without sticky threads. Ovary superior. Carpels 5, fused, with numerous ovules; style long and straight. Pollination is by insects, often by wasps in *E. campanulatus* (Miq.) Nichols. The fruits are elongated capsules with the remains of the calyx at the base and a persistent style, splitting between the ribs. Seeds are few and usually winged.

Key Recognition Features The often elongated, hanging bunches of bell-shaped flowers.

Evolution and Relationships *Enkianthus* belongs to the Vaccinioideae, but is rather isolated within this group. *Menziesia* is superficially similar, but has floral parts usually in groups of 4 and anthers without appendages.

Ecology and Geography On rocky hillsides and in open woods from the Himalayas to China and Japan.

Comment These shrubs are attractive in flower and often spectacular in autumn colour.

Enkianthus campanulatus
½ life size
May 11th

Enkianthus chinensis
fruits, ⅔ life size
December 8th

Enkianthus campanulatus
autumn leaves and fruit
¾ life size, November 29th

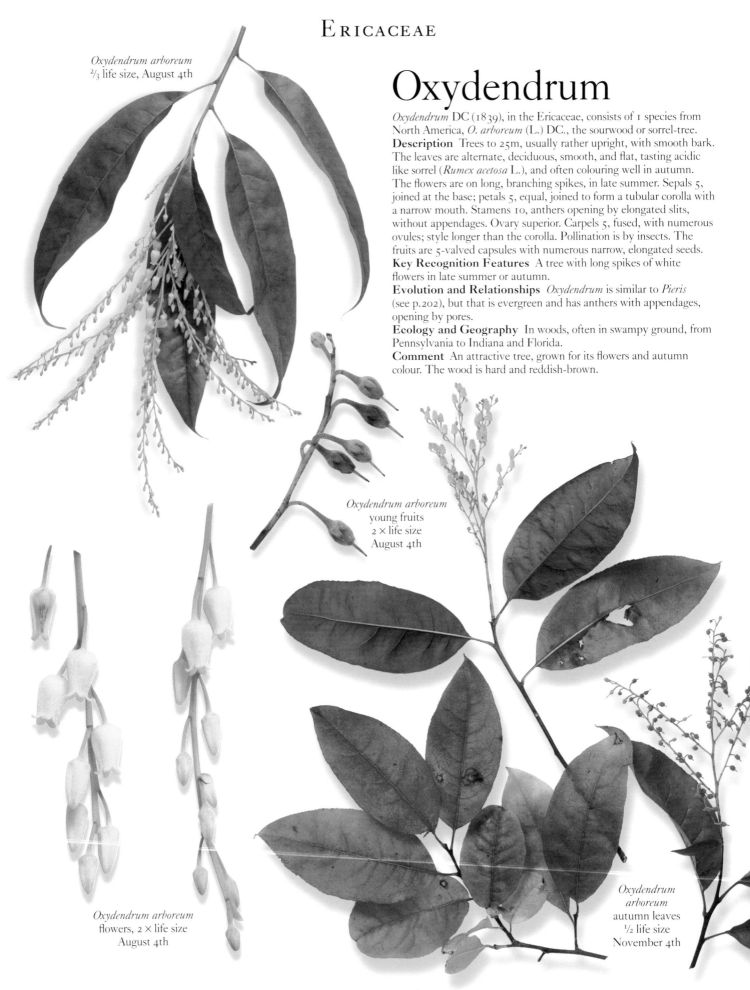

Oxydendrum arboreum
²/₃ life size, August 4th

Oxydendrum

Oxydendrum DC (1839), in the Ericaceae, consists of 1 species from North America, *O. arboreum* (L.) DC., the sourwood or sorrel-tree.
Description Trees to 25m, usually rather upright, with smooth bark. The leaves are alternate, deciduous, smooth, and flat, tasting acidic like sorrel (*Rumex acetosa* L.), and often colouring well in autumn. The flowers are on long, branching spikes, in late summer. Sepals 5, joined at the base; petals 5, equal, joined to form a tubular corolla with a narrow mouth. Stamens 10, anthers opening by elongated slits, without appendages. Ovary superior. Carpels 5, fused, with numerous ovules; style longer than the corolla. Pollination is by insects. The fruits are 5-valved capsules with numerous narrow, elongated seeds.
Key Recognition Features A tree with long spikes of white flowers in late summer or autumn.
Evolution and Relationships *Oxydendrum* is similar to *Pieris* (see p.202), but that is evergreen and has anthers with appendages, opening by pores.
Ecology and Geography In woods, often in swampy ground, from Pennsylvania to Indiana and Florida.
Comment An attractive tree, grown for its flowers and autumn colour. The wood is hard and reddish-brown.

Oxydendrum arboreum
young fruits
2 × life size
August 4th

Oxydendrum arboreum
flowers, 2 × life size
August 4th

*Oxydendrum
arboreum*
autumn leaves
¹/₂ life size
November 4th

Zenobia pulverulenta
flowers, 1¼ × life size
June 24th

Zenobia pulverulenta
½ life size, June 24th

Zenobia pulverulenta
½ life size
October 6th

Zenobia pulverulenta
capsules
2 × life size
October 6th

Zenobia

Zenobia D. Don (1834), in the family Ericaceae, contains 1 variable species, *Z. pulverulenta* (Willd.) Pollard, in eastern North America.

Description Shrubs to 2m, with smooth, reddish-brown twigs. The leaves are alternate, deciduous, broadly to narrowly ovate, sometimes white beneath. The flowers are white, bell-shaped, scented, in elongated bunches at the ends of the shoots and short bunches in the upper leaf axils. Sepals 5, joined at the base; petals 5, equal, joined to form a lobed corolla. Stamens 10, the anthers with appendages, opening by pores. Ovary superior. Carpels 5, fused, with numerous ovules. Pollination is by insects. The fruits are capsules with numerous winged seeds.

Key Recognition Features The broadly bell-shaped, pure white flowers on slender stalks are easy to recognise.

Evolution and Relationships This is close to *Pieris* (see p.202) and other similar genera which were all included at one time under *Andromeda* L.

Ecology and Geography In damp, sandy or peaty pine barrens from southeastern Virginia to South Carolina.

Comment A very attractive, summer-flowering shrub, often cultivated. Zenobia was Queen of Palmyra, in present-day Syria, and led a revolt against Rome, but was defeated and captured by Aurelian in 272AD.

Pieris japonica
'Valley Valentine'
½ life size, March 20th

Pieris japonica, flowers
3 × life size, March 15th

Pieris floribunda
¾ life size, March 20th

Pieris japonica 'Grayswood'
¾ life size, March 15th

Pieris

Pieris D. Don (1834), in the family Ericaceae, contains 7 species in China, Japan, and North America.

Description Trees to 8m, but usually shrubs. The leaves are alternate, evergreen, narrowly ovate or oblanceolate, leathery. The flowers are tubular, narrowed at the mouth, in upright or hanging spikes, white or pinkish, slightly scented. Sepals 5, joined at the base, sometimes coloured; petals 5, equal, joined to form a toothed corolla. Stamens 10, the anthers opening by pores, with spur-like appendages. Ovary superior. Carpels 5, fused, with numerous ovules; style long and curved. Pollination is by insects, usually bumblebees. The fruits are nearly-round capsules, with numerous very small seeds.

Key Recognition Features The narrow, dark green leaves and the spikes of white flowers at the tops of the shoots.

Evolution and Relationships This and related genera, such as *Zenobia* (see p.201) and *Leucothoë* (see p.206), were included by Linnaeus in the genus *Andromeda*, which is still sometimes used as a common name for *Pieris*, the most frequently grown of these genera.

Ecology and Geography On rocky hillsides and in open woods; 2 species in eastern North America from Virginia to Florida, 1 species in western Cuba, and 4 species in eastern Asia from the Himalayas to Taiwan and Japan.

Comment The wild plants are usually white-flowered, but recent cultivars have pink and almost red flowers. When David Don proposed splitting *Andromeda* in 1834, he kept to classical names for his new genera. *Pieris* is another word for a muse; the muses were called *Pierides* as they were said to come from Pieria, in Thessaly.

Pieris japonica 'Grayswood' (top) spikes
and *Pieris japonica* (bottom) flowers
life size, March 15th

Chamaedaphne

Chamaedaphne Moench (1794), in the family Ericaceae, contains 1 species, *C. calyculata* (L.) Moench., the leatherleaf, found around the northern hemisphere.

Description Shrubs to 1.5m. The leaves are alternate, evergreen, dull green, with scurfy scales when young. The flowers are tubular-bell-shaped, solitary in the upper leaf axils. Sepals 5, joined at the base, with small bracts; petals 5, equal, joined to form a toothed corolla. Stamens 10, the filaments swollen at the base, the anthers opening by pores, without appendages. Ovary superior. Carpels 5, fused, with numerous ovules; style long and straight. Pollination is by insects. The fruits are dry, round capsules with unwinged seeds.

Key Recognition Features The very tough, leathery leaves, scaly beneath, and flowers in the leaf axils.

Evolution and Relationships The genus *Lyonia*, with 35 species in North America and eastern Asia, is similar but has flowers in clusters and a capsule with thickened ribs.

Ecology and Geography In bogs and pine barrens around the Arctic and in North America, southwards to Georgia and British Colombia, in Hokkaido in Japan, and in Europe southwards to central Russia and Poland.

Comment Often cultivated, but not particularly showy.

Chamaedaphne calyculata
flowers, 2 × life size
March 15th

Pieris 'Forest Flame'
fruits, ½ life size
October 5th

Pieris 'Forest Flame'
young leaves
⅓ life size, March 23rd

Pieris 'Forest Flame'
fruits, 2 × life size
October 5th

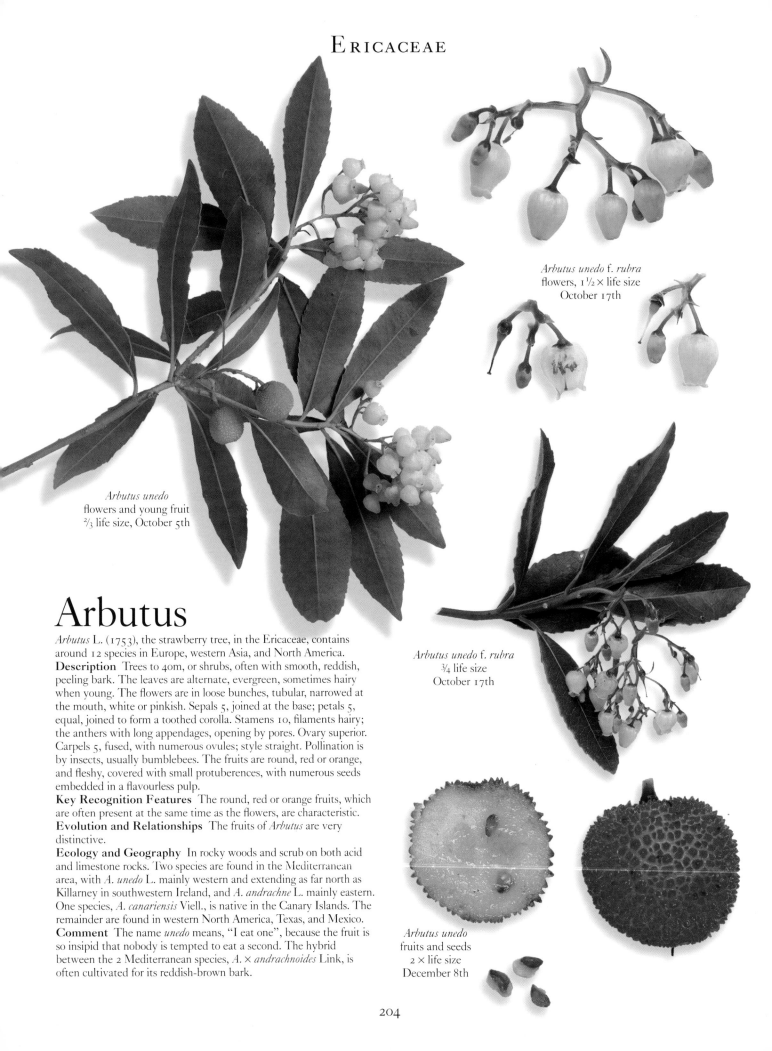

Arbutus unedo f. *rubra*
flowers, 1 ½ × life size
October 17th

Arbutus unedo
flowers and young fruit
⅔ life size, October 5th

Arbutus unedo f. *rubra*
¾ life size
October 17th

Arbutus unedo
fruits and seeds
2 × life size
December 8th

Arbutus

Arbutus L. (1753), the strawberry tree, in the Ericaceae, contains around 12 species in Europe, western Asia, and North America.

Description Trees to 40m, or shrubs, often with smooth, reddish, peeling bark. The leaves are alternate, evergreen, sometimes hairy when young. The flowers are in loose bunches, tubular, narrowed at the mouth, white or pinkish. Sepals 5, joined at the base; petals 5, equal, joined to form a toothed corolla. Stamens 10, filaments hairy; the anthers with long appendages, opening by pores. Ovary superior. Carpels 5, fused, with numerous ovules; style straight. Pollination is by insects, usually bumblebees. The fruits are round, red or orange, and fleshy, covered with small protuberences, with numerous seeds embedded in a flavourless pulp.

Key Recognition Features The round, red or orange fruits, which are often present at the same time as the flowers, are characteristic.

Evolution and Relationships The fruits of *Arbutus* are very distinctive.

Ecology and Geography In rocky woods and scrub on both acid and limestone rocks. Two species are found in the Mediterranean area, with *A. unedo* L. mainly western and extending as far north as Killarney in southwestern Ireland, and *A. andrachne* L. mainly eastern. One species, *A. canariensis* Viell., is native in the Canary Islands. The remainder are found in western North America, Texas, and Mexico.

Comment The name *unedo* means, "I eat one", because the fruit is so insipid that nobody is tempted to eat a second. The hybrid between the 2 Mediterranean species, *A. × andrachnoides* Link, is often cultivated for its reddish-brown bark.

Arctostaphylos uva-ursi
fruits, $2\frac{1}{4}$ × life size
July 28th

Arctostaphylos uva-ursi
var. *leobreweri*
2 × life size, March 1st

Arctostaphylos

Arctostaphylos Adans. (1763), in the family Ericaceae, contains around 50 species, mostly in California.

Description Trees to 6m, or shrubs, often with smooth, red bark. The leaves are alternate, evergreen, sometimes grey or hairy. The flowers are in loose or tight bunches, tubular and usually narrowed at the mouth, white or pink. Sepals 5, rarely 4, not joined at the base; petals 5, equal, joined to form a toothed corolla. Stamens 10, the anthers with long appendages, opening by pores. Ovary superior. Carpels 2–10, fused, with numerous ovules; style straight. Pollination is by insects. The fruits are round and berry-like, usually red, with 2–10 nutlets, which are sometimes fused.

Key Recognition Features The berry-like fruits with hard nutlets; in California, the often smooth bark and bunches of tubular flowers.

Evolution and Relationships Close to *Arbutus*, except for the fruits with nutlets.

Ecology and Geography On rocky hills and bare, gravelly soils. Two species are found in Europe: *A. uva-ursi* (L.) Spreng., a prostrate mat-forming shrub found also throughout North America and Asia, and *A. alpina* (L.) Spreng., found in the Arctic and mountains of Europe and New England. The remainder are native from western North America to Mexico.

Comment Many Californian species, such as *A. manzanita* Parry, are very beautiful but seldom cultivated outside the west coast, where they are often called manzanita, from the Spanish name for the genus.

Arctostaphylos uva-ursi
$\frac{3}{4}$ life size
July 28th

Leucothoë

Leucothoë D. Don (1834), in the family Ericaceae, contains around 8 species, scattered across the world.

Description Shrubs to 2m. The leaves are alternate and evergreen or deciduous. The flowers are white or green, in spikes in the leaf axils, with a small bract and a bracteole at the base of each flower. Sepals 5, not joined; petals 5, equal, joined to form a toothed corolla. Stamens 10, filaments straight, woolly towards the base; the anthers with appendages, opening by pores. Ovary superior. Carpels 5, fused, with numerous ovules; style 5-lobed. Pollination is by insects. The fruits are dry capsules with numerous minute, winged seeds.

Key Recognition Features The spikes of flowers with small bracts in the leaf axils.

Evolution and Relationships Close to *Chamaedaphne* (see p.203). The genus *Agarista* G. Don, found mainly in Africa, including Madagascar, and in North and South America, is very similar, but its seeds are not winged.

Ecology and Geography In moist woods and along streams; 4 species are native in eastern North America, 2 in Japan, and the others in the Himalayas.

Comment These shrubs are grown more for their foliage than for their flowers, which are rather hidden beneath the leaves. Leucothoë was the daughter of a King of Babylon.

Gaultheria procumbens ¾ life size September 16th

Gaultheria procumbens with fruits ¾ life size September 16th

Gaultheria mucronata male flowers 2 × life size May 9th

Leucothoë fontanesiana flowers, just over life size May 2nd

Leucothoë fontanesiana ½ life size, May 2nd

Gaultheria

Gaultheria Kalm ex L. (1753), in the family Ericaceae, contains 134 species of mainly juicy-fruited shrubs.

Description Trees to 8m, but usually shrubs, the bark and leaves often aromatic. The leaves are alternate, evergreen, often sharp-pointed. The flowers are solitary or in spikes in the leaf axils, occasionally unisexual. Sepals 5, joined at the base, usually becoming fleshy in fruit; petals 5, equal, joined to form a bell-shaped corolla. Stamens usually 10, the anthers often with appendages, opening by pores. Ovary superior. Carpels 5, fused, with numerous ovules; style short and straight. Pollination is by insects. The fruits are usually capsules surrounded by a fleshy calyx, but often the capsule itself is fleshy. Seeds small and numerous.

Key Recognition Features The fleshy calyx of most species is easily recognised; in some southern-hemisphere species, however, the calyx is not fleshy, but the fruit itself is berry-like.

Evolution and Relationships Many of the species in which the calyx is not fleshy, such as *G. mucronata* (L. fil.) Hook. & Arn., were formerly put in the genus *Pernettya*. Subsequently, species were found that had a slightly fleshy calyx and a fleshy capsule, so the distinction between the two was considered worthless. Hybrids between the 2 groups, such as *G.* × *wisleyensis*, previously called *Gaulnettya*, have a fleshy calyx partially surrounding a berry.

Ecology and Geography In rocky woods, in bogs, and on open hillsides. Most species are found in Malaysia, eastern Asia, Australia and New Zealand, and Central and South America. Five, including *G. shallon* Pursh and *G. procumbens* L., are found in North America.

Comment *Gaultheria procumbens*, the checkerberry or creeping wintergreen, and *G. shallon* contain oil of wintergreen, of which the active ingredient is methyl salicylate. The berries of *G. insana* (Molina) Middleton are poisonous. *Gaultheria mucronata*, formerly called *Pernettya mucronata*, from southern Chile and Argentina, is often planted for its berries, which may be white, pink, red, or purple, and are abundant if 1 male plant is grown for every 5 or 6 females.

ERICACEAE

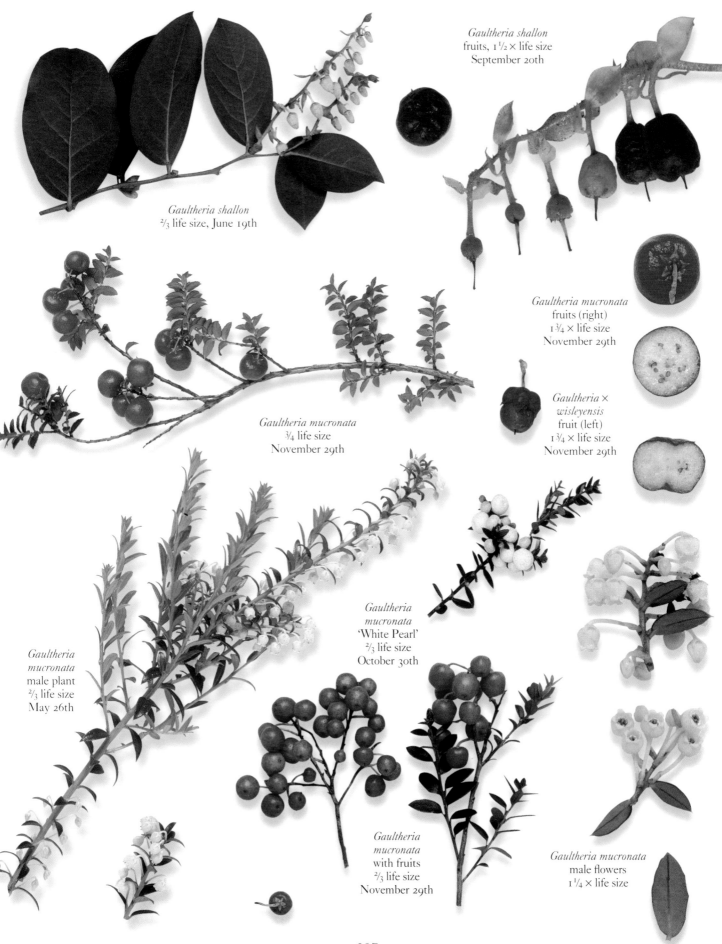

Gaultheria shallon
2/3 life size, June 19th

Gaultheria shallon
fruits, 1 1/2 × life size
September 20th

Gaultheria mucronata
fruits (right)
1 3/4 × life size
November 29th

*Gaultheria ×
wisleyensis*
fruit (left)
1 3/4 × life size
November 29th

Gaultheria mucronata
3/4 life size
November 29th

*Gaultheria
mucronata*
'White Pearl'
2/3 life size
October 30th

*Gaultheria
mucronata*
male plant
2/3 life size
May 26th

*Gaultheria
mucronata*
with fruits
2/3 life size
November 29th

Gaultheria mucronata
male flowers
1 1/4 × life size

Vaccinium

Vaccinium L. (1753), in the family Ericaceae, contains around 450 species, including the cranberries and blueberries of North America and the bilberries of northern Europe.

Description Small trees to 4m, but usually low shrubs. The leaves are alternate, evergreen or deciduous. The flowers are in large or small bunches or solitary, bell-shaped and often narrowed at the mouth, cup-shaped or with reflexed petals. Sepals 4 or 5, joined at the base, often very small; petals 4 or 5, equal, usually joined to form the corolla. Stamens 8–10, the anthers opening by pores, sometimes with appendages. Ovary inferior. Carpels 5, fused, with numerous ovules; style straight. Pollination is by insects, usually bees. The fruits are fleshy berries with numerous seeds.

Key Recognition Features The sweet and juicy fruits from an inferior ovary are characteristic of the *Vaccinium*, which otherwise looks much like other related genera.

Evolution and Relationships *Gaylussacia* Kunth, with around 48 species in North and South America, is close to *Vaccinium*, and also has an inferior ovary, but has fruits with 1 stone, which is made up of 10 hard nutlets.

Ecology and Geography In wet bogs (cranberries), in woods, and on open moorland in temperate areas; many tropical species grow on mossy rocks and trees. Mainly in the northern hemisphere and on mountains in the tropics. There are 65 species in North America, 30 in tropical America, 8 in Europe, 6 in tropical Africa, 22 in Japan, 240 in Malaysia, and others in Asia.

Comment The most commonly cultivated species are the American cranberry, *V. macrocarpon* Ait., and the highbush blueberry *V. corymbosum* L.. The European bilberry or blaeberry, *V. myrtillus* L., is collected from the wild. The North American *V. stramineum* L. is an attractive ornamental bearing white flowers with long, tubular, exserted anthers, which are pollinated by being "buzzed" by bees, to shake out the pollen. *Vaccinium arctostaphylos* L. from northern Turkey makes *broussa* (Bursa) tea. Leaves of the cowberry, *V. vitis-idaea* L., produce a yellow dye. *Vaccinium glaucoalbum* Clarke from the eastern Himalayas is striking for its handsome leaves, whitish beneath. *Vaccinium ovatum* Pursh is a common species in western North America.

Vaccinium glaucoalbum
²/₃ life size
December 8th

Vaccinium stamineum
¾ life size
June 19th

Vaccinium ovatum
1½ × life size
April 2nd

Vaccinium ovatum
fruit, 2 × life size
September 16th

Agapetes buxifolia
¾ life size
February 7th

Agapetes 'Ludgvan Cross'
flowers, 2 × life size
June 15th

Agapetes 'Ludgvan Cross'
½ life size, June 15th

Agapetes

Agapetes D. Don ex G. Don fil (1834), in the family Ericaceae,
contains 95 species, mainly in tropical Asia, just reaching Queensland.
Description Shrubs to 2m, often climbing, the stems often bristly-
hairy. The leaves are alternate, evergreen. The flowers are tubular,
often with zigzag stripes and markings. Sepals 5, joined at the base,
winged or ribbed, often coloured; petals 5, equal, joined to form a
tubular corolla with teeth. Stamens 10, the anthers with elongated
tubes, opening by pores or slits. Ovary inferior. Carpels 5, fused, with
numerous ovules; style long and straight. Pollination is by insects and
probably also by birds. The fruits are berries with numerous seeds.
Key Recognition Features The leathery leaves on long, trailing
stems and the long flowers in the leaf axils or from the stems.
Evolution and Relationships The genus is close to *Vaccinium*, and
some species have smaller, *Vaccinium*-like flowers, but all tend to have
large, winged sepals and fleshy flowers.
Ecology and Geography On mossy rocks and trees from
northeastern India and southwestern China to New Guinea, with a
few species in Fiji, New Caledonia, and Queensland.
Comment A few species are cultivated in cool greenhouses in
Europe, where they survive outside in very mild areas. *Agapetes*
'Ludgvan Cross' is a hybrid between *A. incurvata* (Griffith) Sleumer
and *A. serpens* (Wight) Sleumer, raised by Miss G. Talbot at Ludgvan
in Cornwall. It is hardier than either parent and will survive a few
degrees of frost undamaged. *Agapetes* may sometimes be found under
the old name *Pentapterygium*.

Erica

Erica L. (1753), the heather or heath, in the family Ericaceae, contains around 735 species, mostly in South Africa.

Description Trees to 6m, but mostly shrubs. The leaves are alternate or whorled, evergreen, usually small and narrow, with the margins rolled under, and often lined with stalked glands. The flowers are usually small and tubular. Sepals 4, joined at the base; petals 5, equal, joined to form the corolla, which usually has 4 lobes. Stamens 8, the anthers opening by pores, often with very well-developed spurs, or leafy appendages. Ovary superior. Carpels 4, fused, with numerous ovules; style long with a rounded stigma. Pollination is by insects, usually bees, but by sunbirds in some large-flowered South African species. The fruits are dry capsules, usually enclosed by the dead corolla, with numerous small seeds.

Key Recognition Features The narrow, often glandular leaves in whorls of 3–6, the 4-lobed corolla, and the 8 anthers with appendages.

Evolution and Relationships *Erica* is related to *Calluna* and *Bruckenthalia* Rchb., small heather-like genera; this section of the Ericaceae is confined to Europe, southwestern Asia, and Africa.

Ecology and Geography In peaty, acidic soils on open hillsides, though a few species grow on limestone. Many species are regenerated by fire. Around 16 species are found mainly in western Europe and extending around the Mediterranean area eastwards to Syria; 2 are found in east Africa, including *E. arborea* L., which has an interesting distribution from the Atlantic coast of France to the Canary Islands, in the Tibesti mountains in the Sahara, and in east Africa as far south as Kilimanjaro. The vast majority of the species are found in southern Africa, and particularly in the mountains around Caledon in the Western Cape, where there is a wonderful diversity of flower shape, size, colour, and scent.

Comment European species are valuable as ornamentals, with some species flowering in winter. They are also a good source of nectar for honeybees. South African species are often grown in pots for winter flowering, and will grow outdoors in suitable mild climates. The wood, especially from the roots of the larger species, is used for briar pipes, the name derived from *bruyère*, the French for heather.

Calluna

Calluna Salisb. (1802), in the family Ericaceae, contains 1 species, *C. vulgaris* (L.) Huth, the ling, found in most of Europe and Turkey.

Description Shrubs to 1m. The leaves are small and crowded, evergreen, opposite, in 4 rows. The flowers are small, usually pinkish-purple, on short shoots from elongated branches. Sepals 4, large and petal-like; petals 4, shorter than the sepals, joined at the base. Stamens 8, the anthers with awns, opening by pores. Ovary superior. Carpels 5, fused, with numerous ovules; style long. Pollination is by bees and thrips, and perhaps also by wind in the far north. The fruits are dry capsules, hidden by the persistant calyx, with few seeds.

Key Recognition Features The very small leaves in 4 rows and the flowers with an enlarged, petal-like calyx.

Evolution and Relationships *Calluna* is close to *Erica*, but differs in its enlarged calyx.

Ecology and Geography On peaty hillsides and mountains from Iceland and the Azores to the Urals, northern Turkey, and northwestern Morocco.

Comment This heath is dominant over much of the drier hills of northern England and Scotland, where it forms the main food of the red grouse. It is also a valuable nectar source for honeybees. There is a wide range of cultivars, grown as ornamentals.

Calluna vulgaris
'Kinlochruel'
¾ life size
September 10th

Calluna vulgaris
'Red Star'
¾ life size, September 10th

Calluna vulgaris
'Darkness'
¾ life size
September 10th

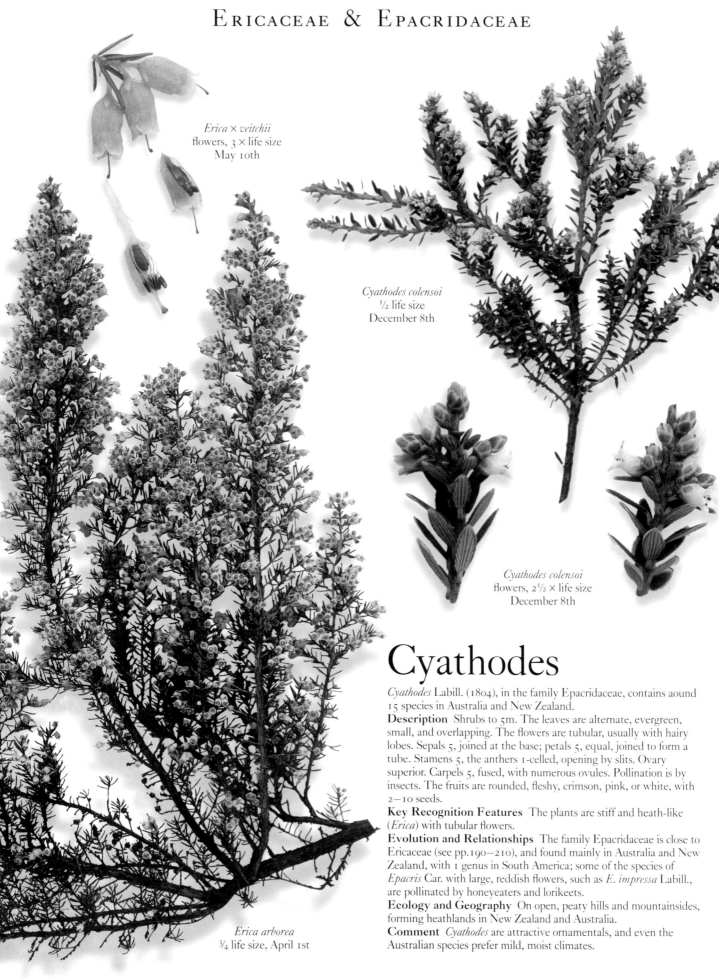

Erica × veitchii
flowers, 3 × life size
May 10th

Cyathodes colensoi
½ life size
December 8th

Cyathodes colensoi
flowers, 2½ × life size
December 8th

Erica arborea
¾ life size, April 1st

Cyathodes

Cyathodes Labill. (1804), in the family Epacridaceae, contains aound 15 species in Australia and New Zealand.

Description Shrubs to 5m. The leaves are alternate, evergreen, small, and overlapping. The flowers are tubular, usually with hairy lobes. Sepals 5, joined at the base; petals 5, equal, joined to form a tube. Stamens 5, the anthers 1-celled, opening by slits. Ovary superior. Carpels 5, fused, with numerous ovules. Pollination is by insects. The fruits are rounded, fleshy, crimson, pink, or white, with 2—10 seeds.

Key Recognition Features The plants are stiff and heath-like (*Erica*) with tubular flowers.

Evolution and Relationships The family Epacridaceae is close to Ericaceae (see pp. 190—210), and found mainly in Australia and New Zealand, with 1 genus in South America; some of the species of *Epacris* Car. with large, reddish flowers, such as *E. impressa* Labill., are pollinated by honeyeaters and lorikeets.

Ecology and Geography On open, peaty hills and mountainsides, forming heathlands in New Zealand and Australia.

Comment *Cyathodes* are attractive ornamentals, and even the Australian species prefer mild, moist climates.

Eucryphia cordifolia
fruits, 4 × life size
September 10th

Eucryphia

Eucryphia Cav. (1797), in the family Eucryphiaceae contains 6 species in the southern hemisphere.

Description Trees to 20m, or shrubs. The leaves are opposite, usually evergreen, simple or pinnately divided. The flowers are white, rarely pale pink, scented, solitary in the leaf axils. Sepals 4, falling together as a cap when the flower opens; petals usually 4. Stamens numerous, the anthers small and pinkish. Ovary superior. Carpels 4–14, fused, each with a simple style. Pollination is by insects. The fruits are dry, splitting capsules with few flattened and winged seeds.

Key Recognition Features The opposite leaves and white flowers with numerous stamens are typical.

Evolution and Relationships The genus is the only one in the family, which is perhaps close to the Cunoniaceae, a southern-hemisphere family, which contains the genus *Weinmannia* L..

Ecology and Geography In temperate rainforest and on moist, rocky slopes. *Eucryphia moorei* F. Muell. is found in New South Wales, *E. lucida* (Labill.) Baillon and *E. milliganii* Hook. fil. in Tasmania, and *E. cordifolia* Cav. and *E. glutinosa* (Poepp. & Endl.) Baillon in Chile.

Comment These attractive ornamental trees and shrubs are commonly grown in gardens along the coast of western Europe, and valued especially for their late-summer flowering; they need good drainage and ample water in summer, as well as protection from freezing wind. *Eucryphia moorei* and *E. cordifolia* are exploited commercially for their timber.

Eucryphia glutinosa
⅔ life size
August 4th

Eucryphia cordifolia
flower back, ⅔ life size
September 10th

EUCRYPHIACEAE

Eucryphia glutinosa
just over life size
August 4th

Eucryphia moorei
²/₃ life size
September 10th

Eucryphia moorei
fruit and flowers
²/₃ life size
September 10th

Pittosporum

Pittosporum Banks ex Solander (1788), in the family Pittosporaceae, contains around 150 species in Africa, Asia, and Australasia.

Description Trees to 30m, or shrubs. The leaves are alternate, evergreen, often with wavy edges. The flowers are usually scented, solitary or in bunches, in the leaf axils or on the tip of the shoot, white, blackish-purple, pink, yellow, or green. Sepals 5, sometimes joined at the base; petals 5, equal, rather short, often reflexed, joined at the base to form a short tube. Stamens 6, alternating with the petals. Carpels 2–4, fused, with numerous ovules and 1 style, often persisting in fruit. Pollination is by insects. The fruits are dry, rounded, woody capsules, splitting into 2 or 3, with a very sticky, reddish-brown resin around the seeds.

Key Recognition Features The 5-petalled, scented flowers on an evergreen tree or shrub, and the sticky coating around the seeds.

Evolution and Relationships The family Pittosporaceae, with 9 genera found mainly in Australasia, is related to the Grossulariaceae (see pp.224–27) and especially to *Escallonia* (see p.226). *Pittosporum* itself is close to *Hymenosporum flavum* (R. Br.) Muell., a beautiful tree with scented, yellow flowers, commonly planted in subtropical areas.

Ecology and Geography On rocky hills and woods, often near the sea. From the Canaries (1 species) to Africa, and from the Himalayas and southwestern China, Japan, Australia, and New Zealand.

Comment Many species are grown as ornamentals. *Pittosporum undulatum* Vent., the Victorian box or cheesewood, is a native of New South Wales and Tasmania, and a common garden tree in southern California; it can become naturalised and a pest, as it has in Jamaica. Its wood is used for golf clubs, and a fragrant oil can be extracted from the flowers. *Pittosporum tobira* Ait., the *tobira* from Japan, is commonly planted near the coast for its orange-blossom scent. *Pittosporum tenuifolium* Banks & Solander from New Zealand is one of the hardier species, grown for its attractive small, silvery or variegated leaves on slender, black twigs.

Pittosporum tenuifolium
'Limelight'
½ life size, April 18th

Pittosporum tobira
2 × life size, May 15th

Pittosporum tenuifolium
'Variegatum'
½ life size, April 18th

Pittosporum tobira
½ life size, May 15th

Pittosporum tobira
fruits, 2 × life size
November 12th

Billardiera longiflora
seeds, 1½ × life size
September 16th

Sollya heterophylla
life size
June 19th

Billardiera longiflora
fruits, 1½ × life size
September 16th

Pittosporum tenuifolium
'Purpureum'
life size, March 25th

Pittosporum tenuifolium 'Garnettii'
fruits (above) seeds (below), life size
December 8th

Billardiera

Billardiera J.E. Smith (1793), in the family Pittosporaceae, contains 30 species, all from Australia.

Description Woody, twining climbers to 6m, or low shrubs. The leaves are alternate, evergreen, usually rather narrow, sometimes lobed. The flowers are tubular, often reflexed at the mouth, but sometimes starry, often scented, white, cream, green, orange, or blue. Sepals 5, joined at the base; petals 5, equal, usually joined towards the base. Stamens 5. Ovary superior; style slender. Carpels 5, fused, with numerous ovules. Pollination is by insects. The fruits are often fleshy, blue, purple, pink, or white berries, sometimes a flattish capsule.

Key Recognition Features The twining stems, narrow leaves, and tubular flowers of most species are easily recognised.

Evolution and Relationships The genus *Billardiera* was formerly split into *Billardiera*, with berries, and *Marianthus* Huegel ex Endl., with capsules. *Rhytidosporum*, a genus of dwarf shrubs, is now also united with *Billardiera*. Another climber in the Pittosporaceae is *Sollya* Lindl., a native of Western Australia, but naturalised elsewhere; it has starry, dangling blue flowers with the anthers in a ring around the style and blue berries with black seeds. In the genus *Bursaria* Cav. in the same family, most species are spiny shrubs with small, whitish flowers, like *Bursaria spinosa* Cav. the sweet bursaria or blackthorn.

Ecology and Geography In rocky, shady places, open forest, and heathland. Most of the species are found in Western Australia, but *B. longiflora* Labill., the hardiest species, often cultivated in Europe, is from New South Wales, Victoria, and Tasmania.

Comment Several species are cultivated in Australia, notably the Chapman river climber, *B. ringens* (Drumm. ex Harv.) E.M.Bennett, which has clusters of bright orange flowers. The genus is named after J.J.H. de la Billardière, (1755–1834), a French botanist and traveller, who sailed on d'Entrecasteaux's expedition in 1791–94.

Hydrangea serrata 'Blue Bird'
fertile flowers, 1½ × life size
August 10th

Hydrangea serrata 'Blue Bird' male
flower, 2 × life size, August 10th

Hydrangea macrophylla
'Générale Vicomtesse
de Vibraye'
⅔ life size, June 26th

Hydrangea paniculata
capsules and autumn colour
life size, November 24th

*Hydrangea
macrophylla*
autumn colour
⅔ life size,
November 24th

Hydrangea

Hydrangea L. (1753), in the family Hydrangeaceae, contains around 100 species in eastern Asia and the Americas.

Description Small trees to 6m, shrubs, or climbers to 30m. The leaves are opposite or in whorls of 3, usually deciduous. The flowers are usually in flat-topped or pyramidal bunches, white, pink, purplish, or blue, often of 2 kinds: sterile outer flowers with large sepals, and small, fertile inner flowers. Sometimes dioecious. Sepals 4 or 5, very small in the fertile flowers; petals 4 or 5. Stamens 8 or 10. Ovary inferior. Carpels 2–5, fused, with numerous ovules, with 1 style per carpel. Pollination is by insects. The fruits are small capsules with numerous small seeds.

Key Recognition Features The flattish, rounded, or pyramidal bunches of flowers, the outer flowers usually larger than the rest. In the mophead garden hydrangeas all the flowers are large and sterile.

Evolution and Relationships The family Hydrangeaceae is sometimes united with the Saxifragaceae (see Volume 2), but here the woody genera are kept separate and divided into the Hydrangeaceae, which includes the Philadelphaceae, and the the Grossulariaceae (see pp.224–27), which includes the Escalloniaceae. All this confusion indicates how closely these families are related. There are also indications from DNA studies that Hydrangeaceae is related to Cornaceae (see pp.324–29). Other genera closely related to *Hydrangea* include the almost herbaceous *Cardiandra* Sieb. & Zucc. from China and Japan, which has alternate leaves and *Hydrangea*-like flowers, and the strange *Platycrater arguta* Sieb. & Zucc., which has a loose head of a few showy, sterile flowers with fused sepals and less showy, fertile ones in the centre, with numerous stamens.

Ecology and Geography On rocky, wooded hillsides, on the sides of gorges, and in open places near the sea; the climbing species on forest trees and cliffs. Found in North and South America and from the Himalayas eastwards to Indonesia.

Comment Many species are grown as ornamentals. Some have flowers that are pink in alkaline or neutral soil and blue in acid soil or where aluminium ions are available; a dressing of aluminium sulphate turns pink hydrangeas blue in all but the most alkaline soils. Mophead hydrangeas, mutants with sterile flowers only, have been found in Ohio in *H. arborescens* L. and also in Japan in *H. macrophylla* (Thunb.) Seringe, the hortensia long cultivated by the Japanese, *H. involucrata* Sieb., and *H. paniculata* Sieb, a variable shrub with pyramidal heads of white flowers. *Hydrangea quercifolia* Bartram, from southeastern North America, has oak-shaped leaves. *Hydrangea anomala* D. Don subsp. *petiolaris* (Sieb. & Zucc.) McClintock, from eastern Asia, is the most commonly grown climbing hydrangea; *H. serratifolia* (Hook & Arn.) Philippi is a climber from Chile and Argentina with male and female flowers on separate plants, at first enclosed in papery bracts.

HYDRANGEACEAE

Hydrangea serratifolia
½ life size, July 1st

Hydrangea aspera
subsp. *sargentiana*
½ life size
September 2nd

Hydrangea quercifolia
½ life size, June 26th

Hydrangea paniculata
'Brussels Lace'
½ life size, August 4th

Hydrangea anomala
subsp. *petiolaris*
½ life size, May 15th

Schizophragma

Schizophragma Sieb. & Zucc. (1835), in the family Hydrangeaceae, contains 2 or 3 species in eastern Asia.

Description Climbing shrubs to 12m. The leaves are opposite, deciduous, with long and often red stalks. The flowers are in loose, flat heads, both sterile and fertile, white or pinkish. Sterile flowers with 1 large, petal-like bract. Sepals 4 or 5; petals 4 or 5, equal. Stamens 10. Ovary inferior. Carpels 10, fused, with numerous ovules; style with a lobed stigma. Pollination is by insects. The fruits are ribbed capsules with several seeds, opening between the ribs.

Key Recognition Features A climbing, *Hydrangea*-like shrub (see pp.216–17) with single, petal-like bracts on the outer, sterile flowers.

Evolution and Relationships Close to the climbing hydrangeas.

Ecology and Geography On rocks, cliffs, and trees, climbing by aerial roots, *S. hydrangeoides* Sieb. & Zucc. in Japan and Korea, *S. integrifolium* (Franch.) Oliver in China and Taiwan.

Comment These are attractive shrubs, like refined climbing hydrangeas. They need rather more moist and sheltered conditions than *Hydrangea anomala* subsp. *petiolaris*.

Schizophragma hydrangeoides
⅔ life size, June 23rd

Dichroa febrifuga
1¼ × life size, May 17th

Dichroa febrifuga
½ life size
May 17th

Dichroa

Dichroa Lour. (1790), in the family Hydrangeaceae, contains around 13 species in eastern Asia.

Description Shrubs to 2.5m. The leaves are opposite, usually evergreen. The flowers are in rather flat or pyramidal, loose heads, white or, depending on the soil, pink or blue. Sepals usually 5; petals 5 or sometimes 6. Stamens 10. Ovary mostly inferior. Carpels 4, fused, with numerous ovules; styles 4. Pollination is by insects. The fruits are small, blue or red berries with numerous seeds.

Key Recognition Features *Hydrangea*-like plants (see pp.216–17) with all the flowers fertile and fleshy fruit.

Evolution and Relationships The genus is close to *Hydrangea*.

Ecology and Geography On shrubby hillsides and in damp areas from Nepal eastwards to Malaysia.

Comment Shoots and bark of the most common species, *D. febrifuga* Lour., are used to treat fever in the Himalayas.

Pileostegia

Pileostegia Hook. & Thoms. (1858), in the family Hydrangeaceae, contains 3 species in eastern Asia.

Description Climbing shrubs to 6m. The leaves are opposite, evergreen, leathery, not toothed. The flowers are small, white, with long stamens, in a loose, branching inflorescence. Sepals 4 or 5, joined at the base, petals 4 or 5, falling without separating, as the flower opens. Stamens 8–10. Ovary inferior. Carpels 4 or 5, fused, with numerous ovules. Pollination is probably by insects, but perhaps also by wind. The fruits are ribbed capsules, opening between the ribs, with numerous seeds.

Key Recognition Features The smooth-edged, evergreen leaves and long stamens are characteristic.

Evolution and Relationships Close to the climbing species of *Hydrangea* (see pp.216–17), but without sterile flowers and without the papery bracts found in *Hydrangea serratifolia*.

Ecology and Geography On rocks, cliffs, or trees, climbing by aerial roots. The commonly cultivated *P. viburnoides* Hook. & Thoms. is found from eastern India to Sichuan and Taiwan.

Comment Attractive evergreen climbers with handsome leaves.

Pileostegia viburnoides
²/₃ life size, September 12th

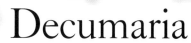

Decumaria sinensis
young flowers, 2 × life size, April 16th

Decumaria barbara
¾ life size, June 21st

Decumaria

Decumaria L. (1762), in the family Hydrangeaceae, contains 2 species in North America and China.

Description Climbing shrubs to 10m with aerial roots. The leaves are opposite, evergreen or deciduous, with shallow teeth. The flowers are in flattish heads, whitish, all fertile. Sepals 7–10, reduced to small teeth, petals 7–10, equal. Stamens 20–30. Ovary inferior. Carpels 7–10, fused, with numerous ovules; style very short with a round stigma. Pollination is by insects. The fruits are ribbed capsules with several seeds, opening between the ribs.

Key Recognition Features A climbing, *Hydrangea*-like shrub (see pp.216–17) with white flowers, no enlarged sepals or petals, and 7–10 petals and numerous stamens.

Evolution and Relationships Close to *Pileostegia*, which has only 4 or 5 petals. A third genus, *Broussaisia* Gaudich., with 1 species, *B. arguta* Gaudich. from Hawaii, is very similar, but has a fleshy fruit.

Ecology and Geography In woods, climbing on trees, by aerial rootlets. *Decumaria barbara* L., in eastern North America from Virginia southwards to Florida, has sweetly scented flowers; the other, *D. sinensis* Oliver from Hubei in China, has unpleasantly scented, greenish flowers.

Comment These *Hydrangea*-like climbing shrubs are sometimes grown in botanical collections; the distribution of species between China and eastern North America is often seen in large genera, but is more remarkable in a small genus such as this.

Carpenteria

Carpenteria Torr. (1854), in the family Hydrangeaceae, contains 1 species in California, *C. californica* Torr., sometimes called the tree-anemone.

Description Shrubs to 5m, with shredding bark. The leaves are opposite, evergreen, lanceolate-oblong. The flowers are large, around 6cm across, white, solitary or a few together. Sepals 5–7, joined at the base, persisting to fruiting; petals 5–7, equal, rounded. Stamens many, with slender filaments. Ovary superior. Carpels 5–7, fused, with numerous ovules; style short with a 5- to 7-lobed stigma. Pollination is by insects. The fruits are leathery, beaked capsules with numerous small seeds.

Key Recognition Features The simple, narrow, evergreen leaves and large, white flowers on an upright shrub.

Evolution and Relationships The genus has no near relatives, but is probably an ancient relict genus, closest to *Philadelphus*. It combines many primitive characteristics, such as the numerous stamens, few, large flowers, and superior ovary; other similarly isolated Californian genera include *Romneya* (see p.90) and *Fremontodendron* (see p.152).

Ecology and Geography On dry, granite slopes in the foothills in Fresno County, between the San Joaquin and King rivers.

Comment A very attractive shrub for warm, dry climates. Named after Professor William Carpenter (1811–48) of Louisiana.

Carpenteria californica
young fruits
⅔ life size, July 28th

Carpenteria californica
⅔ life size, July 3rd

Carpenteria californica
flowers and buds
life size, July 3rd

Philadelphus

Philadelphus L. (1753), in the family Hydrangeaceae, contains around 40 species in the northern hemisphere.

Description Small trees to 7m or shrubs, sometimes climbing. The leaves are opposite, evergreen or deciduous, usually with 3 main veins from the base, with simple hairs. The flowers are white or creamy, usually scented, solitary or in loose, pyramidal heads. Sepals 4, joined at the base, petals 4, equal, sometimes with pinkish spots at the base. Stamens numerous, the filaments not winged. Ovary mostly inferior. Carpels 4, fused; styles 4, partly or wholly fused from the base. Pollination is by insects. The fruits are woody capsules, splitting into 8, with numerous narrow seeds, winged at 1 end.

Key Recognition Features The scented, white flowers with 4 petals and numerous stamens, and an inferior ovary.

Evolution and Relationships The genus is close to *Carpenteria*, with which it shares the numerous stamens and, in many species, large, single flowers, and to *Deutzia* (see p.222).

Ecology and Geography In rocky woods, semi-desert, or openings in wet forest. One species, *P. coronarius* L., is found in eastern Europe and the Caucasus, several in the Himalayas, and many from western China eastwards to Japan. Many other species are found in North America from British Columbia southwards to Mexico.

Comment *Philadelphus coronarius*, commonly called mock orange or syringa, is most commonly grown in its golden-leaved form 'Aureus'; its flowers are particularly well-scented. Many hybrids, such as 'Sybille', were raised in France by Victor Lemoine of Nancy in the late 19th century by crossing *P. coronarius*, *P. microphyllus* Gray from Texas, and *P. mexicanus* Schlecht. (probably 'Rose Syringa') from Mexico. They are still the best smaller cultivars, with large, scented flowers, often with a pinkish base to the petals. *Philadelphus mexicanus* 'Rose Syringa' is a climber that can scramble to the tops of tall trees. *Philadelphus madrensis* from eastern Mexico, is close to P. microphyllus and is especially well-scented. *Philadelphus sericanthus* Koehne is a representative of a group from in western China, of which the finest is *P. delavayi* Franch., which often has purple stems and sepals.

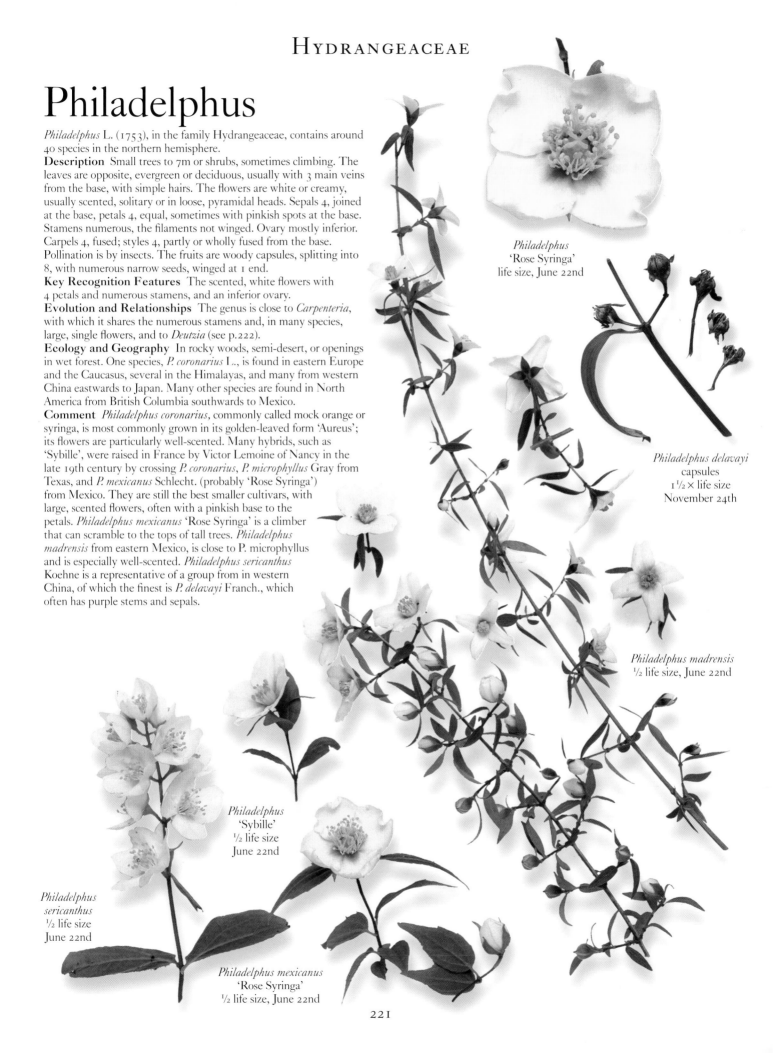

Philadelphus
'Rose Syringa'
life size, June 22nd

Philadelphus delavayi
capsules
1½ × life size
November 24th

Philadelphus madrensis
½ life size, June 22nd

Philadelphus
'Sybille'
½ life size
June 22nd

Philadelphus
sericanthus
½ life size
June 22nd

Philadelphus mexicanus
'Rose Syringa'
½ life size, June 22nd

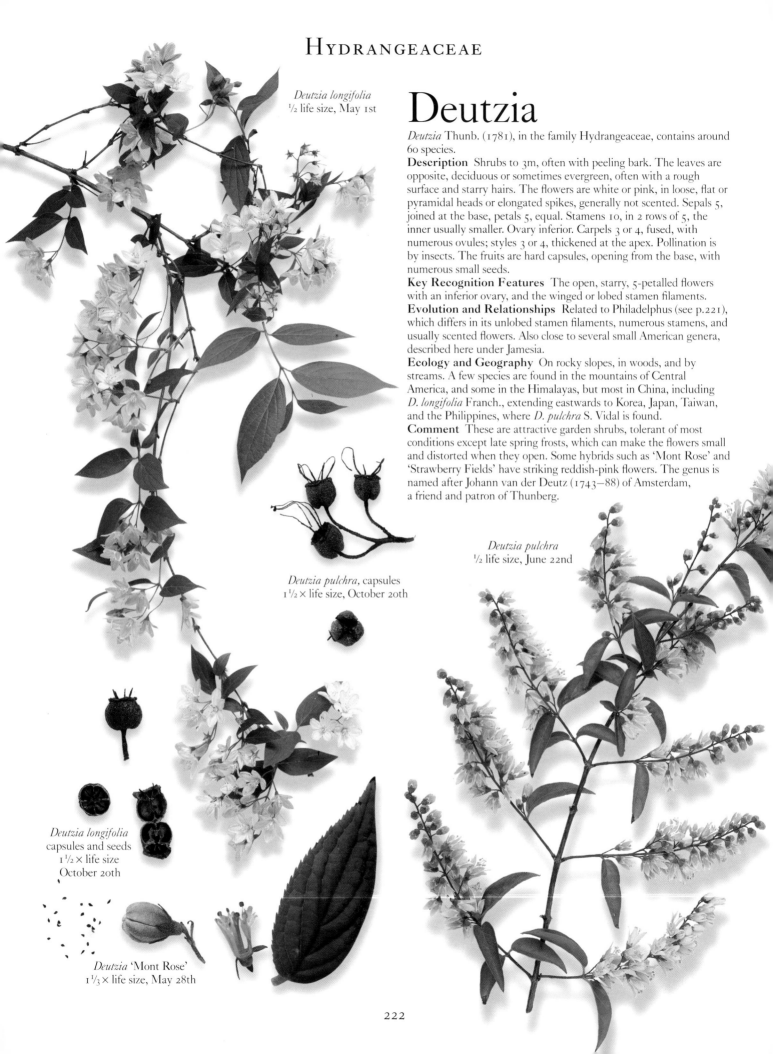

Deutzia longifolia
½ life size, May 1st

Deutzia

Deutzia Thunb. (1781), in the family Hydrangeaceae, contains around 60 species.

Description Shrubs to 3m, often with peeling bark. The leaves are opposite, deciduous or sometimes evergreen, often with a rough surface and starry hairs. The flowers are white or pink, in loose, flat or pyramidal heads or elongated spikes, generally not scented. Sepals 5, joined at the base, petals 5, equal. Stamens 10, in 2 rows of 5, the inner usually smaller. Ovary inferior. Carpels 3 or 4, fused, with numerous ovules; styles 3 or 4, thickened at the apex. Pollination is by insects. The fruits are hard capsules, opening from the base, with numerous small seeds.

Key Recognition Features The open, starry, 5-petalled flowers with an inferior ovary, and the winged or lobed stamen filaments.

Evolution and Relationships Related to Philadelphus (see p.221), which differs in its unlobed stamen filaments, numerous stamens, and usually scented flowers. Also close to several small American genera, described here under Jamesia.

Ecology and Geography On rocky slopes, in woods, and by streams. A few species are found in the mountains of Central America, and some in the Himalayas, but most in China, including *D. longifolia* Franch., extending eastwards to Korea, Japan, Taiwan, and the Philippines, where *D. pulchra* S. Vidal is found.

Comment These are attractive garden shrubs, tolerant of most conditions except late spring frosts, which can make the flowers small and distorted when they open. Some hybrids such as 'Mont Rose' and 'Strawberry Fields' have striking reddish-pink flowers. The genus is named after Johann van der Deutz (1743–88) of Amsterdam, a friend and patron of Thunberg.

Deutzia pulchra
½ life size, June 22nd

Deutzia pulchra, capsules
1½ × life size, October 20th

Deutzia longifolia
capsules and seeds
1½ × life size
October 20th

Deutzia 'Mont Rose'
1⅓ × life size, May 28th

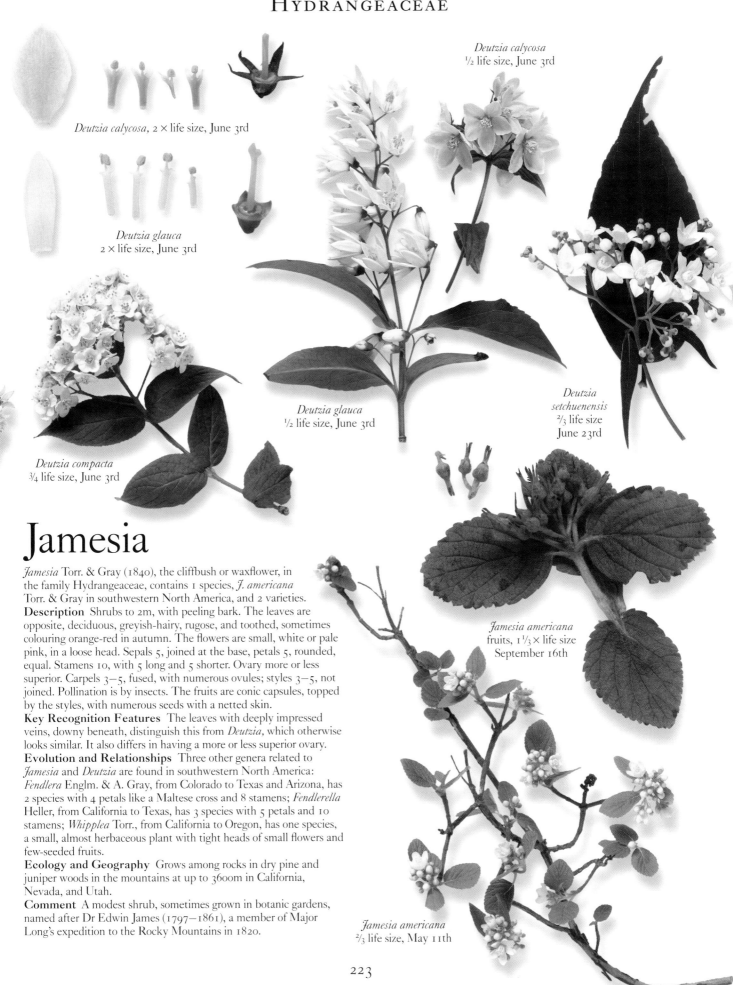

Deutzia calycosa, 2 × life size, June 3rd

Deutzia glauca
2 × life size, June 3rd

Deutzia calycosa
½ life size, June 3rd

Deutzia glauca
½ life size, June 3rd

Deutzia setchuenensis
⅔ life size
June 23rd

Deutzia compacta
¾ life size, June 3rd

Jamesia

Jamesia Torr. & Gray (1840), the cliffbush or waxflower, in the family Hydrangeaceae, contains 1 species, *J. americana* Torr. & Gray in southwestern North America, and 2 varieties.

Description Shrubs to 2m, with peeling bark. The leaves are opposite, deciduous, greyish-hairy, rugose, and toothed, sometimes colouring orange-red in autumn. The flowers are small, white or pale pink, in a loose head. Sepals 5, joined at the base, petals 5, rounded, equal. Stamens 10, with 5 long and 5 shorter. Ovary more or less superior. Carpels 3–5, fused, with numerous ovules; styles 3–5, not joined. Pollination is by insects. The fruits are conic capsules, topped by the styles, with numerous seeds with a netted skin.

Key Recognition Features The leaves with deeply impressed veins, downy beneath, distinguish this from *Deutzia*, which otherwise looks similar. It also differs in having a more or less superior ovary.

Evolution and Relationships Three other genera related to *Jamesia* and *Deutzia* are found in southwestern North America: *Fendlera* Englm. & A. Gray, from Colorado to Texas and Arizona, has 2 species with 4 petals like a Maltese cross and 8 stamens; *Fendlerella* Heller, from California to Texas, has 3 species with 5 petals and 10 stamens; *Whipplea* Torr., from California to Oregon, has one species, a small, almost herbaceous plant with tight heads of small flowers and few-seeded fruits.

Ecology and Geography Grows among rocks in dry pine and juniper woods in the mountains at up to 3600m in California, Nevada, and Utah.

Comment A modest shrub, sometimes grown in botanic gardens, named after Dr Edwin James (1797–1861), a member of Major Long's expedition to the Rocky Mountains in 1820.

Jamesia americana
fruits, 1⅓ × life size
September 16th

Jamesia americana
⅔ life size, May 11th

Ribes speciosum
²⁄₃ life size, March 17th

Ribes speciosum
1¼ × life size
March 17th

Ribes

Ribes L. (1753), in the family Grossulariaceae, contains around 150 species including the flowering and culinary currants and the gooseberry.

Description Shrubs to 4m, often spiny. The leaves are alternate, deciduous or sometimes evergreen, usually lobed and often aromatic, as in the blackcurrant. The flowers are in loose spikes or solitary, often greenish, sometimes white, yellow, purple, or red, male and female flowers, sometimes on different plants. Sepals 5, rarely 4, joined at the base; petals 5, usually shorter than the sepals. Stamens 5. Ovary inferior. Carpels 2, fused, with several ovules; style 2-lobed or divided. Pollination is by insects or, according to Mabberley, by hummingbirds. The fruits are fleshy and juicy with several seeds, with the dried remains of the flower remaining on the tip.

Key Recognition Features The 1-celled ovary forming a berry is typical of *Ribes*. The flowers are of 2 main shapes: a cup-shaped flower with 5 rounded sepals and 5 smaller petals is found in subgenus Ribes, the currants, which do not have spines; a more tubular flower, in which the sepals are sometimes reflexed, is found in subgenus Grossularia, the gooseberries, which also have spiny stems.

Evolution and Relationships As treated here, Grossulariaceae includes Escalloniaceae and Iteaceae. *Ribes* is the only genus in Grossulariaceae in the more narrow sense.

Ecology and Geography In rocky places in the mountains, on dry hillsides, and in wet woods and swamps. Species are found all around the northern hemisphere, and extend into the Andes.

Comment Many species are grown for their fruit, notably the redcurrant and whitecurrant, both *R. rubrum* L., and the blackcurrant, *R. nigrum* L., which has particularly large amounts of vitamin C and is the basis of cassis and the popular drink Ribena. *Ribes uva-crispa* L. is the gooseberry, commonly made into pies. An old hybrid between the gooseberry and the blackcurrant, *R. × culverwellii* Macfarlane, is sometimes found in abandoned gardens; the fruits are like small, hairless, black gooseberries. *Ribes sanguineum* Pursh, from northern California to British Columbia, is the popular "flowering currant", with red or pink flowers in hanging bunches and a rather catty smell. The Californian fuchsia *R. speciosum* Pursh, common on coastal hills near Los Angeles, usually loses its leaves in summer and flowers in early spring, when it is much visited by Anna hummingbirds, which nest earlier than other hummingbird species. *Ribes odoratum* Wendl., the buffalo currant, from the American midwest and the Rocky Mountains, is a very attractive and hardy ornamental shrub.

Ribes uva-crispa
fruit, ¾ life size
July 4th

Ribes nigrum 'Ben Nevis'
fruit, ¾ life size
July 4th

GROSSULARIACEAE

Ribes longeracemosum
²⁄₃ life size
May 11th

Ribes odoratum
just under life size
April 1st

Ribes sanguineum
2 × life size, March 10th

Ribes sanguineum
¾ life size, March 10th

Ribes menziesii
life size,
March 17th

225

Escallonia

Escallonia Mutis ex L. fil. (1781), in the family Grossulariaceae, contains around 40 species in South America.

Description Trees to 12m, or shrubs. The leaves are alternate, sometimes whorled, evergreen or sometimes deciduous, usually shining above, and finely toothed. The flowers are in small or large clusters, white, pink, or red, sometimes scented. Sepals 5, joined at the base, petals 5, equal, sometimes elongated, forming a tubular flower, sometimes rounded, forming an open flower. Stamens 5. Ovary mostly inferior. Carpels 2 or 3, fused, with numerous ovules; style 1, with a rounded stigma, or sometimes 2-fid. Pollination is by insects, often by butterflies in the case of white, open-flowered species, and possibly by hummingbirds in the case of red, tubular-flowered species. The fruits are capsules with numerous seeds.

Key Recognition Features The evergreen species have distinctive, finely-toothed leaves, often combined with trumpet-shaped, pink or white flowers.

Evolution and Relationships The family Escalloniaceae is now generally put in the Grossulariaceae, though in many ways it is also closely related to the Pittosporaceae (see pp.214–15). Genera related to *Escallonia* and formerly included in the Escalloniaceae include *Anopterus* Labill. from Australia and *Carpodetus* Forster & Forster fil. from New Zealand. *Itea*, which was at one time put in its own family, the Iteaceae, is now put here.

Ecology and Geography In scrub, on cliffs, and on open hillsides by streams in Chile, Argentina, and Uruguay.

Comment The genus is named after Señor Escallon, who travelled in South America in the late 18th century. Many species are grown as wind-tolerant ornamentals on the coasts of western Europe. *Escallonia* 'Iveyi' is a particularly good cultivar which appeared as a seedling at Caerhays Castle, Cornwall in the 1920s; it is probably a seedling of *E. bifida*.

Escallonia 'Iveyi'
2 × life size, July 9th

Escallonia bifida
²/₃ life size, October 3rd

Escallonia 'Iveyi'
¹/₂ life size, July 9th

Escallonia 'Red Elf'
2 × life size, November 12th

Escallonia 'Red Elf'
fruits and seeds
2 × life size, November 29th

Escallonia rubra
life size, June 23rd

Itea virginica
¾ life size
June 19th

Itea virginica
¾ life size
June 19th

Itea ilicifolia
½ life size, September 2nd

Itea

Itea L. (1753), in the family Grossulariaceae, contains 15 species.
Description Trees to 4m, and in the cultivated species shrubs, the branches with chambered pith. The leaves are alternate, evergreen and sometimes holly-like (*Ilex*, see p.179) or deciduous. The flowers are small, green or white, sometimes scented, in upright or hanging spikes. Sepals 5, persisting to fruiting, petals 5, linear. Stamens 5. Ovary superior. Carpels 2, fused, with numerous ovules; styles 2, fused. Pollination is by insects. The fruits are capsules with numerous seeds.
Key Recognition Features The distinctive, holly-like leaves and long, hanging, catkin-like spikes of green flowers in summer are typical of the commonly cultivated *I. ilicifolia* Oliver. *Itea virginica* L. from North America has upright spikes of fragrant, white flowers.
Evolution and Relationships Now included in Grossulariaceae, Iteaceae was formerly put in Saxifragaceae (see Volume 2).
Ecology and Geography *Itea virginica* is found in swamps and pine barrens in eastern North America, the rest of the species on wooded hills in eastern Asia, especially China.
Comment In addition to the 2 species mentioned, *I. yunnanensis* Franch. with narrower, less spiny leaves and dull, white flowers in shorter spikes, is sometimes cultivated.

Rosa

Rosa L. (1753), the Rose, in the family Rosaceae subfamily Rosoideae, contains around 150 species in the northern hemisphere.
Description Shrubs to 3m, or climbers reaching 30m or more when supported. Stems usually with curved or straight thorns or spines. The leaves are alternate, evergreen or deciduous, pinnate, with 1 terminal lobe and up to 9 pairs of lateral lobes; the lobes usually toothed. The flowers are usually scented, red, pink, white, or yellow, solitary or in groups on the ends of short shoots. Sepals 5, unequal, 2 lobed, 2 not lobed, and the last lobed on 1 side, all joined at the base to the top of the ovary wall (receptacle). Petals 5, nearly equal, usually falling as the flowers fade. Stamens many, the anthers opening by slits. Ovary inferior. Carpels many, fused, each with 1 ovule and 1 style; styles sometimes united in a column. Pollination is by insects, usually by bees or beetles, which visit the flowers for their ample pollen. The fruits are hips, with the 1-seeded, hard achenes formed on the fleshy wall.
Key Recognition Features The 5 petals with numerous stamens, inferior ovary, and hips with seeds on the inside of the receptacle.
Evolution and Relationships The family Rosaceae is close to Saxifragaceae and Crassulaceae (see Volume 2), but has many more woody genera than either, and much larger seeds. Most genera have alternate leaves and many have an epicalyx, like an extra row of sepals. Fossil flowers ancestral to Rosaceae have been found in the Cretaceous in Nebraska, and leaves of *Rosa* in the mid-Tertiary in Colorado and Oregon. Rosaceae is usually divided into 4 sections: Rosoideae (roses), Spiraeoideae (spiraea, see pp.240–45), Maloideae (apples, see pp.246–65), and Prunoideae (plums, see pp.266–71). The Rosoideae contains the genera that have more than 2 styles with 1 ovule each, the seeds being dry achenes or small, fleshy drupes; these are as diverse as *Polylepis* (see p.236) or *Alchemilla* or *Fragaria*, the strawberry (see Volume 2).
Ecology and Geography In woods, scrub, and especially in hedgerows, throughout the northern hemisphere, as far south as Mexico, Ethiopia, and southern India.
Comment Wild rose species are often divided into 4 subgenera: Rosa, Hesperhodos, Hulthemia, and Platyrhodon. Garden roses come almost entirely from subgenus Rosa, which is split into 10 sections, the most important of which are illustrated here. Section Rosa, often called Cinnamomae, includes *R. moyesii* Hemsl. & Wils., grown primarily for its large hips, and *R. rugosa* Thunb. (see p.232). This section has been little used in modern roses, but is becoming important in recent breeding because of its resistance to blackspot. Section Caninae, the dog rose, is little used for breeding, apart from the Alba roses (see p.230), because of its breeding system of partial apomixis – that is, the ability to set seed almost identical to the mother plant; Caninae have unusual chromosome numbers, and hybrids involving them are often sterile. Section Synstylae, the musk roses, includes *R. soulieana* Crep., *R. arvensis* Huds., *R. moschata* Herrm., possibly a parent of the Damasks (see p.230), and *R. multiflora* Thunb. ex Murray., which is important in the ancestry of Ramblers and Floribundas (see p.232). Section Pimpinellifoliae contains the Scotch roses and yellow roses, such as *R. ecae* Aitch. and *R. foetida* L., which brought the colour yellow into modern roses. Section Carolinae contains many American species, including *R. nutkana* Presl (see p.232); these are little used for breeding modern roses. Section Gallicanae contains only *R. gallica* L., ancestor of all the major groups of modern roses, valued for its red colour and excellent scent. Section Chinenses contains *R. chinensis* L. and *R. gigantea* Collett ex Crép., vital ancestors of modern roses through the Teas and Chinas (see p.230); their hips are large but not the most striking. Chinese species were often originally described from cultivated double forms, which were the first to be brought to the notice of botanists in Europe; later the wild, single forms were discovered by travellers and therefore named as varieties of the doubles.

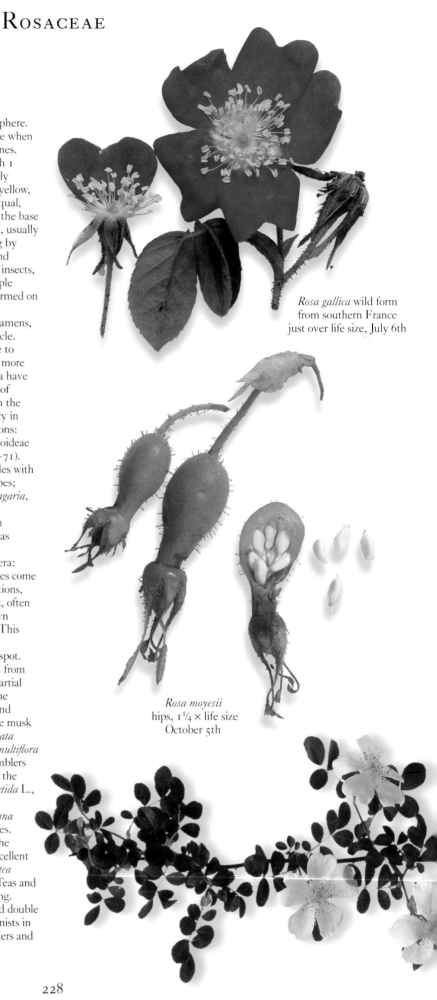

Rosa gallica wild form
from southern France
just over life size, July 6th

Rosa moyesii
hips, 1¼ × life size
October 5th

ROSACEAE

Rosa arvensis
showing the styles
united into a column
just over life size
July 6th

Rosa chinensis
var. *spontanea*
⅔ life size
April 12th

Rosa canina
⅔ life size
June 9th

Rosa soulieana
⅔ life size
June 23rd

Rosa ecae
life size
May 23rd

Old Roses

Roses were cultivated in both the Middle East and China in ancient times for their scent and beautiful flowers — usually double forms rather than the single species (see pp.228–229). Modern rose breeding began with the introduction of Chinese cultivated roses to Europe at the end of the 18th century, becoming immensely fashionable in 19th-century France, producing the types now known as Old Roses.

Gallicas An ancient group, varieties of *R. gallica* L., grown by the Romans but reaching the height of their development in early 19th century France, with intricately double flowers in shades of red and purple, on low, suckering shrubs. 'Tuscany' is an old variety.

Damasks These were probably grown by the Romans, or at least by the Arabs in the middle ages, and are now cultivated in Turkey for their scent. 'Madame Hardy' was raised in France in 1832. Damasks flower only in spring, but the Autumn Damasks (the original being *R. × damascena* 'Bifera') have a second, lesser flowering in autumn.

Albas Thought to derive from a white-flowered dog rose crossed with either a Gallica or a Damask, Albas are tall and very hardy, and usually sterile. *Rosa × alba* 'Semiplena' syn. *R.* 'Alba Semiplena' is one of the most ancient, grown at least since medieval times.

Centifolias Also called cabbage roses, these appeared in the Netherlands in the latter half of the 17th century; they are thought to have originated from a hybrid between an Alba and an Autumn Damask, but are sterile, so new varieties depend on mutations or sports, which Centifolias tend to produce. 'Cristata' is an unusual mutation, often called 'Chapeau de Napoléon', said to have been found in Switzerland in 1820.

Mosses Centifolia roses often sported to produce stems and sepals covered with numerous fine prickles and glands, so called moss roses; they were very popular in the mid-19th century. 'Louis Gimard' was raised in 1877, and possibly has some China rose in its ancestry.

Chinas *Rosa chinensis* is a cultivated double rose that will flower almost throughout the year, and has been grown in China for over 1000 years. The wild form, *R. chinensis* var. *spontanea*, is a climber flowering only in spring. Its flowers open pale cream and become pink and red as they fade, a quality also found in *R. chinensis* 'Mutabilis', another old perpetual-flowering variety.

Teas These are derived from the Chinese *R. gigantea*, which has large, single, white or pale yellow flowers. Most are probably hybrids with *R. chinensis*; many are low-growing, some are climbers, and most flower throughout the summer and autumn. Many were raised in China and in France in the 19th century and grow best in a warm or subtropical climate. 'Lady Hillingdon' is one of the hardiest.

Noisettes These originated in 1802 in South Carolina with 'Champneys' Pink Cluster', a cross between *R. moschata* and *R. chinensis* 'Old Blush' with branched heads of small, pink flowers. Seeds of this were sown by Phillipe Noisette in Charleston and produced 'Blush Noisette', also with small, pink flowers. A cross with the yellow Tea rose 'Parks' Yellow Tea-scented China' produced a large-flowered race of Noisettes, of which 'Rêve d'Or', raised in France in 1817, is a typical example. Later Noisettes became large-flowered and very close to Teas.

Bourbons Hybrids of the Autumn Damask and *R. chinensis*, both planted by French colonists, were found on the Ile de Bourbon, now called Réunion, in the Indian Ocean. Seeds of the hybrids were sent to France in 1817 and became the originators of this new group with the long flowering season of the China roses and the wonderful scent of the Damasks. 'Madame Isaac Pereire' was raised in France in 1881.

Hybrid Perpetuals Crosses in the 1830s of Bourbons and China hybrids with 'Rose du Roi', a tough, red rose of Gallica and Damask ancestry that flowers in spring and autumn, produced Hybrid Perpetuals. Rather coarse, with large flowers in summer and autumn, they were popular around the end of the 19th century, but are now uncommon, though still important as parents of the Hybrid Teas (see p.232). 'Mrs John Laing' was raised in England in 1887.

Rosa 'Madame Hardy'
just under life size
May 22nd

Rosa × centifolia
'Cristata'
¾ life size, June 28th

Rosa × alba
'Semiplena'
¾ life size, May 22nd

Rosa gallica
'Tuscany'
¾ life size
June 2nd

Rosa 'Mrs John Laing'
²⁄₃ life size, July 3rd

Rosa 'Louis Gimard'
just under life size, June 9th

Rosa 'Madame Isaac Pereire'
²⁄₃ life size, May 22nd

Rosa chinensis
'Mutabilis'
¾ life size, May 22nd

Rosa 'Reve d'Or'
²⁄₃ life size
May 22nd

Rosa 'Cupid' (see p.232), hips
¾ life size, October 17th

Rosa
'Lady Hillingdon'
½ life size
May 22nd

Modern Roses

Modern roses, produced in the greatest numbers in the 20th century, are the result of crossing some of the old groups (see pp.230–31) and species (see pp.228–29) to achieve a combination of tall-budded flowers, clear colours, and continuous flowering. The Hybrid Teas and Floribundas dominated breeding until the 1980s, when miniatures and David Austin's English Roses began to gain in popularity. Ramblers, Rugosas, and Shrub Roses have remained as minor groups.

Hybrid Teas These are the modern large-flowered roses, the most successful of all groups. They are the result of crossing Teas with Hybrid Perpetuals, themselves complex crosses between Gallicas, Damasks, and Chinas. The first were raised in France in 1867, and some are low shrubs, others are climbers. 'Paul's Lemon Pillar', a strong climber, dates from 1916. 'Cupid' is a prolific bearer of hips, (see p.231) dating from 1915. 'Glendora' was raised by Kordes in 1995.

Floribundas Sometimes called cluster-flowered roses, these are the other very large modern group after Hybrid Teas. They originated with Poulsen's nursery in Denmark from crosses of Hybrid Teas with Polyantha Roses, themselves crosses between dwarf Chinas and a dwarf, repeat-flowering form of *R. multiflora*. Genes from other species have now been introduced into the group, and have resulted in very free-flowering, low-growing roses, popular for bedding. 'Rhythm 'n' Blues' was raised in 1999 by Poulsen.

Ramblers These roses send out long, non-flowering shoots in midsummer to flower once, in great profusion, early the following summer. Most ramblers have been raised by crossing large-flowered roses, such as Hybrid Perpetuals, with wild roses of the Synstylae section, which have masses of small, white flowers. 'Bleu Magenta' is a typical rambler raised in the United States in 1932, with *R. multiflora* as one parent. 'Raubritter' is a more unusual hybrid, raised by Kordes in Germany in 1936, a cross between a rambler and *R.* × *macrantha*, itself probably a hybrid of *R. gallica* and *R.* × *alba*.

English Roses A relatively recent group raised by David Austin in central England, aiming to combine the good scents and beautiful, fully double flowers of the old Gallicas and Damasks with the long flowering and general health of modern roses. Most English Roses are tall shrubs with fully double flowers in subtle shades of apricot to pale pink or deep red. 'John Clare' was raised in 1994.

Rugosa Roses These are derived from *R. rugosa*, a native of the coasts of Japan and eastern China, now found wild on sand dunes in other parts of the world. 'Roseraie de l'Haÿ', raised in France in 1910 and named after the great rose garden near Paris, is possibly a hybrid with a double *R. gallica*.

Shrub Roses Any rose that does not belong to one of the other sections is loosely called a shrub rose. They are generally large shrubs with one main flowering, and often close to a wild species. *Rosa nutkana* Presl. 'Plena', a semi-double form of the species, noted in 1894, is a good example.

Rosa 'Roseraie de l'Haÿ'
⅔ life size, June 3rd

Rosa rugosa
hips, just under
life size
October 25th

Rosa 'Rhythm 'n' Blues'
⅔ life size, July 1st

Rosa 'Paul's Lemon Pillar'
½ life size, May 22nd

Rosa 'Glendora'
²/₃ life size
July 1st

Rosa nutkana
'Plena'
²/₃ life size
June 3rd

Rosa 'John Clare'
¹/₂ life size, June 9th

Rosa 'Bleu Magenta'
²/₃ life size
July 3rd

Rosa 'Raubritter'
¹/₂ life size, June 9th

Kerria japonica 'Simplex'
just over life size
April 9th

Kerria

Kerria DC (1817), in the family Rosaceae subfamily Rosoideae, contains 1 species *K. japonica* (L.) DC.

Description Shrubs to 3m, with green twigs and small, narrow stipules. The leaves are alternate, deciduous, ovate or narrowly ovate, toothed. The flowers are orange-yellow to almost white, not scented. Sepals 5, joined at the base; petals 5, equal, or numerous in the commonly cultivated double forms. Stamens many. Ovary superior. Carpels 5–8, fused, with 1 ovule each; styles 5–8, very slender. Pollination is by insects. The fruits are usually 5, ovate-globose, smooth, green achenes surrounded by persistent sepals.

Key Recognition Features The slender, green twigs are characteristic in winter; the orange-yellow flowers are conspicuous in summer, like small roses but with separate achenes.

Evolution and Relationships *Kerria* is close to *Rhodotypos* Sieb. & Zucc., also from Japan and China, but that has opposite leaves (unique in the Rosaceae), large sepals, white flowers, and 1–4 black achenes.

Ecology and Geography On rocky slopes in warm valleys and in woods in the mountains. In Japan and China, as far west as Sichuan.

Comment The double-flowered form 'Pleniflora' is commonly grown and was popular in Victorian gardens; it sends up long, upright shoots. The single-flowered form, 'Simplex', is usually smaller and more spreading in habit.

Kerria japonica
'Pleniflora'
⅔ life size, April 24th

Kerria japonica 'Simplex'
⅔ life size, April 9th

Potentilla

Potentilla L. (1753), in the family Rosaceae subfamily Rosoideae, contains around 500 species, mainly in the northern hemisphere and mainly herbaceous, with 1 very variable shrubby species, *P. fruticosa* L..
Description Shrubs to 1.5m. The leaves are alternate, deciduous, with 3, 5, or 7 leaflets, with persistant stipules. The flowers are yellow or white, rarely red, not scented. Sepals 5, joined at the base and subtended by a sepal-like epicalyx; petals 5, equal. Stamens many. Ovary superior. Carpels many, each with 1 ovule; styles many. Pollination is by insects. The fruits are dry, 1-seeded achenes, covered with long hairs.
Key Recognition Features The small, pinnate leaves with persistent stipules, the epicalyx, and the dry achenes.
Evolution and Relationships *Potentilla* is close to *Fragaria* (strawberry, see Volume 2) and has even been hybridised with it, but differs in the dry and hairy, rather than sweet and juicy, fruit.
Ecology and Geography In rocky, damp places, on mountain cliffs or limestone pavement throughout the northern hemisphere from Alaska and Greenland to western Ireland, the Himalayas, and northern Japan. It is particularly variable in the northern Himalayas.
Comment *Potentilla fruticosa* is sometimes put in the separate genus *Dasiphora* Raf. It is reported as a weed in parts of New England. Many different forms are cultivated; the most distinct are 'Beesii', a dwarf with silver leaves, from southern Tibet; 'Red Ace' with red or orange flowers, originating in northern Burma, and var. *dahurica* f. *rhodocalyx* with nodding, white flowers, from Yunnan. 'Vilmoriniana' originated from seed sent to the firm Vilmorin from Sichuan in 1905.

Potentilla fruticosa
from northeastern Turkey
⅔ life size, July 6th

Potentilla fruticosa
1¼ × life size
July 6th

Potentilla fruticosa
'Vilmoriniana'
⅔ life size, July 27th

Polylepis

Polylepis Ruíz & Pavón (1794), in the family Rosaceae subfamily Rosoideae, contains around 35 species of trees and shrubs from South America, of which *P. australis* Bitter is sometimes cultivated.

Description Small trees to 6m, or shrubs, with reddish bark peeling in long strips. The leaves are alternate or crowded, evergreen or deciduous, pinnate with 3–7 elliptic, toothed, bluish-green leaflets. The flowers are small, green, in branched and hanging spikes, usually bisexual. Sepals 3–5, small and lanceolate, joined at the base to form a calyx, narrow at the mouth; petals absent. Stamens numerous, with large anthers on slender filaments. Ovary inferior; style short and feathery. Pollination is by wind. The fruits are dry and 3-winged or spiny, containing 1 seed, and probably dispersed by wind or llamas.

Key Recognition Features The bluish-green, pinnate leaves, very shaggy, peeling bark, and hanging spikes of small, green flowers.

Evolution and Relationships *Polylepis* belongs to the group of Rosaceae which includes the wind-pollinated *Sanguisorba*, *Alchemilla*, (see Volume 2), and *Acaena* Mutis. ex L.. Some authorities such as Hutchinson have postulated that the catkin-bearing plants, such as hazels (*Corylus*, see p.119), might have originated from the ancestral Rosaceae via wind-pollinated ancestors similar to *Polylepis*.

Ecology and Geography On rocky slopes and cliffs from Tierra del Fuego to the high Andes, with *P. australis* throughout Argentina.

Comment In cultivation an unusual shrub or small tree, grown for its interesting bark and leaves. *Polylepis* reaches the highest altitude of any woody plant in the world, to over 5000m in the Andes.

Polylepis australis
½ life size
July 6th

Polylepis australis
fruits, 2½ × life size
October 6th

Polylepis australis
papery bark
½ life size, July 6th

Polylepis australis
fruits, ¾ life size
October 6th

Polylepis australis
autumn leaves
life size, October 8th

Polylepis australis
female flowers
1 ¹/₂ × life size, July 6th

Polylepis australis
male flowers, 1 ¹/₄ × life size
July 6th

Lyonothamnus

Lyonothamnus A. Gray (1823), in the family Rosaceae
subfamily Rosoideae, contains 1 species, *L. floribundus* A. Gray, the
Catalina ironwood, in southwestern California.

Description Small trees to 15m, or shrubs, often with reddish,
peeling bark. The leaves are opposite, more or less evergreen, simple
or pinnate, entire or toothed and lobed. The flowers are small and
white, in large bunches. Sepals 5, joined at the base to form a short,
wide tube; petals 5, rounded, to 5mm. Stamens 15. Ovary superior;
carpels 2, each with 4 ovules. Pollination is presumed to be by insects.
The fruits are 2 small woody capsules, with usually 4 seeds in each.

Key Recognition Features The divided, leathery leaves and
peeling, reddish bark.

Evolution and Relationships An isolated genus, which has no
near relatives in the Rosaceae. Two subspecies are recognised,
subsp. *floribundus*, with leaflets that are simple or toothed, and
subsp. *asplenifolius* (E. Greene) Raven, with leaves that are
2-pinnate and again pinnatifid into oblique lobes.

Ecology and Geography On dry slopes in chaparral, found only
on Santa Catalina island, off southwestern California.

Comment *Lyonothamnus floribundus* and especially subsp.
asplenifolius is grown for its interesting leaves and bark. Though it
grows and survives well in mild areas in western Europe, it seldom
flowers; flowering is regular, however, in the Mediterranean area. The
name commemorates W.S. Lyon, an early resident of Los Angeles,
who discovered the plant.

Lyonothamnus floribundus
subsp. *asplenifolius*
¹/₂ life size, May 31st

237

Rubus

Rubus L. (1753), the brambles and raspberries, in the family Rosaceae subfamily Rosoideae, contains around 250 species and many more apomictic microspecies throughout the world.

Description Shrubs to 4m or more, often climbing or scrambling, usually with hooked prickles, often with peeling bark. The leaves are alternate, evergreen or deciduous, simple, lobed, or variously divided. The flowers are usually in bunches, occasionally hanging down below the canes. Sepals 5, joined at the base; petals 5, equal, white, red, pink, or dark maroon, sometimes very small or absent. Stamens many. Ovary superior. Carpels many, separate, each with 1 ovule; styles slender. Pollination is by insects, often butterflies in wild blackberries, bees in raspberries. The fruit are composed of 1-seeded, juicy drupelets, sometimes separating easily from the receptacle, as in the raspberry, sometimes staying attached to it, as in the blackberry.

Key Recognition Features The prickly or bristly stems of most species and the blackberry-like fruit.

Evolution and Relationships The genus has great diversity in leaf form, cane form, and flowers. In some, such as *R. deliciosus* Torr. and the hybrid 'Benenden', the leaves are simple, shallowly lobed, with palmate veining, and the flowers are rose-like, to 7cm across. In others the leaves are pinnate or, as in *R. lineatus* Reinwart, palmate with parallel-veined leaflets. In *R. chamaemorus* L., the cloudberry, which grows in bogs in the Arctic, the stems creep underground and only the leaves and flowers emerge. In the New Zealand *R. cissoides* A. Cunn., juvenile leaflets are very narrow, adult leaflets rounded on long stalks.

Ecology and Geography In hedges, on rough slopes and in woods from subtropical forests to the Arctic, throughout the world.

Comment Many species are cultivated for their fruit. Apart from the familiar raspberries, *R. idaeus* L., and blackberries, *R. fruticosus* L., the genus includes Japanese wineberries, *R. phoenicolasius* Maxim., and cloudberries, and numerous hybrids have been produced, including loganberries, boysenberries, marionberries, and tayberries. The thimbleberry, *R. odoratus* L., has large leaves and scented pink flowers on upright canes. *R. spectabilis* Pursh, the salmonberry, has deep pink flowers before the leaves in early spring; a form with double flowers is often cultivated. *R. cockburnianus* Hemsl. from China, is grown for its canes, waxy white in winter. The unusual *R. calophyllus* Clarke, from Bhutan, has single leaflets with parallel veins, and claret-red flowers; the distant *R. lineatus* Reinw. has 5 leaflets.

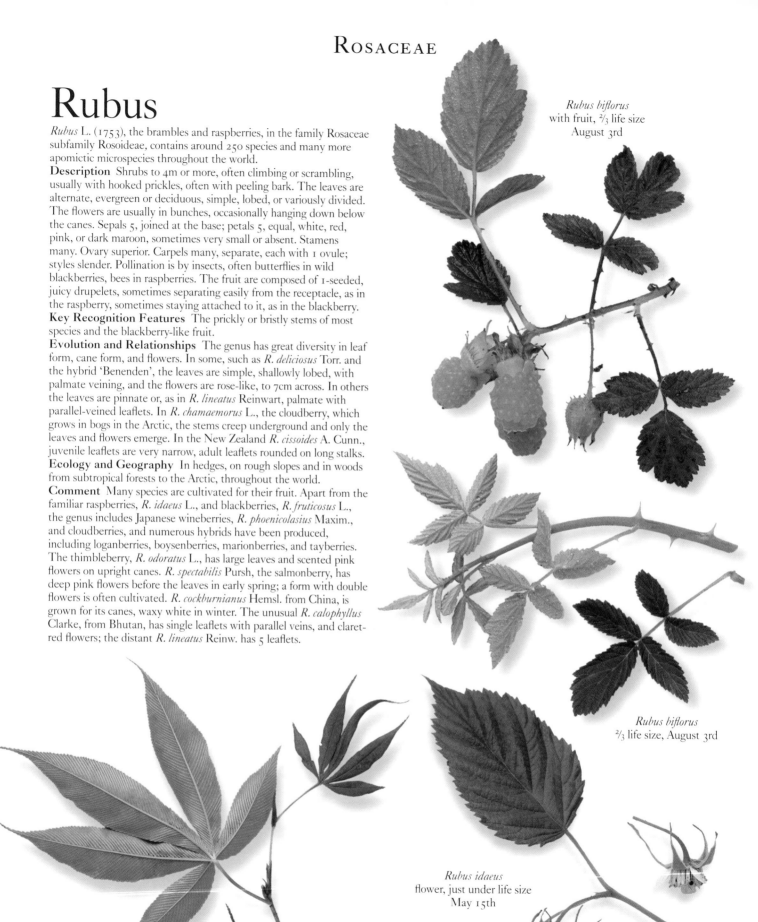

Rubus biflorus
with fruit, ²/₃ life size
August 3rd

Rubus biflorus
²/₃ life size, August 3rd

Rubus idaeus
flower, just under life size
May 15th

Rubus lineatus
½ life size, July 27th

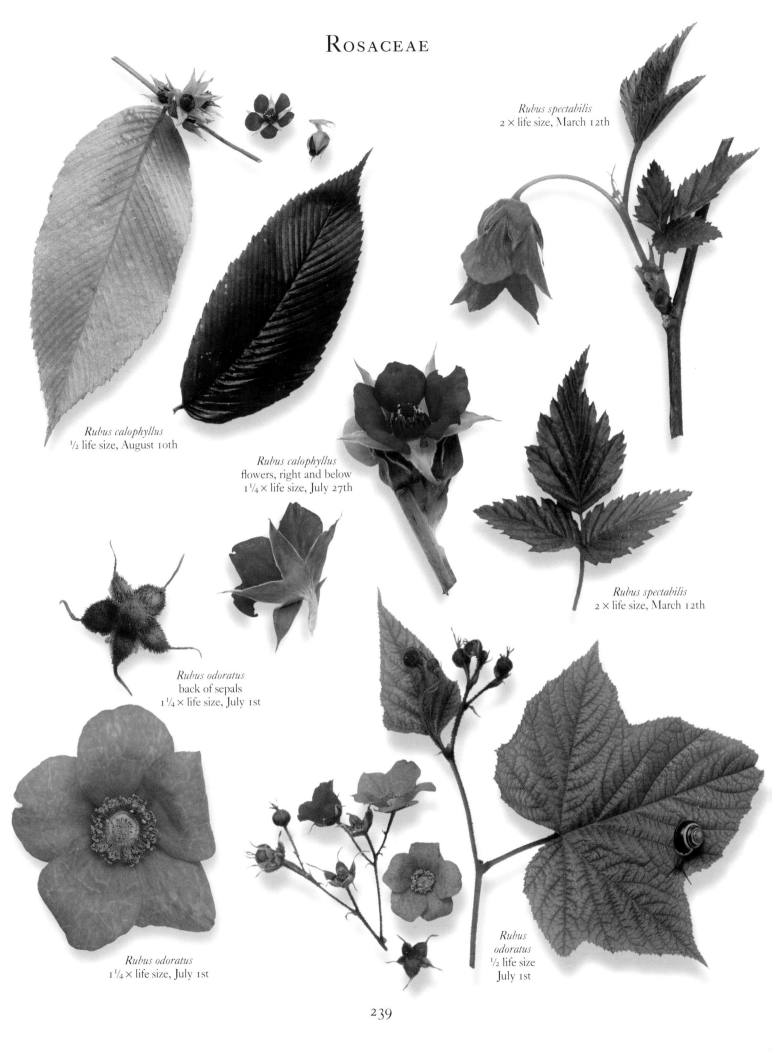

ROSACEAE

Rubus spectabilis
2 × life size, March 12th

Rubus calophyllus
½ life size, August 10th

Rubus calophyllus
flowers, right and below
1¼ × life size, July 27th

Rubus spectabilis
2 × life size, March 12th

Rubus odoratus
back of sepals
1¼ × life size, July 1st

Rubus odoratus
1¼ × life size, July 1st

*Rubus
odoratus*
½ life size
July 1st

Stephanandra

Stephanandra Sieb. & Zucc. (1843), in the family Rosaceae subfamily Spiraeoideae, contains around 4 species.

Description Shrubs to 2m, with graceful, spreading stems. The leaves are alternate, deciduous, with sharp teeth and long-pointed lobes, and with ovate stipules, colouring well in autumn. The flowers are very small and greenish or whitish, in loose, branching heads. Sepals 5, joined at the base, forming a cup; petals 5, narrow, alternating with the sepals. Stamens 10—20. Ovary inferior. Carpel 1; style attached at the side. Pollination is probably by insects. The ripe carpel opens only at the base, with 1 or 2 seeds.

Key Recognition Features The long-pointed lobes of the leaves and the small flowers.

Evolution and Relationships *Stephanandra* is close to *Spiraea* (see p.242), which differs in having no stipules, usually 5 carpels, and generally larger flowers.

Ecology and Geography In mountain scrub in eastern China, Korea, and Japan.

Comment This is usually grown for its elegance of habit, leaf, and autumn colour, since the flowers are insignificant.

Stephanandra incisa
½ life size
June 12th

Neillia

Neillia D. Don (1825), in the family Rosaceae subfamily Spiraeoideae, contains around 11 species of low, spreading shrubs.

Description Shrubs to 3m. The leaves are alternate, deciduous, coarsely toothed and lobed, often with a long, slender point. The flowers are small, usually pink, in elongated spikes. Sepals 5, joined at the base to form a cup-shaped calyx; petals 5, equal. Stamens 8—25, with short filaments. Ovary inferior. Carpels 1 or 2, with a terminal style. Pollination is by insects. The ripe carpel is hidden by the calyx and splits along the inner edge, with 2—10 but usually 5 glossy seeds.

Key Recognition Features The long-pointed and lobed leaves and terminal spikes of small flowers with a cup-shaped calyx.

Evolution and Relationships Closely related to the mainly American genus *Physocarpus*, but that has flat, umbel-like heads of flowers with larger petals and about 5 swollen carpels, which split along both edges. *Neillia torreyi* S. Wats. is now included in *Physocarpus monogynus* (Torr.) Coult.

Ecology and Geography On rocky slopes and in moist forest from Nepal to southwestern China, Korea, and Indonesia.

Comment *Neillia longiracemosa* Hemsl. is cultivated for its graceful spikes of bright pink flowers; in *N. thibetica* Franch. the spikes are more compact.

Neillia thibetica
⅓ life size, June 22nd

Neillia sinensis
var. *ribesoides*
flowers and young fruit
1½× life size, July 10th

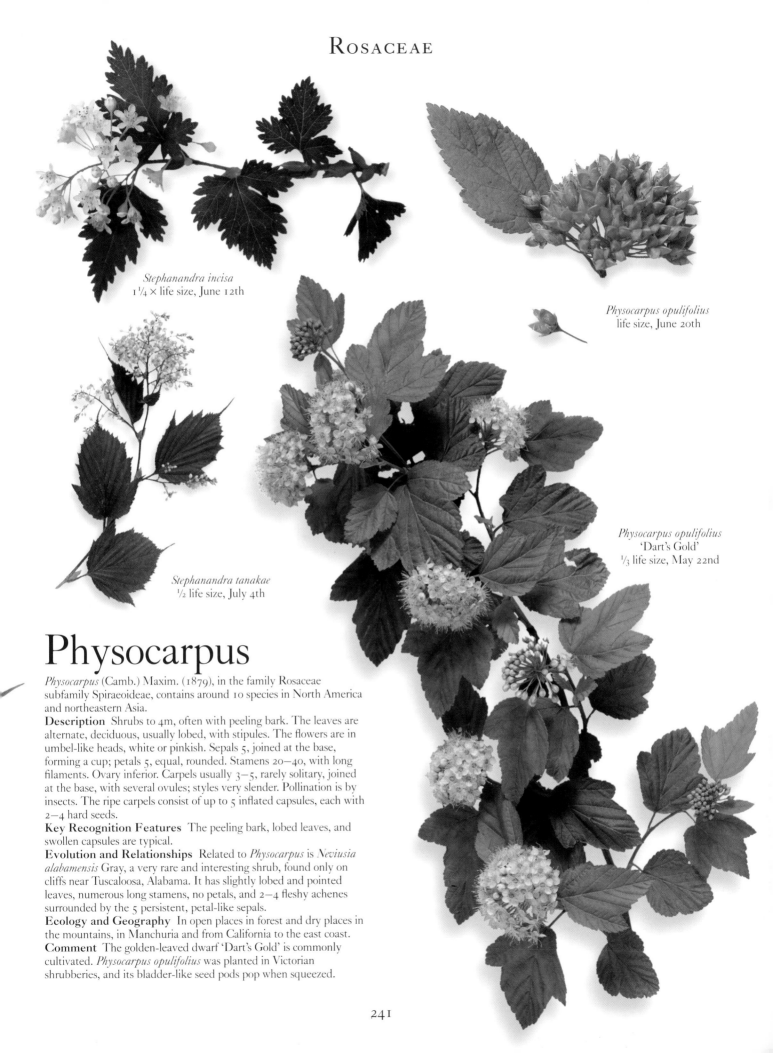

Stephanandra incisa
1¼ × life size, June 12th

Physocarpus opulifolius
life size, June 20th

Stephanandra tanakae
½ life size, July 4th

Physocarpus opulifolius
'Dart's Gold'
⅓ life size, May 22nd

Physocarpus

Physocarpus (Camb.) Maxim. (1879), in the family Rosaceae subfamily Spiraeoideae, contains around 10 species in North America and northeastern Asia.

Description Shrubs to 4m, often with peeling bark. The leaves are alternate, deciduous, usually lobed, with stipules. The flowers are in umbel-like heads, white or pinkish. Sepals 5, joined at the base, forming a cup; petals 5, equal, rounded. Stamens 20–40, with long filaments. Ovary inferior. Carpels usually 3–5, rarely solitary, joined at the base, with several ovules; styles very slender. Pollination is by insects. The ripe carpels consist of up to 5 inflated capsules, each with 2–4 hard seeds.

Key Recognition Features The peeling bark, lobed leaves, and swollen capsules are typical.

Evolution and Relationships Related to *Physocarpus* is *Neviusia alabamensis* Gray, a very rare and interesting shrub, found only on cliffs near Tuscaloosa, Alabama. It has slightly lobed and pointed leaves, numerous long stamens, no petals, and 2–4 fleshy achenes surrounded by the 5 persistent, petal-like sepals.

Ecology and Geography In open places in forest and dry places in the mountains, in Manchuria and from California to the east coast.

Comment The golden-leaved dwarf 'Dart's Gold' is commonly cultivated. *Physocarpus opulifolius* was planted in Victorian shrubberies, and its bladder-like seed pods pop when squeezed.

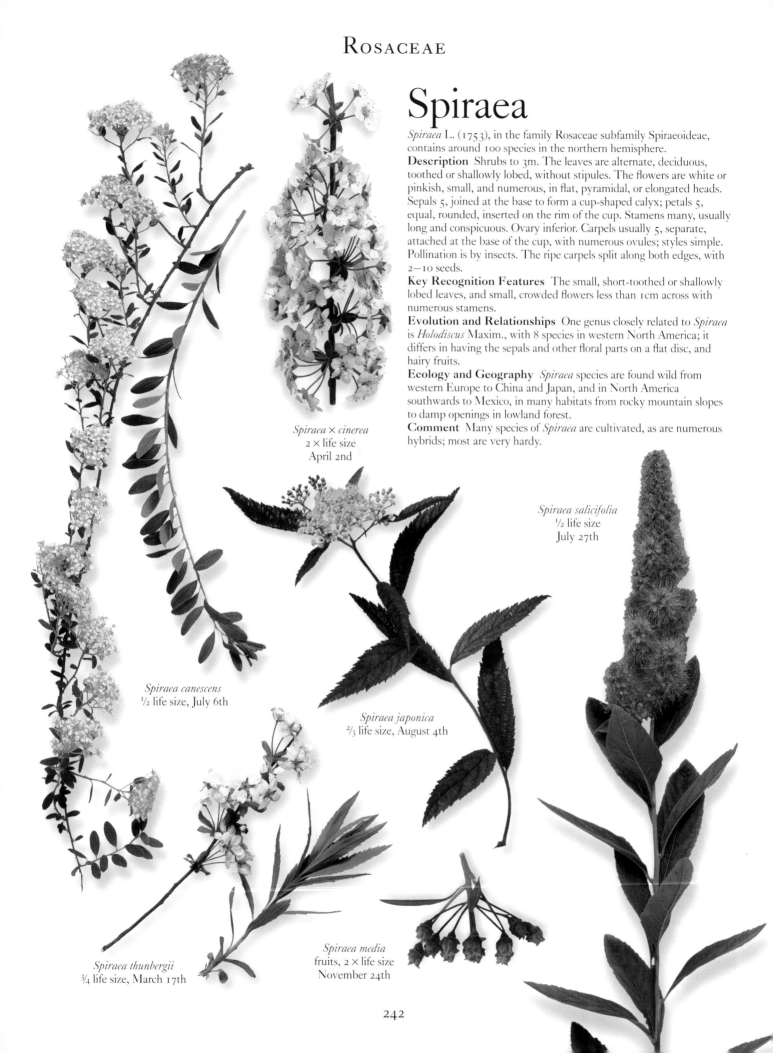

Spiraea

Spiraea L. (1753), in the family Rosaceae subfamily Spiraeoideae, contains around 100 species in the northern hemisphere.

Description Shrubs to 3m. The leaves are alternate, deciduous, toothed or shallowly lobed, without stipules. The flowers are white or pinkish, small, and numerous, in flat, pyramidal, or elongated heads. Sepals 5, joined at the base to form a cup-shaped calyx; petals 5, equal, rounded, inserted on the rim of the cup. Stamens many, usually long and conspicuous. Ovary inferior. Carpels usually 5, separate, attached at the base of the cup, with numerous ovules; styles simple. Pollination is by insects. The ripe carpels split along both edges, with 2–10 seeds.

Key Recognition Features The small, short-toothed or shallowly lobed leaves, and small, crowded flowers less than 1cm across with numerous stamens.

Evolution and Relationships One genus closely related to *Spiraea* is *Holodiscus* Maxim., with 8 species in western North America; it differs in having the sepals and other floral parts on a flat disc, and hairy fruits.

Ecology and Geography *Spiraea* species are found wild from western Europe to China and Japan, and in North America southwards to Mexico, in many habitats from rocky mountain slopes to damp openings in lowland forest.

Comment Many species of *Spiraea* are cultivated, as are numerous hybrids; most are very hardy.

Spiraea × cinerea
2 × life size
April 2nd

Spiraea salicifolia
½ life size
July 27th

Spiraea canescens
½ life size, July 6th

Spiraea japonica
⅔ life size, August 4th

Spiraea thunbergii
¾ life size, March 17th

Spiraea media
fruits, 2 × life size
November 24th

Exochorda × macrantha
'The Bride'
½ life size, May 9th

Exochorda

Exochorda Lindl. (1858), in the family Rosaceae subfamily Spiraeoideae, contains around 4 species in Asia.

Description Shrubs to 4m. The leaves are alternate, deciduous, without stipules, usually oblanceolate, and rarely toothed. The flowers are large, pure white, often unisexual, in few-flowered, elongated heads on the tips of the branches. Sepals 5, joined only at the base to form a tube, the lobes falling as the flowers open; petals 5, equal, narrowed at the base. Stamens 15–30. Ovary inferior. Carpels 5, fused when young, with few ovules; styles 5. Pollination is by insects. The fruits are 5-lobed, eventually splitting into 5 hard, 1- or 2-seeded sections.

Key Recognition Features The large, white flowers with 5 very separate petals in early spring, and the 5-lobed fruits combined with oblanceolate, bluish-green leaves.

Evolution and Relationships Closely related is *Sibiraea* Maxim., with 5 species from southeastern Europe to Central Asia and China; it has untoothed leaves, and very small flowers with carpels joined at the base.

Ecology and Geography On rocky slopes in the mountains from Central Asia to China and Korea.

Comment *Exochorda* species are most attractive, hardy shrubs for early flowering. 'The Bride', raised by Grootendorst in around 1938, is commonly cultivated; it is a selection of *E. × macrantha* (Lem.) Schneid., a hybrid between *E. racemosa* (Lindl.) Rehd. and *E. korolkowii* Lav., and has weeping branches often covered with white flowers.

Exochorda × macrantha
'The Bride'
1¼ × life size, May 9th

Exochorda × macrantha
'The Bride', fruits
1½ × life size, May 9th

243

Sorbaria sorbifolia
capsules, 2 × life size
September 16th

Sorbaria kirilowii
1²/₃ × life size, July 27th

Sorbaria

Sorbaria (DC) A. Br. (1864), in the family Rosaceae
subfamily Spiraeoideae, contains around 10 species in Asia.
Description Robust shrubs to 6m. The leaves are alternate,
deciduous, pinnate, with narrow, sharply toothed leaflets. The
flowers are small and white, in very large, pyramidal heads at the
ends of new shoots. Sepals 5, joined at the base to form a cup-shaped
calyx; petals 5, equal. Stamens 20–50, usually longer than the petals.
Ovary inferior. Carpels 5, joined at the base, with numerous ovules;
styles 1 per carpel. Pollination is by insects. The ripe carpels split
along the inner edge, each with several seeds.
Key Recognition Features The pinnate leaves and large,
pyramidal heads of white flowers.
Evolution and Relationships Few other genera of the Rosaceae,
especially of the subfamily Spiraeoideae, have pinnate leaves, although
they are found in *Rosa* (see pp.228–33) and *Sorbus* (see pp.262–65).
Ecology and Geography On rocky hills and in forests from
Afghanistan and Kashmir to China, Korea, Japan, and eastern Siberia.
Comment Many of the species, especially the large *S. kirilowii* (Reg.)
Maxim., are fine hardy shrubs for late summer, good on chalky soils.

Sorbaria kirilowii
²/₃ life size, July 27th

244

Chamaebatiaria

Chamaebatiaria (Brewer & Watson) Maxim. (1879), in the family Rosaceae subfamily Spiraeoideae, contains 1 species, *C. millefolium* (Torr.) Maxim., the fernbush, in western North America.

Description Low, aromatic shrubs to 2m. The leaves are alternate, deciduous, 2-pinnate, with undivided stipules. The flowers are white, in elongated heads in the upper leaf axils and at the ends of the shoots. Sepals 5, joined at the base to form a wide tube; petals 5, equal. Stamens many. Carpels 5, joined at the base; styles 5. Pollination is by insects. The fruits are split along the inner edge, each with few seeds.

Key Recognition Features The finely divided leaves, the white flowers, and the 5 carpels, leathery when ripe.

Evolution and Relationships *Chamaebatia* Benth., the mountain misery, from California and southwest Oregon, is similar but has larger flowers, each with 1 carpel and 1 seed. *Lyonothamnus* Gray, the Catalina ironwood, is an upright, evergreen tree with opposite, undivided or pinnate leaves and loose heads of small, white flowers; it is confined to the Santa Barbara Islands off southern California.

Ecology and Geography On rocky slopes in dry pine scrub and semi-desert from California to Oregon, Wyoming, and Arizona.

Comment A modest shrub for a dry position.

*Chamaebatiaria
millefolium*
1 ½ × life size, May 5th

*Chamaebatiaria
millefolium*
¾ life size, May 5th

245

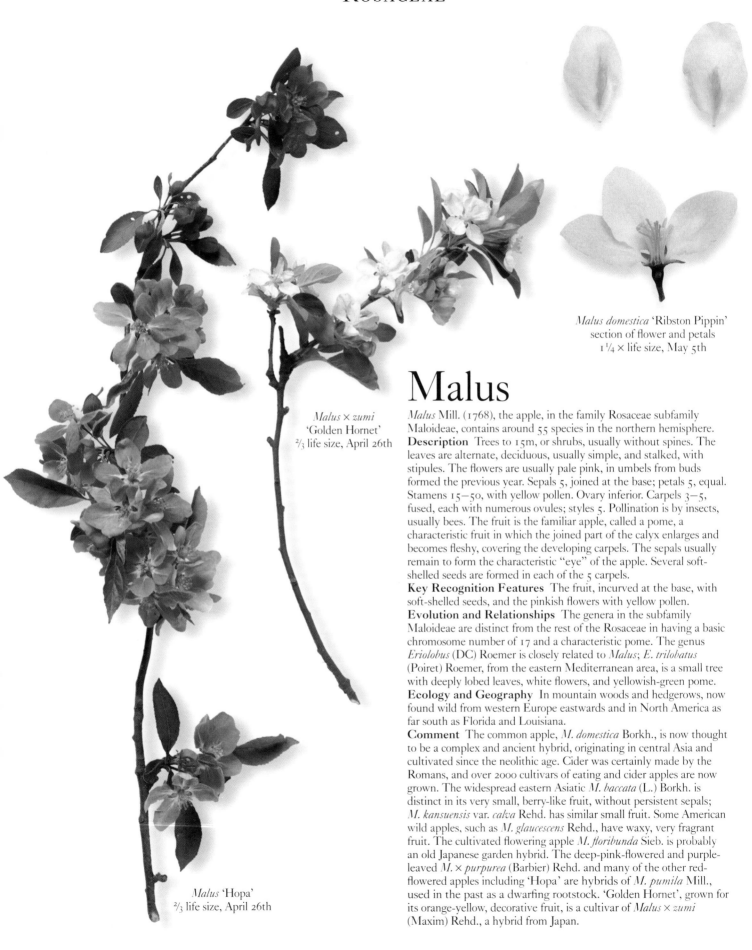

Malus domestica 'Ribston Pippin'
section of flower and petals
1 ¼ × life size, May 5th

Malus × *zumi*
'Golden Hornet'
²/₃ life size, April 26th

Malus 'Hopa'
²/₃ life size, April 26th

Malus

Malus Mill. (1768), the apple, in the family Rosaceae subfamily Maloideae, contains around 55 species in the northern hemisphere.

Description Trees to 15m, or shrubs, usually without spines. The leaves are alternate, deciduous, usually simple, and stalked, with stipules. The flowers are usually pale pink, in umbels from buds formed the previous year. Sepals 5, joined at the base; petals 5, equal. Stamens 15–50, with yellow pollen. Ovary inferior. Carpels 3–5, fused, each with numerous ovules; styles 5. Pollination is by insects, usually bees. The fruit is the familiar apple, called a pome, a characteristic fruit in which the joined part of the calyx enlarges and becomes fleshy, covering the developing carpels. The sepals usually remain to form the characteristic "eye" of the apple. Several soft-shelled seeds are formed in each of the 5 carpels.

Key Recognition Features The fruit, incurved at the base, with soft-shelled seeds, and the pinkish flowers with yellow pollen.

Evolution and Relationships The genera in the subfamily Maloideae are distinct from the rest of the Rosaceae in having a basic chromosome number of 17 and a characteristic pome. The genus *Eriolobus* (DC) Roemer is closely related to *Malus*; *E. trilobatus* (Poiret) Roemer, from the eastern Mediterranean area, is a small tree with deeply lobed leaves, white flowers, and yellowish-green pome.

Ecology and Geography In mountain woods and hedgerows, now found wild from western Europe eastwards and in North America as far south as Florida and Louisiana.

Comment The common apple, *M. domestica* Borkh., is now thought to be a complex and ancient hybrid, originating in central Asia and cultivated since the neolithic age. Cider was certainly made by the Romans, and over 2000 cultivars of eating and cider apples are now grown. The widespread eastern Asiatic *M. baccata* (L.) Borkh. is distinct in its very small, berry-like fruit, without persistent sepals; *M. kansuensis* var. *calva* Rehd. has similar small fruit. Some American wild apples, such as *M. glaucescens* Rehd., have waxy, very fragrant fruit. The cultivated flowering apple *M. floribunda* Sieb. is probably an old Japanese garden hybrid. The deep-pink-flowered and purple-leaved *M.* × *purpurea* (Barbier) Rehd. and many of the other red-flowered apples including 'Hopa' are hybrids of *M. pumila* Mill., used in the past as a dwarfing rootstock. 'Golden Hornet', grown for its orange-yellow, decorative fruit, is a cultivar of *Malus* × *zumi* (Maxim) Rehd., a hybrid from Japan.

Malus hupehensis
fruit, just over life size,
September 16th

Malus floribunda
⅔ life size, September 20th

Malus × zumi
'Golden Hornet'
fruit, ⅔ life size
September 16th

Malus kansuensis var. *calva*
fruit, ⅔ life size
September 16th

Malus sieboldii
autumn leaves
½ life size, November 29th

247

Pyrus

Pyrus L. (1753), the pear, in the family Rosaceae subfamily Maloideae, contains around 25 species in the northern hemisphere.

Description Trees to 20m, or shrubs, often with spiny branchlets. The leaves are alternate, deciduous, simple, and stalked. The flowers are white, in umbels, from buds formed the previous year. Sepals 5, joined at the base; petals 5, equal. Stamens 20–30, with purple pollen. Ovary inferior. Carpels 5, fused, each with 2 ovules; styles usually 5. Pollination is by insects, usually bees. The fruit is the familiar pear, a pome (see *Malus*, p.246), with numerous woody cells; 1 or 2 soft-shelled seeds are formed in each of the carpels.

Key Recognition Features The white flowers with purple pollen and pear-shaped fruit with woody cells are typical of most species.

Evolution and Relationships A genus closely related to *Malus*.

Ecology and Geography On rocky hillsides from western Europe across Asia to China and Japan, with 9 species in Turkey.

Comment Pears derived from *P. communis* L. are grown mainly for fruit; unlike nearly all other pears, the yellow- and orange-fruited 'Glow Red Williams' has pink flowers. Chinese and Japanese cultivated pears, derived from *P. pyrifolia* (Burm.) Nakai, are often very large and apple-like in shape, but have the crisp, watery flesh and woody pits of an unripe European pear. The ornamental pear, *P. salicifolia* Pallas, is wild in the Caucasus and Turkey; its weeping form 'Pendula' is commonly cultivated. *Pyrus pashia* Hamilt. is a large ornamental tree from the Himalayas and western China. *Pyrus cordata* Desf. is native of southern Europe and Cornwall. Pearwood, called fruitwood in the furniture trade, is very stable; it is used for turning, for mathematical and musical instruments, and for bread boards.

Pyrus ussuriensis
fruit, ⅔ life size
September 16th

Pyrus cordata
fruit, ¾ life size
September 16th

Pyrus pashia
⅔ life size
April 16th

Pyrus communis
1½× life size, April 5th

248

Cydonia

Cydonia Mill. (1768), the quince, in the family Rosaceae subfamily Maloideae, contains 1 species, *C. oblonga* Mill., a native of southwestern Asia.

Description Trees to 8m or shrubs, with dark, smooth bark. The leaves are alternate, deciduous, ovate or rounded, simple, and stalked, densely hairy beneath. The flowers are 4–6cm across, usually white shaded with pink, single, on short shoots, from buds formed the previous year. Sepals 5, joined at the base, reflexed; petals 5, equal. Stamens 15–25. Ovary inferior. Carpels 5, fused, each with numerous ovules; styles 5. Pollination is by insects, usually bees. The fruit is the quince, a pome (see *Malus*, p.246), yellow, slightly scurfy, aromatic, and pear-shaped. Several soft-shelled seeds are formed in each of the 5 carpels.

Key Recognition Features The rounded leaves, hairy beneath, solitary, large flowers, and pear-shaped, aromatic fruit.

Evolution and Relationships The genus is very closely related to *Pyrus*. *Docynia* Decne, closely related to *Cydonia*, contains 2 species from the Himalayas and South East Asia. They have evergreen leaves, lobed in *D. indica* Decne, umbels of a few flowers, and very woolly, edible fruit, used in China, according to Mabberley, to speed the bletting of persimmons (*Diospyros*, see p.178).

Ecology and Geography In forests and scrub, from the Caucasus to northern Iran, the Kopet Dag, and perhaps northern Iraq.

Comment The quince has long been cultivated for its fruit, which imparts an excellent aromatic flavour to stewed apples and makes a good jam or jelly. In France, Spain, and Portugal quince jelly is made into a solid paste the consistency of Turkish delight (*lokoum*), which is variously called *cotignac*, *membrillo*, *marmelo*, *marmelda*, or *mermelada*. Quince rootstock is commonly used for grafting pears.

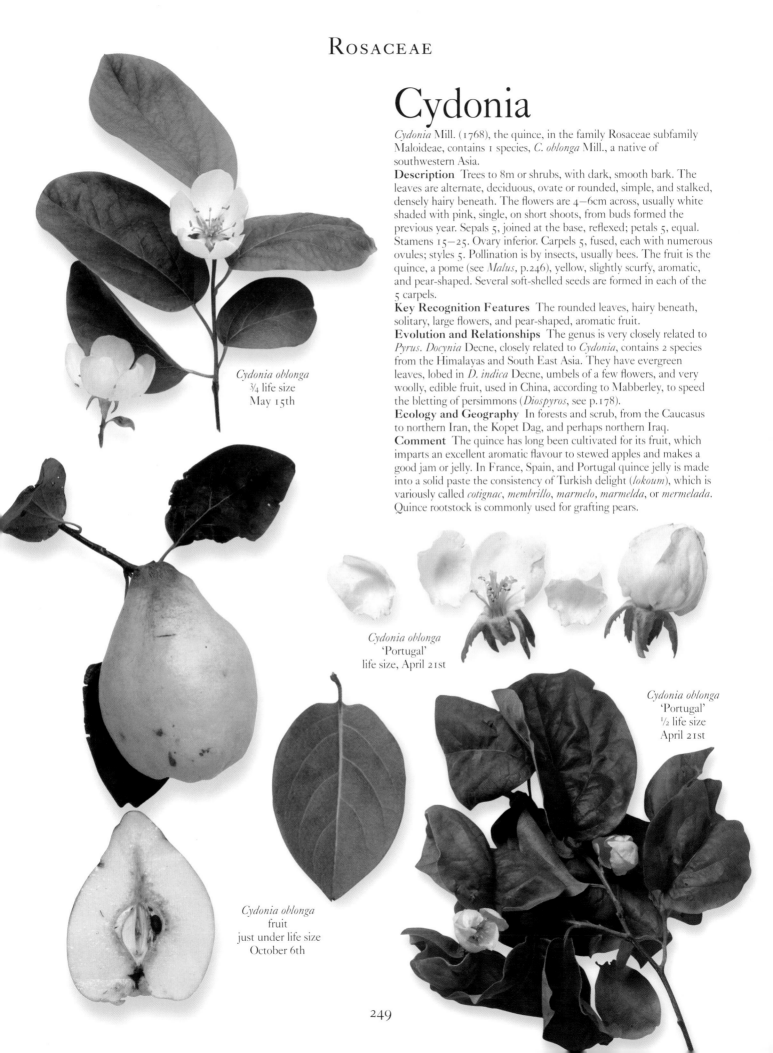

Cydonia oblonga
¾ life size
May 15th

Cydonia oblonga
'Portugal'
life size, April 21st

Cydonia oblonga
'Portugal'
½ life size
April 21st

Cydonia oblonga
fruit
just under life size
October 6th

249

Pseudocydonia

Pseudocydonia (C. Schneid.) C. Schneid (1906), in the family Rosaceae subfamily Maloideae, contains 1 species, *P. sinensis* Schneid, in China, often included in *Cydonia* (see p.249) or *Chaenomeles*.

Description Tree to 12m, or shrub, with peeling bark. The leaves are alternate, deciduous, ovate, usually simple, stalked, ciliate and finely toothed, with pointed tips; stipules glandular. The flowers are pink, borne singly from buds formed the previous year. Sepals 5, reflexed, joined at the base; petals 5, equal. Stamens many, the filaments in a ring, with yellow pollen. Ovary inferior. Carpels 5, fused, each with numerous ovules; styles 5. Pollination is by insects, usually bees. The fruit is a green pome (see *Malus*, p.246) similar to that of *Chaenomeles*. Several soft-shelled seeds are formed in each of the carpels.

Key Recognition Features The solitary pink flowers and ovoid, green fruit.

Evolution and Relationships This genus combines characteristics of *Cydonia* and *Chaenomeles*.

Ecology and Geography In rocky woods; perhaps native in Hubei, but cultivated elsewhere in China and in Japan.

Comment An attractive, hardy tree, seldom cultivated.

Pseudocydonia sinensis
1½ × life size, May 5th

Chaenomeles

Chaenomeles Lindl. (1821), the japonica or Japanese quince, in the family Rosaceae subfamily Maloideae, contains around 3 species in eastern Asia, formerly included in *Cydonia* (see p.249).

Description Trees to 15m, or shrubs, often with spines and with smooth bark. The leaves are alternate, deciduous, usually simple and stalked, with kidney-shaped stipules on strong shoots. The flowers are usually pale pink, red, or orange, in stalkless umbels, from buds formed the previous year. Sepals 5, joined at the base; petals 5, equal. Stamens many, with yellow pollen. Ovary inferior. Carpels 5, fused, each with numerous ovules; styles 5, joined at the base. Pollination is by insects, usually bees. The fruit is a pome (see *Malus*, p.246), apple-shaped, with a large, deep eye, yellowish to red, sometimes mottled and aromatic when ripe. Several soft-shelled seeds are formed in each of the carpels.

Key Recognition Features The usually hairless leaves and the stalkless umbels of flowers with rounded petals. The fruits are very hard and long-lasting, and may remain on the branch until the following spring.

Evolution and Relationships Closely related to *Pyrus* (see p.248) and *Cydonia*.

Ecology and Geography In rocky woods, by streams, and in grassy places in Japan and in China, where it is widely cultivated.

Comment The familiar japonica is one of the most popular of all spring-flowering shrubs. Confusingly, the name japonica became attached to the pink or crimson-flowered Chinese species *C. speciosa* (Sweet) Nakai, which has been grown in China since at least the 16th century. The true *C. japonica* (Thunb.) Lindl. is a straggling shrub with orange flowers and smaller fruit, less often cultivated.

Pseudocydonia sinensis
⅔ life size, May 5th

Chaenomeles japonica
sections of flowers
2 × life size
May 3rd

Chaenomeles japonica
²⁄₃ life size, May 3rd

Chaenomeles cathayensis
¾ life size, May 9th

Chaenomeles cathayensis
section of fruit with seeds
¾ life size, May 9th

Chaenomeles cathayensis
fruit, ¾ life size
May 9th

*Chaenomeles
speciosa*
life size
May 9th

Eriobotrya

Eriobotrya Lindl. (1821), in the family Rosaceae subfamily Maloideae, contains around 26 species in subtropical eastern Asia, including *E. japonica* (Thunb.) Lindl., the loquat.

Description Trees and shrubs to 10m, with thick branches. The leaves are large, alternate, evergreen, usually simple, with strong, parallel veins ending in teeth. The flowers are small and usually white, scented, in loose, pyramidal heads, produced in autumn and winter on the tips of the branches. Sepals 5, joined at the base, finely hairy; petals 5, equal. Stamens 20. Ovary inferior. Carpels 2–5, fused, each with 2 ovules; styles 2–5. Pollination is by insects. The fruit is a pear-shaped pome (see *Malus*, p.246). A few large, dark brown seeds are formed in each fruit.

Key Recognition Features The large, evergreen leaves and the loose heads of flowers, followed by orange fruit in spring.

Evolution and Relationships The fruit of *Eriobotrya* is similar to a large, orange haw; the seeds, however, are not woody, and it has many superficial similarities with the whitebeams (*Sorbus*, see pp.262–65). *Rhaphiolepis* is close in details of the fruit.

Ecology and Geography In woods. *Eriobotrya japonica* is native of southern China and the southern half of Japan, while the other species are found further south.

Comment The loquat is unusual among edible temperate fruits in that it flowers in autumn and winter, and the fruit ripens in late spring. Good specimens are sweet and juicy with an excellent sharp flavour.

Eriobotrya japonica
1/3 life size, May 25th

Eriobotrya japonica
fruit and seeds, 1/2 life size, May 15th

Rhaphiolepis umbellata
2 1/4 × life size, November 15th

Rhaphiolepis

Rhaphiolepis Lindl. (1821), in the family Rosaceae subfamily Maloideae, contains around 9 species in eastern Asia.

Description Shrubs to 2m, usually around 1m. The leaves are alternate, evergreen, leathery, usually simple, and short-stalked. The flowers are white or pink, few to many, in loose, pyramidal heads. Sepals 5, narrow, joined at the base; petals 5, obovate, equal, sometimes dark at the base. Stamens many. Ovary inferior. Carpels 2, fused, each with 2 ovules; styles 2, thickened near the apex. Pollination is by insects. The fruit is black and nearly round, a pome (see *Malus*, p.246), with 1 or 2 rather large seeds.

Key Recognition Features The tough, leathery leaves, usually narrowed into the stalk, and the pyramidal heads of small flowers.

Evolution and Relationships Closely related to *Amelanchier* (see p.254) in flower and fruit, but always evergreen.

Ecology and Geography On rocky seashores and in scrub, mainly in China and Japan.

Comment *Rhaphiolepis* are tough evergreens, widely planted in the warmer parts of North America and in the Mediterranean in places where a tough and drought-resistant, low shrub is needed. Many of the modern cultivars have bright pink or red flowers.

Rhaphiolepis × delacourii
'Coates' Crimson'
1 1/2 × life size, May 18th

Mespilus

Mespilus L. (1753), in the family Rosaceae subfamily Maloideae, contains 2 species in the northern hemisphere, including *M. germanica* L., the medlar.

Description Trees to 6m, and shrubs, sometimes with spines. The leaves are alternate, deciduous, usually simple, and stalked. The flowers are usually white, solitary, from buds formed the previous year. Sepals 5, joined at the base, longer than the petals; petals 5, equal. Stamens 20–30, with red anthers. Ovary inferior. Carpels 5, fused, each with 2 ovules; styles 5. Pollination is by insects, usually bees. The fruit is the medlar, a pome (see *Malus*, p.246), with 1 or 2 hard-shelled seeds forming in each of the carpels.

Key Recognition Features The large, solitary, white flowers and large, brownish fruit with a flat apex.

Evolution and Relationships A genus closely related to *Crataegus* (see pp.260–61), but with solitary flowers and large fruit.

Ecology and Geography In rocky mountain woods, *M. germanica* native from southeastern Europe to the Caucasus and often cultivated and escaping elsewhere, *M. canescens* Phipps found in Arkansas.

Comment Medlars are usually eaten "bletted", after they have been frosted or begun to rot, when they become sweeter; they are edible, but no more than that. Long cultivated in Europe; medlar seeds have been found in Roman deposits in Silchester.

Mespilus germanica
'Nottingham'
fruit, ⅔ life size
September 16th

Mespilus germanica
life size, May 15th

Mespilus germanica
½ life size, May 15th

Rhaphiolepis umbellata
flowers, fruits and seed
just over life size
November 15th

253

Amelanchier lamarckii
½ life size, autumn leaves
October 14th

Amelanchier lamarckii
just under life size
April 25th

Amelanchier lamarckii
fruit, ¾ life size
June 23rd

Amelanchier

Amelanchier Medik. (1789), the serviceberry or snowy mespilus, in the family Rosaceae subfamily Maloideae, contains 20–30 species in the northern hemisphere, particularly in North America.

Description Trees to 10m, and shrubs. The leaves are alternate, deciduous, usually ovate, simple, stalked, toothed, usually turning a good red in autumn. The flowers are white, in elongated clusters, from buds formed the previous year. Sepals 5, joined at the base; petals 5, equal, usually rather narrow. Stamens 10–20. Ovary inferior. Carpels 2–5, fused, each with 2 ovules; styles 2–5. Pollination is by insects. The fruit is small and black or red, a pome (see *Malus*, p.246). A few small, soft-shelled seeds are formed in each of the carpels.

Key Recognition Features The ovate or round, bluntly toothed leaves on a delicately branching shrub, and the white flowers with rather narrow petals.

Evolution and Relationships *Peraphyllum* Nutt. has 1 species, *P. ramosissimum* Nutt., the squaw-apple from western North America, and is closely related to *Amelanchier* but differs in having flowers in groups of up to 3, with 1 style, 2 carpels, and very bitter fruit. It is a low shrub with oblanceolate leaves and pink petals 7–8mm long.

Ecology and Geography On screes and rocky slopes, in dry and wet woods, and in swamps. There is 1 species in Europe and 2 in Turkey; most of the remaining 18 are found in North America, where there are many closely related species.

Comment These are very attractive trees for spring flowering, especially on wet soils. The fruit of many species are good to eat, but small. *Amelanchier lamarckii* F.G. Schroed. is naturalised in southern England and commonly grown in gardens.

Amelanchier lamarckii
½ life size, April 25th

Aronia melanocarpa
fruit, 2 × life size
September 15th

Aronia

Aronia Medik. (1789), the chokeberry, in the family Rosaceae subfamily Maloideae, contains around 3 species in North America.
Description Shrubs to 4m, without spines. The leaves are alternate, deciduous, usually simple, and short-stalked. The flowers are usually white, occasionally pink, in loose heads, from buds formed the previous year. Sepals 5, joined at the base; petals 5, equal. Stamens many, with purple pollen. Ovary inferior. Carpels 3–5, fused, each with numerous ovules; styles 3–5. Pollination is by insects, usually bees. The fruit is small, red or black, a pome (see *Malus*, p.246), with 1 or 2 soft-shelled seeds in each of the carpels.
Key Recognition Features The flowers with short, rounded petals and the red or black fruit in hanging bunches.
Evolution and Relationships *Aronia* is closely related to *Amelanchier*, but with smaller flowers. It is also sometimes included in *Photinia* (see p.259).
Ecology and Geography In swamps and wet woods from Newfoundland and Nova Scotia to Florida.
Comment Attractive shrubs for wet places, grown for their berries and their bright red and purplish autumn leaves.

Aronia melanocarpa
just under life size
May 11th

Aronia melanocarpa
⅓ life size, May 11th

Aronia arbutifolia
fruit and autumn leaves
⅔ life size, October 8th

255

Cotoneaster salicifolius
fruits, ¾ life size
November 22nd

Cotoneaster salicifolius
⅔ life size, June 15th

Cotoneaster melanocarpus
fruits, ⅔ life size
September 16th

Cotoneaster franchetii
fruits, ⅔ life size
September 16th

Cotoneaster × watereri
fruits, ⅔ life size
September 16th

Cotoneaster
horizontalis
flowers
1⅓ × life size
May 10th

Cotoneaster serotinus
life size, May 11th

Cotoneaster horizontalis
with fruits, ⅓ life size
September 12th

Cotoneaster

Cotoneaster Medik. (1789), in the family Rosaceae subfamily Maloideae, contains around 260 species in Europe and temperate Asia.

Description Shrubs to 5m, often creeping and ground-hugging, usually without spines. The leaves are alternate, evergreen or deciduous, usually simple, and sessile or only short-stalked. The flowers are reddish, pale pink, or white, solitary or in cymes or corymbs, from buds formed the previous year. Sepals 2–5, joined at the base; petals 5, equal. Stamens around 20. Ovary inferior. Carpels 2–5, fused, each with 2 ovules; styles 2–5. Pollination is by insects, usually by bees, but by queen wasps in *C. horizontalis* Decne and related species, which flower before the workers have emerged. The fruits are red or black pomes (see *Malus*, p.246). One hard-shelled seed, called a pyrene, is formed in each carpel.

Key Recognition Features The usually untoothed, small leaves, often solitary flowers, and stony-seeded fruit.

Evolution and Relationships The genus *Dichotomanthes* has 1 species, *D. tristaniicarpa* Kurz from southwestern China, and is closely related to *Cotoneaster*, but differs in having a fleshy calyx surrounding a dry fruit. Other genera with pyrenes are *Pyracantha* (see p.258) and *Crataegus* (see pp.260–61), both of which are often spiny and have toothed or lobed leaves. *Cotoneaster* divides into 2 groups according to the shape of the flower: in some species, of which *C. salicifolius* Franch. is an example, the petals are white and spreading, forming a relatively conspicuous flower; in other species, including *C. horizontalis*, the petals are upright and pink, and the flowers inconspicuous; it is these that are visited by wasps.

Ecology and Geography On cliffs and in dry, stony places and rocky woods; from western Europe (north Wales) to eastern Asia. Several Himalayan species have become naturalised in Europe.

Comment Many species are grown for their bright red fruits and their red autumn leaves. *Cotoneaster horizontalis*, with spreading, ferny branches, is often used for covering unsightly banks.

Cotoneaster salicifolius
¹/₂ life size
June 2nd

257

Pyracantha 'Orange Glow'
just under life size
May 15th

Pyracantha 'Mohave'
fruit, life size
October 25th

Pyracantha rogersiana 'Flava'
⅔ life size, October 30th

Pyracantha

Pyracantha M. Roem. (1847), in the family Rosaceae subfamily Maloideae, contains around 9 species in the northern hemisphere.

Description Spiny shrubs to 6m. The leaves are alternate, usually evergreen, shallowly toothed. The flowers are usually white, in umbel-like clusters from buds formed the previous year. Sepals 5, joined at the base; petals 5, rounded, equal. Stamens 20, with yellow pollen. Ovary inferior. Carpels 5, fused, each with 2 ovules; styles 5. Pollination is by insects, usually bees. The fruit is a small, shining, red, orange, or yellow pome (see *Malus*, pp.246–47) with 5 hard-shelled seeds (pyrenes) in each fruit.

Key Recognition Features The evergreen, shallow-toothed leaves, masses of small, white flowers, and fruits with hard-coated seeds.

Evolution and Relationships A genus closely related to *Crataegus* (see pp.260–61), but differing in its usually evergreen leaves and smaller fruits.

Ecology and Geography On rocky hillsides and in hedges, ranging from southern Europe, in Spain and France, eastwards to China.

Comment Pyracanthas are commonly grown for their spectacular show of berries, where the climate is suitable; in northwestern Europe, flowering and fruiting are often better when the shrubs are trained on a wall.

Photinia davidiana
²/₃ life size
December 15th

Photinia

Photinia Lindl. (1821), in the family Rosaceae subfamily Maloideae, contains around 60 species in the northern hemisphere, mainly in eastern Asia.

Description Trees to 15m, and shrubs. The leaves are alternate, deciduous or evergreen, leathery, usually simple, lanceolate, and short-stalked. The flowers are white, in wide, rounded heads, from buds formed the previous year. Sepals 5, joined at the base; petals 5, equal. Stamens many, with yellow pollen. Ovary usually inferior. Carpels 2–5, fused, each with 2 ovules; styles usually 2–4. Pollination is by insects, usually bees. The fruit is a small, red pome (see *Malus*, pp.246–47), with 1 or 2 soft-shelled seeds in each carpel.

Key Recognition Features The often evergreen, lanceolate leaves and large, rounded heads of small, white flowers.

Evolution and Relationships The genus *Photinia* now includes plants previously classified as *Heteromeles* M. Roem., especially *H. arbutifolia* (Lindl.) M. Roem., and *Stranvaesia* Lindl., especially *S. davidiana* Decne, as well as *Pourthiaea* Decne, of which the most familiar is the small tree, *P. villosa* (Thunb.) Decne; even *Aronia* (see p.255) is included in *Photinia* by some authorities; *Photinia*, in the wide sense, is also closely related to *Crataegus* (see pp.260–61), but that has hard-shelled seeds.

Ecology and Geography In woods and on hillsides. Most species are from China; *P. glabra* Maxim. and *P. serrulata* Lindl. are from Japan, and *P. arbutifolia* Lindl. is found on dry hills in California.

Comment Some species are grown for the red colour of their young leaves. 'Red Robin', a hybrid between *P. glabra* and *P. serrulata*, is often planted on chalky soils that are not tolerated by other spring-flowering and red-leaved shrubs such as *Pieris* (see p.202).

Photinia
'Robusta', showing
young red foliage
¹/₃ life size
April 18th

Photinia arbutifolia
¹/₂ life size, August 4th

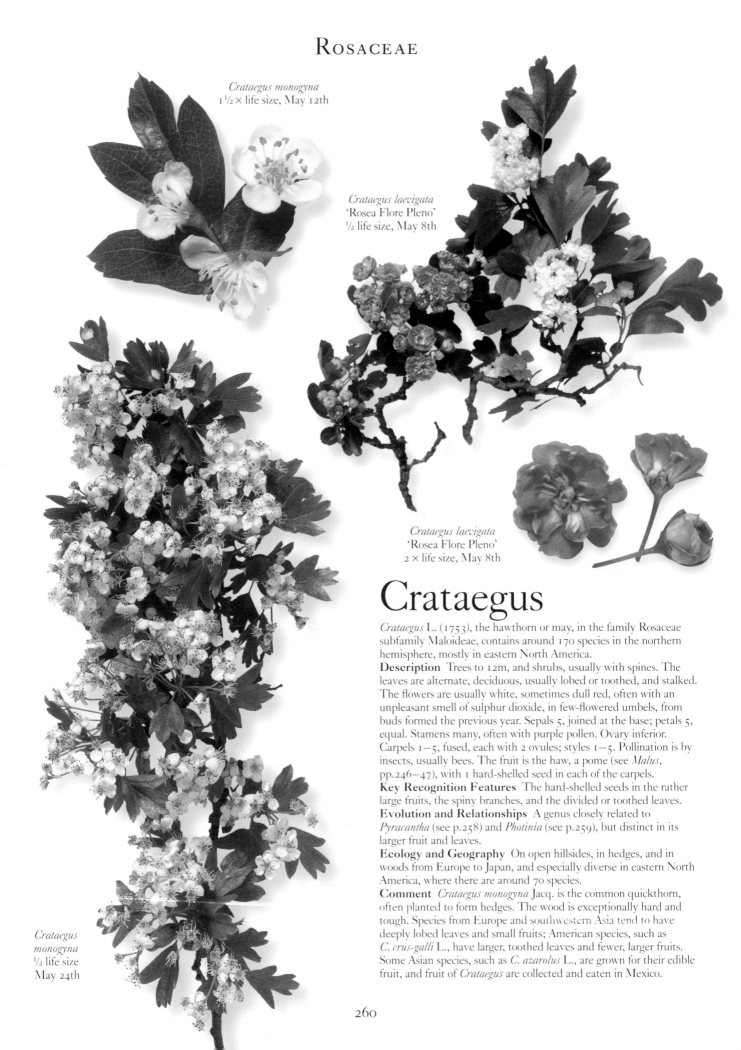

Crataegus monogyna
1¹⁄₂ × life size, May 12th

Crataegus laevigata
'Rosea Flore Pleno'
¹⁄₂ life size, May 8th

Crataegus laevigata
'Rosea Flore Pleno'
2 × life size, May 8th

Crataegus monogyna
¹⁄₂ life size
May 24th

Crataegus

Crataegus L. (1753), the hawthorn or may, in the family Rosaceae subfamily Maloideae, contains around 170 species in the northern hemisphere, mostly in eastern North America.

Description Trees to 12m, and shrubs, usually with spines. The leaves are alternate, deciduous, usually lobed or toothed, and stalked. The flowers are usually white, sometimes dull red, often with an unpleasant smell of sulphur dioxide, in few-flowered umbels, from buds formed the previous year. Sepals 5, joined at the base; petals 5, equal. Stamens many, often with purple pollen. Ovary inferior. Carpels 1–5, fused, each with 2 ovules; styles 1–5. Pollination is by insects, usually bees. The fruit is the haw, a pome (see *Malus*, pp.246–47), with 1 hard-shelled seed in each of the carpels.

Key Recognition Features The hard-shelled seeds in the rather large fruits, the spiny branches, and the divided or toothed leaves.

Evolution and Relationships A genus closely related to *Pyracantha* (see p.258) and *Photinia* (see p.259), but distinct in its larger fruit and leaves.

Ecology and Geography On open hillsides, in hedges, and in woods from Europe to Japan, and especially diverse in eastern North America, where there are around 70 species.

Comment *Crataegus monogyna* Jacq. is the common quickthorn, often planted to form hedges. The wood is exceptionally hard and tough. Species from Europe and southwestern Asia tend to have deeply lobed leaves and small fruits; American species, such as *C. crus-galli* L., have larger, toothed leaves and fewer, larger fruits. Some Asian species, such as *C. azarolus* L., are grown for their edible fruit, and fruit of *Crataegus* are collected and eaten in Mexico.

ROSACEAE

Crataegus crus-galli
fruit, 1 ½ × life size
September 23rd

Crataegus monogyna
fruit, ½ life size
September 15th

Crataegus monogyna
fruit and seed
2 × life size
September 15th

Crataegus atrocarpa
fruit and seeds
just under life size
October 8th

Crataegus orientalis
fruit, ⅔ life size
October 3rd

261

Sorbus gonggashanica
fruits, 2 × life size
September 16th

Sorbus × thuringiaca
fruits, 2 × life size
September 16th

Sorbus

Sorbus L. (1753), in the family Rosaceae subfamily Maloideae, contains around 200 species in the northern hemisphere.

Description Trees to 20m, and shrubs. The leaves are alternate, deciduous, pinnate, simple or variously lobed. The flowers are usually white, rarely pinkish or yellowish, in large numbers on flattish heads or corymbs, from buds formed the previous year. Sepals 5, joined at the base; petals 5, equal, rounded. Stamens 15−20, often with purple pollen. Ovary inferior or partly inferior. Carpels 2−5, fused, each with numerous ovules; styles 5, free or joined at the base. Pollination is by insects. The fruit is small, usually less than 15mm across, a round or rarely pear-shaped pome, (see *Malus*, pp.246−47) with 1 or 2 soft-shelled seeds in each of the carpels.

Key Recognition Features Pinnate or simple leaves together with white flowers in large, flattish heads and fruits with 2−10 soft seeds.

Evolution and Relationships Sorbus has formed hybrids with *Pyrus* (see pp.248−49), *Aronia* (see p.255), and *Cotoneaster* (see p.256−57), which have persisted in cultivation (see p.265). The genus has often been divided into sections. Section Sorbus, the mountain ashes, with pinnate leaves and small fruit, is the largest group, with many species throughout the northern hemisphere. Section Cormus contains 1 species, the service tree *S. domestica* L. from southern Europe and southwestern Asia, with pinnate leaves and edible, apple- or pear-shaped fruit, large for a *Sorbus*, around 3cm long. Section Aria, the whitebeams, with simple leaves, usually silvery beneath, and fruits with the calyx lobes persisting, is the second largest group in Europe and throughout temperate Asia. Section Torminalis, the wild service trees, with lobed leaves, has 2 species from Europe to Iran, including *S. torminalis* (L.) Crantz. Section Chamaemespilus contains 1 species, the dwarf whitebeam *S. chamaemespilus* (L.) Crantz, from the mountains of central Europe. Section Micromeles, with green, undivided leaves and small fruits, the calyx lobes soon falling off, has around 7 species in eastern Asia, including *S. meliosmifolia* Rehd.. Hybrids between the sections are common and may continue to breed true through becoming apomictic; the resulting hybrid species are often rare and restricted in the wild.

Ecology and Geography On rocky hills and mountains, often on limestone, and in woods; *S. americana* Marsh is unusual in growing in wet places. The range extends from western Europe to the Himalayas and Japan, and in North America southwards to Arizona.

Comment Many species are grown as ornamentals for their silver leaves, beautiful autumn colour, or large heads of fruit. A few species have fruit that is edible when overripe (such as *S. devoniensis* E.F. Warb.), or made into jelly (such as *S. aucuparia* L., the rowan.) Geoffrey Grigson records that the fruits of *S. torminalis* were used to settle the stomach, and made into a cider-like drink called "checkers" in Kent and Sussex, still a common name for pubs in that area.

The illustrations of Sorbus *continue on pp.264−265.*

Sorbus commixta
²⁄₃ life size, May 11th

Sorbus 'Kirsten Pink'
just over life size
August 4th

Rosaceae

Sorbus × thuringiaca
¾ life size
September 28th

Sorbus gonggashanica
¾ life size
September 28th

Sorbus 'Ethel's Gold'
¾ life size, September 28th

Sorbus hupehensis
var. *obtusa*
¾ life size
September 28th

Sorbus decora
¾ life size
September 28th

Sorbus americana
autumn leaves
⅔ life size, October 8th

ROSACEAE

Sorbus 'Wilfrid Fox'
1⅓ × life size
September 3rd

Sorbus aria
just over life size
September 28th

Sorbus aria 'Magnifica'
½ life size
May 11th

Sorbus aria 'Magnifica'
¾ life size, May 11th

Sorbus meliosmifolia
½ life size
May 15th

264

× *Sorbopyrus auricularis*
½ life size, May 5th

Sorbus megalocarpa
⅔ life size
April 2nd

× *Sorbaronia dippelii*
½ life size
May 5th

× *Pyronia veitchii luxemburgiana*
½ life size, May 5th

× *Pyronia veitchii luxemburgiana*
fruits, ⅔ life size, July 27th

INTERGENERIC HYBRIDS

Several hybrids have been made over the centuries between *Sorbus* (see pp.262–64) and other genera, and are grown in gardens as curiosities. The 2 largest sections of *Sorbus* have been crossed with *Aronia* (see p.255) to form the hybrid genus × *Sorbaronia*; × *Sorbaronia dippelii* (Zabel) Schneid. is a hybrid between *Sorbus aria* (L.) Crantz and *Aronia melanocarpa*; × *Sorbaronia hybrida* (Moench.) Schneid., a hybrid with *Sorbus aucuparia*, has leaves divided at the base. × *Sorbopyrus auricularis* (Kroup.) Schneid. is a hybrid between *Sorbus aria* and *Pyrus communis* (see pp.248–49) known since 1619; it has *Sorbus*-like leaves and edible, red, pear-shaped fruit around 3cm long. × *Sorbocotoneaster pozdnjakovii* Pojark is a most unusual hybrid between *Sorbus sibirica* Hedl. and *Cotoneaster melanocarpa* (see pp.256–57); it has variably cut leaves and red fruit. × *Pyronia veitchii* Guill., a hybrid of *Aronia* and *Pyrus*, is a shrub or small tree with white flowers and greenish-yellow fruit with red spots when ripe.

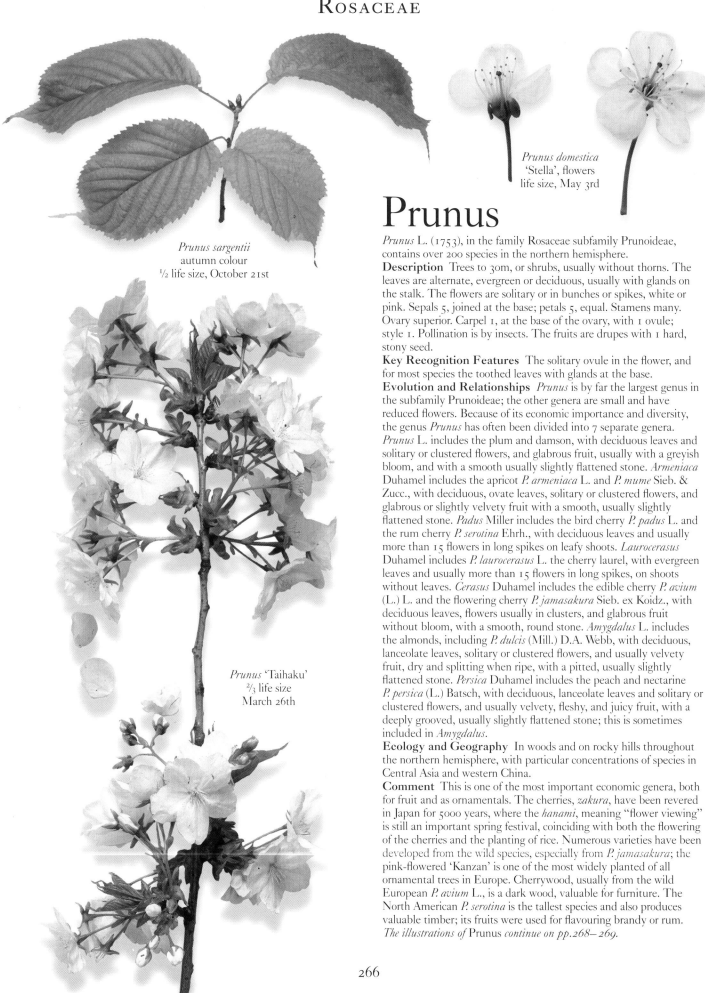

Prunus sargentii
autumn colour
½ life size, October 21st

Prunus domestica
'Stella', flowers
life size, May 3rd

Prunus

Prunus L. (1753), in the family Rosaceae subfamily Prunoideae, contains over 200 species in the northern hemisphere.

Description Trees to 30m, or shrubs, usually without thorns. The leaves are alternate, evergreen or deciduous, usually with glands on the stalk. The flowers are solitary or in bunches or spikes, white or pink. Sepals 5, joined at the base; petals 5, equal. Stamens many. Ovary superior. Carpel 1, at the base of the ovary, with 1 ovule; style 1. Pollination is by insects. The fruits are drupes with 1 hard, stony seed.

Key Recognition Features The solitary ovule in the flower, and for most species the toothed leaves with glands at the base.

Evolution and Relationships *Prunus* is by far the largest genus in the subfamily Prunoideae; the other genera are small and have reduced flowers. Because of its economic importance and diversity, the genus *Prunus* has often been divided into 7 separate genera. *Prunus* L. includes the plum and damson, with deciduous leaves and solitary or clustered flowers, and glabrous fruit, usually with a greyish bloom, and with a smooth usually slightly flattened stone. *Armeniaca* Duhamel includes the apricot *P. armeniaca* L. and *P. mume* Sieb. & Zucc., with deciduous, ovate leaves, solitary or clustered flowers, and glabrous or slightly velvety fruit with a smooth, usually slightly flattened stone. *Padus* Miller includes the bird cherry *P. padus* L. and the rum cherry *P. serotina* Ehrh., with deciduous leaves and usually more than 15 flowers in long spikes on leafy shoots. *Laurocerasus* Duhamel includes *P. laurocerasus* L. the cherry laurel, with evergreen leaves and usually more than 15 flowers in long spikes, on shoots without leaves. *Cerasus* Duhamel includes the edible cherry *P. avium* (L.) L. and the flowering cherry *P. jamasakura* Sieb. ex Koidz., with deciduous leaves, flowers usually in clusters, and glabrous fruit without bloom, with a smooth, round stone. *Amygdalus* L. includes the almonds, including *P. dulcis* (Mill.) D.A. Webb, with deciduous, lanceolate leaves, solitary or clustered flowers, and usually velvety fruit, dry and splitting when ripe, with a pitted, usually slightly flattened stone. *Persica* Duhamel includes the peach and nectarine *P. persica* (L.) Batsch, with deciduous, lanceolate leaves and solitary or clustered flowers, and usually velvety, fleshy, and juicy fruit, with a deeply grooved, usually slightly flattened stone; this is sometimes included in *Amygdalus*.

Ecology and Geography In woods and on rocky hills throughout the northern hemisphere, with particular concentrations of species in Central Asia and western China.

Comment This is one of the most important economic genera, both for fruit and as ornamentals. The cherries, *zakura*, have been revered in Japan for 5000 years, where the *hanami*, meaning "flower viewing" is still an important spring festival, coinciding with both the flowering of the cherries and the planting of rice. Numerous varieties have been developed from the wild species, especially from *P. jamasakura*; the pink-flowered 'Kanzan' is one of the most widely planted of all ornamental trees in Europe. Cherrywood, usually from the wild European *P. avium* L., is a dark wood, valuable for furniture. The North American *P. serotina* is the tallest species and also produces valuable timber; its fruits were used for flavouring brandy or rum.

The illustrations of Prunus *continue on pp.268–269.*

Prunus 'Taihaku'
⅔ life size
March 26th

ROSACEAE

Prunus campanulata
just over life size
March 18th

Prunus avium
¹/₂ life size
May 3rd

Prunus 'Okumiyako'
flowers, ¹/₂ life size
March 27th

Prunus avium cultivar
fruit, life size, June 28th

Prunus × *amygdalopersica*
½ life size
February 19th

Prunus persica
'Flat China'
½ life size
July 21st

Prunus persica
'Nectarella'
flower details
1 ½ × life size
March 18th

Prunus mume
1 ⅓ × life size
February 26th

Prunus dulcis
just under life size
September 16th

*Prunus
laurocerasus*
²/₃ life size
April 1st

*Prunus
laurocerasus*
fruits, just over
life size
August 15th

Prunus insititia
flower details
1¼ × life size, April 7th

Prunus padus 'Watereri'
½ life size
April 29th

plum stone (above) and peach stone
(below), just over life size, July 20th

Prunus spinosa
½ life size
April 7th

Prunus insititia
½ life size, April 7th

Oemleria

Oemleria Reichenb. (1841), the oso berry, in the family Rosaceae subfamily Prunoideae, contains 1 species, *O. cerasiformis* (Hook. & Arn.) Landon in western North America. It is often called *Osmaronia* E. Greene, or *Nuttallia* Torr. & Gray.

Description Small trees to 5m, or suckering shrubs, without thorns. The leaves are alternate, deciduous, and oblong or oblanceolate. The flowers are small, white, in hanging spikes, sometimes bisexual, but usually with males and females on different plants, produced in early spring, and almond-scented. Sepals 5, joined at the base; petals 5, equal. Male flowers with 15 stamens in 3 series, and with obovate petals 5–6mm long; female flowers with superior ovary, shorter, narrower petals, abortive stamens, and 5 carpels each with 1 ovule and style. Pollination is by insects. The fruits are 1–5 drupes, usually only 2 developing, black, glaucous, and bitter, with hard stones.

Key Recognition Features The narrow leaves and hanging spikes of small, white flowers.

Evolution and Relationships An isolated genus, close to *Prunus*, (see pp.266–69), but differing in having 5 carpels, and 1 or 2 fruits from a single flower.

Ecology and Geography In chaparral and open places in the forest in California, from Santa Barbara County northwards to British Columbia in the Coast Ranges and the northwestern Sierra Nevada.

Comment In cultivation a modest shrub, grown for its very early flowering and almond scent.

Oemleria cerasiformis
⅓ life size
June 21st

Maddenia hypoleuca
flowers
2 × life size
March 19th

Oemleria cerasiformis
male flowers, 1⅔ × life size
February 6th

Oemleria cerasiformis
male flowers, ¾ life size
February 6th

Maddenia

Maddenia Hook. fil. & Thomson (1854), in the family Rosaceae subfamily Prunoideae, contains 4 or 5 species in eastern Asia.

Description Shrubs to 6m. The leaves are alternate, deciduous, toothed, and strongly parallel-veined, whitish or hairy beneath. The flowers are small, in short spikes, produced in early spring before the leaves, the males and females usually on separate plants. Sepals 10, unequal, in 2 series; petals very small or absent. Stamens many. Ovary superior. Carpel 1, with 1 ovule; style 1. Pollination is presumed to be by insects. The fruits are solitary, black drupes around 9mm long, with 1 large stone.

Key Recognition Features The small flowers without petals produced before the strongly veined and toothed leaves.

Evolution and Relationships *Maddenia* is close to *Prunus* (see pp.266–69), but differs in having 10 sepals and no petals.

Ecology and Geography In mountain scrub in the Himalayas and western China.

Comment Sometimes grown as a curiosity in collections. The genus is named after Colonel Edward Madden, (1805–56), of the Bengal Artillery, who sent seed collected in the high Himalayas between 1841 and 1849 to the botanical garden at Glasnevin in Dublin, Ireland; from them several now-familar plants, including *Cardiocrinum giganteum* (see Volume 2) were introduced to cultivation.

Prinsepia

Prinsepia Royle (1834), in the family Rosaceae subfamily Prunoideae, contains around 4 species in the Himalayas and eastern Asia.

Description Shrubs to 3m, with long, arching stems, the spiny twigs with the pith not continuous but reduced to thin segments. The leaves are alternate, deciduous, and lanceolate or linear. The flowers are solitary or in elongated bunches, white or yellow, produced in late autumn, winter, or early spring, before or with the leaves. Sepals 5, unequal, joined at the base to form a cup; petals 5, equal. Stamens 10 or more. Ovary superior. Carpel 1, with 1 ovule; style 1. Pollination is by insects. The fruits are red or purplish-black, sometimes elongated drupes with 1 stone.

Key Recognition Features The long, green, spiny shoots, with a slender spine at each joint, and the narrow leaves.

Evolution and Relationships Related to *Prunus*, but differing in the spines and interrupted pith.

Ecology and Geography In hedges and on bare hills, from the Himalayas in Pakistan to northeastern China and Taiwan.

Comment In the Himalayas oil is made from the crushed seeds of *P. utilis* Royle. The genus is named after James Prinsep (1800–40), secretary of the Asiatic Society of Bengal, and a friend of Royle.

Prinsepia utilis
½ life size
March 1st

Prinsepia utilis
fruits, 2 × life size
May 5th

Maddenia hypoleuca
flowers and young
leaves, ⅔ life size
March 19th

Prinsepia utilis
flower details
2 × life size, March 1st

Prinsepia uniflora
½ life size
April 25th

Caesalpinia

Caesalpinia L. (1753), in the family Leguminosae subfamily Caesalpinioideae, contains around 150 species in the tropics of America, Asia, and Africa, with a few species extending into temperate areas.

Description Trees to 10m, or more in tropical species, shrubs, or climbers, often with thorns. The leaves are alternate, evergreen or deciduous, usually 2-pinnate. The flowers are in elongated bunches, usually yellow. Sepals 5, unequal, joined at the base to form a tubular calyx; petals 5, more or less equal, the upper often the smallest. Stamens 10, often much longer than the petals, the filaments often hairy at the base. Ovary superior, with 1 carpel containing several ovules; style 1, very short. Pollination is by bees and butterflies, and by hummingbirds in *C. gilliesii* (Hook.) D. Dietr. and *C. pulcherrima* (L.) Sw., which have very long stamens. The fruits are flattened, often woody or prickly legumes with 1 or more seeds.

Key Recognition Features The ferny, 2-pinnate leaves and the flowers with almost equal petals, the lowest sepal partially or completely enclosing the others.

Evolution and Relationships Around 180 genera belong to the subfamily Caesalpinioideae, including the commonly planted tropical trees *Delonix regia* (Bojer) Raf., which has bright red flowers and is called the flamboyant, and *Bauhinia* L., with white or pink, orchid-like flowers and characteristic leaves that have 1 leaflet with 2 rounded lobes. The Caesalpinioideae has the least specialised flowers of the 3 subfamilies of Leguminosae, and DNA studies suggest that some genera included in it are more closely related to the other traditional subfamilies than they are to each other.

Ecology and Geography In open woods and scrub and on rocky hillsides in South America and South East Asia. The almost hardy climber *C. decapetala* (Roth) Alston var. *japonica* (Sieb. & Zucc.) Isley is found in China and Japan.

Comment A diverse genus, with many species planted throughout the tropics.

Caesalpinia gillesii
²/₃ life size
July 28th

Senna

Senna Mill. (1768), in the family Leguminosae subfamily Caesalpinioideae, contains around 350 species in tropical Asia, Australia, Africa, and tropical and temperate America. Many of its species are often included in *Cassia* L..

Description Trees to 40m, but usually small trees or shrubs, rarely herbaceous. The leaves are alternate, evergreen or deciduous, pinnate, with up to 14 pairs of leaflets without a terminal leaflet. The flowers are usually in elongated bunches, or large, branching heads, usually yellow. Sepals 5, unequal, separate nearly to the base; petals 5, the lowest sometimes the smallest. Stamens 10, the upper 3 usually small and sterile; 2 or 3 of the remaining 7 are usually longer than the others. Ovary superior, with 1 carpel containing many ovules; style 1. Pollination is by bees. The fruits are legumes, often woody, with divisions between the seeds.

Key Recognition Features The pinnate leaves without a terminal leaflet and the rather cup-shaped, yellow flowers are typical.

Evolution and Relationships *Senna* and *Cassia* may be told apart by their stamens; in *Senna* the 2 or 3 lower stamens are often longer than the others, but not more than twice as long, and the anthers are hairless. In *Cassia* in the strict sense the 3 lower stamens have long curved filaments and are much more than twice as long as the short, hairy anthers. *Cassia* contains around 30 tropical trees from Asia and Africa, including the lovely *C. fistula* L., the Indian laburnum or golden shower, with long, hanging spikes of flowers, which is commonly planted in the tropics. A third genus, *Chamaecrista* Moench., which includes the prairie senna, *C. fasciculata* (Mich.) E. Greene, has also been included in *Cassia*; it has straight anthers and distinct bracteoles.

Ecology and Geography In deserts, scrub, and forests throughout the tropics and into temperate parts of Australia and North and South America.

Comment Many members of the genus are often planted in gardens. Senna leaves, valued as a laxative in Europe since medieval times, and earlier among the Arabs, from whom the name senna originated, come from various tropical species. *Senna alata* (L.) Roxb. has been used for skin diseases, especially ringworm. Other species, such as *S. septentrionalis* (Viv.) Irwin & Barnaby, also often listed as *S. septemtrionalis*, are grown for ornament.

Senna septentrionalis
½ life size
July 28th

Senna septentrionalis
unripe (green) and ripe (brown) pods
¾ life size, July 28th

Senna septentrionalis
showing two stamens
longer than the rest,
and the curving green
ovary and style
¾ life size, July 28th

Cercis siliquastrum
2 × life size, May 11th

Cercis siliquastrum 'Alba'
¾ life size, May 9th

Cercis siliquastrum
⅔ life size, May 11th

Cercis siliquastrum
pods and seeds
⅔ life size, December 15th

Cercis

Cercis L. (1753), the Judas tree or redbud, in the family Leguminosae subfamily Caesalpinioideae, contains around 6 species in the northern hemisphere.

Description Trees to 10m, or shrubs. The leaves are alternate, deciduous, simple, and almost round or heart-shaped. The flowers are in umbel-like clusters or elongated bunches, usually purplish-pink, rarely white, somewhat pea-shaped. Sepals 5, unequal, joined at the base to form a wide, cup-shaped, blunt-toothed calyx; petals 5, the upper 3 curved back, the lower 2 larger, protecting the stamens and ovary. Stamens 10, not joined at the base. Ovary superior, with 1 carpel containing several ovules; style 1. Pollination is by bees. The fruits are legumes, reddish when ripe, with numerous seeds, often remaining on the tree after the leaves have fallen.

Key Recognition Features The pea-like, purplish-pink flowers, often produced directly on the trunk and branches, and the simple, rounded leaves. In the Chinese *C. racemosa* Oliver the flowers are in hanging bunches.

Evolution and Relationships A rather isolated genus, one of the few mainly hardy members of the subfamily, and showing the transition from regular flowers to pea-like flowers. The distribution is that of a relict from Tertiary times, with 1 formerly widespread species surviving in widely separated areas.

Ecology and Geography In woods and on dry hills. North America has *C. canadensis* L., the redbud, with 2 varieties in the east, and another species from Utah to California. There is 1 species in the Mediterranean area, another very similar in the western Himalayas, and 2 species (of which *C. racemosa* is the most distinctive) in China.

Comment Very attractive trees for their early flowering, usually before the leaves unfurl. *Cercis canadensis* 'Forest Pansy' has wonderful, deep purple leaves. The red buds emerging on the trunk have inspired the name Judas tree, suggesting that the tree bled when Judas hanged himself from it.

Ceratonia

Ceratonia L. (1753), in the family Leguminosae subfamily Caesalpinioideae, contains 2 species, including *C. siliqua* L., the carob.

Description Trees to 10m, often wide-spreading. The leaves are alternate, evergreen, pinnate, with around 4 pairs of almost-round leaflets. The flowers are small, greenish, in elongated, catkin-like bunches, often unisexual, males and females sometimes on different trees, rarely together on the same tree or in the same bunch. Sepals 5, soon falling; petals absent. Stamens 5, with the filaments separate. Ovary superior, with 1 carpel containing several ovules; style 1. Pollination is presumed to be by bees. The fruits are legumes, leathery and dark brown when ripe, to 20cm long, with numerous oval seeds.

Key Recognition Features The pinnate, leathery leaves and the catkin-like flower spikes produced in autumn. The beans have a characteristic sweet, sickly, chocolate-like flavour.

Evolution and Relationships Related to tropical genera from eastern Asia, and to *Gleditsia* (see p.276), with bunches of small flowers often growing directly on the trunk.

Ecology and Geography On dry, rocky hills; now found commonly in the Mediterranean region, but it may be an ancient cultivated plant from further south, possibly Oman. A second species is found in the Arabian Peninsula and Somalia.

Comment The carob is said to be the locust eaten by John the Baptist, and the husks eaten by the prodigal son. Nowadays carob pods are used as a substitute for chocolate and are common in animal feed. Carob is also said to be the the origin of the carat of jewellers, from the use of the beans for weighing. They weigh 189–205mg, closely approximating to the official carat weight of 200mg.

Ceratonia siliqua
flower buds, 2 × life size
October 12th

Cercis canadensis
'Forest Pansy'
autumn leaves
½ life size
November 4th

Ceratonia siliqua
just under life size
October 12th

Gleditsia triacanthos
pod, ⅔ life size
October 2nd

Gleditsia triacanthos 'Sunburst'
flowers, 1⅓ × life size
June 3rd

Gleditsia triacanthos
'Sunburst'
½ life size, June 3rd

Gleditsia sinensis
thorns, ⅓ life size
June 22nd

Gleditsia

Gleditsia L. (1753), the honey locust, in the family Leguminosae
subfamily Caesalpinioideae, contains around 14 species mostly in
central and eastern Asia and North America.

Description Trees to 30m, or shrubs, often with spines. The leaves
are alternate, deciduous, pinnate or 2-pinnate, with numerous pairs of
leaflets and no terminal leaflet. The flowers are small, greenish or
reddish, in elongated, catkin-like or branching bunches, often bisexual
or unisexual on the same tree or in the same bunch. Sepals 3–5, small;
petals 3–5, similar to the sepals. Stamens 6–10, with the filaments
separate. Ovary superior, with 1 carpel containing 1 to several ovules;
style 1, short. Pollination is presumed to be by bees. The fruits are
legumes, often twisted, to 20cm long, with 1 to many flattened seeds.

Key Recognition Features The pinnate and sometimes 2-pinnate
leaves, small flowers, and usually spiny branches; groups of spines,
often branched, grow directly from the trunk.

Evolution and Relationships Related to *Gymnocladus*, with its
very small flowers, and to other tropical genera. It is a relict tree of the
Tertiary forests.

Ecology and Geography In forests by the Caspian, in China,
Japan, eastern North America, and with 1 species in northeastern
Argentina, very similar to a Chinese species.

Comment *G. triacanthos* L. from eastern North America is often
cultivated, especially in the 2 recent cultivars, 'Sunburst' from
around 1954 with golden leaves, and 'Rubylace' from around 1961
with purplish young leaves.

Gymnocladus

Gymnocladus Lam. (1783), in the family Leguminosae subfamily Caesalpinioideae, contains 4 species in China and eastern North America.

Description Trees to 25m, without spines, with thick twigs. The leaves are alternate, deciduous, 2-pinnate, and very large, to 80cm long, with numerous leaflets. The flowers are in branching bunches, unisexual, with males and females on the same tree, white or lilac. Sepals 5, joined at the base to form a tubular, 5-toothed calyx; petals 5, sometimes 4, slightly wider than the sepals, hairy. Stamens 10, in 2 whorls. Ovary superior, with 1 carpel containing several ovules; style 1. Pollination is presumed to be by bees. The fruits are thick and leathery, wide, curved pods, with rather few seeds.

Key Recognition Features The huge, 2-pinnate leaves on thick twigs. The trees seldom flower in the cool summers of northern Europe.

Evolution and Relationships Related to *Gleditsia* and with other tropical relatives. The pod structure is especially primitive.

Ecology and Geography In rich woods; 1 species, *G. dioica* (L.) Koch, the Kentucky coffee-tree, in eastern North America from southern Ontario southwards to Tennessee; 3 species in China.

Comment *Gymnocladus dioica* was used as a substitute for coffee. The light, reddish-brown wood was called Kentucky mahogany.

Gymnocladus dioica
mature leaves, ½ life size
August 4th

Gymnocladus dioica
young leaves
½ life size
August 4th

Acacia

Acacia Willd. (1805), in the family Leguminosae subfamily Mimosoideae, contains around 1200 species mainly in the tropics and subtropics in Australia and Africa.

Description Trees to 3m, or shrubs, often with spiny twigs. The leaves are alternate, evergreen or deciduous, pinnate, or reduced to variously shaped phyllodes. The flowers are small, in spherical or elongated bunches, spikes, or few-flowered heads on a long axis, fluffy with long stamens. Sepals 4 or 5, joined at the base to form a cup; petals 4 or 5, very small, equal. Stamens numerous, not joined at the base, longer than the petals. Ovary superior, with 1 carpel containing several ovules; style 1. Pollination is by insects. The fruits are legumes, often interestingly contorted, with several seeds.

Key Recognition Features The fluffy flowerheads are typical of *Acacia* and all members of the subfamily Mimosoideae.

Evolution and Relationships The pod or legume is typical of all the family Leguminosae, which is often considered to be related to, and more advanced than, the Rosaceae (see pp.228–71), and parallel to the Myrtaceae (see pp.313–21) and related families. Both Myrtaceae and Leguminosae are particularly diverse in Australia.

Ecology and Geography *Acacia* species are most common in seasonally dry areas, particularly in Australia and tropical Africa. The temperate species from the colder parts of Australia and Tasmania are commonly planted in Europe, California, South Africa, and other mild climates. Without their natural insect predators, they have often become serious pests in these areas.

Comment Many species of *Acacia* are grown as ornamentals, especially *A. dealbata* Link, which is grown in France and sold by florists as mimosa. *Acacia farnesiana* (L.) Willd. from Dominica is grown in Europe for its scent. Many species, and especially *A. saligna* (Labill.) H.L. Wendl., are valuable for stabilising sandy soils in dry areas. The most cold-tolerant species are probably *A. pravissima* F. Muell. from New South Wales and Victoria, and the hardier forms of *A. dealbata* from New South Wales, Victoria, and Tasmania.

Acacia dealbata
½ life size,
February 14th

Acacia dealbata
flowers, 1¼ × life size
February 14th

LEGUMINOSAE

Acacia longifolia
½ life size
February 14th

Acacia verticillata
just under life size
March 15th

Acacia longifolia
showing different
leaf form, ¾ life size
February 10th

Acacia longifolia
pods and seeds
2 × life size
December 4th

Acacia Exeter hybrid
⅔ life size
March 15th

Acacia pravissima
⅓ life size, March 25th

Albizia

Albizia Durazz. (1772), in the family Leguminosae subfamily Mimosoideae, contains 100—150 species in Asia, Australia, Africa, and the Americas.

Description Trees to 40m, or shrubs, without spines. The leaves are alternate, evergreen or deciduous, 2-pinnate, with small leaflets. The flowers are in umbel-like or elongated bunches or in spikes, fluffy with very long stamens, sometimes with 1 or 2 flowers in each head larger than the rest. Sepals 5, joined at the base to form a toothed cup; petals 5, joined to make a bell-shaped corolla. Stamens 19—50, joined at the base to form a tube, longer than the petals. Ovary superior, with 1 carpel containing several ovules; style thread-like, with a minute stigma. Pollination is by insects. The fruits are legumes, thin and papery or leathery when ripe, with flattened seeds.

Key Recognition Features The fluffy flowerheads are typical of the subfamily Mimosoideae. The stamens fused at the base and the large, ferny leaves are typical of *Albizia*.

Evolution and Relationships Close to *Acacia* (see pp.278—79) but much less diverse, and even closer to *Calliandra* Benth., in which the flowers in the head are all equal and the pods split from the base.

Ecology and Geography In rainforest and open woods, mainly in the tropics and subtropics.

Comment The name commemorates Fillipo degli Albizzi, an Italian naturalist. The most commonly cultivated temperate species is *A. julibrissin* (Willd.) Durazz., native of Asia eastwards from Iran, and of Ethiopia. It forms a flat-topped tree with pink flowers, and is hardy once it is woody. *Albizia lophantha* (Willd.) Benth. from Western Australia is now put in the genus *Paraserianthes* L. Murray; it has long spikes of creamy-white flowers, produced within a year from seed. It survives a few degrees of frost.

Calliandra calothyrsus
buds and flowers
just under life size
June 26th

Albizia julibrissin
flowering branch
1¼ × life size, July 29th

Cladrastis

Cladrastis Raf. (1825), the yellow-wood, in the family Leguminosae subfamily Papilionoideae, contains around 6 species in the northern hemisphere.

Description Trees to 25m, or shrubs, without spines. The leaves are alternate, deciduous, pinnate, with 7–13 alternate leaflets and a terminal leaflet; the swollen base of the leaf stalk encloses the leaf bud. The flowers are pea-like, in elongated, upright or hanging, branched bunches, white or pinkish, sometimes marked with yellow. Sepals 5, equal, joined at the base to form a bell-shaped calyx; petals 5, unequal, the uppermost a standard, the 2 outer wings, the 2 lowest forming a keel that encloses the stamens, style, and ovary. Stamens 10, their filaments almost separate. Ovary superior, with 1 carpel containing several ovules; style 1. Pollination is by bees. The pods are flattened and sometimes winged, often constricted between the seeds.

Key Recognition Features Trees with alternate leaflets, the swollen base of the leaf stalk enclosing the leaf bud, and the *Wisteria*-like flowers (see pp.284–85) in pyramidal heads.

Evolution and Relationships The pea-flowered subfamily of the Leguminosae, called the Papilionoideae, are very easy to recognise. Their fossil flowers first appear in the late Paleocene, together with more primitive, *Mimosa*-like flowers. *Cladrastis* itself is related to *Sophora* (see p.283).

Ecology and Geography In open woods: 1 species, the Kentucky yellow-wood *C. kentukea* (Dumont de Courset) Rudd, commonly called *C. lutea* (Michx.) Koch, in eastern North America; 2 species, including *C. platycarpa* (Maxim.) Mak. in Japan; the remainder, including *C. sinensis* Hemsl., in China.

Comment The hard wood was used for gunstocks, and a dye was extracted from the heartwood of *C. kentukea*. Species are sometimes planted as ornamentals and form rather open, upright trees.

Albizia julibrissin
young pods, ¾ life size
October 22nd

Cladrastis kentukea
½ life size, July 28th

Albizia julibrissin
pods and seeds, life size
October 22nd

Maakia chinensis
½ life size, July 28th

Sophora microphylla
pods, ½ life size
April 1st

Maakia amurensis var. *buergeri*
young leaves, life size
May 17th

Maakia amurensis var. *buergeri*
pods and seeds, 1¾ × life size
December 15th

Maakia

Maakia Rupr. & Maxim. (1856), in the family Leguminosae subfamily Papilionoideae, contains around 6 species in eastern Asia.

Description Trees to 20m, but usually shrubs in cultivation, often with peeling bark. The leaves are alternate, deciduous, pinnate, with 5–17 opposite leaflets and a terminal leaflet, the leaf stalk not covering the bud. The flowers are small, pea-like, in upright spikes, whitish. Sepals 5, unequal, joined at the base to form a tubular calyx; petals 5, unequal, the uppermost a standard, the 2 outer wings, the 2 lowest forming a keel that encloses the stamens, style, and ovary. Stamens 10, their filaments joined only at the base. Ovary superior, with 1 carpel containing 1–5 ovules; style 1. Pollination is presumed to be by bees. The pods are flattened, rather narrow, with few seeds.

Key Recognition Features The numerous opposite leaflets and the groups of upright spikes of small flowers.

Evolution and Relationships Related to *Castanospermum* A. Cunn. ex Mudie, the Moreton Bay chestnut, which is sometimes planted as a street tree in Australia.

Ecology and Geography In open woods and scrub. *Maakia amurensis* Rupr. is found from eastern Siberia to Taiwan, the other species in China.

Comment The genus is named after Richard Maak, (1825–86), a Russian naturalist. The widespread *M. amurensis* from northeastern Asia is sometimes grown in collections; var. *buergeri* (Max.) Schneid. has leaves that are very silky when young, and longer flower spikes.

Sophora microphylla
pod and seeds
1¼ × life size
April 1st

Sophora japonica
½ life size
September 16th

Sophora microphylla
⅔ life size, April 1st

Sophora japonica, stamens and style,
keel petals, and flowers, 1½ × life size,
September 16th

Sophora

Sophora L. (1753), in the family Leguminosae subfamily Papilionoideae, contains around 50 species in both the northern and southern hemispheres.

Description Trees to 30m, or shrubs. The leaves are alternate, evergreen or deciduous, pinnate, with 5–43 usually opposite leaflets and a terminal leaflet. The flowers are pea-like, in elongated bunches or branched heads, white, blue, or yellow. Sepals 5, unequal, joined to form a tubular, toothed calyx; petals 5, unequal, the uppermost a broad, reflexed standard, the 2 outer wings, the 2 lowest forming a keel that encloses the stamens, style, and ovary. Stamens 10, their filaments joined only at the base. Ovary superior, with 1 carpel containing several ovules; style 1. Pollination is by bees. The pods are constricted between the seeds, often breaking into 1-seeded segments.

Key Recognition Features The pods with strong constrictions between the seeds are typical of *Sophora*; the genus is very diverse in other characteristics.

Evolution and Relationships Seed pods constricted between the seeds are particularly well-developed in *Sophora* and typical of the tribe Sophoreae, which includes *Cladrastris* (see p.281).

Ecology and Geography In woods and scrub; a group of very similar species, with mostly evergreen leaves and large, yellow flowers, is found in New Zealand and Chile; other species with white or blue flowers are found in China and southern North America. Herbaceous species are common in eastern Europe and Central Asia.

Comment *Sophora japonica* L., native of China and Korea but not Japan, is commonly planted near shrines or in the courtyards of *madressahs*, the Muslim colleges, in Central Asia. *Sophora davidii* Franch. from western China is an attractive, hardy, low shrub with blue flowers. The herbaceous *S. alopecuroides* L. is common in Turkey and Central Asia, in disturbed areas where grazing is heavy; it is very poisonous to stock. *Sophora secundiflora* (Ortega) DC, from southwestern North America, was formerly used as a hallucinogen. Kowhai, *S. tetraptera* Miller, is a tree with evergreen leaves and large, golden-yellow flowers; 'Gnome' is a low-growing cultivar of it.

Wisteria floribunda 'Alba'
¾ life size, 15th May

Wisteria sinensis
buds, life size
March 2nd

Wisteria floribunda, pods and seeds
⅔ life size, December 15th

Wisteria

Wisteria Nutt. (1818), in the family Leguminosae subfamily Papilionoideae, contains around 6 species in eastern Asia and North America.

Description A climber on trees or cliffs to over 40m, or kept as a shrub by pruning. The leaves are alternate, deciduous, pinnate, with 3–19 opposite leaflets and a terminal leaflet. The flowers are pea-like, scented, in long, hanging bunches, white or blue, rarely pinkish. Sepals 5, unequal, joined to form a tubular, toothed calyx; petals 5, unequal, the uppermost a broad standard, the 2 outer wings, the 2 lowest forming a keel that encloses the stamens, style, and ovary. Stamens 10, of which 9 have their filaments joined and the last is free. Ovary superior, with 1 carpel containing few to several ovules; style 1. Pollination is by bees. The fruits are large, usually velvety pods, with rather few seeds.

Key Recognition Features The pinnate leaves and large pea-flowers in hanging bunches.

Evolution and Relationships Related to a diverse group of genera including the shrubby *Tephrosia* Pers. and *Derris* Lour., used to produce an insecticide and the fish-poison rotenone. The spectacular tropical climbers *Mucuna* Adans. and *Strongylodon* Vogel are more closely related to the familiar climbing beans.

Ecology and Geography Climbing into trees in forests. Two species from southeastern North America, including *W. frutescens* (L.) Poir. with short bunches of large flowers, are found as far north as New York. The remainder are native in China and Japan, and long cultivated in both countries.

Comment *Wisteria*, in Japanese *fuji*, is one of the most popular of all woody climbers, grown by the Japanese at least since the 8th century. *Wisteria sinensis* (Sims) Sweet is now particularly common in warmer parts of North America and Europe, where it was introduced from China in 1816. The longest flower spikes are found in *W. floribunda* (Willd.) DC 'Shiro-kapitan' or 'Multijuga' syn. 'Macrobotrys', and have reached 2m in specimens in Japan. It is interesting to note that *W. floribunda* climbs clockwise while *W. sinensis* climbs anticlockwise. The genus is named after Caspar Wistar (1761–1818), professor of anatomy at the University of Pennsylvania. It was first included in *Glycine* Willd; this name has survived in the French *glycine*.

Wisteria floribunda 'Rosea'
¾ life size, June 10th

Wisteria floribunda
stems, ¾ life size
December 4th

Wisteria sinensis
flower details
1½ × life size, May 3rd

Wisteria sinensis
⅔ life size
May 3rd

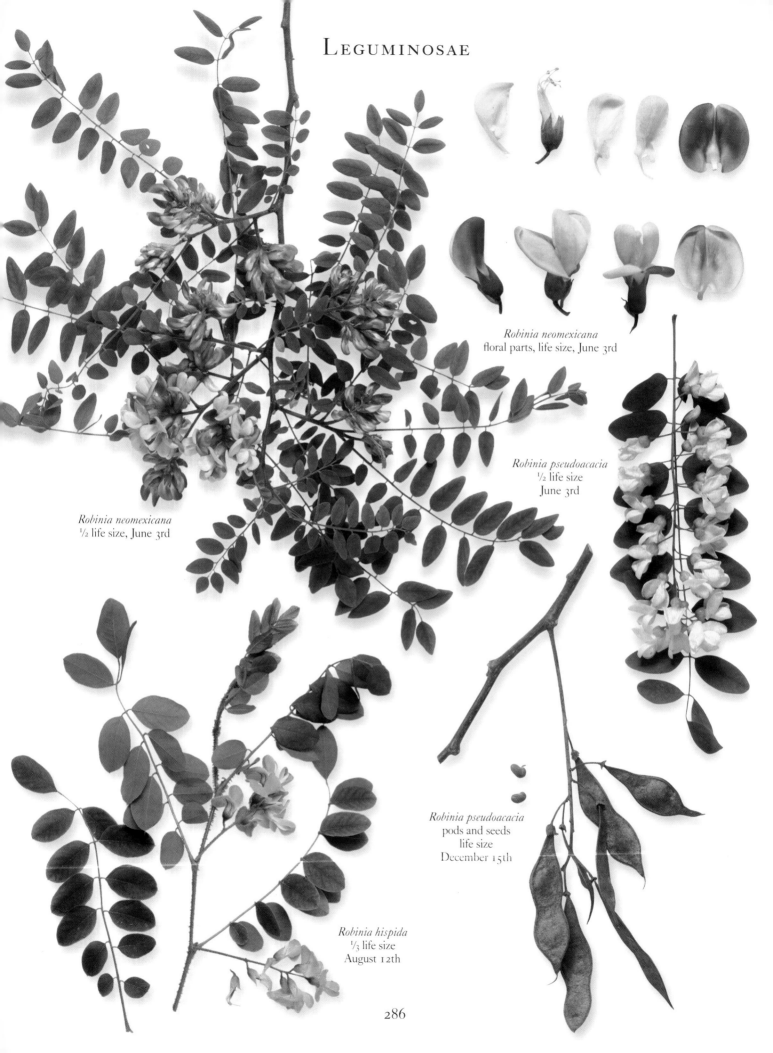

Robinia neomexicana
floral parts, life size, June 3rd

Robinia neomexicana
¹/₂ life size, June 3rd

Robinia pseudoacacia
¹/₂ life size
June 3rd

Robinia pseudoacacia
pods and seeds
life size
December 15th

Robinia hispida
¹/₃ life size
August 12th

Indigofera heterantha
1 1/2 × life size
June 23rd

Robinia

Robinia L. (1753), the false acacia or black locust, in the family Leguminosae subfamily Papilionoideae, contains around 4 species with numerous varieties, all from North America.

Description Trees to 25m, or shrubs, often with pairs of spines. The leaves are alternate, deciduous, pinnate, with 5–25 opposite or alternate leaflets and a terminal leaflet. The flowers are pea-like, scented, in elongated bunches, white or pink. Sepals 5, unequal, joined to form a bell-shaped calyx. Petals 5, unequal, the uppermost a broad, reflexed standard, the 2 outer wings, the 2 lowest forming a keel that encloses the stamens, style, and ovary. Stamens 10, of which 9 have their filaments joined and 1 is free. Ovary superior, with 1 carpel containing numerous ovules; style 1. Pollination is by bees. The fruits are flattened pods, often bristly, with several seeds.

Key Recognition Features The pinnate leaves and hanging flowers like those of *Wisteria* (see pp.284–85). *Robinia pseudoacacia* L. has dark brown bark with vertical grooves. Many of the other species have bristly or sticky stems.

Evolution and Relationships *Robinia* belongs to a group of mainly American tropical genera, of which only *Sesbania* Scop. is found in other tropical areas.

Ecology and Geography In woods, waste places, and scrub throughout North America east of the Rockies and in Arizona.

Comment The genus is named after Jean Robin (d.1629), gardener and herbalist to Henri IV of France. The original plant survived in the Jardin des Plantes until the 1980s. *Robinia pseudoacacia*, especially the golden-leaved 'Frisia', is commonly planted and is naturalised over much of southern Europe. It suckers widely and has powerful surface roots to prevent competition. The pink-flowered species and hybrids are most attractive small trees or shrubs; many are triploid, and spread by suckers rather than seed.

Indigofera

Indigofera L. (1753), indigo, in the family Leguminosae subfamily Papilionoideae, contains around 700 species, mainly in the tropics, with temperate species in eastern Asia and South Africa.

Description Shrubs to 4m, or herbaceous with a woody base, often sparsely hairy, without spines. The leaves are alternate, evergreen or deciduous, pinnate with 7–27 opposite leaflets, with a terminal leaflet. The flowers are pea-like, in slender spikes in the leaf axils, sometimes hanging, usually purplish-pink. Sepals 5, unequal, joined at the base to form a bell-shaped calyx. Petals 5, unequal, the uppermost a broad standard enfolding the 2 outer wings, the 2 lowest forming a keel that encloses the stamens, style, and ovary. Stamens 10, of which 9 have the filaments joined and the uppermost is free. Ovary superior, with 1 carpel containing numerous ovules; style 1. Pollination is by bees. The pods are slender, usually cylindrical, with thin partitions between the seeds.

Key Recognition Features The numerous slender, tapering spikes of flowers in the axils of pinnate leaves.

Evolution and Relationships Related to *Desmodium* (see p.288) and *Lespedeza* Mich., though not very closely.

Ecology and Geography On open, rocky hillsides and in waste places; the greatest concentrations of species are in southern Africa and eastern Asia, and around 30 species are found in Australia.

Comment The genus is one of the most important for blue dye, the colour of blue jeans. *Indigofera tinctoria* L., of uncertain origin, was the main species cultivated for dyeing. Several species are cultivated as attractive, late-flowering, small shrubs.

Indigofera heterantha
1/2 life size
June 23rd

Desmodium

Desmodium L. (1753), in the family Leguminosae subfamily Papilionoideae, contains around 300 species, mostly in the tropics and subtropics.

Description Subshrubs or shrubs to 4m, or herbaceous perennials. The leaves are alternate, evergreen or deciduous, pinnate, with 3 leaflets or sometimes with only the terminal leaflet. The flowers are pea-like, in elongated bunches, usually purple to pink. Sepals 5, unequal, joined at the base to form a funnel-shaped calyx. Petals 5, unequal, the uppermost a broad standard, the 2 outer wings, the 2 lowest forming a keel that encloses the stamens, style, and ovary. Stamens 10, of which 9 have the filaments joined, and the uppermost is free at the base but joined to the others above the base. Ovary superior, with 1 carpel containing a few ovules; style 1. Pollination is by bees. The pods are often lobed and generally break into 1-seeded segments, which may form burrs that catch in the wool of animals and socks.

Key Recognition Features The few, broad leaflets on an elegant shrub, and the lobed pods that break into the 1-seeded burrs of the weedy species.

Evolution and Relationships Related to *Campylotropis* Bunge from western China, and *Lespedeza* Mich. from eastern Asia and North America, both of which are sparse, low shrubs with pinkish-magenta flowers and 1-seeded pods.

Ecology and Geography On rocky slopes and in scrub, with many species in waste ground, throughout the tropics and into the temperate parts of North America.

Comment The cultivated ornamentals *D. elegans* DC and *D. praestans* Forrest are from the Himalayas and China. They are useful for their late flowering.

Desmodium praestans
floral parts and pod
2 × life size, October 5th

Desmodium praestans
1 ¼ × life size
October 5th

Desmodium praestans
½ life size, October 5th

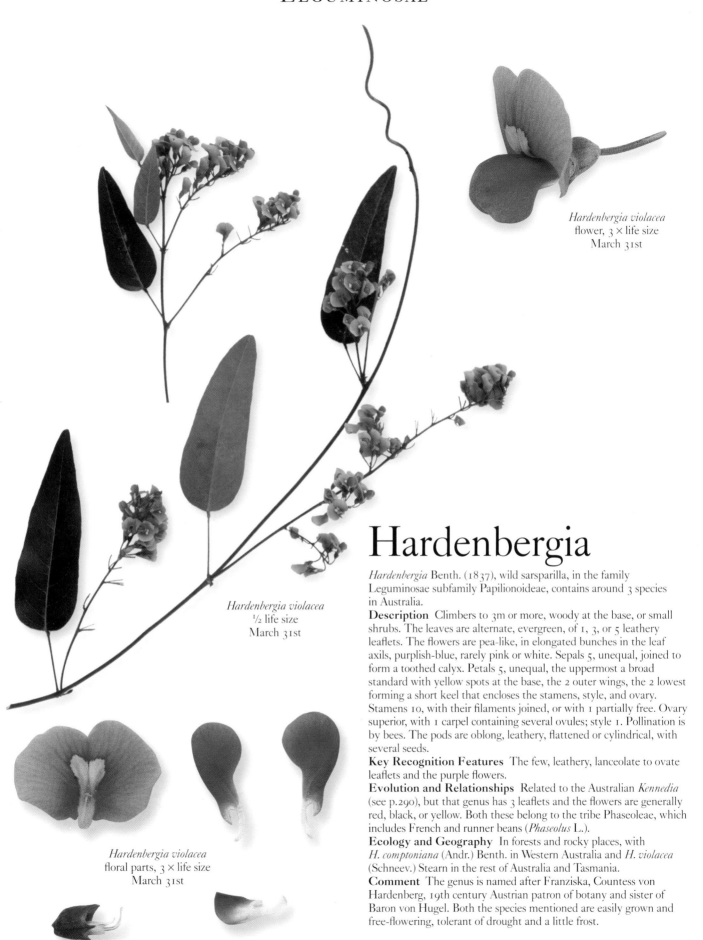

Hardenbergia violacea
flower, 3 × life size
March 31st

Hardenbergia violacea
½ life size
March 31st

Hardenbergia violacea
floral parts, 3 × life size
March 31st

Hardenbergia

Hardenbergia Benth. (1837), wild sarsparilla, in the family Leguminosae subfamily Papilionoideae, contains around 3 species in Australia.

Description Climbers to 3m or more, woody at the base, or small shrubs. The leaves are alternate, evergreen, of 1, 3, or 5 leathery leaflets. The flowers are pea-like, in elongated bunches in the leaf axils, purplish-blue, rarely pink or white. Sepals 5, unequal, joined to form a toothed calyx. Petals 5, unequal, the uppermost a broad standard with yellow spots at the base, the 2 outer wings, the 2 lowest forming a short keel that encloses the stamens, style, and ovary. Stamens 10, with their filaments joined, or with 1 partially free. Ovary superior, with 1 carpel containing several ovules; style 1. Pollination is by bees. The pods are oblong, leathery, flattened or cylindrical, with several seeds.

Key Recognition Features The few, leathery, lanceolate to ovate leaflets and the purple flowers.

Evolution and Relationships Related to the Australian *Kennedia* (see p.290), but that genus has 3 leaflets and the flowers are generally red, black, or yellow. Both these belong to the tribe Phaseoleae, which includes French and runner beans (*Phaseolus* L.).

Ecology and Geography In forests and rocky places, with *H. comptoniana* (Andr.) Benth. in Western Australia and *H. violacea* (Schneev.) Stearn in the rest of Australia and Tasmania.

Comment The genus is named after Franziska, Countess von Hardenberg, 19th century Austrian patron of botany and sister of Baron von Hugel. Both the species mentioned are easily grown and free-flowering, tolerant of drought and a little frost.

Erythrina

Erythrina L. (1753), in the family Leguminosae subfamily Papilionoideae, contains around 120 species in the tropics and subtropics.

Description Trees to 20m, or shrubs, often with short, stiff spines. The leaves are alternate, usually deciduous, pinnate, with 3 leaflets. The flowers are large, pea-like, in elongated bunches or long, stiff spikes, on the ends of the branches, usually red, sometimes twisted so as to be held upside down. Sepals 5, unequal, joined to form a tubular calyx. Petals 5, unequal, the uppermost a broad standard, often covering the other smaller petals, sometimes reflexed; the 2 outer small wings, the 2 lowest forming an often greenish keel that encloses the stamens, style, and ovary. Stamens 10, of which 9 have their filaments joined and 1 is free. Ovary superior, with 1 carpel containing several ovules; style 1. Pollination is by sunbirds and hummingbirds. The pods are woody, flat or cylindrical, usually narrow between the often red-and-black seeds.

Key Recognition Features The red flowers in large heads on a thick-twigged tree or large shrub.

Evolution and Relationships Related to the beans (*Phaseolus* L.), but adapted for bird pollination and seed dispersal.

Ecology and Geography In seasonally dry climates on hills and plains, with 12 species in Asia, 31 in Africa, 1 in Australia, and around 70 in the Americas.

Comment The genus has some fascinating interactions with birds. In Asia, the stems are stiff to act as perches for sunbirds, and the very watery nectar is a source of water for birds in the dry season. In the Americas, some species with high-sucrose nectar are adapted for hummingbirds, others with low-sucrose nectar for passerines. The seeds are generally very poisonous, but are used as beads.

Kennedia

Kennedia Vent. (1804) in the family Leguminosae subfamily Papilionoideae, contains around 16 species, mainly in Australia.

Description Climbers to 3m or more, often woody at the base, or creepers. The leaves are alternate, evergreen, of usually 3 leathery leaflets, rarely 1 or 5, often with conspicuous stipules. The flowers are pea-like, in pairs or in elongated bunches in the leaf axils, red, black-and-yellow, purple, or pink. Sepals 5, unequal, joined to form a toothed calyx. Petals 5, unequal, the standard with yellow spots at the base, the 2 outer wings, the 2 lowest forming a short or long keel that encloses the stamens, style, and ovary. Stamens 10, of which 9 have their filaments joined and 1 is free. Ovary superior, with 1 carpel containing several ovules; style 1. Pollination is by birds and bees. The pods are oblong, leathery, flattened, with several seeds.

Key Recognition Features The few, leathery, lanceolate to ovate leaflets and purple flowers.

Evolution and Relationships Species of the Leguminosae are particularly diverse and beautiful in Western Australia, and are mainly shrubs; the tribe Phaseoleae, which includes French and runner beans (*Phaseolus* L.), and to which *Kennedia* belongs, is one of the few climbers.

Ecology and Geography In jarrah forests (*Eucalyptus marginata* see p.320) and rocky places; 11 species in Western Australia, including the black-flowered *K. nigricans* Lindl.; *K. coccinea* Vent. in the rest of Australia and Tasmania; 1 species in New Guinea.

Comment The genus is named after Lewis Kennedy (1775–1818), a founder of Lee and Kennedy, nurserymen of Hammersmith, who introduced many new Australian plants into cultivation in Europe. Kennedias are beautiful and easily grown climbers with flowers in a variety of striking colours; many can survive a little frost.

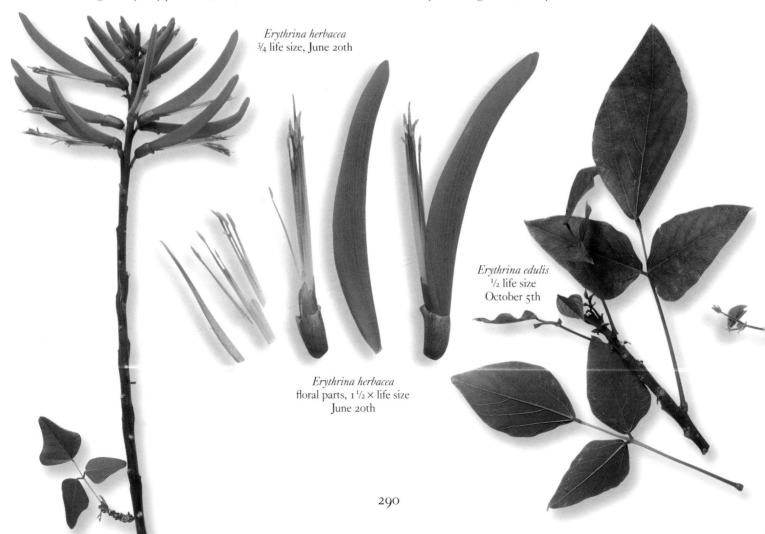

Erythrina herbacea
¾ life size, June 20th

Erythrina herbacea
floral parts, 1½ × life size
June 20th

Erythrina edulis
½ life size
October 5th

Kennedia coccinea
floral parts, 1¹⁄₂ × life size
April 16th

Amorpha fruticosa
¹⁄₂ life size
June 21st

Kennedia rubicunda
¹⁄₂ life size
April 16th

Kennedia macrophylla
¹⁄₂ life size
April 16th

Amorpha fruticosa
flowers, 1¹⁄₃ × life size
June 21st

Kennedia retrorsa
¹⁄₂ life size, April 16th

Amorpha

Amorpha L. (1753), in the family Leguminosae subfamily Papilionoideae, contains around 15 species in North America.

Description Shrubs to 3m. The leaves are alternate, deciduous, pinnate, with 11–51 leaflets, with a terminal leaflet. The flowers are very small and numerous, often scented, in long, upright spikes, not pea-like, usually purplish or bluish. Sepals 5, unequal, joined at the base to form a tubular, toothed calyx. Petals 1, only the standard, which encloses lower parts of the stamens, style, and ovary. Stamens 10, with their filaments all joined at the base. Ovary superior, with 1 carpel containing 1 or 2 ovules; style 1, long and slender. Pollination is presumed to be by insects. The pods are small with 1 or 2 seeds.

Key Recognition Features The upright or spreading spikes of minute, dull-purplish or bluish flowers.

Evolution and Relationships The flowers are very reduced, but produced in huge numbers. In the related, vetch-like genus *Dalea* L., which is common on the American prairies, the small flowers are in clover-like heads (*Trifolium* L.), and have wings and keel mostly longer than the standard.

Ecology and Geography In sandy woods, especially by streams, and on river banks and floodplains in North America, extending into Mexico.

Comment The genus is unusual in its very reduced flowers, and is sometimes cultivated in collections of shrubs.

Clianthus

Clianthus Sol. ex Lindl. (1835), in the family Leguminosae subfamily Papilionoideae, contains 1 species, *C. puniceus* (G. Don fil.) Lindl., the kaka beak or parrot's bill, in New Zealand.

Description Shrubs to 2m, with spreading branches. The leaves are alternate, evergreen, pinnate, with up to 15 pairs of alternate leaflets and a terminal leaflet, all soft and blunt at the apex. The flowers are large, pea-like, in elongated hanging bunches, red, pink, or greenish-white, to 8cm long. Sepals 5, equal, joined to form a loose, short, sharp-toothed calyx. Petals 5, unequal, the uppermost a broad, pointed, and bent-back standard, the 2 outer small and incurved wings, the 2 lowest forming a long, slender-pointed keel that encloses the stamens, style, and ovary. Stamens 10, the lowest 9 joined for around half their length, the uppermost free. Ovary superior, with 1 carpel containing numerous ovules; style 1, stiff, just emerging from the keel. Pollination is by birds. The pods are slightly swollen, with numerous small, kidney-shaped seeds.

Key Recognition Features The soft leaves with alternate leaflets and the large, usually red flowers.

Evolution and Relationships Sturt's desert pea, *Swainsona formosa* (G. Don fil.) J. Thompson from the deserts of Western Australia, was formerly included in *Clianthus* on account of its large red flowers, but these are now considered to have evolved separately as an adaptation to pollination by birds.

Ecology and Geography In scrub and forest; on the North Island, in the islets of the Bay of Islands, and inland near lake Waikairemoana.

Comment A spectacular plant for flowering in early spring in mild areas with little frost. In cold areas the plants can be grown in large pots and brought under glass in winter, as they will not tolerate freezing wind.

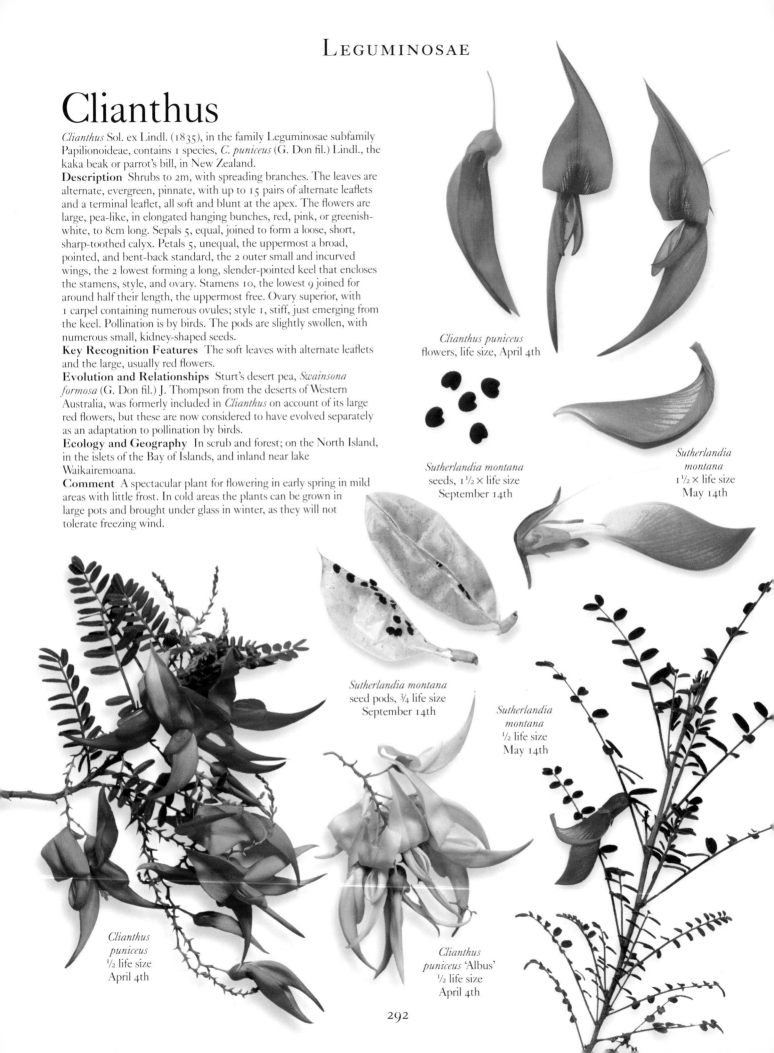

Clianthus puniceus
flowers, life size, April 4th

Sutherlandia montana
seeds, 1½ × life size
September 14th

Sutherlandia montana
1½ × life size
May 14th

Sutherlandia montana
seed pods, ¾ life size
September 14th

Sutherlandia montana
½ life size
May 14th

Clianthus puniceus
½ life size
April 4th

Clianthus puniceus 'Albus'
½ life size
April 4th

Colutea arborescens
flowers, just over life size
July 16th

Colutea arborescens
pods and seeds
just over life size
July 16th

Colutea arborescens
½ life size
July 16th

Sutherlandia

Sutherlandia R. Br. (1812), the *kanker bos*, *gansie*, or balloon pea, in the family Leguminosae subfamily Papilionoideae, contains around 3 rather similar species in South Africa,

Description Shrubs to 1.5m. The leaves are alternate, partially deciduous or evergreen, pinnate, with up to 12 pairs of opposite and alternate leaflets and a terminal leaflet, all soft and blunt at the apex. The flowers are large, pea-like, up to 5 in an umbel, red with white markings, sometimes purplish, to 5cm long. Sepals 5, equal, joined to form a tubular, toothed calyx. Petals 5, unequal, the uppermost a broad, blunt, and bent-back standard, the 2 outer wings very small and hidden, the 2 lowest forming a long, curved, and pointed keel that encloses the stamens, style, and ovary. Stamens 10, the lowest 9 joined, and the uppermost free. Ovary superior, with 1 carpel containing numerous ovules; style 1, stiff. Pollination is by sunbirds. The pods are swollen, papery when dry, with numerous small, kidney-shaped seeds.

Key Recognition Features The soft, greyish leaves with small leaflets and the usually red flowers, followed by whitish, papery, transparent seed pods.

Evolution and Relationships Related to *Colutea*, but with larger, red flowers adapted to bird pollination.

Ecology and Geography In dry, open places, particularly along roads, throughout the drier parts of South Africa and naturalised in South America, East Africa, and New Zealand.

Comment Sutherlandias are easily grown from seed, but are short-lived, needing very dry, well-drained soil. Infusions of the leaves were used for cancer, as a cough remedy, and for stomach, intestinal, and uterine problems.

Colutea

Colutea L. (1753), bladder senna, in the family Leguminosae subfamily Papilionoideae, contains around 26 species in eastern Europe, Asia, and northeast Africa.

Description Shrubs to 5m, with slender arching branches. The leaves are alternate, usually deciduous, pinnate, with 2–6 pairs of rounded, opposite and alternate leaflets and a terminal leaflet. The flowers are pea-like, solitary or few in short bunches, yellow, reddish, or brownish-orange. Sepals 5, unequal, joined to form a 5-toothed, bell-shaped calyx. Petals 5, unequal, the uppermost a short, broad standard with 2 small swellings at the base, the 2 outer wings with lobes or sometimes a spur, about as long as the keel formed by the 2 lowest, which is round or beaked at the apex and encloses the stamens, style, and ovary. Stamens 10, the lowest 9 joined, the uppermost free. Ovary superior, with 1 carpel containing several ovules; style 1. Pollination is by bees. The pods are swollen and papery, with several seeds.

Key Recognition Features The small, yellow to orange-red flowers, followed by papery seed pods.

Evolution and Relationships The related genus *Halimodendron* Fischer ex DC, with 1 species *H. halodendron* (Pallas) Voss, differs in having purplish-pink or magenta flowers and more leathery pods; it usually grows on saline soils in the steppes of Russia and Central Asia. *Amicia* H. B. & K., has around 7 species in Mexico and South America; the only species commonly cultivated, *A. zygomeris* DC, has *Colutea*-like flowers and very large, rounded stipules on the stems.

Ecology and Geography On dry hills and rocky slopes from France and Germany eastwards to northwestern China.

Comment Modestly attractive and very hardy ornamental shrubs.

Caragana

Caragana Lam. (1783), in the family Leguminosae subfamily Papilionoideae, contains around 65 species in Asia.

Description Trees to 7m, or shrubs, often with short, spiny stipules at the leaf base, with short side shoots. The leaves are alternate, evergreen or deciduous, pinnate, with 4–12 leaflets, often with the terminal leaflet replaced by a spine, or with 4 leaflets in a cluster. The flowers are pea-like, solitary or in small bunches, usually yellow, sometimes pinkish. Sepals 5, unequal, joined to form a toothed calyx. Petals 5, unequal, long and narrow at the base, the uppermost a standard with reflexed margins, the 2 outer wings, the 2 lowest forming a keel that encloses the stamens, style, and ovary. Stamens 10, the lowest 9 joined, the uppermost free. Ovary superior, with 1 carpel containing several ovules; style 1. Pollination is by bees. The pods are long and narrow, sometimes slightly inflated, with several seeds.

Key Recognition Features The spiny stems and remains of leaves, and the short side shoots.

Evolution and Relationships Most closely related to *Astragalus* L., a very large genus containing over 2000 species of herbs and dwarf shrubs, mainly from the drier parts of the northern hemisphere; this has similar spiny leaves but lacks the short side shoots.

Ecology and Geography On dry slopes from eastern Bulgaria eastwards to Mongolia and northeastern China.

Comment Caraganas are sometimes grown as ornamentals; they are drought-resistant and hardy.

Caragana sinica
⅔ life size, April 1st

Caragana arborescens
⅔ life size, April 29th

Caragana brevispina
pods and seeds, 1¼ × life size
October 5th

Caragana arborescens
life size, April 29th

294

Dorycnium

Dorycnium Mill. (1758), in the family Leguminosae subfamily Papilionoideae, contains around 8 species in the Mediterranean basin and western Asia, sometimes included in the large and mainly herbaceous genus *Lotus* L. (see Volume 2).

Description Shrubs to 50cm, with upright stems, without spines. The leaves are alternate, evergreen, pinnate, with 5 leaflets. The flowers are pea-like, in flat-topped heads, pink, purplish, or whitish. Sepals 5, equal or unequal, joined to form a toothed calyx. Petals 5, unequal, the uppermost the standard, the 2 outer wings, the 2 lowest forming a keel that encloses the stamens, style, and ovary. Stamens 10, the lowest 9 joined, the uppermost free. Ovary superior, with 1 carpel containing several ovules; style 1. Pollination is by bees. The pods are dark and slightly swollen, with up to 8 seeds.

Key Recognition Features The greyish, hairy leaves with 5 leaflets and the heads of pinkish flowers.

Evolution and Relationships Related to *Lotus*, which differs in being mostly yellow-flowered and herbaceous, not shrubby.

Ecology and Geography On rocky slopes and other well-drained places, rarely in woods and damp scrub, from southern France to Turkey and the Caucasus; 1 species in the Canary Islands.

Comment *Dorycnium hirsutum* (L.) Ser. is attractive and easily grown in a dry, sunny site.

Dorycnium hirsutum
life size, June 20th

Dorycnium hirsutum
pods and seeds
2½ × life size
November 29th

Dorycnium hirsutum
seed head, 1¼ × life size
November 29th

Dorycnium hirsutum
flowers and floral parts
1¾ × life size, June 20th

Medicago

Medicago L. (1753), in the family Leguminosae subfamily Papilionoideae, contains around 50 species in Europe and Asia. Most are annuals or small perennials; only *M. arborea* L. is shrubby.

Description Shrub to 2m, without spines. The leaves are alternate, evergreen, pinnate, with 3 leaflets. The flowers are pea-like, in elongated bunches of 4–8, yellow. Sepals 5, equal, joined to form a toothed calyx; petals 5, unequal, the uppermost a broad standard, the 2 outer wings, the 2 lowest forming a keel, shorter than the wings. Stamens 10, the lower 9 joined, the uppermost free. Ovary superior, with 1 carpel containing several ovules; style 1. Pollination is by bees. The pods are coiled, open spirals of ½–1½ turns, with several seeds.

Key Recognition Features The crowded heads of yellow flowers and coiled seed pods.

Evolution and Relationships The related genus *Ononis* L. is mainly herbaceous but contains a few low shrubs with toothed, glandular leaflets and pink or yellow, veined flowers with a broad standard, all filaments united, and oblong or ovate pods.

Ecology and Geography On rocky slopes and in other well-drained places from southern France to western Turkey and in the Canary Islands.

Comment *Medicago arborea* has long been cultivated as a curiosity for its coiled pods.

Coronilla

Coronilla L. (1753), in the family Leguminosae subfamily Papilionoideae, contains around 25 species in the Mediterranean basin and western Asia.

Description Shrubs to 2m, or perennial herbs, without spines. The leaves are alternate, evergreen or deciduous, pinnate, with up to 8 usually obovate leaflets. The flowers are pea-like, in heads, scented, usually yellow in the shrubby species. Sepals 5, equal or unequal, joined to form a toothed calyx; petals 5, unequal, the uppermost the standard, the 2 outer wings, the 2 lowest forming a keel that encloses the stamens, style, and ovary. Stamens 10, the lowest 9 joined, the uppermost free. Ovary superior, with 1 carpel containing several ovules; style 1. Pollination is by bees. The pods break up into 1-seeded segments.

Key Recognition Features The glaucous leaves with 5 leaflets and the heads of yellow, scented flowers in early spring.

Evolution and Relationships Related to *Hippocrepis* L., which also has pods that break up, but segments that are curved or horseshoe shaped.

Ecology and Geography On rocky slopes and other well-drained places in most of Europe to Turkey and the Caucasus.

Comment The genus is often planted for its sweetly scented flowers, appearing in early spring.

Medicago arborea
1 ¾ × life size
March 17th

Coronilla emerus
just under life size
March 17th

Medicago arborea
½ life size
March 17th

Medicago arborea
life size, July 20th

Piptanthus

Piptanthus Sweet (1838), in the family Leguminosae subfamily Papilionoideae, contains 2 variable species in the Himalayas and China.

Description Shrubs to 3m, without spines, with smooth, green twigs. The leaves are alternate, deciduous, pinnate, with 3 leaflets. The flowers are pea-like, in a loose, upright head, yellow. Sepals 5, unequal, joined to form a toothed calyx, with the 2 upper teeth joined for most of their length. Petals 5, unequal, the uppermost a reflexed, broad, notched standard, the 2 outer wings, the 2 lowest forming a keel that encloses the stamens, style, and ovary. Stamens 10, the filaments not joined. Ovary superior, with 1 carpel containing several ovules; style 1. Pollination is by bees. The fruits are flattened pods with several seeds.

Key Recognition Features The smooth, blackish-green twigs, leathery leaflets, and yellow flowers.

Evolution and Relationships The related genus *Anagyris* L. from the Mediterranean region has smaller, greenish flowers with the standard around half as long as the other petals. The related herbaceous genera *Baptisia* Vent. and *Thermopsis* R. Br. are found in North America and eastern Asia.

Ecology and Geography On open slopes and in scrub in the Himalayas from northern India to western China, in Yunnan and Sichuan.

Comment Attractive, rather stiff but soft, upright shrubs for gardens in mild areas.

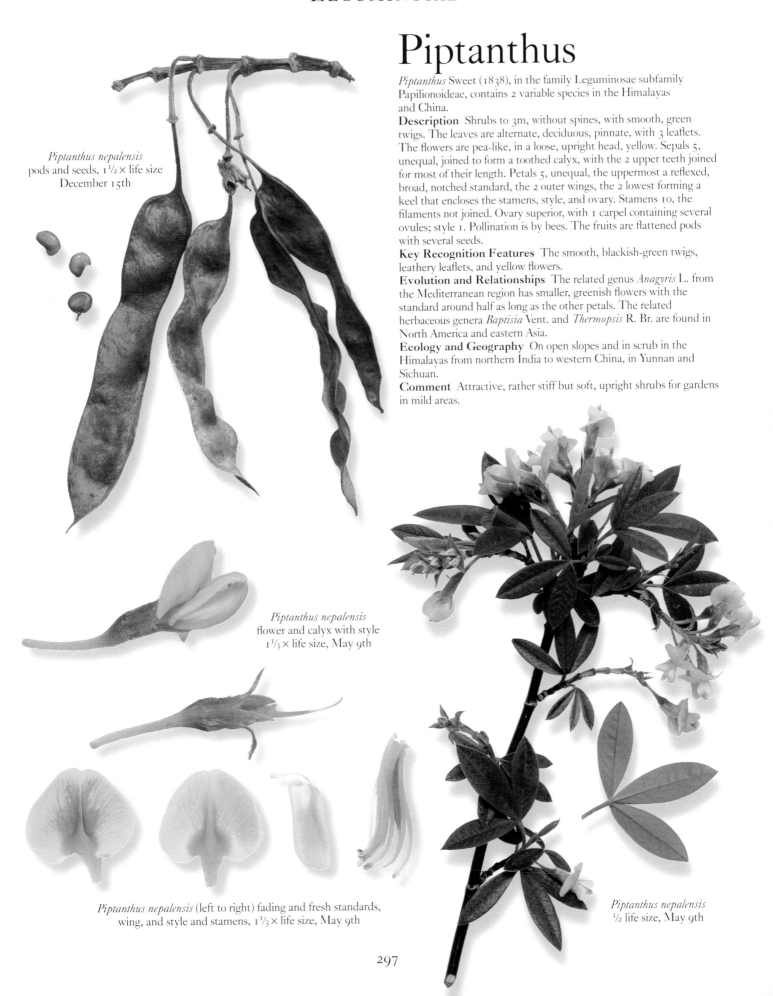

Piptanthus nepalensis
pods and seeds, 1½ × life size
December 15th

Piptanthus nepalensis
flower and calyx with style
1⅓ × life size, May 9th

Piptanthus nepalensis (left to right) fading and fresh standards,
wing, and style and stamens, 1⅓ × life size, May 9th

Piptanthus nepalensis
½ life size, May 9th

Lupinus

Lupinus L. (1753), in the family Leguminosae subfamily Papilionoideae, contains around 200 species, mainly in North America, of which a few are shrubby and described here, but most are annuals or herbaceous perennials (see Volume 2).

Description Shrubs to 2m, without spines. The leaves are alternate, evergreen or deciduous, palmate, with 5–12 leaflets. The flowers are pea-like, in elongated spikes, yellow, blue, or white, usually scented. Sepals 5, unequal, joined to form a tubular, 2-lipped calyx. Petals 5, unequal, the uppermost a broad standard with the sides folded back, the 2 outer wings enclosing the keel formed by the 2 lowest, which contains the stamens, style, and ovary. Stamens 10, all joined into a tube at the base. Ovary superior, with 1 carpel containing several ovules; style 1. Pollination is by bees. The pods are usually silky and contain numerous seeds.

Key Recognition Features The palmate leaves and the flower with the standard folded back and large, inflated wings.

Evolution and Relationships Related to *Laburnum* and the brooms (see pp. 300–302), rather than the superficially similar *Baptisia* Vent..

Ecology and Geography On dunes and open grasslands, mainly in North America and extending southwards along the Andes, with a few mainly annual species in southern Europe and southwestern Asia. The shrubby species are mainly found along the Pacific coast of the Americas.

Comment The shrubby species make excellent garden plants; they are fast-growing and easy to grow, though short-lived. Many species are cultivated for fodder and for protein, though most wild species contain poisonous alkaloids.

Laburnum

Laburnum Medik. (1787), in the family Leguminosae subfamily Papilionoideae, contains 2 species in Europe.

Description Trees to 10m, or shrubs. The leaves are alternate, deciduous, pinnate, with 3 leaflets. The flowers are pea-like, in elongated hanging bunches, yellow. Sepals 5, unequal, joined at the base to form a toothed calyx. Petals 5, unequal, the uppermost a broad standard enfolding the 2 outer wings, the 2 lowest forming a keel that encloses the stamens, style, and ovary. Stamens 10, all the filaments joined into a tube. Ovary superior, with 1 carpel containing several ovules; style 1. Pollination is by bees. The pods are flattened, slightly narrowed between the seeds.

Key Recognition Features The 3 leaflets and hanging bunches of yellow flowers.

Evolution and Relationships *Petteria ramentacea* (Sieb.) C. Presl., from the mountains of the Balkans, is rather similar, but has short, upright spikes of flowers, as does *Podocytisus caramanicus* Boiss. & Heldr., which was sometimes included in *Laburnum*, but which has a winged pod.

Ecology and Geography From France to eastern Europe. *Laburnum alpinum* (Mill.) Bercht. & C. Presl on moist, gravelly slopes, *L. anagyroides* Medic. in subalpine woods on limestone.

Comment Laburnums are commonly grown ornamental trees; the seeds and wood contain the very poisonous alkaloid cytisine. The longest bunches of flowers are produced by *L. × watereri* 'Vossii', a hybrid between the 2 wild species, which is mainly sterile. Laburnum wood is yellowish in colour and durable, and was popular as a veneer in English furniture in the late 17th century.

Lupinus albifrons
floral details: note the wings attached at their tips just over life size
May 15th

Lupinus albifrons
½ life size
May 15th

+ Laburnocytisus

+ *Laburnocytisus adamii* (Poit.) C. K. Schneid. This unusual plant, called a graft chimera, was created by chance in 1826, when the low-growing *Cytisus purpureus* Scop. was grafted onto *Laburnum anagyroides* in Adams nursery in Vitry, near Paris. The resulting tree is like a laburnum, with the pinkish flowers of the chimera, as well as bearing shoots of yellow laburnum flowers and shoots of pure purplish-pink *Cytisus* flowers. This frequent reversion to the parental types shows that the hybrid shoots are *Cytisus* (see p. 300) on the surface, *Laburnum* inside, and that fusion of the cells has not taken place, as it would if the plant were a sexual cross between the genera.

LEGUMINOSAE

Petteria ramentacea
⅓ life size
June 21st

Laburnum anagyroides
⅔ life size, May 9th

+ *Laburnocytisus adamii*
⅔ life size, May 9th

*Cytisus
purpureus*
⅔ life size
May 9th

Laburnum
pods and seeds
life size
December 20th

flowers of:
+ *Laburnocytisus adamii* (top)
Cytisus purpureus (bottom left)
Laburnum anagyroides (bottom right)
just under life size, May 9th

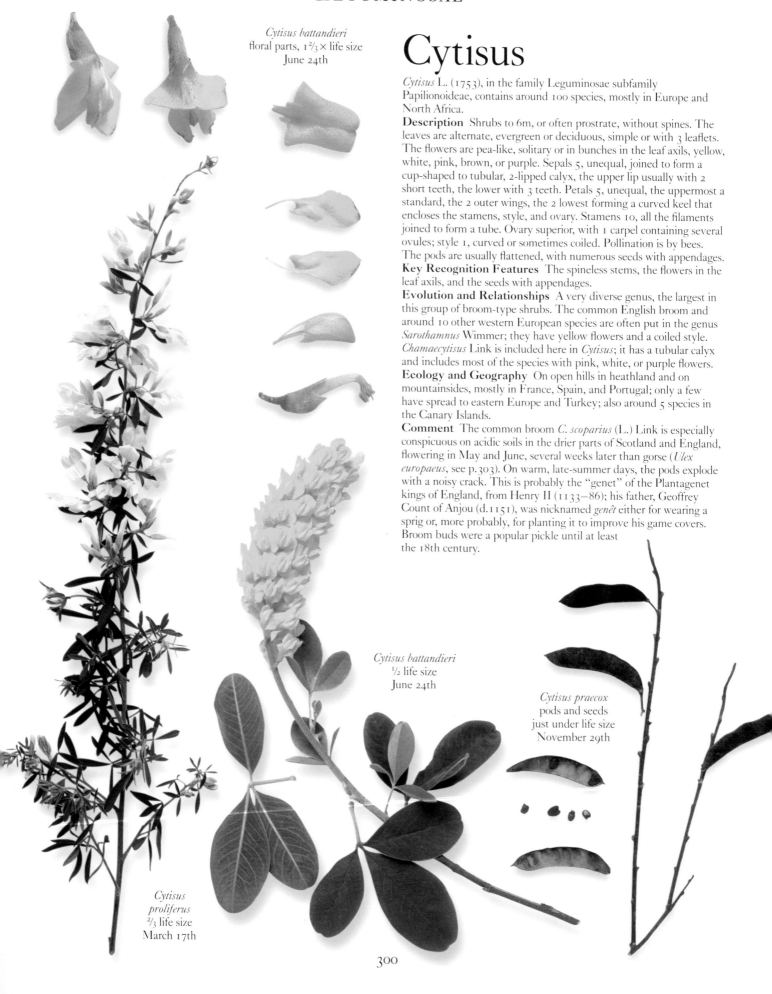

Cytisus battandieri
floral parts, 1²/₃ × life size
June 24th

Cytisus

Cytisus L. (1753), in the family Leguminosae subfamily Papilionoideae, contains around 100 species, mostly in Europe and North Africa.

Description Shrubs to 6m, or often prostrate, without spines. The leaves are alternate, evergreen or deciduous, simple or with 3 leaflets. The flowers are pea-like, solitary or in bunches in the leaf axils, yellow, white, pink, brown, or purple. Sepals 5, unequal, joined to form a cup-shaped to tubular, 2-lipped calyx, the upper lip usually with 2 short teeth, the lower with 3 teeth. Petals 5, unequal, the uppermost a standard, the 2 outer wings, the 2 lowest forming a curved keel that encloses the stamens, style, and ovary. Stamens 10, all the filaments joined to form a tube. Ovary superior, with 1 carpel containing several ovules; style 1, curved or sometimes coiled. Pollination is by bees. The pods are usually flattened, with numerous seeds with appendages.

Key Recognition Features The spineless stems, the flowers in the leaf axils, and the seeds with appendages.

Evolution and Relationships A very diverse genus, the largest in this group of broom-type shrubs. The common English broom and around 10 other western European species are often put in the genus *Sarothamnus* Wimmer; they have yellow flowers and a coiled style. *Chamaecytisus* Link is included here in *Cytisus*; it has a tubular calyx and includes most of the species with pink, white, or purple flowers.

Ecology and Geography On open hills in heathland and on mountainsides, mostly in France, Spain, and Portugal; only a few have spread to eastern Europe and Turkey; also around 5 species in the Canary Islands.

Comment The common broom *C. scoparius* (L.) Link is especially conspicuous on acidic soils in the drier parts of Scotland and England, flowering in May and June, several weeks later than gorse (*Ulex europaeus*, see p.303). On warm, late-summer days, the pods explode with a noisy crack. This is probably the "genet" of the Plantagenet kings of England, from Henry II (1133–86); his father, Geoffrey Count of Anjou (d.1151), was nicknamed *genêt* either for wearing a sprig or, more probably, for planting it to improve his game covers. Broom buds were a popular pickle until at least the 18th century.

Cytisus battandieri
½ life size
June 24th

Cytisus praecox
pods and seeds
just under life size
November 29th

Cytisus
proliferus
²/₃ life size
March 17th

Spartium

Spartium L. (1753), in the family Leguminosae subfamily Papilionoideae, contains 1 species, *S. junceum* L. in southern Europe, sometimes called Spanish broom.

Description Shrubs to 3m, without spines and with upright, green, rush-like twigs. The leaves are scattered, deciduous, with 1 narrow leaflet, soon falling. The flowers are yellow, scented, pea-like, in elongated heads at the tips of the branches. Sepals 5, equal, joined to form a sheath-like, split calyx with 5 small teeth. Petals 5, unequal, the uppermost a broad, upright standard, the 2 outer curved wings, the 2 lowest forming a long keel that encloses the stamens, style, and ovary. Stamens 10, the filaments all joined. Ovary superior, with 1 carpel containing many ovules; style 1. Pollination is by bees. The pods are flattened with many seeds.

Key Recognition Features The rush-like, green, tapering, mainly leafless shoots and large, scented, yellow flowers in an elongated head.

Evolution and Relationships Some species of *Cytisus* with green shoots have been put in the genus *Spartocytisus* Webb; they are beautiful shrubs with white flowers from the Canary Islands. The genus *Lygos* Adanson, also classified as *Retama* Boiss., from Spain, North Africa, and the southeastern Mediterranean, also has mainly leafless stems, but has small flowers and 1-seeded pods.

Ecology and Geography On dry hills and roadsides; native from Portugal, Spain, and North Africa eastwards to Turkey and western Syria; naturalised in dry areas elsewhere.

Comment The genus *Spartium* is distinctive and easy to recognise. The flowers are narcotic, and there have been cases of poisoning when *Spartium* flowers have been used in error for common broom, *Cytisus scoparius*, when making broom-flower wine.

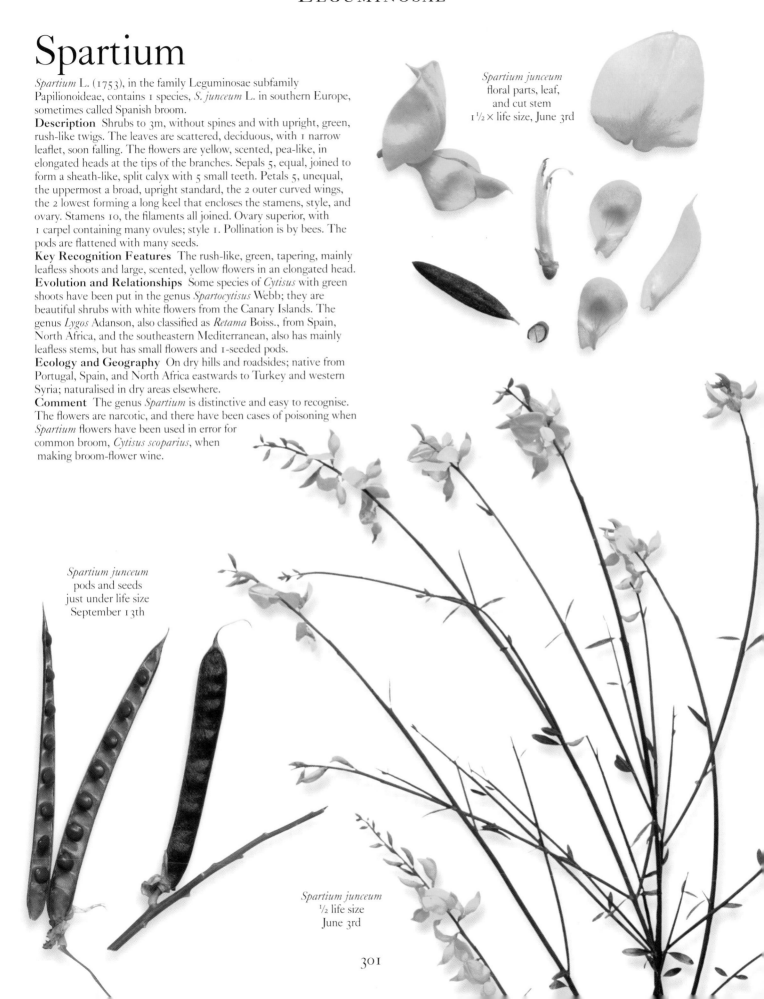

Spartium junceum
floral parts, leaf,
and cut stem
1 ½ × life size, June 3rd

Spartium junceum
pods and seeds
just under life size
September 13th

Spartium junceum
½ life size
June 3rd

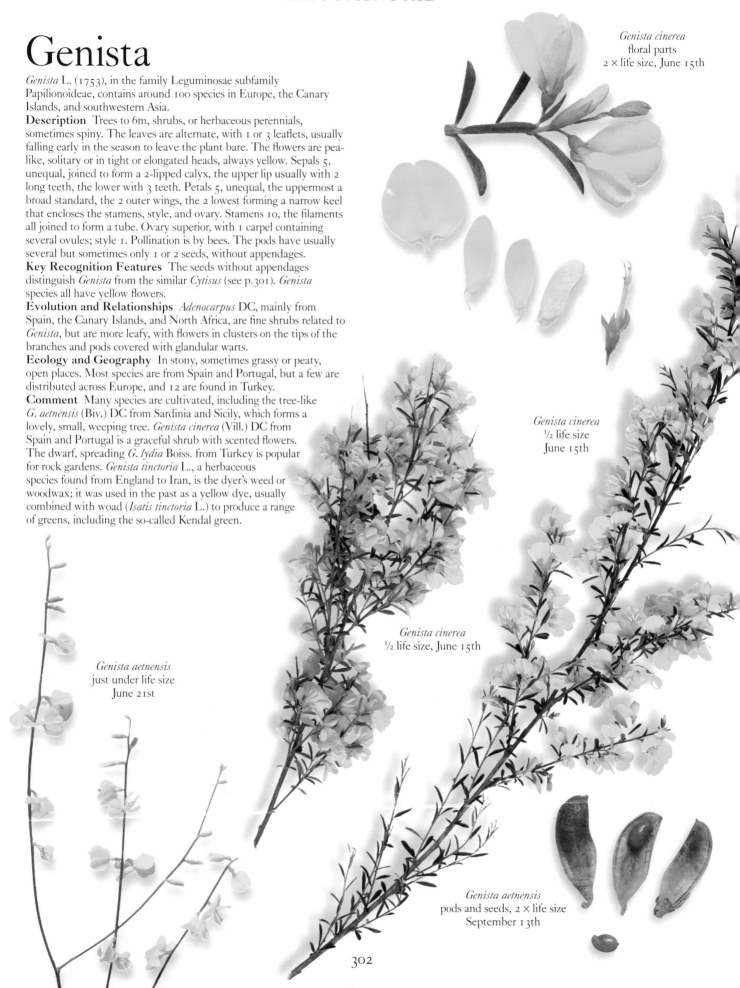

Genista

Genista L. (1753), in the family Leguminosae subfamily Papilionoideae, contains around 100 species in Europe, the Canary Islands, and southwestern Asia.

Description Trees to 6m, shrubs, or herbaceous perennials, sometimes spiny. The leaves are alternate, with 1 or 3 leaflets, usually falling early in the season to leave the plant bare. The flowers are pea-like, solitary or in tight or elongated heads, always yellow. Sepals 5, unequal, joined to form a 2-lipped calyx, the upper lip usually with 2 long teeth, the lower with 3 teeth. Petals 5, unequal, the uppermost a broad standard, the 2 outer wings, the 2 lowest forming a narrow keel that encloses the stamens, style, and ovary. Stamens 10, the filaments all joined to form a tube. Ovary superior, with 1 carpel containing several ovules; style 1. Pollination is by bees. The pods have usually several but sometimes only 1 or 2 seeds, without appendages.

Key Recognition Features The seeds without appendages distinguish *Genista* from the similar *Cytisus* (see p.301). *Genista* species all have yellow flowers.

Evolution and Relationships *Adenocarpus* DC, mainly from Spain, the Canary Islands, and North Africa, are fine shrubs related to *Genista*, but are more leafy, with flowers in clusters on the tips of the branches and pods covered with glandular warts.

Ecology and Geography In stony, sometimes grassy or peaty, open places. Most species are from Spain and Portugal, but a few are distributed across Europe, and 12 are found in Turkey.

Comment Many species are cultivated, including the tree-like *G. aetnensis* (Biv.) DC from Sardinia and Sicily, which forms a lovely, small, weeping tree. *Genista cinerea* (Vill.) DC from Spain and Portugal is a graceful shrub with scented flowers. The dwarf, spreading *G. lydia* Boiss. from Turkey is popular for rock gardens. *Genista tinctoria* L., a herbaceous species found from England to Iran, is the dyer's weed or woodwax; it was used in the past as a yellow dye, usually combined with woad (*Isatis tinctoria* L.) to produce a range of greens, including the so-called Kendal green.

Genista cinerea
floral parts
2 × life size, June 15th

Genista cinerea
½ life size
June 15th

Genista cinerea
½ life size, June 15th

Genista aetnensis
just under life size
June 21st

Genista aetnensis
pods and seeds, 2 × life size
September 13th

Ulex europaeus
floral parts
1¾ × life size
January 29th

Ulex europaeus
fruit and seeds, 1½ × life size, July 3rd

Ulex

Ulex L. (1753), the gorse, in the family Leguminosae subfamily Papilionoideae, contains around 20 species in Europe and North Africa.

Description Shrubs to 3m, with sharp spines formed by short shoots. The leaves are alternate, pinnate, with 3 leaflets on seedlings, later reduced to narrow scales or spines, falling early in the season to leave the plant bare. The flowers are pea-like, solitary or in small clusters, yellow, scented. Sepals 5, joined and split to form 2 usually hairy, petal-like, pointed lobes. Petals 5, unequal, the uppermost a broad, folded standard, the 2 outer narrow wings, asymmetrical at the base, the 2 lowest forming a rounded keel that encloses the stamens, style, and ovary. Stamens 10, joined in the lower half. Ovary superior, with 1 carpel containing 1–6 ovules; style 1. Pollination is by bees, which release the trigger-like style and are dusted with pollen at the same time. The pods are hairy, with 1–6 seeds, depending on the species.

Key Recognition Features The spiny shoots and the petal-like calyx.

Evolution and Relationships *Stauracanthus* Link, with 2 species from Spain, Portugal, and North Africa, is spiny like *Ulex*, but has opposite or subopposite leaves and the calyx tubular at the base.

Ecology and Geography On open hillsides and moorland, especially in areas subject to fire; 7 species in southwestern Europe, of which 3 extend to Britain; others in North Africa.

Comment Common gorse (*Ulex europaeus* L.) is a conspicuous flower of poor soils in early spring from Ireland eastwards to Italy; the flowers have a heavy, sweet, and buttery scent, reminiscent of coconut. Small gorse (*U. minor* Roth.) and western gorse (*U. gallii* Planch.) flower in late summer and autumn; they are generally lower shrubs, and are especially striking when mixed in and flowering with the magenta-flowered bell heather, *Erica cinerea* (see p.210).

Ulex europaeus
just under life size
January 29th

Elaeagnus parvifolia
flowers
just over life size
May 1st

Elaeagnus ebbingei
'Gilt Edge'
with fruit, ²/₃ life size
March 19th

*Elaeagnus
macrophylla*
fruits
1¼ × life size
March 19th

Elaeagnus macrophylla flowers,
just under life size
September 25th

Elaeagnus macrophylla
¹/₃ life size
September 25th

Elaeagnus

Elaeagnus L. (1753), in the family Elaeagnaceae, contains around 40 species around the northern hemisphere.

Description Trees to 7m, or shrubs, sometimes climbing and with spines. The leaves are alternate, evergreen or deciduous, simple, often silvery and scaly beneath. The flowers are solitary or in small clusters, white or yellowish, usually scented. Sepals 4, equal, joined at the base to form a tube; petals absent. Stamens 4, on the throat of the tube, alternating with the sepals. Ovary superior, with 1 carpel containing 1 ovule; style 1, with an elongated stigma. Pollination is by bees. The fruits are mealy or fleshy and juicy berries, with 1 stone-like seed.

Key Recognition Features The silvery, scaly, or hairy back of the simple leaves and the small, 4-lobed, scented flowers. *Daphne* (see p.170) has similar flowers but never has scaly leaves.

Evolution and Relationships In flower and in the 1-seeded fruit the Eleagnaceae is similar to the Thymeliaceae, which includes the familiar *Daphne*. It is here associated with the southern-hemisphere Proteaceae (see pp.306–309) with which it has in common the lack of petals and the single carpel, but the Proteaceae has diversified into a large number of remarkable shrubs, especially in Australia and South Africa. DNA evidence, however, now suggests that Eleagnaceae is closer to families such as Rhamnaceae (see pp.338–343) and Ulmaceae (see pp.160–63), in the order Rosales.

Ecology and Geography In open habitats and semi-deserts, and in scrub in the mountains; many species can exploit poor soils because of their nitrogen-fixing root nodules containing actinomycetes. *Elaeagnus* is found from eastern Europe across Asia to Japan and North America.

Comment Many species are cultivated for their scented flowers and attractive, silvery leaves; the scent of the early summer-flowering *E. angustifolia* L., sometimes called Russian olive, is especially arousing. The species *E. macrophylla* Thunb. and *E. pungens* Thunb. from Japan and their hybrid *E. × ebbingii* Boom are popular evergreens, their cultivars often having variegated leaves, small flowers with a sharp, penetrating scent in autumn, and juicy, reddish berries in spring.

Hippophae

Hippophae L. (1753), sea buckthorn, in the family Eleagnaceae, contains 3 species in Europe and Asia.

Description Trees to 12m, or shrubs, often suckering, with spine-tipped side branches. The leaves are alternate, deciduous, simple, and linear to lanceolate. The flowers are very small and brownish-green, the males in small clusters, the females solitary, the sexes on separate plants. Sepals 2, equal, joined at the base to form a tubular flower; petals absent. Stamens 4, on the throat of the tube. Ovary superior, with 1 carpel containing 1 ovule; style 1. Pollination is by wind. The fruits are orange, fleshy berries, with 1 stone-like seed.

Key Recognition Features The narrow, silver- or brown-scaled leaves and the masses of orange berries in autumn.

Evolution and Relationships Related to *Elaeagnus*, but with flowers adapted to wind-pollination.

Ecology and Geography On dunes, in the bare ground left by retreating glaciers, and in stony river valleys. *Hippophae* was an important coloniser of bare soils at the end of the ice ages, helped to thrive in sterile, mineral soils by its ability to fix nitrogen from the atmosphere. Now found from western Europe across Asia to the Himalayas.

Comment *Hippophae* is often planted to stabilise sandy soils and is valuable near the sea as it can tolerate salt-laden wind. It is also grown, especially in eastern Europe, for its berries, which are a good source of vitamin C. Male and female plants need to be planted nearby to get a good set of berries.

Hippophae rhamnoides
fruit, 2 × life size
September 12th

Hippophae rhamnoides
female flowers
just over life size, April 24th

Shepherdia argentea
½ life size
June 3rd

Shepherdia argentea
flowers, life size
March 5th

Shepherdia

Shepherdia Nutt. (1818), buffalo-berry, in the family Eleagnaceae, contains 3 species in North America.

Description Trees to 6m, or shrubs, often with spiny twigs. The leaves are opposite, deciduous, broadly elliptic to lanceolate, scaly or with stellate hairs beneath. The flowers are in small clusters or spikes, greenish, opening before the leaves. Sepals usually 4, sometimes 2 or 6, equal, joined at the base only to form a starry flower; petals absent. Stamens usually 8, on the throat of the tube, in groups alternating with the sepals. Ovary superior, but appearing inferior because the floral tube is blocked by a fleshy disc at the base of the stamens, with 1 carpel containing 1 ovule; style 1. Pollination is by wind. The fruits are fleshy, red or yellowish berries, topped by the persistent sepals, with 1 stone-like seed.

Key Recognition Features The opposite leaves and 8 stamens distinguish *Shepherdia* from the very similar *Hippophae*.

Evolution and Relationships Related to *Hippophae*, which it replaces in North America.

Ecology and Geography By streams and in open ground, throughout northern North America from Newfoundland to Alaska, southwards to California and New Mexico in the mountains.

Comment Occasionally planted as a slow-growing, silvery shrub. The berries were eaten by the American Indians. The genus is named after John Shepherd (c. 1764–1836) the first curator of Liverpool Botanic Garden, 1803–36, and friend of Nuttall and other botanists.

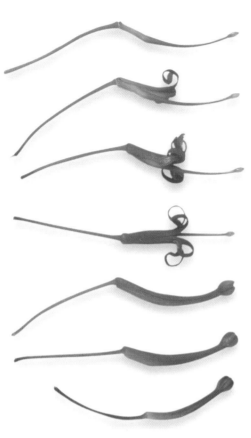

Embothrium coccineum
'Norquinco'
flowers at successive stages
from a bud (bottom) to a
flower from which the sepals
have fallen (top)
1 1/4 × life size, May 2nd

*Embothrium
coccineum*
leaves
1/2 life size
May 2nd

Embothrium coccineum
'Norquinco'
1/2 life size, May 2nd

Embothrium

Embothrium Forster & Forster fil. (1776), the Chilean firebush, in the family Proteaceae, contains 1 species in Chile and southwestern Argentina. Other species are now placed in *Oreocallis* R. Br..

Description Trees to 15m, or suckering shrubs. The leaves are alternate, evergreen or deciduous, lanceolate to ovate, smooth, hairless, and undivided. The flowers are in pairs, in loose heads, red or yellowish, very rarely pale yellow or white. The flower structure is unusual; sepals 4, equal, joined at the base to form a tubular flower, recurving when the flower opens; petals absent. Stamens 4, without stalks, attached to the cup-shaped tips of the sepals. Ovary superior, with 1 carpel containing several ovules; style 1, curved, with a conical pollen-presenter, which picks up the pollen from the stamens as it unbends. Pollination is by hummingbirds. The fruits are capsules topped by a persistent style, with several winged seeds.

Key Recognition Features The simple, leathery leaves and the masses of red flowers along the branches in early summer.

Evolution and Relationships The family Proteaceae is almost totally confined to the southern hemisphere, with 1 species, *Helicia cochinchinensis* Lour., reaching Japan and China and another, *Protea gaguedi*, in Africa as far north as Ethiopia. The greatest diversity is reached in South Africa with 115 species of *Protea* L., and in Australia with 71 species of *Banksia* L. fil.. Few species in the family are hardy enough to survive the frosty winters of the northern hemisphere, and only 2 species are found in New Zealand. The family is an isolated one, traditionally considered close to the Elaeagnaceae, although DNA evidence now suggests a very radical reassessment grouping it with Trochodendraceae and Tetracentraceae (see p.94), Platanaceae (see p.98), Buxaceae (see pp.129–30), and Nelumbonaceae (the lotus).

Ecology and Geography *Embothrium* is found in open, rocky places and on the margins of forest in Chile as far north as Concepción and in Argentina in the province of Neuquen.

Comment *Embothrium* is one of the most spectacular flowering trees to grow in the open in Europe and on the Pacific coast of North America. It requires good drainage at the root, moisture in summer and shelter from hot, dry or freezing wind.

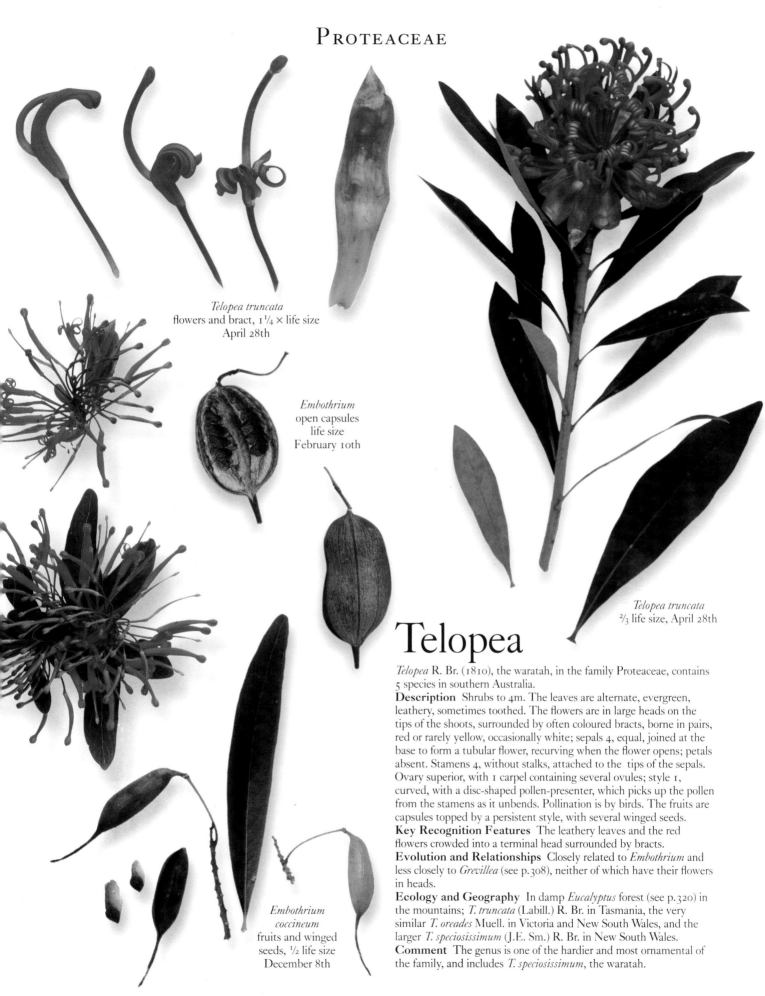

Telopea truncata
flowers and bract, 1¼ × life size
April 28th

Embothrium
open capsules
life size
February 10th

Telopea truncata
²⁄₃ life size, April 28th

Embothrium
coccineum
fruits and winged
seeds, ½ life size
December 8th

Telopea

Telopea R. Br. (1810), the waratah, in the family Proteaceae, contains 5 species in southern Australia.

Description Shrubs to 4m. The leaves are alternate, evergreen, leathery, sometimes toothed. The flowers are in large heads on the tips of the shoots, surrounded by often coloured bracts, borne in pairs, red or rarely yellow, occasionally white; sepals 4, equal, joined at the base to form a tubular flower, recurving when the flower opens; petals absent. Stamens 4, without stalks, attached to the tips of the sepals. Ovary superior, with 1 carpel containing several ovules; style 1, curved, with a disc-shaped pollen-presenter, which picks up the pollen from the stamens as it unbends. Pollination is by birds. The fruits are capsules topped by a persistent style, with several winged seeds.

Key Recognition Features The leathery leaves and the red flowers crowded into a terminal head surrounded by bracts.

Evolution and Relationships Closely related to *Embothrium* and less closely to *Grevillea* (see p.308), neither of which have their flowers in heads.

Ecology and Geography In damp *Eucalyptus* forest (see p.320) in the mountains; *T. truncata* (Labill.) R. Br. in Tasmania, the very similar *T. oreades* Muell. in Victoria and New South Wales, and the larger *T. speciosissimum* (J.E. Sm.) R. Br. in New South Wales.

Comment The genus is one of the hardier and most ornamental of the family, and includes *T. speciosissimum*, the waratah.

Lomatia ferruginea
floral parts, $1\frac{2}{3}\times$ life size, June 18th

Grevillea rosmarinifolia, flowers
¾ life size
April 18th

Grevillea rosmarinifolia
½ life size, April 18th

Grevillea

Grevillea R. Br. ex J. Knight (1809), in the family Proteaceae, contains around 250 species in Australia, with a few reaching New Guinea and Indonesia.

Description Trees to 30m, or shrubs, sometimes creeping. The leaves are alternate, evergreen, simple or deeply dissected. The flowers are in small or large clusters or spikes, white, red, pink, or yellow, sometimes scented. Sepals 4, equal, joined at the base to form a tube, recurving when the flower opens; petals absent. Stamens 4, attached to the tips of the sepals. Ovary superior, with 1 carpel containing 1 or 2 ovules; style 1, straight, curved, or hooked. Pollination is by birds such as honeyeaters and lorikeets, mostly in the red-flowered species, and by insects in white-flowered species. The fruits are small but often woody capsules with 1 or 2 seeds.

Key Recognition Features The leaves, usually silvery beneath, the stalked heads of paired flowers, and the small, usually thin-walled capsules.

Evolution and Relationships Related to *Hakea*, but less often stiff and spiny.

Ecology and Geography In sandy areas, deserts, heathland, or open *Eucalyptus* forest (see p. 320). The species are concentrated in Western Australia, where there are 135 species; there are 3 species in New Caledonia and 3 in New Guinea.

Comment The genus is named after the Hon. Charles Francis Greville (1749–1809), one of the founders of the Horticultural Society of London, now the Royal Horticultural Society.

Lomatia ferruginea
½ life size
August 10th

Lomatia

Lomatia R. Br. (1810), in the family Proteaceae, contains 12 species in Australia and South America.

Description Trees to 20m, or shrubs. The leaves are alternate, rarely opposite, evergreen, leathery, sometimes divided. The flowers are in pairs in small clusters or spikes, red, white, or yellowish. Sepals 4, equal, joined at the base to form a tube, recurving when the flower opens; petals absent. Stamens 4, attached to the tips of the sepals. Ovary superior, with 1 carpel containing 1 or 2 ovules; style 1, straight, curved, or hooked. Pollination is perhaps by hummingbirds in the red-flowered South American species, and by insects in the white-flowered species. The fruits are woody capsules with numerous seeds.

Key Recognition Features The 3 or 4 scales in the flower, and the numerous seeds in each capsule.

Evolution and Relationships Related to *Gevuina* Molina from South America, which has pinnate, leathery leaves, long spikes of white, yellow-green, or red, radially symmetrical flowers, and red then black, woody fruit with 1 edible seed.

Ecology and Geography In damp, peaty soils; 8 species in eastern Australia and Tasmania, 4 species in South America.

Comment Most species are rather dull shrubs with narrow leaves and small heads of whitish flowers. *Lomatia ferruginea* R. Br. from Chile is the most striking.

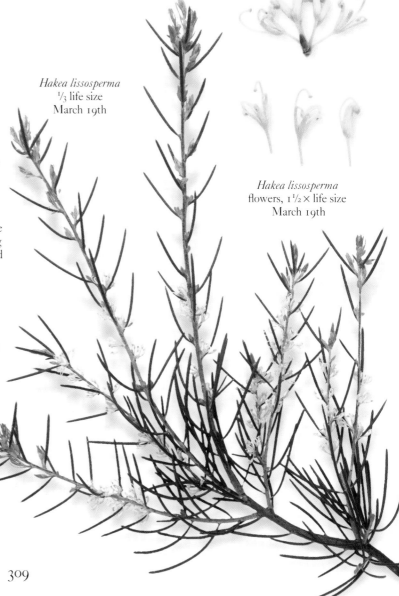

Hakea lissosperma
⅓ life size
March 19th

Hakea lissosperma
flowers, 1½ × life size
March 19th

Hakea

Hakea Schrader (1797), in the family Proteaceae, contains around 150 species in Australia.

Description Trees to 10m, or shrubs. The leaves are alternate, evergreen, often stiff and pointed, or leathery, flat, or holly-like, sometimes divided. The flowers are usually whitish, sometimes pink or red, in clusters or in dense, elongated spikes, along the shoots in the leaf axils. Sepals 4, joined at the base to form a tubular flower, curving as the flower opens; petals absent. Stamens 4, without stalks, attached to the tips of the sepals. Ovary superior, with 1 carpel containing several ovules; style 1, curved, with a conical pollen-presenter, which picks up the pollen from the stamens as it unbends. Pollination is by birds in the red-flowered species, mainly by butterflies in the white-flowered species. The fruits are large, thick-walled, woody capsules, often beaked or horned, with 1 or 2 winged seeds.

Key Recognition Features The clusters of flowers in the leaf axils and the large, woody, 1- or 2-seeded fruits.

Evolution and Relationships Related to *Grevillea*, but distinctive in its woody fruits and its stiff leaves, which are never silvery beneath.

Ecology and Geography Throughout Australia, but with most species in southwestern Western Australia. The hardiest species, including *H. sericea* Schrader, are from Tasmania and the mountains of southeastern Australia.

Comment A few *Hakea* species are sometimes cultivated in northern Europe as a curiosity. The more spectacular species with red flowers can be grown outside in the Mediterranean and California. *Hakea victoria* Drumm., the royal hakea, from Western Australia, has prickly, white-and-red variegated leaves on the flowering shoots.

Fuchsia fulgens
fruit, life size
September 24th

Fuchsia denticulata
flower cross-sections
life size, September 24th

Fuchsia denticulata
²/₃ life size
September 24th

Fuchsia magellanica
var. *molinae*
²/₃ life size, July 27th

*Fuchsia
procumbens*
²/₃ life size
July 28th

Fuchsia

Fuchsia L. (1753), in the family Onagraceae, contains around 105 species, mainly in South America and New Zealand.

Description Trees to 12m, or shrubs, sometimes climbing or creeping. The leaves are opposite, deciduous or evergreen. The flowers hang down singly in the leaf axils or in terminal clusters, red, orange, green, white, pink, or purple, with sepals, calyx tube, and petals often of contrasting colours. Sepals 4, usually reflexed, joined at the base to form an often tubular calyx; petals absent or 4, often overlapping each other. Stamens usually 8, longer than the petals. Ovary inferior, with 4 fused carpels containing numerous ovules; style 1, with a 4-lobed stigma. Pollination is usually by hummingbirds. The fruits are juicy berries, eaten by birds, which distribute the small seeds.

Key Recognition Features The opposite leaves and the flowers with 4 coloured sepals and long stamens.

Evolution and Relationships The Onagraceae is closely related to the Myrtaceae (see pp.313–21), but most genera are herbaceous perennials or annuals, and are particularly well represented in the Americas. The weedy willowherb, *Epilobium* L., is found in the temperate parts of both hemispheres. *Zauschneria* C. Presl, from California, often included in *Epilobium*, is closest to *Fuchsia*, being subshrubby with red flowers adapted to hummingbird pollination, though its narrow capsules and silky winged fruit are typical of *Epilobium*. The New Zealand fuchsias have small, dull-coloured flowers, which are upright and without petals in the creeping *F. procumbens* R. Cunn., and often produced in early spring directly out of the trunk in the tree *F. excorticata* Forster & Forster fil.. All the New Zealand species have flowers of 2 kinds, larger bisexual flowers with blue pollen and a style that matures before the anthers, and smaller flowers, which are female with abortive anthers; flowers that function as male only are also found.

Ecology and Geography In forests and scrub, mainly in the Andes, with several species in Mexico and the West Indies, 1 in Tahiti, and 4 in New Zealand.

Comment Many species and thousands of hybrids are cultivated for their flowers. The frost-hardy cultivars are derived from *F. magellanica* Lam. from southern Chile and Argentina. The genus is named after the Bavarian Leonart Fuchs (1501–66), sometime professor of medicine at Tübingen. His *De historia stirpium* (1542), was the outstanding illustrated herbal of its day, and its excellent illustrations (by one Albrecht Meyer) continued to be printed until the late 18th century.

ONAGRACEAE

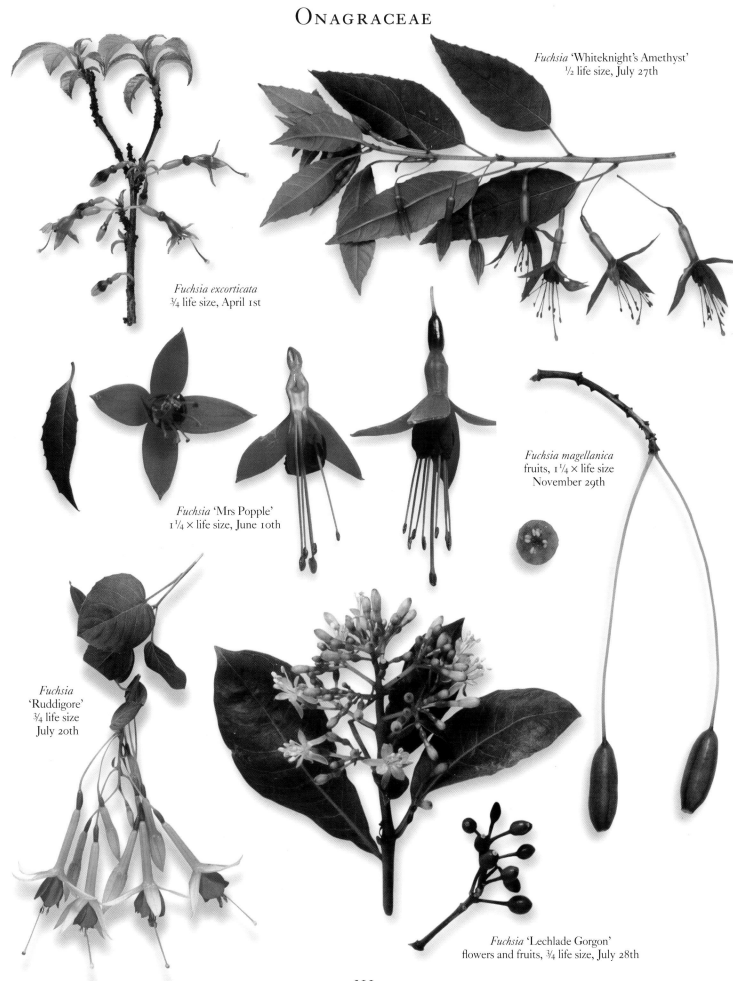

Fuchsia 'Whiteknight's Amethyst'
½ life size, July 27th

Fuchsia excorticata
¾ life size, April 1st

Fuchsia 'Mrs Popple'
1¼ × life size, June 10th

Fuchsia magellanica
fruits, 1¼ × life size
November 29th

Fuchsia
'Ruddigore'
¾ life size
July 20th

Fuchsia 'Lechlade Gorgon'
flowers and fruits, ¾ life size, July 28th

Punica granatum var. *nana*
1¼ × life size, October 5th

Punica

Punica L. (1753), the sole genus in the family Punicaceae, contains 2 species, *P. granatum* L. the pomegranate, from the eastern Mediterranean area to the Himalayas, and *P. protopunica* Balf. fil. from Socotra.

Description Trees to 6m, or shrubs, often with spiny twigs. The leaves are almost opposite, deciduous, simple, entire, and shining on the upper surface, exuding nectar from the tip. The flowers are solitary or in clusters of 2–4. Sepals 5–7, equal, joined at the base to form a tube, red; petals 5–7, red, rarely white, delicate, and crinkled. Stamens numerous. Ovary inferior, with 8–12 fused carpels containing numerous ovules; style 1, with a lobed stigma. Pollination is presumed to be by bees and beetles collecting the pollen. The fruits are red to yellowish, topped by the persistent sepals, with a juicy coating on the numerous seeds and a leathery shell.

Key Recognition Features The bright red flowers with crinkly petals and the large and beautiful fruit.

Evolution and Relationships Punicaceae is related to the mainly herbaceous family Lythraceae, which includes the common magenta-flowered *Lythrum salicaria* L.; woody members of the Lythraceae include the common ornamental tree *Lagerstroemia indica*, L. and the shrubby, yellow-flowered *Heimia* Link from South America. It also has similarities in flower and fruit to Myrtaceae (see pp.313–21).

Ecology and Geography On cliffs and rocky hillsides, often forming ancient, gnarled trees; the common species is now found from the Mediterranean to the Himalayas, but is probably native only along the south of the Caspian and in northeastern Turkey. *Punica protopunica* from Socotra is perhaps a more ancient species, with smaller flowers and fruit.

Comment The pomegranate tree has been valued since ancient times and its seeds have been found in Bronze Age Jericho; it is both refreshing in the drought of late summer, when the fruit is ripe, and medicinal. The fruit, which look delicious, but are full of seeds, were a symbol of fertility; the seeds do indeed contain oestrone. Persephone was condemned to remain for part of the year in the underworld because she had eaten the seed of a pomegranate there, and so had involuntarily married Hades. Paris is also supposed to have given Venus a pomegranate. Grenadine syrup is made from the fruit.

Punica granatum
½ life size
October 5th

Punica granatum
fruit, ⅔ life size
November 24th

Acca

Acca Berg (1855), in the family Myrtaceae, contains 6 species in South America, including the pineapple guava, *A. sellowiana* (Berg) Burret, formerly called *Feijoa sellowiana* (Berg) Berg.

Description Trees to 3m, or shrubs. The leaves are opposite, ovate, silvery beneath, evergreen. The flowers are solitary in the leaf axils. Sepals 4, equal, reflexed, joined at the base only to form a tube; petals 4, pinkish and spotted inside, white and hairy outside, somewhat crinkled, reflexed. Stamens numerous, crimson, longer than the petals. Ovary inferior, with 2 fused carpels containing numerous ovules; style 1. Pollination is perhaps by hummingbirds or butterflies. The fruits are green or yellowish, fleshy, and juicy, and contain numerous seeds.

Key Recognition Features The silvery twigs and undersides of the rounded leaves, the 4 petals, and the long, red stamens.

Evolution and Relationships *Psidium* L., the guava, is related to *Acca*, but has 5 petals and sepals and in the cultivated species, *P. guayava* L. from tropical America, much larger fruit with persistent green sepals. The relationships of the family Myrtaceae are discussed under *Myrtus* (see p.314).

Ecology and Geography In scrub at low altitudes in southern Brazil, northern Argentina, Paraguay, and Uruguay.

Comment The fruits of *Acca* are are sometimes sold as feijoas. They are made into jam, and used to make a fizzy drink in southern Russia.

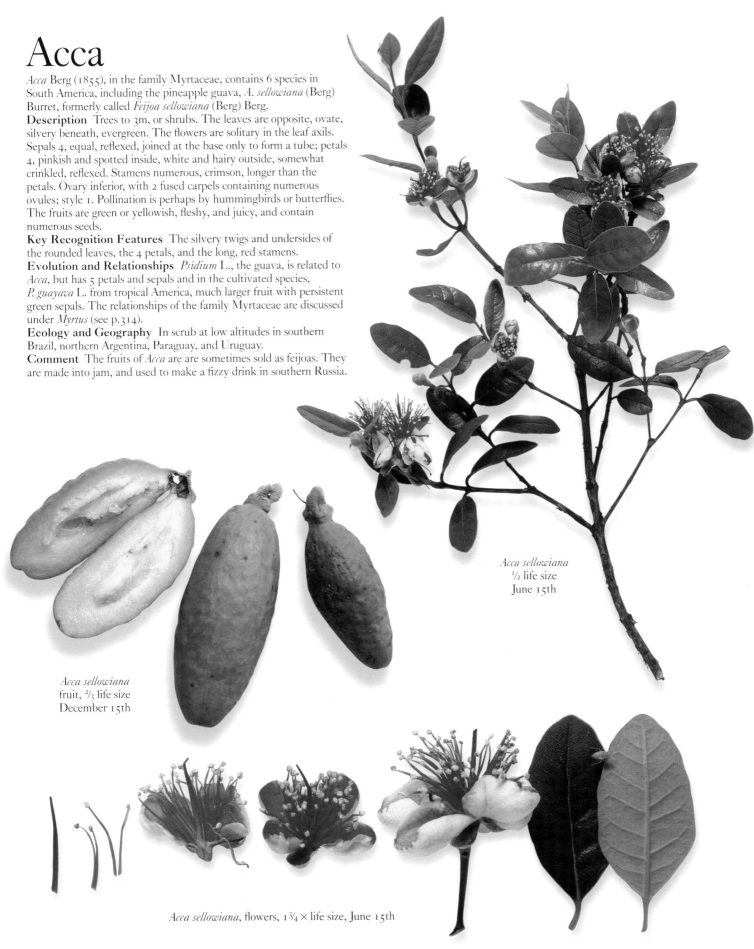

Acca sellowiana
½ life size
June 15th

Acca sellowiana
fruit, ⅔ life size
December 15th

Acca sellowiana, flowers, 1¾ × life size, June 15th

Myrtus

Myrtus L. (1753), in the family Myrtaceae, contains 2 species in the Mediterranean area, *M. communis* L., and *M. tarentina* L., the latter often ranked as a subspecies or variety of *M. communis*. The South American and New Zealand species formerly included in *Myrtus* are now placed in other genera, including *Amomyrtus*, *Luma*, and *Ugni* (see p.316).

Description Shrubs to 5m. The leaves are opposite, spirally arranged, simple, evergreen, and aromatic. The flowers are solitary in the leaf axils. Sepals 4 or 5, equal, often reddish, joined at the base to form a tube; petals 4, white, rounded. Stamens white, numerous. Ovary inferior, with fused carpels containing numerous ovules; style 1. Pollination is by bees. The fruits are purplish to black berries, rarely whitish, topped by the persistent sepals, with numerous seeds.

Key Recognition Features The aromatic, evergreen leaves and solitary, white flowers.

Evolution and Relationships Myrtaceae is associated with Onagraceae (see pp.310–11), Punicaceae (see p.312), and Lythracae in the order Myrtales. It is a mainly southern-hemisphere family, well represented in Australia, tropical Asia, and South America, but with *Myrtus* the only representative in Europe.

Ecology and Geography In scrub on dry hills, with *M. communis* around the Mediterranean eastwards to central Asia and Pakistan, and *M. tarentina* mostly in western Europe.

Comment In classical times myrtle was greatly loved as a symbol of beauty and youth; Aphrodite hid behind a myrtle bush when she arose naked from the sea. A spray of myrtle is traditionally carried in a bridal bouquet. The berries were used medicinally for indigestion, and twigs of *M. tarentina* have been found in Roman tombs.

Myrtus communis
'Variegata'
1 ½ × life size, October 5th

Myrtus tarentina
2 × life size, September 16th

Myrtus tarentina
½ life size
September 16th

Amomyrtus

Amomyrtus (Burret) Legrand & Kausel (1947), in the family Myrtaceae, contains 2 species in South America, of which one, *A. luma* (Molina) Legrand & Kaus., often known as *Myrtus lechleriana* Miq., is commonly cultivated.

Description Trees to 7m, or shrubs, with smooth and whitish or scaly bark. The leaves are opposite, simple, evergreen, and aromatic, reddish when young. The flowers are scented, solitary or up to 6 in a cluster, in the leaf axils. Sepals 5, equal, joined at the base; petals 5, creamy white, rounded. Stamens white, numerous. Ovary inferior, with 2 or 3 fused carpels containing few ovules; style 1. Pollination is presumed to be by bees. The fruits are red to black berries with 4–6 hard, woody seeds.

Key Recognition Features The 5-lobed calyx and clusters of creamy white flowers, which open flat.

Evolution and Relationships Very similar to *Luma*, which differs in its larger leaves with shorter stalks, and an always 2-celled ovary usually with numerous seeds. *Amomyrtus* flowers in spring, *Luma* in late summer.

Ecology and Geography In open or shady riversides and moist places in southern Chile and southwestern Argentina.

Comment *Amomyrtus luma* is an attractive tree, without the striking bark of the more familiar *Luma apiculata*, but producing more numerous flowers. It is good in gardens in the milder parts of western Europe, and in colder areas will do well in an unheated glasshouse.

Luma

Luma Gray (1854), in the family Myrtaceae, contains 2 species from South America, of which *Luma apiculata* (DC) Burret, often known as *Myrtus luma* Molina, is commonly cultivated.

Description Trees to 20m, or shrubs, often with bright orange-brown, smooth bark, peeling to reveal a smooth, grey underlayer. The leaves are opposite, almost round, and pointed, with very short stalks. The flowers are solitary or in clusters of 3. Sepals 4, equal, joined at the base; petals 4, white, usually incurved. Stamens numerous. Ovary inferior, with 2 fused carpels containing numerous ovules; style 1. Pollination is presumed to be by bees. The fruits are dark purple, fleshy berries, with 1–16 seeds.

Key Recognition Features The grey and red-brown bark of old trees, and the pairs of very short-stalked leaves.

Evolution and Relationships Close to *Amomyrtus* and the New Zealand genus *Lophomyrtus* Burret, in which the flowers are always solitary.

Ecology and Geography In moist, temperate forests in the Andes of southern Chile and Argentina.

Comment *Luma apiculata* is a most attractive tree, often seen in mild gardens on the western seaboard of Europe. The variety 'Glanleam Gold' has irregular pale and white edges to the leaves. The other species, *L. chequen* (Molina) Gray, has greyish-brown bark, smaller, glandular leaves, and solitary flowers.

Luma apiculata
fruit and flowers
life size
October 5th

Luma apiculata
fruit cross-sections and seeds
1 1/3 × life size, December 8th

Luma apiculata
2/3 life size
December 8th

Amomyrtus luma
1/2 life size, April 6th

315

Ugni

Ugni Turcz. (1848), in the family Myrtaceae, contains around 10 species in South America, of which *U. molinae* Turcz. is often cultivated and is described here.

Description Shrub to 2m. The leaves are opposite, ovate, dark green above and pale beneath. The flowers are solitary, cup-shaped, pointing downwards, pinkish, waxy, and scented. Sepals 5, equal, narrow, and pointed, joined at the base, the lobes reflexed in bud; petals usually 5. Stamens numerous, shorter than the petals. Ovary inferior, with 3 fused carpels containing numerous ovules; style 1. Pollination is presumed to be by insects. The fruits are dark red, fleshy, aromatic berries, smelling of wild strawberries (*Fragaria vesca* L.), with few seeds.

Key Recognition Features The myrtle-like, aromatic leaves and nodding, pinkish flowers.

Evolution and Relationships Previously called *Myrtus ugni* Molina, but distinct from the myrtles in its cup-shaped flowers and short stamens.

Ecology and Geography In scrub and on the edges of forest, in southern Chile.

Comment An attractive shrub with unusual flowers and delicious fruit.

Ugni molinae, fruit and seeds (above)
flowers (below), 2¼ × life size
October 6th

Ugni molinae
½ life size
October 6th

Ugni molinae
½ life size, December 8th

316

Leptospermum

Leptospermum Forster & Forster fil. (1776), the tea tree, in the family Myrtaceae, contains around 83 species in Australia, New Zealand. and South East Asia.

Description Trees to 18m, or shrubs, often with peeling bark. The leaves are alternate, small, simple, mostly narrowly elliptic, entire, often silvery, evergreen. The flowers are solitary or in clusters of 2 or 3, usually white, rarely pink or red, sometimes unisexual. Sepals 5–7, equal, joined to form a cup-shaped base; petals 5, usually rounded. Stamens numerous, usually shorter than the petals, in 5 groups opposite the petals, with versatile anthers. Ovary inferior or semi-inferior, with 5 fused carpels containing numerous ovules; style 1. Pollination is mainly by bees, but in some species mainly by beetles. The capsules are hard and brown, topped by the often persistent sepals, opening to release the seeds after a fire.

Evolution and Relationships Myrtaceae is divided into 2 groups according to whether the fruit is a fleshy berry or a dry capsule. The genera with dry capsules, (around 70 in all), such as *Leptospermum*, *Callistemon* and *Melaleuca* (see pp.318–19), *Eucalyptus* (see p.320), and *Kunzea* Reichb., are all from Australia and New Zealand; the only exceptions are *Tepualia* Griseb. from Chile and western Argentina and 1 species of *Metrosideros* (see p.321) in South Africa.

Key Recognition Features The small leaves and 5 rounded petals, with the old capsules still on the older twigs.

Ecology and Geography On rocks and heathland, in swamps, and by streams; 79 species in Australia, 3 in New Zealand, including *L. scoparium* Forster & Forster fil., and 4 extending through Indonesia to Malaysia and the Philippines. *Leptospermum laevigatum* (Gaertn.) F. Muell. is a serious weed in parts of the Cape.

Comment Several species, especially the red-flowered and double varieties of *L. scoparium*, are cultivated for ornament. *Leptospermum petersonii* F.M. Baill. is grown for its lemon-scented oils. The flowers of *Chamelaucium uncinatum* Schauer, the Geraldton wax, are rather similar to *Leptospermum*, but they are more waxy, with a ring of short stamens joined at the base; it is a popular cut flower throughout the world.

Leptospermum scoparium
'Fascination'
²/₃ life size
June 3rd

Leptospermum minutifolium
fruit and seeds, 2 × life size
October 3rd

Leptospermum lanigerum
1¹/₂ × life size, June 23rd

Leptospermum obovatum
¹/₃ life size, June 3rd

Callistemon

Callistemon, R. Br. (1814), the bottlebrush, in the family Myrtaceae, contains around 30 species in Australia.

Description Trees to 6m, or shrubs, often with papery bark. The leaves are alternate, simple, usually narrow, evergreen, often aromatic. The flowers are clustered on the stems below the current year's growth, usually red, but sometimes white, pink, or green, the colour produced by the stamens. Sepals 5, equal, joined to form a bell- or cup-shaped base; petals 5, usually small and rounded. Stamens numerous, longer than the petals. Ovary inferior, with 3 or 4 fused carpels containing numerous ovules; style 1, as long as the stamens. Pollination is usually by birds. The capsules are hard and brown, often remaining closed for many years and opening to release the seeds after a fire.

Key Recognition Features The narrow leaves and the long stamens of the cylindrical spikes of flowers, with the groups of old capsules still on the older twigs.

Evolution and Relationships Close to *Kunzea* Reichb., but that has flowers in small, terminal heads and often has shorter leaves and larger petals, with flowers very like a *Leptospermum* (see p.317).

Ecology and Geography On rocks, in sandy heathland, and in dry areas along streams around the coasts of Australia.

Comment Bottlebrushes are some of the most spectacular subtropical plants suitable for cultivation in climates with hot, dry summers and mild winters.

Melaleuca

Melaleuca L. (1753), in the family Myrtaceae, contains around 200 species, throughout Australia and northwards to Indomalesia.

Description Trees to 12m, or shrubs, often with many-layered, papery bark. The leaves are alternate or opposite, sometimes whorled, simple, evergreen, sometimes heath-like (*Erica*, see p.210) or narrowly lanceolate. The flowers are sometimes clustered on the stems below the current year's growth, sometimes in rounded heads, usually white but sometimes red, purple, pink, or green, the colour produced by the stamens. Sepals 5, equal, joined to form a bell- or cup-shaped tube; petals 5, usually small and rounded. Stamens numerous, longer than the petals, joined to form 5 bundles. Ovary inferior, with 3 fused carpels containing numerous ovules; style 1, as long as or longer than the stamens. Pollination is usually by birds. The capsules are hard and brown, often remaining closed for many years and opening to release the seeds after a fire.

Key Recognition Features The *Callistemon*-like trees or shrubs with the stamens joined into 5 bundles.

Evolution and Relationships Other smaller, closely related genera are *Lamarchia* Gaud., with 2 species in Western Australia, in which the staminal bundles of the large, solitary flowers are joined to form a tube, and *Conothamnus* Lindl., with 3 species in Western Australia, in which the carpels each have a single ovule. *Calothamnus* Labill. with 38 species, and *Regelia* Schauer with 6 species, both from Western Australia, also have the stamens joined into bundles, but have basifixed not versatile anthers.

Ecology and Geography On rocks, in sandy heathland and swamps, sometimes in seasonally flooded or saline areas, throughout Australia and Tasmania. A few species also in New Guinea, northwards to the Philippines and eastwards to Sumatra, mainland Malaysia, and India.

Comment Melaleucas are more diverse than callistemons, but often equally spectacular. The layers of loose bark protect the trunks of some species from fire, and can also hold rain, as I found on Tresco, when poking an overhead branch; my sleeve was filled with water.

Callistemon citrinus
⅓ life size
June 10th

Callistemon pallidus
½ life size, June 15th

Callistemon citrinus
'Splendens'
⅓ life size
June 24th

Callistemon
'Jeffersii'
⅓ life size
June 24th

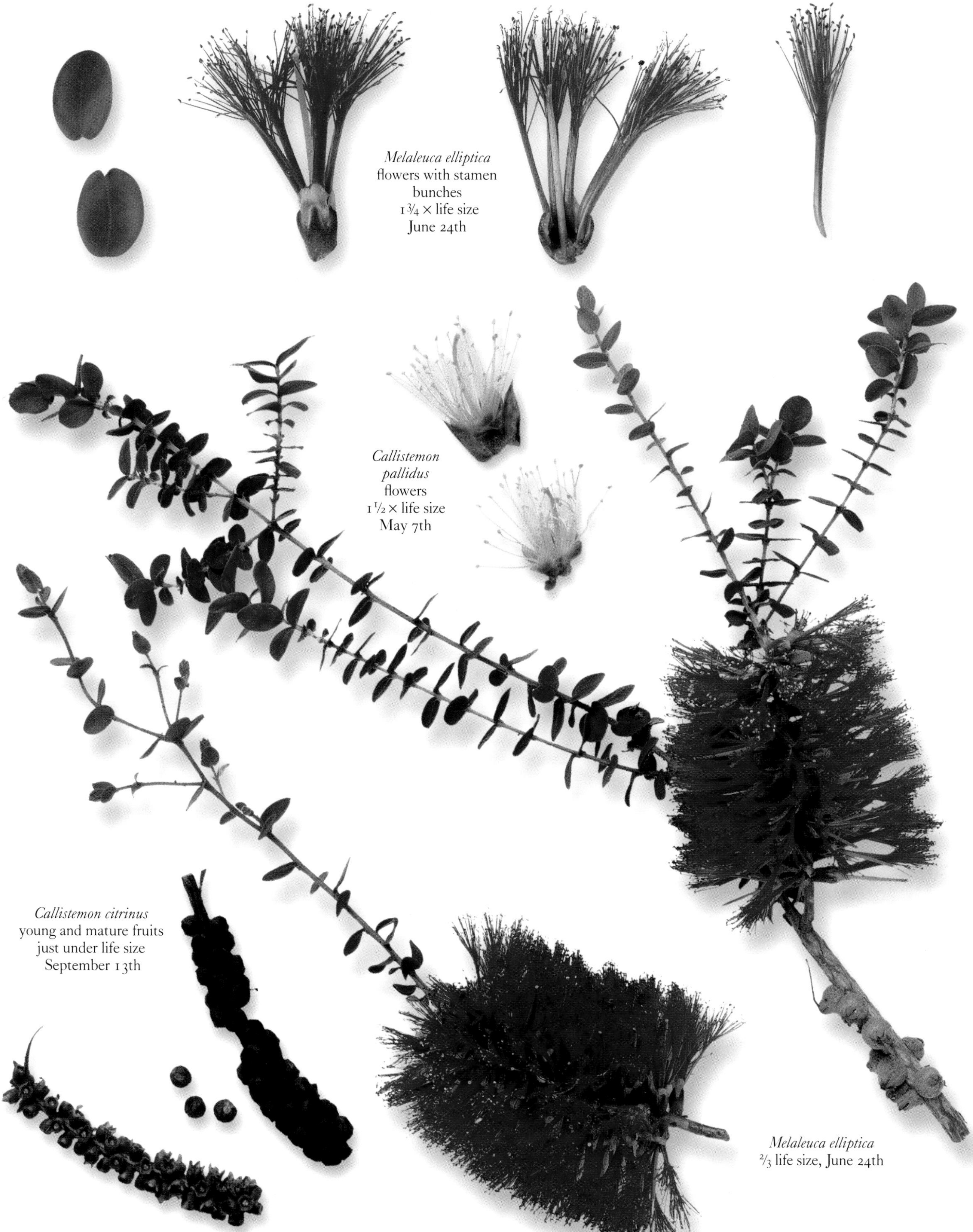

Melaleuca elliptica
flowers with stamen
bunches
1¾ × life size
June 24th

*Callistemon
pallidus*
flowers
1½ × life size
May 7th

Callistemon citrinus
young and mature fruits
just under life size
September 13th

Melaleuca elliptica
⅔ life size, June 24th

Eucalyptus

Eucalyptus L'Hérit. (1788), in the family Myrtaceae, contains around 700 species, mostly in Australia.

Description Trees to 97m, or shrubs, often with silvery or peeling bark. The leaves are evergreen and aromatic; on adult shoots, they are alternate, usually lanceolate or sickle-shaped; on juvenile shoots leaves are often opposite and almost round. The flowers are solitary or in umbels of 3 or more, with conspicuous, coloured stamens. Sepals and petals joined to form a cap, which falls as the stamens expand. Stamens numerous. Ovary inferior or partly superior, with 2—7 fused carpels containing numerous ovules; style 1, with a small stigma. Pollination is by insects, especially bees and beetles, and by birds. The fruits are hard and woody, opening by flaps to release the seeds.

Key Recognition Features The leathery leaves and the buds with a pointed cap.

Evolution and Relationships *Eucalyptus* has evolved in Australia to be the dominant tree or shrub throughout the continent. Some of the large-flowered species in Western Australia are now placed in the genus *Corymbia* K. Hill & L. Johnson, distinguished by having their flowers not in umbels but in flat-topped corymbs, and by their urn-shaped fruit; they include the ghostwoods and bloodgums, notably *C. ficifolia* (F. Muell.) K. Hill & L. Johnson, commonly planted for its beautiful red flowers.

Ecology and Geography On most soils and in most habitats, according to the species, throughout Australia and Tasmania, with a few species in eastern Malaysia and the Philippines.

Comment Most *Eucalyptus* require climates with little frost, but a few species from the mountains of southern Australia and Tasmania grow well in western Europe. *Eucalyptus* are widely planted and often naturalised in Mediterranean and subtropical climates worldwide. Many are valuable in the tropics as the fastest-growing source of domestic firewood. *Eucalyptus marginata* Sm. is the jarrah, used for flooring, panelling, and high-quality furniture. *Eucalyptus regnans* F. Muell. has reached 97m and *E. diversicolor* F. Muell. from Western Australia is almost as tall, reaching around 90m.

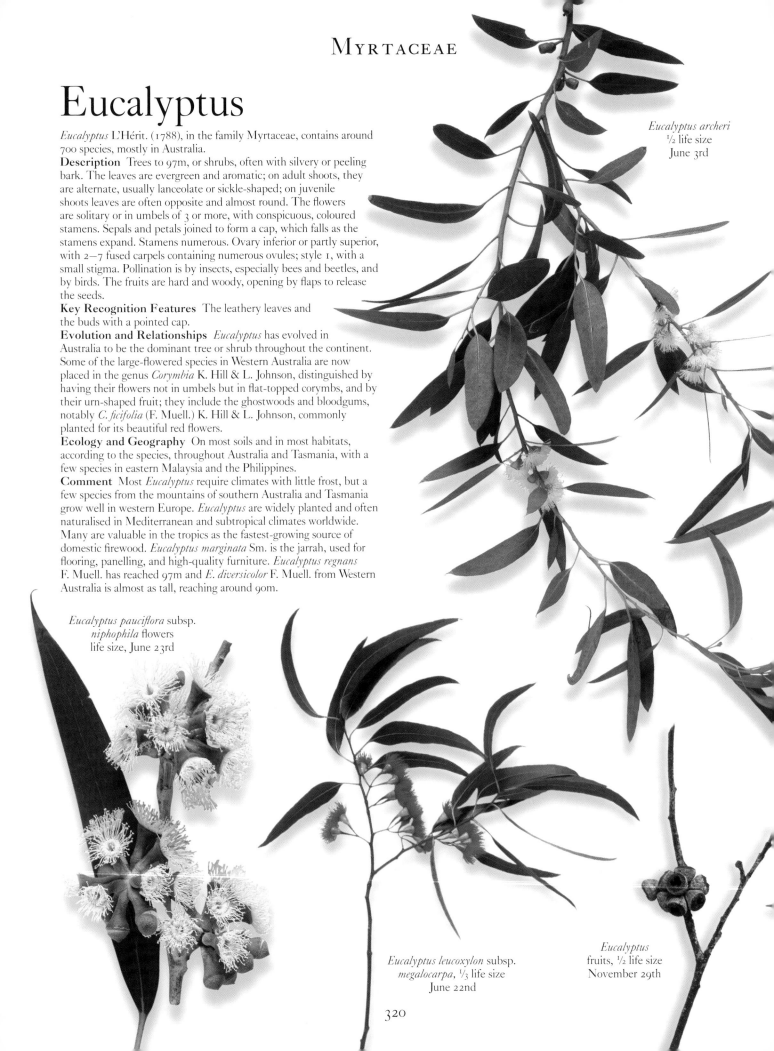

Eucalyptus archeri
½ life size
June 3rd

Eucalyptus pauciflora subsp.
niphophila flowers
life size, June 23rd

Eucalyptus leucoxylon subsp.
megalocarpa, ⅓ life size
June 22nd

Eucalyptus
fruits, ½ life size
November 29th

Eucalyptus leucoxylon
subsp. *megalocarpa*
flowers, 1¼ × life size
June 22nd

Metrosideros

Metrosideros Banks ex Gaertn. (1788), in the family Myrtaceae, contains around 50 species in Australia, New Zealand, and Malesia.

Description Trees to 25m, or shrubs, sometimes creeping or climbing like a small-leaved ivy (*Hedera*, see p.380). The leaves are opposite, evergreen. The flowers are in terminal clusters, white, scarlet or crimson, with conspicuous, coloured stamens. Sepals 5, overlapping, joined at the base only to form a cup-shaped calyx; petals 5, small, spreading. Stamens numerous, with versatile anthers. Ovary inferior or partly superior, with 3 fused carpels containing numerous ovules; style 1, with a small stigma. Pollination is by both insects and especially birds. The fruits are leathery capsules, with 3 valves, opening to release the seeds.

Key Recognition Features The opposite, often rounded leaves and heads of flowers with long stamens.

Evolution and Relationships Myrtaceae is closely related to Callistemon (see p.318), but differs in having opposite leaves and its flowers on stalks and in heads at the tips of the branches.

Ecology and Geography In forests; 11 species in New Zealand, many epiphytic as seedlings, 1 species, *M. angustifolia* (L.) Sm., in the Cape region of South Africa, 1 in Hawaii, the rest from Australia to New Guinea, northwards to the Philippines and mainland Malaysia eastwards to Sumatra, and in the Hawaiian Islands.

Comment *Metrosideros excelsa* Sol. ex Gaertn. is the *pohutukawa* or New Zealand Christmas tree, flowering in midsummer, especially near the coast; it is a spectacular tree in mild, maritime climates. *Metrosideros polymorpha* Gaud. from Hawaii is said to be especially resistant to sulphur dioxide in volcanic fumes.

Eucalyptus
cross sections of fruits
2 × life size
November 29th

Metrosideros
kermadecensis
¾ life size, May 5th

Metrosideros excelsa
¾ life size, May 5th

Metrosideros
umbellata
¾ life size
May 5th

Metrosideros kermadecensis
⅔ life size, May 5th

Alangium

Alangium Lam. (1783), the only genus in the family Alangiaceae, contains 21 species in eastern Asia, Africa, and Australasia.

Description Trees to 17m, or shrubs. The leaves are alternate, deciduous or evergreen, sometimes lobed. The flowers are in loose, branched clusters in the leaf axils, usually white, rarely yellow, scented. Sepals 4–10, often very small and apparently lacking; petals 4–10, narrow, curled back in the open flower. Stamens 4–30, with long, basifixed anthers and short, often hairy filaments. Ovary inferior or partly superior, with 2 fused carpels each containing 1 ovule; style 1, with a rounded stigma. Pollination is presumed to be by bees. The fruits are small, rounded, and juicy, with only 1 seed developing.

Key Recognition Features The small flowers with curled back petals in the leaf axils, and the lobed, alternate leaves.

Evolution and Relationships Alangiaceae is related to the Cornaceae (see pp.324–29); this relationship is traditional in botanical systems and has been confirmed by DNA studies. Alangiaceae, Cornaceae, and Nyssaceae are grouped together in the Cornales, most of which have small flowers and 1-seeded fruits.

Ecology and Geography In forests; mostly in tropical Africa, with 2 or 3 species in northern Australia and New Caledonia, and around 3 species in China. The evergreen *A. chinense* (Lour.) Harms is found in East Africa and from India eastwards to China.

Comment *Alangium platanifolium* (Sieb. & Zucc.) Harms, from China, Korea, and Japan, is sometimes grown as an ornamental. *Alangium villosum* (Blume) Wangerin, the Australian muskwood, has scented timber when freshly cut.

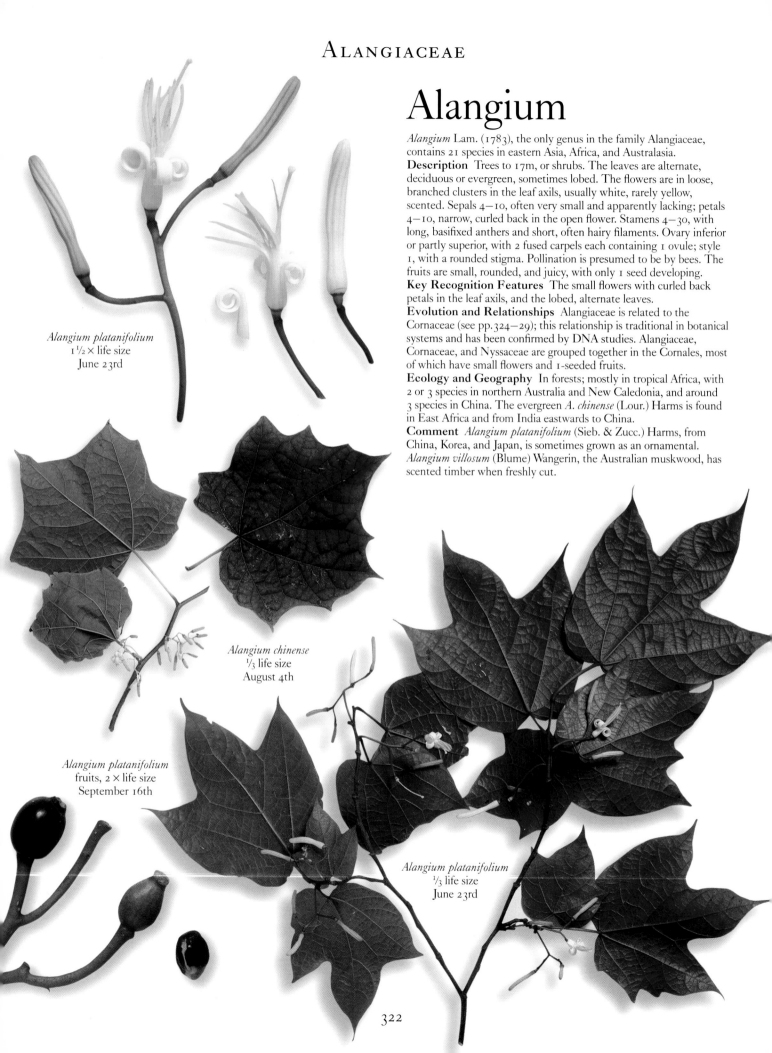

Alangium platanifolium
1 1/2 × life size
June 23rd

Alangium chinense
1/3 life size
August 4th

Alangium platanifolium
fruits, 2 × life size
September 16th

Alangium platanifolium
1/3 life size
June 23rd

Garrya

Garrya Dougl. ex Lindl. (1834), the only genus in the family
Garryaceae, contains 13 species in western North America and
Central America.

Description Trees to 15m, or shrubs. The leaves are opposite,
evergreen, simple. The flowers are unisexual, greenish, in hanging
catkins, with the males and females on different plants. Male flowers
in groups of 3 in the axils of cup-shaped bracts, without sepals and
with 4 very small petals, often joined at the tips, open towards the
base. Stamens 4, with large anthers. Female flowers solitary in the
axils of 2−4 small bracts (or petals) but otherwise without sepals or
petals. Ovary inferior and often hairy, with 2 or 3 fused carpels, each
containing 1 ovule, and 2 divergent styles. Pollination is by wind. The
fruits are dark blue or grey, at first juicy and bitter, but dry when ripe,
with 1 or 2 black seeds.

Key Recognition Features The rounded, evergreen leaves and the
silvery catkins in winter or early spring.

Evolution and Relationships Although superficially similar to
catkin-bearing trees such as hazels (*Corylus*, see p.119), and
traditionally associated with the Cornaceae, recent DNA studies
suggest that *Garrya* is an isolated genus and family, closest to the
Solanaceae (see pp.388−393).

Ecology and Geography In scrub on dry hills from Oregon and
California southwards to Mexico, Guatemala, and the West Indies.

Comment The genus is named after Nicholas Garry (1781−1856)
of the Hudson Bay Company, a friend of the plant collector David
Douglas who introduced *Garrya* to Europe in 1827. *Garrya* is often
cultivated for its silky male catkins; the plants respond well to
clipping or pruning in spring as soon as the flowers have ceased to be
beautiful.

Garrya elliptica
catkins, just under life size
January 22nd

Garrya elliptica
fruits, ¾ life size
August 4th

Garrya elliptica
⅓ life size, January 22nd

Nyssa

Nyssa L. (1753), the tupelo, in the family Cornaceae, contains 8 species in eastern Asia and America.

Description Trees to 30m, or shrubs. The leaves are alternate, deciduous, simple, smooth, and shining, crowded at the ends of the branches. The flowers are unisexual, greenish. Male flowers numerous, with 5 minute sepals and 5 very small petals. Stamens 8–16, in 2 whorls, with short anthers. Female flowers in few-flowered clusters, with 5–8 minute petals, vestigial stamens, and an inferior ovary with 1 carpel containing 1 ovule; style 1, forked. Pollination is by bees and perhaps also by wind. The fruits are small, oblong, and juicy, but bitter, with 1 seed.

Key Recognition Features The smooth and shining leaves and the very small, green flowers followed by black berries.

Evolution and Relationships Fossilised ribbed seeds, called *Nyssidium*, which possibly belonged to ancestral *Nyssa*, have been found in the lower Cretaceous and are among the oldest fosssils that may be of flowering plants. *Nyssa* is often included in the Nyssaceae, sometimes with *Camptotheca* Decne, a genus of 1 species, *C. acuminata* Decne. from China and South East Asia, with simple, broad leaves and spherical clusters of flowers and fruit, and with *Davidia*, but these 3 very distinct genera are now thought close to *Cornus* (see p.326).

Ecology and Geography In forests, often in areas subject to floods; 5 species in North America, 1 in Central America, 1 in China, and 1 from mainland Malaysia to the Philippines and New Guinea.

Comment The 2 commonly cultivated species, *N. sinensis* Oliver and *N. sylvatica* Marsh from eastern North America, are valued for their bright red colour in autumn.

Nyssa sylvatica
autumn leaves and fruits
1/3 life size, November 29th

Nyssa sinensis, fruits and seeds
1 1/4 × life size, December 8th

Nyssa sylvatica
flowers, 3/4 life size, June 3rd

Nyssa sylvatica
1/2 life size
May 18th

Davidia involucrata
1/3 life size
April 27th

Davidia involucrata
4 seedlings from 1 fruit
1/3 life size, April 18th

Davidia involucrata
young fruit
1 1/4 × life size
July 13th

Davidia involucrata
mature flowers and
bract, 1/2 life size
May 4th

Davidia involucrata
section of young
flowerhead with female
flower on the top
1 1/4 × life size, April 27th

Davidia

Davidia Baillon (1871), in the family Cornaceae, contains 1 species, *D. involucrata* Baillon from western China, sometimes called dove tree, handkerchief tree, or ghost tree.

Description Trees to 20m. The leaves are alternate, deciduous, with strong veins ending in sharp teeth, and an abruptly acuminate tip. The spherical head of flowers is backed by 2 leaf-like bracts, and has a functionally female flower surrounded by numerous male flowers. The male flowers have no sepals or petals, and 1–7 stamens. The female flowers have an inferior ovary with 6–10 carpels, each with 1 ovule and a short, tufted style, surrounded by a ring of sterile stamens. Pollination is by bees and perhaps also by wind. The fruits are green with a thin, fleshy coating around the ridged nut, which contains 3–5 seeds. The seeds may germinate either all simultaneously (as shown here) or in different years.

Key Recognition Features The simple leaves with strong, parallel veins ending in teeth, and the hanging flowers backed by 2 white, leaf-like bracts.

Evolution and Relationships *Davidia* is sometimes placed in its own family, the Davidiaceae, or associated with *Nyssa* and *Camptotheca* Decne. in the Nyssaceae. Recent work suggests they are all close to *Cornus* (see pp. 326–29). Its unique flowers suggest that *Davidia* is a very ancient genus, long isolated in the forests of western China, in the same habitats as the living fossils *Ginkgo* (see p.18) and *Metasequoia* (see p.38).

Ecology and Geography In dense, moist forests at 1500–2200m in the mountains of Sichuan and Hubei, often as isolated trees.

Comment The genus is named after Pére Armand David (1826–1900), French naturalist and missionary in China. He spent most of the summer of 1869 in Moupine, then a semi-independent principality, now Baoxing in Sichuan, and found hundreds of new species of plants, animals (including the giant panda), and birds. *Davidia*, named after him by Baillon, still grows in the forest near the mission where David stayed.

Cornus

Cornus L. (1753), in the family Cornaceae, contains around 65 species throughout the northern hemisphere.

Description Trees to 20m, or shrubs, sometimes small and suckering. The leaves are usually opposite, rarely alternate, simple, deciduous or evergreen, with distinct veins at an acute angle to the midrib. The flowers are usually bisexual, yellow, white, or greenish, sometimes in a tight head surrounded by white or pinkish, petal-like bracts. Sepals 4; petals 4; stamens 4; style 1, simple. Ovary inferior, 2-celled. Pollination is presumed to be by insects. The fruits are small, oblong, and juicy but sour, with a 2-celled stone, sometimes aggregated into a spherical, strawberry-like head.

Key Recognition Features The opposite leaves with distinct veins and the flower parts in groups of 4.

Evolution and Relationships Recent studies suggest that Cornaceae and related families are close to Hydrangeaceae (see pp.216—23) and Loasaceae (see Volume 2). *Cornus* in the narrow sense covers the European *C. mas* L. and related species in eastern Asia with small umbels of around 8 yellow flowers surrounded by small, green bracts and followed by cherry-like fruit (illustrated on pp.328—9). In the wider sense, used here, it includes the following, which are sometimes considered seperate genera: *Chamaepericlymenum* Hill, including the dwarf arctic *C. suecica* L., with a tight head of small flowers surrounded by white bracts and followed by tight bunches of red berries; *Swida* Opiz, syn. *Thelycrania* (Dumort.) Fourr., covering the species with flat-topped clusters of white flowers followed by rounded heads of berries, such as *C. rugosa* Lam. and *C. alba* L., often with colourful twigs (illustrated on pp.328—9); *Benthamidia* Spach., syn. *Benthamia* Lindl. and *Dendrobenthamia* Hutch., covering the species with white or pink bracts around a tight, round head of flowers followed by strawberry-like fruits, such as the flowering dogwood, *C. florida* L. and *C. kousa* (Miq.) Hance.

Ecology and Geography In forests, swamps, and dry scrub throughout the northern hemisphere. *Cornus* in the strict sense is found in Europe and Asia; *Benthamidia* in North America and eastern Asia; *Chamaepericlymenum* in acid bogs in the mountains of Britain, Europe, and North America; *Swida* is the least specialised of the groups, with species found throughout the northern hemisphere.

Comment A diverse and popular genus: *C. florida, C. kousa*, and their relatives are grown for their flowers, actually minute flowers with petal-like bracts; *C. stolonifera* Michx., *C. alba*, and related species for their winter twigs; and *C. controversa* Hemsl. and *C. alternifolia* L. fil. for their tiered branches and, in the forms generally cultivated, variegated leaves. *Cornus mas*, which also has a variegated form, is grown for its yellow flowers in early spring, and for its red fruit, which can be made into jam. Mabberley records that the name dogwood is derived from the use of the wood for skewers or "dogs".

The illustrations of Cornus *continue on pp.328—29.*

Cornus capitata
fruits and seeds
just under life size
November 15th

Cornus nuttallii
autumn leaves
⅓ life size
November 4th

Cornus florida
½ life size, May 11th

Cornus florida
f. *rubra*
½ life size
May 11th

CORNACEAE

Cornus nuttallii
'Ascona'
⅔ life size, April 8th

Cornus capitata
⅓ life size
June 15th

Cornus kousa
var. *chinensis*
bracts and open flowers
just under life size
June 23rd

Cornus canadensis
flowers, 2¼ × life size
May 1st

Cornus canadensis, ¾ life size
May 1st

Cornus canadensis
flowers and bract
2¼ × life size, May 1st

Cornus kousa
var. *chinensis*
½ life size, June 23rd

327

CORNACEAE

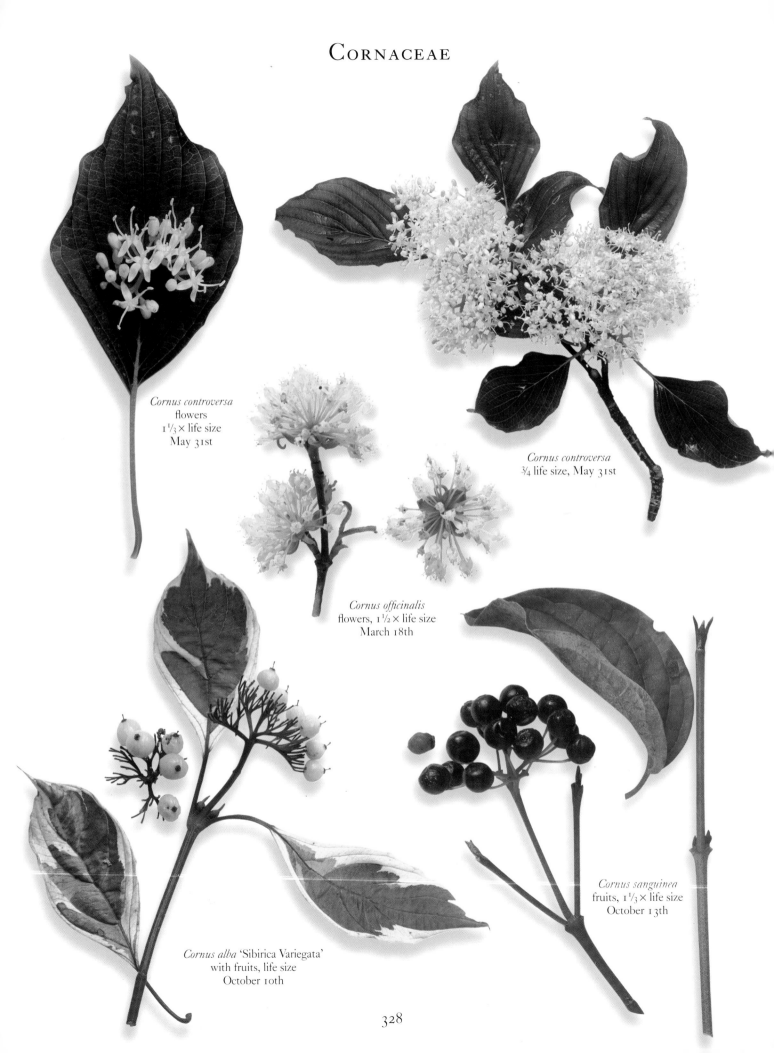

Cornus controversa
flowers
$1\frac{1}{3}\times$ life size
May 31st

Cornus controversa
¾ life size, May 31st

Cornus officinalis
flowers, $1\frac{1}{2}\times$ life size
March 18th

Cornus sanguinea
fruits, $1\frac{1}{3}\times$ life size
October 13th

Cornus alba 'Sibirica Variegata'
with fruits, life size
October 10th

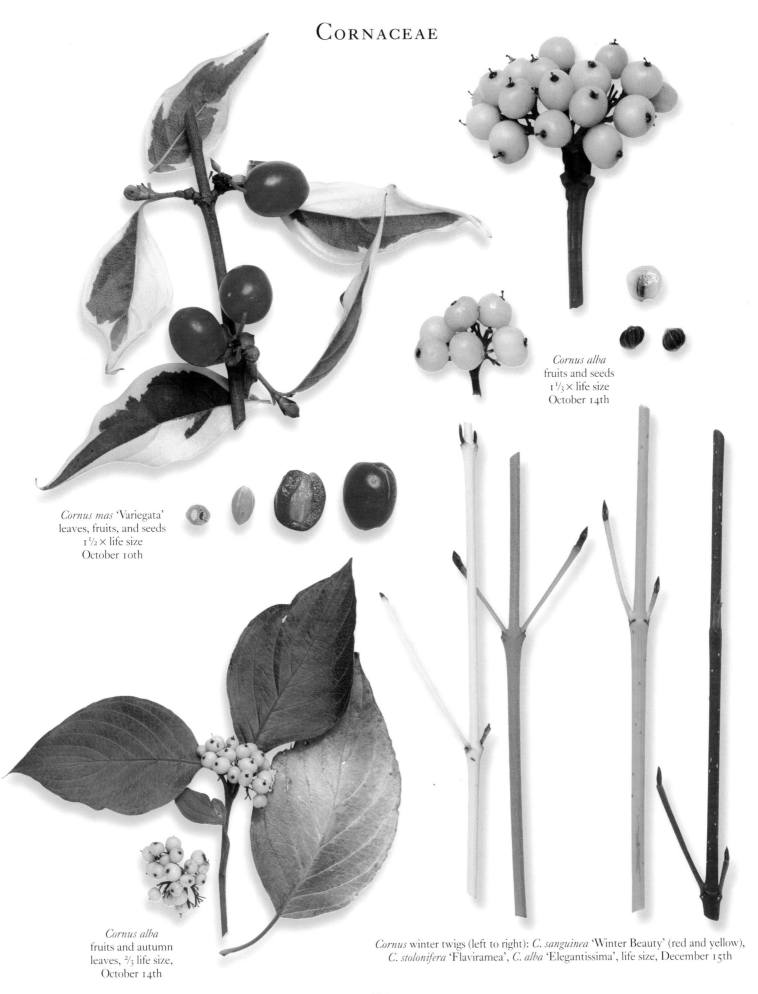

Cornus alba
fruits and seeds
$1^{1}/_{3}\times$ life size
October 14th

Cornus mas 'Variegata'
leaves, fruits, and seeds
$1^{1}/_{2}\times$ life size
October 10th

Cornus alba
fruits and autumn
leaves, $^{2}/_{3}$ life size,
October 14th

Cornus winter twigs (left to right): *C. sanguinea* 'Winter Beauty' (red and yellow),
C. stolonifera 'Flaviramea', *C. alba* 'Elegantissima', life size, December 15th

HELWINGIACEAE

Helwingia chinensis, male flowers
2 × life size, May 13th

Helwingia japonica
1/3 life size
May 17th

Helwingia chinensis, leaves and male flowers
1 1/2 × life size, May 13th

Helwingia chinensis
1/2 life size, May 13th

Helwingia

Helwingia Willd. (1865), in the family Helwingiaceae, contains
3 species from the Himalayas and eastern Asia.

Description Shrubs to 2m, often suckering. The leaves are opposite,
deciduous or evergreen, toothed and shining. The flowers are
unisexual, the sexes usually on separate plants, greenish, with usually
3–5 small petals, and come out of the centre of the leaves. Male
flowers about 5 in an umbel, stalked, with 3–5 stamens. Female
flowers stalkless, in groups of 1–3, with an inferior ovary with 3 or 4
carpels, each containing 1 ovule; style with 3–5 stigmas. Pollination is
presumed to be by small insects. The fruits are small, spherical and
red or shining black, with 3 or 4 stones.

Key Recognition Features The umbel of small, green or brown
flowers emerging from the centre of the leaves.

Evolution and Relationships *Helwingia* was often put in the
Cornaceae (see pp. 324–29), but DNA evidence suggests that it is not
closely related to *Cornus* (see pp. 326–29), but to Aquifoliaceae (see
p.179). It is similar to *Cornus*, however, in that the fruit is a drupe,
but similar to *Aucuba* (see p.332) in its brown, insignificant flowers.

Ecology and Geography In forests and scrub from Bhutan and
Darjeeling eastwards to China and Japan.

Comment The genus is named after G.A. Helwing (1666–1748),
a Prussian botanist. Both the narrow-leaved, evergreen *H. chinensis*
Batalin and the broad-leaved, deciduous *H. japonica* (Thunb.) Dietr.
are cultivated as curiosities.

Helwingia japonica
female flowers and
leaves, 1 1/3 × life size
May 17th

Griselinia

Griselinia Forster & Forster fil. (1786), in the family Griseliniaceae contains 7 species in South America and New Zealand.

Description Trees to 15m, or shrubs. The leaves are alternate, evergreen, simple, smooth, and leathery, usually asymmetric at the base. The flowers are unisexual, greenish, in branched clusters. Male flowers minute, with 5 sepals and 5 very small petals. Stamens 5, with short anthers. Female flowers have 5 sepals and either 5 very small petals or none, rarely with vestigial stamens, with 1 or 2 carpels and 3 styles. Pollination is presumed to be by insects. The fruits are small, fleshy, and dark purple with 1 seed.

Key Recognition Features The rounded, rather pale, evergreen leaves and green twigs in the commonly cultivated New Zealand species. The leaves curl and become black if frosted.

Evolution and Relationships Often included in the Cornaceae (see pp. 324–29), but recent DNA studies suggest that it is best kept apart in its own family, the Griseliniaceae.

Ecology and Geography In forests and scrub, with 2 species in New Zealand, including the commonly cultivated *G. littoralis* (Raoul) Raoul, and the remainder in Chile.

Comment Good evergreen shrubs for mild areas, especially near the sea. *Griselinia littoralis* is a much less oppressive green than most evergreens, and there are forms with variegated leaves. The genus is named after the Italian botanist Franc Griselini (1717–83).

Griselinia littoralis
fruits, life size
September 25th

Griselinia littoralis
flowers, just under life size
May 4th

Griselinia littoralis
⅔ life size, May 4th

Aucuba

Aucuba Thunb. (1783), in the family Aucubaceae, contains 3 species in the Himalayas and China,

Description Shrubs to 6m, with thick, green twigs. The leaves are alternate or grouped at the ends of the branches, evergreen, smooth, and leathery. The flowers are unisexual, brownish, the males and females on different plants. Male flowers numerous, in upright, branched bunches on the tips of the branches, with 4 minute sepals joined to form a ring and 4 small petals. Stamens 4, with conspicuous anthers. Female flowers in fewer-flowered clusters, with 4 petals, a short, thick style, and an inferior ovary with 1 carpel containing 1 ovule. Pollination is presumed to be by insects. The fruits are oblong and bright red, with 1 seed.

Key Recognition Features The leathery, shallow-toothed leaves, acrid when crushed, and often spotted with white, and the heads of small, dark brown flowers in spring.

Evolution and Relationships *Aucuba* was often put in the Cornaceae (see pp.324–29), but DNA studies suggest that it is not closely related. *Corokia* Cunn. is another genus formerly included in Cornaceae, but now considered separate, or even put in the Saxifragaceae. Here it is included in the Argophyllaceae (see p.452).

Ecology and Geography In forests and woods from the eastern Himalayas, in Bhutan and around Darjeeling, eastwards to Japan.

Comment The spotted laurel, *A. japonica* Thunb. 'Variegata', is common in Victorian shrubberies, as it tolerates urban pollution and thrives under plane trees (*Platanus*, see p.98)

Aucuba japonica leaves (left to right): 'Golden King', 'Crotonifolia', 'Lance Leaf', and *Aucuba japonica* ½ life size, April 30th

Aucuba japonica fruits and seeds just over life size, March 8th

Aucuba japonica female flowers 1½ × life size, April 18th

Aucuba japonica male flowers, ¾ life size April 18th

Aucuba japonica 'Variegata' ½ life size, March 8th

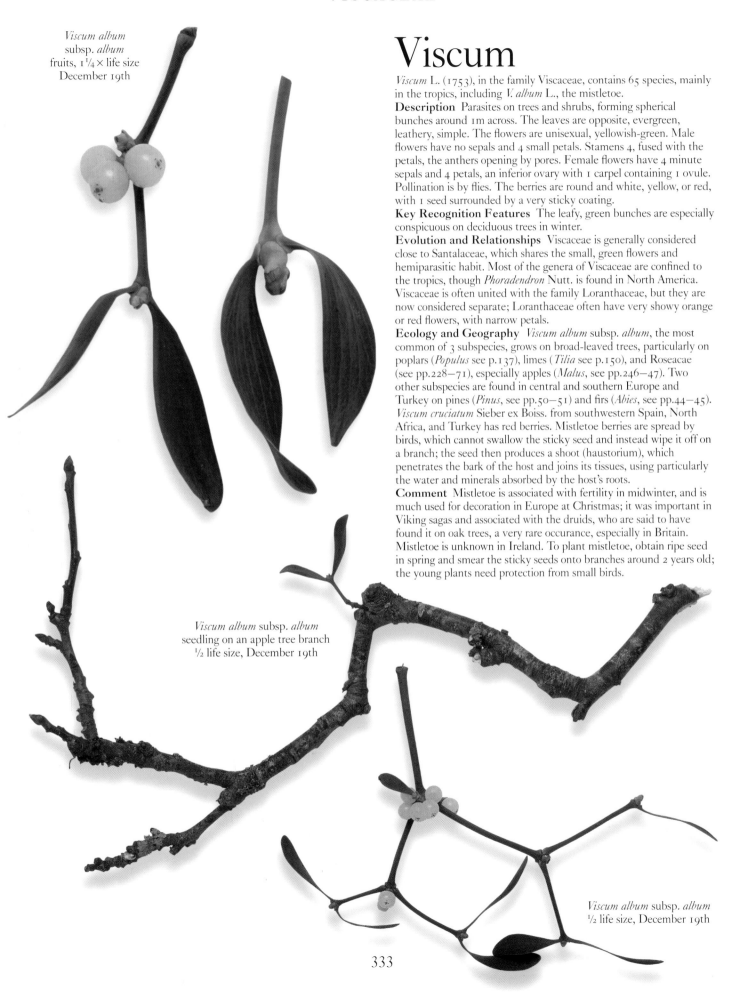

Viscum album
subsp. *album*
fruits, 1¼ × life size
December 19th

Viscum

Viscum L. (1753), in the family Viscaceae, contains 65 species, mainly in the tropics, including *V. album* L., the mistletoe.

Description Parasites on trees and shrubs, forming spherical bunches around 1m across. The leaves are opposite, evergreen, leathery, simple. The flowers are unisexual, yellowish-green. Male flowers have no sepals and 4 small petals. Stamens 4, fused with the petals, the anthers opening by pores. Female flowers have 4 minute sepals and 4 petals, an inferior ovary with 1 carpel containing 1 ovule. Pollination is by flies. The berries are round and white, yellow, or red, with 1 seed surrounded by a very sticky coating.

Key Recognition Features The leafy, green bunches are especially conspicuous on deciduous trees in winter.

Evolution and Relationships Viscaceae is generally considered close to Santalaceae, which shares the small, green flowers and hemiparasitic habit. Most of the genera of Viscaceae are confined to the tropics, though *Phoradendron* Nutt. is found in North America. Viscaceae is often united with the family Loranthaceae, but they are now considered separate; Loranthaceae often have very showy orange or red flowers, with narrow petals.

Ecology and Geography *Viscum album* subsp. *album*, the most common of 3 subspecies, grows on broad-leaved trees, particularly on poplars (*Populus* see p.137), limes (*Tilia* see p.150), and Roseacae (see pp.228–71), especially apples (*Malus*, see pp.246–47). Two other subspecies are found in central and southern Europe and Turkey on pines (*Pinus*, see pp.50–51) and firs (*Abies*, see pp.44–45). *Viscum cruciatum* Sieber ex Boiss. from southwestern Spain, North Africa, and Turkey has red berries. Mistletoe berries are spread by birds, which cannot swallow the sticky seed and instead wipe it off on a branch; the seed then produces a shoot (haustorium), which penetrates the bark of the host and joins its tissues, using particularly the water and minerals absorbed by the host's roots.

Comment Mistletoe is associated with fertility in midwinter, and is much used for decoration in Europe at Christmas; it was important in Viking sagas and associated with the druids, who are said to have found it on oak trees, a very rare occurance, especially in Britain. Mistletoe is unknown in Ireland. To plant mistletoe, obtain ripe seed in spring and smear the sticky seeds onto branches around 2 years old; the young plants need protection from small birds.

Viscum album subsp. *album*
seedling on an apple tree branch
½ life size, December 19th

Viscum album subsp. *album*
½ life size, December 19th

Celastrus

Celastrus L. (1753), in the family Celastraceae, contains around 30 species mainly in eastern Asia and North America.

Description Climbers to 20m. The leaves are alternate, deciduous, simple, usually rounded, colouring gold in autumn. The flowers are often unisexual, greenish, in loose bunches at the ends of the shoots and in the leaf axils. Petals 5. Male flowers have 5 stamens. Female flowers have 3 styles and 3 carpels. Pollination is presumed to be by flies. The fruits are small, spherical, often yellow, splitting into 3 to reveal the seeds in a red or orange, fleshy aril.

Key Recognition Features The twining stems, alternate leaves, and masses of yellow fruit, with orange-covered seeds inside.

Evolution and Relationships The family Celastraceae, with 88 genera, is largely tropical and is isolated; it has relationships, surprisingly, with *Parnassia* L.. It has also been associated with the Aquifoliaceae (see p.179). *Celastrus* itself is close to *Euonymus* (see pp.336–337), but has climbing stems, alternate leaves, and spherical fruit. The fresh leaves of *Catha edulis* (Vahl) Endl., a member of the Celastraceae from Arabia, Somalia, Ethiopia, and especially Yemen, are called *qat* or *khat* and chewed for their mild narcotic effects.

Ecology and Geography In forests; from China to Japan, with 1 species, *C. scandens* L., in eastern North America.

Comment *Celastrus* are sometimes cultivated for their ornamental fruit; *C. orbiculatus* Thunb. is the species most commonly grown, with masses of berries that remain on the branches into winter, after the leaves have fallen.

Celastrus scandens
½ life size
June 21st

Celastrus orbiculatus
flowers, 2 × life size
June 21st

Celastrus orbiculatus
fruits, ⅓ life size
December 5th

*Celastrus
orbiculatus*
⅓ life size
June 21st

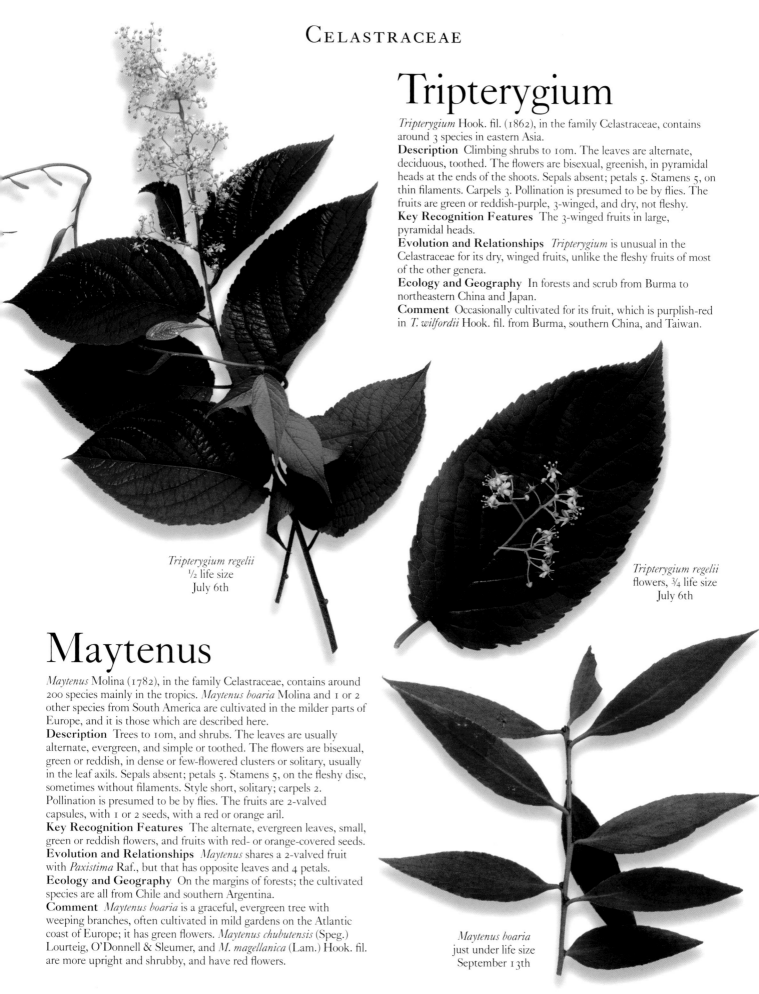

Tripterygium

Tripterygium Hook. fil. (1862), in the family Celastraceae, contains around 3 species in eastern Asia.

Description Climbing shrubs to 10m. The leaves are alternate, deciduous, toothed. The flowers are bisexual, greenish, in pyramidal heads at the ends of the shoots. Sepals absent; petals 5. Stamens 5, on thin filaments. Carpels 3. Pollination is presumed to be by flies. The fruits are green or reddish-purple, 3-winged, and dry, not fleshy.

Key Recognition Features The 3-winged fruits in large, pyramidal heads.

Evolution and Relationships *Tripterygium* is unusual in the Celastraceae for its dry, winged fruits, unlike the fleshy fruits of most of the other genera.

Ecology and Geography In forests and scrub from Burma to northeastern China and Japan.

Comment Occasionally cultivated for its fruit, which is purplish-red in *T. wilfordii* Hook. fil. from Burma, southern China, and Taiwan.

Tripterygium regelii
½ life size
July 6th

Tripterygium regelii
flowers, ¾ life size
July 6th

Maytenus

Maytenus Molina (1782), in the family Celastraceae, contains around 200 species mainly in the tropics. *Maytenus boaria* Molina and 1 or 2 other species from South America are cultivated in the milder parts of Europe, and it is those which are described here.

Description Trees to 10m, and shrubs. The leaves are usually alternate, evergreen, and simple or toothed. The flowers are bisexual, green or reddish, in dense or few-flowered clusters or solitary, usually in the leaf axils. Sepals absent; petals 5. Stamens 5, on the fleshy disc, sometimes without filaments. Style short, solitary; carpels 2. Pollination is presumed to be by flies. The fruits are 2-valved capsules, with 1 or 2 seeds, with a red or orange aril.

Key Recognition Features The alternate, evergreen leaves, small, green or reddish flowers, and fruits with red- or orange-covered seeds.

Evolution and Relationships *Maytenus* shares a 2-valved fruit with *Paxistima* Raf., but that has opposite leaves and 4 petals.

Ecology and Geography On the margins of forests; the cultivated species are all from Chile and southern Argentina.

Comment *Maytenus boaria* is a graceful, evergreen tree with weeping branches, often cultivated in mild gardens on the Atlantic coast of Europe; it has green flowers. *Maytenus chubutensis* (Speg.) Lourteig, O'Donnell & Sleumer, and *M. magellanica* (Lam.) Hook. fil. are more upright and shrubby, and have red flowers.

Maytenus boaria
just under life size
September 13th

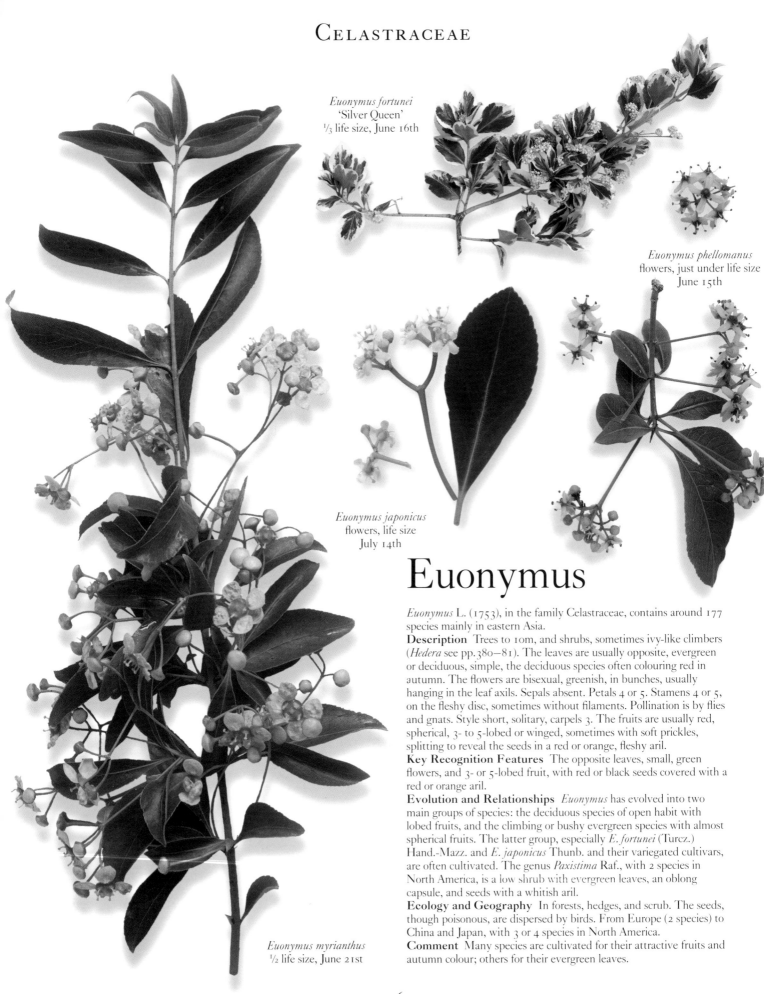

Euonymus fortunei
'Silver Queen'
1/3 life size, June 16th

Euonymus phellomanus
flowers, just under life size
June 15th

Euonymus japonicus
flowers, life size
July 14th

Euonymus myrianthus
1/2 life size, June 21st

Euonymus

Euonymus L. (1753), in the family Celastraceae, contains around 177 species mainly in eastern Asia.

Description Trees to 10m, and shrubs, sometimes ivy-like climbers (*Hedera* see pp. 380–81). The leaves are usually opposite, evergreen or deciduous, simple, the deciduous species often colouring red in autumn. The flowers are bisexual, greenish, in bunches, usually hanging in the leaf axils. Sepals absent. Petals 4 or 5. Stamens 4 or 5, on the fleshy disc, sometimes without filaments. Pollination is by flies and gnats. Style short, solitary, carpels 3. The fruits are usually red, spherical, 3- to 5-lobed or winged, sometimes with soft prickles, splitting to reveal the seeds in a red or orange, fleshy aril.

Key Recognition Features The opposite leaves, small, green flowers, and 3- or 5-lobed fruit, with red or black seeds covered with a red or orange aril.

Evolution and Relationships *Euonymus* has evolved into two main groups of species: the deciduous species of open habit with lobed fruits, and the climbing or bushy evergreen species with almost spherical fruits. The latter group, especially *E. fortunei* (Turcz.) Hand.-Mazz. and *E. japonicus* Thunb. and their variegated cultivars, are often cultivated. The genus *Paxistima* Raf., with 2 species in North America, is a low shrub with evergreen leaves, an oblong capsule, and seeds with a whitish aril.

Ecology and Geography In forests, hedges, and scrub. The seeds, though poisonous, are dispersed by birds. From Europe (2 species) to China and Japan, with 3 or 4 species in North America.

Comment Many species are cultivated for their attractive fruits and autumn colour; others for their evergreen leaves.

Euonymus oxyphyllus
fruits, ½ life size
October 8th

Euonymus europaeus
'Red Cascade'
½ life size
October 8th

Euonymus phellomanus
fruits, ½ life size
October 3rd

Euonymus oxyphyllus
fruits and seeds
just over life size
October 8th

Euonymus alatus var.
apterus, ½ life size
October 8th

Euonymus europaeus
'Red Cascade'
fruits and seeds
just over life size
October 8th

Euonymus alatus
autumn leaves and winged stems
½ life size, October 12th

Euonymus cornutus
var. *quinquecornutus*
fruit, ¾ life size
September 10th

Ceanothus

Ceanothus L. (1753), the California lilac, in the family Rhamnaceae, contains around 55 species in North America.

Description Small trees to 7m, or shrubs, often thorny and sometimes prostrate. The leaves are alternate, evergreen or deciduous, shallowly toothed, pinnately veined or with 3 main veins from the base. The flowers are bisexual, blue or white, in pyramidal or elongated heads in the leaf axils. Sepals 5, coloured, pointed, joined at the base to a fleshy disk. Petals 5, hooded and narrow at the base. Stamens 5, opposite the petals, with flat filaments. Pollination is by bees and flies. Ovary superior, with 3 carpels and a 3-fid style or 3 short styles. The fruits are 3-lobed capsules, breaking into 3 when ripe.

Key Recognition Features The heads of small, blue flowers and the leathery leaves; the white-flowered species usually have thorns.

Evolution and Relationships *Ceanothus* is close to *Pomaderris* Labill. from Australia and New Zealand, which has yellow flowers.

Ecology and Geography In scrub, especially on open hillsides in California; it is successful on bare soils because the roots contain the actinomycete *Frankia*, which fixes nitrogen. Mainly in western North America, from British Columbia southwards to Guatemala, with 2 species in eastern North America from Maine and Ontario southwards.

Comment The western, blue-flowered species and the many hybrids derived from them are excellent and popular ornamental shrubs, thriving in poor, dry soils. Leaves of *C. americanus* L., the New Jersey tea, were used as tea by native Americans and by the rebel troops during the American War of Independence.

Ceanothus 'Puget Blue'
½ life size, April 4th

Ceanothus arboreus
½ life size, April 20th

338

RHAMNACEAE

Ceanothus × delineanus
'Henri Desfossé'
$2/3$ life size, June 23rd

Ceanothus megacarpus
flowers, $2\frac{1}{4}$ × life size
May 4th

Ceanothus 'Snow Flurries'
just over life size, April 4th

Ceanothus megacarpus
leaves, fruits, and seeds
$1\frac{1}{2}$ × life size, October 5th

Ceanothus megacarpus
fruits, just over life size
June 23rd

Ceanothus megacarpus
$2/3$ life size, April 4th

Ceanothus × delineanus
'Gloire de Versailles'
$2/3$ life size, June 23rd

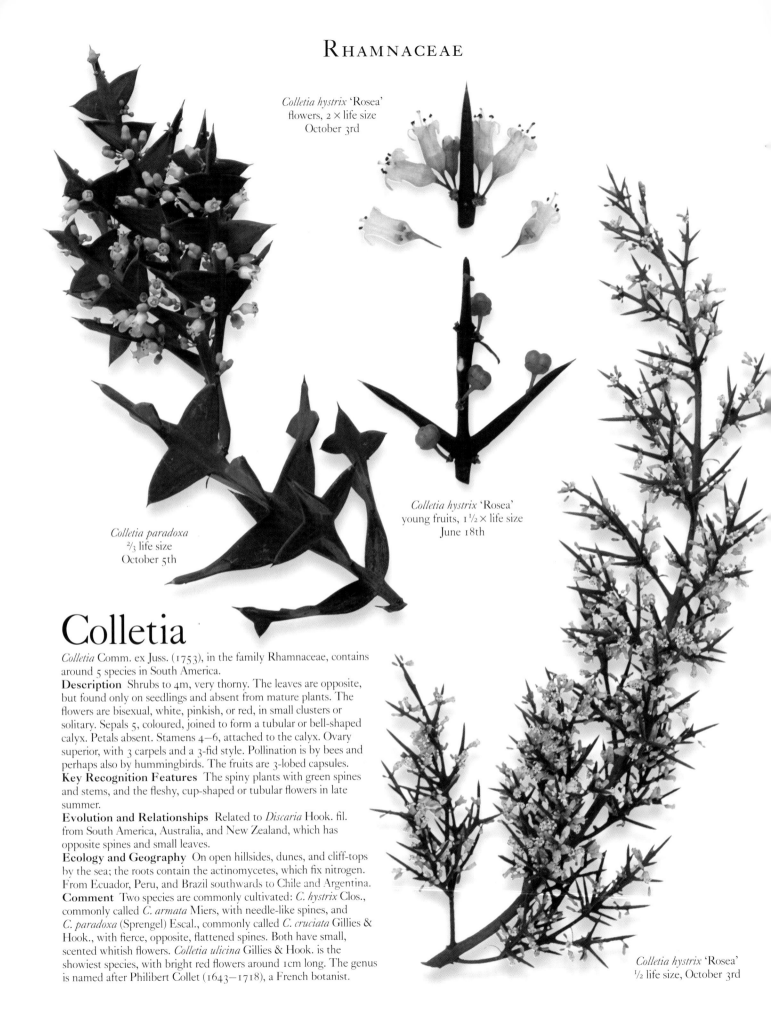

Colletia hystrix 'Rosea'
flowers, 2 × life size
October 3rd

Colletia hystrix 'Rosea'
young fruits, 1 ½ × life size
June 18th

Colletia paradoxa
⅔ life size
October 5th

Colletia

Colletia Comm. ex Juss. (1753), in the family Rhamnaceae, contains around 5 species in South America.

Description Shrubs to 4m, very thorny. The leaves are opposite, but found only on seedlings and absent from mature plants. The flowers are bisexual, white, pinkish, or red, in small clusters or solitary. Sepals 5, coloured, joined to form a tubular or bell-shaped calyx. Petals absent. Stamens 4–6, attached to the calyx. Ovary superior, with 3 carpels and a 3-fid style. Pollination is by bees and perhaps also by hummingbirds. The fruits are 3-lobed capsules.

Key Recognition Features The spiny plants with green spines and stems, and the fleshy, cup-shaped or tubular flowers in late summer.

Evolution and Relationships Related to *Discaria* Hook. fil. from South America, Australia, and New Zealand, which has opposite spines and small leaves.

Ecology and Geography On open hillsides, dunes, and cliff-tops by the sea; the roots contain the actinomycetes, which fix nitrogen. From Ecuador, Peru, and Brazil southwards to Chile and Argentina.

Comment Two species are commonly cultivated: *C. hystrix* Clos., commonly called *C. armata* Miers, with needle-like spines, and *C. paradoxa* (Sprengel) Escal., commonly called *C. cruciata* Gillies & Hook., with fierce, opposite, flattened spines. Both have small, scented whitish flowers. *Colletia ulicina* Gillies & Hook. is the showiest species, with bright red flowers around 1cm long. The genus is named after Philibert Collet (1643–1718), a French botanist.

Colletia hystrix 'Rosea'
½ life size, October 3rd

Discaria

Discaria Hook. (1830), in the family Rhamnaceae, contains around 8 species in the southern hemisphere.

Description Small trees or shrubs to 5m, very thorny. The leaves and thorns are opposite, narrow, mainly on the young shoots. The flowers are bisexual, white or greenish, in dense clusters or solitary. Sepals 4 or 5, coloured, joined to form a tubular or bell-shaped calyx. Petals very small or absent. Stamens 4 or 5, attached to the calyx. Ovary superior, with 3 carpels and a 3-fid style. Pollination is presumed to be by bees and flies. The fruits are 3-lobed capsules, either exploding or floating and dispersed by water.

Key Recognition Features Usually spiny plants with green spines and stems, and the fleshy, cup-shaped or tubular flowers in late summer.

Evolution and Relationships Closely related to *Colletia*.

Ecology and Geography On open hills and dunes, and in scrub and dry riverbeds, with 5 species in South America, 2 in Australia, and 1, *D. toumatou* Raoul, in New Zealand.

Comment *Discaria toumatou* is sometimes cultivated as a curiosity. *Discaria chacaye* (G. Don) Tortosa, syn. *D. discolor* Dusen, from Chile and Argentina has scented flowers.

Hovenia dulcis
½ life size
October 12th

Hovenia dulcis
just under life size
September 13th

Discaria chacaye
flowers, 1¾ × life size
June 3rd

Discaria chacaye
½ life size, June 3rd

Hovenia

Hovenia Thunb. (1781), the Chinese raisin tree, in the family Rhamnaceae, contains 2 species in eastern Asia.

Description Trees to 20m, or shrubs, without thorns. The leaves are alternate, 3-veined, wavy-edged, stalked. The flowers are bisexual, white or greenish, in dense clusters in the leaf axils and on the ends of shoots. Sepals 5, purplish or greenish. Petals 5, very small, folded around the stamens. Stamens 5. Ovary superior, with 3 carpels and a 3-lobed style. The fruits are 3-celled berries with fleshy stalks. Pollination is presumed to be by bees and flies. The stalks become red, edible, and sweet after frost. Seeds flat.

Key Recognition Features The wavy-edged, stalked leaves with 3 veins, and the fleshy fruit stalks.

Evolution and Relationships Closely related to the tropical *Colubrina* Rich. ex Brogn, which includes *C. arborescens* (Mill.) Sarg. from the West Indies and central America.

Ecology and Geography In woods in China, Korea and Japan.

Comment The edible fruit-stalks are said to help hangovers. The tree needs a hot summer to flower and fruit well.

Paliurus

Paliurus Mill. (1768), in the family Rhamnaceae, contains 8 species in Europe and Asia.

Description Trees to 7m, or shrubs, sometimes creeping, usually with thorns. The leaves are deciduous, alternate, 3-veined, in 2 rows on an often zig-zag, green twig. The flowers are bisexual, yellowish or greenish, in dense clusters in the leaf axils and on the ends of shoots. Sepals 5; petals 5, shorter than the sepals. Stamens 5. Ovary superior, with 2 or 3 carpels. Pollination is presumed to be by bees and flies. The fruits are 2- or 3-celled, flattened discs, with a wing around the edge and 1 seed in each cell.

Key Recognition Features The 3-nerved leaves in 2 rows and the green, disk-like fruit.

Evolution and Relationships Similar to *Ziziphus* Mill. in leaf, but that has juicy, edible, cherry-like fruit.

Ecology and Geography On dry hills and in scrub from southeastern Europe eastwards to China, Korea, and Japan.

Comment *Paliurus spina-christi* Mill., called Christ's thorn and by tradition used for the crown of thorns at Calvary, is a common feature of dry hills in the eastern Mediterranean. It is sometimes planted as an ornamental, or as a thorny hedge.

Paliurus spina-christi
fruits, ½ life size
October 5th

Paliurus spina-christi
flowers, 2 × life size
June 22nd

Paliurus spina-christi
1¼ × life size
June 22nd

Paliurus spina-christi
fruits and seed
life size, October 5th

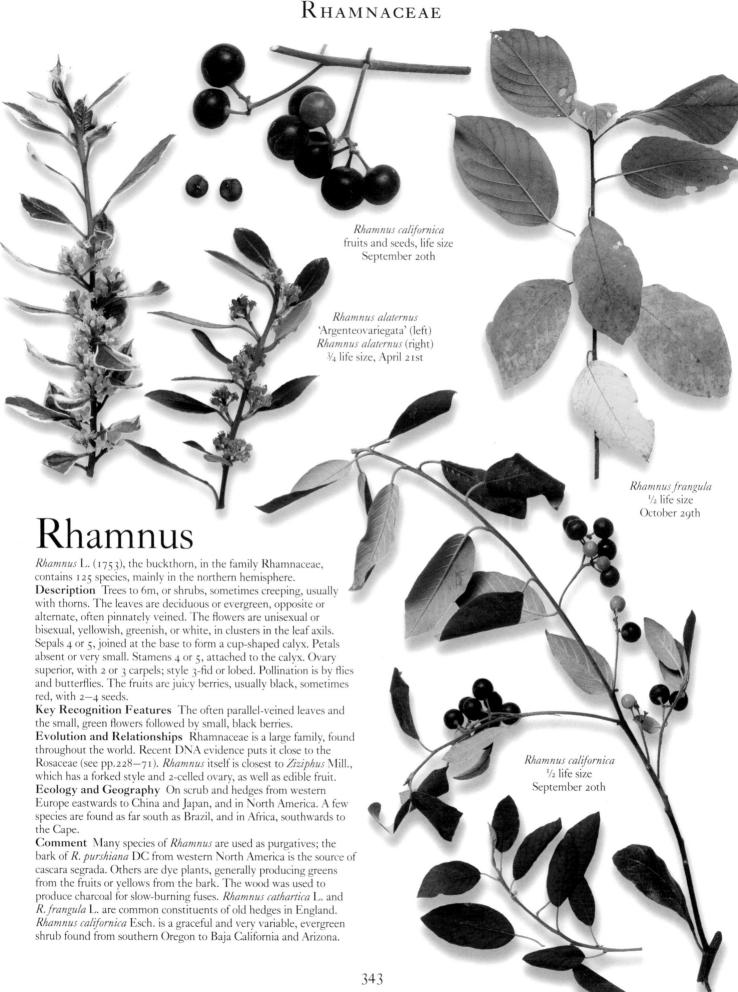

Rhamnus californica
fruits and seeds, life size
September 20th

Rhamnus alaternus
'Argenteovariegata' (left)
Rhamnus alaternus (right)
¾ life size, April 21st

Rhamnus frangula
½ life size
October 29th

Rhamnus californica
½ life size
September 20th

Rhamnus

Rhamnus L. (1753), the buckthorn, in the family Rhamnaceae, contains 125 species, mainly in the northern hemisphere.

Description Trees to 6m, or shrubs, sometimes creeping, usually with thorns. The leaves are deciduous or evergreen, opposite or alternate, often pinnately veined. The flowers are unisexual or bisexual, yellowish, greenish, or white, in clusters in the leaf axils. Sepals 4 or 5, joined at the base to form a cup-shaped calyx. Petals absent or very small. Stamens 4 or 5, attached to the calyx. Ovary superior, with 2 or 3 carpels; style 3-fid or lobed. Pollination is by flies and butterflies. The fruits are juicy berries, usually black, sometimes red, with 2–4 seeds.

Key Recognition Features The often parallel-veined leaves and the small, green flowers followed by small, black berries.

Evolution and Relationships Rhamnaceae is a large family, found throughout the world. Recent DNA evidence puts it close to the Rosaceae (see pp.228–71). *Rhamnus* itself is closest to *Ziziphus* Mill., which has a forked style and 2-celled ovary, as well as edible fruit.

Ecology and Geography On scrub and hedges from western Europe eastwards to China and Japan, and in North America. A few species are found as far south as Brazil, and in Africa, southwards to the Cape.

Comment Many species of *Rhamnus* are used as purgatives; the bark of *R. purshiana* DC from western North America is the source of cascara segrada. Others are dye plants, generally producing greens from the fruits or yellows from the bark. The wood was used to produce charcoal for slow-burning fuses. *Rhamnus cathartica* L. and *R. frangula* L. are common constituents of old hedges in England. *Rhamnus californica* Esch. is a graceful and very variable, evergreen shrub found from southern Oregon to Baja California and Arizona.

Vitis vinifera 'Schiava Grossa', ½ life size
October 3rd

Vitis vinifera 'Schiava Grossa'
fruit and seeds, just over life size
October 3rd

Vitis coignetiae
young leaf and flowers
⅔ life size
May 23rd

Vitis

Vitis L. (1753), the grape, in the family Vitaceae, contains around 65 species, mainly in the northern hemisphere.
Description Climbers to 20m, usually with tendrils opposite the leaves. The leaves are deciduous, alternate, often lobed. The flowers are unisexual or bisexual, greenish, in stalked bunches in the leaf axils. Sepals minute. Petals 5, joined to form a cap and falling together as the flower opens. Stamens 5. Ovary superior, with 2 cells, each with 2 ovules; style short. Pollination is by flies. The fruits are juicy berries, usually black or purple, with 1–4 seeds.
Key Recognition Features The often maple-like leaves (*Acer*, see pp. 354–58) and small, green flowers followed by small, black or green berries. *Vitis* is distinguished from other genera in the Vitaceae by having the petals falling as a cap.
Evolution and Relationships Recent DNA evidence indicates that Vitaceae is an isolated family, despite many resemblances to to Rhamnaceae (see pp. 338–43). It differs in its climbing habit, and in most species by having tendrils. Of the 13 genera of Vitaceae *Vitis*, *Parthenocissus*, *Ampelopsis* Mich., and *Cayratia* Juss. are temperate, the rest tropical or subtropical.
Ecology and Geography In scrub and rocky places, and climbing high into forest trees from southern Europe eastwards to China and Japan, and in North America.
Comment The grapevine, *V. vinifera* L., probably originated in the foothills of eastern Anatolia; it has been cultivated for over 5000 years in Syria and Egypt, and probably made into wine for almost as long. The wild subspecies has male and female flowers on separate plants, the cultivated one has bisexual flowers. 'Schiava Grossa', more often called 'Black Hamburg', is an old and reliable dessert variety. Several cultivars are grown as ornamentals, including 'Purpurea' with dark purple leaves and 'Incana' with whitish, cobwebby young leaves. 'Brant', a hybrid with the American variety 'Clinton', is a very hardy grape with good, sweet fruit and beautiful red and yellow autumn colour. The ornamental *V. coignetiae* Planch. from north Japan and Korea has deep purple leaves in autumn; I have seen it in forests on Hokkaido, climbing to the top of tall lime trees (*Tilia*, see p. 150). *Vitis vulpina* L. from North America has scented flowers and fruit that become sweet after having been frozen.

Vitis vinifera 'Purpurea'
⅓ life size
October 3rd

Vitis coignetiae
autumn leaves
⅓ life size, October 3rd

Parthenocissus quinquefolia
fruits, ¾ life size
September 16th

Parthenocissus tricuspidata
⅓ life size
September 24th

Parthenocissus quinquefolia
½ life size
September 24th

Parthenocissus

Parthenocissus Planch. (1906), the Virginia creeper, in the family Vitaceae, contains around 10 species in North America and eastern Asia.

Description Climbers to 20m, usually with tendrils ending in adhesive pads. The leaves are deciduous, alternate, often lobed or divided into 3 or 5 leaflets. The flowers are unisexual or bisexual, greenish, in small bunches in the leaf axils. Sepals minute; petals 4 or 5, separate. Stamens 5. Ovary superior, with 2 or rarely 3 cells; style short. Pollination is by flies. The fruits are juicy berries, usually black or purple, with 1–4 seeds.

Key Recognition Features The rather thin stems and tendrils with pads. The leaf shape is variable, the fruits small and hard.

Evolution and Relationships *Parthenocissus* differs from others in this family by the absence of a nectar-producing disc in the flower. *Ampelopsis* Mich. has similar variations in leaf shape, from lime-like (*Tilia*, see p.150) to compound and pinnatifid, but has a 4-lobed calyx and a disc. *Cissus* L. has around 200 species mainly in the tropics; *C. discolor* Blume, with elongated, heart-shaped leaves with silvery markings, is a commonly grown houseplant.

Ecology and Geography On rocks and climbing high into trees in forests from the Himalayas eastwards to China and Japan, and in eastern North America southwards to Mexico.

Comment Names have been the subject of some confusion; Virginia creeper, *P. quinquefolia* (L.) Planch. is a native of North America and has leaves divided into 5 separate leaflets. Boston ivy, sometimes also called Virginia creeper, *P. tricuspidata* (Sieb. & Zucc.) Planch., is a native of China and Japan and has 3-lobed leaves, sometimes divided into separate leaflets. Both grow fast and have beautiful autumn colour. *Parthenocissus henryana* (Hemsl.) Diels & Gilg is one of the most beautiful, with 5 reddish leaflets marked with silver veins.

Polygala

Polygala L. (1753), the milkwort, in the family Polygalaceae, contains around 500 species through much of the world.

Description Trees (in the tropics), shrubs, or herbaceous perennials, often creeping. The leaves are alternate, occasionally opposite, simple, evergreen or deciduous. The flowers are generally in loose spikes at the ends of the branches. Sepals 5, unequal, the inner 2 petal-like, the rest smaller. Petals 3, rarely 5, the upper 2 joined to the staminal tube, the lower boat-shaped, often with a 2-lobed and fimbriated crest. Stamens usually 8, the filaments joined into a split tube. Ovary superior, with 2 cells; style short. Pollination is by bees. The fruits are flattened, often notched capsules with 1 seed in each cell. The seeds have an appendage, an aril or caruncle, which is sometimes reduced to a tuft of hairs.

Key Recognition Features The pea-like flowers with a pair of petal-like sepals, and a fringed lip.

Evolution and Relationships The flowers of *Polygala* show interesting parallels with the flowers of Leguminosae (see pp.272–303) and recent DNA studies show that the 2 families are closely related.

Ecology and Geography Mostly in heath and rocky places but a few species, such as the Himalayan *P. arillata* D. Don, in forests; throughout the world, apart from New Zealand.

Comment The shrubby *Polygala* species from South Africa, such as the broom-like (see pp.300–302) *P. virgata* Thunb., are very different from the dwarf herbaceous species of European moorlands and mountains, and from the woodland species of eastern North America. Another group of species are clover-like annuals, characteristic of the American prairies.

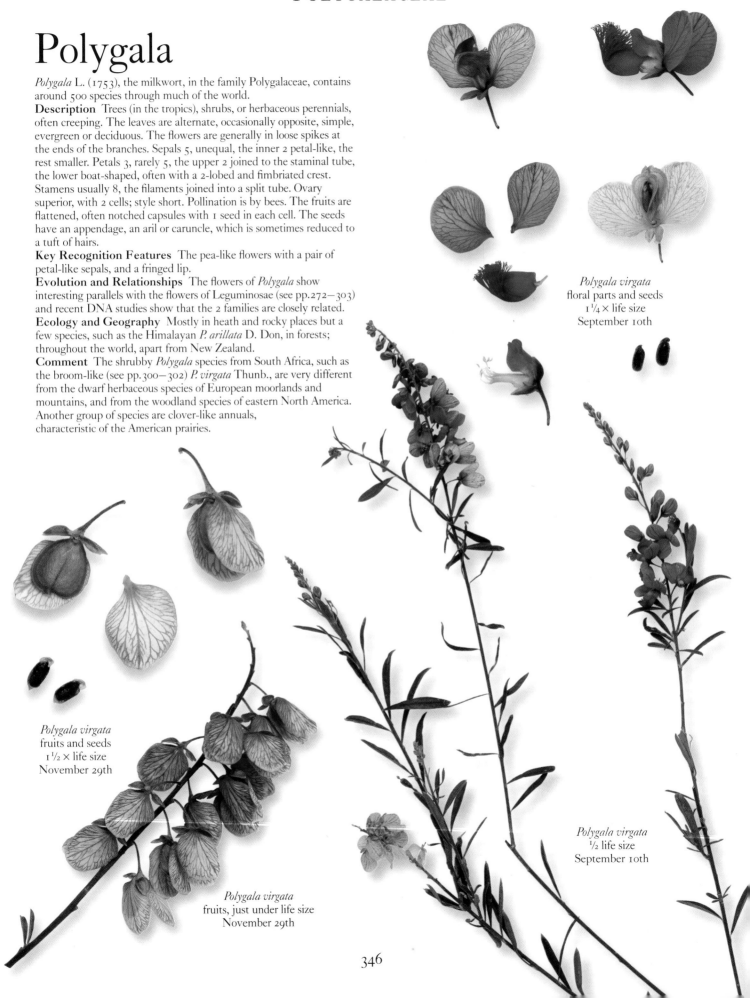

Polygala virgata
floral parts and seeds
1¼ × life size
September 10th

Polygala virgata
fruits and seeds
1½ × life size
November 29th

Polygala virgata
fruits, just under life size
November 29th

Polygala virgata
½ life size
September 10th

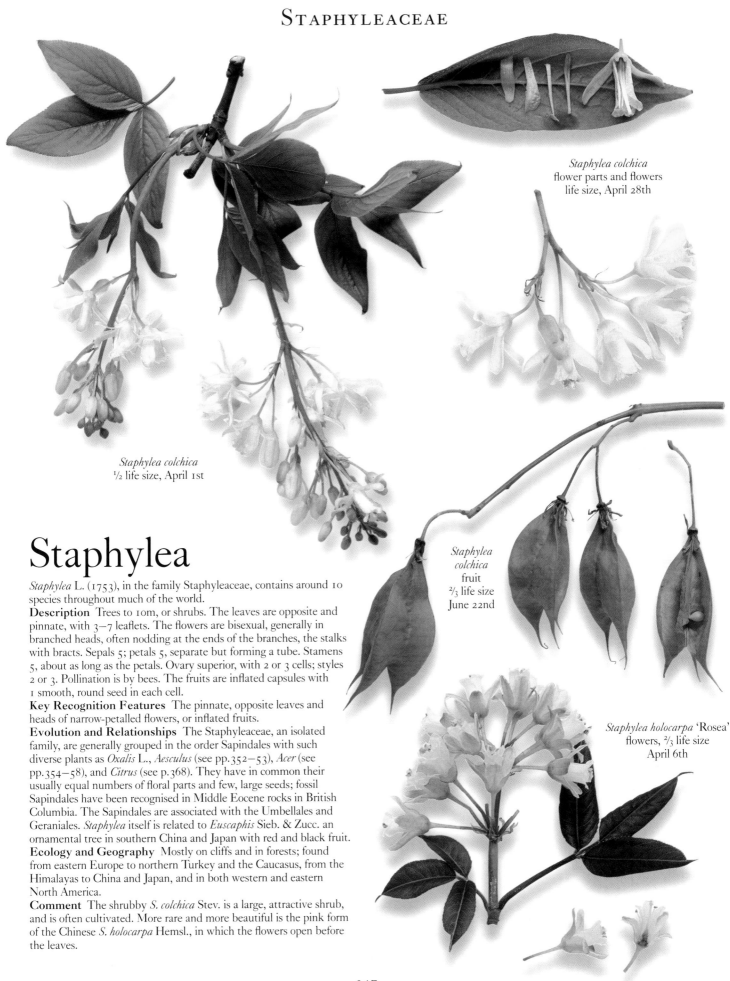

Staphylea colchica
flower parts and flowers
life size, April 28th

Staphylea colchica
½ life size, April 1st

Staphylea

Staphylea L. (1753), in the family Staphyleaceae, contains around 10 species throughout much of the world.

Description Trees to 10m, or shrubs. The leaves are opposite and pinnate, with 3–7 leaflets. The flowers are bisexual, generally in branched heads, often nodding at the ends of the branches, the stalks with bracts. Sepals 5; petals 5, separate but forming a tube. Stamens 5, about as long as the petals. Ovary superior, with 2 or 3 cells; styles 2 or 3. Pollination is by bees. The fruits are inflated capsules with 1 smooth, round seed in each cell.

Key Recognition Features The pinnate, opposite leaves and heads of narrow-petalled flowers, or inflated fruits.

Evolution and Relationships The Staphyleaceae, an isolated family, are generally grouped in the order Sapindales with such diverse plants as *Oxalis* L., *Aesculus* (see pp.352–53), *Acer* (see pp.354–58), and *Citrus* (see p.368). They have in common their usually equal numbers of floral parts and few, large seeds; fossil Sapindales have been recognised in Middle Eocene rocks in British Columbia. The Sapindales are associated with the Umbellales and Geraniales. *Staphylea* itself is related to *Euscaphis* Sieb. & Zucc. an ornamental tree in southern China and Japan with red and black fruit.

Ecology and Geography Mostly on cliffs and in forests; found from eastern Europe to northern Turkey and the Caucasus, from the Himalayas to China and Japan, and in both western and eastern North America.

Comment The shrubby *S. colchica* Stev. is a large, attractive shrub, and is often cultivated. More rare and more beautiful is the pink form of the Chinese *S. holocarpa* Hemsl., in which the flowers open before the leaves.

*Staphylea
colchica*
fruit
⅔ life size
June 22nd

Staphylea holocarpa 'Rosea'
flowers, ⅔ life size
April 6th

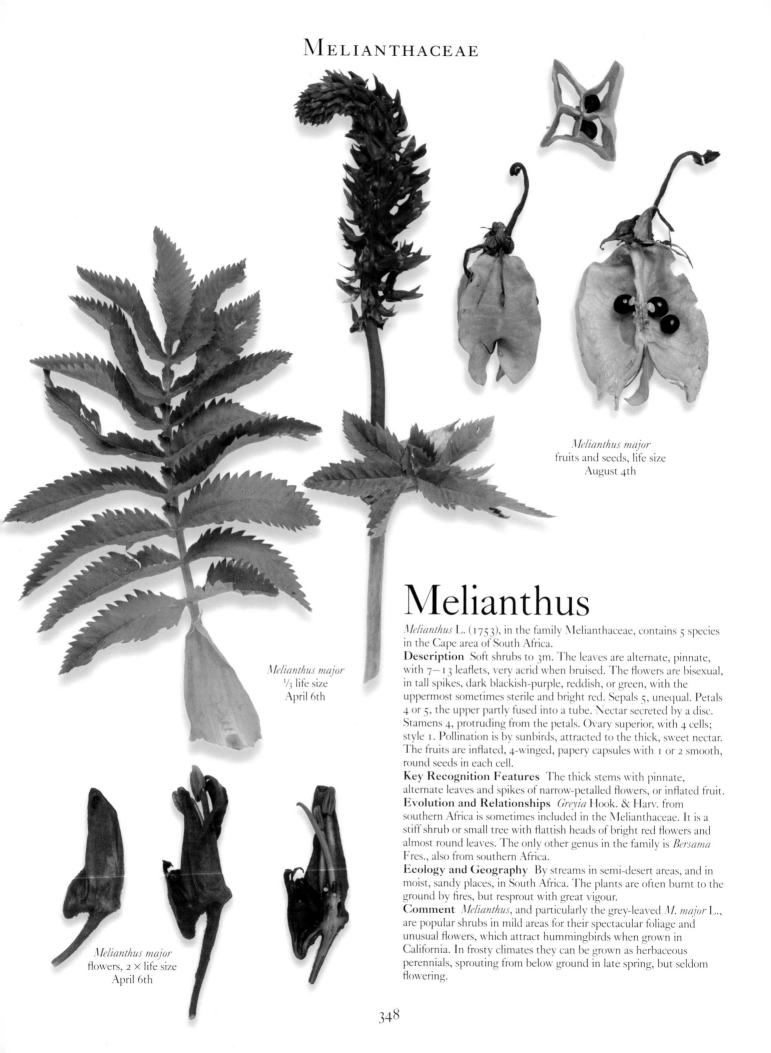

Melianthus major
fruits and seeds, life size
August 4th

Melianthus major
⅓ life size
April 6th

Melianthus

Melianthus L. (1753), in the family Melianthaceae, contains 5 species in the Cape area of South Africa.

Description Soft shrubs to 3m. The leaves are alternate, pinnate, with 7–13 leaflets, very acrid when bruised. The flowers are bisexual, in tall spikes, dark blackish-purple, reddish, or green, with the uppermost sometimes sterile and bright red. Sepals 5, unequal. Petals 4 or 5, the upper partly fused into a tube. Nectar secreted by a disc. Stamens 4, protruding from the petals. Ovary superior, with 4 cells; style 1. Pollination is by sunbirds, attracted to the thick, sweet nectar. The fruits are inflated, 4-winged, papery capsules with 1 or 2 smooth, round seeds in each cell.

Key Recognition Features The thick stems with pinnate, alternate leaves and spikes of narrow-petalled flowers, or inflated fruit.

Evolution and Relationships *Greyia* Hook. & Harv. from southern Africa is sometimes included in the Melianthaceae. It is a stiff shrub or small tree with flattish heads of bright red flowers and almost round leaves. The only other genus in the family is *Bersama* Fres., also from southern Africa.

Ecology and Geography By streams in semi-desert areas, and in moist, sandy places, in South Africa. The plants are often burnt to the ground by fires, but resprout with great vigour.

Comment *Melianthus*, and particularly the grey-leaved *M. major* L., are popular shrubs in mild areas for their spectacular foliage and unusual flowers, which attract hummingbirds when grown in California. In frosty climates they can be grown as herbaceous perennials, sprouting from below ground in late spring, but seldom flowering.

Melianthus major
flowers, 2 × life size
April 6th

348

Koelreuteria

Koelreuteria Laxm. (1772), in the family Sapindaceae, contains 3 species in China.

Description Trees to 12m. The leaves are alternate, pinnate or 2-pinnate, with deeply and irregularly toothed leaflets. The flowers are unisexual, with males and females together in large, branched, pyramidal heads. Sepals 5, with 3 longer than the other 2, joined at the base. Petals 4 or 5, narrow towards the base. Stamens usually 8, with hairy filaments. Ovary superior, with 3 cells and 2 ovules per cell. Pollination is presumed to be by bees. The fruits are inflated, often reddish, papery capsules with 1 smooth, round seed in each cell.

Key Recognition Features The pinnate or 2-pinnate, alternate leaves and large, loose heads of small, yellow flowers or reddish capsules, often conspicuous on the trees at the same time.

Evolution and Relationships *Dodonea* (see p. 351) is closely related but has simple leaves and flowers without petals.

Ecology and Geography In dry river valleys in the mountains, with 2 species in southwestern China, 1 in Taiwan to Fiji.

Comment *Koelreuteria paniculata* Laxm. is easily grown in dry gardens, where it makes an attractive, wide-spreading, and gnarled-looking tree. It requires a hot summer to flower well, but the bright pink young leaves are an attractive feature. The yellow flowers are used as a dye. *Koelreuteria bipinnata* Franch. has 2-pinnate leaves.

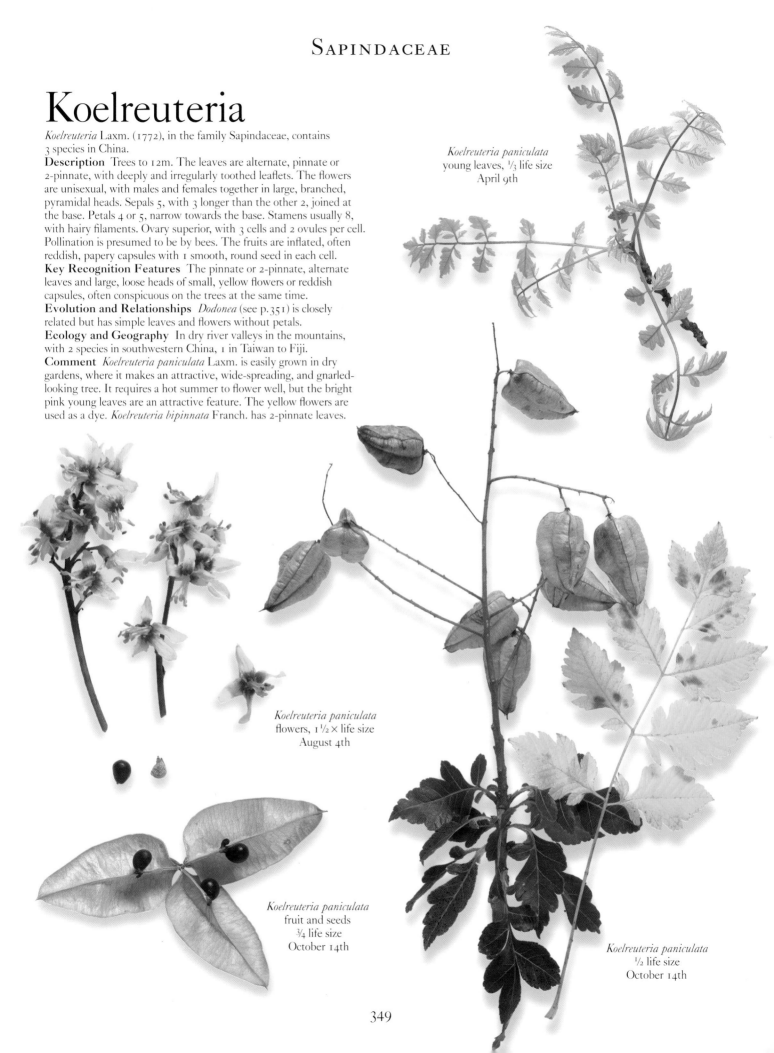

Koelreuteria paniculata
young leaves, ⅓ life size
April 9th

Koelreuteria paniculata
flowers, 1 ½ × life size
August 4th

Koelreuteria paniculata
fruit and seeds
¾ life size
October 14th

Koelreuteria paniculata
½ life size
October 14th

349

Sapindus

Sapindus L. (1753), the soapberry, in the family Sapindaceae, contains around 13 species, mainly in the tropics.

Description Trees to 15m, or shrubs. The leaves are evergreen or deciduous, alternate, pinnate, with up to 18 untoothed or finely toothed leaflets. The flowers are small, unisexual, generally in branched heads, males and females sometimes on separate plants, yellowish white. Sepals 4 or 5, small; petals 4 or 5, separate. Stamens 8–10, about as long as the petals. Ovary superior, with 2 or 3 cells; style 1. Pollination is presumed to be by bees. The fruits are round and fleshy with 1 smooth, round seed.

Key Recognition Features The pinnate leaves with no terminal leaflet and small, round fruit, yellow, becoming black; the berries often remain on the tree after the leaves have fallen.

Evolution and Relationships The Sapindaceae is a large, mainly tropical family; most genera have poisonous saponins. Some have delicious fruit, such as litchis (*Litchi chinensis* Sonn.) and rambutans (*Nephelium lappaceum* L.). Sapindaceae is closely related to Hippocastanaceae (see pp.352–53) and Aceraceae (see pp.354–59).

Ecology and Geography Mostly on cliffs and in forests. In tropical Asia, India, and America; the hardiest species, *S. drummondii* Hook. & Arn., is from southwestern North America, from Kansas to Arizona and northern Mexico.

Comment Many species are used as fish, slug, and snail poisons, and also as soaps, hence the common name.

Xanthoceras

Xanthoceras Bunge (1834), in the family Sapindaceae, contains 1 species, *X. sorbifolium* Bunge from China.

Description Trees to 8m, or shrubs. The leaves are deciduous, alternate, pinnate with 9–17 toothed leaflets including a terminal leaflet. The flowers are unisexual, in short spikes, the terminal flowers usually female, the lower flowers male. Sepals 5; petals 5, white, at first veined yellowish or greenish at the base, later becoming deep red. Stamens 8, about as long as the petals. Floral disc with horn-like appendages. Ovary superior, with 3 cells and a short, thick style. Pollination is presumed to be by bees. The fruits are capsules with several nut-like seeds in each cell.

Key Recognition Features The pinnate leaves and spikes of white flowers with the petals deep red at the base.

Evolution and Relationships As with so many of the genera of the Sapindaceae, *Xanthoceras* is a rather isolated genus. It is interesting that the colour change of the petals is also seen in *Aesculus* (see pp.352–53).

Ecology and Geography On dry hills in northern China.

Comment The seeds are said to be edible. This is a very pretty shrub, but needs warm summers to form the buds for the following spring, and is susceptible to damage by late frosts in spring. It was introduced to Paris by Père David in 1866.

Xanthoceras sorbifolium
young fruit, 1½ × life size
May 18th

Sapindus saponaria
⅓ life size
October 5th

Sapindus drummondii
⅓ life size, October 5th

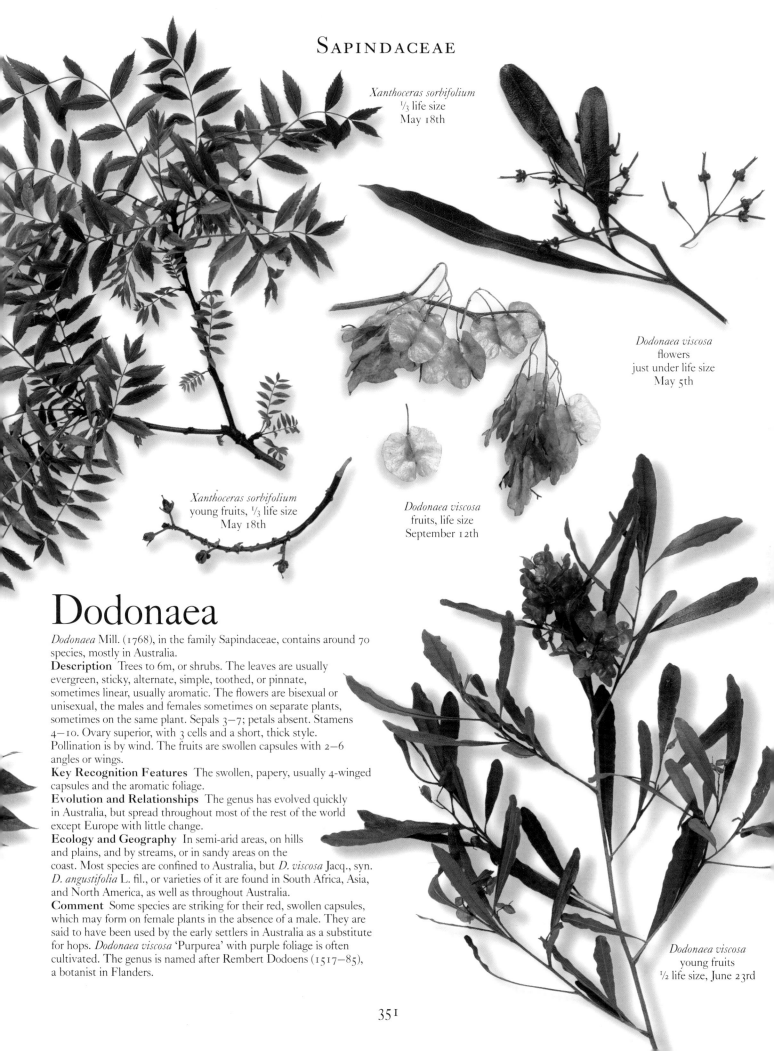

Xanthoceras sorbifolium
1/3 life size
May 18th

Dodonaea viscosa
flowers
just under life size
May 5th

Xanthoceras sorbifolium
young fruits, 1/3 life size
May 18th

Dodonaea viscosa
fruits, life size
September 12th

Dodonaea

Dodonaea Mill. (1768), in the family Sapindaceae, contains around 70 species, mostly in Australia.

Description Trees to 6m, or shrubs. The leaves are usually evergreen, sticky, alternate, simple, toothed, or pinnate, sometimes linear, usually aromatic. The flowers are bisexual or unisexual, the males and females sometimes on separate plants, sometimes on the same plant. Sepals 3–7; petals absent. Stamens 4–10. Ovary superior, with 3 cells and a short, thick style. Pollination is by wind. The fruits are swollen capsules with 2–6 angles or wings.

Key Recognition Features The swollen, papery, usually 4-winged capsules and the aromatic foliage.

Evolution and Relationships The genus has evolved quickly in Australia, but spread throughout most of the rest of the world except Europe with little change.

Ecology and Geography In semi-arid areas, on hills and plains, and by streams, or in sandy areas on the coast. Most species are confined to Australia, but *D. viscosa* Jacq., syn. *D. angustifolia* L. fil., or varieties of it are found in South Africa, Asia, and North America, as well as throughout Australia.

Comment Some species are striking for their red, swollen capsules, which may form on female plants in the absence of a male. They are said to have been used by the early settlers in Australia as a substitute for hops. *Dodonaea viscosa* 'Purpurea' with purple foliage is often cultivated. The genus is named after Rembert Dodoens (1517–85), a botanist in Flanders.

Dodonaea viscosa
young fruits
1/2 life size, June 23rd

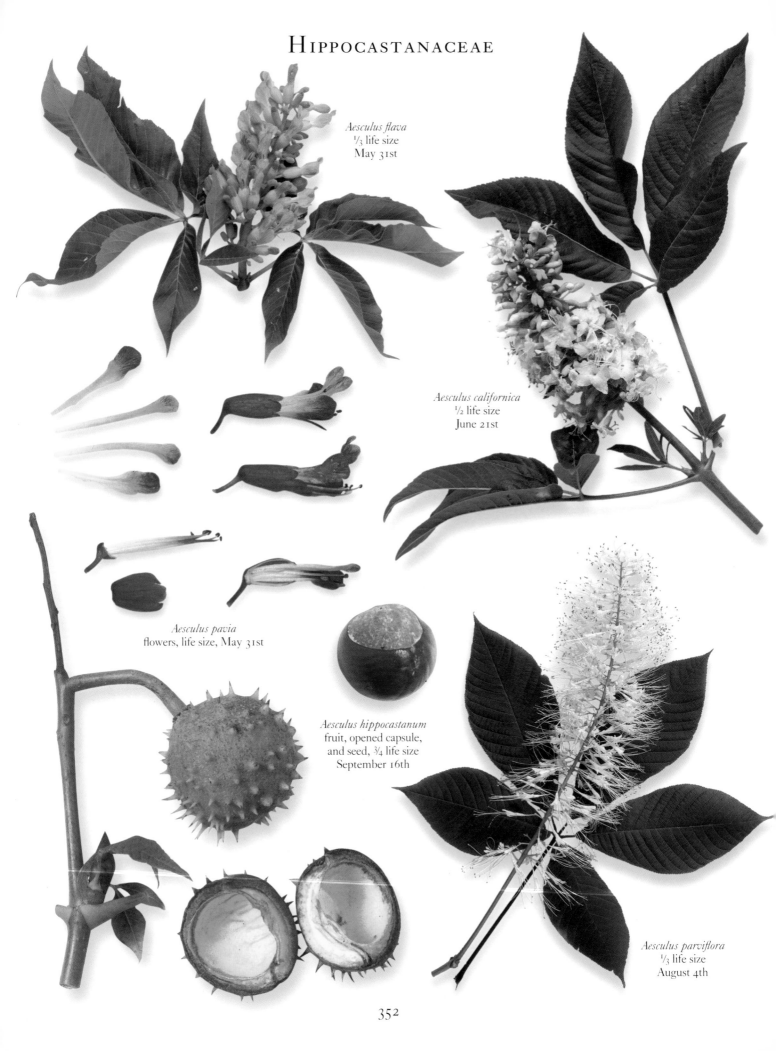

Hippocastanaceae

Aesculus flava
⅓ life size
May 31st

Aesculus californica
½ life size
June 21st

Aesculus pavia
flowers, life size, May 31st

Aesculus hippocastanum
fruit, opened capsule,
and seed, ¾ life size
September 16th

Aesculus parviflora
⅓ life size
August 4th

Aesculus

Aesculus L. (1753), the horse chesnut or buckeye, in the family Hippocastanaceae, contains 13 species in the northern hemisphere.

Description Trees to 35m, or shrubs. The leaves are deciduous, opposite, palmately divided into 5–7 leaflets. The flowers are bisexual, in large, pyramidal or elongated heads, on the tips of the branches. Sepals 4 or 5, joined at the base. Petals 4 or 5, with a narrow base, often white with a yellow blotch that changes to red, otherwise red throughout. Stamens 5–8, longer than the petals, often curled. Ovary superior, with 3 cells, and 2 ovules in each cell; style long and simple. Pollination is by bees. The fruits are thick-walled, often spiny or leathery capsules with 1 or 2 nut-like seeds in each.

Key Recognition Features The palmate leaves and pyramidal or elongated spikes of white, red, or yellow flowers. Also the large, brown, sticky buds in winter.

Evolution and Relationships The Hippocastanaceae contains only 2 genera, *Aesculus* and *Billia* Peyr.; *Billia* has 2 species of small evergreen trees or shrubs in Mexico and South America, with narrow-petalled flowers and small, chesnut-like seeds (*Castanea*, see p.118).

Ecology and Geography In forests and on dry hills, often by streams; 1 species, the familiar *A. hippocastanum* L., in Albania and northern Greece, 5 species from the Himalayas to China and Japan, and 7 species in North America, of which one is the shrubby *A. californica* (Spach) Nutt. from dry hills in California.

Comment The seeds were used by the Turks to help the wind of horses, hence the name; some American species were used to stupefy fish. Many species are cultivated for ornament, and their dry seeds are the conkers of the children's game played in Britain.

Aesculus indica
½ life size
June 3rd

Acer

Acer L. (1753), in the family Aceraceae, contains around 120 species throughout the northern hemisphere.

Description Trees to 40m, or shrubs. The leaves are opposite, deciduous or evergreen, simple, 3- to 5-lobed, palmate or pinnate, with 3–5 or rarely 9 leaflets. The flowers are small, unisexual, bisexual or functionally unisexual, in short spikes or rounded or flat heads. Sepals 5 or rarely 4. Petals 5, rarely 4, 6, or absent, usually green or reddish. Stamens 8, rarely 4 or 5, or 10–12. Pollination is by insects, often bees or small, black gnats, or rarely by wind. Ovary usually superior, with 2 cells and 2 styles, each cell with 2 ovules. The fruits are winged on 1 side and usually paired, with 1 seed developing in each fruit.

Key Recognition Features The opposite leaves and paired fruits with spreading wings.

Evolution and Relationships Aceraceae is close to Sapindaceae, and consists of only 2 genera, *Acer* and *Dipteronia* (see p.359). Fossil remains of *Acer* have been found in deposits in western North America ranging from the Paleocene to the Pliocene, and have shown that Aceraceae probably evolved from Sapindaceae (see pp.349–51). *Acer* has evolved great diversity of floral arrangement and leaf shape.

Ecology and Geography On dry hills and cliffs, in woods, and in swamps from western Europe, across Asia to Japan, and throughout North America; the greatest diversity is found in China.

Comment Many species are grown for ornament, especially for their red and orange autumn colour. Maple syrup is produced by bleeding the bark of *A. saccharum* Marshall in the early spring. The sycamore, *A. pseudoplatanus* L. is often regarded as a weed, but its wood is good for veneers, furniture, and making violins. The Japanese maples are particularly variable in leaf shape and colour, and many selected forms with coloured or finely dissected leaves are cultivated in Japan and in other parts of the world. Many of the cultivated species of *Acer* fall into natural groups (the main ones detailed opposite), others are isolated with no close relatives.

Acer shirasawanum
'Aureum', young fruits
½ life size, May 20th

Acer palmatum
'Heptalobum'
flowers, ¾ life size
May 5th

Acer rubrum, flowers
just under life size, March 5th

Acer palmatum f. *atropurpureum*
flowers, ⅔ life size, May 5th

Acer platanoides
flowers, ¾ life size
April 29th

Acer palmatum
'Bloodgood'
½ life size
April 18th

ACERACEAE

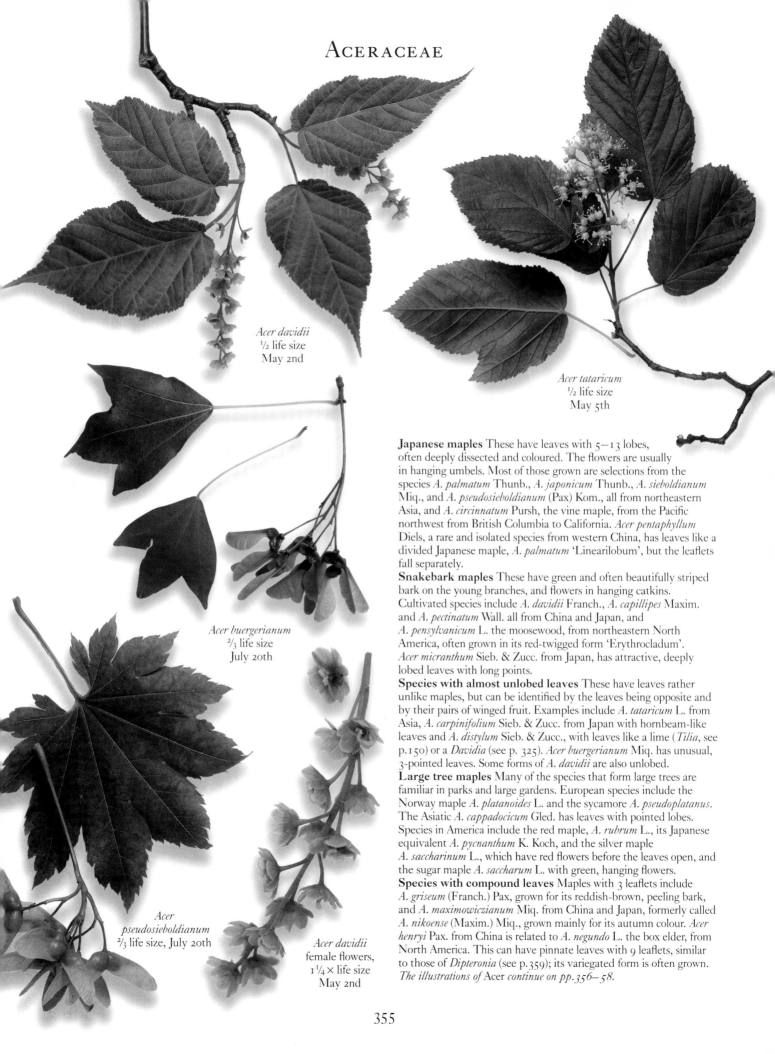

Acer davidii
½ life size
May 2nd

Acer tataricum
½ life size
May 5th

Acer buergerianum
⅔ life size
July 20th

*Acer
pseudosieboldianum*
⅔ life size, July 20th

Acer davidii
female flowers,
1¼ × life size
May 2nd

Japanese maples These have leaves with 5–13 lobes, often deeply dissected and coloured. The flowers are usually in hanging umbels. Most of those grown are selections from the species *A. palmatum* Thunb., *A. japonicum* Thunb., *A. sieboldianum* Miq., and *A. pseudosieboldianum* (Pax) Kom., all from northeastern Asia, and *A. circinnatum* Pursh, the vine maple, from the Pacific northwest from British Columbia to California. *Acer pentaphyllum* Diels, a rare and isolated species from western China, has leaves like a divided Japanese maple, *A. palmatum* 'Linearilobum', but the leaflets fall separately.

Snakebark maples These have green and often beautifully striped bark on the young branches, and flowers in hanging catkins. Cultivated species include *A. davidii* Franch., *A. capillipes* Maxim. and *A. pectinatum* Wall. all from China and Japan, and *A. pensylvanicum* L. the moosewood, from northeastern North America, often grown in its red-twigged form 'Erythrocladum'. *Acer micranthum* Sieb. & Zucc. from Japan, has attractive, deeply lobed leaves with long points.

Species with almost unlobed leaves These have leaves rather unlike maples, but can be identified by the leaves being opposite and by their pairs of winged fruit. Examples include *A. tataricum* L. from Asia, *A. carpinifolium* Sieb. & Zucc. from Japan with hornbeam-like leaves and *A. distylum* Sieb. & Zucc., with leaves like a lime (*Tilia*, see p.150) or a *Davidia* (see p. 325). *Acer buergerianum* Miq. has unusual, 3-pointed leaves. Some forms of *A. davidii* are also unlobed.

Large tree maples Many of the species that form large trees are familiar in parks and large gardens. European species include the Norway maple *A. platanoides* L. and the sycamore *A. pseudoplatanus*. The Asiatic *A. cappadocicum* Gled. has leaves with pointed lobes. Species in America include the red maple, *A. rubrum* L., its Japanese equivalent *A. pycnanthum* K. Koch, and the silver maple *A. saccharinum* L., which have red flowers before the leaves open, and the sugar maple *A. saccharum* L. with green, hanging flowers.

Species with compound leaves Maples with 3 leaflets include *A. griseum* (Franch.) Pax, grown for its reddish-brown, peeling bark, and *A. maximowiczianum* Miq. from China and Japan, formerly called *A. nikoense* (Maxim.) Miq., grown mainly for its autumn colour. *Acer henryi* Pax. from China is related to *A. negundo* L. the box elder, from North America. This can have pinnate leaves with 9 leaflets, similar to those of *Dipteronia* (see p.359); its variegated form is often grown. *The illustrations of* Acer *continue on* *pp.356–58.*

Aceraceae

Acer pycnanthum
½ life size
December 4th

Acer pensylvanicum
½ life size
October 20th

Acer micranthum
⅔ life size
December 15th

Acer carpinifolium
½ life size
November 10th

Acer buergerianum
½ life size
October 8th

Acer palmatum
½ life size
October 8th

Acer japonicum
½ life size,
November 10th

ACERACEAE

Acer rubrum
½ life size
September 16th

Acer pentaphyllum
½ life size
December 4th

Acer saccharum, ½ life size
September 20th

Acer davidii
⅓ life size
December 4th

357

ACERACEAE

Acer negundo var. *interius*
male flowers, ¾ life size
April 24th

Acer henryi
young fruits, ⅓ life size
July 6th

Acer griseum
½ life size
May 11th

Acer henryi
fruits, ⅔ life size
July 6th

358

Dipteronia sinensis
½ life size
June 21st

Dipteronia

Dipteronia Oliver (1903), in the family Aceraceae, contains
2 species in China.

Description Trees to 16m, or shrubs. The leaves are opposite,
deciduous, pinnate with 7–11 pairs of leaflets, the leaf stalks with
latex. The flowers are small, unisexual, in large branched heads, with
up to 200 flowers, at the tips of the branches. Sepals 5; petals 5,
white. Stamens 8. Ovary superior, with 2 cells and 2 styles, each cell
with 2 ovules. Pollination is by insects, or perhaps by wind. The fruits
are winged all round and paired, with 1 seed developing in each fruit.

Key Recognition Features The opposite, pinnate leaves with
latex and the wings encircling the seeds.

Evolution and Relationships *Dipteronia* is probably more
primitive than *Acer* (see pp. 354–58), as it retains the charcters of
having the seed winged all round and the pinnate leaves of *Bohlenia*,
a primitive fossil genus in the Sapindaceae (see pp. 349–51).

Ecology and Geography In woods in central and southwestern
China, along with other ancient genera such as *Cercidiphyllum*
(see p.96) and *Davidia* (see p.325)

Comment *Dipteronia sinensis* Oliver, the only species generally
cultivated, is grown in a few botanical collections.

Dipteronia sinensis, male and female flowers
just under life size, June 21st

359

Coriaria

Coriaria L. (1753), in the family Coriariaceae, contains around 5 species in southwestern Europe, eastern Asia, South America, and New Zealand.

Description Shrubs to 3m, or herbaceous plants with a woody base. The leaves are opposite, simple, deciduous. The flowers are small, bisexual or unisexual, in dense spikes or solitary. Sepals 5, persistent. Petals 5, 3-angled, becoming fleshy in fruit. Stamens 10, the filaments sometimes joined to the petals, often pendent. Ovary superior, with 5 or 10 cells, each with a long, slender style. Pollination is perhaps by wind as well as by insects. The fruits are heads of achenes surrounded by the fleshy petals; the seeds are flattened.

Key Recognition Features The opposite or whorled leaves on long, arching shoots and the small flowers followed by fleshy fruits.

Evolution and Relationships *Coriaria* is the only genus in the Coriariaceae; its relationships are uncertain, but it is usually now associated with the Sapindaceae (see pp. 349–51). Some have suggested it is close to Ranunculaceae (see pp. 86–89).

Ecology and Geography In open woods and hedges, and on moist rocks in forested areas. Found in America from Mexico to Chile, in eastern Europe, and from the Himalayas to Japan, New Guinea, and New Zealand.

Comment The seeds are poisonous and hallucinogenic; the roots fix nitrogen by symbiosis with an actinomycete.

Coriaria plumosa
young fruits
$2^{1}/_{4} \times$ life size
July 28th

Cotinus coggygria
'Royal Purple'
$^{2}/_{3}$ life size, June 3rd

Cotinus coggygria
$^{2}/_{3}$ life size
June 3rd

Coriaria microphylla
$^{1}/_{2}$ life size, June 21st

Cotinus

Cotinus Mill. (1768), the smoke tree, in the family Anacardiaceae, contains 3 species in North America, Europe, and Asia.

Description Trees to 10m, or shrubs. The leaves are aromatic, alternate, deciduous, simple and rounded, often purple in cultivars and colouring red in autumn, with long leaf stalks. The flowers are small, yellow, unisexual, in branched heads, the males and females sometimes on different plants. Sepals 5; petals 5, white. Stamens 5. Ovary superior, with 2 cells and 2 styles, each cell with 2 ovules. Pollination is by insects. The fruits develop a plume-like stalk and contain 1 seed.

Key Recognition Features The smooth, thin, rounded, aromatic leaves and feathery fruit stalks, many of which lack seeds.

Evolution and Relationships Close to *Rhus* (see p. 362), and formerly often called *Rhus cotinus* L. *Rhus* proper has pinnate leaves and crowded clusters of fruit. Both genera have excellent red leaf colour in autumn.

Ecology and Geography On rocky hills and in scrub, *C. coggygria* Scop. from France eastwards to the Himalayas and China, *C. obovatus* Raf. in southeastern North America, and the remaining species in southwestern China.

Comment *Cotinus coggygria* is commonly cultivated for its good colour in the autumn, and for its purple-leaved cultivars. Hybrids between the American and European species are particularly vigorous. The bark of *C. coggygria* produces a yellow dye, that of *C. obovatus* an orange dye.

Pistacia

Pistacia L. (1753), in the family Anacardiaceae, contains 9 species in North and Central America, southern Europe, and Asia.

Description Trees to 8m, or shrubs. The leaves are alternate, usually deciduous, pinnate with 1–12 leaflets, with or without a terminal leaflet. The flowers are small, unisexual, the males and females on different plants. Sepals 5; petals absent. Stamens 3–5. Ovary superior, with 1 cell and 1 style. Pollination is by small insects. The fruits are 1-seeded, often reddish becoming brown or black.

Key Recognition Features The pinnate, rather leathery leaves and the flowers in branching heads in the leaf axils.

Evolution and Relationships *Pistacia* is close to *Rhus* (see p. 362) but has smaller leaves, and flowers without petals.

Ecology and Geography On rocky hills and in dry, open woods, with 3 species in Europe, mainly in the Mediterranean area, and the rest in Central Asia, China, and North and Central America.

Comment The seeds of *P. vera* L., from Iran and Central Asia, provide the pistachio nut. The resin of *P. lentiscus* L. from the Mediterranean area is used for chewing and as mastic varnish; it is also put in ouzo. The young shoots of *P. chinensis* Bunge are eaten as a vegetable in China. The cashew, *Anacardium occidentale* L., and the mango, *Mangifera indica* L., also belong to the family Anacardiaceae.

Cotinus 'Grace'
autumn leaves
⅔ life size
September 16th

Pistacia chinensis, male flowers
1¼ × life size, May 5th

Pistacia lentiscus
life size, August 10th

Schinus molle
½ life size, July 20th

Schinus polygamus
subsp. *ovatus*
½ life size, May 5th

Schinus

Schinus L. (1753), in the family Anacardiaceae, contains 27 species, mostly in tropical South America.

Description Trees to 8m, or shrubs. The leaves are alternate, evergreen, usually pinnate, with 7–13 pairs of leaflets, often hanging down, occasionally simple. The flowers are small, white, unisexual, the males and females usually on different plants, in large, branched heads, both terminal and in the leaf axils. Sepals 5; petals 5, white. Stamens 10. Ovary superior, with 1 cell and 3 styles. Pollination is by small insects. The fruits are 1-seeded, round, often reddish, hanging in large bunches.

Key Recognition Features The alternate pinnate leaves and round, pinkish or red, smooth fruit.

Evolution and Relationships Close to *Rhus*, but usually glabrous, and with more stamens.

Ecology and Geography In rocky valleys and along streams, from Mexico to Chile, Argentina, and Uruaguay.

Comment *Schinus molle* L., the Brazilian pepper tree, is commonly grown for ornament around the Mediterranean, and in other subtropical areas of the world; it makes an exceptionally graceful tree, and may become naturalised. *Schinus polygamus* (Cav.) Cabrera is unusual in its simple leaves.

Schinus polygamus subsp. *ovatus*
flowers, 1¼ × life size
May 5th

Rhus

Rhus L. (1753), in the family Anacardiaceae, contains around 200 species, found in North and Central America, southern Europe, Africa, and Asia.

Description Trees to 10m, or shrubs. The leaves are alternate, deciduous or evergreen, pinnate with up to 15 leaflets, or simple. The flowers are small, white or green, unisexual or bisexual, in large, branched heads, usually at the tips of the branches. Sepals 5, joined at the base; petals 5. Stamens 5. Ovary superior, with 1 cell and 3 styles. Pollination is by small insects. The fruits are 1-seeded, often with thin, red flesh.

Key Recognition Features The alternate, usually pinnate leaves and usually hairy inflorescence.

Evolution and Relationships *Rhus* is the largest genus in the family Anacardiaceae. Poison oak and poison ivy are now again separated in the genus *Toxicodendron*, as they were by Miller in 1768.

Ecology and Geography In woods in southern Europe and South Africa, in Asia southwards to northern Australia, and in North America.

Comment Many species are grown for their fine autumn colour. The fruit of the stag's horn sumach, *R. typhina* L. may be used to make a cordial. The leaves of several species are used in tanning, and others are a valuable source of Chinese laquer and copal varnish.

ANACARDIACEAE

Rhus chinensis
⅓ life size
June 22nd

Rhus coriaria
fruits, ½ life size
October 8th

Rhus trichocarpa
twig showing leaf base
concealing young bud
2 × life size
October 29th

Rhus trichocarpa
½ life size
June 15th

Rhus trichocarpa
flowers, 2 × life size
June 15th

Rhus trichocarpa
autumn leaves
⅔ life size, October 8th

Meliosma

Meliosma Blume (1823), in the family Sabiaceae, contains around 55 species, mainly in tropical Asia and America.

Description Trees to 20m, or shrubs. The leaves are alternate, deciduous, simple or pinnate with 2–11 pairs of leaflets, the leaves with numerous parallel veins. The flowers are small, white or cream, scented, bisexual, in large, branched heads, at the tips of the branches. Sepals 3–5. Petals 5, the 3 outer unequal, much larger than the inner, which are forked. Stamens 5, only 2 fertile, with flat filaments forming a cup in which the anther sits. Ovary superior, with 2 cells and 2 styles, each cell with 2 ovules. Pollination is by insects. The fruits are fleshy, with 1 seed.

Key Recognition Features The leaves with pinnate veins and the branched inflorescence of small flowers with unusual stamens.

Evolution and Relationships Fossils of *Meliosma* species dating from the Tertiary are known from North America.

Ecology and Geography In woods from the Himalayas to China and Japan, and in tropical America.

Comment A few species are grown in collections; *M. dilleniifolia* subsp. *cuneifolia* (Franch.) Beusekom from western China makes an attractive small tree. The leaves have reddish, hairy patches beneath.

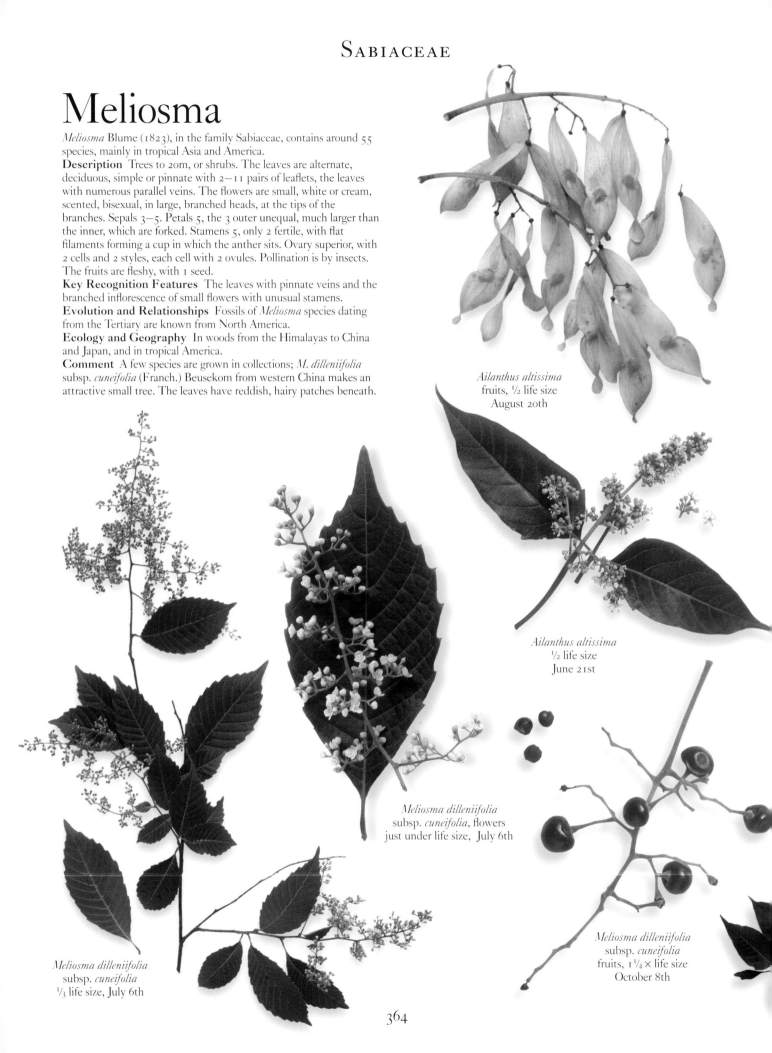

Ailanthus altissima
fruits, ½ life size
August 20th

Ailanthus altissima
½ life size
June 21st

Meliosma dilleniifolia
subsp. *cuneifolia*, flowers
just under life size, July 6th

Meliosma dilleniifolia
subsp. *cuneifolia*
⅓ life size, July 6th

Meliosma dilleniifolia
subsp. *cuneifolia*
fruits, 1¼× life size
October 8th

Ailanthus

Ailanthus Desf. (1766), in the family Simaroubaceae, contains around 5 species in tropical Asia and Australia.

Description Trees to 30m, with greyish bark. The leaves are alternate, deciduous, pinnate with 11−35 leaflets, the terminal leaflet solitary. The flowers are small, usually unisexual, in branched heads, at the ends of the branches. Sepals 5, rarely 6; petals 5, rarely 6, white. Stamens 2−5 in bisexual flowers, 10 in male flowers. Ovary superior, with 5 cells and 5 styles, each cell with a solitary ovule; after pollination the cells divide into separate fruits. Pollination is by insects. The fruits are winged samaras, often reddish, with 1 seed developing in each.

Key Recognition Features The alternate, pinnate leaves and winged, reddish fruit make the tree similar to a large ash (*Fraxinus*, see p.416).

Evolution and Relationships The family Simaroubaceae is considered close to Anacardiaceae (see pp.361−63) and Meliaceae, which contains mahogany, *Swietenia mahogani* (L.) Jacq., from the West Indies, and the ornamental *Melia azedarach* L. with shining, much-divided leaves, small, purple flowers, and yellow-orange berries, commonly planted around the Mediterranean. *Leitneria floridana* Chapman, an isolated species from southeastern North America, is now considered to belong to the Simaroubaceae, although it is wind-pollinated, unlike the other genera. Its fossils have been found in Eocene deposits near London.

Ecology and Geography Found in woods in central and southwestern China.

Comment *Ailanthus altissima* (Mill.) Swingle is commonly planted as a street tree in cities.

Ailanthus altissima
flowers, 2 × life size
August 4th

Picrasma quassioides
buds, life size
May 1st

Ailanthus altissima
¼ life size
June 21st

Picrasma quassioides
½ life size, June 3rd

Picrasma

Picrasma Blume. (1825), in the family Simaroubaceae, contains around 6 species in tropical America and Asia.

Description Trees to 12m, or shrubs. The leaves are alternate, deciduous, pinnate with 9−15 leaflets, with a terminal leaflet. The flowers are small, in loose, branched clusters in the leaf axils. Sepals 4 or 5, joined at the base; petals 4 or 5. Stamens 4 or 5, hairy. Ovary superior, with 3−5 cells and a style with 3−5 branches. Pollination is by small insects. The fruits are a cluster of 1−3 fleshy or leathery, 1-seeded berries, attached to the receptacle.

Key Recognition Features The alternate, pinnate leaves and blue, purplish, or red, berry-like fruits.

Evolution and Relationships Related to *Ailanthus*, but differing in its fleshy fruits.

Ecology and Geography In woods in Asia, with the common *Picrasma quassioides* (D. Don) Benn. from India to Japan and Korea.

Comment *Picrasma quassioides* (D. Don) Bennett, is sometimes grown as an ornamental for its good autumn colour. *Picrasma excelsa* (Sweet) Planch. from the West Indies is the source of quassia chips, a traditional insecticide.

Acradenia
frankliniae
1½ × life size
June 15th

Acradenia frankliniae
capsules and leaves
1¼ × life size
December 8th

Acradenia

Acradenia Kipp. (1852), in the family Rutaceae, contains 2 species in eastern Australia.

Description Trees to 30m, and shrubs. The leaves are opposite, evergreen, with 3 leaflets. The flowers are bisexual, white, generally in flattish heads at the ends of the branches. Sepals 5–7, petals 5–7, with velvety hairs. Stamens 10–14. Ovary superior, with around 5 cells; style short. Pollination is presumed to be by bees. The fruits are separate, 1-seeded capsules around 8mm long.

Key Recognition Features The evergreen, 3-foliolate, aromatic leaves and the white flowers with velvety petals and many stamens.

Evolution and Relationships The Rutaceae is characterised by the oil-bearing cells in the leaves; these are especially conspicuous in the skins of fruit such as oranges and tangerines (*Citrus*, see p. 368–69).

Ecology and Geography In rainforest and by streams in Queensland, New South Wales, and Tasmania.

Comment *Acradenia frankliniae* Kipp., from Tasmania, is an attractive, evergreen shrub, often grown in gardens in mild areas. The second species, *A. euodiiformis* (F. Muell.) T.G. Hartley, is an evergreen tree for warm climates.

Acradenia frankliniae
½ life size, June 15th

Choisya ternata
'Sundance'
1 ¼ × life size
June 15th

Choisya 'Aztec Pearl'
½ life size, April 18th

Choisya dumosa
½ life size, April 29th

Choisya

Choisya Kunth. (1823), in the family Rutaceae, contains
around 6 species in southwestern North America and Mexico.
Description Shrubs to 3m. The leaves are opposite,
evergreen, aromatic, with 3–13 leaflets. The flowers are
bisexual, white, generally in flattish heads at the ends of the branches
and in the upper leaf axils. Sepals usually 5; petals usually 5. Stamens
usually 10. Ovary superior, with around 5 cells; style short. Pollination
is by bees. The fruits have 5 carpels, each with 1 seed and joined at
the base.
Key Recognition Features The evergreen, many-foliolate,
aromatic leaves and the white flowers with many stamens.
Evolution and Relationships *Murraya paniculata* (L.) Jack, the
orange jessamine, commonly planted as a low hedge, has similar
trifoliolate leaves, but scented flowers and small, bright orange fruit.
Choisya is very close to *Acradenia*, but that has petals with velvety
hairs.
Ecology and Geography In deserts and open woods, from New
Mexico, Arizona, and Texas southwards to central Mexico.
Comment *Choisya ternata* Kunth from central Mexico is commonly
cultivated, and is tolerant of dry shade in cities. Its golden form
'Sundance' is commonly planted, as is the hybrid with *C. dumosa*
(Torr.) Gray var. *arizonica* (Standley) Benson, called 'Aztec Pearl'; a
yellow-leaved variety of 'Aztec Pearl' has recently appeared. *Choisya* is
named after the Swiss botanist M.J.C. Choisy (1799–1859).

Choisya ternata
½ life size, April 8th

Citrus × meyeri
'Meyer'
fruit and flowers
$^1/_2$ life size
April 18th

Citrus limon 'Quatre Saison'
$^2/_3$ life size, April 15th

Citrus × meyeri 'Meyer'
leaf and flowers
life size, April 18th

Citrus

Citrus L. (1753), in the family Rutaceae, contains around 16 species in South East Asia.

Description Trees to 15m or shrubs, often spiny. The leaves are alternate, evergreen, aromatic, simple, often with winged stalks. The flowers are bisexual, white, in the upper leaf axils, sweetly scented. Sepals usually 5; petals usually 5, thick-textured, white or purplish. Stamens at least 4 times as many as the petals. Ovary superior, with around 5 cells; style short. Pollination is by bees. The fruit are oranges, lemons, and other citrus fruit, with seeds embedded in a juicy pulp, and a leathery skin with aromatic oil cells.

Key Recognition Features The evergreen, simple, aromatic leaves, the white, scented flowers with many stamens, and the familiar fruit.

Evolution and Relationships Very close to *Ponciris* and to *Fortunella*, both of which form hybrids with *Citrus*.

Ecology and Geography In forests from India and China to Malaysia and Polyesia, but long cultivated, so that the native ranges of the species are uncertain.

Comment Most species are cultivated in subtropical areas for their fruit; the flowers are also wonderful for their scent in winter and spring. The hardiest *Citrus* is Meyer's lemon, *C. × meyeri* Tan 'Meyer', from China, which can survive around -5°C of frost; it is perhaps a hybrid between an orange and a lemon. *Citrus medica* L. 'Ethrog', the citron, is an old variety thought to have been introduced to the Mediterranean by the returning armies of Alexander the Great. The fruit is used in the feast of the Tabernacles, and the thick, fragrant rind is often candied for peel.

Citrus medica
fruit, $^2/_3$ life size
June 14th

Fortunella

Fortunella Swingle (1915), the kumquat, in the family Rutaceae, contains around 5 species in south East Asia.

Description Trees to 5m or shrubs, sometimes spiny. The leaves are alternate, evergreen, aromatic, simple. The flowers are bisexual, white, in the upper leaf axils, sweetly scented. Sepals 5; petals 5, thick-textured, white. Stamens 16–20. Ovary superior, with around 5 cells, each with 2 ovules; style short. Pollination is by bees. The fruit are kumquats, with seeds embedded in a juicy pulp and a thin skin with aromatic oil cells.

Key Recognition Features The evergreen, simple, aromatic leaves, the white, scented flowers with many stamens, and the small, usually elongated fruit.

Evolution and Relationships Very close *Citrus*, probably not really distinct from it, and sometimes included in it.

Ecology and Geography In forests in China.

Comment Most species are cultivated in subtropical areas for their fruit, which are eaten whole and commonly candied whole, producing an interesting combination of sweet flesh and sour, aromatic skin. The genus commemorates Robert Fortune (1812–80), who made several plant collecting journeys to China for the Horticultural Society and the East India Company between 1843 and 1861.

Poncirus trifoliata
fruit, ²⁄₃ life size
June 20th

Poncirus trifoliata
life size, May 5th

Fortunella × *crassifolia*
'Fukushu'
fruit, ¾ life size
January 6th

Poncirus trifoliata
½ life size, May 5th

Fortunella × *crassifolia* 'Fukushu'
⅓ life size, January 6th

Poncirus

Poncirus Raf. (1838), in the family Rutaceae, contains 1 species in China.

Description Shrubs to 7m, very spiny. The leaves are alternate, deciduous, aromatic, with 3–5 leaflets. The flowers are bisexual, white, in the upper leaf axils, slightly scented. Sepals 5; petals 5, thin-textured, white. Stamens 20–60. Ovary hairy, superior, with 6–8 cells, each with numerous ovules; style short. Pollination is by bees. The fruits are downy, yellow, with seeds embedded in a juicy pulp, very aromatic.

Key Recognition Features The spiny, green branches, compound leaves, and white flowers.

Evolution and Relationships Very close to *Citrus* and probably not really distinct from it.

Ecology and Geography In scrub in northern China and Korea.

Comment The hardiest of the citrus group, sometimes planted as an impenetrable hedge. The hybrid of *Poncirus* with the orange, the citrange, × *Citroncirus webberi* Ingram & Moore, is often planted as a hardy stock for citrus cultivars.

Skimmia japonica
female flowers
½ life size
April 10th

Skimmia japonica 'Rubella'
½ life size, April 10th

Skimmia japonica
male flowers
½ life size, April 10th

Skimmia japonica
flowers and fruits
⅔ life size, April 10th

Skimmia japonica
fruits and seeds
1⅓ × life size, December 12th

Skimmia

Skimmia Thunb. (1788), in the family Rutaceae, contains around 4 species in eastern Asia.

Description Trees to 13m, or shrubs, with green twigs. The leaves are alternate, evergreen, aromatic, simple and untoothed, near the ends of each year's growth. The flowers are usually unisexual, green, reddish, or white, slightly scented, in bunches at the tips of the shoots, the males and females generally on different plants. Sepals 4 or 5; petals 4 or 5. Stamens 4 or 5. Ovary superior, with 2—5 fused cells, each with 1 ovule; style short. Pollination is by bees. The fruits are red or black, with 1—4 seeds.

Key Recognition Features The smooth leaves at the tips of the branches and the pyramidal heads of small flowers or berries.

Evolution and Relationships *Skimmia* is not close to any of the other hardy Rutaceae.

Ecology and Geography In forests from the western Himalayas to China and Japan.

Comment Many species and cultivars are grown as small ornamental evergreens for their flowers in spring and, in female plants, showy fruits through the winter.

Skimmia japonica
½ life size, December 12th

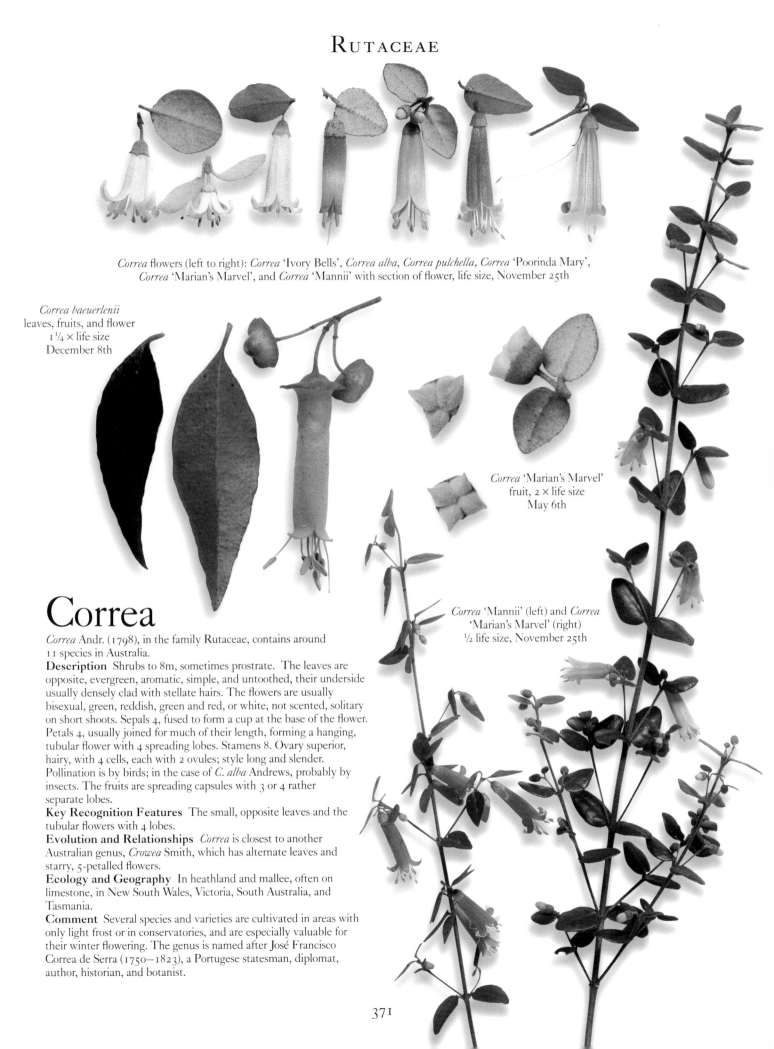

Correa flowers (left to right): *Correa* 'Ivory Bells', *Correa alba*, *Correa pulchella*, *Correa* 'Poorinda Mary', *Correa* 'Marian's Marvel', and *Correa* 'Mannii' with section of flower, life size, November 25th

Correa baeuerlenii
leaves, fruits, and flower
1 ¼ × life size
December 8th

Correa 'Marian's Marvel'
fruit, 2 × life size
May 6th

Correa 'Mannii' (left) and *Correa*
'Marian's Marvel' (right)
½ life size, November 25th

Correa

Correa Andr. (1798), in the family Rutaceae, contains around 11 species in Australia.

Description Shrubs to 8m, sometimes prostrate. The leaves are opposite, evergreen, aromatic, simple, and untoothed, their underside usually densely clad with stellate hairs. The flowers are usually bisexual, green, reddish, green and red, or white, not scented, solitary on short shoots. Sepals 4, fused to form a cup at the base of the flower. Petals 4, usually joined for much of their length, forming a hanging, tubular flower with 4 spreading lobes. Stamens 8. Ovary superior, hairy, with 4 cells, each with 2 ovules; style long and slender. Pollination is by birds; in the case of *C. alba* Andrews, probably by insects. The fruits are spreading capsules with 3 or 4 rather separate lobes.

Key Recognition Features The small, opposite leaves and the tubular flowers with 4 lobes.

Evolution and Relationships *Correa* is closest to another Australian genus, *Crowea* Smith, which has alternate leaves and starry, 5-petalled flowers.

Ecology and Geography In heathland and mallee, often on limestone, in New South Wales, Victoria, South Australia, and Tasmania.

Comment Several species and varieties are cultivated in areas with only light frost or in conservatories, and are especially valuable for their winter flowering. The genus is named after José Francisco Correa de Serra (1750–1823), a Portugese statesman, diplomat, author, historian, and botanist.

371

Ptelea trifoliata
'Aurea'
$1/3$ life size
June 21st

Orixa

Orixa Thunb. (1783), in the family Rutaceae, contains 1 species, *O. japonica* Thunb., in China, Korea, and Japan.

Description Shrubs to 3m, often low and spreading, without spines, the old branches with flaking bark. The leaves are alternate, deciduous, dark green, aromatic, simple, and untoothed. The flowers are unisexual, green, males in elongated clusters in the leaf axils, females solitary. Sepals 4, fused at the base. Petals 4, spreading. Stamens 4. Ovary superior, hairy, with 4 cells; style with a 4-lobed stigma. Pollination is by insects. The fruits are spreading capsules with 4 separate lobes, 1 seed per lobe.

Key Recognition Features The aromatic leaves and small, green flowers with 4 of each part.

Evolution and Relationships *Orixa* is not close to any other genus.

Ecology and Geography In woods in China, Korea, and Japan.

Comment Often grown for hedging in Japan, because of its aromatic leaves and good autumn colour; 'Variegata', with cream-edged leaves, is often cultivated in Europe.

Ptelea trifoliata, fruits
just under life size
November 15th

Ptelea trifoliata
'Aurea'
flowers
$2 \times$ life size
June 21st

Ptelea

Ptelea L. (1753), in the family Rutaceae, contains around 11 species in North America, but as many as 60 minor variations have been described as species.

Description Trees to 8m, and shrubs, without spines. The leaves are alternate, deciduous, aromatic, with 3–5 stalkless leaflets. The flowers are mostly unisexual, green or whitish, in clusters at the tips of the twigs. Sepals 4 or 5, minute. Petals 4 or 5, spreading. Stamens 4 or 5, the filaments hairy on the inner surface. Ovary superior, hairy, with 2 cells, each with 2 ovules. Pollination is by insects. The fruits are dry with a flat wing around the 2 seeds.

Key Recognition Features The aromatic leaves with 3–5 leaflets and the winged, 2-seeded fruits.

Evolution and Relationships The winged fruits are unusual in the family.

Ecology and Geography In woods and canyons and on plains in North America, from the east coast to California.

Comment The fruits of *P. trifoliata* L., the hop tree, were used by the early Europeans in America as a substitute for hops in brewing. The golden-leaved variety 'Aurea' makes an attractive small tree.

Orixa japonica
$1/2$ life size
April 28th

Orixa japonica
flowers, $1\frac{1}{4} \times$ life size
April 28th

Zanthoxylum

Zanthoxylum L. (1753), in the family Rutaceae, contains around 250 species worldwide. The temperate species are trees or shrubs, and it is these which are described below.

Description Trees to 20m, and shrubs, usually with spines. The leaves are alternate, deciduous, aromatic, pinnate, with 3–30 stalkless leaflets, the midrib sometimes winged. The flowers are mostly unisexual, green, in loose or compact clusters in the axils of the upper leaves. Sepals 3–5, small. Petals up to 5, spreading. Stamens 3–5. Ovary superior, with 1–5 cells, each with 2 ovules. Pollination is by insects. The fruits or sections of fruits usually have 1 seed.

Key Recognition Features The aromatic, pinnate leaves with spines often in pairs at the base, and red fruits with often black seeds.

Evolution and Relationships Some of the larger species from eastern Asia were formerly put in the genus *Fagara* L. or in *Phellodendron* (see p.374).

Ecology and Geography In woods in eastern North America, and in east Asia from the Himalayas to Japan and Indonesia.

Comment The seeds of *Z. piperitum* (L.) DC are used in China and Japan as pepper; they cause a numbing sensation in the mouth when chewed. The young leaves are also eaten.

Zanthoxylum piperitum
fruits and seeds
2 × life size, October 6th

*Zanthoxylum
schinifolium*
flowers, 1 ¾ × life size
October 3rd

Zanthoxylum schinifolium
½ life size, October 3rd

Zanthoxylum americanum
fruits, ⅔ life size, October 5th

Phellodendron

Phellodendron Rupr. (1857), in the family Rutaceae, contains around 10 species in eastern Asia.

Description Trees to 25m, with corky bark. The leaves are opposite, deciduous, aromatic, and pinnate, with 5–13 stalkless leaflets. The flowers are small, unisexual, green, in loose clusters in the axils of the upper leaves. Sepals 5–8, small. Petals 5–8, spreading. Stamens 5–6 in the male flowers. Ovary superior, with 5 cells, a short style, and a 5-lobed stigma. Pollination is by insects. The fruits usually have 5 seeds and a black rind.

Key Recognition Features A widely branching tree with corky bark, aromatic pinnate leaves, and loose bunches of small, black fruits. The buds in the leaf axils are hidden by the swollen base of the leaf stalk.

Evolution and Relationships *Phellodendron* is similar to the large species of *Zanthoxylum* (see p.373), but differing in the berry-like, several-seeded fruits.

Ecology and Geography In woods in northeastern China, eastern Siberia, Japan, and Korea.

Comment The Amur cork tree, *P. amurense* Rupr., is sometimes seen in tree collections.

Phellodendron amurense
fruits, ¾ life size
June 21st

Phellodendron amurense
½ life size, June 21st

Phellodendron amurense
var. *sachalinense*, flowers
¾ life size, June 3rd

374

Tetradium daniellii
½ life size, October 5th

Tetradium daniellii
fruits and seeds
1½ × life size, October 5th

Tetradium

Tetradium Lour. (1790), in the family Rutaceae, contains around 9 species from the Himalayas to eastern Asia, formerly included in *Euodia* Forster & Forster fil..

Description Trees to 20m. The leaves are opposite, deciduous, aromatic, and pinnate, with 5–19 stalkless leaflets. The flowers are small, unisexual, green, in loose clusters at the tips of the branches. Sepals 4 or 5, small; petals 4 or 5, spreading. Stamens 4 or 5 in the male flowers. Ovary superior, with 4 or 5 cells and a short style. Pollination is by insects. The fruits are composed of 4 or 5 radiating capsules, each with 1 or 2 shiny, black seeds.

Key Recognition Features The pinnate leaves and starry fruit with black seeds.

Evolution and Relationships *Euodia* in the narrow sense has 1 or 3 leaflets and bisexual flowers. *Phellodendron* differs in its berry-like fruits, and in having the buds in the leaf axils hidden. *Zanthoxylum* (see p.373) has thorns.

Ecology and Geography In woods from Nepal eastwards to China, Korea, and Japan, and southwards to Java.

Comment *Tetradium daniellii* (Bennett) Hartley now includes what was formerly called *Euodia hupehensis* Dode, and is sometimes planted in collections of trees. Other species have been used medicinally as stimulants and against worms.

375

Aralia

Aralia L. (1753), in the family Araliaceae, contains around 55 species in North America, eastern Asia, and from mainland Malaysia eastwards to the Philippines and New Guinea.

Description Trees to 14m, shrubs, or large herbaceous perennials, often with spiny stems, and a few climbers. The leaves are alternate, deciduous, simple or compound, with many, usually toothed leaflets. The flowers are bisexual or unisexual, white or greenish, in umbels or heads at the ends of the branches. Sepals 5, joined to form a shallow-toothed calyx. Petals usually 5, overlapping in bud. Stamens 5. Ovary inferior, generally with 2–5 cells; styles 5. Pollination is presumed to be by insects. The fruits are fleshy berries, usually black when ripe, with 2–5 large, hard seeds.

Key Recognition Features Recognised by its thick stems, large, usually compound leaves and inflorescences, and small, black fruit.

Evolution and Relationships The family Araliaceae is characterised by umbels of small flowers, usually with an inferior ovary, and by its fleshy fruit; it is now often included with the Umbelliferae (see pp. 382–83, also called Apiaceae), as there are genera that are intermediate between the 2 families. DNA studies of the relationships of the families suggest that Araliaceae is close to Pittosporaceae (see pp.214–15), in a group which includes Aquifoliaceae (see p.179), Caprifoliaceae (see pp.453–63), and Compositae (see pp. 438–47).

Aralia is close to *Oplopanax* (Torr. & Gray) Miq. from western North America and northeastern Asia, but that has spiny, deciduous stems, large, lobed leaves, and elongated sprays of red berries.

Ecology and Geography In woods, scrub, or clearings in forest in eastern and western North America, and from the Himalayas eastwards to Japan and the Kuril Islands.

Comment *Aralia elata* (Miq.) Seeman from Japan is a large shrub or tree with huge, compound leaves and fine heads of flowers in late summer; the variegated forms are especially valued in gardens. The young shoots of *A. chinensis* L. and *A. cordata* L. are eaten as vegetables. *Aralia spinosa* L. is the prickly Hercules club from North America.

Eleutherococcus gracilistylus
(right)
²/₃ life size
June 20th

Aralia elata
flowers (above)
life size
August 4th

Aralia cachemirica
fruit, 1½ × life size
September 16th

Aralia elata
stem, ²/₃ life size
August 4th

Aralia elata
⅓ life size
August 4th

376

Araliaceae

Eleutherococcus setchuenensis 1/3 life size October 5th

Eleutherococcus setchuenensis fruits and seeds, just under life size October 5th

Pseudopanax

Pseudopanax Koch. (1859), in the family Araliaceae, contains around 20 species in New Zealand, Tasmania, and southern South America.

Description Trees to 15m, with non-spiny twigs. The leaves are alternate, evergreen, thick and leathery, simple or palmate, often narrowly linear and sharply toothed in the juvenile phase. The flowers are greenish, in small umbels or clusters at the tips of a compound inflorescence, usually unisexual, the males and females on different plants. Sepals 4 or 5, joined to form a minutely toothed calyx. Petals 4 or 5. Stamens 4 or 5. Ovary inferior, with 2–5 cells; style 1, branched. Pollination is presumed to be by insects. The fruits are fleshy berries, usually black when ripe, with 2–5 seeds.

Key Recognition Features *Pseudopanax* is a leathery-leaved, branched tree, its leaves simple to palmate with 3–5 leaflets. In the juvenile stage the plants look quite different, with a single upright stem and greyish, linear leaves, toothed like a saw.

Evolution and Relationships *Pseudopanax* now includes the species formerly called *Neopanax* Allan and the New Zealand species of *Nothopanax* Miq., while *Metapanax* Frodin includes 2–4 species from China and northern Vietnam formerly in *Nothopanax* and *Pseudopanax*, including *M. davidii* (Franch.) Frodin; these relationships are complex and subject to some differences of opinion. All are related to *Schefflera* (see p.379).

Ecology and Geography In forests, around 12 species in New Zealand, the rest in Tasmania, Chile, and southern Argentina.

Comment The strange phenomenon of trees having a juvenile form totally distinct from the adult form is found in several unrelated species in New Zealand; apart from *Pseudopanax*, juvenile forms are found in some *Podocarpus* (see p.21) and in some *Metrosideros* (see p.321), in which the juvenile phase is an ivy-like climber; in the northern hemisphere less distinct juvenile phases are found in climbers such as *Hedera* (see p.380) and the fig *Ficus repens* (see p.165).

Eleutherococcus

Eleutherococcus Maxim. (1859), in the family Araliaceae, contains around 30 species in eastern Asia. Plants formerly in *Acanthopanax* (Decne & Planch.) Miq. are now included in *Eleutherococcus*.

Description Trees to 6m, shrubs, and a few climbers, often with prickly stems. The leaves are alternate, deciduous, palmately compound with 3–5 toothed leaflets. The flowers are bisexual or unisexual, white or greenish, in umbels or heads at the ends of main or side branches. Sepals 5, joined to form a shallow-toothed calyx. Petals usually 5, not overlapping in the bud. Stamens usually 5. Ovary inferior, with around 2–5 cells and 1–5 styles. Pollination is presumed to be by insects. The fruits are fleshy berries, usually black or purplish-black when ripe, with 2–5 large, hard seeds.

Key Recognition Features The relatively small, palmate leaves and inflorescences, on a much-branched shrub.

Evolution and Relationships The affinities of *Eleutherococcus* seem to be with *Hedera* and *Fatsia* (see p.380), rather than *Aralia*, as the petals do not overlap in bud, a characteristic used to divide the family.

Ecology and Geography In woods and scrub from the Himalayas eastwards to Japan and northeastern Asia.

Comment *Eleutherococcus sieboldianus* (Mak.) Koidz., often called *Acanthopanax sieboldianus* Mak., is often grown as an ornamental, especially in its variegated form. It makes a low, rather dense shrub, often scrambling and forming thickets.

Pseudopanax crassifolius leaf of juvenile state, 1/2 life size June 18th

Pseudopanax arboreus 1/2 life size, July 28th

377

Kalopanax septemlobus
fruit, 1/3 life size
April 3rd

Kalopanax

Kalopanax Miq. (1863), in the family Araliaceae, contains 1 species in China and eastern Asia, *K. septemlobus* (Murray) Koidz., often called *K. pictus* (Thunb.) Nakai.

Description Trees to 31m, with thick spines on the stiff twigs and branches. The leaves are alternate, deciduous, palmately 5- to 7-lobed, on long, slender stalks to 50cm. The flowers are bisexual or unisexual, white or greenish, in small umbels at the tips of a large, compound inflorescence. Sepals 5, joined to form a shallow-toothed calyx. Petals usually 5, edge-to-edge in bud, spreading in the open flower. Stamens 5. Ovary inferior, with 2 cells; style 1, forked. Pollination is presumed to be by insects. The fruits are fleshy berries, usually black when ripe, containing 2 seeds.

Key Recognition Features *Kalopanax* is a thick-twigged tree rather like *Aesculus hippocastanum* (horse chestnut, see pp. 352–53) but with spines and lobed leaves.

Evolution and Relationships *Kalopanax* is close to *Eleutherococcus* (see p. 377). The leaves vary in the depth of the lobes and in hairiness; young trees tend to have deeper lobes.

Ecology and Geography In forests from western China eastwards to Japan, Sakhalin, and the southern Kuril Islands.

Comment *Kalopanax septemlobus* is a fine ornamental tree, fast-growing but little-branched when young. It may be propagated easily by planting pieces of the fleshy roots.

Kalopanax septemlobus
leaves and stem
1/3 life size
November 24th

Schefflera

Schefflera Forster & Forster fil. (1776), in the family Araliaceae, contains over 900 species throughout the tropics and into temperate New Zealand, and a few in the mountains of Asia. It is the temperate species that are described and illustrated here.

Description Trees to 25m, without spines. The leaves are alternate, evergreen, usually thick and leathery, palmate with 4–9 or more, often stalked leaflets, with the bases forming sheaths around the twig. The flowers are greenish, in small umbels, clusters, or spikes, in a compound inflorescence, usually bisexual, sometimes unisexual with the males and females on different plants. Sepals joined to form a minutely toothed calyx or just a ring. Petals usually 5, often fused into a cap. Stamens as many as the petals or numerous. Ovary inferior or partly superior, with 2–30 cells; styles 1 or several, branched. Pollination is presumed to be by insects. The fruits are fleshy berries, red or orange and finally black when ripe, with 2–5 seeds.

Key Recognition Features *Schefflera* is usually recognised by its palmate, evergreen leaves and spike-like or umbellate inflorescences.

Evolution and Relationships A very large and diverse genus; *Pseudopanax* (see p. 377) is close to *Schefflera* but has the flower stalks jointed below the flower.

Ecology and Geography In forests; 1 temperate species, *S. digitata* Forster & Forster fil., in New Zealand; others, such as *S. arboricola* (Hayata) Merrill, in China and the Himalayas.

Comment A few species are grown for ornament in mild gardens in western Europe and the Mediterranean. The commonly cultivated houseplant *S. elegantissima* (Masters) Lowry & Frodin, often called *Dizygotheca*, is endemic to New Caledonia. *Schefflera actinophylla* (Endl.) Harms from New Guinea and Australia is also cultivated in mild areas.

Schefflera impressa
fruit, ½ life size
December 8th

Schefflera impressa
⅓ life size
September 10th

Schefflera impressa
fruit and seeds
1½ × life size
December 8th

Schefflera impressa
female flowers, 2 × life size
September 10th

379

Fatsia

Fatsia Decne & Planch. (1776), in the family Araliaceae, contains 3 species in eastern Asia, from Taiwan to Japan.

Description Shrubs to 5m, with thick twigs, without spines. The leaves are alternate, evergreen, thick and leathery, palmately lobed with 7–11 lobes. The flowers are white, in small umbels, usually bisexual, sometimes unisexual, in a compound inflorescence, with white branches. Sepals joined to form a minutely toothed calyx or just a ring. Petals usually 5, spreading when open. Stamens usually 5. Ovary inferior, with 3–10 cells; styles 3–10. Pollination is presumed to be by insects. The fruits are fleshy berries, usually black when ripe, with 3–10 seeds.

Key Recognition Features *Fatsia* is usually recognised by its shining, palmately lobed, evergreen leaves and inflorescence of white flowers or black fruit.

Evolution and Relationships *Fatsia* is an isolated genus, confined to islands in the Pacific. *Dendropanax* Decne & Planch. is often similar, with evergreen, shining leaves, but the inflorescence is a small, simple umbel of green flowers.

Ecology and Geography In forests and scrub near the sea, with *F. japonica* (Murray) Decne & Planch. in the southern half of Japan, on the Ryukyu Islands, and in Korea, and *F. oligocarpella* (Nakai) syn. *Boninofatsia oligocarpella* Nakai on the Bonin Islands. The last species is found on Taiwan.

Comment *Fatsia japonica* is commonly grown in western Europe and the milder parts of North America; it thrives in the shade of buildings, and the shining surface of the leaves throws off pollution.

Hedera

Hedera L. (1753), in the family Araliaceae, contains around 22 species in Europe, North Africa, and parts of Asia.

Description Climbers to 10m or more, the stems attaching themselves to bark or rocks by short roots, and becoming shrubby when adult. The leaves are alternate, evergreen, thick and leathery, simple, especially when mature, or palmately lobed with 3–7 lobes, especially when young. The flowers are green, in spherical umbels, bisexual. Sepals joined to form a 5-lobed calyx. Petals 5, spreading when open. Stamens 5. Ovary inferior, with 4 or 5 cells; style 1, lobed. Pollination is by insects, especially bees and flies. The fruits are fleshy berries, usually black or orange when ripe, with 4 or 5 seeds.

Key Recognition Features *Hedera* is recognised by its climbing, rooting stems and evergreen leaves.

Evolution and Relationships *Hedera* is related to *Fatsia*, *Dendropanax* Decne & Planch., and other shrubby genera.

Ecology and Geography In forests and on cliffs from the Azores, Canaries, and Madeira to Spain and North Africa, and from northwestern Europe to southwestern Asia, the Caucasus, and Iran; also from eastern Asia westwards to the Hindu Kush.

Comment Many varieties are grown for their attractive leaves. The flowers, produced in autumn, are a popular source of nectar for flies and bees approaching hibernation; the berries, which ripen in spring, are loved by birds; and the leaves are avidly eaten by deer and sheep in cold weather.

× Fatshedera

× *Fatshedera lizei* (C.-Cochet) Guillaumin is a hybrid between *Fatsia* and *Hedera* which arose in the nursery of Lizé Frères in Nantes in 1910, said to be between *F. japonica* 'Moseri' and *H. hibernica* (Kirchner) Bean. This hybrid is sterile and has never been repeated. It is a sprawling shrub with wavy stems to 2.5m and greenish-white flowers, the anthers without pollen.

Hedera helix
fruits, ½ life size
April 29th

Hedera helix
flowers, life size
December 4th

Hedera helix
½ life size
December 2nd

*Fatsia
japonica*
flowers
⅔ life size
October 20th

ARALIACEAE

Fatsia japonica
fruits and seeds
⅔ life size
April 18th

Hedera helix leaves (left to right): 'Pedata',
'Manda's Crested', and 'Glacier'
⅔ life size, December 2nd

× *Fatshedera lizei*
⅓ life size
January 6th

Fatsia japonica
¼ life size
October 20th

Bupleurum

Bupleurum L. (1753), in the family Umbelliferae, contains around 100 species in Europe, North Africa, and Asia, of which 1 or 2 are shrubby and are described here.

Description Shrubs to 2.5m. The leaves are alternate, evergreen, thin and leathery, simple, narrowly elliptic to obovate. The flowers are green, bisexual, in flat-topped umbels with distinct bracts. Sepals absent; petals 5. Stamens 5. Ovary inferior, with 2 cells and 1 ovule per cell; styles 2. Pollination is by flies. The fruits are dry and split into halves, each with 1 seed, when ripe.

Key Recognition Features *Bupleurum* is recognised by its simple, leathery leaves and umbels of green flowers; the distinct bracts of the herbaceous species soon fall off in *B. fruticosum* L..

Evolution and Relationships *Bupleurum* is one of the few hardy, shrubby members of the Umbelliferae.

Ecology and Geography On dry hills in the Mediterranean area of southern Europe and northwestern Africa.

Comment *Bupleurum fruticosum* is sometimes grown as an ornamental by those who appreciate green flowers.

Bupleurum
fruticosum
fruits
$1\frac{1}{2} \times$ life size
October 5th

Bupleurum fruticosum
$\frac{1}{2}$ life size
September 10th

Heteromorpha

Heteromorpha Cham. & Schldl. (1826), in the family Umbelliferae, contains around 5 species in Africa and the Arabian peninsula.

Description Trees to 10m, and shrubs. The leaves are opposite, evergreen, thin and leathery, simple or with 3 leaflets, narrowly elliptic. The flowers are green, bisexual, in rounded, compound umbels, without bracts. Sepals absent; petals 5. Stamens 5. Ovary inferior, with 2 cells and 1 ovule per cell; styles 2. Pollination is presumed to be by flies. The fruits are dry and split into halves, each with 1 seed, when ripe.

Key Recognition Features The narrowly elliptic leaves and leaflets and the compound umbels without bracts are characteristic.

Evolution and Relationships Tree-like members of the true Umbelliferae are very unusual; most trees with umbellate inflorescences belong to the fleshy-fruited Araliaceae (see pp.376–81). However, recent work, backed up by DNA studies, suggests that the Umbelliferae and Araliaceae should be combined.

Ecology and Geography In forests in the Yemen, tropical Africa, and South Africa.

Comment *Heteromorpha trifoliata* (Wendl.) Ecklon & Zeyher, syn. *H. arborescens* (Spreng.) Cham. & Schldl. is the parsley tree of Africa, found from the Cape to Kenya.

Heteromorpha
trifoliata
¹/₂ life size
October 5th

Heteromorpha trifoliata
flowers, 1¹/₄ × life size
October 5th

Heteromorpha
trifoliata
¹/₂ life size
October 5th

Nerium oleander
flower parts, life size
July 20th

Nerium

Nerium L. (1753), in the family Apocynaceae, contains 1 species,
N. oleander L., in the Mediterranean region.

Description Trees to 3m, and shrubs. The leaves are opposite or
in whorls of 3, evergreen, leathery, simple, narrowly elliptic, with
a distinct, pale midrib. The flowers are pink in wild plants, white,
yellow, red, and apricot in cultivars, in loose bunches on the ends of
the shoots. Sepals 5, joined at the base. Petals 5, twisted around each
other in bud, joined into a tube for more than half their length, with a
corona of narrow, forked scales in the mouth of the tube. Stamens 5,
inserted about half way up the tube, the anthers with long, feathery
appendages, and attached to the stigma. Ovary superior,
with 2 cells and numerous ovules per cell; style 1,
with a large complex stigma. Pollination is by
insects, but the flowers are without nectar and offer no
reward to the insect visitor. The fruits are dry and narrowly
elliptic, splitting to release the silky, winged seeds.

Key Recognition Features The narrow, leathery leaves and pink,
red, white, or orange tubular flowers with spreading petals.

Evolution and Relationships The Apocynaceae is a mainly
tropical family, and many genera are cultivated for their attractive
flowers. *Nerium* is one of the few shrubby genera that will tolerate any
frost, and the only truly temperate genus is *Vinca*, the periwinkle.
Apocynaceae and Asclepiadaceae (see pp. 386–87) have always been
considered closely related, and some recent authorities unite them
under Apocynaceae. The more complex Asclepiadaceae probably
evolved from the simpler Apocynaceae.

Ecology and Geography By streams in dry areas in the
Mediterranean area of southern Europe and northwestern Africa, and
in Asia eastwards to India and central Nepal. The eastern plants
are sometimes called *N. indicum* Mill. and are scented. The
seeds need running water to germinate, but after that the
plants are very drought tolerant.

Comment *Nerium* is an attractive shrub, widely planted in warm
climates; it needs a cool winter of around 5–8°C to flower well. The
leaves and stalks of the plant are extremely poisonous; just 1 leaf can
be fatal to a human.

Nerium oleander
½ life size
July 20th

384

Trachelospermum

Trachelospermum Lemaire (1851), in the family Apocynaceae, contains around 20 species in Asia and southeastern North America.

Description Evergreen shrubby climbers to 15m, sometimes free-standing. The leaves are opposite, leathery, simple, elliptic to broadly oblanceolate. The flowers are scented, white, often changing to yellow, in small, loose bunches on the ends of the shoots and in the leaf axils. Sepals 5, joined at the base. Petals 5, twisted around each other in bud, joined into a tube for more than half their length, without scales in the throat. Stamens 5, partially emerging from the throat, the anthers attached to the stigma. Ovary superior, with 2 cells and numerous ovules per cell; style 1. Pollination is by insects, probably moths. Fruits are long and hanging, bean-like, often red, splitting to release seeds with a tuft of silky hairs at the apex.

Key Recognition Features The leathery leaves and white or pale yellow, jasmine-like flowers (*Jasminum*, see pp.420–21) with petals arranged like a propeller.

Evolution and Relationships The genus *Strophanthus* DC is vegetatively similar to *Trachelospermum* but has long, thread-like petals, which are often green.

Ecology and Geography In forests and gorges, climbing up trees and rocks: 3 species in Japan, around 11 in China, others in South East Asia, and 1 species, *T. difforme*, the Confederate jasmine, in the southeastern United States from Delaware and Missouri southwards.

Comment *Trachelospermum jasminoides* (Lindl.) Lem. and *T. asiaticum* (Sieb. & Zucc.) Nakai are both cultivated for their scented flowers. They will tolerate -10°C for short periods, but not prolonged freezing conditions.

Trachelospermum jasminoides
flowers, 1 ½ × life size
June 22nd

*Trachelospermum
asiaticum*
flowers
1 ½ × life size
June 22nd

*Trachelospermum
asiaticum*
½ life size
June 22nd

Trachelospermum jasminoides
½ life size, June 22nd

385

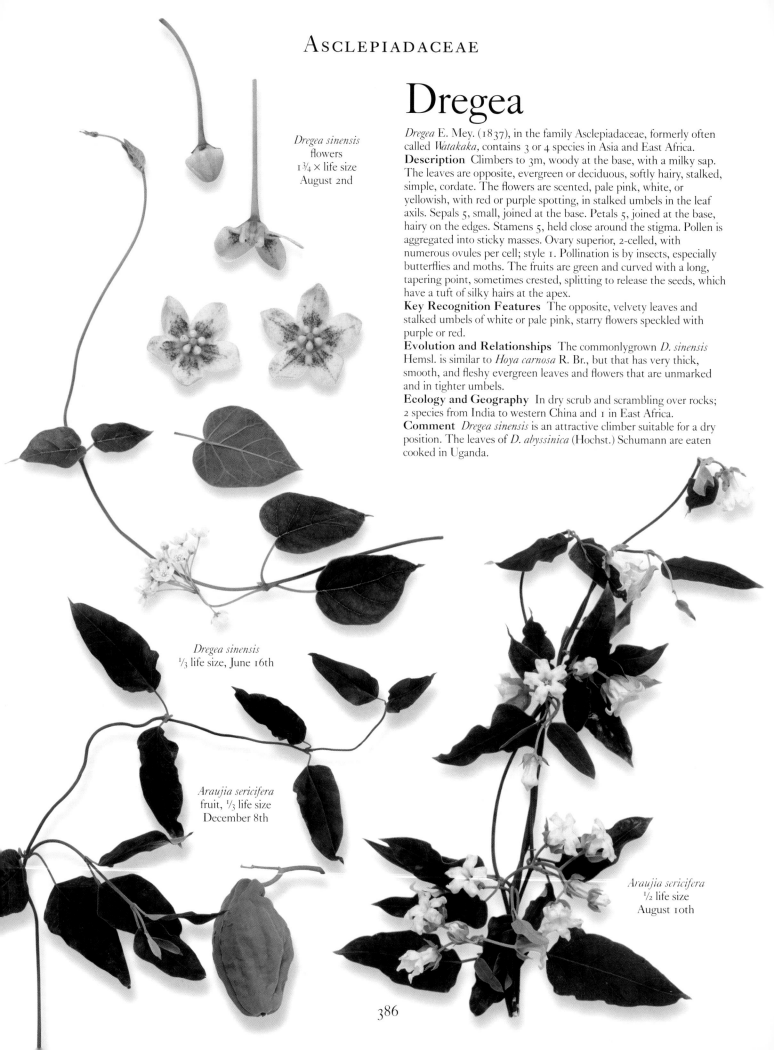

Dregea

Dregea sinensis
flowers
1¾ × life size
August 2nd

Dregea E. Mey. (1837), in the family Asclepiadaceae, formerly often called *Watakaka*, contains 3 or 4 species in Asia and East Africa.
Description Climbers to 3m, woody at the base, with a milky sap. The leaves are opposite, evergreen or deciduous, softly hairy, stalked, simple, cordate. The flowers are scented, pale pink, white, or yellowish, with red or purple spotting, in stalked umbels in the leaf axils. Sepals 5, small, joined at the base. Petals 5, joined at the base, hairy on the edges. Stamens 5, held close around the stigma. Pollen is aggregated into sticky masses. Ovary superior, 2-celled, with numerous ovules per cell; style 1. Pollination is by insects, especially butterflies and moths. The fruits are green and curved with a long, tapering point, sometimes crested, splitting to release the seeds, which have a tuft of silky hairs at the apex.
Key Recognition Features The opposite, velvety leaves and stalked umbels of white or pale pink, starry flowers speckled with purple or red.
Evolution and Relationships The commonlygrown *D. sinensis* Hemsl. is similar to *Hoya carnosa* R. Br., but that has very thick, smooth, and fleshy evergreen leaves and flowers that are unmarked and in tighter umbels.
Ecology and Geography In dry scrub and scrambling over rocks; 2 species from India to western China and 1 in East Africa.
Comment *Dregea sinensis* is an attractive climber suitable for a dry position. The leaves of *D. abyssinica* (Hochst.) Schumann are eaten cooked in Uganda.

Dregea sinensis
⅓ life size, June 16th

Araujia sericifera
fruit, ⅓ life size
December 8th

Araujia sericifera
½ life size
August 10th

386

Marsdenia

Marsdenia R. Br. (1809), in the family Asclepiadaceae, contains around 100 species, mainly in the tropics; 1 species, *M. oreophila* W.W. Sm. from China, is sometimes cultivated and is described here.

Description Climber to 3m, woody at the base, with copious milky sap. The leaves are opposite, evergreen, rather fleshy, softly hairy beneath, stalked, simple, cordate. The flowers are strongly and sweetly scented, white or yellowish, unspotted, in stalked umbels in the leaf axils. Sepals 5, small, joined at the base. Petals 5, the edges bent back and slightly twisted, hairy on the surface, joined at the base to form a cup. Stamens 5, held close around the swollen base of the style. The pollen is aggregated into sticky masses. Ovary superior, 2-celled, with numerous ovules per cell; style 1, long and sinous, bottle-shaped at the base. Pollination is by insects, especially butterflies and moths. The fruits are curved and green, with a long, tapering point, splitting to release the seeds, which have a tuft of silky hairs at the apex.

Key Recognition Features The opposite, fleshy leaves and stalked umbels of scented, hairy, creamy white flowers.

Evolution and Relationships *Marsdenia* is related to *Dregea, Hoya* R. Br., and other tropical, climbing Asclepiadaceae. *Cionura* Griseb. is sometimes considered a synonym of *Marsdenia*; it is based on *C. erecta* Griseb, a shrubby or shortly climbing species from southeastern Europe and from Turkey to Afghanistan. The familiar *Stephanotis floribunda* A. Brogn., a tropical species from Madagascar with hairless leaves and sweetly scented, white, waxy flowers with a long tube, much used by florists at weddings, is now included in *Marsdenia*. Apart from the climbing tropical Asclepiadaceae, of which *Hoya* and *Marsdenia* are the most often cultivated, a group of 42 genera, the so-called stapeliads, are desert succulents from Africa and the Canary Islands, with large, starry, brown flowers that smell of rotting meat and attract blowflies as pollinators.

Ecology and Geography In scrub and open forest: *M. oreophila* in Yunnan in western China, other temperate species in the Himalayas.

Comment The genus is named after William Marsden (1754–1836) Orientalist and numismatist, who worked for the East India Company and collected plants in Sumatra.

Marsdenia oreophila
½ life size
August 2nd

Marsdenia oreophila
flowers, 2 × life size
August 2nd

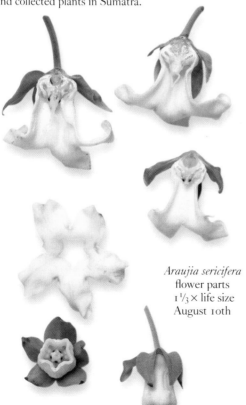

Araujia sericifera
flower parts
1⅓ × life size
August 10th

Araujia

Araujia Brot. (1818), in the family Asclepiadaceae, contains 2 or 3 species in South America.

Description Climbers to 5m, sometimes woody at the base. The leaves are opposite, evergreen, softly hairy, stalked, simple, triangular. The flowers are scented, pale pink, becoming white, in small, loose umbels in the leaf axils. Sepals 5, large, joined at the base. Petals 5, fleshy, joined into a tube for around half their length, with 5 scales at the middle of the tube. Stamens 5, in the throat of the tube, the anthers attached to the stigma. The pollen is aggregated into sticky masses. Ovary superior, 2-celled, with numerous ovules per cell; style 1. Pollination is by insects, especially moths, which become trapped on the stamens by their proboscis. Fruits large, curved, and green, with soft prickles, splitting to release the seeds, which have a tuft of silky hairs at the apex.

Key Recognition Features The opposite, velvety leaves and white or pale pink flowers with large sepals; moths are often found trapped by the flowers in the morning.

Evolution and Relationships The genus *Araujia* is related to milkweed, *Asclepias* L., and the starry, sky-blue-flowered *Oxypetalum caeruleum* (D. Don) Decne, syn. *Tweedia caerulea* D. Don.

Ecology and Geography In forests and scrub in Brazil and Peru.

Comment *Araujia sericifera* Brot., which is commonly cultivated in warm areas and has become naturalised in parts of Australia, is called the cruel plant because it traps moths.

Solanum

Solanum L. (1753), in the family Solanaceae, contains around 1700 species worldwide. A few species from temperate South America are shrubby, ornamental climbers, and these are described here.

Description Shrubby climbers to 6m. The leaves are alternate, evergreen or deciduous, simple or pinnate. The flowers are purplish, yellow or white, bisexual. Sepals 5, joined at the base. Petals 5, not twisted in bud, joined for around half their length, often opening to form a star. Stamens 5, often pressed together around the style, opening by slits or apical pores. Ovary superior, 2-celled, with numerous ovules per cell; style 1, simple, slender, with a small stigma. Pollination is by insects, which visit the flowers for pollen. The fruits are fleshy berries, black, orange, or red when ripe.

Key Recognition Features The purplish, white, or yellow, starry flowers with spreading petals, and the stamens held tightly around the style.

Evolution and Relationships The Solanaceae, with around 3000 species, is a mainly tropical family, close to Convolvulaceae (see p. 393). Two groups are generally recognised: the Solanoideae, mostly with berries, and the Cestroideae, usually with capsules. *Solanum* itself is a very large genus, many of its species being potato-like plants from the Andes, others weedy annuals. DNA studies suggest that *Lycopersicon* Miller, the tomatoes, and *Cyphomandra* Mart. ex Sendtner, the tree tomato, should be included in *Solanum*.

Ecology and Geography The climbers in woods and scrub, other species in many habitats. The majority of species in South America; 3 species in Europe, including *Solanum dulcamara* L., the woody nightshade or bittersweet.

Comment Of the shrubby, temperate *S. crispum* Ruíz & Pavón 'Glasnevin' and *S. jasminoides* Paxton 'Album', syn. *S. laxum* Spreng. 'Album' are most commonly cultivated. *Cyphomandra betacea* Cav. is grown for its egg-shaped and very tasty orange fruit, the tree tomato or tamarillo.

Solanum laciniatum
fruit, 1¼ × life size
October 5th

Lycium barbarum
¾ life size, July 28th

Lycium

Lycium L. (1753), in the family Solanaceae, contains around 100 species worldwide.

Description Shrubs to 4m, often spiny. The leaves are alternate, deciduous, simple, often small, and oblanceolate. The flowers are purple, reddish, greenish, or white, bisexual, solitary or in small clusters. Sepals 5, joined at the base. Petals 5, joined for half their length or more, tubular at the base. Stamens 5, often exserted from the flower. Ovary superior, 2-celled, with numerous ovules per cell; style 1, simple, slender. Pollination is by insects. The fruits are fleshy berries, usually red when ripe.

Key Recognition Features The narrow leaves on a twiggy, spiny bush, and the tubular or starry, purple or greenish flowers with spreading petals.

Evolution and Relationships *Lycium* is similar to *Iochroma* (see p. 390), but has smaller flowers with larger petals and smaller leaves.

Ecology and Geography Generally in dry or semi-desert areas, or near the sea; many species tolerate saline soil. Found in Europe and across Asia to China, in South Africa, in northwestern America (with 10 species in Arizona), and along the Andes to Chile.

Comment *Lycium barbarum* L., the Duke of Argyll's tea tree, is used in Chinese medicine; the fruit of several species were eaten in times of food shortage, particularly in North America, and the young shoots may be eaten as a vegetable.

Lycium barbarum
1⅓ × life size, July 28th

Solanum laciniatum
1⅓ × life size, May 15th

Solanum crispum
¾ life size, May 15th

Solanum crispum
flowers, 2¼ × life size
May 15th

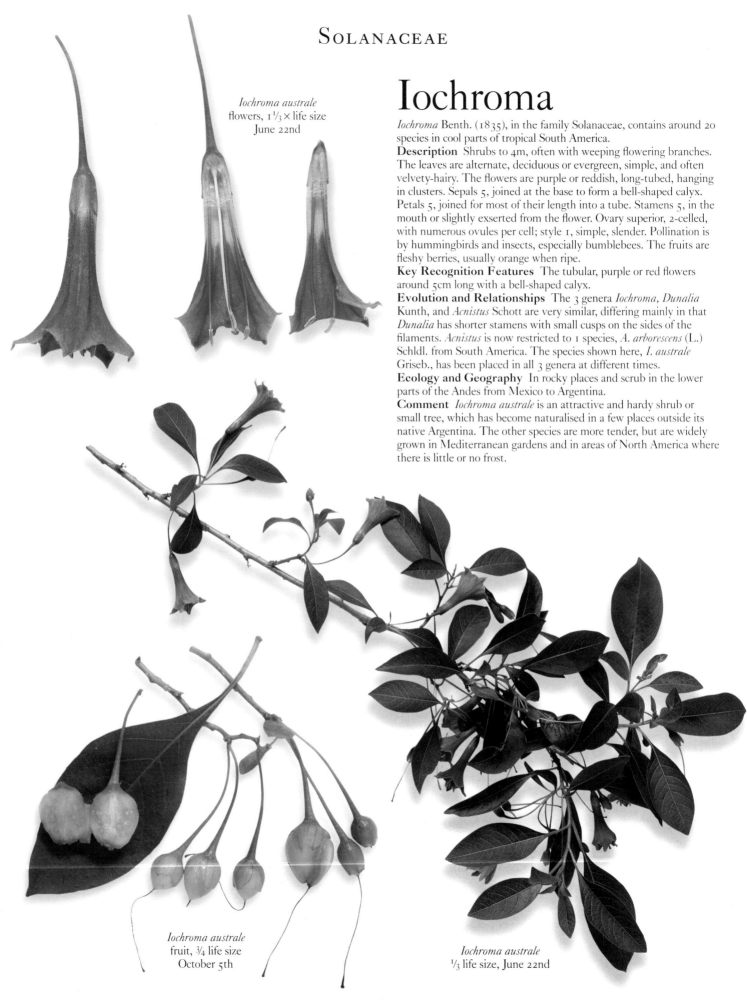

Iochroma

Iochroma Benth. (1835), in the family Solanaceae, contains around 20 species in cool parts of tropical South America.

Description Shrubs to 4m, often with weeping flowering branches. The leaves are alternate, deciduous or evergreen, simple, and often velvety-hairy. The flowers are purple or reddish, long-tubed, hanging in clusters. Sepals 5, joined at the base to form a bell-shaped calyx. Petals 5, joined for most of their length into a tube. Stamens 5, in the mouth or slightly exserted from the flower. Ovary superior, 2-celled, with numerous ovules per cell; style 1, simple, slender. Pollination is by hummingbirds and insects, especially bumblebees. The fruits are fleshy berries, usually orange when ripe.

Key Recognition Features The tubular, purple or red flowers around 5cm long with a bell-shaped calyx.

Evolution and Relationships The 3 genera *Iochroma*, *Dunalia* Kunth, and *Acnistus* Schott are very similar, differing mainly in that *Dunalia* has shorter stamens with small cusps on the sides of the filaments. *Acnistus* is now restricted to 1 species, *A. arborescens* (L.) Schldl. from South America. The species shown here, *I. australe* Griseb., has been placed in all 3 genera at different times.

Ecology and Geography In rocky places and scrub in the lower parts of the Andes from Mexico to Argentina.

Comment *Iochroma australe* is an attractive and hardy shrub or small tree, which has become naturalised in a few places outside its native Argentina. The other species are more tender, but are widely grown in Mediterranean gardens and in areas of North America where there is little or no frost.

Iochroma australe
flowers, 1⅓ × life size
June 22nd

Iochroma australe
fruit, ¾ life size
October 5th

Iochroma australe
⅓ life size, June 22nd

Vestia foetida
½ life size, April 1st

Vestia foetida
fruit, 1 ¼ × life size

Vestia foetida
flowers, 1 ¾ × life size
April 1st

Vestia

Vestia Willd. (1809), in the family Solanaceae, contains 1 species, *V. foetida* (Ruíz & Pavón) Hoffsgg., syn. *V. lycioides* Willd., in Chile.

Description Shrubs to 3.6m, with soft, green branches. The leaves are elliptic, alternate, evergreen, glabrous, foetid when crushed. The flowers are pale yellow, long-tubed, usually pendent. Sepals 5, joined at the base into a bell-shaped calyx. Petals 5, joined for most of their length into a greenish tube, with triangular tips. Stamens 5, attached to the inside of the tube, exserted from the flower. Ovary superior, 2-celled, with numerous ovules per cell; style 1, simple, slender. Pollination is by insects and hummingbirds. The fruits are yellow capsules with numerous seeds.

Key Recognition Features The tubular, yellow flowers with exserted stamens and green stems.

Evolution and Relationships Most closely related to *Cestrum*, but with capsules rather than berries.

Ecology and Geography In scrub from Valparaiso to Valdivia in Chile.

Comment Only *V. foetida* is cultivated, and it survives longest in mild maritime gardens with good drainage. The genus is named after L.C. de Vest (1776–1840) a professor at Graz University in Austria.

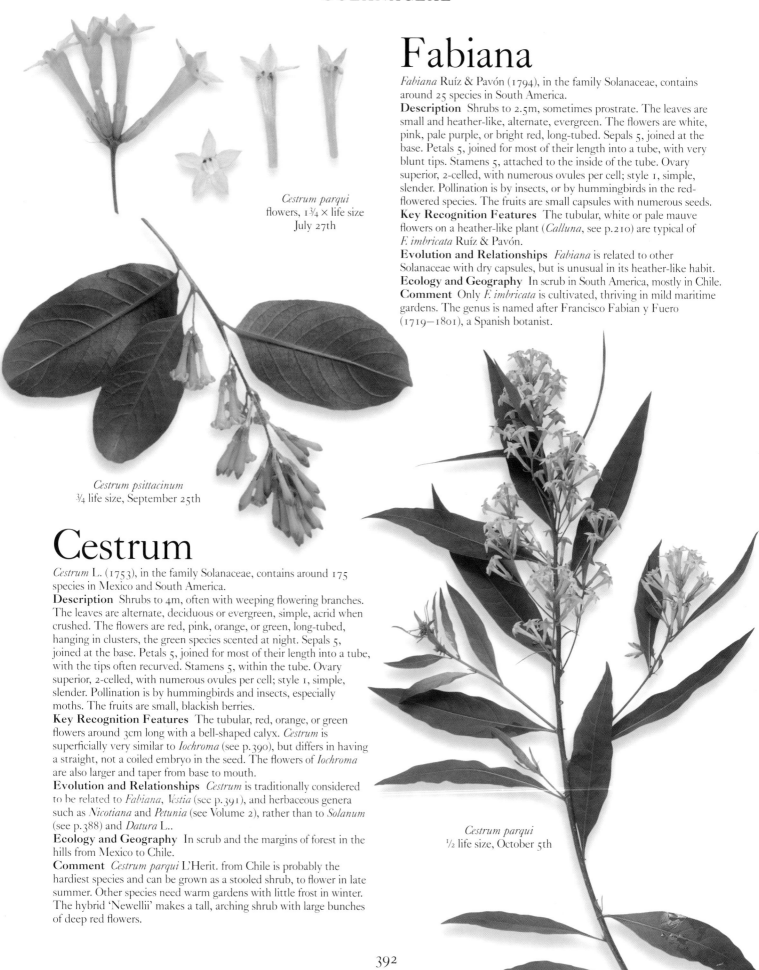

Fabiana

Fabiana Ruíz & Pavón (1794), in the family Solanaceae, contains around 25 species in South America.

Description Shrubs to 2.5m, sometimes prostrate. The leaves are small and heather-like, alternate, evergreen. The flowers are white, pink, pale purple, or bright red, long-tubed. Sepals 5, joined at the base. Petals 5, joined for most of their length into a tube, with very blunt tips. Stamens 5, attached to the inside of the tube. Ovary superior, 2-celled, with numerous ovules per cell; style 1, simple, slender. Pollination is by insects, or by hummingbirds in the red-flowered species. The fruits are small capsules with numerous seeds.

Key Recognition Features The tubular, white or pale mauve flowers on a heather-like plant (*Calluna*, see p.210) are typical of *F. imbricata* Ruíz & Pavón.

Evolution and Relationships *Fabiana* is related to other Solanaceae with dry capsules, but is unusual in its heather-like habit.

Ecology and Geography In scrub in South America, mostly in Chile.

Comment Only *F. imbricata* is cultivated, thriving in mild maritime gardens. The genus is named after Francisco Fabian y Fuero (1719–1801), a Spanish botanist.

Cestrum parqui
flowers, 1¾ × life size
July 27th

Cestrum psittacinum
¾ life size, September 25th

Cestrum

Cestrum L. (1753), in the family Solanaceae, contains around 175 species in Mexico and South America.

Description Shrubs to 4m, often with weeping flowering branches. The leaves are alternate, deciduous or evergreen, simple, acrid when crushed. The flowers are red, pink, orange, or green, long-tubed, hanging in clusters, the green species scented at night. Sepals 5, joined at the base. Petals 5, joined for most of their length into a tube, with the tips often recurved. Stamens 5, within the tube. Ovary superior, 2-celled, with numerous ovules per cell; style 1, simple, slender. Pollination is by hummingbirds and insects, especially moths. The fruits are small, blackish berries.

Key Recognition Features The tubular, red, orange, or green flowers around 3cm long with a bell-shaped calyx. *Cestrum* is superficially very similar to *Iochroma* (see p.390), but differs in having a straight, not a coiled embryo in the seed. The flowers of *Iochroma* are also larger and taper from base to mouth.

Evolution and Relationships *Cestrum* is traditionally considered to be related to *Fabiana*, *Vestia* (see p.391), and herbaceous genera such as *Nicotiana* and *Petunia* (see Volume 2), rather than to *Solanum* (see p.388) and *Datura* L..

Ecology and Geography In scrub and the margins of forest in the hills from Mexico to Chile.

Comment *Cestrum parqui* L'Herit. from Chile is probably the hardiest species and can be grown as a stooled shrub, to flower in late summer. Other species need warm gardens with little frost in winter. The hybrid 'Newellii' makes a tall, arching shrub with large bunches of deep red flowers.

Cestrum parqui
½ life size, October 5th

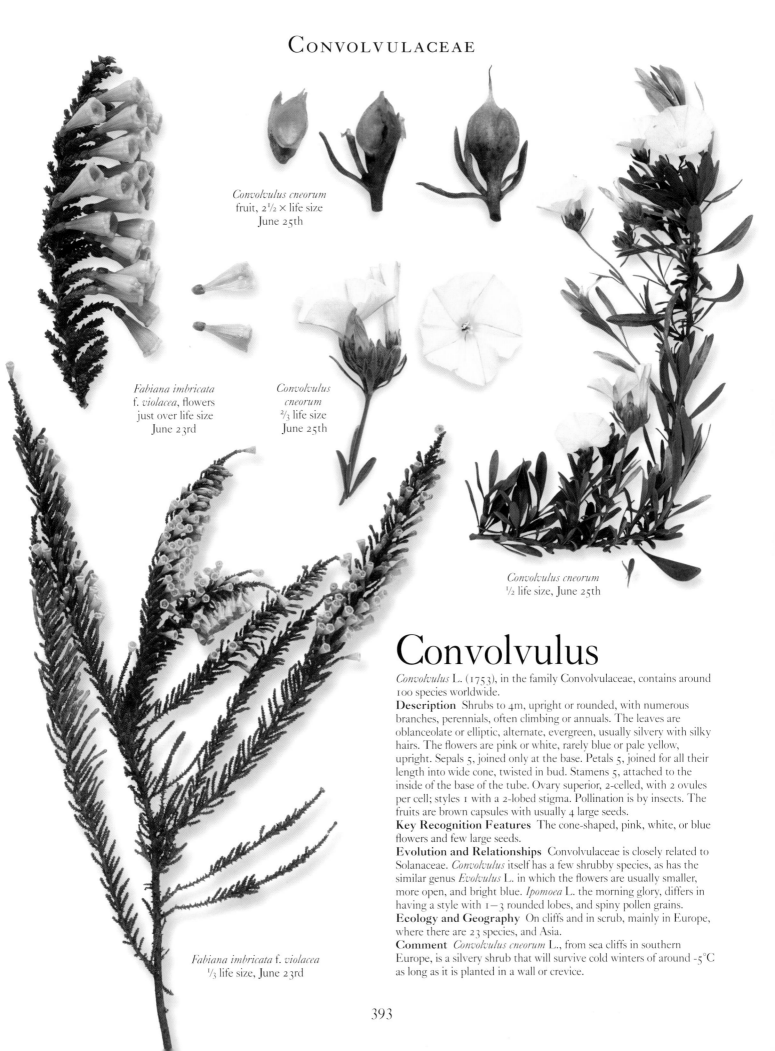

Convolvulus cneorum
fruit, 2½ × life size
June 25th

Fabiana imbricata
f. *violacea*, flowers
just over life size
June 23rd

*Convolvulus
cneorum*
⅔ life size
June 25th

Convolvulus cneorum
½ life size, June 25th

Fabiana imbricata f. *violacea*
⅓ life size, June 23rd

Convolvulus

Convolvulus L. (1753), in the family Convolvulaceae, contains around 100 species worldwide.

Description Shrubs to 4m, upright or rounded, with numerous branches, perennials, often climbing or annuals. The leaves are oblanceolate or elliptic, alternate, evergreen, usually silvery with silky hairs. The flowers are pink or white, rarely blue or pale yellow, upright. Sepals 5, joined only at the base. Petals 5, joined for all their length into wide cone, twisted in bud. Stamens 5, attached to the inside of the base of the tube. Ovary superior, 2-celled, with 2 ovules per cell; styles 1 with a 2-lobed stigma. Pollination is by insects. The fruits are brown capsules with usually 4 large seeds.

Key Recognition Features The cone-shaped, pink, white, or blue flowers and few large seeds.

Evolution and Relationships Convolvulaceae is closely related to Solanaceae. *Convolvulus* itself has a few shrubby species, as has the similar genus *Evolvulus* L. in which the flowers are usually smaller, more open, and bright blue. *Ipomoea* L. the morning glory, differs in having a style with 1–3 rounded lobes, and spiny pollen grains.

Ecology and Geography On cliffs and in scrub, mainly in Europe, where there are 23 species, and Asia.

Comment *Convolvulus cneorum* L., from sea cliffs in southern Europe, is a silvery shrub that will survive cold winters of around -5°C as long as it is planted in a wall or crevice.

393

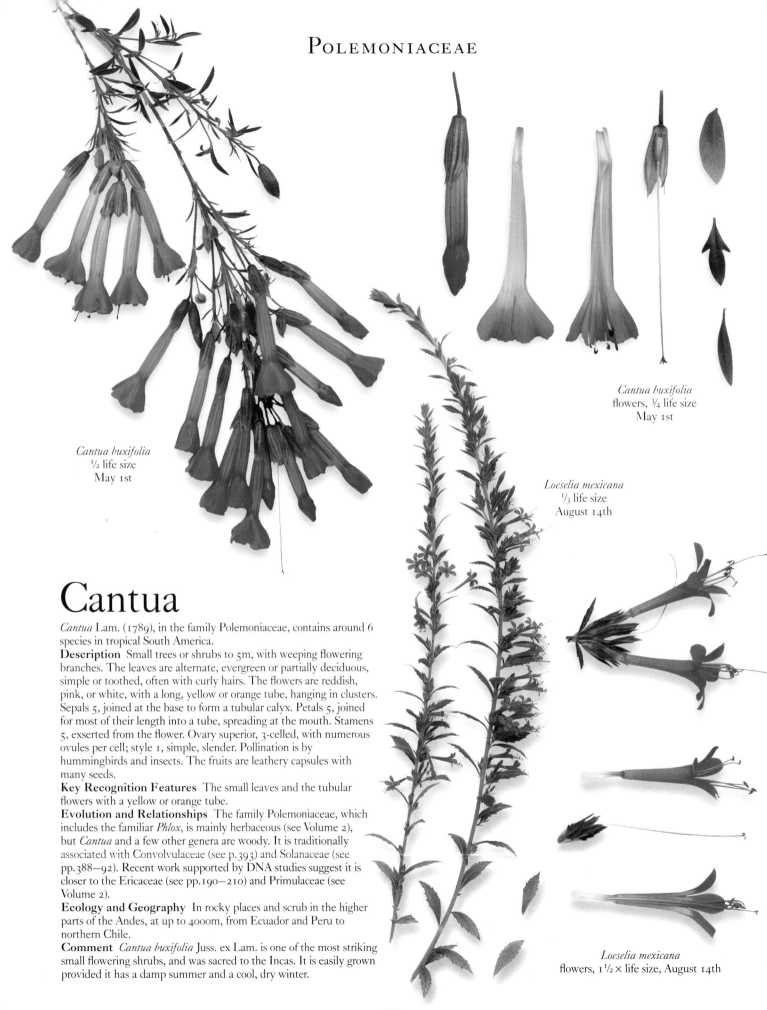

Cantua buxifolia
flowers, ³⁄₄ life size
May 1st

Cantua buxifolia
¹⁄₂ life size
May 1st

Loeselia mexicana
¹⁄₃ life size
August 14th

Cantua

Cantua Lam. (1789), in the family Polemoniaceae, contains around 6 species in tropical South America.

Description Small trees or shrubs to 5m, with weeping flowering branches. The leaves are alternate, evergreen or partially deciduous, simple or toothed, often with curly hairs. The flowers are reddish, pink, or white, with a long, yellow or orange tube, hanging in clusters. Sepals 5, joined at the base to form a tubular calyx. Petals 5, joined for most of their length into a tube, spreading at the mouth. Stamens 5, exserted from the flower. Ovary superior, 3-celled, with numerous ovules per cell; style 1, simple, slender. Pollination is by hummingbirds and insects. The fruits are leathery capsules with many seeds.

Key Recognition Features The small leaves and the tubular flowers with a yellow or orange tube.

Evolution and Relationships The family Polemoniaceae, which includes the familiar *Phlox*, is mainly herbaceous (see Volume 2), but *Cantua* and a few other genera are woody. It is traditionally associated with Convolvulaceae (see p.393) and Solanaceae (see pp.388–92). Recent work supported by DNA studies suggest it is closer to the Ericaceae (see pp.190–210) and Primulaceae (see Volume 2).

Ecology and Geography In rocky places and scrub in the higher parts of the Andes, at up to 4000m, from Ecuador and Peru to northern Chile.

Comment *Cantua buxifolia* Juss. ex Lam. is one of the most striking small flowering shrubs, and was sacred to the Incas. It is easily grown provided it has a damp summer and a cool, dry winter.

Loeselia mexicana
flowers, 1¹⁄₂ × life size, August 14th

Desfontainia spinosa flowers 1¼ × life size 27th July

Desfontainia spinosa fruit, life size August 11th

Desfontainia

Desfontainia Ruíz & Pavón (1794), in the family Desfontainiaceae, contains 1 species, *D. spinosa* Ruíz & Pavón, in South America.

Description Shrub to 3m, with peeling bark. The leaves are opposite, evergreen, holly-like and spiny toothed, smooth. The flowers are scarlet with yellow lobes and a red tube, thick and waxy, solitary at the ends of the shoots. Sepals 5, joined at the base. Petals 5, joined for most of their length into a tube, straight or slightly wider at the mouth, rounded. Stamens 5, with short filaments, inserted in a ring at the mouth of the flower. Ovary superior, 5-celled, with numerous ovules per cell; style 1, long and slender. Pollination is by green-backed firecrown hummingbirds. The fruits are short, greenish-purple, fleshy berries, surrounded by persistent sepals.

Key Recognition Features The holly-like, opposite leaves and tubular flowers.

Evolution and Relationships The affinities of *Desfontainia* are still unclear; sometimes it is associated with *Buddleja* (see pp.422–23) in the Loganiaceae, but now it is placed in its own family.

Ecology and Geography In moist, cool forest with *Drimys winteri* (see p.60) and *Nothofagus betuloides* (see p.111); from Colombia to Patagonia and the western islands of Tierra del Fuego.

Comment *Desfontainia* is most often seen in mild gardens on the western coasts of Europe and North America; it thrives in New Zealand. It has been used in the past for a yellow dye, and a tea reported to be hallucinogenic can be made from the leaves. The genus is named after R.L. Desfontaines (1752–1833) a French botanist.

Loeselia

Loeselia L. (1753), in the family Polemoniaceae, contains around 9 species from North America to northern South America.

Description Subshrubs to 2m, with peeling bark and upright flowering branches. The leaves are alternate, evergreen, simple or spiny toothed, often spine-tipped and glandular-hairy. The flowers are scarlet with a white throat and a red tube, or bluish, solitary or in pairs on the ends of short shoots in the leaf axils, with bracts scarious at the base. Sepals 5, joined at the base to form a tube. Petals 5, rounded at the apex, joined for some of their length into a tube, spreading at the mouth. Stamens 5, exserted from the flower. Ovary superior, with 3 cells and numerous ovules per cell; style 1, slender, 3-lobed at the apex. Pollination is by hummingbirds in the red-flowered species and by various insects in the blue-flowered species. The fruits are short, 3-celled capsules with winged seeds.

Key Recognition Features The small, spine-tipped leaves and tubular flowers on short shoots surrounded by spiny bracts.

Evolution and Relationships In its variation in flower from purplish-blue and open to red and tubular, *Loeselia* is similar to other genera of the Polemoniaceae such as *Gilia* Ruíz & Pavón, *Leptodactylon* Hook. & Arn., the prickly phlox from California, is also shrubby at the base.

Ecology and Geography In rocky places and scrub from Arizona and Mexico to Venezuela.

Comment *Loeselia mexicana* (Lam.) Brand, the species illustrated here, is sometimes cultivated; it requires a dry sunny climate with little winter frost.

Desfontainia spinosa ½ life size, 27th July

Ehretia

Ehretia L. (1759), in the family Boraginaceae, contains around 75 species, mainly in the tropics; 3 or 4 species are found in temperate Asia, and it is these that are described below.

Description Trees to 15m, or shrubs. The leaves are alternate, deciduous, simple, often toothed. The flowers are small, white, short-tubed, sometimes scented, in upright, branched, pyramidal or rounded clusters. Sepals 5, forming a toothed calyx. Petals 4, about equalling the tube in length. Stamens 5, exserted from the flower. Ovary superior, 4-celled, with 1 ovule per cell; style 1, deeply forked. Pollination is by insects. The fruits are small, orange or black, 1-seeded berries.

Key Recognition Features The branching clusters of small, white flowers and the alternate leaves.

Evolution and Relationships The family Boraginaceae contains many familiar herbaceous plants, such as forget-me-not, *Myosotis*, and comfrey, *Symphytum* (see Volume 2), but few temperate trees or shrubs. Boraginaceae is close to Convolvulaceae (see p.393) and Solanaceae (see pp.388–92). *Ehretia* itself belongs to a mainly tropical group which includes *Cordia* L., a coastal genus of trees from Central America. It is sometimes put in a distinct family, the Ehretiaceae.

Ecology and Geography In forests and warm, rocky valleys; the temperate species from Nepal and western China eastwards to Taiwan and Japan.

Comment The genus is named after G.D. Ehret (1708–70), a native of Heidelberg and most accomplished flower painter, who worked in London from 1735, mostly at the Chelsea Physic garden. Ehret drew the plates of plants in P. Browne's *Civil and Natural History of Jamaica* (1756). Poles of *Ehretia* wood were used for carrying loads in China.

Ehretia acuminata
flower buds, ¾ life size
July 28th

Ehretia acuminata
flowers, ¾ life size
July 28th

Ehretia acuminata
½ life size
July 28th

Aloysia chamaedrifolia
½ life size
September 13th

Aloysia

Aloysia Palau (1784), in the family Verbenaceae, contains around 37 species in America.

Description Shrubs to 5m, but usually less. The leaves are in whorls of 4, deciduous or evergreen, rough to the touch, sometimes hairy. The flowers are small, pale purple, pink, or white, short-tubed, sometimes scented, in upright, branched spikes. Sepals 2–4, forming a toothed calyx. Petals 4, about equalling the tube in length. Stamens 4, slightly exserted from the flower. Ovary superior, 2-celled, with 1 ovule per cell; style 1, simple, slender. Pollination is by insects. The fruits are pairs of small nutlets.

Key Recognition Features The tubular, purple or red flowers around 5cm long with a bell-shaped calyx.

Evolution and Relationships The families Verbenaceae and Labiatae (see pp. 398–409) are closely related, and recently many genera formerly in Verbenaceae, including *Clerodendrum* and *Callicarpa* (see pp. 398–99), have been transferred to Labiatae. *Aloysia* was formerly included in the much larger genus *Lippia* L..

Ecology and Geography In dry, rocky places and scrub from Texas and California southwards and along the Andes to Argentina and Chile.

Comment The lemon verbena, *A. citriodora* Palau, often called *A. triphylla* (L'Herit.) Britt. or *Lippia citriodora* (Palau) Kunth, is commonly grown for its scented leaves, which may be brewed into a sedative tea; in the Andes of northwestern Argentina, where the species is frequent, both lemon-scented and anise-scented plants grow together.

Aloysia chamaedrifolia
2 × life size
September 13th

Aloysia citriodora
1 ½ × life size, August 1st

Aloysia citriodora
½ life size, August 1st

Rhaphithamnus spinosus
life size, May 5th

Rhaphithamnus

Rhaphithamnus Miers (1870), in the family Verbenaceae, contains 2 species in South America.

Description Small trees or shrubs to 8m, twiggy and spiny. The leaves are opposite or in whorls of 3, evergreen, simple. The flowers are bluish-purple, long-tubed, solitary or in pairs in the upper leaf axils. Sepals 5, joined at the base to form a bell-shaped calyx. Petals 4 or 5, joined for most of their length. Stamens 4. Ovary superior, 2-celled, with 2 ovules per cell; style 1, simple. Pollination is by insects, especially bumblebees. The fruits are fleshy, light blue berries with few hard seeds.

Key Recognition Features The tubular, bluish-purple flowers on a spiny bush with simple, dark green leaves and spines.

Evolution and Relationships The blue berries of *R. spinosus* (Juss.) Small, which is the species generally cultivated, are reminiscent of those of *Callicarpa* (see pp. 398–99), which has now been transferred to the Labiatae (see pp. 398–409). Fleshy berries are common in the Verbenaceae, for example in the tropical genera *Lantana* L. and *Duranta* L., but less common in the Labiatae.

Ecology and Geography In scrub in the Andes in Chile, on the Juan Fernandes Islands (traditionally the landfall of Robinson Crusoe), and in Argentina.

Comment *Rhaphithamnus spinosus* is sometimes grown for its unusual berries.

397

Clerodendrum trichotomum var. *fargesii*
flowers, life size, August 20th

Clerodendrum

Clerodendrum L. (1753), in the family Labiatae, contains around
400 species worldwide, mainly in the tropics, but a few temperate.
Description Trees to 8m, or shrubs, sometimes climbing, often
suckering. Leaves opposite, simple, deciduous or evergreen,
sometimes hairy, acrid or smelling of roasted nuts. The flowers are
usually white, pink, or pale purple, long-tubed, scented, in flattish
heads or large sprays. Sepals 5, sometimes enlarging and becoming
coloured and starry in fruit. Petals 5, about equalling or shorter than
the tube. Stamens 4, exserted from the flower. Ovary superior,
2-celled, with 2 ovules per cell; style 1, simple, slender. Pollination is
by insects, mainly butterflies, and possibly also by birds. The fruits
are fleshy berries with 4 seeds.
Key Recognition Features The soft, acrid leaves and tubular,
scented flowers in a flat head. In fruit the blue berries and red sepals
of *Clerodendrum trichotomum* Thunb. are unique.
Evolution and Relationships *Clerodendrum* was formerly put in
the Verbenaceae (see p.397), but has recently been moved to the
Labiatae with other genera such as *Callicarpa*, *Vitex* (see p.401), and
Tectona L. fil., the teak tree. Within the Labiatae, *Clerodendrum* is
related to herbaceous genera such as *Ajuga* L. and *Teucrium* (see p.400).
Ecology and Geography In scrub and forest clearings, mainly in
the tropics and subtropics, with the temperate species found in China
and Japan.
Comment *Clerodendrum trichotomum* is grown for its scented, white
flowers and colourful fruits; *C. philippinum* Schauer for its scented,
often double flowers. Many tropical species, such as *C. paniculatum* L.,
the pagoda flower, have large heads of scarlet flowers. *Clerodendrum
bungei* Steud. has dense, rounded heads of deep pink flowers, and is
noted for its particularly rampant suckering habit.

Callicarpa

Callicarpa L. (1753), in the family Labiatae, contains around
140 species, mainly in the tropics and subtropics.
Description Shrubs to 3m, or small trees. Leaves opposite, finely
toothed and slender pointed, deciduous, usually softly hairy. The
flowers are small, pinkish or pale blue, scented, in flattish or rounded
heads. Sepals 4, joined to form a cup-shaped calyx. Petals 4, about
equalling or shorter than the tube. Stamens 4, exserted from the flower.
Ovary superior, 2-celled, with 2 ovules per cell; style 1, simple, slender.
Pollination is by insects. The fruits are fleshy berries with 2 or 4 seeds.
Key Recognition Features The soft leaves and small, pale pinkish
or bluish, scented flowers in a head. In fruit the crowded heads of blue
or pink, shining berries are easily recognised.
Evolution and Relationships *Callicarpa*, previously included in
the Verbenaceae (see p.397), is associated with *Vitex* (see p.401).
Ecology and Geography In scrub, from the Himalayas to China
and Japan. *Callicarpa americana* L. is found in southeastern North
America, and other tropical species are found in Central America and
northern Australia.
Comment A few *Callicarpa* species, and particularly *C. bodinieri*
var. *giraldii* (Hesse) Rehd., are grown for their masses of violet berries,
3–4mm across.

Callicarpa bodinieri
½ life size
September 29th

LABIATAE

Clerodendrum trichotomum
ripe (left) and unripe (right) fruits
1½ × life size, September 29th

Clerodendrum trichotomum
⅔ life size
September 29th

Callicarpa bodinieri
fruits, 1½ × life size
September 29th

Clerodendrum trichotomum
(above), ½ life size
August 20th

*Clerodendrum
bungei* (right)
buds and flowers
½ life size
August 20th

Callicarpa bodinieri
flowers, just under life
size, June 22nd

399

Caryopteris

Caryopteris Bunge. (1835), in the family Labiatae, contains around 6 species in eastern Asia.

Description Small shrubs to 1m, sometimes woody only at the base. Leaves sweetly aromatic, opposite, usually toothed, deciduous, grey beneath. The flowers are blue to lilac, in rounded, terminal heads and in the upper leaf axils. Sepals 5, joined to form a toothed calyx. Petals 5, about equalling or shorter than the tube. Stamens 4, exserted from the flower. Ovary superior, 2-celled, with 2 ovules per cell; style 1, simple, slender. Pollination is by insects. The fruits are capsules with 4 seeds.

Key Recognition Features The soft, often coarse-toothed leaves and the blue flowers in late summer.

Evolution and Relationships Apart from having a capsule rather than 4 nutlets, *Caryopteris* is close in many characters to *Teucrium* L. *Caryopteris* was formerly included in Verbenaceae, but has many characters in common with typical Labiatae, such as sharp-toothed, aromatic leaves and clusters of blue flowers in the upper leaf axils.

Ecology and Geography In dry, open scrub and rock crevices in Central Asia and rainshadow valleys in the Himalayas, and eastwards to Japan.

Comment *Caryopteris incana* (Houtt.) Miq. and *C.* × *clandonensis* Simmonds ex Rehder, its hybrid with *C. mongholica* Bunge, are grown for their late flowering. They are tolerant of poor soil and drought.

Teucrium

Teucrium L. (1753), in the family Labiatae, contains around 100 species around the world, mainly in the Mediterranean area.

Description Shrubs to 2m, often scrambling, or herbaceous perennials, rarely annuals. Leaves aromatic, opposite, usually undivided, greyish, sometimes toothed. The flowers are blue, white, or yellowish, solitary or in groups in the upper leaf axils. Sepals 5, joined to form a toothed calyx. Petals joined at the base, forming a tube, the upper lip very small or absent, the lower lip with a rounded central lobe and 2 teeth on each side. Stamens 4, exserted from the flower, curving downwards. Ovary superior, 2-celled, with 2 ovules per cell; style 1, forked, slender. Pollination is mainly by bees. The fruits are 4 nutlets.

Key Recognition Features The flowers with the upper lip apparently absent.

Evolution and Relationships Recent studies suggest that *Teucrium* is related to *Caryopteris* and *Clerodendrum*, (see p.398), traditionally in Verbenaceae (see p.397), rather than the superficially similar *Ajuga* L..

Ecology and Geography In dry, open scrub, or seasonally wet places, from Europe, where there are 49 species, across Asia to Japan and southwards to Australia and New Zealand.

Comment The most shrubby species, *T. fruticans* L., with whitish or blue flowers, is found in southern Spain and Portugal; it is only hardy in the mildest climates with dry winters and little frost.

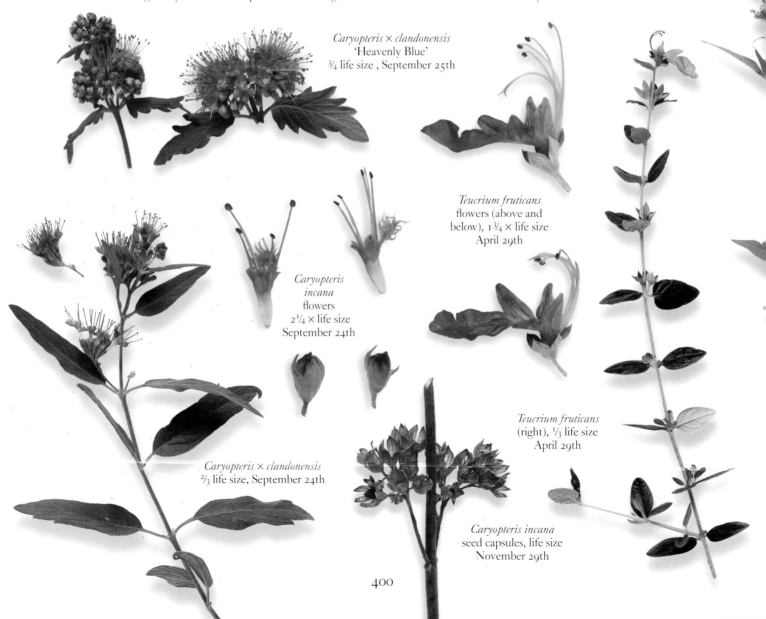

Caryopteris × *clandonensis*
'Heavenly Blue'
¾ life size , September 25th

Caryopteris incana flowers
2¼ × life size
September 24th

Teucrium fruticans flowers (above and below), 1¾ × life size
April 29th

Caryopteris × *clandonensis*
⅔ life size, September 24th

Teucrium fruticans (right), ⅓ life size
April 29th

Caryopteris incana seed capsules, life size
November 29th

Vitex negundo var. *heterophylla*
flowers, 2 × life size, October 5th

Vitex agnus-castus
flowers, 2 × life size
October 6th

Vitex negundo var.
heterophylla
½ life size, October 5th

Vitex agnus-castus
½ life size, October 6th

Vitex

Vitex L. (1753), in the family Labiatae, contains around 250 species, mainly in the tropics; the description here covers the temperate species.

Description Trees to 20m, and shrubs, sometimes creeping. Leaves aromatic, opposite, usually palmately divided into 3–7 narrow, toothed leaflets, deciduous or evergreen, often greyish. The flowers are blue to lilac, pink, white, or reddish, usually in narrow, upright, compound spikes. Sepals 5, joined to form a toothed calyx. Petals 5, about equalling or shorter than the tube. Stamens 4, exserted from the flower, 2 long and 2 short. Ovary superior, 2-celled, with 2 ovules per cell; style 1, forked, slender. Pollination is by insects. The fruits are bright red or black, fleshy berries with 4 seeds.

Key Recognition Features The 3- to 7-palmate leaves and spikes of blue flowers in late summer.

Evolution and Relationships *Vitex* was formerly placed in the Verbenaceae (see p.297) on account of its berry-like fruit; it is related to *Callicarpa* (see p.298).

Ecology and Geography In dry, open scrub, river gravel, seashore, and rock crevices from southern Europe across Asia to Japan and southwards to Australia and in forest in New Zealand.

Comment *Vitex agnus-castus* L., the chaste tree, is found around the Mediterranean, and was called *agnos,* meaning chaste or sacred, in pre-Hellenic Greek and by Homer. The tough, flexible, willow-like stems were used for bindings; to affirm their chastity, women would lie on couches covered with its branches at the festival of Demeter. By an irony that was not lost on early herbalists, the seeds were used against venereal disease. *Vitex lucens* Kirk from New Zealand is a stout tree with dark green, shining leaves and reddish flowers around 2.5cm long in small clusters beneath the leaves.

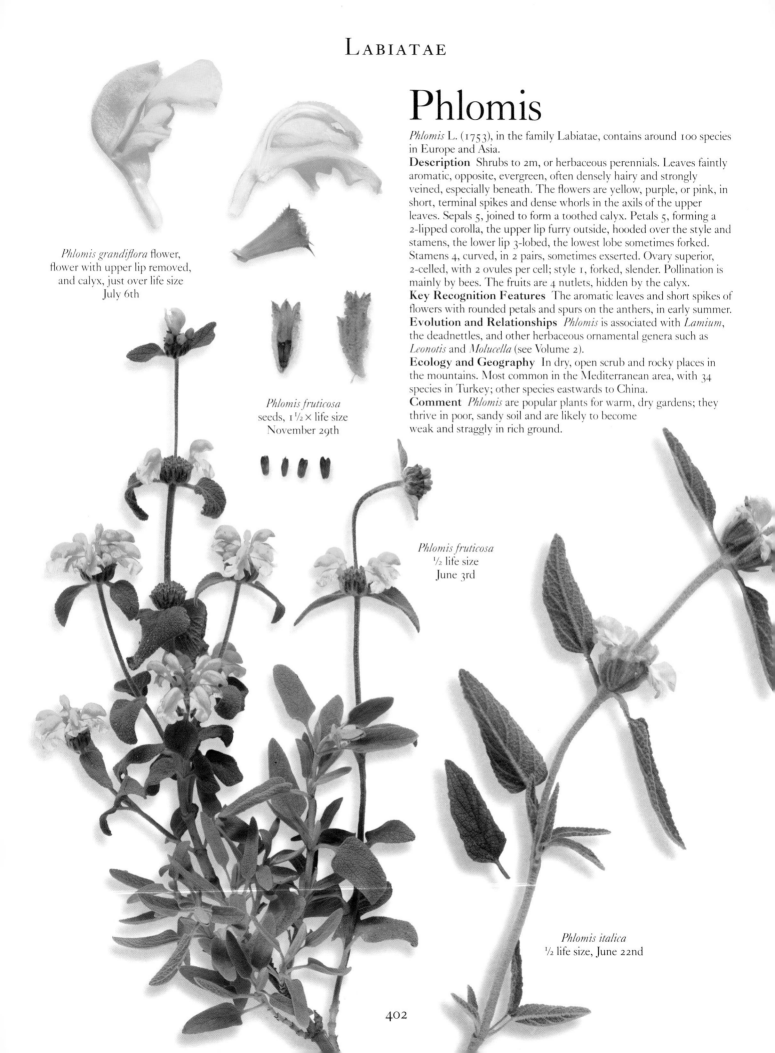

Phlomis

Phlomis L. (1753), in the family Labiatae, contains around 100 species in Europe and Asia.

Description Shrubs to 2m, or herbaceous perennials. Leaves faintly aromatic, opposite, evergreen, often densely hairy and strongly veined, especially beneath. The flowers are yellow, purple, or pink, in short, terminal spikes and dense whorls in the axils of the upper leaves. Sepals 5, joined to form a toothed calyx. Petals 5, forming a 2-lipped corolla, the upper lip furry outside, hooded over the style and stamens, the lower lip 3-lobed, the lowest lobe sometimes forked. Stamens 4, curved, in 2 pairs, sometimes exserted. Ovary superior, 2-celled, with 2 ovules per cell; style 1, forked, slender. Pollination is mainly by bees. The fruits are 4 nutlets, hidden by the calyx.

Key Recognition Features The aromatic leaves and short spikes of flowers with rounded petals and spurs on the anthers, in early summer.

Evolution and Relationships *Phlomis* is associated with *Lamium*, the deadnettles, and other herbaceous ornamental genera such as *Leonotis* and *Molucella* (see Volume 2).

Ecology and Geography In dry, open scrub and rocky places in the mountains. Most common in the Mediterranean area, with 34 species in Turkey; other species eastwards to China.

Comment *Phlomis* are popular plants for warm, dry gardens; they thrive in poor, sandy soil and are likely to become weak and straggly in rich ground.

Phlomis grandiflora flower,
flower with upper lip removed,
and calyx, just over life size
July 6th

Phlomis fruticosa
seeds, 1¹/₂ × life size
November 29th

Phlomis fruticosa
¹/₂ life size
June 3rd

Phlomis italica
¹/₂ life size, June 22nd

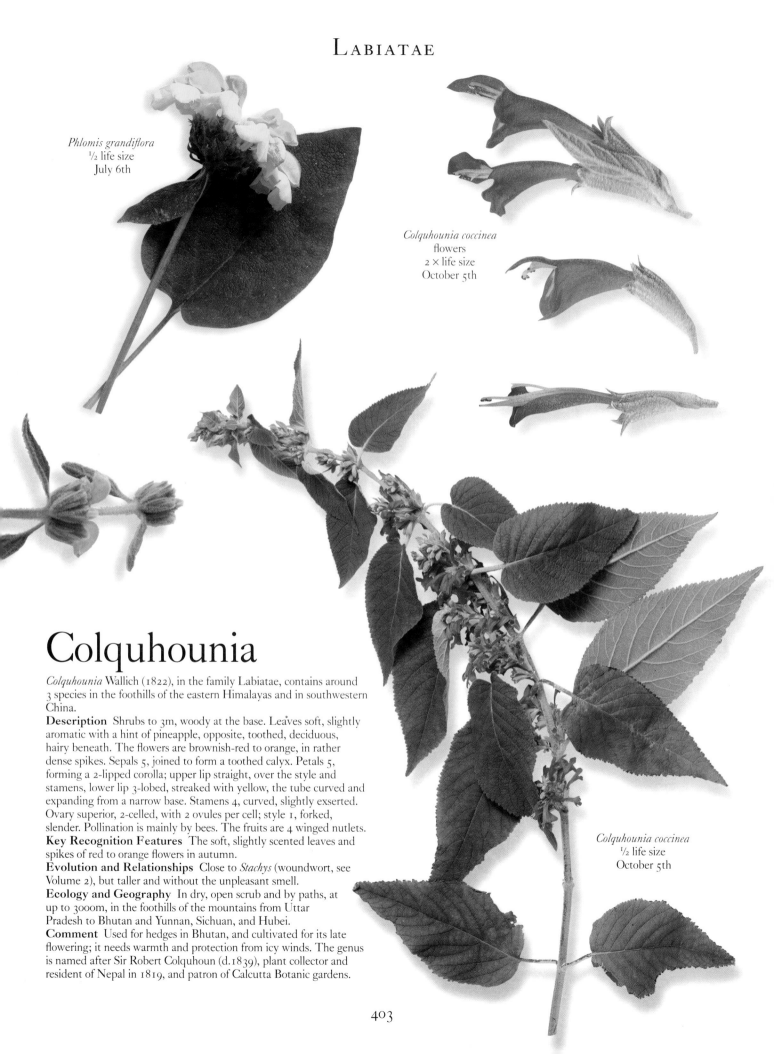

Phlomis grandiflora
¹/₂ life size
July 6th

Colquhounia coccinea
flowers
2 × life size
October 5th

Colquhounia

Colquhounia Wallich (1822), in the family Labiatae, contains around 3 species in the foothills of the eastern Himalayas and in southwestern China.

Description Shrubs to 3m, woody at the base. Leaves soft, slightly aromatic with a hint of pineapple, opposite, toothed, deciduous, hairy beneath. The flowers are brownish-red to orange, in rather dense spikes. Sepals 5, joined to form a toothed calyx. Petals 5, forming a 2-lipped corolla; upper lip straight, over the style and stamens, lower lip 3-lobed, streaked with yellow, the tube curved and expanding from a narrow base. Stamens 4, curved, slightly exserted. Ovary superior, 2-celled, with 2 ovules per cell; style 1, forked, slender. Pollination is mainly by bees. The fruits are 4 winged nutlets.

Key Recognition Features The soft, slightly scented leaves and spikes of red to orange flowers in autumn.

Evolution and Relationships Close to *Stachys* (woundwort, see Volume 2), but taller and without the unpleasant smell.

Ecology and Geography In dry, open scrub and by paths, at up to 3000m, in the foothills of the mountains from Uttar Pradesh to Bhutan and Yunnan, Sichuan, and Hubei.

Comment Used for hedges in Bhutan, and cultivated for its late flowering; it needs warmth and protection from icy winds. The genus is named after Sir Robert Colquhoun (d.1839), plant collector and resident of Nepal in 1819, and patron of Calcutta Botanic gardens.

Colquhounia coccinea
¹/₂ life size
October 5th

Prostanthera

Prostanthera Labill. (1804), the mintbushes, in the family Labiatae, contains around 70 species in Australia.

Description Small trees to 8m or shrubs. Leaves aromatic, often mint- or eucalyptus-scented, opposite, usually toothed, evergreen, often greyish or sticky. The flowers are blue, greenish, white, or red, in short spikes or paired in the axils of the upper leaves. Sepals 5, joined to form a 2-lipped calyx, the lips sometimes toothed. Petals 5, often rounded, forked, or reflexed, about equalling or longer than the tube. Stamens 4, with 1 or 2 spurs, sometimes exserted from the flower, in 2 pairs. Ovary superior, 2-celled, with 2 ovules per cell; style 1, forked, slender. Pollination is by insects. The fruits are 4 nutlets, hidden by the calyx.

Key Recognition Features The aromatic leaves and the short spikes of flowers in spring and summer, with rounded petals and spurs on the anthers.

Evolution and Relationships *Prostanthera* is closely related to *Westringia* Sm., a rosemary-like shrub with 25 species in Australia, but generally duller flowers with narrow lobes.

Ecology and Geography In dry, open scrub and open forest and by streams in Australia and Tasmania.

Comment Mintbushes are very attractive shrubs for frost-free gardens; the only species which regularly survives frost is *P. cuneata* Benth. from southeastern Australia and Tasmania. It has rounded, dark-green leaves and white flowers. The taller *P. incisa* R. Br and *P. rotundifolia* R. Br will tolerate a few degrees of frost, especially against a wall.

Prostanthera cuneata
½ life size
May 15th

Prostanthera cuneata
1⅓ × life size, May 15th

Prostanthera incisa
¾ life size, April 20th

Prostanthera nivea
¾ life size, April 20th

Rosmarinus

Rosmarinus L. (1753), the rosemary, in the family Labiatae, contains 2 species in the Mediterranean region.

Description Shrubs to 2m, sometimes creeping. Leaves aromatic, opposite, narrow, evergreen, with the edges rolled under, white beneath. The flowers are blue to white or rarely pink, in small spikes towards the ends of the branches. Sepals 5, joined to form a 3-toothed calyx. Petals 5, joined at the base, forming a tube, with upper lip forked, the lower lip with a rounded central lobe and 2 narrow lobes on each side. Stamens 2, exserted from the flower, curving downwards. Ovary superior, with 4 ovules; style 1, forked, slender. Pollination is mainly by bees. The fruits are 4 brown nutlets.

Key Recognition Features The narrow, crowded leaves with the characteristic scent and masses of blue to white flowers in early spring.

Evolution and Relationships *Rosmarinus* is closely related to other herbs such as *Salvia* (see pp.408–409) *Mentha* (mint), and *Origanum* (see Volume 2).

Ecology and Geography In dry, open scrub, usually not far from the sea, throughout the Mediterranean area.

Comment Rosemary is commonly used as a herb in cooking, especially with lamb, potatoes, or fish. The aromatic oils from the leaves are a constituent of eau de Cologne. The nectar is valuable for early foraging bees. The plants will survive only a few days below freezing; upright, white varieties seem to be the hardiest.

Rosmarinus officinalis 'Miss Jessopp's Upright'
flowers and leaf, 1¾ × life size, March 29th

Rosmarinus officinalis
'Benenden Blue'
flowers and leaf
1¾ × life size, March 29th

Rosmarinus
officinalis
'Benenden Blue'
½ life size
March 29th

Rosmarinus officinalis
'Majorca Pink'
⅔ life size, March 29th

Rosmarinus officinalis
Prostratus Group
½ life size, March 29th

Rosmarinus officinalis
'Miss Jessopp's Upright'
½ life size, March 29th

Perovskia

Perovskia Karelin (1841), in the family Labiatae, contains around 7 species in Central Asia.

Description Subshrubs to 1.5m, woody only at the base, stems silvery. Leaves powerfully aromatic, with a hint of disinfectant, opposite, usually deeply and jaggedly toothed and pinnate, deciduous. The flowers are blue, furry, in loose whorls on branching and leafless spikes. Sepals 5, joined to form a toothed calyx, covered with golden glands. Petals 5, forming a 2-lipped corolla, the upper lip furry outside, sometimes 3-toothed, the lower lip 2-toothed. Stamens 4, with 2 fertile and 2 small sterile ones hidden in the upper lip. Ovary superior, 2-celled, with 2 ovules per cell; style 1, forked, slender. Pollination is mainly by bees. The fruits are 4 nutlets.

Key Recognition Features The soft and very pungent, often dissected leaves, and the tall, slender spikes of furry, blue flowers in late summer.

Evolution and Relationships *Perovskia* is allied to *Salvia* (see pp.408–409) and *Nepeta* (see Volume 2), and adapted to climates with a wet spring and dry summer.

Ecology and Geography On dry steppe from Central Asia to Afghanistan and Pakistan.

Comment A few species and hybrids are grown for ornament; they are especially valuable for their late flowering and for tolerating dry summers. The genus is named after V.A. Perovski (1794–1857), a Russian provincial governor in Turkestan in the 19th century.

Perovskia atriplicifolia
flower parts
1 ½ × life size
September 22nd

Lavandula multifida
subsp. *canariensis*
²⁄₃ life size
September 20th

Perovskia atriplicifolia
½ life size
September 22nd

Lavandula

Lavandula L. (1753), the lavender, in the family Labiatae, contains around 30 species in the Mediterranean area.

Description Shrubs to 1.5m. Leaves aromatic, opposite, narrow, simple or deeply toothed or pinnate, and evergreen. The flowers are blue, rarely white or pink, in leafless, compact or interrupted spikes, sometimes with a tuft of petal-like bracts at the top. Sepals 5, joined to form a coloured calyx, the upper teeth often with auricles. Petals 5, forming a 2-lipped corolla, the upper lip 2-lobed and slightly larger than the 3-lobed lower lip. Stamens 4, hidden in the tube. Ovary superior, 2-celled, with 2 ovules per cell; style 1, forked, slender. Pollination is mainly by bees. The fruits are 4 nutlets.

Key Recognition Features The aromatic leaves and compact spikes of flowers with equal lobes.

Evolution and Relationships *Lavandula* is allied to *Thymus* L., *Salvia* (see pp.408–409), and other similar herbs. Two main groups are grown: those with a tuft of coloured bracts at the apex of the inflorescence, such as *L. stoechas* L., which tend to flower in spring; those without a tuft, such as *L. angustifolia* Mill., which tend to flower from mid-summer onwards.

Ecology and Geography On dry hills in the Mediterranean region, the Canary Islands, and from North Africa to Somalia and India.

Comment Many species and hybrids are grown for ornament and for perfume; the name lavender comes from the Latin *lavare*, to wash. Most species survive some frost, but the species from the Canary Islands are very tender.

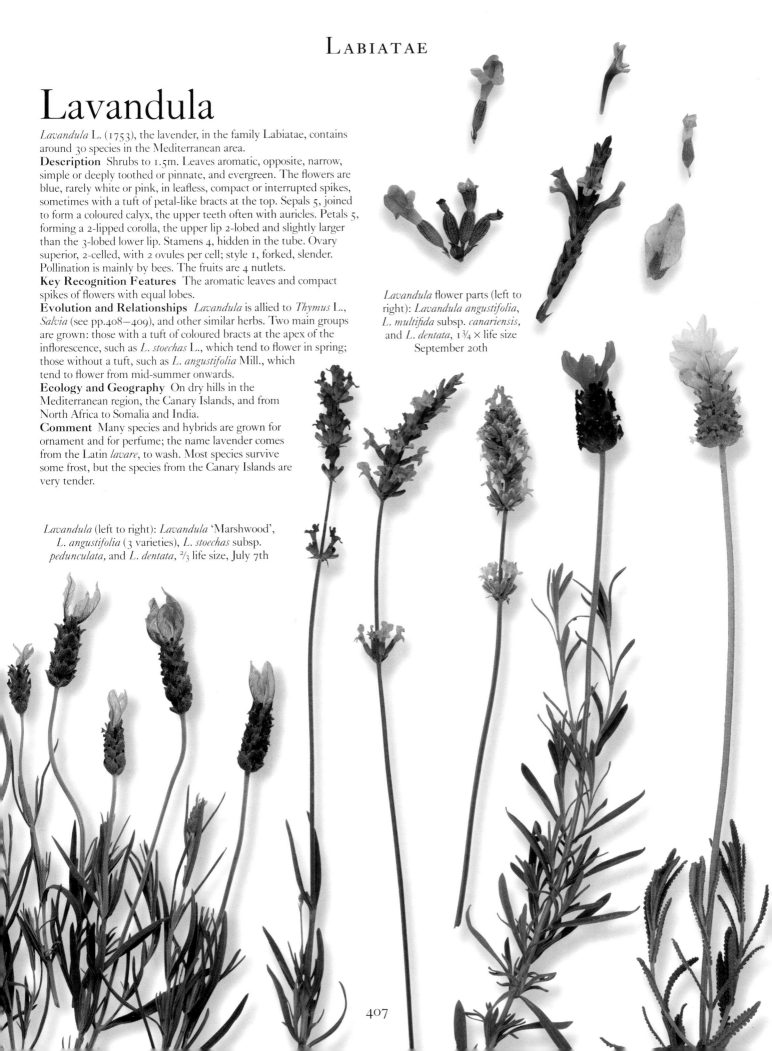

Lavandula flower parts (left to right): *Lavandula angustifolia*, *L. multifida* subsp. *canariensis*, and *L. dentata*, 1¾ × life size September 20th

Lavandula (left to right): *Lavandula* 'Marshwood', *L. angustifolia* (3 varieties), *L. stoechas* subsp. *pedunculata*, and *L. dentata*, ⅔ life size, July 7th

407

Salvia

Salvia L. (1753), in the family Labiatae, contains over 900 species worldwide.

Description Subshrubs to 3m, woody at the base, herbaceous perennials, or annuals. Leaves aromatic, with various scents, opposite, evergreen or deciduous. The flowers are blue, white, red, yellow, purple, or pink, in whorls on simple or compound spikes. Sepals 5, joined to form a 4- or 5-toothed calyx. Petals 5, forming a 2-lipped corolla, the upper lip often furry outside, sometimes forked, the lower lip 3-lobed, the large, lowest lobe sometimes divided. Stamens 2, often forked, with a long connective between the fertile cell of the stamen and the sterile cell, which forms a conspicuous staminode. Ovary superior, 2-celled, with 2 ovules per cell; style 1, usually unequally forked. Pollination is mainly by bees, or by hummingbirds in the red-flowered species. The fruits are 4 nutlets.

Key Recognition Features The flowers with forked stamens and an unequally forked style.

Evolution and Relationships Most of the shrubby species are from Central and South America, where the genus is very diverse and spectacular, with numerous red- or blue-flowered, hummingbird-pollinated species. The staminodes are positioned in the mouth of the tube, and when depressed they pitch the pollen onto the head of the hummingbird or the back of the bee.

Ecology and Geography In meadows, open scrub, and forest margins throughout the world, but with interesting concentrations of species in Turkey, where there are 86 species, and in Mexico.

Comment Many species and hybrids are grown for ornament; they are especially valuable for their late flowering. *Salvia officinalis* L. is commonly used for cooking. The Mexican *S. splendens* Sellow, with bright red flowers, was formerly planted by the million in public places throughout the Soviet Union. *Salvia sclarea* L. is used medicinally and in scent; it has colourful bracts longer than the flowers.

Salvia atrocyanea
flowers, 1 ¹⁄₂ × life size
October 5th

Salvia atrocyanea
fruits, 1 ¹⁄₂ × life size
October 5th

Salvia buchananii
²⁄₃ life size
September 2nd

Salvia atrocyanea
¹⁄₂ life size, October 5th

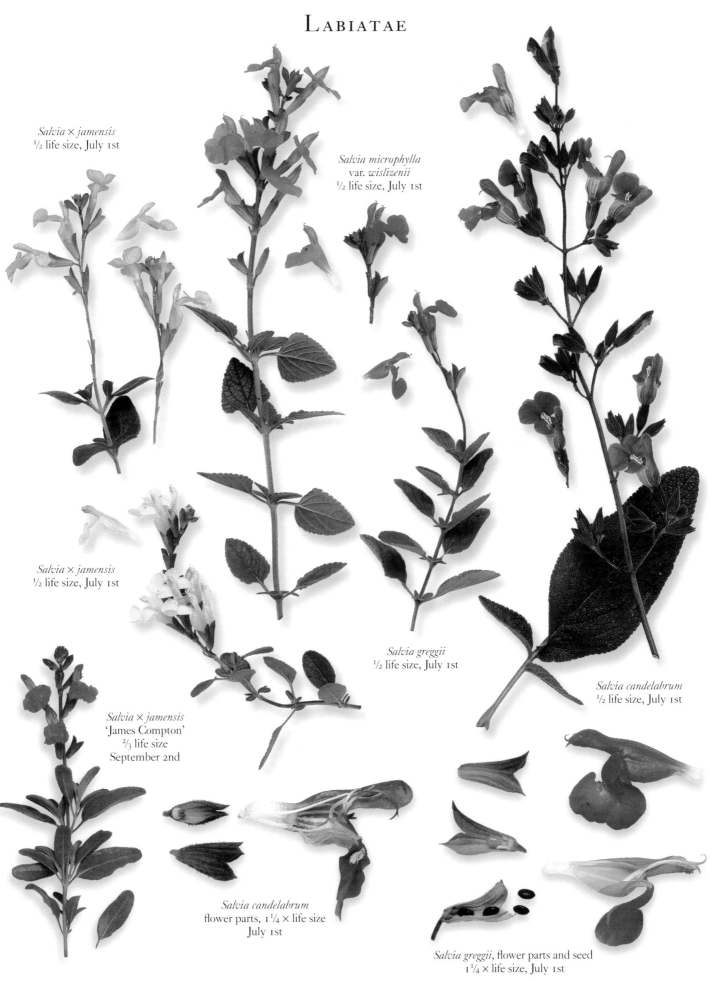

Salvia × jamensis
½ life size, July 1st

Salvia microphylla
var. *wislizenii*
½ life size, July 1st

Salvia × jamensis
½ life size, July 1st

Salvia greggii
½ life size, July 1st

Salvia candelabrum
½ life size, July 1st

Salvia × jamensis
'James Compton'
⅔ life size
September 2nd

Salvia candelabrum
flower parts, 1¼ × life size
July 1st

Salvia greggii, flower parts and seed
1¼ × life size, July 1st

Olea europea, stone and fruit,
1½ × life size, July 20th

Olea

Olea L. (1753), in the family Oleaceae, contains around 20 species in southern Europe, Africa, and Asia.

Description Trees to 15m, or shrubs, sometimes spiny. The leaves are opposite, evergreen, elliptic, rarely toothed, often with silvery scales. The flowers are small and white or greenish, unisexual or bisexual, in clusters. Sepals 4, joined at the base. Petals 4, joined at the base into a short tube. Stamens 2, inserted in the tube. Ovary superior. Pollination is by insects. The fruits are greenish-purple, fleshy berries with 1 large seed.

Key Recognition Features The greyish, narrow, opposite, evergreen leaves and the small, green flowers followed by blue or yellow fruit.

Evolution and Relationships The affinities of Oleaceae are traditionally with Buddlejaceae (see pp.422–23), Scrophulariaceae (see pp.424–428), and Plantaginaceae: recent DNA studies support this. *Olea* itself is close to *Chionanthus* and *Osmanthus* (see p.412) both of which also have fleshy fruit.

Ecology and Geography On dry hillsides and in forest; from the Mediterranean region to South Africa and across Asia to Australia and New Zealand.

Comment The olive, *O. europea* L. is one of the most valuable of all trees for its oil and edible fruit. Seed-raised plants are usually inedible, but several cultivars are grown. Cultivated olives probably originated in Arabia or India, and there is evidence of olive cultivation dating from around 3600 BC in the eastern Mediterranean.

Olea europea
½ life size, June 22nd

Olea europea, leaves and flowers
just over life size, July 20th

Chionanthus virginicus
flowers, 1²/₃ × life size
May 24th

Chionanthus retusus
½ life size, June 3rd

Chionanthus virginicus
½ life size, May 24th

Chionanthus

Chionanthus L. (1753), in the family Oleaceae, contains around 100 species mainly in the tropics (formerly placed in the genus *Linociera* Sw. ex Schreber), but with 1 temperate species in America and 1 in eastern Asia.

Description Trees to 10m, or shrubs. The leaves are opposite, deciduous, narrowly ovate or obovate with a blunt apex. The flowers are small and white, unisexual or bisexual, in clusters. Sepals 4, joined at the base. Petals 4, joined at the base into a short tube, long and narrow. Stamens 2, inserted in the tube. Ovary superior. Pollination is by insects. The fruits are purple or dark blue, ovoid, fleshy berries with 1 large seed.

Key Recognition Features The long, narrow, white petals and the simple, opposite leaves, followed by bluish or purplish fruits.

Evolution and Relationships *Chionanthus* is closest to *Osmanthus* (see p.412); both have fleshy fruit, but *Osmanthus* is evergreen.

Ecology and Geography In woods and forest. *Chionanthus virginicus* L., the fringe tree, is found from Pennsylvania southwards to Florida; *C. retusus* Lindl. is found in China from Yunnan and western Sichuan eastwards and in Korea on Quelpart Island.

Comment Both these temperate species are attractive ornamentals. *Chionanthus virginicus* needs hot summers and cold winters to flower well, and is then a most attractive large shrub or small tree.

Osmanthus

Osmanthus Lour. (1790), in the family Oleaceae, contains around 15 species in Asia and southern North America.

Description Trees to 14m, or shrubs. The leaves are opposite, evergreen, sometimes spiny and holly-like, sometimes toothed or simple. The flowers are small, white to yellow and orange, strongly scented, bisexual or unisexual, in clusters in the leaf axils. Sepals 4, joined at the base. Petals 4, rounded, joined at the base into a long or short tube. Stamens 2, inserted in the tube. Ovary superior, 2-celled, with 2 ovules per cell. Pollination is by insects. The fruits are purple or dark blue, fleshy berries with 1 large seed.

Key Recognition Features The opposite, evergreen leaves, often variably spiny, and the scented, usually white flowers followed by bluish or purplish fruits.

Evolution and Relationships *Osmanthus* is close to *Phillyrea*, but that has small, greenish flowers and round fruit. Also close to *Picconia* DC, from the Canary Islands and the Azores, but that has conspicuous bracts.

Ecology and Geography In forest and scrub, with many species in China and eastern Asia; 1 species, *O. decorus* (Boiss. & Bal.) Kasapigil from the southern coast of the Black Sea; and 1 species, *O. americanus* (L.) Gray, in southeastern North America from Virginia to Mexico.

Comment These are attractive evergreens, valuable for their scented flowers, often opening in autumn, winter, or spring. *Osmanthus heterophyllus* (G. Don) Green has leaves very like those of a holly, sometimes spiny, sometimes smooth, with white flowers in autumn. *Osmanthus* × *burkwoodii* is an attractive shrub with dull green leaves and white, scented flowers in spring, a hybrid between *O. decorus* and the Chinese *O. delavayi* Franch. *Osmanthus fragrans* Lour. is widely grown in China, Japan, and the warmer parts of America for its powerfully scented flowers.

Osmanthus heterophyllus
flowers, 2 × life size
December 8th

Osmanthus delavayi
1 1/3 × life size
April 2nd

Osmanthus delavayi
1/3 life size, April 2nd

Osmanthus heterophyllus
1/2 life size, December 8th

Phillyrea

Phillyrea L. (1753), in the family Oleaceae, contains 2 species in the Mediterranean area.

Description Trees to 10m, or shrubs. The leaves are opposite, evergreen, usually toothed. The flowers are small and greenish-white, not well scented, bisexual, in clusters in the leaf axils. Sepals 4, joined at the base. Petals 4, joined at the base into a short tube. Stamens 2, exserted from the tube. Ovary superior, 2-celled, with 2 ovules per cell. Pollination is by various insects. The fruits are purple or dark blue, fleshy berries with 1 large seed.

Key Recognition Features The opposite, evergreen leaves and small, 4-petalled, greenish-white flowers followed by bluish or purplish fruits. Old trees often have an attractive curving and leaning trunk.

Evolution and Relationships *Phillyrea* is close to *Osmanthus* but restricted to the Mediterranean area.

Ecology and Geography In dry forest and scrub in southern Europe from Portugal westwards to North Africa and western Turkey.

Comment *Phillyrea* are slow-growing trees with inconspicuous flowers, often surviving in old gardens; before the arrival of hardy evergreens from Japan and China in the early 19th century, *Phillyrea* were valued as evergreens for sunny gardens; their cultivation was recorded in 1597.

Phillyrea angustifolia
fruits and seed
2 × life size
December 15th

Phillyrea latifolia
just over life size
April 2nd

Osmanthus × burkwoodii
⅓ life size, April 24th

413

Ligustrum

Ligustrum L. (1753), the privet, in the family Oleaceae, contains around 50 species in Europe and from eastern Asia southwards to Australia.

Description Trees to 15m, or shrubs. The leaves are opposite, rather fleshy, evergreen or deciduous, usually not toothed. The flowers are white, heavily but often unpleasantly scented, bisexual, in dense clusters or sprays at the ends of the shoots. Sepals 4, small, joined at the base. Petals 4, joined at the base into a short or long tube. Stamens 2, enclosed in or exserted from the tube. Ovary superior, 2-celled, with 2 ovules in each cell. Pollination by various insects. The fruits are black or dark blue fleshy berries, with 1–4 seeds.

Key Recognition Features Usually shrubs with opposite, evergreen leaves and clusters or sprays of 4-petalled, white flowers followed by blackish fruit.

Evolution and Relationships *Ligustrum* is related to *Syringa*, the lilac, but has fleshy fruit and usually smaller, less sweetly-scented flowers.

Ecology and Geography In scrub and hedgerows, usually on limestone; from northern Europe (1 species), eastwards to China, where the genus is most diverse, and Japan. One species in Queensland.

Comment Privet is sometimes planted as a hedge, and the golden-leaved *L. ovalifolium* Hassk. 'Aureum', as an evergreen shrub. *Ligustrum lucidum* Ait. slowly forms a large evergreen tree with conspicuous white flowers in late summer; it is common as a street tree, but a conspicuous one around 20m tall, which I have seen in the Min valley in Sichuan, is exceptional.

Ligustrum lucidum
fruits, ²⁄₃ life size
April 18th

Ligustrum vulgare
fruits
¾ life size
October 13th

Ligustrum sinense
⅓ life size, June 22nd

Ligustrum lucidum
½ life size, June 23rd

Syringa × chinensis
flower section
1¾ × life size
May 6th

Syringa reflexa
fruit, ⅔ life size
September 9th

Syringa vulgaris
'Katherine Havemeyer'
½ life size, May 15th

Syringa × chinensis
⅓ life size, April 18th

Syringa emodi
⅔ life size
June 3rd

Syringa

Syringa L. (1753), the lilac, in the family Oleaceae, contains around 30 species in Europe and Asia.

Description Small trees to 7m, or shrubs. The leaves are opposite, deciduous, entire or rarely pinnate. The flowers are pink, purple or white, heavily and usually pleasantly scented, bisexual, in dense or elongated clusters at the ends of the shoots. Sepals 4, small, joined at the base. Petals 4, usually spreading, joined at the base into a short or long tube. Stamens 2, enclosed in or exserted from the tube. Ovary superior, 2-celled, with 2 ovules in each cell; style with a 2-lobed stigma. Pollination is by various insects including hawkmoths. The fruits are oblong capsules with 2 winged seeds in each cell.

Key Recognition Features Usually shrubs with opposite deciduous leaves and clusters or sprays of 4-petalled, pinkish or purplish, scented flowers followed by green capsules.

Evolution and Relationships *Syringa* is close to *Ligustrum* in flower and to *Forsythia* (see p.148) in fruit.

Ecology and Geography In scrub and on cliffs, usually on limestone; from southeastern Europe (2 species) eastwards to China, where the genus is most diverse, and in Japan.

Comment The common lilac, *S. vulgaris* L. from southern Europe, has been one of the most popular of all flowering shrubs since it was first cultivated in the 16th century. Chinese species and hybrids from them have extended the flowering period into the summer, and often have long-tubed flowers. *Syringa pekinensis* Rupr. is closer to *Ligustrum*, and has white flowers, but deciduous leaves and capsules.

Fraxinus ornus
⅓ life size, May 11th

Fraxinus excelsior
⅓ life size, April 28th

Fraxinus excelsior
flowers, 1¾ × life size
April 28th

Fraxinus americana
autumn leaves
½ life size
October 12th

Fraxinus

Fraxinus L. (1753), the ash, in the family Oleaceae, contains around 65 species in Europe, North America, and Asia.

Description Trees to 40m, or shrubs. The leaves are opposite, deciduous, pinnate or rarely reduced to a single leaflet. The flowers are green or white, sometimes scented, bisexual or unisexual, in dense or elongated clusters in the upper leaf axils or at the ends of the shoots. Sepals 4, small, joined at the base, or absent. Petals 2–6, usually 4, joined at the base, or in many species, absent. Stamens 2. Ovary superior, 2-celled, with 2 ovules in each cell; style with 2 stigmas. Pollination is by insects and by wind. The fruits are so-called keys, winged nutlets with 1 seed.

Key Recognition Features Trees with opposite, deciduous, pinnate leaves, and sometimes with sprays of feathery, white, scented flowers.

Evolution and Relationships *Fraxinus* is a diverse genus with 2 main sections: the common ashes in which the inconspicuous, wind-pollinated flowers open before the leaves, and the flowering ashes, of which *F. ornus* L. is the most common, in which the white, feathery flowers appear with the leaves.

Ecology and Geography In woods and disturbed ground in North America southwards to Mexico, throughout Europe, and from China southwards to Java. Species in both main groups are found in all 3 areas.

Comment Ash is an important timber tree, both in Europe and in North America, but at the same time it is fast-growing and can become a weed. The strong, white, straight-grained wood is used for furniture, broom handles, and in the past for car bodies; it is also valued for burning. The unripe fruits were sometimes pickled.

416

Fontanesia

Fontanesia Labill. (1791) in the family Oleaceae, contains 2 very similar species in the eastern Mediterranean and China.

Description Shrubs to 5m. The leaves are opposite, deciduous, simple, entire, with a tapering point. The flowers are greenish-white, bisexual, in clusters in the upper leaf axils and at the ends of the shoots. Sepals 4, very small, joined at the base. Petals 4, joined at the base, narrow and small. Stamens 2, longer than the petals. Ovary superior, 2-celled; style with 2-lobed stigma. Pollination is presumed to be by insects. The fruits are nutlets, winged all round.

Key Recognition Features Shrubs with opposite, deciduous, simple leaves and numerous small, 4-petalled flowers in midsummer.

Evolution and Relationships The isolation of 2 such similar species in a genus in this way is unusual, but paralleled in part by *Liquidambar* (see p. 99), which is found in North America, as well as in the eastern Mediterranean and in China. In fruit *Fontanesia* is close to *Fraxinus*.

Ecology and Geography In scrub on dry hills, with *F. phillyreoides* Labill. in southern Turkey, northern Syria, and 1 locality in Sicily, and *F. fortunei* Carr. in China.

Comment The genus is named after Réné-Louiche Desfontaines (1753–1813) a French botanist and director of the Jardin des Plantes, who was working in Paris at the time the shrub was discovered by Labillardiere in Syria, in around 1789. The Chinese use the plant for making graceful hedges.

Fontanesia fortunei
½ life size, June 21st

Fontanesia fortunei
flowers, ¾ life size
June 21st

Fraxinus excelsior
fruits, life size
September 18th

Forsythia

Forsythia Vahl. (1805) in the family Oleaceae, contains around 7 species in southern Europe, and eastern Asia.

Description Shrubs to 3m. The leaves are opposite, deciduous, simple, usually toothed, and occasionally with 3 leaflets. The flowers are yellow, bisexual, long- or short-styled, in clusters of 1–6 in the axils of the previous year's leaves. Sepals 4, joined at the base. Petals 4, joined at the base, sometimes reflexed. Stamens 2, usually in the mouth of the tube. Ovary superior, 2-celled; style short or long, with 2-lobed stigma. Pollination is by insects. The fruits are 2-celled capsules with many winged seeds.

Key Recognition Features Shrubs with opposite, deciduous, toothed leaves, usually squarish twigs, and numerous yellow, 4-petalled flowers in spring before the leaves.

Evolution and Relationships Related to *Abeliophyllum* and *Jasminum* (see pp.420–21), rather than other members of the family.

Ecology and Geography In scrub on dry hills, with 1 species in southern Europe, the rest in China, Korea, and Japan.

Comment The genus is named after William Forsyth (1737–1804) of Oldmeldrum, a Scottish horticulturist who was gardener at Syon in 1763, later at the Chelsea Physic Garden and St James' and Kensington Palaces, and a founder of what became the Royal Horticultural Society. Many species and hybrids are spectacular for their yellow flowers in spring.

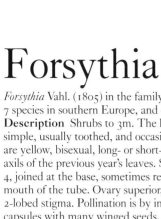

Forsythia 'Spectabilis'
sepals and leaves
¾ life size
April 29th

Forsythia 'Spectabilis'
1¼ × life size
March 28th

Forsythia 'Spectabilis'
½ life size
March 28th

Forsythia 'Beatrix Farrand'
fruits and seeds, just over life size,
December 15th

Forsythia 'Spectabilis'
buds, life size
November 24th

418

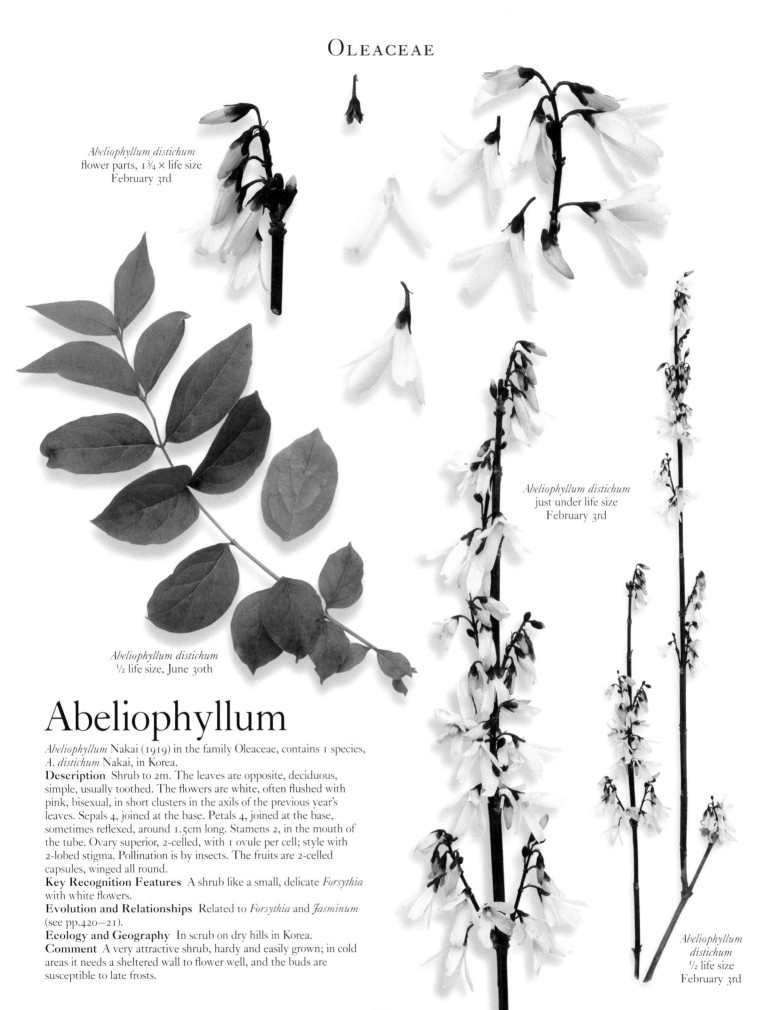

Abeliophyllum distichum
flower parts, 1¾ × life size
February 3rd

Abeliophyllum distichum
just under life size
February 3rd

Abeliophyllum distichum
½ life size, June 30th

Abeliophyllum
distichum
½ life size
February 3rd

Abeliophyllum

Abeliophyllum Nakai (1919) in the family Oleaceae, contains 1 species, *A. distichum* Nakai, in Korea.

Description Shrub to 2m. The leaves are opposite, deciduous, simple, usually toothed. The flowers are white, often flushed with pink, bisexual, in short clusters in the axils of the previous year's leaves. Sepals 4, joined at the base. Petals 4, joined at the base, sometimes reflexed, around 1.5cm long. Stamens 2, in the mouth of the tube. Ovary superior, 2-celled, with 1 ovule per cell; style with 2-lobed stigma. Pollination is by insects. The fruits are 2-celled capsules, winged all round.

Key Recognition Features A shrub like a small, delicate *Forsythia* with white flowers.

Evolution and Relationships Related to *Forsythia* and *Jasminum* (see pp.420–21).

Ecology and Geography In scrub on dry hills in Korea.

Comment A very attractive shrub, hardy and easily grown; in cold areas it needs a sheltered wall to flower well, and the buds are susceptible to late frosts.

Jasminum

Jasminum L. (1753), the jasmine, in the family Oleaceae, contains around 200 species, mainly tropical, in Europe, Africa, Asia, and Australia, with 1 species in North America.

Description Shrubs or climbers to 10m or more, with green twigs. The leaves are opposite or alternate, evergreen or deciduous, sometimes 3-foliate or pinnate. The flowers are white to yellow or pinkish-red, often sweetly scented, bisexual, borne singly or in clusters in the leaf axils, or in sprays at the ends of the branches. Sepals 4–9, joined at the base. Petals 4–9, twisted in the bud, rounded, joined at the base into a tube. Stamens 2, inserted in the tube. Ovary superior, 2-celled, with 1–4 ovules per cell. Pollination is by insects. The fruits are blackish-purple, fleshy, 2-lobed berries, with 1 or 2 large seeds in each lobe.

Key Recognition Features The long-tubed flowers, twisted in bud, followed by blackish fruit.

Evolution and Relationships *Jasminum* is rather isolated within the family; in general the twining species have scented, white flowers, the shrubby species have unscented, yellow flowers. *Jasminum* is superficially very similar to *Trachelospermum* in the Apocynaceae (see p. 385), but that has 5 stamens and totally different fruit.

Ecology and Geography In scrub, with around 50 species found in the Himalayas and China, and 1 species, *J. fruticans* L., found in southern Europe.

Comment Jasmines have long been cultivated for their scent, particularly in the Arabian Peninsula and India. *Jasminum officinale* L., the common white jasmine, is the most often seen; *J. grandiflorum* L. is sold in summer as a pot of flowering cuttings, and *J. polyanthum* Franch. as a twining plant for winter flowering; both survive outside in Mediterranean climates. The yellow-flowered winter jasmine, *J. nudiflorum* Lindl. from northern China, is often planted around cottage doors, and can be clipped into an archway. *Jasminum sambac* (L.) Ait. from India is a tropical shrub with particularly well-scented flowers, used dried to perfume tea.

Jasminum humile
young fruit, 1¾ × life size
September 24th

Jasminum polyanthum
½ life size, June 2nd

Jasminum polyanthum
flower parts, 1½ × life size
June 2nd

Jasminum primulinum
½ life size, March 17th

Jasminum beesianum
(below), ⅔ life size
May 20th

Jasminum primulinum
just over life size
March 17th

Jasminum officinale f. *affine*
⅔ life size, June 22nd

Jasminum officinale f. *affine*
⅓ life size, June 22nd

Buddleja

Buddleja L. (1753), in the family Buddlejaceae, contains around 100 species in Africa, Asia, and South America.

Description Trees, shrubs, or herbaceous perennials. The leaves are opposite or rarely alternate, deciduous or evergreen, usually covered with dense, starry hairs or scales, especially beneath. The flowers are small and purple, white, yellow, or orange, often sweetly scented, bisexual, in dense, rounded or spike-like heads. Sepals 4, joined at the base. Petals 4, rounded, joined at the base into a long or short tube. Stamens 4, inserted in the tube. Ovary superior; style with 2-lobed stigma. Pollination is by insects, especially butterflies. The fruits are 2-celled, often elongated capsules with numerous very small, wind-dispersed seeds or rarely juicy berries.

Key Recognition Features The opposite leaves and dense heads of small, honey-scented flowers with 4 petals.

Evolution and Relationships The family Buddlejaceae was sometimes included in the Loganiaceae, a mainly tropical family with around 57 genera. Buddlejaceae in the narrow sense has 8 genera, which are also mainly tropical; DNA studies indicate that it is close to Scrophulariaceae (see pp.426–28), and not to other members of the Loganiaceae.

Ecology and Geography On rocky hills and cliffs and in river shingle; concentrations of species are found in Central and South America and in western China.

Comment The genus is named after the Rev. Adam Buddle, (c.1660–1715), an early collector of grasses and mosses. Most species are especially popular with butterflies. *Buddleja davidii* Franch. from western China is commonly naturalised on waste ground in Europe, and quickly colonised bomb sites in London after the World War II; its natural habitat is on cliffs and river shingle in dry mountain valleys; its flowering in July and August in the British Isles coincides with the arrival of migratory red admirals and other butterflies from southern Europe, and the hatching of the first brood of small tortoiseshells and peacocks. Many of the Chinese species, such as *B. asiatica* Lour., flower in midwinter; *B. madagascariensis* Lam. has orange flowers and purple berries and is naturalised in Bermuda.

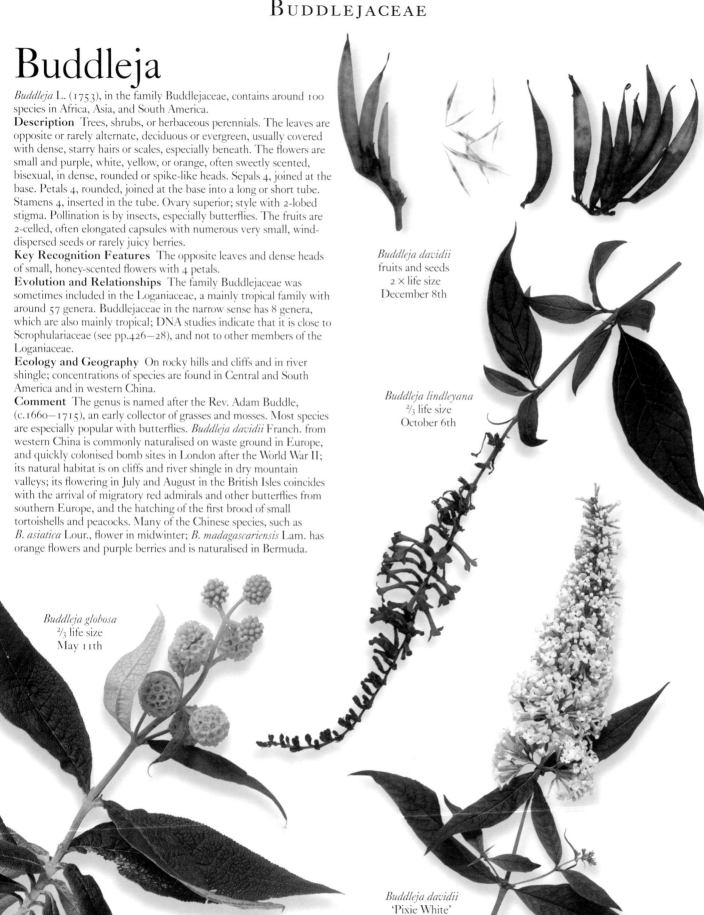

Buddleja davidii
fruits and seeds
2 × life size
December 8th

Buddleja lindleyana
²⁄₃ life size
October 6th

Buddleja globosa
²⁄₃ life size
May 11th

Buddleja davidii
'Pixie White'
½ life size
August 4th

BUDDLEJACEAE

Buddleja colvilei
flower parts, 2 × life size
October 5th

Buddleja alternifolia
½ life size
June 3rd

Buddleja colvilei
⅔ life size, October 5th

Buddleja officinalis
½ life size, April 1st

Buddleja salviifolia
½ life size
April 1st

Hebe 'Rosie' (pink) and
Hebe seedling (mauve)
flower parts, 1²⁄₃× life size
July 1st

Hebe seedling
½ life size
July 1st

Hebe 'Red Edge'
½ life size
July 1st

Hebe

Hebe Comm. ex Juss. (1789), in the family Scrophulariacaceae, contains around 30 species in New Zealand, Australia, New Guinea, and South America.

Description Small trees or shrubs, often dwarf and *Cupressus*-like (see p.26). The leaves are opposite, usually in 2 ranks, evergreen and leathery. The flowers are small, purple to white, bisexual, in short, dense, spike-like heads in the upper leaf axils. Sepals 4, equal, joined at the base. Petals 4, often bluntly pointed, joined at the base into a short tube. Stamens 2, inserted near the base of the tube. Ovary superior; style long, with an unlobed stigma. Pollination is by insects. The fruits are 2-celled capsules with numerous small seeds.

Key Recognition Features The opposite pairs of leathery, usually overlapping leaves and dense heads of small flowers with 4 petals.

Evolution and Relationships DNA studies indicate that the family Scrophulariacaceae should be split; if it is, the smaller part, which contains *Scrophularia* L., *Verbascum* L., and some other South African genera, retains the name Scrophulariacaceae. The larger part, which is called *Plantaginaceae*, contains most of the other familiar genera, such as *Mimulus* L., *Penstemon* Mitch., *Digitalis* L. and *Antirrhinum* L., and includes *Plantago* L. the plantains. *Hebe* is close to *Veronica* L., but that has distinctly 2-lobed capsules with fewer, often large seeds. (For herbaceous Scrophulariacaceae see Volume 2.)

Ecology and Geography On rocky hills, in woods and by streams, mainly in New Zealand, where there are around 70 species and numerous hybrids. Two of the New Zealand species are also found in South America.

Comment Many species and hybrids are grown as ornamentals in maritime climates, and some are used for low hedges on the Atlantic coast of Europe.

Hebe cupressoides
²⁄₃ life size
June 23rd

Hebe 'Rosie'
½ life size
July 1st

Hebe fruit
life size
September 4th

Parahebe

Parahebe W.R.B. Oliver (1944), in the family Scrophulariacaceae, contains around 30 species in New Zealand, Australia, and New Guinea.

Description Subshrubs, often with creeping and rooting stems. The leaves are opposite, evergreen, and sometimes leathery. The flowers are bluish to white, bisexual, in loose spikes in the upper leaf axils. Sepals 4, equal, joined at the base. Petals 4, rounded, joined at the base into a short tube. Stamens 2, inserted near the base of the tube. Ovary superior; style long, with an unlobed stigma. Pollination is by insects. The fruits are 2-celled capsules containing few, rather large seeds.

Key Recognition Features The opposite pairs of evergreen or leathery leaves and the loose spikes of small flowers with rounded petals.

Evolution and Relationships *Parahebe* is close to *Hebe*, but differs in having the stems sprawling and rooting, and in the septum being across the narrowest part of the 2-lobed capsule. In general appearence it is closer to *Veronica* (see Volume 2) in flower.

Ecology and Geography On rocks and by streams, with around 11 species in New Zealand, 1 species, *P. perfoliata* (R. Br.) B.G. Briggs, in Australia, and the remainder in New Guinea.

Comment A few species, including *P. perfoliata*, are grown as ornamentals.

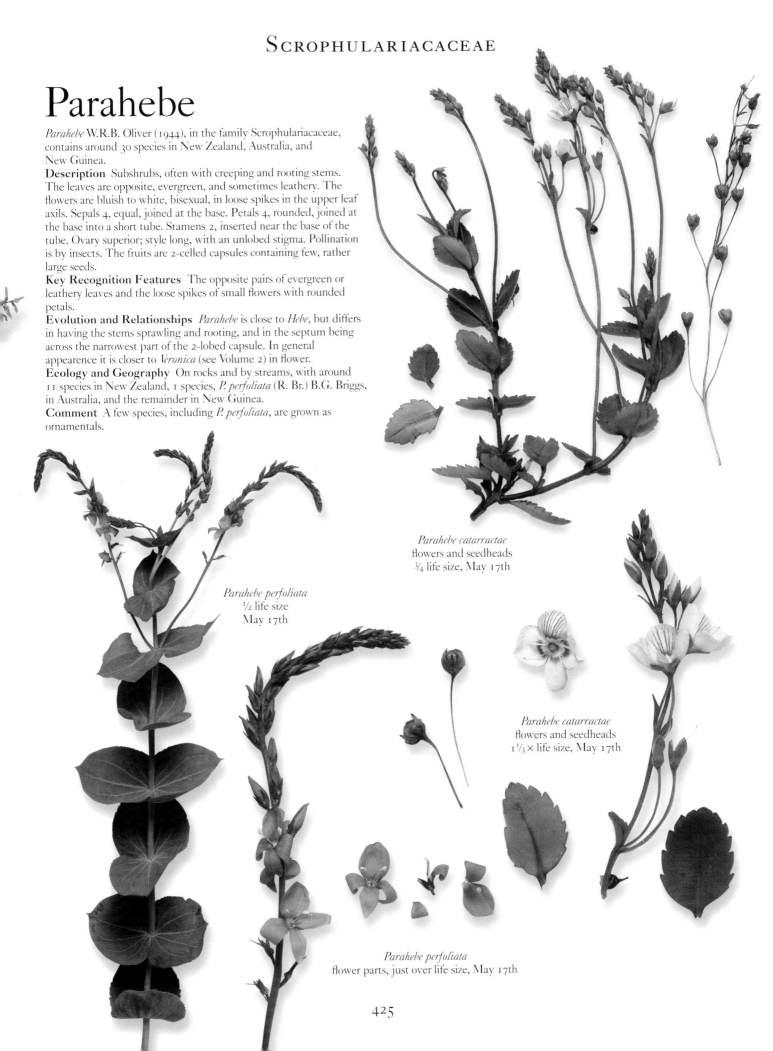

Parahebe catarractae
flowers and seedheads
¾ life size, May 17th

Parahebe perfoliata
½ life size
May 17th

Parahebe catarractae
flowers and seedheads
1⅓ × life size, May 17th

Parahebe perfoliata
flower parts, just over life size, May 17th

Phygelius

Phygelius E. Mey. ex Benth. (1836), the Cape figwort or Cape fuchsia, in the family Scrophulariaceae, contains 2 species in South Africa.

Description Subshrubs to 2m, often suckering. The leaves are opposite, evergreen or deciduous, and stalked, with a triangular blade. The flowers are red, orange, purplish, or pale yellow, bisexual, in loose, branching sprays at the tops of the stems. Sepals 5, equal, joined at the base. Petals 5, unequal, joined into a long, curved tube, often yellow inside; the base of the tube has swollen nectar pouches. Stamens 4, inserted near the middle of the tube. Ovary superior; style long and curved, with an unlobed stigma. Pollination is by sunbirds. The fruits are 2-celled capsules with numerous small seeds.

Key Recognition Features The opposite pairs of stalked leaves and tubular, curved, hanging flowers.

Evolution and Relationships *Phygelius* is close to *Scrophularia* L. the figwort, which is specialised for wasp pollination. A second shrubby genus of Scrophulariaceae from South Africa is *Freylinia* Colla, which has 4 species; the most common, *F. lanceolata* (L. fil.) G. Don, has willow-like leaves and bears nodding sprays of small, orange flowers.

Ecology and Geography On rocks and in grassland, usually by mountain streams, in South Africa, mainly in the Drakensberg in Natal.

Comment Both species and several hybrids between them are commonly cultivated. Plants are often attacked by the figwort weevil, *Cionus scrophulariae*, which can ruin the early flowers of *Phygelius*. The adult beetles are small and greyish with a dark spot, like a minute bird-dropping; the larvae, which eat the young buds, are black and slimy; the cocoons resemble a figwort seed capsule.

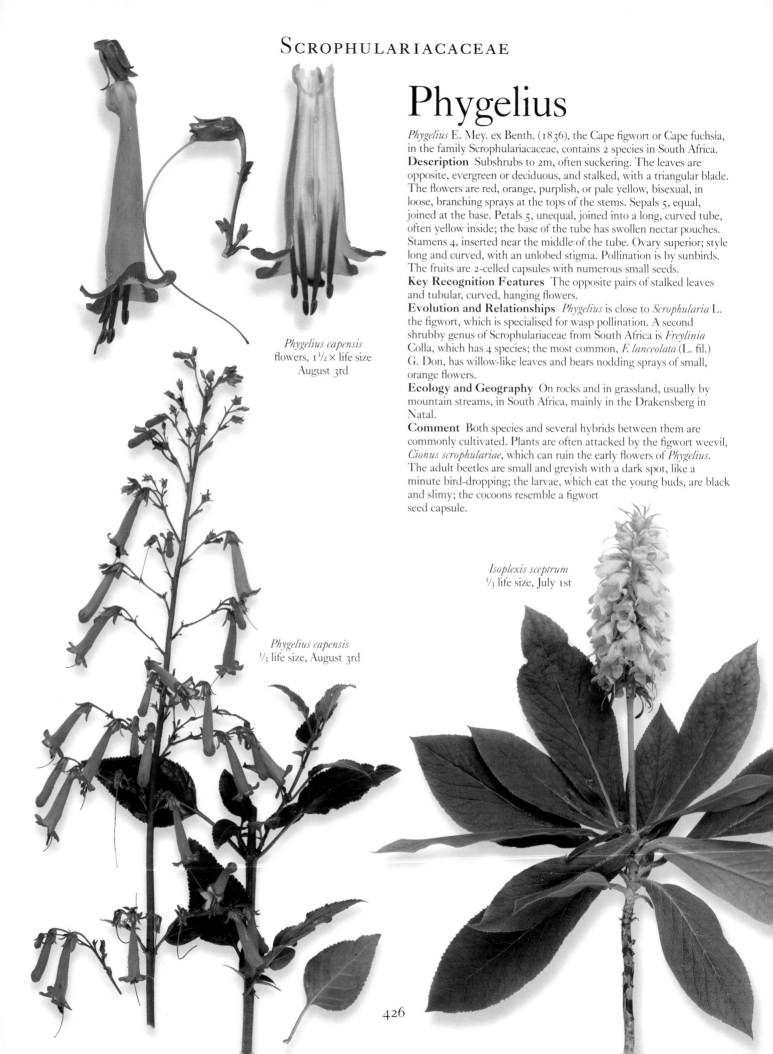

Phygelius capensis
flowers, 1½ × life size
August 3rd

Phygelius capensis
⅓ life size, August 3rd

Isoplexis sceptrum
⅓ life size, July 1st

426

Isoplexis

Isoplexis (Lindl.) Loud. (1835), in the family Scrophulariacaceae, contains around 4 species in the Canary Islands and Madeira.

Description Shrubs to 2m. The leaves are alternate and crowded on the tops of the branches, evergreen, not stalked. The flowers are reddish-brown or orange, bisexual, in spikes at the tops of the stems. Sepals 5, equal, joined at the base. Petals 5, unequal, joined into a long tube. Stamens 4, inserted near the middle of the tube. Ovary superior; style long and curved, with an unlobed stigma. Pollination is by birds. The fruits are 2-celled capsules with numerous small seeds.

Key Recognition Features The lanceolate leaves and spikes of orange or reddish, foxglove-like flowers.

Evolution and Relationships *Isoplexis* is close to *Digitalis* (foxgloves, see Volume 2), but is specialised for bird pollination. There are no sunbirds on the Canary Islands, but birds that are normally insectivorous have been observed to visit the flowers.

Ecology and Geography In evergreen laurel forests on the larger Canary Islands, and 1 species, *I. sceptrum* Loud., on Madeira.

Comment *Isoplexis sceptrum* is a spectacular shrub when in flower, often grown in frost-free gardens or cool greenhouses.

Mimulus aurantiacus
½ life size, July 20th

Mimulus aurantiacus
⅓ life size,
June 23rd

Isoplexis sceptrum
flower parts, 1½ × life size, July 1st

Mimulus aurantiacus
1¼ × life size
July 20th

Mimulus

Mimulus L. (1753), in the family Scrophulariacaceae, contains around 150 species, mostly herbaceous, but with a few shrubby species in western North America; the shrubby species, sometimes called *Diplacus* Jepson, are described here.

Description Spreading shrubs or subshrubs to 2m. The leaves are opposite, evergreen, lanceolate, not stalked, usually sticky, and dark shining green. The flowers are red, reddish-brown, orange, yellow, or white, bisexual, in the upper leaf axils. Sepals 5, unequal, joined to form a tube. Petals 5, unequal, joined into a long tube, spreading and forming a 2-lipped flower. Stamens 4, inserted near the middle of the tube. Ovary superior; style long and curved, with a 2-lobed stigma. Pollination is possibly by hummingbirds. The fruits are 2-celled capsules with numerous small seeds.

Key Recognition Features The dark green, sticky leaves and orange or reddish, 2-lipped flowers.

Evolution and Relationships *Mimulus* is a large genus in California, ranging from dwarf annuals to these shrubs. Other shrubby genera not illustrated here are *Keckiella* Straw, with small flowers, and related to *Penstemon* (see Volume 2) and *Galvezia* Domb. ex Juss., with snapdragon-like red flowers similar to *Antirrhinum* (see Volume 2).

Ecology and Geography On dry hills and cliffs from western Oregon to northwestern Mexico.

Comment All the species in this group are good garden plants, but will survive only a few degrees of frost.

Paulownia

Paulownia Sieb. & Zucc. (1835), in the family Scrophulariaceae, contains around 17 species, in eastern Asia.

Description Trees to 20m, exceptionally fast-growing when young. The leaves are opposite, deciduous, long-stalked, usually large and velvety. The flowers are bluish-lilac to whitish, in large, pyramidal clusters at the tips of the branches, opening in spring before the leaves from brown, velvety buds formed in autumn. Sepals 5, joined at the base. Petals 5, joined for most of their length into a tube, 2-lipped at the mouth, usually yellowish inside. Stamens 4, with distinct, 2-celled anthers. Ovary superior, with 2 cells and numerous ovules per cell; style 1. Pollination is by insects. The fruits are 2-valved capsules with very numerous small, winged seeds.

Key Recognition Features The large, soft, opposite leaves and large clusters of bluish, tubular flowers.

Evolution and Relationships *Paulownia* is exceptional in the family Scrophulariaceae in being a tree; in habit it has many affinities with *Catalpa* in the family Bignoniaceae (see pp.429–31). It is perhaps best placed in a family of its own; on the basis of DNA evidence, this appears to be most closely related to the parasitic families in the Orobanchaceae.

Ecology and Geography In warm temperate forest from western China to Korea. Naturalised and appearing wild in eastern North America, southwards from southern New York state.

Comment This is a very beautiful and striking tree when covered with its sweetly scented flowers. Shoots of young trees may reach 3m or more in a year, with huge leaves around 50cm across. The wood is used in Japan for the traditional 13-stringed *koto*, a curved instrument around 2m long. The genus is named after Anna Paulowna (1795–1865), daughter of Paul I, Czar of Russia.

Paulownia tomentosa
flowers, ½ life size
April 1st

Paulownia tomentosa
seed pods, ¾ life size
August 4th

Paulownia tomentosa
seed pods, ¼ life size
August 4th

Paulownia tomentosa
section through
seed pod and
seeds, (left)
1½ × life size
September 9th

Paulownia tomentosa
⅓ life size, July 14th

Catalpa bignonioides
seeds, 2 × life size
October 14th

Catalpa bignonioides
½ life size
August 4th

Catalpa bignonioides
pods and seeds
½ life size
October 14th

Catalpa

Catalpa Scop. (1777), in the family Bignoniaceae, contains around 10 species in eastern Asia, eastern North America, and the West Indies.

Description Trees to 30m, fast-growing when young. The leaves are opposite, deciduous or rarely evergreen, long-stalked, usually large, sometimes lobed, with a purple spot in the axils of the veins on the underside. The flowers are white, pink, or lilac, in pyramidal clusters at the tips of the branches, opening with the leaves in midsummer. Sepals 5, joined to form an irregularly split tube. Petals 5, joined at the base, 2-lipped at the mouth, usually with yellow or orange markings and dark spots inside. Stamens 5, with 2 fertile, and the remaining 3 reduced to thin, sterile staminodes. Ovary superior, with 2 cells and numerous ovules per cell; style 1, 2-lobed at the tip. Pollination is by insects. The fruits are long, bean-like, 2-valved capsules with numerous flattened seeds with thread-like wings.

Key Recognition Features The large, opposite leaves and clusters of white flowers in summer.

Evolution and Relationships *Catalpa* is unusual in the Bignoniaceae in having simple, not pinnate leaves. The family Bignoniaceae is mainly tropical, with 113 genera and around 800 species, many of them climbers. *Chilopsis* D. Don, the desert willow from southern California, is closely related to *Catalpa*, but is a shrub with linear-lanceolate leaves; an unusual hybrid between the two genera, × *Chitalpa taskentensis* hort. has recently appeared in cultivation.

Ecology and Geography In warm temperate forest and in open areas in western and central China, and in eastern North America, southwards from Georgia and southern Illinois.

Comment These are beautiful summer-flowering trees for warm climates, and good shade trees in large gardens; the pink- and purple-flowered Chinese species flower there in late May, the white-flowered species in late June or July.

Catalpa bignonioides
flowers, ⅔ life size
August 4th

Campsis

Campsis Lour. (1790), in the family Bignoniaceae, contains 2 species, 1 in eastern Asia, the other in eastern North America.

Description Climbers to 10m or more, clinging by aerial rootlets. The leaves are opposite, deciduous, pinnate with 7–11 leaflets. The flowers are in loose heads, red or orange, tubular, thick in texture. Sepals 5, joined to form a pale orange tube. Petals 5, joined to form a long tube, 2-lipped at the mouth. Stamens 4, on the inside of the tube. Ovary superior, with 2 cells and numerous ovules per cell; style 1, 2-lobed at the tip. Pollination is by birds. The fruits are long, bean-like, 2-valved capsules with numerous flattened seeds with large wings.

Key Recognition Features Self-clinging climber with pinnate leaves and clusters of tubular, orange flowers in summer.

Evolution and Relationships Both species of *Campsis* are pollinated by birds; the American species, *C. radicans* (L.) Seem. is a typical hummingbird-pollinated flower with thick, sucrose-rich nectar; the Chinese species *C. grandiflora* (Thunb.) K. Schum. has more open flowers and hexose-rich nectar for other birds. *Tecoma* Juss. (which now includes *Tecomaria* Spach), is a genus of around 13 species of upright shrubs with curved, tubular flowers, with the 3 or 4 African species polliniated by sunbirds, and the remaining American species polliniated by hummingbirds.

Ecology and Geography On trees in warm temperate forest in central China, and in eastern North America, southwards from Pennsylvania to Florida and Texas.

Comment *Campsis* are commonly cultivated under the name trumpet vine or bignonia, the genus in which the American species was described by Linnaeus. The hybrid between the species, *Campsis × tagliabuana* (Vis.) Rehder, is also cultivated, particularly the clone 'Madame Galen'.

Campsis × tagliabuana 'Madame Galen'
flower parts, ¾ life size, September 16th

Campsis × tagliabuana
'Madame Galen'
⅓ life size, September 16th

Campsis radicans
pods and seeds (below)
½ life size
December 15th

Eccremocarpus scaber
⅓ life size, June 22nd

430

Pandorea

Pandorea (Endl.) Spach (1840), in the family Bignoniaceae, contains around 6 species from New Guinea to New Caledonia and Australia.

Description Slender climbers to 10m or more, with twining stems. The leaves are opposite, evergreen, pinnate, without tendrils. The flowers are brownish, yellow, or white with a pink throat. Sepals 5, joined to form a tube. Petals 5, joined to form a tube at the base, spreading at the mouth. Stamens 4, with 2 long and 2 short, on the inside of the tube. Ovary superior, with 1 cell and numerous ovules; style 1, 2-lobed at the tip. Pollination is presumed to be by insects. The fruits are oblong, thick-valved capsules with numerous small, flattened seeds with wings.

Key Recognition Features Climbers with pinnate leaves without tendrils, woody at the base. The 2 cultivated species look very different: *P. jasminoides* (Lindl.) K. Schum. has large, white flowers with a deep pink throat, while *P. pandorana* (Andr.) Van Steenis, the wonga-wonga vine, has masses of small brownish or golden-yellow flowers, hairy in the throat.

Evolution and Relationships Related to *Tecomanthe* Baill. which is found from New Guinea to Queensland and Three King's Island, New Zealand; it has a larger, deeply toothed calyx and flowers with pointed lobes.

Ecology and Geography In forest and along the coast, *P. jasminoides* in Queensland and New South Wales, *P. pandorana* from New Guinea through eastern Australia to Tasmania.

Comment These are attractive climbers for essentially frost-free climates, cultivated in Australia and elsewhere.

Pandorea pandorana
'Golden Rain'
¹/₂ life size, April 10th

Eccremocarpus scaber
seeds, 2 × life size
November 29th

Eccremocarpus scaber f. *carmineus*
just under life size
September 16th

Eccremocarpus scaber
seed pods, ¹/₃ life size
June 22nd

Eccremocarpus

Eccremocarpus Ruíz & Pavón (1794), in the family Bignoniaceae, contains 5 species in South America.

Description Slender climbers to 4m or more, with clinging, branched tendrils. The leaves are opposite, deciduous, pinnate or 2-pinnate. The flowers are small, red, orange, yellow, or pinkish, tubular. Sepals 5, joined to form a tube. Petals 5, joined to form a tube, narrowed just below the mouth. Stamens 4, on the inside of the tube. Ovary superior, with 1 cell and numerous ovules; style 1, 2-lobed at the tip. Pollination is by hummingbirds. The fruits are 1-valved capsules with numerous small, flattened seeds with wings.

Key Recognition Features A delicate climber, woody only at the base, with pinnate leaves and tendrils and masses of small tubular flowers. The short, broad seed pods are unusual in the family.

Evolution and Relationships *Eccremocarpus* is unusual in the family by being almost herbaceous. *Bignonia* L. from eastern North America, southwards from Virginia, contains 1 species, *B. capreolata* L., which has 2 leaflets and branching tendrils ending in small pads; the flowers are reddish-orange, paler inside, tubular, and 2-lipped at the mouth.

Ecology and Geography In temperate forest Chile and Peru.

Comment *Eccremocarpus scaber* Ruíz & Pavón is the only species commonly cultivated; in frost-prone climates it may be grown from seed as an annual.

431

Sarmienta

Sarmienta Ruíz & Pavón (1794), in the family Gesneriaceae, contains 1 species, *S. repens* Ruíz & Pavón, from southern South America.

Description A creeping subshrub, with stems rooting at the nodes. The leaves are opposite, evergreen, rounded, thick, and fleshy. The flowers are scarlet-red, solitary on slender stalks in the leaf axils. Sepals 5, joined at the base. Petals 5, short, spreading, joined to form a swollen tube, which is narrowed just below the mouth. Stamens 2, extending beyond the mouth of the tube. Ovary superior, with 2 cells and numerous ovules; style 1, simple. Pollination is by hummingbirds. The fruits are rounded berries with numerous minute seeds.

Key Recognition Features A shrubby scrambler with toothed, slightly fleshy leaves and tubular, scarlet flowers.

Evolution and Relationships Related to *Asteranthera* and *Mitraria*. The fruits are eaten by yellow-headed hummingbirds.

Ecology and Geography In temperate rainforest; epiphytic, and often climbing high into trees. Found in Chile and southwestern Argentina; also growing with *Desfontainia* (see p.395).

Comment A beautiful miniature shrub; although it tolerates some frost it is not easy to grow outdoors, but does best in a humid, shaded greenhouse.

Sarmienta repens
flowers, 2 × life size, June 24th

Sarmienta repens
½ life size, June 24th

Asteranthera

Asteranthera Hanst. (1853), in the family Gesneriaceae, contains 1 species, *A. ovata* (Cav.) Hanst. from southern South America.

Description Slender climbers to 3m, with stems rooting at the nodes. The leaves are opposite, evergreen, rounded, sparsely bristly, with a few large teeth. The flowers are red, whitish in the throat, solitary in the leaf axils. Sepals 5, toothed, joined at the base. Petals 5, wide-spreading at the mouth, joined to form a tube at the base. Stamens 4, the anthers joined into a star-like cluster. Ovary inferior, with 2 cells and numerous ovules; style 1. Pollination is by hummingbirds. The fruits are fleshy, purple and green, with numerous minute seeds.

Key Recognition Features Climbers with toothed, slightly bristly leaves and large, red, 2-lipped flowers.

Evolution and Relationships The family Gesneriaceae, with 126 genera and nearly 3000 species, is almost exclusively tropical and herbaceous; the genera of 3 small, red-flowered subshrubs shown here are closely related hummingbird-pollinated flowers from temperate South America. The taurepo, *Rhabdothamnus solandri* Cunn. from New Zealand is rather similar to *Asteranthera*, but has 5 distinct petals; it is the only representative of the family in New Zealand.

Ecology and Geography In temperate rainforest in Chile and southwestern Argentina, south from Nequen (40°S). Often growing beneath *Desfontainia spinosa* (p.395), and climbing on deciduous trees. The fruits are eaten by hummingbirds.

Comment A beautiful climber, rarely cultivated successfully, and only in warm, very humid gardens. I have found that the young stems are eaten by wood mice as well as slugs.

Asteranthera ovata
¾ life size, June 16th

Mitraria

Mitraria Cav. (1801), in the family Gesneriaceae, contains 1 species from southern South America.

Description Scrambling shrub to 6m or more, with stems rooting at the nodes. The leaves are opposite, evergreen, ovate, slightly fleshy, with few blunt teeth. The flowers are scarlet-red, solitary on slender stalks in the leaf axils. Sepals 4 or 5, joined at the base. Petals 5, short, spreading, joined to form a swollen tube, which is narrowed just below the mouth and above the base. Stamens 4, in 2 pairs, extending beyond the mouth of the tube. Ovary inferior, with 2 cells and numerous ovules; style 1, simple. Pollination is by hummingbirds. The fruits are rounded berries with numerous minute seeds.

Key Recognition Features A shrubby scrambler with toothed, slightly fleshy leaves and tubular, scarlet flowers.

Evolution and Relationships Related to *Asteranthera* and *Sarmienta*. Another isolated species, *Fieldia australis* Cunn. from Queensland, New South Wales, and Victoria, with greenish-yellow flowers, is closely related to *Mitraria*; it climbs on tree-fern trunks in moist, sheltered gullies.

Ecology and Geography In temperate rainforest, on tree trunks and rocks in Chile, mainly around the Magellan Straits and southwestern Argentina, and in the mist forest south of Coquimbo.

Comment A beautiful and free-flowering shrub, if not grown in too much shade.

Mitraria coccinea
flowers, 1²/₃ × life size
June 25th

Asteranthera ovata
flower parts and leaf
1 ¹/₂ × life size, June 16th

Mitraria coccinea
¹/₂ life size, June 25th

Lysionotus

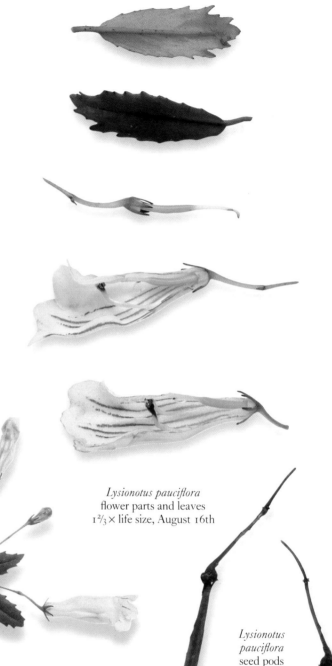

Lysionotus D. Don (1822), in the family Gesneriaceae, contains around 30 species from eastern Asia.

Description Shrubs to 25cm or more. The leaves are opposite or in whorls of 3–6, evergreen, elliptic to ovate-lanceolate, fleshy, with few blunt teeth. The flowers are purplish or white, solitary or in small clusters, on slender stalks in the leaf axils. Sepals 5, of which 2 are joined at the base. Petals 5, joined to form a tube, 2-lipped at the mouth. Stamens 2, inside the tube, with a tooth at the apex. Ovary superior, with 2 cells and numerous ovules; style 1, with 2 stigmas. Pollination is by insects. The fruits are narrow, hanging capsules, splitting into 4 parts, with numerous minute, narrow seeds, with a hair at each end.

Key Recognition Features A shrub with whorled, fleshy leaves, jointed twigs, and usually pale flowers.

Evolution and Relationships Related to other Himalayan genera of Gesneriaceae such as *Aeschynanthus* Jack.

Ecology and Geography On trees in temperate rainforest from Japan to western China and the central Himalayas.

Comment *Lysionotus* are unusual and modest shrubs for woodland or humid shade. *Lysionotus pauciflora* Maxim. is found from central Japan to Taiwan and in western Hubei, growing on large trees in the mountains.

Lysionotus pauciflora
flower parts and leaves
1²⁄₃ × life size, August 16th

Lysionotus pauciflora
½ life size, August 16th

Lysionotus pauciflora
seed pods
1¾ × life size
November 29th

Justicia carnea
⅓ life size, August 31st

Justicia

Justicia L. (1753), in the family Acanthaceae, contains around 400 species, mainly in the tropics.

Description Shrubs to 3m, woody at the base. Leaves opposite, usually evergreen, often softly hairy. The flowers are usually in rather dense spikes, with overlapping bracts. Sepals 5, joined to form a toothed calyx. Petals forming a 2-lipped corolla; upper lip straight, over the style and stamens, the lower lip sometimes 3-lobed. Stamens 2, curved. Ovary superior, with 2 cells and 1 or 2 ovules per cell; style 1, with a round stigma. Pollination is by bees or hummingbirds. The fruits are 2- or 4-seeded capsules.

Key Recognition Features The stamens are attached inside the tube in *Justicia*; in the closely related *Pachystachys* Rich. ex DC they are at the base of the tube

Evolution and Relationships The smaller genera *Jacobinia* Nees ex Moric., *Adhatoda* Mill., and *Beloperone* Nees are here included in *Justicia*, which is related to *Ruellia* L. and *Strobilanthes* Blume. The family Acanthaceae is related to Bignoniaceae (see p.429–31) and Gesneriaceae (see pp.432–34), and recognised by its often spiny or colourful bracts and explosive capsules.

Ecology and Geography In dry desert scrub, and in moist forest, mainly in Central and South America.

Comment Several species are commonly cultivated, and will survive a few degrees of frost. *Justicia brandegeeana* Wassh. & L.B. Sm. is the familiar shrimp plant, formerly called *Beloperone guttata* Brandeg. *Justicia carnea* Lindl. is particularly tolerant of low light levels, and will flower in very shady situations. *Justicia californica* (Benth.) D. Gibson is a wiry shrub with red flowers found in southern Californian deserts. The genus is named after James Justice (1698–1763), a Scottish amateur botanist and gardener who specialised in bulbs and the cultivation of exotic fruit.

Justicia carnea, flowers
⅔ life size, August 31st

Serissa

Serissa Comm. ex Juss. (1789), in the family Rubiaceae, contains 2 species in China and Japan.

Description Much-branched, small shrubs to 1m. The leaves are opposite, evergreen, not toothed, foetid when bruised. The flowers are white or pink, scented, solitary or clustered. Sepals usually 5. Petals usually 5, forming a radially symmetrical corolla, joined at the base to form a short tube. Stamens 5. Ovary inferior, with 2 cells and 2 ovules; style 1, forked. Pollination is by insects. The fruits are berries with 2 seeds.

Key Recognition Features A densely twiggy bush with small leaves and white or pink flowers.

Evolution and Relationships Related to *Leptodermis* Wall. and the climbing *Paedaria* L., which smells of faeces when bruised. In the light of DNA studies, the family Rubiaceae is now considered close to the Apocynaceae (see pp.384–85) and Gentianaceae within the Gentianales, not close to the Caprifoliaceae (see pp.438–47) and Compositae (see pp.453–63) as was formerly thought. The family contains such different plants as *Coffea arabica* L. the coffee tree, *Cinchona* L. the source of quinine, and *Rubia* L. the madder, as well as the tropical climbing *Mussaenda* L. with orange flowers and white or red, petal-like sepals, the scented *Gardenia* Ellis, and *Galium verum* L. the wild lady's bedstraw.

Ecology and Geography In scrub and on cliffs, in China and Japan.

Comment *Serissa japonica* (Thunb.) Thunb. is often cultivated in mild areas, and can be clipped into a small hedge; both variegated and double-flowered forms have long been cultivated in China and Japan.

Serissa japonica 'Flore Pleno'
flowers, 2 × life size
May 17th

Serissa japonica 'Flore Pleno'
⅔ life size, May 17th

Coprosma robusta
flowers, 2 × life size
April 1st

Coprosma robusta
fruits and seed
2 × life size, April 1st

Coprosma

Coprosma Forster & Forster fil. (1776), in the family Rubiaceae, contains around 90 species from the western Pacific to Australia and New Zealand.

Description Upright shrubs or rarely trees, to 15m. The leaves are opposite, usually evergreen, not toothed. The flowers are small, usually unisexual, often in short-stalked heads in the leaf axils. Sepals 4 or 5, minute or absent in male flowers. Petals 5, very small, joined at the base to form a tube. Stamens 5, on long filaments. Ovary inferior, with 2 cells and numerous ovules; styles 2, long. Pollination is usually by wind. The fruits are berries, red or blue when ripe, with 2–4 large seeds.

Key Recognition Features The often glossy, evergreen leaves and the inconspicuous flowers followed by often crowded berries.

Evolution and Relationships Very unusual in the family in having evolved wind pollination, which is also found in the tropical African genus *Anthospermum* L.

Ecology and Geography In woods and open places in the mountains; 45 species in New Zealand, around 20 in Hawaii, the rest scattered from Borneo to New Guinea, Australia, and Tasmania.

Comment Some species of *Coprosma* are grown as ornamental evergreens, particularly in mild maritime climates; *C. lucida* Forster & Forster fil. and *C. robusta* Roaul are striking for their very shiny leaves and orange-red berries.

Coprosma robusta
½ life size, April 1st

437

Abelia

Abelia R. Br. (1818), in the family Caprifoliaceae, contains around 30 species in eastern Asia and 1 or 2 in Mexico.

Description Upright or scrambling shrubs to 4m. The leaves are opposite, evergreen or deciduous, ovate to lanceolate, usually without teeth. The flowers are white, purplish, or crimson, often yellowish in the throat, often scented, solitary or few in the upper leaf axils. Sepals 2–5, joined at the base. Petals 5, short, spreading, forming a 2-lipped corolla, joined at the base to form a tube. Stamens 4, in 2 pairs, attached at the base of the tube. Ovary inferior, with 3 cells, but only 1 cell fertile, with 1 ovule; style 1, simple, with a capitate stigma. Pollination is by bees, moths, or hummingbirds. The fruits are leathery, with 1 seed, topped by the persistent sepals.

Key Recognition Features The large, often paired and persistent sepals are characteristic, combined with the 2-lipped flowers.

Evolution and Relationships The family Caprifoliaceae is now considered to include the traditional Dipsacaceae, which covered such genera as *Dipsacus*, the teasel, *Valeriana*, and *Scabiosa* (see Volume 2). But it excludes *Viburnum* (see pp.448–50), and *Sambucus* (elder, see p.451), which are now placed in the Adoxaceae. Within Caprifoliaceae, *Abelia* is close to *Dipelta* (see p.440) and *Kolkwitzia* (see p.441).

Ecology and Geography In scrub and on cliffs; most species are from China, with 1 species, *A. triflora* R. Br., in the northwestern Himalayas. *Abelia floribunda* Decne is from Mexico; it has tubular, crimson flowers, and it is this species that is pollinated by hummingbirds.

Comment The garden hybrid *A. × grandiflora* (André) Rehd. is very commonly planted in warm areas, where it will flower almost throughout the year. The genus was named after Dr Clarke Abel (1760–1826), botanist and surgeon who visited China with Lord Amhurst in 1816–17 and died at Cawnpore. His plant collections, which survived the wreck of the Alceste, were described by Robert Brown in 1818.

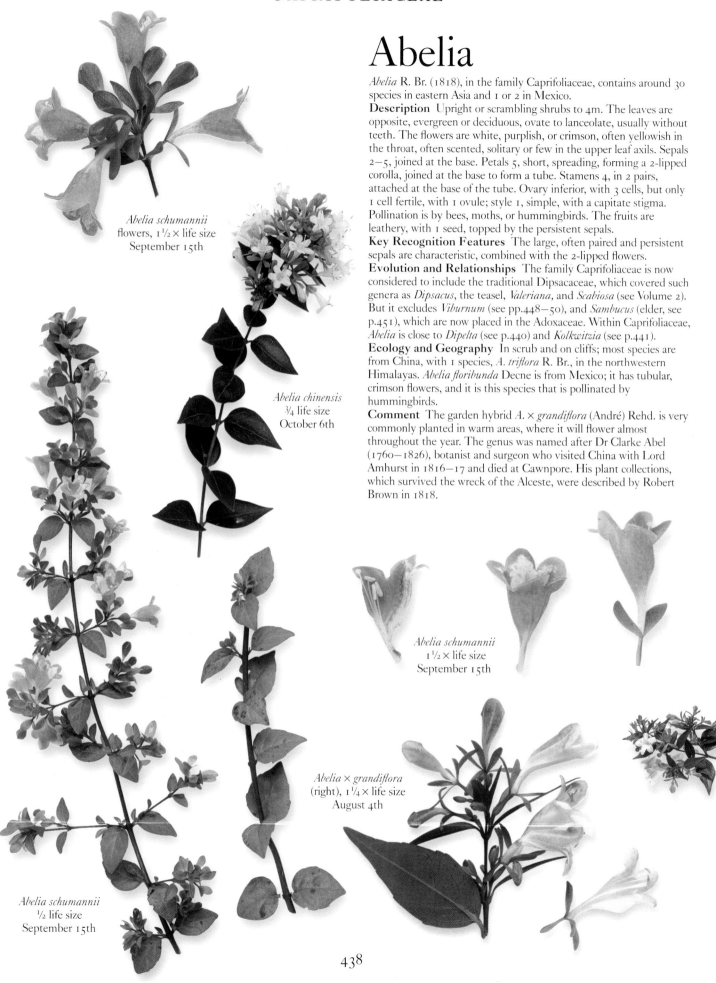

Abelia schumannii
flowers, 1 ½ × life size
September 15th

Abelia chinensis
¾ life size
October 6th

Abelia schumannii
1 ½ × life size
September 15th

Abelia × grandiflora
(right), 1 ¼ × life size
August 4th

Abelia schumannii
½ life size
September 15th

Heptacodium

Heptacodium Rehd. (1916), in the family Caprifoliaceae, contains 1 species, *H. miconioides* Rehd., in China.

Description A large shrub to 5m. The leaves are opposite, deciduous, curved, with 3 strong veins from the base, without teeth. The flowers are white, scented, in groups of 3, in repeatedly branching sprays at the ends of branches of the current year's growth. Sepals 5, enlarging and becoming reddish in fruit. Petals 5, rather narrow, spreading, joined at the base to form a tube. Stamens 5, longer than the petals. Ovary inferior; style 1, simple, with a capitate stigma. Pollination is presumed to be by bees and moths. The fruits are capsules with few large seeds.

Key Recognition Features The curved, 3-veined leaves and small, white flowers in groups of 3 are easily recognised.

Evolution and Relationships A rather distinct genus, probably closest to *Abelia*.

Ecology and Geography In rocky woods in western China.

Comment This distinctive shrub was introduced to cultivation in the west only in the 1980s. It is tough and easily grown, conspicuous in flower in late summer, and with the red sepals in autumn.

Heptacodium miconioides
fruits with enlarged sepals
(above), just over life size
October 5th

Heptacodium miconioides
flowers, 1⅓ × life size, September 15th

Heptacodium miconioides
½ life size, September 15th

*Abelia ×
grandiflora*
⅓ life size
August 4th

Heptacodium miconioides
½ life size
September 15th

Dipelta floribunda
fruiting branch
¹/₃ life size, June 15th

Dipelta floribunda (left)
¹/₃ life size, May 9th

Dipelta floribunda
fruiting calyces
just under life size
June 15th

Dipelta floribunda, flower section
flower and fruit, life size, May 9th

Dipelta

Dipelta Maxim. (1878), in the family Caprifoliaceae, contains
4 species in China.

Description Upright, arching shrubs to 5m. The leaves are opposite,
deciduous, sometimes with fine teeth. The flowers are white or
pinkish, often yellowish-orange in the throat, not scented, solitary or
few in the upper leaf axils. Bracts large and round, the upper
2 covering the ovary. Sepals 5, narrow, joined at the base. Petals 5,
spreading, forming a 2-lipped corolla, joined at the base to form a tube.
Stamens 4, in 2 pairs, attached at the base of the tube. Pollination is
by bees. Ovary inferior, with 4 cells: 2 cells with 1 fertile ovule each,
2 with many sterile ovules. Style 1, simple, with a capitate stigma.
The fruits are 2-seeded capsules, topped by the persistent bracts.

Key Recognition Features The large, round, paired, persistent
bracts are characteristic, combined with the wide, 2-lipped flowers.

Evolution and Relationships *Dipelta* is close to *Abelia* (see p.438)
and *Kolkwitzia*.

Ecology and Geography In scrub and on cliffs in central and
western China.

Comment These are unusual and attractive shrubs; the 2 large
bracts give the genus its name, from *pelte*, the Greek for a small,
round shield.

Kolkwitzia amabilis
flower parts, 1½ × life size
June 21st

Kolkwitzia amabilis
young fruits, 2 × life size
June 21st

Kolkwitzia

Kolkwitzia Graebn. (1901), in the family Caprifoliaceae, contains 1 species, *K. amabilis* Graebn., in China.

Description Upright, arching shrub to 4m. The leaves are opposite, deciduous, broadly ovate, long-pointed, sometimes with few teeth. The flowers are in pairs on short branches, white or pinkish, yellowish in the throat, not scented. Sepals 5, narrow, spreading and long-hairy. Petals 5, spreading, forming a 2-lipped corolla, joined in the lower half to form a tube. Stamens 4, in 2 pairs, attached at the base of the tube. Ovary inferior, bristly-hairy, with 3 cells: 1 cell with 1 fertile ovule and 2 with many sterile ovules; style 1, simple, with a capitate stigma. Pollination is by bees. The fruits are 2-seeded capsules topped by the persistent bracts.

Key Recognition Features The bristly-hairy ovaries combined with the wide, 2-lipped flowers, often borne in great abundance in late spring.

Evolution and Relationships *Kolkwitzia* is close to *Abelia* (see p.438) and *Dipelta*.

Ecology and Geography In scrub and on cliffs in central China, in northwestern Hubei, on the watershed between the Yangtze and the Han rivers.

Comment Named after Richard Kolkwitz (1873–1956), professor of botany in Berlin around 1910.

Kolkwitzia amabilis
½ life size
June 21st

441

Diervilla sessilifolia
flowers, 2 × life size
June 23rd

Diervilla

Diervilla Mill. (1754), in the family Caprifoliaceae, contains 3 or 4 species in eastern North America.

Description Upright shrubs to 2m. The leaves are opposite, deciduous, long-pointed, sometimes with few teeth. The flowers are in pairs or groups of 3 or more, on short branches, yellowish, not scented. Sepals 5, narrow. Petals 5, spreading, forming a 2-lipped corolla, joined at the base to form a short tube. Stamens 5, longer than the petals. Ovary inferior, with 2 cells and many ovules; style 1, simple, with a capitate stigma. Pollination is presumed to be by various insects. The fruits are capsules with numerous small seeds.

Key Recognition Features The curved and beaked ovaries with 5 very narrow sepals, and yellow flowers with rather narrow petals.

Evolution and Relationships *Diervilla* is close to the more familiar *Weigela*.

Ecology and Geography In rocky woods in eastern North America, from Newfoundland southwards to Georgia and Alabama.

Comment Named after M. Dierville, a French surgeon, who visited Canada in 1699–1700.

Weigela

Weigela Thunb. (1780), in the family Caprifoliaceae, contains 10 species in eastern Asia.

Description Upright or spreading shrubs to 5m. The leaves are opposite, deciduous, with teeth. The flowers are solitary or in groups of 3 or more, on short branches, white, pink, purple, or yellow with an orange throat, usually scented. Sepals 5, narrow. Petals 5, spreading, forming a 2-lipped or almost regular corolla, joined at the base to form a tube. Stamens 5, shorter than the petals. Ovary inferior, with 2 cells and many ovules; style 1, simple, with a capitate stigma. Pollination is presumed to be by bees. The fruits are capsules with numerous minute, often winged seeds.

Key Recognition Features The narrow ovaries with 5 sepals, and the usually pinkish flowers with rounded petals.

Evolution and Relationships There are 2 rather distinct types of *Weigela*; the commonly cultivated species such as *W. florida* (Bunge) DC and *W. praecox* (Lem.) Bailey, which have almost radially symmetrical flowers, and the yellow-flowered species such as *W. middendorfiana* (Carr.) Lem. and *W. maximowiczii* (S. Moore) Rehd. which have distinctly 2-lipped flowers.

Ecology and Geography In moist, rocky woods in China, Korea, northeastern Siberia, and Japan.

Comment *Weigela* is a popular ornamental genus, particularly in cold-winter areas; many cultivars were raised in France in the late 19th century. The genus is named after C.E. von Weigel, (1748–1831), professor of botany in Greifswald.

Diervilla sessilifolia
½ life size, June 23rd

Weigela middendorfiana
just over life size, April 28th

Caprifoliaceae

Weigela maximowiczii
flowers, life size, May 11th

Weigela florida
'Foliis Purpureis'
flowers, 2¼ × life size
May 15th

Weigela florida
'Foliis Purpureis'
½ life size, May 15th

Weigela florida
½ life size, May 28th

Weigela florida 'Foliis Purpureis'
½ life size, May 15th

Caprifoliaceae

Leycesteria crocothyrsos
cross sections of fruit
$2\frac{1}{4}$ × life size
November 15th

Leycesteria formosa
$\frac{1}{3}$ life size, August 3rd

Leycesteria crocothyrsos
$\frac{1}{2}$ life size, June 21st

Leycesteria crocothyrsos
young fruits (right)
and flowers (below)
just over life size
June 21st

Leycesteria crocothyrsos
fruits (left)
$\frac{1}{2}$ life size
November 15th

444

Symphoricarpos albus
fruits, 1 ¼ × life size,
August 5th

Symphoricarpos albus
flowers, 2 ¼ × life size
June 1st

Leycesteria
formosa
fruits and flowers
1 ⅓ × life size,
August 3rd

Symphoricarpos albus
1 ⅓ × life size, June 1st

Leycesteria

Leycesteria Wall. (1824), in the family Caprifoliaceae, contains 6 species from the Himalayas and southwestern China.

Description Upright or pendulous shrubs to 4m. The leaves are opposite, deciduous, long-pointed, without teeth. The flowers are in whorls of 3 or more, white, purplish, or yellow, not scented, often subtended by large, heart-shaped, sometimes claret-red bracts. Sepals 5, narrow. Petals 5, spreading, forming a radially symmetrical corolla, joined at the base to form a long tube. Stamens 5. Ovary inferior, with 5–8 cells, and many ovules; style 1, simple, with a capitate stigma. Pollination is by bees. The fruits are berries with numerous small seeds.

Key Recognition Features The whorls of radially symmetrical flowers followed by berries, and the heart-shaped, coloured bracts in *L. formosa* Wall..

Evolution and Relationships *Leycesteria* is close to *Lonicera* (see pp.446–47) and *Symphoricarpos*, which also have berries.

Ecology and Geography In wet, rocky woods and on cliffs in the eastern Himalayas and western China.

Comment Two species are cultivated; the rare and tender yellow-flowered *L. crocothyrsos* Airy Shaw, introduced by Kingdon Ward from cliffs in Assam, and the commonly planted white-flowered and claret-bracted *L. formosa* Wall., a frequent species in wet woods throughout the Himalayas to western China. The genus is named after William Leycester (1775–1831), a judge in the Bengal Civil Service.

Symphoricarpos

Symphoricarpos Duhamel (1755), in the family Caprifoliaceae, contains 17 species from North America and China.

Description Upright or creeping shrubs to 3m, often with a characteristic scent. The leaves are opposite, deciduous, usually rounded, sometimes with a few lobes or teeth. The flowers are in groups of 3 or more, in the leaf axils or in short spikes, white or pinkish. Sepals 4 or 5, joined at the base. Petals 4 or 5, joined at the base to form a bell-shaped or tubular corolla, usually hairy inside. Stamens 4 or 5, longer or shorter than the petals. Ovary inferior, with 4 cells: 2 cells with 1 fertile ovule each, 2 with many sterile ovules. Style 1, simple, with a capitate stigma. Pollination is by bees. The fruits are white, pink, or blackish-purple berries with 2 large seeds.

Key Recognition Features The rounded, opposite leaves, small flowers, and very pithy berries with 2 seeds.

Evolution and Relationships *Symphoricarpos* is related to *Lonicera* (see pp.446–47).

Ecology and Geography In rocky woods and scrub; 16 species in North America and 1 species, *S. sinensis* Rehder, in western Hubei in northwestern China.

Comment Several species are cultivated for their fruits, which may remain on the leafless bushes through the winter. *Symphoricarpos albus* (L.) Blake, the snowberry, is often planted as a quick-growing hedge. *Symphoricarpos orbiculatus* Moench., with purplish-red berries, is called Indian currant.

Lonicera

Lonicera L. (1753), the honeysuckle, in the family Caprifoliaceae, contains around 180 species, from Europe to Asia and North America.

Description Upright or arching shrubs, or rarely small trees, to 5m, or twining climbers to 10m or more. The leaves are opposite, deciduous or evergreen, long-pointed, usually without teeth. The flowers are white, purplish, red, or yellow, often scented, in pairs or whorls, often subtended by large, paired or fused, sometimes reddish bracts. Sepals 5, usually inconspicuous. Petals 5, spreading, forming a radially symmetrical or 2-lipped corolla, joined at the base to form a short or long tube. Stamens 5. Ovary inferior, with 2, 3, or 5 cells and many ovules; style 1, simple, with a capitate stigma. Pollination is by bees, moths, or hummingbirds. The fruits are berries with few or numerous seeds.

Key Recognition Features The paired or whorled flowers followed by berries.

Evolution and Relationships *Lonicera* is a large and varied genus; in general the shrubby species have rather small flowers, the climbing species larger flowers, culminating in the subtropical *L. hildebrandiana* Collett & Hemsl. from the southeastern Himalayas, which has flowers around 15cm long.

Ecology and Geography In woods, scrub, and hedges in North America southwards to Mexico, in Europe and North Africa, and in Asia eastwards to Japan, the Philippines, and Java.

Comment Over a hundred species are cultivated; shrubby, winter-flowering species, such as *L. fragrantissima* Lindl. & Paxt., are particularly valued for their strong scent, and some evergreen species such as *L. nitida* Wils. are clipped as hedges. The climbing species are the most showy, and most also have sweet scent, particularly at night. The American red-flowered species, such as *L. sempervirens* L., are scentless, and pollinated by hummingbirds.

Lonicera × tellmanniana
just under life size, June 3rd

Lonicera maackii
⅓ life size, April 29th

Lonicera fragrantissima
fruits and seeds
just over life size
April 2nd

CAPRIFOLIACEAE

Lonicera × italica
flower parts
life size, May 15th

Lonicera standishii
just under life size
March 5th

Lonicera × italica
⅓ life size, May 15th

Lonicera fragrantissima
¾ life size
March 18th

Lonicera sempervirens
½ life size
August 12th

Lonicera involucrata
(left) ½ life size
July 1st

Lonicera chaetocarpa
flowers and bracts, 1½ × life size, June 21st

Viburnum

Viburnum L. (1753), in the family Adoxaceae (traditionally in the Caprifoliaceae, see pp.438–47), contains around 150 species distributed around the northern hemisphere.

Description Upright shrubs, or rarely small trees, to 10m. The leaves are opposite, deciduous or evergreen, and often toothed. The flowers are small, white or pinkish, often scented, crowded into flat, rounded, or pyramidal heads, sometimes with sterile outer florets larger than the fertile inner ones. Sepals 5, inconspicuous. Petals usually 5, spreading, forming a radially symmetrical corolla, joined at the base to form a tube. Stamens 5. Ovary inferior, with 1 cell and 1 ovule; style 1. Pollination is by various insects. The fruits are berries with 1 hard, usually flattened seed.

Key Recognition Features The opposite leaves and the flat, pyramidal, or rounded heads of small flowers, followed by 1-seeded berries.

Evolution and Relationships Related to *Sambucus* (see p.451) and now included with it in the Adoxaceae. Enlarged, sterile florets very similar to those found in *V. plicatum* Thunb. and *V. opulus* L. are also found in *Hydrangea* (see pp.216–17); less similar ones in *Scabiosa* L. and of course in the Compositae (see pp.453–463). *Viburnum* is a large and diverse genus, with species that flower in winter, spring, or summer. It is divided into 9 sections. Section Thyrsosma includes the winter-flowering *V. farreri* Stearn and the commonly planted *V. × bodnantense* Aberc. ex Stearn, as well as *V. erubescens* Wall. Section Lantana includes the wild European *V. lantana* L., called the wayfaring tree, as well as the scented *V. carlesii* Hemsl. and its hybrids. Section Pseudotinus includes the American *V. lantanoides* Michx., with enlarged outer florets. Section Pseudopulus includes *V. plicatum* Thunb. and the Chinese species with enlarged florets. Section Lentago includes the American *V. lentago* L., the sheep-berry. Section Tinus includes the Mediterranean *V. tinus* L., the laurustinus, commonly planted in Victorian shrubberies, and also the Chinese evergreen *V. davidii* Franch. Section Megalotinus includes the evergreen Himalayan *V. cylindricum* D. Don. Section Odontotinus includes *V. betulifolium* Batal., grown for its spectacular autumn berries. Section Opulus includes *V. opulus* L., the guelder rose, and *V. trilobum* Marsh, the cranberry-bush.

Ecology and Geography In woods, fens, and scrub. Found in North America and southwards along the Andes to Chile, in Europe and North Africa, and in Asia eastwards to China, Japan, Java, and New Guinea.

Comment Selected forms of the common species *V. opulus* and *V. plicatum* have "snowball" flowers, in which all the flowers are sterile, forming a rounded head. Many species are grown for their fruit as much as for their flowers; some species have edible fruit, but many are poisonous. The spring-flowering *V. carlesii* and its hybrids are among the best-scented of all shrubs. Many species are notable for their straight shoots; *V. acerifolium* L. is the American arrowwood, and arrows made of *V. lantana* were found in 1991 with a neolithic man preserved in the ice of the Ötztal in the Alps.

The illustrations of Viburnum *continue on p.450.*

Viburnum × bodnantense
flowers, life size, January 8th

Viburnum carlesii
'Diana'
½ life size
April 2nd

Viburnum × bodnantense
½ life size, January 8th

ADOXACEAE

Viburnum plicatum
'Mariesii', flowers with
sterile outer florets
just over life size
June 11th

Viburnum plicatum 'Mariesii'
¹/₃ life size, June 11th

Viburnum tinus
flowers
1 ¹/₂ × life size
September 5th

Viburnum rhytidophyllum
¹/₃ life size
March 14th

Viburnum opulus 'Sterile'
¹/₂ life size, May 25th

Viburnum × *burkwoodii*
¹/₃ life size
March 14th

449

Viburnum opulus
fruits and autumn
colour, ½ life size
September 4th

Viburnum betulifolium
fruits, ¾ life size
September 16th

Viburnum opulus
fruits and seed
1 ¼ × life size
September 4th

Viburnum sargentii
fruits and autumn
colour, ½ life size
October 30th

Viburnum henryi
fruits, ⅔ life size
October 30th

Viburnum setigerum
fruits, ⅔ life size, October 30th

Viburnum tinus, fruits
life size, October 5th

Sambucus nigra
⅓ life size, June 20th

Sambucus racemosa
'Sutherland Gold'
½ life size, May 15th

Sambucus racemosa
½ life size
June 22nd

Sambucus nigra
'Guincho Purple'
⅓ life size, June 20th

Sambucus nigra
fruit, ½ life size
September 12th

Sambucus

Sambucus L. (1753), the elder, in the family Adoxaceae (traditionally in the Caprifoliaceae, see pp.438–47), contains 9 species from around the northern hemisphere.

Description Upright shrubs, or rarely small trees, to 15m, or sometimes suckering perennials. The leaves are opposite, deciduous, pinnate with 5–7 toothed leaflets, acrid when crushed. The flowers are small, white or yellowish-green, rarely purplish, often scented, crowded into flat or pyramidal heads. Sepals 5, inconspicuous. Petals usually 5, spreading, forming a radially symmetrical corolla, joined at the base to form a short tube. Stamens 5. Ovary inferior, with 3–5 cells and as many ovules; style 1, with 3–5 lobes. Pollination is by insects. The fruits are berries with 3–5 hard seeds.

Key Recognition Features The flat or pyramidal heads of very small flowers and the pinnate leaves.

Evolution and Relationships Both *Sambucus* and *Viburnum* (see pp.448–50) are now considered separate from the rest of the traditional Caprifoliaceae and are included in the Adoxaceae, along with *Adoxa moschatelina* L., the small, spring-flowering herb moschatel.

Ecology and Geography In waste places and scrub in North America southwards to Mexico, in Europe and North Africa, and in Asia eastwards to Japan and Java.

Comment Several selected forms of the common species of *Sambucus*, *S. nigra* L. and *S. racemosa* L., are cultivated for their ornamental leaves. The flowers of *S. nigra* are used to flavour a cordial drink.

451

Corokia

Corokia Cunn. (1839), in the family Argophyllaceae, contains 6 species, mainly in New Zealand.

Description Trees to 6m or shrubs. The leaves are usually alternate, evergreen, simple, dark green and shining above, silvery beneath. The flowers are unisexual or bisexual, yellow, in bunches, or solitary in the leaf axils. Sepals 5. Petals 5. Stamens 5. Ovary 1 or 2 celled, with a 2-lobed stigma. Pollination is by presumed to be by insects. The fruit is a red or yellow berry with 1 seed.

Key Recognition Features The leathery leaves, silvery beneath, on a twiggy shrub, and the small, starry, yellow flowers.

Evolution and Relationships *Corokia* has in the past been considered to belong to the Cornaceae (see pp. 324–29), but DNA evidence suggests that it is distinct. The other genus in the family Argophyllaceae is *Argophyllum* Forster & Forster fil. from tropical Australia and New Caledonia, most of which have leaves silvery beneath. Two possible, and very different, relationships have been suggested: firstly, that *Corokia* is close to *Escallonia* (see p.226) in the Grossulariaceae; secondly that it is closer to the Compositae (see pp.453–463). We have put *Corokia* here until a more definite position is agreed.

Ecology and Geography In rocky places, by rivers, and on the edges of forest, with 3 species in New Zealand and 1 on the Austral Islands in the south Pacific.

Comment Many species are cultivated for their attractive leaves, which colour orange in the autumn, reinforcing the effect of the orange berries.

*Corokia
cotoneaster*
1 1/2 × life size
April 8th

Corokia macrocarpa
2 × life size
December 8th

Corokia macrocarpa
fruits and seeds
2 × life size, December 8th

Corokia macrocarpa
1/2 life size, December 8th

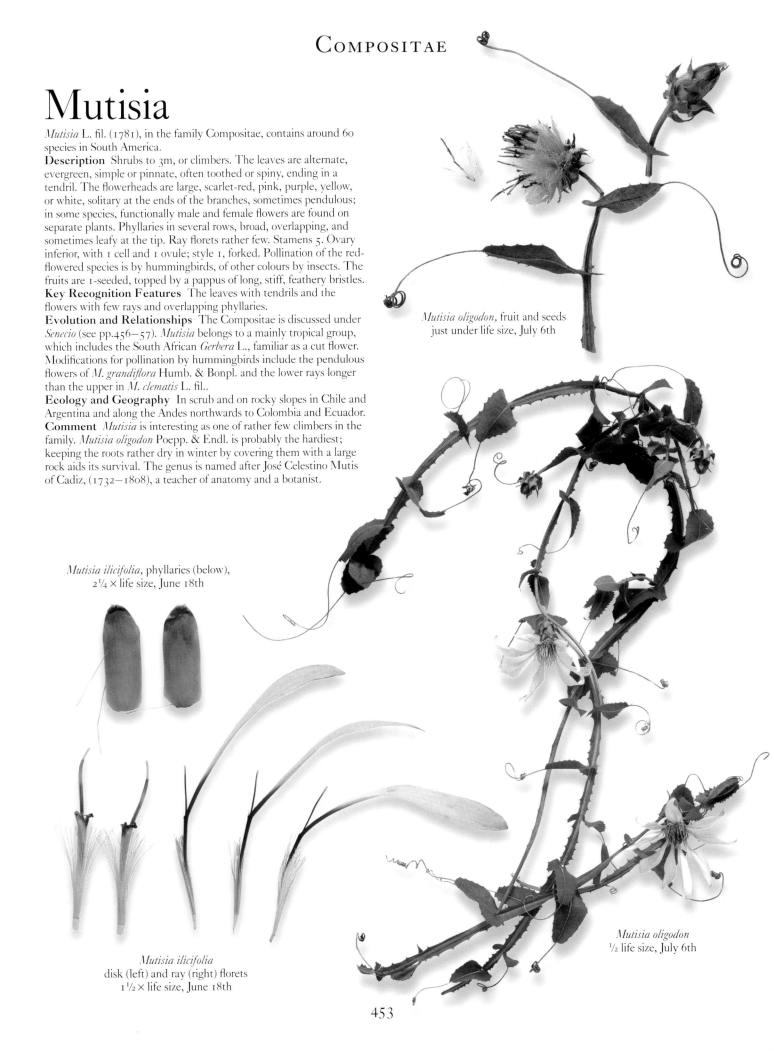

Mutisia

Mutisia L. fil. (1781), in the family Compositae, contains around 60 species in South America.

Description Shrubs to 3m, or climbers. The leaves are alternate, evergreen, simple or pinnate, often toothed or spiny, ending in a tendril. The flowerheads are large, scarlet-red, pink, purple, yellow, or white, solitary at the ends of the branches, sometimes pendulous; in some species, functionally male and female flowers are found on separate plants. Phyllaries in several rows, broad, overlapping, and sometimes leafy at the tip. Ray florets rather few. Stamens 5. Ovary inferior, with 1 cell and 1 ovule; style 1, forked. Pollination of the red-flowered species is by hummingbirds, of other colours by insects. The fruits are 1-seeded, topped by a pappus of long, stiff, feathery bristles.

Key Recognition Features The leaves with tendrils and the flowers with few rays and overlapping phyllaries.

Evolution and Relationships The Compositae is discussed under *Senecio* (see pp.456–57). *Mutisia* belongs to a mainly tropical group, which includes the South African *Gerbera* L., familiar as a cut flower. Modifications for pollination by hummingbirds include the pendulous flowers of *M. grandiflora* Humb. & Bonpl. and the lower rays longer than the upper in *M. clematis* L. fil..

Ecology and Geography In scrub and on rocky slopes in Chile and Argentina and along the Andes northwards to Colombia and Ecuador.

Comment *Mutisia* is interesting as one of rather few climbers in the family. *Mutisia oligodon* Poepp. & Endl. is probably the hardiest; keeping the roots rather dry in winter by covering them with a large rock aids its survival. The genus is named after José Celestino Mutis of Cadiz, (1732–1808), a teacher of anatomy and a botanist.

Mutisia oligodon, fruit and seeds just under life size, July 6th

Mutisia ilicifolia, phyllaries (below), 2¼ × life size, June 18th

Mutisia ilicifolia disk (left) and ray (right) florets 1½ × life size, June 18th

Mutisia oligodon ½ life size, July 6th

453

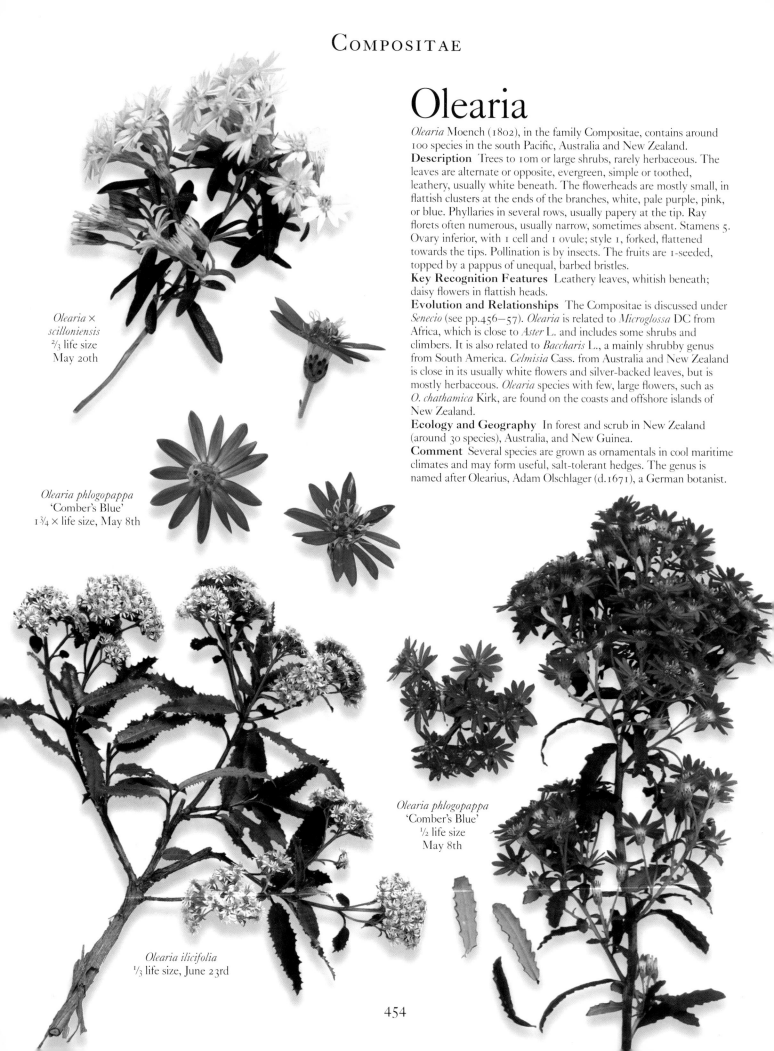

Olearia

Olearia Moench (1802), in the family Compositae, contains around 100 species in the south Pacific, Australia and New Zealand.

Description Trees to 10m or large shrubs, rarely herbaceous. The leaves are alternate or opposite, evergreen, simple or toothed, leathery, usually white beneath. The flowerheads are mostly small, in flattish clusters at the ends of the branches, white, pale purple, pink, or blue. Phyllaries in several rows, usually papery at the tip. Ray florets often numerous, usually narrow, sometimes absent. Stamens 5. Ovary inferior, with 1 cell and 1 ovule; style 1, forked, flattened towards the tips. Pollination is by insects. The fruits are 1-seeded, topped by a pappus of unequal, barbed bristles.

Key Recognition Features Leathery leaves, whitish beneath; daisy flowers in flattish heads.

Evolution and Relationships The Compositae is discussed under *Senecio* (see pp.456–57). *Olearia* is related to *Microglossa* DC from Africa, which is close to *Aster* L. and includes some shrubs and climbers. It is also related to *Baccharis* L., a mainly shrubby genus from South America. *Celmisia* Cass. from Australia and New Zealand is close in its usually white flowers and silver-backed leaves, but is mostly herbaceous. *Olearia* species with few, large flowers, such as *O. chathamica* Kirk, are found on the coasts and offshore islands of New Zealand.

Ecology and Geography In forest and scrub in New Zealand (around 30 species), Australia, and New Guinea.

Comment Several species are grown as ornamentals in cool maritime climates and may form useful, salt-tolerant hedges. The genus is named after Olearius, Adam Olschlager (d.1671), a German botanist.

Olearia ×
scilloniensis
⅔ life size
May 20th

Olearia phlogopappa
'Comber's Blue'
1¾ × life size, May 8th

Olearia ilicifolia
⅓ life size, June 23rd

Olearia phlogopappa
'Comber's Blue'
½ life size
May 8th

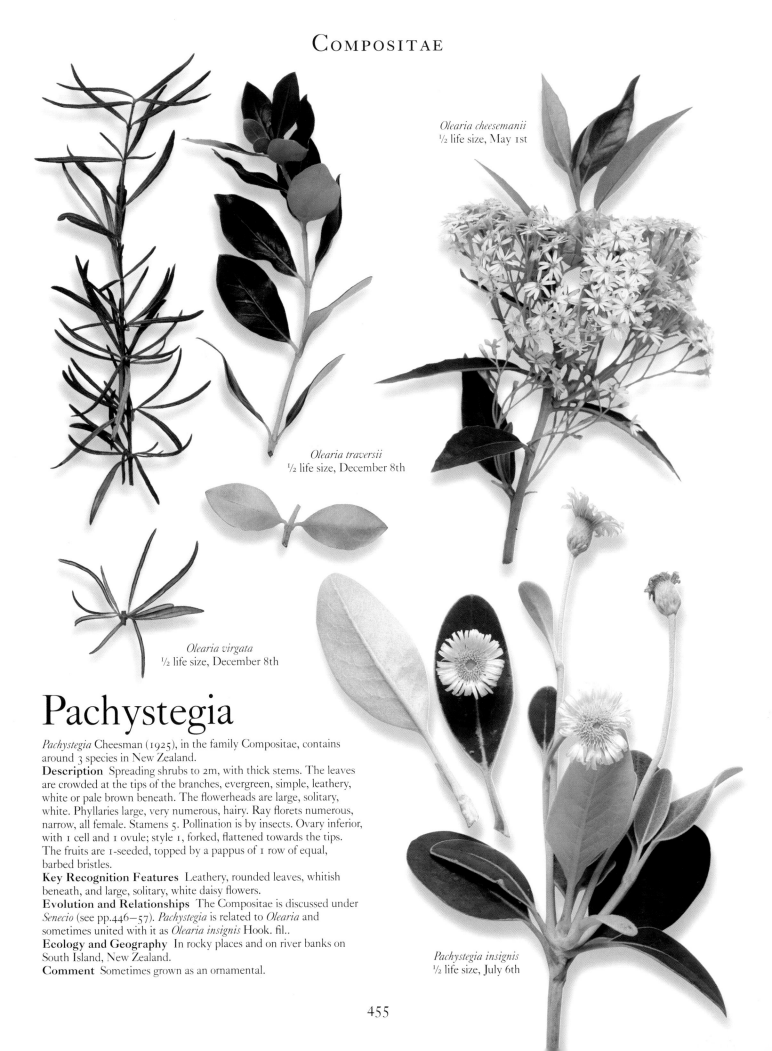

Olearia cheesemanii
½ life size, May 1st

Olearia traversii
½ life size, December 8th

Olearia virgata
½ life size, December 8th

Pachystegia

Pachystegia Cheesman (1925), in the family Compositae, contains
around 3 species in New Zealand.
Description Spreading shrubs to 2m, with thick stems. The leaves
are crowded at the tips of the branches, evergreen, simple, leathery,
white or pale brown beneath. The flowerheads are large, solitary,
white. Phyllaries large, very numerous, hairy. Ray florets numerous,
narrow, all female. Stamens 5. Pollination is by insects. Ovary inferior,
with 1 cell and 1 ovule; style 1, forked, flattened towards the tips.
The fruits are 1-seeded, topped by a pappus of 1 row of equal,
barbed bristles.
Key Recognition Features Leathery, rounded leaves, whitish
beneath, and large, solitary, white daisy flowers.
Evolution and Relationships The Compositae is discussed under
Senecio (see pp.446–57). *Pachystegia* is related to *Olearia* and
sometimes united with it as *Olearia insignis* Hook. fil..
Ecology and Geography In rocky places and on river banks on
South Island, New Zealand.
Comment Sometimes grown as an ornamental.

Pachystegia insignis
½ life size, July 6th

Brachyglottis

Brachyglottis Forster & Forster fil. (1776), in the family Compositae, contains around 29 species in New Zealand and Tasmania.

Description Trees to 6m, or spreading shrubs, with a few climbers or perennials. The leaves are alternate, evergreen, simple or toothed, often leathery, white or pale brown beneath. The flowerheads are yellow to white, in few- to many-flowered, flattish clusters. Phyllaries few. Ray florets usually female, may be numerous, few, or absent. Stamens 5. Pollination is by insects. Ovary inferior, with 1 cell and 1 ovule; style 1, forked, not flattened towards the tips. Pollination is by insects. The fruits are 1-seeded, topped by a pappus of barbed bristles.

Key Recognition Features Leathery, usually rounded leaves, whitish beneath, and heads of yellow, or rarely white, daisy flowers. White-flowered *Brachyglottis* are distinguished from *Olearia* (see p.454) by having the style arms not flattened, but truncate or pointed.

Evolution and Relationships The Compositae is discussed under *Senecio*. *Brachyglottis* is very closely related to *Senecio*, and indeed most species of *Brachyglottis* were described as *Senecio*. *Brachyglottis* now consists of the shrubby species of *Senecio* from New Zealand and Tasmania and a few related perennials, which have a stiff, bristly pappus rather than the soft, hairy pappus of *Senecio* proper. The African *Chrysanthemoides monilifera* (L.) Norlindh. is similar in general appearance to *Brachyglottis* 'Sunshine', but its outer fruits are juicy, blackish, and berry-like.

Ecology and Geography In woods and rocky places and on river banks in New Zealand and Tasmania.

Comment Many species are grown as ornamentals; particularly common is *Brachyglottis* 'Sunshine' formerly grown as *Senecio greyi*, one of a group of hybrids between *B. greyi* (Hook. fil.) R. Nordenstam, *B. compacta* (T. Kirk) R. Nordenstam, and *B. laxifolia* (Buch.) R. Nordenstam, originating in Dunedin Botanic Garden.

Senecio

Senecio L. (1753), in the family Compositae, contains around 1250 species worldwide.

Description Trees, shrubs, perennials, annuals, and a few climbers. The leaves are alternate, often divided. The flowerheads are yellow to white, red, or purple, usually in few- to many-flowered, flattish clusters. Phyllaries mainly in one row. Ray florets usually female or absent. Stamens 5. Ovary inferior, with 1 cell and 1 ovule; style 1, forked, not flattened towards the tips. Pollination is by insects, rarely by birds. The fruits are 1-seeded, topped by a pappus of usually simple hairs.

Key Recognition Features The usually yellow-centred flowers, with phyllaries in 1 row.

Evolution and Relationships The daisy family, Compositae, sometimes called Asteraceae, is one of the largest, containing over 1500 genera and 22,000 species. The minute individual flowers are crowded together into a head called a capitulum, which behaves as a single entity, often with petal-like rays on the outer, or all the flowers. Each flower produced a 1 seed, often topped by a pappus, which is either feathery to aid distribution by wind, or has barbed spines which stick to the coats of animals. The family is most closely related to the Campanulaceae (see Volume 2), which has a similar arrangement of style and stamens, the stamens forming a tube around the style, the pollen being presented on hairs on the outside of the style. Campanulaceae, however, has numerous small seeds, not the 1 seed per flower of the Compositae. The genus *Senecio* is one of the largest in the family, with many weedy species such as ragwort, *S. jacobaea* L.

Ecology and Geography In mainly open habitats worldwide.

Comment A few species are grown as ornamentals; *S. cineraria* DC from southern Europe is a low shrub, grown for its silvery leaves.

Brachyglottis monroi
seed heads and leaves
½ life size, July 28th

Senecio cineraria
½ life size, August 10th

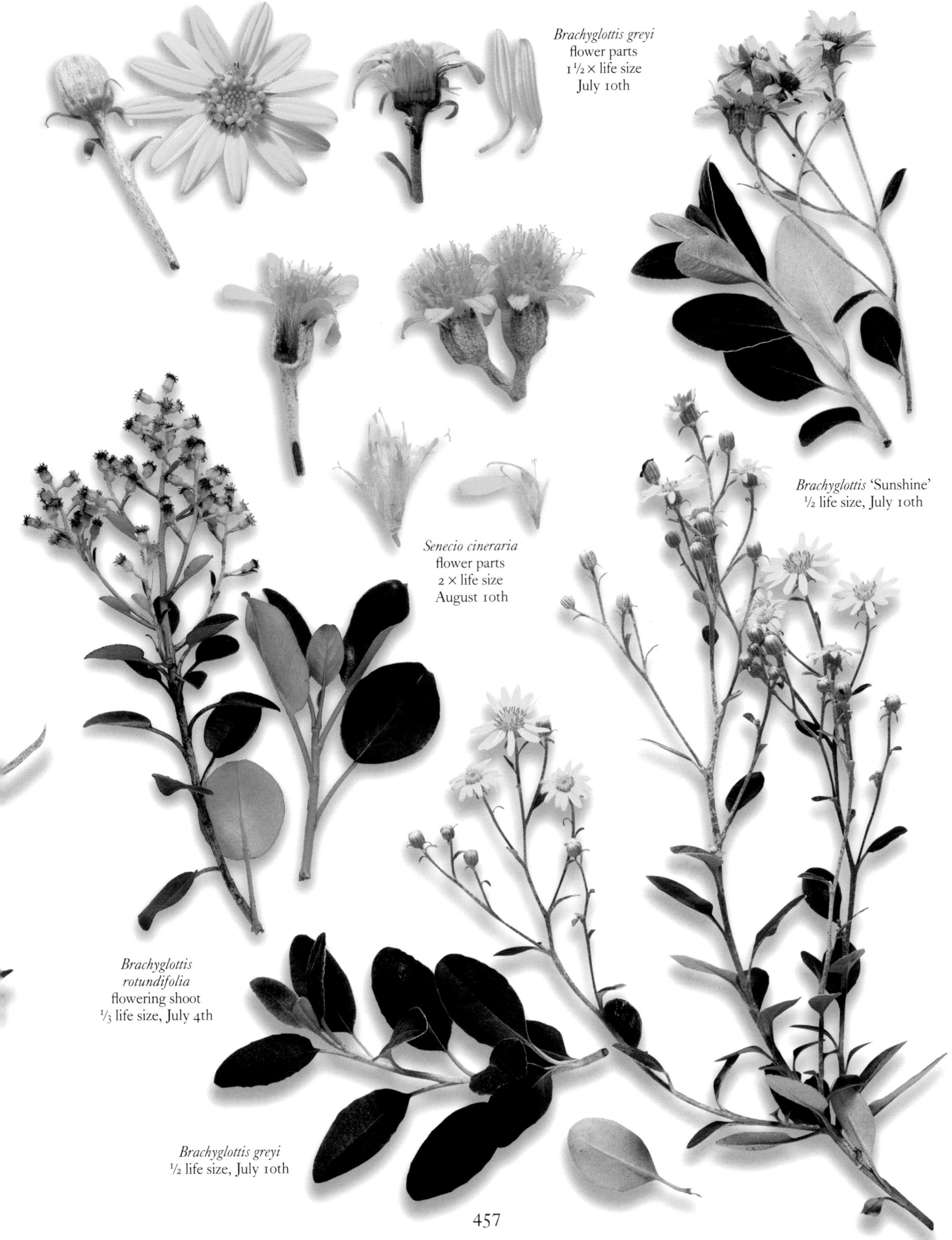

COMPOSITAE

Brachyglottis greyi
flower parts
1 ½ × life size
July 10th

Brachyglottis 'Sunshine'
½ life size, July 10th

Senecio cineraria
flower parts
2 × life size
August 10th

Brachyglottis
rotundifolia
flowering shoot
⅓ life size, July 4th

Brachyglottis greyi
½ life size, July 10th

Euryops

Euryops (Cass.) Cass. (1818), in the family Compositae, contains around 97 species in Africa and the Arabian Peninsula.

Description Shrubs to 3m. The leaves are often divided, alternate, spirally arranged and concentrated at the tips of the shoots. The flowerheads are usually yellow, solitary or in loose clusters. Phyllaries in 1–3 rows. Ray florets usually female or absent. Stamens 5. Ovary inferior, with 1 cell and 1 ovule; style 1, forked, not flattened towards the tips. Pollination is by insects. The fruits are 1-seeded, topped by a pappus of white or brown bristles, or the pappus absent.

Key Recognition Features The yellow, daisy-like flowers and the toothed or divided leaves concentrated at the tips of the shoots.

Evolution and Relationships *Euryops* is related to *Senecio* (see pp.456–57), but differs in having usually solitary flowers and a pappus of bristles rather than hairs.

Ecology and Geography In mainly open habitats, with 46 species in the Cape region of South Africa and others northwards to the island of Socotra and the southern Arabian Peninsula.

Comment A few species are grown as ornamentals, notably *E. pectinatus* (L.) Cass., a shrub with deeply divided leaves that is widely planted in California, and *E. acraeus* M. D. Henderson, a dwarf and almost hardy shrublet from the high Drakensberg with silvery, 3-toothed leaves.

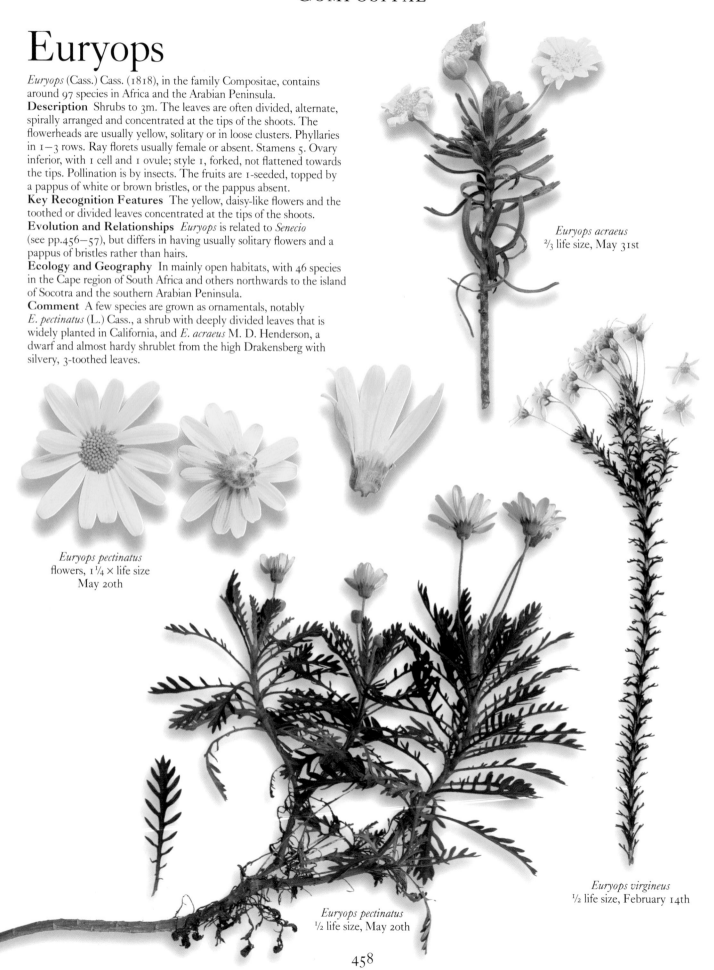

Euryops acraeus
²/₃ life size, May 31st

Euryops pectinatus
flowers, 1¼ × life size
May 20th

Euryops virgineus
½ life size, February 14th

Euryops pectinatus
½ life size, May 20th

Cassinia

Cassinia R. Br. (1817), in the family Compositae, contains around 21 species in Australia and New Zealand.

Description Shrubs to 5m. The leaves are small and often heath-like (see *Erica* pp.210–11), alternate, sometimes yellowish or whitish, crowded and often sticky. The flowerheads are small and white, in dense, flat clusters. Phyllaries in several rows, papery. Ray florets usually absent. Stamens 5. Ovary inferior, with 1 cell and 1 ovule; style 1, forked, short. Pollination is presumed to be by insects. The fruits are 1-seeded, topped by a pappus of slender bristles.

Key Recognition Features The small, often sticky leaves and small, white, papery flowers concentrated at the tops of the shoots.

Evolution and Relationships *Cassinia* is related to *Helichrysum* Mill., and both have papery outer phyllaries, familiar in "everlasting" flowers such as *Bracteantha bracteata* (Vent.) Anderb. & Haegi. It is particularly close to *Ozothamnus* R. Br., which contains 53 species in Australia, New Caledonia, and New Zealand; whereas *Cassinia* is generally aromatic and has a receptacle with scales and the tips of the phyllaries straight or incurved, *Ozothamnus* is generally not aromatic and has the receptacle without scales and the tips of the phyllaries curved outwards. Another closely related shrub, *Tenrhynea phylicifolia* (DC) Hilliard & Burtt, syn. *Cassinia phylicifolia* (DC) Wood, is found in Natal, and is probably the source of records of *Cassinia* in Africa.

Ecology and Geography In mainly open scrub and heathland and on coastal hills in Australia and New Zealand.

Comment *Cassinia leptophylla* (Forst. fil.) R. Br. and several species of *Ozothamnus* are often cultivated. The genus *Cassinia* is named after Viscomte Alexandre Henri Gabriel Cassini, (1781–1832) a French botanist.

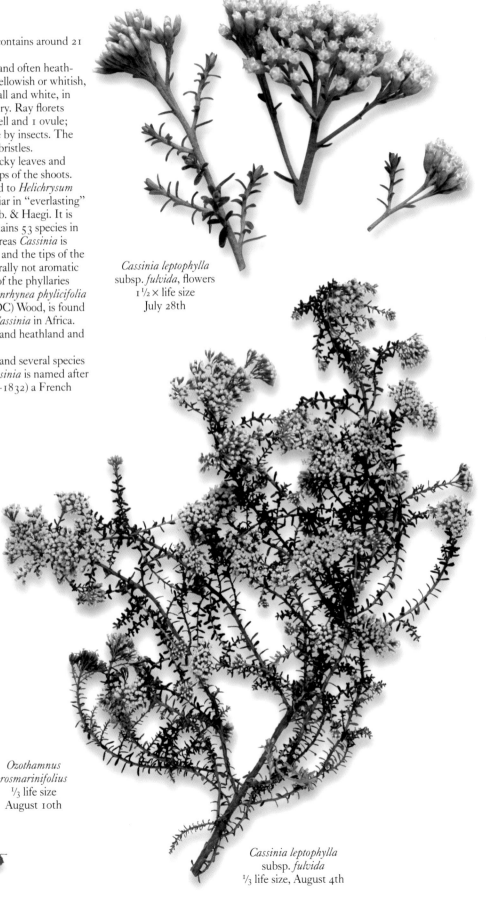

Cassinia leptophylla
subsp. *fulvida*, flowers
1 ½ × life size
July 28th

*Ozothamnus
rosmarinifolius*
⅓ life size
August 10th

Cassinia leptophylla
subsp. *fulvida*
⅓ life size, August 4th

Ageratina

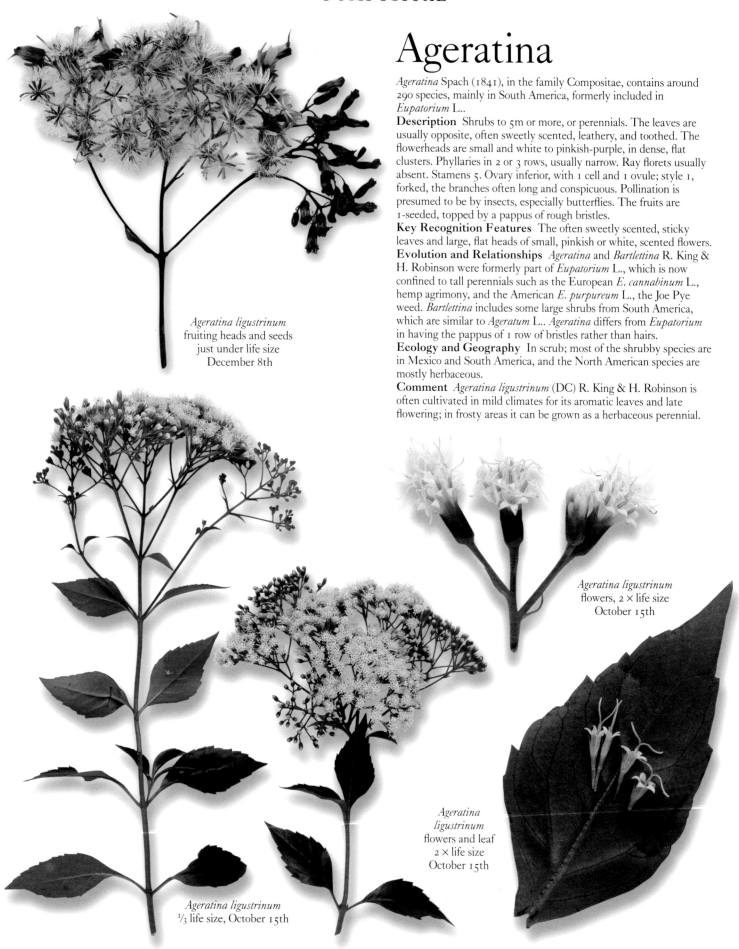

Ageratina Spach (1841), in the family Compositae, contains around 290 species, mainly in South America, formerly included in *Eupatorium* L..

Description Shrubs to 5m or more, or perennials. The leaves are usually opposite, often sweetly scented, leathery, and toothed. The flowerheads are small and white to pinkish-purple, in dense, flat clusters. Phyllaries in 2 or 3 rows, usually narrow. Ray florets usually absent. Stamens 5. Ovary inferior, with 1 cell and 1 ovule; style 1, forked, the branches often long and conspicuous. Pollination is presumed to be by insects, especially butterflies. The fruits are 1-seeded, topped by a pappus of rough bristles.

Key Recognition Features The often sweetly scented, sticky leaves and large, flat heads of small, pinkish or white, scented flowers.

Evolution and Relationships *Ageratina* and *Bartlettina* R. King & H. Robinson were formerly part of *Eupatorium* L., which is now confined to tall perennials such as the European *E. cannabinum* L., hemp agrimony, and the American *E. purpureum* L., the Joe Pye weed. *Bartlettina* includes some large shrubs from South America, which are similar to *Ageratum* L.. *Ageratina* differs from *Eupatorium* in having the pappus of 1 row of bristles rather than hairs.

Ecology and Geography In scrub; most of the shrubby species are in Mexico and South America, and the North American species are mostly herbaceous.

Comment *Ageratina ligustrinum* (DC) R. King & H. Robinson is often cultivated in mild climates for its aromatic leaves and late flowering; in frosty areas it can be grown as a herbaceous perennial.

Ageratina ligustrinum
fruiting heads and seeds
just under life size
December 8th

Ageratina ligustrinum
flowers, 2 × life size
October 15th

Ageratina ligustrinum
flowers and leaf
2 × life size
October 15th

Ageratina ligustrinum
⅓ life size, October 15th

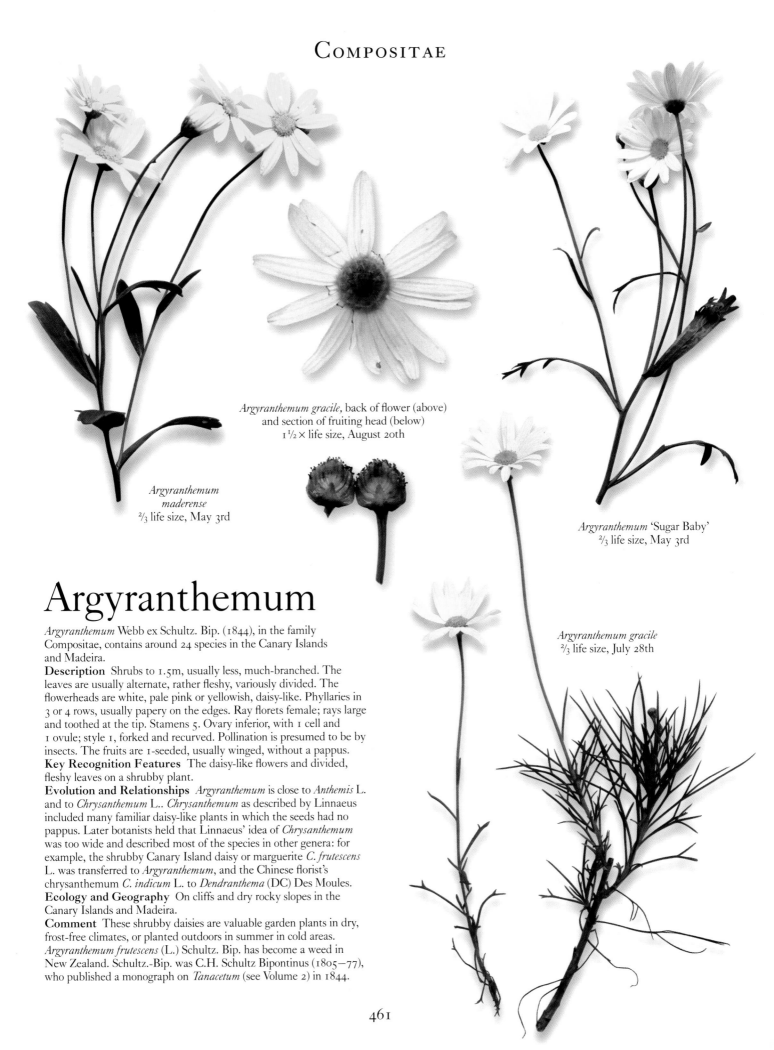

Argyranthemum gracile, back of flower (above)
and section of fruiting head (below)
1½ × life size, August 20th

*Argyranthemum
maderense*
⅔ life size, May 3rd

Argyranthemum 'Sugar Baby'
⅔ life size, May 3rd

Argyranthemum gracile
⅔ life size, July 28th

Argyranthemum

Argyranthemum Webb ex Schultz. Bip. (1844), in the family
Compositae, contains around 24 species in the Canary Islands
and Madeira.

Description Shrubs to 1.5m, usually less, much-branched. The
leaves are usually alternate, rather fleshy, variously divided. The
flowerheads are white, pale pink or yellowish, daisy-like. Phyllaries in
3 or 4 rows, usually papery on the edges. Ray florets female; rays large
and toothed at the tip. Stamens 5. Ovary inferior, with 1 cell and
1 ovule; style 1, forked and recurved. Pollination is presumed to be by
insects. The fruits are 1-seeded, usually winged, without a pappus.

Key Recognition Features The daisy-like flowers and divided,
fleshy leaves on a shrubby plant.

Evolution and Relationships *Argyranthemum* is close to *Anthemis* L.
and to *Chrysanthemum* L.. *Chrysanthemum* as described by Linnaeus
included many familiar daisy-like plants in which the seeds had no
pappus. Later botanists held that Linnaeus' idea of *Chrysanthemum*
was too wide and described most of the species in other genera: for
example, the shrubby Canary Island daisy or marguerite *C. frutescens*
L. was transferred to *Argyranthemum*, and the Chinese florist's
chrysanthemum *C. indicum* L. to *Dendranthema* (DC) Des Moules.

Ecology and Geography On cliffs and dry rocky slopes in the
Canary Islands and Madeira.

Comment These shrubby daisies are valuable garden plants in dry,
frost-free climates, or planted outdoors in summer in cold areas.
Argyranthemum frutescens (L.) Schultz. Bip. has become a weed in
New Zealand. Schultz.-Bip. was C.H. Schultz Bipontinus (1805–77),
who published a monograph on *Tanacetum* (see Volume 2) in 1844.

COMPOSITAE

Santolina

Santolina L. (1753), in the family Compositae, contains around 5 species in the western Mediterranean area.

Description Shrubs to 50cm, usually less, rounded and much branched. The leaves are very aromatic, alternate, with short, narrow segments, sometimes in 4 rows, whitish or green. The flowerheads are yellowish or whitish, rounded, without rays. Phyllaries in 3 or 4 rows, usually papery on the edges. Florets all bisexual. Stamens 5. Ovary inferior, with 1 cell and 1 ovule; style 1, forked and recurved. Pollination is presumed to be by insects. The fruits are 1-seeded, usually angled, without a pappus.

Key Recognition Features The narrow, divided, aromatic leaves on a rounded bush, and the yellow or white, rayless flowerheads.

Evolution and Relationships *Santolina* is close to *Achillea* (yarrow, see Volume 2). The number of species recognised varies with the opinion of the author, from around 5 to as many as 18.

Ecology and Geography On cliffs and dry, rocky slopes in the Mediterranean area from Portugal to Italy, but with most species in Spain.

Comment *Santolina* are popular shrubs for dry, rocky slopes and walls. The aromatic leaves were used as an insecticide, and the grey-leaved *S. chamaecyparissus* L. is still commonly called cotton lavender.

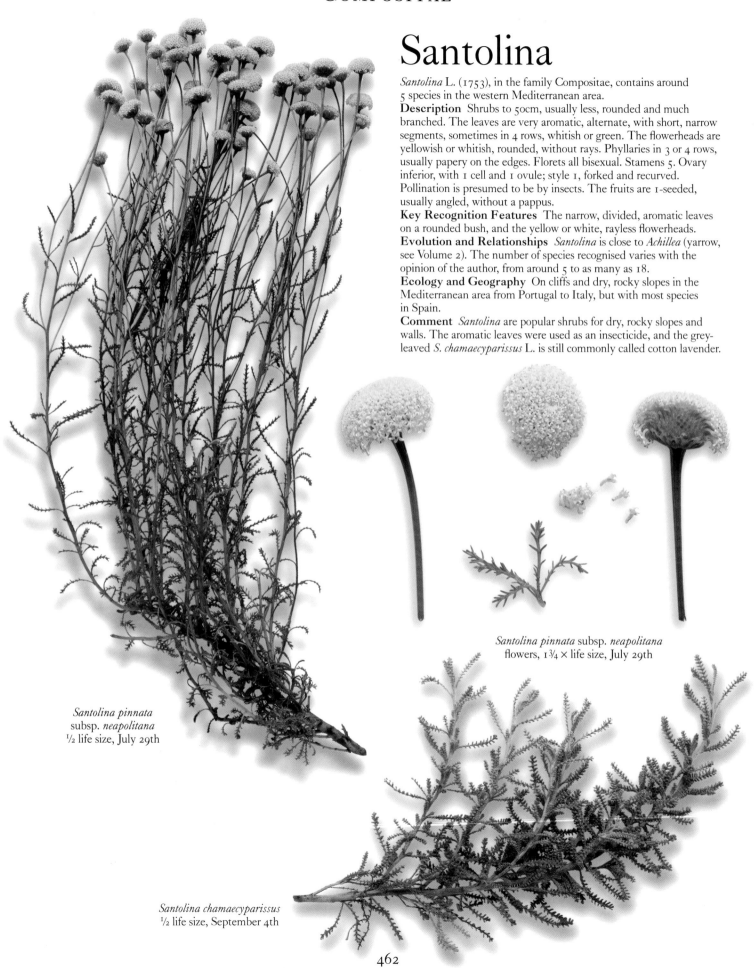

Santolina pinnata subsp. *neapolitana*
flowers, 1¾ × life size, July 29th

Santolina pinnata
subsp. *neapolitana*
½ life size, July 29th

Santolina chamaecyparissus
½ life size, September 4th

Artemisia absinthium
flowerheads
1¾ × life size
September 4th

Artemisia 'Powis Castle'
½ life size, September 4th

Artemisia

Artemisia L. (1753), sagebrush, in the family Compositae, contains around 350 species mainly in dry parts of the northern hemisphere.

Description Shrubs to 2m, usually less. The leaves are very aromatic, alternate, often with long, narrow segments, usually greyish or silvery, hairy. The flowerheads are greenish or brownish, without rays. Phyllaries in 1 or 2 rows, usually papery on the edges. Florets all bisexual, or the outer sometimes female. Stamens 5. Ovary inferior, with 1 cell and 1 ovule; style 1, forked and recurved. Pollination is by wind. The fruits are 1-seeded, usually flattened or ribbed, and without a pappus.

Key Recognition Features The greyish, divided, aromatic leaves on a rounded bush with small flowerheads.

Evolution and Relationships *Artemisia* is related to the florists' chrysanthemum *Dendranthema* (DC) Des Moules.

Ecology and Geography On cliffs and dry slopes, often dominant in cold, semi-desert areas; many species are salt-tolerant and found in coastal habitats. The range is mainly in North America and Asia, with 1 species in South Africa.

Comment Several species and many cultivars are grown for ornament. The cultivar 'Powis Castle' is probably a hybrid of the Mediterranean *A. arborescens* L.. The herb tarragon is *A. dracunculus* L., a herbaceous species with narrow, almost undivided leaves. *Artemisia absinthium* L. is used to flavour absinthe.

Artemisia absinthium
½ life size
September 4th

Trachycarpus

Trachycarpus Wendland (1861), in the family Palmae or Arecaceae, contains around 6 species in eastern Asia.

Description Trees to 20m, usually with fibrous leaf sheaths covering the unbranched trunk. The leaves are fan-shaped, divided to the middle or almost to the base. The flowers are produced in large, hanging sprays among the leaves; individual flowers small, yellow, unisexual or bisexual. Sepals 3; petals 3. Stamens 6; ovary superior, with 3 cells and 3 styles. Pollination is presumed to be by wind. The fruits are 1-seeded, rounded, bluish when ripe.

Key Recognition Features The fan-shaped leaves and usually shaggy trunk.

Evolution and Relationships *Trachycarpus* is close to the European *Chamaerops* L., which is usually short-stemmed and suckering and has strongly spiny leaf stalks.

Ecology and Geography In forest and on open slopes in the Himalayas and China.

Comment *Trachycarpus fortunei* (Hook.) Wendland is the most common frost-hardy palm, often planted in the milder parts of western Europe as well as in China, where the fibrous leaf sheaths are used to make capes. The much rarer *T. martianus* (Wall.) Wendland has a smooth trunk. *Trithrinax* C. Martius, from temperate South America, is now being imported to Europe; some species will tolerate 10°C of frost without damage.

Trachycarpus fortunei
fruits and seeds, 2 × life size
December 15th

Trachycarpus fortunei
fruits, just under life size
December 15th

Palmae

Trachycarpus fortunei
½ life size
November 29th

Trachycarpus fortunei
flowers, ½ life size
May 18th

465

Yucca

Yucca L. (1753), in the family Agavaceae, contains around 30 species in North America.

Description Trees to 15m, or shrubs, sometimes stemless and suckering. Leaves sword-shaped, usually stiff and ending in a sharp spine. Flowers in tall, upright sprays; individual flowers large, white or purplish, bisexual, nodding. Sepals and petals similar, 6, waxy. Stamens 6, with small, short anthers. Ovary superior, with 3 cells and 1 thick style. Pollination is by moths. The fruits are capsules, sometimes fleshy, with numerous flat, black seeds.

Key Recognition Features The stiff, sword-shaped leaves on a thick trunk, and the white, hanging flowers.

Evolution and Relationships *Yucca* is related to *Agave* L., which has yellow, green, or brownish flowers and an inferior ovary, and to the large succulents *Furcraea* Vent. and *Beschorneria* Kunth. The pollination of *Yucca* is unusually specialised; the flowers are visited by the female of the yucca moth, *Tegeticula,* which collects pollen from the reduced anthers and carries it in special tentacles under her head. She then visits another flower, and if it is at a suitable stage, lays an egg among the young ovules, before stuffing the pollen into a cavity in the stigma of the flower; 1 egg is generally laid in each cell, and the stigma is pollinated each time. She then collects more pollen before moving on to the next flower. The developing larvae eat some of the seeds at the apical end of the capsule, which develop abnormally, but leave the lower seeds to develop normally. One species of *Tegeticula* pollinates yuccas east of the Rockies; another species pollinates *Y. whipplei* Torr., which has glutinous pollen, and another, which looks more like a sawfly, pollinates the tall, desert species *Y. brevifolia* Englm.

Ecology and Geography In deserts, on dunes, and in other open, sandy places in western North America northwards as far as Monterey County in California, and in eastern North America, on the coast northwards as far as Maryland.

Comment Several yuccas are grown for ornament, both for their spectacular, branching spikes of flowers and, in cultivars of some species, for their striped leaves.

Yucca recurvifolia
1/3 life size, August 31st

Yucca recurvifolia
flowers, 3/4 life size
August 31st

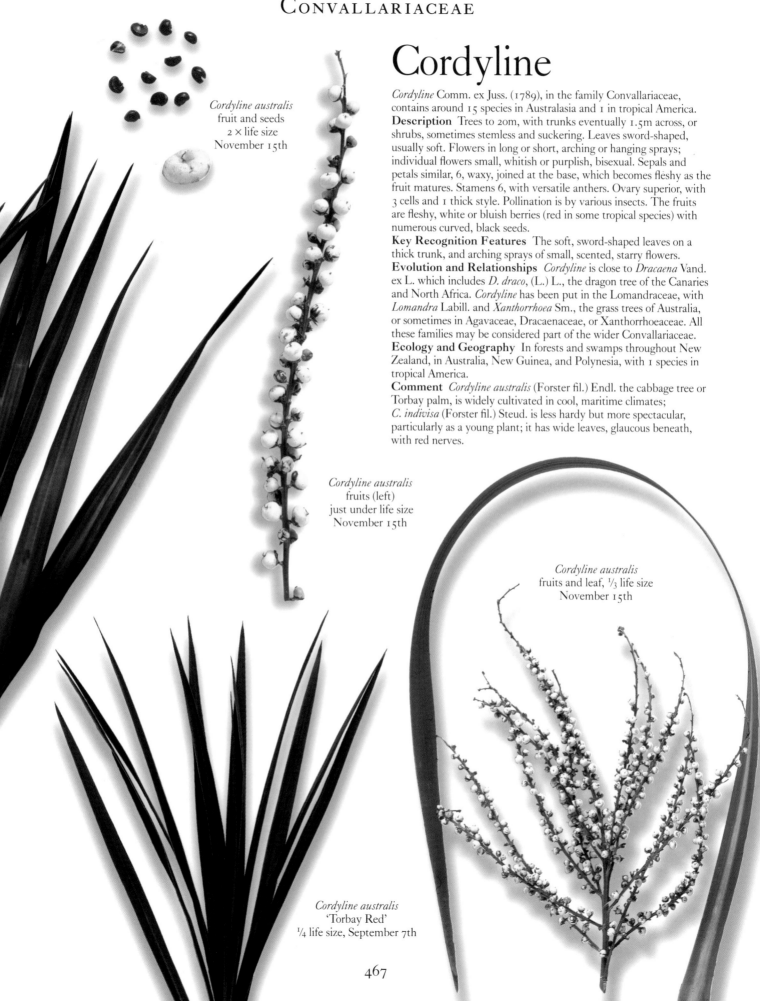

Cordyline

Cordyline australis
fruit and seeds
2 × life size
November 15th

Cordyline Comm. ex Juss. (1789), in the family Convallariaceae, contains around 15 species in Australasia and 1 in tropical America.
Description Trees to 20m, with trunks eventually 1.5m across, or shrubs, sometimes stemless and suckering. Leaves sword-shaped, usually soft. Flowers in long or short, arching or hanging sprays; individual flowers small, whitish or purplish, bisexual. Sepals and petals similar, 6, waxy, joined at the base, which becomes fleshy as the fruit matures. Stamens 6, with versatile anthers. Ovary superior, with 3 cells and 1 thick style. Pollination is by various insects. The fruits are fleshy, white or bluish berries (red in some tropical species) with numerous curved, black seeds.
Key Recognition Features The soft, sword-shaped leaves on a thick trunk, and arching sprays of small, scented, starry flowers.
Evolution and Relationships *Cordyline* is close to *Dracaena* Vand. ex L. which includes *D. draco*, (L.) L., the dragon tree of the Canaries and North Africa. *Cordyline* has been put in the Lomandraceae, with *Lomandra* Labill. and *Xanthorrhoea* Sm., the grass trees of Australia, or sometimes in Agavaceae, Dracaenaceae, or Xanthorrhoeaceae. All these families may be considered part of the wider Convallariaceae.
Ecology and Geography In forests and swamps throughout New Zealand, in Australia, New Guinea, and Polynesia, with 1 species in tropical America.
Comment *Cordyline australis* (Forster fil.) Endl. the cabbage tree or Torbay palm, is widely cultivated in cool, maritime climates; *C. indivisa* (Forster fil.) Steud. is less hardy but more spectacular, particularly as a young plant; it has wide leaves, glaucous beneath, with red nerves.

Cordyline australis
fruits (left)
just under life size
November 15th

Cordyline australis
fruits and leaf, 1/3 life size
November 15th

Cordyline australis
'Torbay Red'
1/4 life size, September 7th

Danae racemosa
flowers, 2 × life size
June 23rd

Danae

Danae Medik. (1787), in the family Convallariaceae, contains
1 species in southwestern Asia.

Description Slender shrub to 2m, with tough green stems. Leaves
reduced to scales, but replaced by lanceolate cladodes (flattened
branchlets). Flowers small and hanging in a short spike at the top of
the stem, green and globose. Sepals and petals similar, fleshy, reduced
to 6 lobes. Stamens 6. Ovary superior, with 1 or 2 cells and 1 short
style. Pollination mechanism is unknown, but the flowers are probably
self-pollinated. The fruits are fleshy, red berries with usually 1 seed.

Key Recognition Features The flat, shiny, leaf-like cladodes and
spikes of small, round, green flowers.

Evolution and Relationships The *Liliaceae*, which included nearly
all genera with 6 stamens and an inferior ovary, is now divided into
several smaller families, the exact delimitation of which is still being
studied. One is Convallariaceae, with berries with few seeds and
without the black skin found in other groups, distinctions supported
by DNA evidence. *Danae* is close to *Ruscus* and to *Semele* Kunth, a
robust, twining climber from the Canary Islands and Madeira, which
has small groups of flowers on the margins of the cladodes.

Ecology and Geography In oak woods in the Amanus Mountains
in southern Turkey and in adjacent Syria; also in northern Iran and
the Talish Mountains.

Comment An unusual evergreen, long cultivated in Turkey and the
rest of southern Europe, as well as in old gardens in the southeastern
United States.

Danae racemosa
½ life size, June 23rd

Ruscus

Ruscus L. (1753), in the family Convallariaceae, contains 6 species in the Atlantic islands, Europe, and southwestern Asia.

Description Low shrubs to 50cm, with tough, green stems. Leaves reduced to scales, but replaced by cladodes (flattened branchlets), which are sometimes stiff and end in a sharp spine. Flowers small, greenish, in small clusters on the surface of the cladodes, usually unisexual, with the males and females on different plants. Sepals and petals similar, 6. Stamens 3, with the filaments joined. Ovary superior, with 1 or 2 cells and 1 short style. Pollination is presumed to be by insects. The fruits are large, fleshy, red berries with 1–4 seeds.

Key Recognition Features The flat, shiny, leaf-like cladodes with flowers on the upper or lower surface.

Evolution and Relationships *Ruscus* is close to *Danae* (see for more detail on the Convallariaceae) and to *Semele* Kunth.

Ecology and Geography In dry woods from England and the Azores to northwestern Africa, the Caucasus, and northern Iran.

Comment *Ruscus aculeatus* L. is the spiny butcher's broom, often cultivated; only hermaphrodite clones have a good number of berries.

Ruscus aculeatus
flowers, fruit, and seeds
2¼ × life size, April 9th

Ruscus aculeatus
½ life size, April 9th

SMILACACEAE

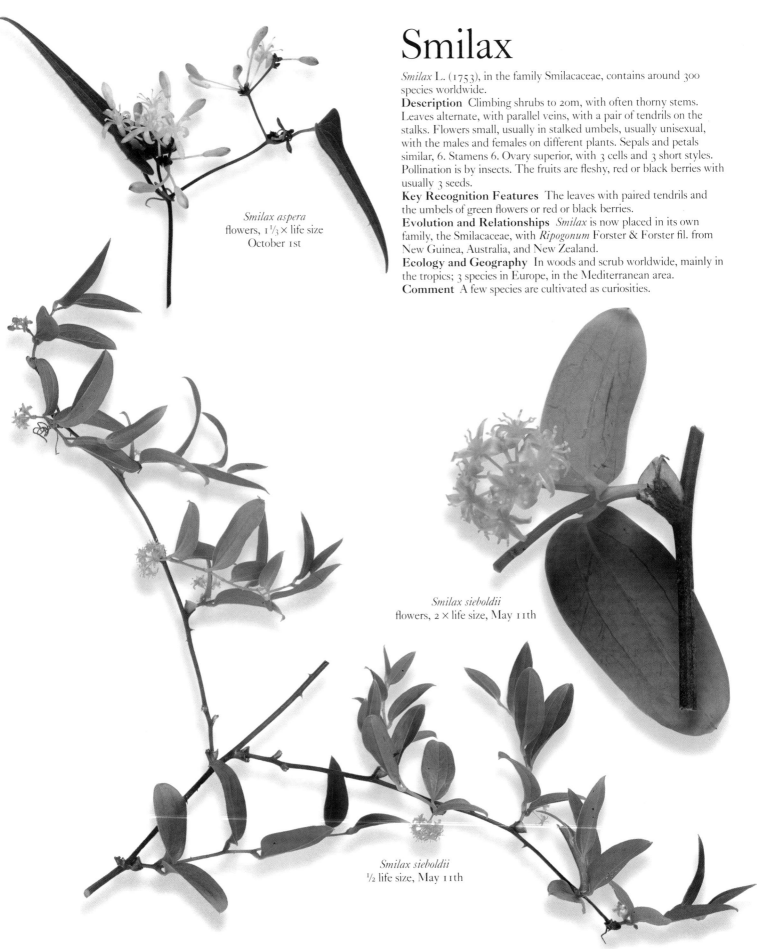

Smilax

Smilax L. (1753), in the family Smilacaceae, contains around 300 species worldwide.

Description Climbing shrubs to 20m, with often thorny stems. Leaves alternate, with parallel veins, with a pair of tendrils on the stalks. Flowers small, usually in stalked umbels, usually unisexual, with the males and females on different plants. Sepals and petals similar, 6. Stamens 6. Ovary superior, with 3 cells and 3 short styles. Pollination is by insects. The fruits are fleshy, red or black berries with usually 3 seeds.

Key Recognition Features The leaves with paired tendrils and the umbels of green flowers or red or black berries.

Evolution and Relationships *Smilax* is now placed in its own family, the Smilacaceae, with *Ripogonum* Forster & Forster fil. from New Guinea, Australia, and New Zealand.

Ecology and Geography In woods and scrub worldwide, mainly in the tropics; 3 species in Europe, in the Mediterranean area.

Comment A few species are cultivated as curiosities.

Smilax aspera
flowers, 1⅓ × life size
October 1st

Smilax sieboldii
flowers, 2 × life size, May 11th

Smilax sieboldii
½ life size, May 11th

Lapageria

Lapageria Ruíz. & Pavón (1802), in the family Philesiaceae, contains 1 species, *L. rosea* Ruíz & Pavón, in South America.

Description Twining climber to 5m, stems very tough at the base. Leaves oval, stiff. Flowers large and tubular, hanging, solitary or a few together in the leaf axils, crimson, more rarely pink or white, sometimes slightly tessellated. Sepals and petals similar, 6, waxy, with thick, sticky nectar at the base. Stamens 6, reaching the mouth of the flower. Ovary superior, with 3 cells and 1 thick, 3-lobed style. Pollination is by hummingbirds. The fruits are fleshy, green capsules with round, whitish seeds.

Key Recognition Features The large, waxy, hanging, bell-shaped flowers on a twining plant.

Evolution and Relationships *Lapageria* is close to the dwarf *Philesia magellanica* Gmel. from southern Chile, and the two have been hybridised in cultivation to form × *Philageria veitchii* Masters, which first flowered in 1872, and forms a scrambling shrub. Also sometimes included in the Philesiaceae is the suckering herb *Luzuragia* Ruíz & Pavón, which has 1 species, *Luzuragia parviflora* (Hook. fil.) Kunth, in New Zealand and 3, including *Luzuragia radicans* Ruíz & Pavón, in South America.

Ecology and Geography In warm temperate rainforests in Chile and southwestern Argentina.

Comment This is one of the most spectacular of all temperate climbers, the *copihue*, the national flower of Chile. It is named after the Empress Joséphine (1763–1814), wife of Napoleon Bonaparte, whose maiden name was Joséphine Tascher de la Pagerie.

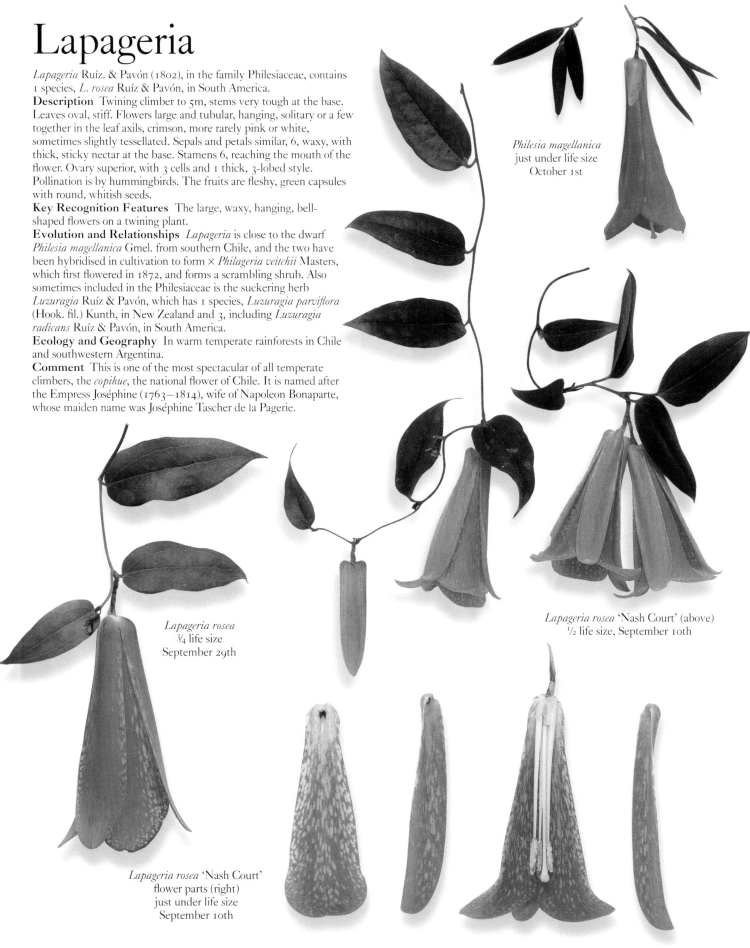

Philesia magellanica
just under life size
October 1st

Lapageria rosea
¾ life size
September 29th

Lapageria rosea 'Nash Court' (above)
½ life size, September 10th

Lapageria rosea 'Nash Court'
flower parts (right)
just under life size
September 10th

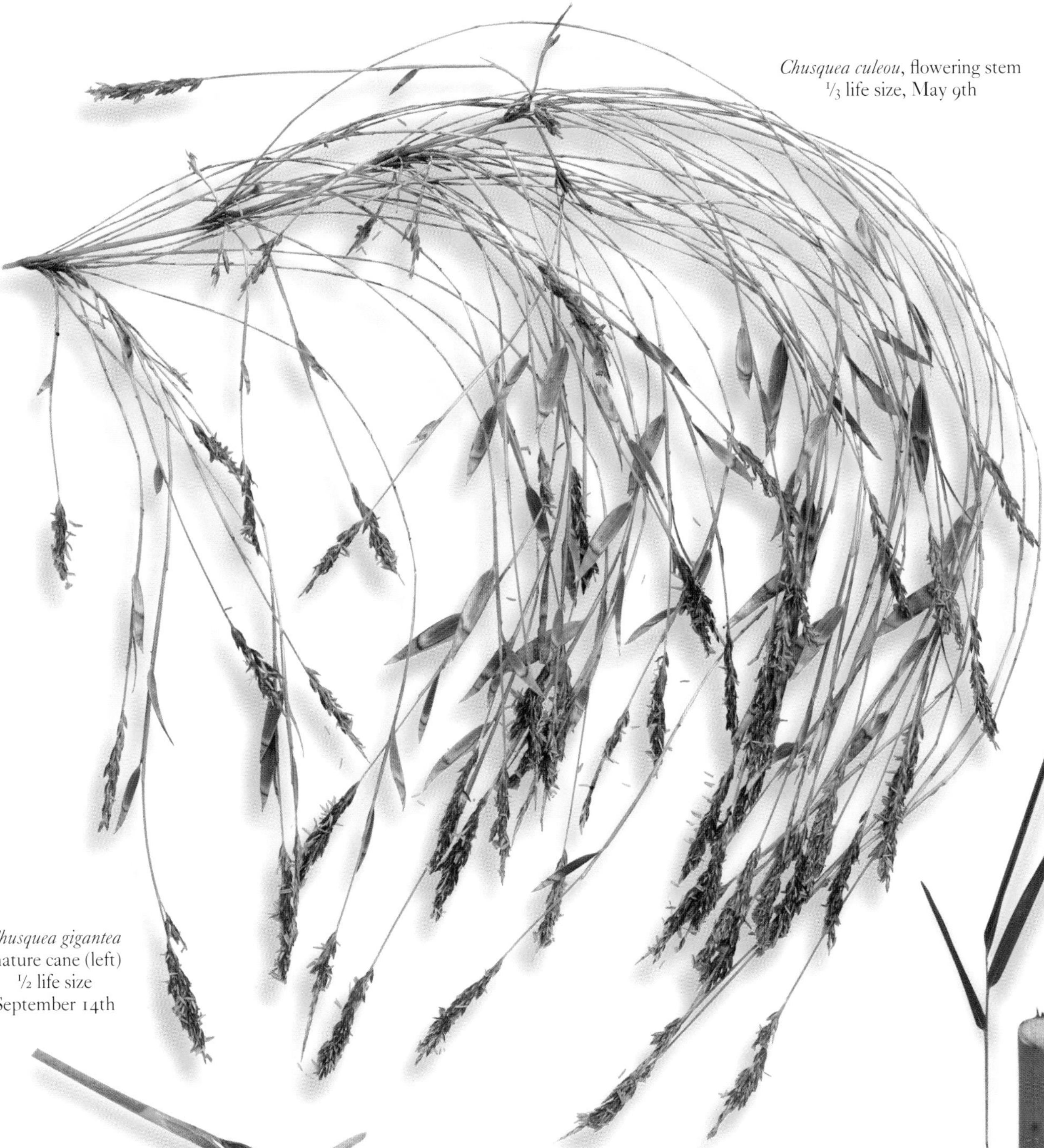

GRAMINEAE

Chusquea culeou, flowering stem
⅓ life size, May 9th

Chusquea gigantea
mature cane (left)
½ life size
September 14th

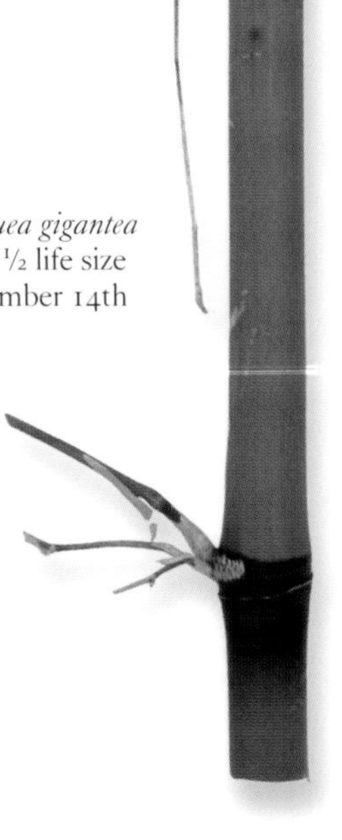

Chusquea gigantea
cane, ½ life size
September 14th

Chusquea culeou pair of florets (left), inflorescence (middle),
and branch (right), 2 × life size, May 9th

472

Chusquea

Chusquea Kunth (1803), in the family Gramineae (sometimes called Poaceae) subfamily Bambusoideae, contains around 120 species in tropical and South America.

Description Stems to 6m in the hardy species, much more in tropical ones, solid with a pithy centre, forming dense clumps of usually yellowish stems. Sheaths persistent. Branches numerous at each node. Leaves small, around 5–10cm long. Bamboo flowers are similar to those of grasses. The inflorescences are made up of spikelets, each with 2 glumes (small bracts) at the base and a few flowers or florets. The florets are each enclosed by further bract-like structures, a palea (outer) and lemma (inner). Sepals and petals are absent or reduced to the small scales, called lodicules, that push apart the palea and lemma to allow the stamens and stigmas to protrude. The usually 3 stamens have very fine filaments which support hinged or versatile anthers. The superior ovary has 1 cell and usually 2 feathery stigmas. Pollination is by wind. The fruits are slender, with 1 seed.

Key Recognition Features The clumps of usually arching stems with short internodes and pith-filled canes.

Evolution and Relationships The bamboos are a distinct subfamily of the grasses, Gramineae. They are found throughout the tropics (though only a few are found in Australia), and in moist temperate areas in Asia and South America, but are particularly diverse in China and Japan. The genera are often difficult to differentiate, a situation complicated by the fact that some so-called species appear to be hybrids between genera. Flowering is sporadic, and there is a tendency for most of the plants of a species to flower within a few years of one another; these mass flowerings may occur as rarely as once in 100 years. Plants are weakened after flowering and often die, but generally set masses of seed.

Ecology and Geography In wet forests from Mexico southwards to Chile.

Comment The commonly cultivated species of *Chusquea*, *C. culeou* Desv., is one of the most elegant and easily manage of garden bamboos, forming a neat clump of arching stems. Some of the subtropical Mexican species have spectacular pendulous canes several metres long. Many plants of *Chusquea culeou* flowered in the late 1990s.

Chusquea culeou
½ life size, August 17th

Chusquea culeou
cane cross-section and leaves
life size, August 17th

Chusquea culeou
cane with sheath
life size, August 17th

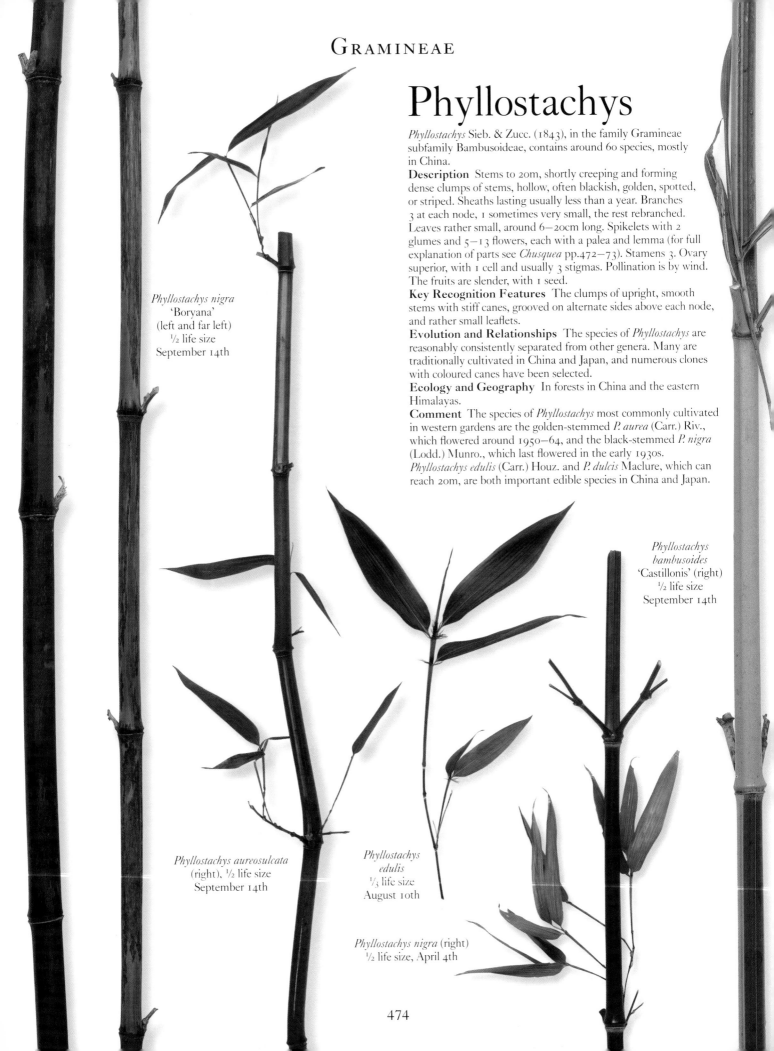

Phyllostachys

Phyllostachys Sieb. & Zucc. (1843), in the family Gramineae subfamily Bambusoideae, contains around 60 species, mostly in China.

Description Stems to 20m, shortly creeping and forming dense clumps of stems, hollow, often blackish, golden, spotted, or striped. Sheaths lasting usually less than a year. Branches 3 at each node, 1 sometimes very small, the rest rebranched. Leaves rather small, around 6–20cm long. Spikelets with 2 glumes and 5–13 flowers, each with a palea and lemma (for full explanation of parts see *Chusquea* pp.472–73). Stamens 3. Ovary superior, with 1 cell and usually 3 stigmas. Pollination is by wind. The fruits are slender, with 1 seed.

Key Recognition Features The clumps of upright, smooth stems with stiff canes, grooved on alternate sides above each node, and rather small leaflets.

Evolution and Relationships The species of *Phyllostachys* are reasonably consistently separated from other genera. Many are traditionally cultivated in China and Japan, and numerous clones with coloured canes have been selected.

Ecology and Geography In forests in China and the eastern Himalayas.

Comment The species of *Phyllostachys* most commonly cultivated in western gardens are the golden-stemmed *P. aurea* (Carr.) Riv., which flowered around 1950–64, and the black-stemmed *P. nigra* (Lodd.) Munro., which last flowered in the early 1930s. *Phyllostachys edulis* (Carr.) Houz. and *P. dulcis* Maclure, which can reach 20m, are both important edible species in China and Japan.

Phyllostachys nigra
'Boryana'
(left and far left)
½ life size
September 14th

Phyllostachys bambusoides
'Castillonis' (right)
½ life size
September 14th

Phyllostachys aureosulcata
(right), ½ life size
September 14th

Phyllostachys edulis
⅓ life size
August 10th

Phyllostachys nigra (right)
½ life size, April 4th

Yushania

Yushania Keng. fil. (1957), in the family Gramineae subfamily Bambusoideae, contains around 4 species mostly in China.

Description Plant basically clump-forming, but sometimes far-running and colonising large areas with new clumps. Stems to 10m, graceful and arching when fully grown. Sheaths usually soon falling, sometimes with auricles and bristles. Branches 3 or 5 at each node, developing low down on mature stems. Leaves rather small, usually around 8–15cm long, less than 2cm wide. Spikelets with 2 or 3 glumes and several flowers, each with a palea and lemma (for full explanation of parts see *Chusquea* pp.472–73). Stamens 3 or 6. Ovary superior, with 1 cell and 3 stigmas. Pollination is by wind. The fruits are slender, with 1 seed.

Key Recognition Features Rampant growers with hanging branches.

Evolution and Relationships *Yushania* is close to *Sinarundinaria* Nakai, and is sometimes included in it, but it is often far-spreading.

Ecology and Geography In forests in China, from Taiwan to the northwestern Himalayas.

Comment *Yushania anceps* (Mitford) Yi, syn. *Arundinaria jaunsarensis* Gamble, is often cultivated and can become a nuisance. It was introduced from seed in the 1860s, and flowered again around 1910. The most recent flowering was in the 1960s, and seedlings from that are shown here. The form 'Pitt White' is taller than the usual form, reaching 10m.

Yushania maling
young shoots
½ life size
September 14th

Yushania anceps
⅓ life size, September 14th

Fargesia

Fargesia Franch. (1893), in the family Gramineae subfamily Bambusoideae, contains around 8 species in western China.

Description Stems to 6m, but usually less, hollow, forming dense clumps of often glaucous stems. Sheaths lasting usually less than a year. Branches numerous at each node. Leaves small, around 5–8cm long. Spikelets with 2 glumes and 2–4 flowers, each with a palea and lemma (for full explanation of parts see *Chusquea* pp.472–73). Stamens 3. Ovary superior, with 1 cell and usually 3 stigmas. Pollination is by wind. The fruits are slender, with 1 seed.

Key Recognition Features The clumps of usually arching stems with slender, hollow canes, and small leaflets.

Evolution and Relationships Species now called *Fargesia* are often found under *Sinarundinaria* Nakai or *Thamnocalamus* Munro.

Ecology and Geography In wet forests in western China.

Comment The commonly cultivated species of *Fargesia* are *F. murieliae* (Gamble) Yi and *F. nitida* (Mitford) Keng & Yi. *F.. Fargesia denudata* is a recent introduction by Roy Lancaster, from northwestern Sichuan. Many plants of *F. murieliae* flowered in the early 1990s. Even thin shoots such as those shown here are collected young for eating in western China.

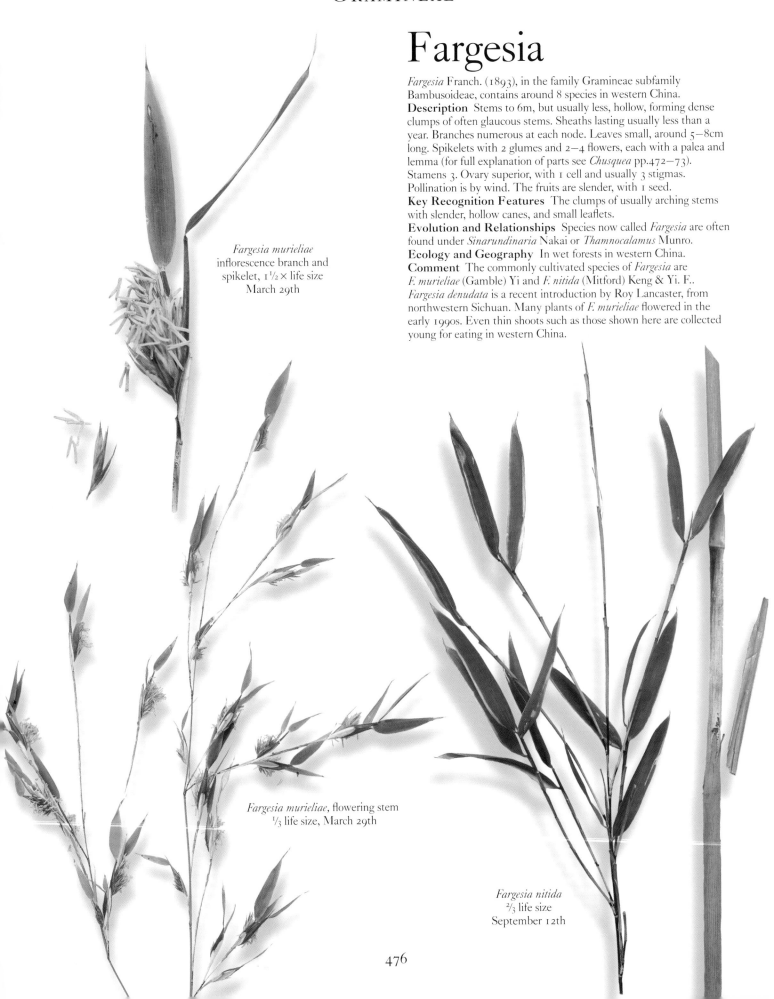

Fargesia murieliae
inflorescence branch and
spikelet, 1½ × life size
March 29th

Fargesia murieliae, flowering stem
⅓ life size, March 29th

Fargesia nitida
⅔ life size
September 12th

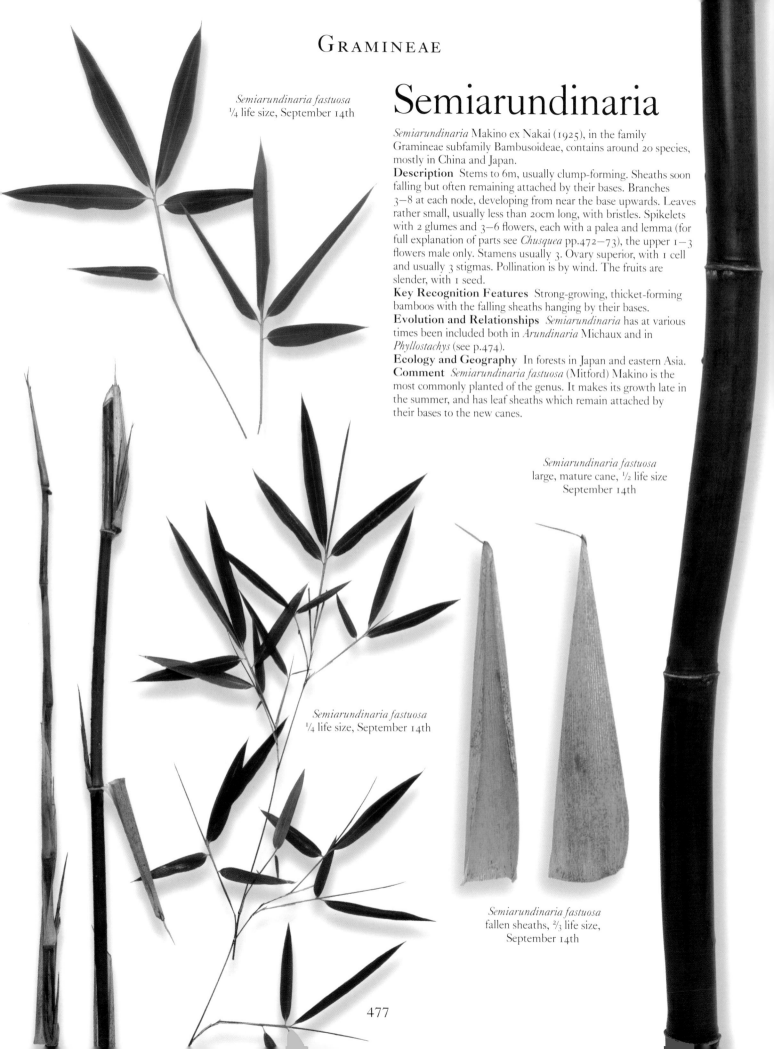

Semiarundinaria fastuosa
¼ life size, September 14th

Semiarundinaria

Semiarundinaria Makino ex Nakai (1925), in the family Gramineae subfamily Bambusoideae, contains around 20 species, mostly in China and Japan.

Description Stems to 6m, usually clump-forming. Sheaths soon falling but often remaining attached by their bases. Branches 3–8 at each node, developing from near the base upwards. Leaves rather small, usually less than 20cm long, with bristles. Spikelets with 2 glumes and 3–6 flowers, each with a palea and lemma (for full explanation of parts see *Chusquea* pp.472–73), the upper 1–3 flowers male only. Stamens usually 3. Ovary superior, with 1 cell and usually 3 stigmas. Pollination is by wind. The fruits are slender, with 1 seed.

Key Recognition Features Strong-growing, thicket-forming bamboos with the falling sheaths hanging by their bases.

Evolution and Relationships *Semiarundinaria* has at various times been included both in *Arundinaria* Michaux and in *Phyllostachys* (see p.474).

Ecology and Geography In forests in Japan and eastern Asia.

Comment *Semiarundinaria fastuosa* (Mitford) Makino is the most commonly planted of the genus. It makes its growth late in the summer, and has leaf sheaths which remain attached by their bases to the new canes.

Semiarundinaria fastuosa
large, mature cane, ½ life size
September 14th

Semiarundinaria fastuosa
¼ life size, September 14th

Semiarundinaria fastuosa
fallen sheaths, ⅔ life size,
September 14th

477

Pleioblastus linearis
cane (left), ²/₃ life size
September 14th

Pleioblastus linearis
spikelets with flowers
2 × life size, August 2nd

Pleioblastus linearis
½ life size, August 2nd

Pleioblastus linearis, flowering branch
½ life size, August 2nd

Pleioblastus

Pleioblastus Nakai (1925), in the family Gramineae subfamily
Bambusoideae, contains around 20 species, mostly in China
and Japan.

Description Stems to 20m, usually long-running, but sometimes
shortly creeping and forming dense clumps of stems, sometimes
almost solid. Sheaths persistent. Branches 1 or 2, or 3—7 at each node.
Leaves medium sized, usually around 15—20cm long. Spikelets with
2 glumes and 5—13 flowers, each with a palea and lemma (for full
explanation of parts see *Chusquea* pp.472—73). Stamens 3. Ovary
superior, with 1 cell and 3 stigmas. Pollination is by wind. The fruits
are slender, with 1 seed.

Key Recognition Features The stems with persistent sheaths, and
often long, narrow leaflets; many of the dwarf, variegated bamboos
are also *Pleioblastus*.

Evolution and Relationships Formerly considered part of
Arundinaria Michaux.

Ecology and Geography In forests in China and Japan.

Comment The most commonly grown species of *Pleioblastus* are
P. auricomus (Mitford) D. McClintock syn. *P. viridi-striatus* (André)
Mak., the narrow-leaved species *P. hindsii* (Munro) Nakai, and
P. linearis (Hack.) Nakai. *Pleioblastus auricomus* has yellowish leaves
striped with green. *Pleioblastus variegatus* (Sieb. ex Mik.) Mak. is a
dwarf with stems to 75cm and striped leaves.

Pleioblastus variegatus
²⁄₃ life size, September 14th

479

Chimonobambusa

Chimonobambusa Makino (1914), in the family Gramineae subfamily Bambusoideae, contains around 10 species, mostly in China and Japan.

Description Stems to 7m, usually short-running, but sometimes far-running, sometimes almost solid, squarish, or with strongly swollen nodes. Sheaths usually soon falling. Branches 3 or more at each node. Leaves small to medium sized, usually around 15–20cm long. Spikelets with up to 2 glumes, sometimes without, and several flowers, each with a palea and lemma (for full explanation of parts see *Chusquea* pp.472–73). Stamens 3. Ovary superior, with 1 cell and 2 stigmas. Pollination is by wind. The fruits are slender, with 1 seed.

Key Recognition Features Many species are notable for their distinctly swollen nodes.

Evolution and Relationships Most species of *Chimonobambusa* were first described in *Arundinaria* Michaux; and the plant formerly grown as *C. hookeriana* (Munro) Nakai is now considered to be a form of *Himalayacalamus falconeri* (Munro) Keng. fil..

Ecology and Geography In forests in China and Japan.

Comment *Chimonobambusa tumidissinoda* has particularly swollen nodes, and its stems are sold as walking sticks to pilgrims on Mount Omei in Sichuan. In cultivation it is very graceful, but far-running when it is established.

Himalayacalamus

Himalayacalamus Keng fil. (1983), in the family Gramineae subfamily Bambusoideae, contains around 2 species, mostly in the Himalayas.

Description Stems to 12m, usually clump-forming. Sheaths rounded at the tip, about equalling the internodes, with a pubescent ligule. Branches around 3 at each node. Leaves medium sized, usually around 15–30cm long. Spikelets with up to 2 glumes, sometimes without, and several flowers, each with a palea and lemma (for full explanation of parts see *Chusquea* pp.472–73). Stamens 3. Ovary superior, with 1 cell and 2 stigmas. Pollination is by wind. The fruits are slender, with 1 seed.

Key Recognition Features The rounded sheaths and pubescent ligule; also a purple-flushed ring below the nodes in *Himalayacalamus falconeri* (Munro) Keng. fil..

Evolution and Relationships Often included in *Drepanostachyum* Keng fil. which is more tropical, or *Thamnocalamus* Munro.

Ecology and Geography In forests in the central and eastern Himalayas.

Comment The plant shown here with its colourful canes (which are even brighter in spring) was formerly grown under the name *H. hookerianus*, a different species; it is now called *H. falconeri* 'Damarapa'.

Chimonobambusa tumidissinoda
½ life size, September 14th

Chimonobambusa tumidissinoda
cane cross-section and leaves
1¼ × life size, August 2nd

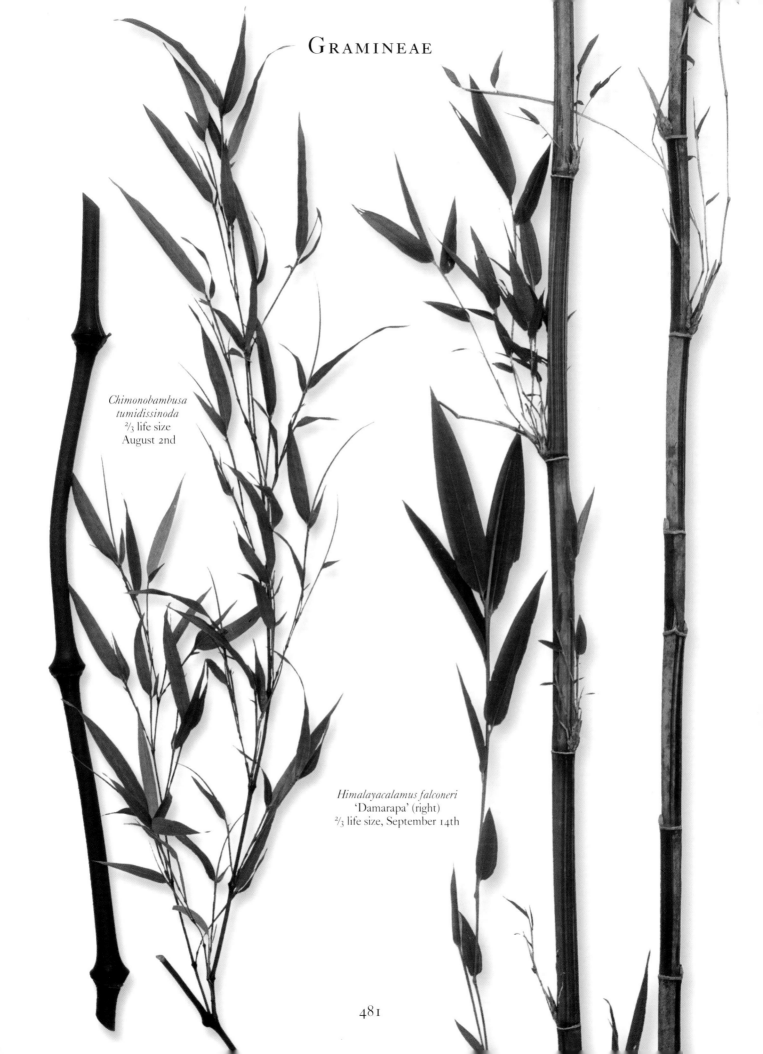

*Chimonobambusa
tumidissinoda*
²/₃ life size
August 2nd

Himalayacalamus falconeri
'Damarapa' (right)
²/₃ life size, September 14th

Sasa palmata
½ life size, September 14th

Sasa palmata 'Nebulosa'
stem (right), ¾ life size
September 14th

Sasa veitchii
stem (right)
½ life size
April 12th

Sasa

Sasa Makino & Shibata (1902), in the family Gramineae subfamily Bambusoideae, contains around 60 species, mostly in Japan.

Description Stems to 4m, mainly far-running and forming extensive thickets. Sheaths usually persistent, shorter than the internodes. Branches 1 or none at each node, as thick as the stems. Leaves large, usually around 20–40cm long, around 3–6cm wide, the undersides ¼ green and ¾ glaucous. Spikelets with 2 glumes and 4–10 flowers, each with a palea and lemma (for full explanation of parts see *Chusquea* pp.472–73). Stamens 6. Ovary superior, with 1 cell and 3 stigmas. Pollination is by wind. The fruits are slender, with 1 seed.

Key Recognition Features Large-leaved, spreading bamboos with slender stems; in the commonly-planted *Sasa veitchii* (Carr.) Rehd. the leaves have a broad white or dead margin.

Evolution and Relationships *Sasa* is related to the smaller genera *Indocalamus* Nakai, *Sasaella* Mak., and *Sasamorpha* Nakai, all of which have only 1 branch at each node.

Ecology and Geography In forests in Japan and Korea.

Comment *Sasa palmata* (Burbridge) Camus and *S. veitchii* were commonly planted in Victorian shrubberies, and often persist to the present; their spreading rhizomes and large leaves can smother most competition. *Sasa palmata* flowered in the 1960s, over 90 years after its introduction to the west, but most colonies have survived.

Sasa palmata
leaf, ½ life size
September 14th

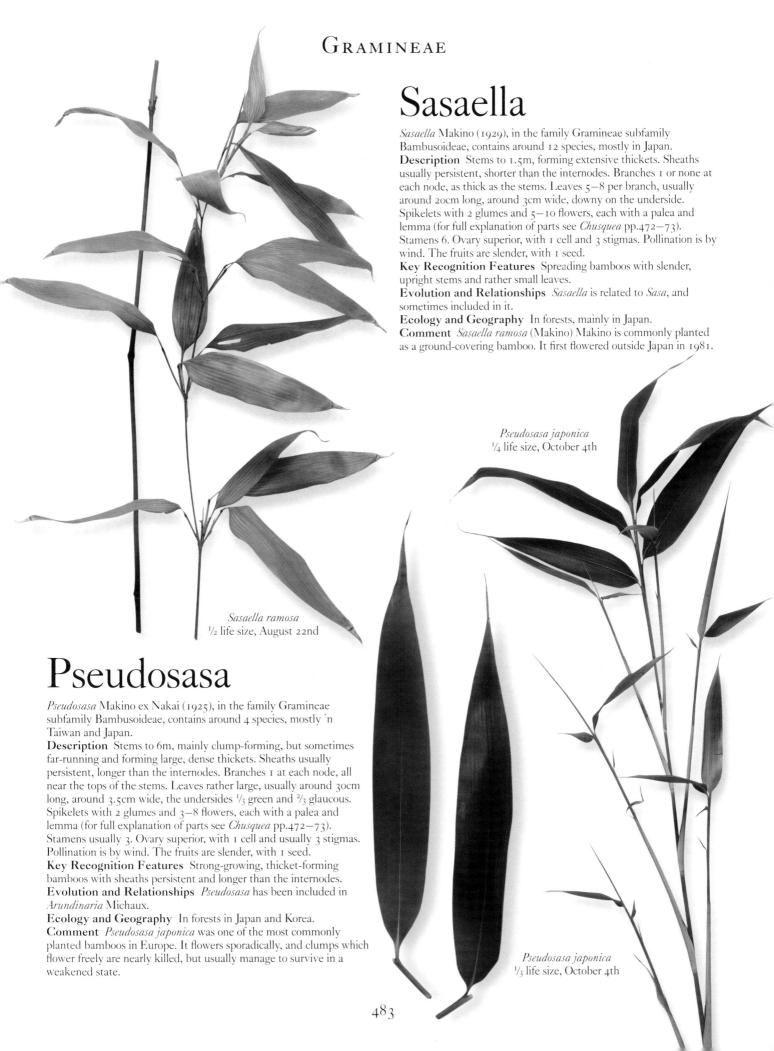

GRAMINEAE

Sasaella

Sasaella Makino (1929), in the family Gramineae subfamily
Bambusoideae, contains around 12 species, mostly in Japan.
Description Stems to 1.5m, forming extensive thickets. Sheaths
usually persistent, shorter than the internodes. Branches 1 or none at
each node, as thick as the stems. Leaves 5–8 per branch, usually
around 20cm long, around 3cm wide, downy on the underside.
Spikelets with 2 glumes and 5–10 flowers, each with a palea and
lemma (for full explanation of parts see *Chusquea* pp.472–73).
Stamens 6. Ovary superior, with 1 cell and 3 stigmas. Pollination is by
wind. The fruits are slender, with 1 seed.
Key Recognition Features Spreading bamboos with slender,
upright stems and rather small leaves.
Evolution and Relationships *Sasaella* is related to *Sasa*, and
sometimes included in it.
Ecology and Geography In forests, mainly in Japan.
Comment *Sasaella ramosa* (Makino) Makino is commonly planted
as a ground-covering bamboo. It first flowered outside Japan in 1981.

Pseudosasa japonica
1/4 life size, October 4th

Sasaella ramosa
1/2 life size, August 22nd

Pseudosasa

Pseudosasa Makino ex Nakai (1925), in the family Gramineae
subfamily Bambusoideae, contains around 4 species, mostly in
Taiwan and Japan.
Description Stems to 6m, mainly clump-forming, but sometimes
far-running and forming large, dense thickets. Sheaths usually
persistent, longer than the internodes. Branches 1 at each node, all
near the tops of the stems. Leaves rather large, usually around 30cm
long, around 3.5cm wide, the undersides 1/3 green and 2/3 glaucous.
Spikelets with 2 glumes and 3–8 flowers, each with a palea and
lemma (for full explanation of parts see *Chusquea* pp.472–73).
Stamens usually 3. Ovary superior, with 1 cell and usually 3 stigmas.
Pollination is by wind. The fruits are slender, with 1 seed.
Key Recognition Features Strong-growing, thicket-forming
bamboos with sheaths persistent and longer than the internodes.
Evolution and Relationships *Pseudosasa* has been included in
Arundinaria Michaux.
Ecology and Geography In forests in Japan and Korea.
Comment *Pseudosasa japonica* was one of the most commonly
planted bamboos in Europe. It flowers sporadically, and clumps which
flower freely are nearly killed, but usually manage to survive in a
weakened state.

Pseudosasa japonica
1/3 life size, October 4th

Bibliography

General plant books:

The New Royal Horticultural Society Dictionary of Gardening, Macmillan (1992). A new version of the old Dictionary.
The Royal Horticultural Society Dictionary of Gardening, Oxford University Press (1976–77). Old but still valuable.
The European Garden Flora I– VI, Cambridge University Press (1986–2001). Scientific account of cultivated plants.
The Plant Book, A portable dictionary of the vascular plants by D.J. Mabberley, 2nd edition, Cambridge University Press (1997). An excellent account of all known genera, full of interesting or strange facts about plants.
The RHS Plant Finder, Dorling Kindersley (2000). Updated annually, a good source of modern plant names, as well as a source list of nurseries for Great Britain.
Flowering Plants of the World, ed. V.H. Heywood, Batsford (1993). Illustrated account of plant families.
100 Families of Flowering Plants, by M. Hickey and C.J. King, Cambridge University Press (1981). Detailed drawings and explanation of the floral parts of 100 important families.
Wild Flowers of the World by Barbara Everard and Brian Morley, Ebury Press & Michael Joseph (1970). A geographical sample of interesting plants, with excellent and fascinating text.
Manual of Cultivated Broad-leaved Trees and Shrubs by Gerd Krüssmann, Batsford (1986).
World Checklist and Bibliography of Conifers by Aljos Farjon, Royal Botanic Gardens, Kew (1998).
Flowering Tropical Climbers by Geoffrey Herklots, Dawson (1976). A clear and detailed account of many genera of climbers, with excellent line drawings.
The Pollination of Flowers by Michael Proctor and Peter Yeo, Collins New Naturalist series, no. 54 (1973).

Plant phylogeny and DNA references:

Plant Systematics, a Phylogenetic Approach, by W.S. Judd et al., Sinauer Associates, Inc. (1999).
Paleobotany and the Evolution of Plants by W.N. Stewart and G.W. Rothwell, 2nd edition, Cambridge University Press (1993).
'Introduction to the Conifers' by Aljos Farjon, in *Curtis's Botanical Magazine*, Volume 16, Part 3, pages 158–72 (1999).

Floras and books on different regions of the world

Europe and southwestern Asia:
Flora Europaea by V.H. Heywood et al., Cambridge University Press (1964–80).
Flora of Turkey by P.H. Davis et al., Edinburgh University Press (1965–87).
Flowers of Greece and the Balkans by Oleg Polunin, Oxford University Press (1980).
Flowers of Southwest Europe by Oleg Polunin, Oxford University Press (1973).

Canary Islands:
Wild Flowers of the Canary Islands by David and Zoë Bramwell, Stanley Thornes (1974).

Africa:
'Plants of the Cape Flora, A Descriptive Catalogue' by Pauline Bond and Peter Goldblatt, in *Journal of South African Botany* suppl. volume 13 (1984).
South African Wild Flower Guides, Botanical Society of South Africa, in association with the the National Botanical Institute:
1. Namaqualand by Annelise Le Roux and Ted Schelpe; photography by Zelda Wahl (1994).
5. Hottentots Holland to Hermanus by Lee Burman and Anne Bean; photography by Jose Burman (1985).
7. West Coast by John Manning and Peter Goldblatt; photography by John Manning (1996).
9. Nieuwoudtville, Bokkeveld Plateau & Hantam by John Manning and Peter Goldblatt (1997).
The Botany of the Southern Natal Drakensberg by O. M. Hilliard and B. L. Burtt, National Botanic Garden (1987).
Wild Flowers of East Africa by Sir Michael Blundell KBE, Collins (1987).

India, China, Japan, and the Himalayas:
Flowers of the Himalaya by Oleg Polunin and Adam Stainton, Oxford University Press(1984); and Supplement, by Adam Stainton Oxford University Press, Delhi (1988).
Flora of Bhutan by A.J.C. Grierson and D.G. Long, Royal Botanic Garden, Edinburgh (1983–94).
Plantae Wilsonianae by J.S. Sargent (1913), reprinted by Dioscorides Press 1988.
Travels in China by Roy Lancaster, Antique Collectors Club (1989).
Flora of Japan by J. Ohwi, Smithsonian (1965).

Australia:
Encyclopaedia of Australian Plants by W. Rodger Elliott and David L. Jones, volumes 1–5, Lothian (1980–90).
Flora of New South Wales ed. Gwen J. Harden, New South Wales University Press, 4 volumes, (1990–93)

New Zealand:
Flora of New Zealand Volume 1 by H.H. Allen, PD Hasselberg (1961)
Flora of New Zealand Volume 2 by L.B .Moore and E. Edgar, PD Hasselberg (1970).

North America:
Flora of North America north of Mexico ed. Flora of North America editorial committee, vols. 1–3, Oxford University Press (1993 and continuing)
A California Flora and Supplement by Philip A. Munz, University of California Press (1973).
Arizona Flora by Thomas H. Kearney, Robert H. Peebles and collaborators, University of California Press (1951).
The Audubon Society Field Guide to Northern American Wild Flowers, western region by R. Spellenberg, Knopf (1979).
Illustrated Flora of the Northern United States and Canada by N.L. Britton and A. Brown, 2nd revised edition (1952).

Geological ages

This table shows the names of the geological periods that have been mentioned in the book with regard to fossils, the dates at which they began in millions of years ago, and, where relevant, the main plant types that appear in each period.

Pre-cambrian	4,700 million years ago: Blue-green bacteria; and green and red algae
Cambrian	570 million years ago: Brown algae
Ordovician	500 million years ago: Dinoflagellates (more advanced algae)
Silurian	435 million years ago: *Rhynia* (first land plants with stems)
Devonian	395 million years ago: Liverworts, tree club mosses
Carboniferous	345 million years ago: Mosses, Ferns, plants with conifer-like cones
Permian	280 million years ago: *Ginkgo* and horsetails
Triassic	225 million years ago: Conifers
Jurassic	195 million years ago: *Taxus* relatives
Cretaceous	141 million years ago: First flowering plants, and towards the end of this period *Magnolia* and *Liriodendron* are well developed.
Tertiary	65 million years ago (including Oligocene, Eocene and Paleocene): By the Eocene period many of the modern genera can be recognized
Quaternary	2.5 million years ago (including Pleistocene, the ice ages, Pliocene, and Miocene): Most modern genera had appeared by this time; during the ice ages many genera disappeared from Europe but survived in the Canary Isles and southern China.

Glossary

In the text we have tried to avoid obscure technical terms wherever possible, but a few are hard to avoid without resorting to a long explanation.

Achene a small, dry, 1-seeded fruit
Actinomycete generally anaerobic bacteria with a filamentous and branching growth pattern, which help fix atmospheric nitrogen
Acuminate gradually tapering to an elongated point
Amplexicaul with the base of the leaf encircling the stem
Androgynophore extension of the flower that bears both the ovary and the stamens *See also Gynophore*
Anther the part of the male *stamen* that contains the pollen
Aril a fleshy attachment or covering on a seed, which often attracts ants
Auricle, Auriculate ear-like projections at the leaf base
Axil the angle between the leaf stalk and the stem
Basic number (of *chromosomes*) the normal number of chromosome pairs in a species or genus *See also Haploid, Diploid, Polyploid*
Basifixed (of an *anther*) attached by the base *See also Versatile*
Biomass Very fast-growing trees cut about every 5 years and used for cheap wood (such as chipboard) or fuel

Bletting allowing fruit to ripen to the point of decay
Bract a modified leaf below a flower
Calyx the outer parts of a flower, usually green, formed by the often fused sepals
Capitate head-like
Capsule a dry fruit containing seeds
Carpel the part of the flower that produces the seeds
Caruncle a fleshy growth on the end of a seed
Chromosome a rod-like structure in the nucleus of a cell, carrying the genetic information; *species* normally have a constant number of chromosomes *See also Diploid, Haploid*
Cladode a flattened, leaf-like stem *See also Phyllode*
Clavate shaped like a club, narrow at the base, swelling towards the apex
Cleistogamous flowers that never open and are self-pollinated
Clone the vegetatively propagated progeny of a single plant
Connective the tissue that connects the 2 sacs of an anther
Corolla the inner parts of the flower, comprising the petals, usually used when the petals are united into a tube
Crenate with shallow, rounded teeth
Cultivar a cultivated variety or hybrid, denoted by a name in inverted commas, such as *Hamamelis* 'Diane' *See also Forma, Microspecies, Subspecies, Variant*
Cuneate wedge-shaped
Dehiscent opening to shed its seeds
Dentate with sharp, regular teeth
Dichotomous branching in 2 equal parts
Diploid containing the usual complement of *chromosomes*, that is twice the *basic number*, also expressed as 2n *See also Haploid, Polyploid*
Erose appearing as if gnawed
Exserted sticking out, usually describing the *style* or *stamens* protruding from the flower
Falcate sickle-shaped
Family A group of related plants, using consisting of several *genera*
-fid split, bifid or 2-fid meaning split in 2, and trifid or 3-fid split in 3
Filament the part of the *stamen* that supports the *anther*
Filiform thread-like
Fl. floruit, given for a date when someone was known to be alive, when their birth or death dates cannot be found
Flagellum the tail on a mobile cell, such as a sperm cell as found in ginkgo, by which it swims (Latin for whip)
Floccose, Flocculose woolly
Forma, f. a minor variant, less different from the basic species than a *Variety See also Cultivar, Microspecies, Subspecies*
Fynbos the South African name for the scrub found on hillsides in the Cape region, a rich community of heathers, pelargoniums, proteas, bulbs etc., which is subject to periodic renewal by fire
Garrigue Vegetation of low, evergreen shrubs, found in the Mediterranean area, usually on thin or shallow soils, the main plants being shrubs of evergreen oak *See also Maquis*
Genome a group of genes, generally a group of *chromosomes* belonging to an ancestral species
Genus, Genera a grouping of related *species* with common features that distinguish them from other plants, such as *Hibiscus, Fuchsia*, or *Pelargonium*
Glabrous without hairs or glands
Glandular with glands, which are usually stalked, like hairs with a sticky blob on the apex
Glaucous with a greyish colour or bloom, especially on the leaves

Glossary

Globose more or less spherical

Glomerule small, crowded, rounded heads of flowers

Gynophore extension of the flower that bears the ovary *See also Androgynophore*

Haploid with a single set of *chromosomes*, the normal state of the reproductive stage of plants, such as pollen or egg cells *See also Basic number, Diploid, Polyploid*

Haustorium a fleshy outgrowth from a parasitic plant, by which it is attached to and receives nourishment from the host

Hispid coarsely and stiffly hairy

Hyaline transparent, often soft or papery

Hybrid the progeny of 2 different *species*

Inferior ovary in which the point of insertion of the sepals and petals is above the *ovary See also Superior ovary*

Inflorescence the flowers and flower stalks, especially when grouped

Keeled with a ridge along the lower side, like the keel of a boat

Laciniate deeply and irregularly toothed and divided into narrow lobes

Lanceolate shaped like a lance blade, widest below the middle, with a tapering point

Latex white, milky, and rubbery juice

Locule parts of a *capsule*

Loess deep deposits of sandy, wind-blown soil

Lyrate leaf with a broad but pointed apex and lobes becoming smaller towards the leaf base

Mallee, mellee Scrubland vegetation of southern Australia, dominated by shrubby eucalyptus and other shrubs with spiny or leathery leaves

Maquis Scrubland vegetation found on the lower slopes of mountains in the Mediterranean area, the main plants being shrubs or small trees with tough, evergreen leaves *See also Garrigue*

Meiosis cell division producing the halving of the number of *chromosomes* during reproduction *See also Diploid, Haploid*

-merous having parts in groups, for example 3-merous or tri-merous, having parts in groups of 3

Microspecies a *species* that is distinguished from others by very small but constant characteristics *See also Cultivar, Forma, Subspecies, Variety*

Monocarpic usually dying after flowering and fruiting

Mucronate with a short, sharp point

Nectary a gland in the flower that produces nectar

Ovary the base of the female part of the flower, which contains the *ovules* and develops into the fruit; may be composed of one or several *carpels*

Ovule the female egg cell that develops into a seed

Palmate with lobes or leaflets, spreading like the fingers of a hand

Panicle a branched *raceme*

Papillose with small, elongated projections

Pappus parachute-like ring of fine hairs

Parietal placentation with ovules attached to the walls of the ovary

Pedicel the stalk of a flower

Peduncle the stalk of an *inflorescence*

Peloric regularity in a normally irregular flower

Peltate shaped like a round shield, with the stalk in the centre

Perfoliate a leaf joined right around the stem, thus looking as if pierced by the stem

Phyllary an incurved, usually narrow *bract*, on the base of a daisy-type flowerhead

Phylloclade *See Cladode*

Phyllode a flattened leaf stalk that functions as a leaf

Pilose hairy, with long soft hairs

Polyploid having more than the usual (*diploid*) number of *chromosomes* for that *genus*, for example triploid, with 3 times the *basic number* of chromosomes, also expressed 3n, or tetraploid, with 4 times the basic number, also expressed 4n

Pome an apple-like fruit

Puberulent with a fine but rather sparse covering of hairs

Pubescent with a fine coating of hairs, denser than *puberulent*

Pyrene a hard-coated seed found within a fruit

Raceme an *inflorescence* with the flowers on a central stem, the oldest at the base

Receptacle part of the stem that bears the flower parts

Reticulate marked with a network, usually of veins

Rugose wrinkled

Saccate with a baggy pouch

Samara a winged seed, usually of a maple

Scarious dry and papery, usually also transparent

Section part of (usually) a *genus*, grouping *species* with particular traits that are not necessarily shared by all the species in the genus *See also Subgenus*

Seta, Setose bristle, bristly

Sinus, Sinuate a deep notch between 2 lobes, towards the centre of a leaf

Species, Sp. group of individuals having common characteristics, distinct from other groups; the basic unit of plant classification *See also Genus*

Spicate like a spike

Spinose with weak spines

Stamen the male part of a flower, consisting of a *filament* supporting an *anther*

Stigma the sticky part of a *style* that receives pollen

Stipule leafy lobes along or near the base of a leaf stalk, found especially in roses

Style the part of the flower that connects the *stigma* to the *ovary*

Subgenus a major division of a *genus*, grouping *species* with particular traits that are not necessarily shared by all the species in the genus *See also Section*

Suborbicular almost round, but usually slightly narrower

Subspecies, Subsp. a division of a species, with minor and not complete differences from other subspecies, usually distinct either ecologically or geographically *See also Cultivar, Forma, Microspecies, Variety*

Succulent fleshy, storing water in the stems or leaves

Superior ovary in which the point of insertion of the sepals and petals is below the *ovary See also Inferior ovary*

Terete not ridged or grooved

Ternate in a group of 3

Tetragonal square in section

Tetraploid *See Polyploid*

Tracheid part of the water-conducting tissue inside a stem

Tribe part of a *family*, usually consisting of several *genera* with common distinguishing characteristics

Triploid *See Polyploid*: triploid plants are usually sterile, but robust growers and good garden plants

Tuberculate warty

Umbel an *inflorescence* in which the branches arise from a single point, usually forming a flat or gently rounded top

Variety, Var., Vars. a group of plants within a *species*, usually differing in one or two minor characteristics, and generally referring to natural variations *See also Cultivar, Forma, Microspecies, Subspecies*

Versatile (of an *anther*) attached in the middle *See also Basifixed*

Index

The entries in roman upper and lower case refer to the main genera covered in this work. The entries in capital letters refer to the families covered, and the entries in italic refer to genera and families only mentioned in the text.

Index

Index